the fragile alliance

fourth edition

the fragile alliance

an orientation to the psychiatric treatment of the adolescent

JOHN E. MEEKS, M.D.

Medical Director
Psychiatric Institute of Montgomery County, Rockville, Maryland
Clinical Associate Professor in the Department of Psychiatry
George Washington University School of Medicine

WILLIAM BERNET, M.D.

Director of Community Services
Charter Lakeside Hospital, Memphis, Tennessee
Clinical Assistant Professor in the Department of Psychiatry
University of Tennessee, Memphis, College of Medicine

ROBERT E. KRIEGER PUBLISHING COMPANY
MALABAR, FLORIDA
1990

Fourth Edition 1990

Printed and Published by
ROBERT E. KRIEGER PUBLISHING COMPANY, INC.
KRIEGER DRIVE
MALABAR, FLORIDA 32950

Library of Congress Cataloging-in-Publication Data
Meeks, John E.
  The fragile alliance : an orientation to the psychiatric treatment
of the adolescent / John E. Meeks, William Bernet. -- 4th ed.
      p.   cm.
  Includes bibliographical references.
  ISBN 0-89464-375-4 (alk. paper)
      1. Adolescent psychotherapy. I. Bernet, William, II. Title.
  RJ503.M44   1990
  616.89'14--dc20   90-4107
                                                       CIP

10 9 8 7 6 5 4 3 2

contents

Part One

Part Three

DEDICATION 1990

By Dr. Meeks: For Anita and my daughters who were Cathy, Julie, and Lindy in 1970 but who have grown to become Catherine, Julia, and Melinda. You still sustain me but you have also taught and inspired me.

By Dr. Bernet: For Susan and the kids, Elizabeth, Daniel, Alice, and Henry.

preface to the fourth edition

In the two decades since the first publication of *The Fragile Alliance*, the field of adolescent psychiatry has matured remarkably. Along with this maturity has come refinement of technical approaches and a major increase in information about adolescents, their problems, and their treatment. Previous editions of this book included basic material—a shell structure to house the adolescent therapist. It is now obvious that there are many new materials, appliances, and conveniences to add to the comfort of the therapist and to provide for the better care of those young troubled travelers who come by for warmth and counsel. We wanted to upgrade the structure for the fourth edition.

There was a problem. A single builder is no longer able to provide the range of expertise, the tools, and the time to construct adequately the needed edifice. Dr. Meeks needed more manpower to join in the construction and renovations of *The Fragile Alliance*. Dr. Meeks's new fellow carpenter is Dr. William Bernet.

Dr. Bernet, an old friend and colleague of Dr. Meeks, has wide experience in child and adolescent psychiatry and a range of special interests that complement his co-author's. Dr. Bernet has contributed four completely new chapters, "The Adolescent at School," "The Adolescent Victim," "Adolescents in Divorced and Remarried Families," and "Medical and Neurological Considerations." In this new edition we added material to almost every chapter, especially to "Group Psychotherapy of the Adolescent," "The Parents of the Adolescent Patient," "Depression, Suicidal Threats, and Suicidal Behavior," and "Homosexuality and Other Issues." In every chapter, the bibliographies have been upgraded and the clinical material made more contemporary.

We both hope that you will find *The Fragile Alliance* helpful as you undertake the difficult but rewarding task of treating adolescents in emotional crisis. The presentation continues to be basically a clinical, "how to" approach offered with the understanding that our suggestions reflect to some extent idiosyncrasies of the authors and will not fit every therapist. However, the suggestions and directions are presented with the hope that they will stimulate thought and provide some sense of direction which individual therapists can then modify to fit their particular patient population and their own personal style. Some of our material, which did not fit comfortably in the text of the chapters, has been organized into sidebars. This material, located in boxes, is the kind of information that a supervisor might say as an aside to a student.

The clinical material in *The Fragile Alliance* has been disguised. The names and other identifying data have been changed. Most of the clinical vignettes are composites of several actual cases.

References are found at the end of each chapter. However, one book is referred to frequently and is not in any of the bibliographies. *DSM-III-R* in the text refers to:

American Psychiatric Association. 1987. *Diagnostic and Statistical Manual of Mental Disorders, Third Edition, Revised.* Washington, D.C.: American Psychiatric Association.

We thank several colleagues for their constructive criticism and suggestions: Ms. Sondra Sutton for reviewing the chapter, "The Adolescent at School"; William Murphy, Ph.D., for material on adolescent sex offenders; Denese Ford-Nepa, Ph.D., for material on sexual trauma; and J. T. Jabbour, M.D., his colleagues at LeBonheur Hospital, Memphis, and Dietrich Blumer, M.D., for reviewing the chapter, "Medical and Neurological Considerations." Thanks to Ms. Gwen Jackson for checking and correcting the bibliographies and to Ms. Karen Williams for helping us stay organized.

acknowledgements

Grateful acknowledgement is made to the following for permission to reprint their material:

1. *Adolescent Psychiatry,* excerpt from D. Anderson, "Family and Peer Relations of Gay Adolescents." 14: 162–178, 1987.

   Excerpt from A. D. Martin, "Learning to Hide: The Socialization of the Gay Adolescent." 10: 52–65, 1982.

2. *American Journal of Orthopsychiatry,* excerpt from P. Barglow et al., "Some Psychiatric Aspects of Illegitimate Pregnancy in Early Adolescence." 38: 672–687, 1968.

3. *American Journal of Psychiatry,* excerpt from A. Heller and H. G. Wittington, "The Colorado Story: Denver General Hospital Experience with the Change in the Law on Therapeutic Abortion." 125: 809–816, 1968.

   Excerpt from R. L. Jenkins, "Classifications of Behavior Problems in Children." 125: 1032–1039, 1969.

   Excerpt from C. J. Newman, "Disaster at Buffalo Creek. Children of Disaster: Clinical Observations at Buffalo Creek." 133: 306–312, 1976.

4. American Psychiatric Association, Washington, D.C., excerpt from S. C. Yudofsky, "Organic Personality Disorder, Explosive Type." In: *Treatments of Psychiatric Disorders, Volume 2,* by American Psychiatric Association Task Force, 1989.

   Excerpts from *Diagnostic and Statistical Manual of Mental Disorders, Third Edition, Revised,* 1987.

5. Brunner/Mazel, Inc., New York, excerpt from E. B. Visher and J. S. Visher, *Stepfamilies: A Guide to Working with Stepparents and Stepchildren,* 1979.

Excerpt from C. J. Sager, *Treating the Remarried Family*, et al., 1983.

6. Doubleday & Company, New York, excerpt from T. Roszak, *The Making of a Counter Culture*, 1969.

7. Harcourt, Brace & World, New York, excerpt from K. Keniston, *The Uncommitted: Alienated Youth in American Society*, 1965.

8. International Universities Press, New York, excerpt from H. Deutsch, *Selected Problems of Adolescence (with special emphasis on group formation)*, 1967.

   Excerpt from I. M. Josselyn, "Psychotherapy of Adolescents at the Level of Private Practice. In: *Psychotherapy of the Adolescent*, edited by B. H. Balser, 1957.

9. Jacob Aronson, New York, excerpt from C. W. Socarides, *Homosexuality*, 1978.

10. *Journal of the American Academy of Child and Adolescent Psychiatry*, excerpt from R. G. Aug and T. P. Bright, "A Study of Wed and Unwed Motherhood in Adolescents and Young Adults." 9: 577–594, 1970.

    Excerpt from W. Bernet, "The Therapist's Role in Child Custody Disputes." 22: 180–183, 1983.

    Excerpt from G. C. Morrison and J. G. Collier, "Family Treatment Approaches to Suicidal Children and Adolescents." 8: 140–153, 1969.

    Excerpt from L. B. Silver, "Psychological and Family Problems Associated with Learning Disabilities: Assessment and Intervention." 28: 319–325, 1989.

11. *Journal of the American Psychoanalytic Association*, excerpt from E. Bibring, "Psychoanalysis and the Dynamic Psychotherapies," 2: 745–770, 1954.

12. *Psychoanalytic Study of the Child*, excerpt from H. Wieder and E. H. Kaplan, "Drug Use in Adolescents: Psychodynamic Meaning and Pharmacogenic Effect," 24: 399–431, 1969.

13. *Seminars in Psychiatry*, excerpt from S. L. Mogul, "Clinical Assessment of Adolescent Development." 1: 24–31, 1969.

14. University of Chicago Press, Chicago, excerpt from F. Fromm-Reichmann, *Principles of Intensive Psychotherapy*, 1950.

15. Vintage Books, New York, excerpt from A. Camus, *The Rebel*, 1956.

Part
One

introduction

At the core of all psychiatric treatment is the therapeutic relationship with the patient. The process of developing an understanding of the adolescent (diagnosis), forming a working relationship or therapeutic alliance, managing the ongoing therapy and then constructively dissolving the therapeutic contract is the subject of Part One. Specific diagnoses and special technical problems will be largely deferred to Part Two. The special applications of therapy to the hospitalized patient will be discussed in Part Three.

The emphasis in Part One will be on general principles of therapy and the primary focus will be on individual therapy. In this section, as in other parts of the book, the discussion of the individual therapist and the individual patient is vital to the structure of the book. To avoid the awkward repetition of *he or she*, the pronoun *he* is understood to refer to either gender.

Part One also includes a chapter discussing the role of the adolescent's family in treatment. The focus of that chapter is on the therapist's relationship with the parents of those adolescents the therapist is seeing in individual therapy.

The remainder of Part One includes brief chapters presenting the basics of group and family psychotherapy. These therapeutic modalities are discussed primarily to show their relationship to the more traditional individual approach and to suggest some of their special applications in planning treatment for adolescent patients.

In short, our hope is that Part One of the book will provide the reader with a general grasp of the aims and methods of psychotherapy with the adolescent in any setting. This basic understanding should never be forgotten whenever a therapist approaches an adolescent patient in any setting. This sense of the therapeutic alliance is the core of the book and the solid grounding of all successful adolescent therapy.

CHAPTER 1

adolescents are different

THE DEVELOPMENTAL STAGE AND ITS IMPACT ON PSYCHOTHERAPY

In recent years, there has been a remarkable growth of interest in adolescence as a discrete phase in the development of the human personality. The information converging from many sources has shown decisively that adolescence cannot be understood completely as merely a recapitulation of previous development. Increasing awareness of the specific role of cultural opportunities and restrictions, the characteristics of adolescent thought processes, the importance of pregenital factors and early introjects, and the synthetic role of the ego during adolescence—to mention only a partial list of recently explored areas—has served to expand our picture of the adolescent toward a three-dimensional view. Blos (1962) has greatly refined our understanding of adolescent intrapsychic process and of the specific dynamic tasks which confront the child during each subphase of adolescence. His careful description of preadolescence, early adolescence, adolescence proper, and late adolescence should be closely reviewed by the serious student. It would be impossible in this introductory chapter to explore the nature of adolescence with any degree of completeness. Instead, primary emphasis is placed on the features which may trouble the competent practicing psychotherapist who is relatively inexperienced in work with adolescents.

Erikson (1968) has offered us an overview of the entire adolescent process as a regression in the service of progression. It is as though the adolescent must drag himself and the adults who care for him through the mud of old conflicts, enmities, and attachments to inoculate himself against both the seductive memories and the frightening dangers of the past. If all goes well, he

5

Peter Blos was a psychoanalyst whose work has become part of the foundation of our understanding of the development and psychopathology of children and adolescents. Many psychotherapists have enjoyed reading *On Adolescence* (Blos, 1962) during training and enjoyed it even more after treating adolescents for twenty years. Blos (1967, 1977, 1979, 1980, 1983) has continued to expand and refine his view of adolescent development. He is a supervisor of child and adolescent analysis at the New York Psychoanalytic Institute.

emerges into adulthood with immunity to some of the more virulent pathogens from his past and the ability to host others without apparent damage to his psychological integrity. The goal is to achieve what Erikson (1968) has called "identity" and what Blos (1967) has called the "second individuation." Both terms refer to the achievement of a workable self-awareness which accepts inner complexity and is able to relate this multifaceted sense of selfhood to others in an interpersonal and larger social context. This sense of self is still tentative and is largely a recognition of potentials, not a static and finalized state. As Erikson has pointed out, the adolescent who is involved in the quest for identity does not actually ask himself, "Who am I?", as we often loosely say. Instead, he asks, "What do I want to make of myself and what do I have to work with?" Recognition of this distinction has implications for defining the goals of psychotherapy with adolescents and setting appropriate end points for therapy which we will consider later.

Perhaps a metaphor based on the world of theatre will help to convey a sense of the adolescent experience. For the adolescent, the external world is sometimes a distant stage on which skillful players are easily producing a successful performance. The young spectator can hardly imagine that he will ever have sufficient skill to handle anything more than a walk-on part. At other times, the world is seen as a cast of faltering and untutored players, totally available to be molded to the adolescent's personal sense of drama. In short, the adolescent shifts from seeing reality as a malleable medium in which he can implant an image of his inner struggles to viewing it as a relatively fixed situation to which he must mold himself. Generally speaking, the younger adolescent tends toward the view of himself as the undiscovered director, whereas the older adolescent gradually comes to accept a less inflated role in the grand production of life.

The theatrical metaphor was deliberately chosen to emphasize the experimental and tentative quality of the adolescent's feelings, attitudes, and relationships. One often has the impression that the adolescent is assuming a role and "playing at" life.

I do not mean to imply that the adolescent is necessarily playful or frivolous in his approach to living. The fact that he is often very serious indeed is revealed by the intense emotions which are typical of adolescence. The adolescent is playing at life with remarkable intensity. What is lacking is a readiness to make permanent commitments or form irreversible loyalties. The adolescent cannot take positions or roles which imply finality because these may prove later to be poorly suited to what he wants to make of himself or what he has to work with. Still, he can only answer these questions by involving himself with life. We cannot expect him to learn to swim without getting into the water. The adolescent's compromise solution involves trial dips which are always undertaken with the option of jumping out if the currents are too swift, if the eddies are too deep, or even if he decides he is a a landlubber after all.

The average adolescent quietly conducts his experiments in living. His surface behavior remains for the most part well within the confines of acceptability. The inner struggle is hardly apparent even to the adolescent himself and is accomplished with only a few exhibitions of artistic temperament. The relative peacefulness of the ordinary adolescent experience is well described by Douvan and Adelson (1966) and Offer (1969, 1987) after large-scale studies of random normative adolescent populations. However, it should be recognized that there is a range of development patterns even within normal adolescence. Some adolescents have a rather obviously turbulent path to adulthood. Others show periodic external distress while others move through the developmental stage with minimal observable evidence of upset.

For the most part, those adolescents who present (or are presented) for psychotherapy are a very different group. Their struggle is desperate and highly visible. For them, adolescence is quite literally a question of life or death. If they cannot find a part in the drama which fits both their sense of personal integrity and their notion of a good show, they refuse to play. The applause of an audience that they would feel they were both exploiting and being exploited by seems to them insufficient reward. They will not be roped into a command performance.

There are three general groups who might be caught in this quandary. One group is composed of those youngsters whose experiences and emotional development have been atypical to a degree which forces them to demand a role which is simply not realistically available.

An 18-year-old boy told his therapist that he was sure his work paralysis would disappear if only he could be entrusted with some worthwhile task. When he was asked to give an example of a worthwhile task, he told at length of his plans for restructuring the executive branch of the United States government.

Other adolescents, even more impaired by their early experience or constitution, are faced with needs and wishes which may be internally inconsistent and even explicitly psychotic. They cannot imagine any role in the real world of adulthood which would even approach a satisfactory level of gratification.

Paul, a 13-year-old, was seen for psychological evaluation during his hospitalization for a crash weight-loss program. His internist insisted on this approach after Paul's weight rose above 300 pounds despite outpatient dietary management. Paul told the evaluating therapist that he saw no reason to lose weight, since it was his plan to establish an absolute monarchy on an uninhabited island. He anticipated that he would be totally cared for by his subjects, emphasizing the gastronomic delights which they would prepare for him. His affect was inappropriate and associations were loose. He appeared to be convinced of the reality of his delusional empire.

When he was released from the hospital, his mother attempted to carry out the dietary restrictions imposed by the internist. She relented, however, when Paul threatened her with a kitchen knife if she did not give him the food he wanted. The mother called the therapist in panic, but explained that she and Paul could not enter therapy since Paul's father "did not believe in psychiatry."

Five years later, the therapist was again contacted by Paul's mother. She wondered if the therapist would testify that Paul was emotionally ill. He was facing trial on charges of air piracy after hijacking an airplane to another country. Paul's psychotic mission in life eventually led him to an extremely dangerous impulsive venture in the real world. He was found to be legally insane and committed to receive the treatment which he should have had five years sooner.

Patients from these two groups are coming to therapy with increasing frequency, as mentioned in the introduction. They require modified treatment approaches which we are gradually improving. These will be discussed in more detail in chapter 5.

A third group of troubled adolescents consists of those who are largely whole within, but who are dismayed by the possibilities which society presents them. Many of the adolescents who come for psychotherapy present a convincing argument for this view of their difficulty. If only society (their parents, their school, their community, their country, their world) were different, everything would be simple for them. They have studied the play and find it to be of inferior quality, lacking any suitable vehicle for their talents. Since social institutions are far from perfect, their argument has surface merit. On closer examination, however, one usually comes to feel that the particular social imperfections which trouble them most are remarkably similar to those features within themselves which they regard as unacceptable. Again, the devil without is easier to abide than the devil within, especially for the conflicted adolescent.

Most adolescents today seem almost too eager to accept society's status quo. Although they may compete vigorously to rise to the top of the "technocracy" (Roszak, 1969) or simply give up and drift into its eddies, there is little sustained and consensual social criticism extant among today's adolescents.

This does not mean that the adolescent no longer battles the adult world. At this time, however, the battle tends to be closer to home, perhaps more interpersonal than political, and less strident. Of course, more seriously disturbed adolescents may be very opposed to society but their rejection tends to be indiscriminate, obviously impassioned, and clearly self-destructive.

However, it does seem that many adolescents come to therapy somewhat more willingly today or at least are prepared to view themselves as unhappy and in need of some kind of assistance. Even when this is true, the adolescent must test the therapist and this test casts the therapist in a variety of roles—mostly adversarial at first. To some extent, though muted, this still represents the adolescent's apprehensive approach to his or her environment.

Naturally, the therapist of the adolescent must expect to be pulled actively into this struggle with the larger world. He will often be cast in roles far removed from his actual attitudes, capabilities, or intentions. Early in therapy, the adolescent tends to utilize the new adult in his life as a screen on which he can externalize the negative aspects of his self-image and his more distressing introjects. The therapist also may be a convenient embodiment of all the social, cultural, and family evils which the adolescent deplores. Later, we will consider more fully both the problems that this tendency poses for the therapist in the establishment of a therapeutic alliance and some of the technical approaches which may be useful in managing this hazard.

Later in therapy, the therapist frequently finds himself unrealistically elevated and venerated to the point of idealization. Although this reaction of the adolescent is not nearly so distressful to the therapist, it can also interfere with the adolescent's emotional growth if it is not properly utilized and eventually dissolved. The countertransference problems which occur when one is faced with adulation are especially marked when this attitude follows upon a previous disdain for the therapist.

These extremes of relating often take different paths which depend on the basic pathology of the adolescent. The capacity to imagine help from others or even to emotionally recognize the separateness of another person may make the passage through this "testing" phase very difficult. At times, with some youngsters it is almost impossible to respond therapeutically to this peculiar style of adolescent relating. The observing ego, with which the therapist has allied himself in working with adults, seems rudimentary or absent in many adolescents. The seasoned psychotherapist expects his patients to distort his intentions and his personality, as long as the patient is able to localize the origins of the distortions within himself and to reflect on their possible meanings. In early therapy with adolescents, one commonly encounters an intensity of feeling and a lack of introspection which produce a degree of uncooperativeness and explosiveness usually seen only in very disturbed individuals in adult psychotherapeutic work. If the adolescent's capacity to relate is seriously impaired or undeveloped before the vicissitudes of this developmental phase, the task can become overwhelming for patient and therapist alike. We will address some of the issues involved in this problem situation and ideas for addressing it in chapter 5.

To understand why even the relatively intact adolescent relates as he does, we will need to consider some of the developmental problems which the adolescent faces and the impact of these problems on the ways in which he deals with other people. The discussion of approaches by which these patterns can be turned to the adolescent's developmental advantage is deferred to the chapters on technique.

THE ADOLESCENT'S STYLE OF RELATING

When adolescence begins, a youngster is subjected to a multipronged attack on his sense of self-esteem. The invading forces include the impact of unpredictable and uneven sudden changes in body configuration and size, an unacceptable upsurge of forbidden impulses, and the adolescent's own need to devalue his parents, thereby losing a valued part of himself. The subjective response to this onslaught is a vague, anxious sense of inner loss and injury. The adolescent, as a result, is eager for new human relationships but is equally driven to use these relationships primarily to bind his psychic wounds. Although he desperately needs human identification patterns to restore a sense of direction, he is unable for several reasons to involve himself in any relationship which requires him to take a consistent interest in the other person. His attachment to other people—other adolescents as well as adults—is primarily narcissistic.

This does not mean that the adolescent will necessarily exploit the people to whom he relates, although he may. It merely means that the tie to others is strongly colored and mainly determined by the adolescent's inner needs. The actual characteristics of the other person are not totally ignored, but they are important primarily as orientation points around which the adolescent weaves complex fantasies and suppositions which are emotionally important to him. Other equally obvious characteristics are simply ignored if they do not fit the adolescent's view.

> An inhibited 14-year-old boy in therapy for six months expressed amazement on learning that his therapist was married.
>
> "You seem more like the 'swinger' type," he exclaimed.
>
> The therapist had worn a clearly visible wedding band throughout his contact with the adolescent. The same therapist had been accused of being hopelessly old-fashioned and an obvious square by other adolescents with different needs.

The adolescent's hunger to merge with an individual who seems to have a workable identity structure must live in uneasy coexistence with the fear that merger may actually occur. The adolescent's opposition to therapy, his therapist, and the therapist's ideas is often a reaction to a fear that the fragile identity he is nurturing may simply be overwhelmed by the strength of the therapist's personality. Perhaps this is the core of the dread of dependency which the adolescent frequently demonstrates. Certainly one is often impressed that youngsters who are most fearful of the dependent role in the psychotherapeutic relationship have parents who frequently intrude into the adolescent's psychological privacy in an attempt to dictate his style of life .

The observable adolescent style of relating to others is the outer manifestation of inward distress. The adolescent often shows an intense but still fleeting and superficial attachment to other people. There is a searching quality, frequently described as fickle, as the adolescent reacts to real or fantasied qualities in new objects which promise an external solution to his inner turmoil. It is also characteristic that he hopes for total solutions and therefore is regularly disillusioned by those to whom he attaches himself. Of course, with the progression of adolescence, the attachments take on an increasingly adult form, although an ebb and flow of mature and immature attitudes toward the loved or admired person will continue until young adulthood. The impact of these characteristic adolescent styles of relating on the problem of establishing a therapeutic alliance will be immediately apparent to the reader. Not only will the styles of relating affect the early phases of therapy, but they must also be considered in attempting to understand "transference" phenomena in this age group.

THE THOUGHT OF THE ADOLESCENT

For many years, the peculiar thought processes of the adolescent have been noted by both the clinician and the creative artist. Prior to the monumental contribution of Jean Piaget, however, the unusual nature of these cognitive processes has been explained on the basis of the emotional changes characteristic of the developmental phase. Piaget has pointed out that we must also consider the way in which the intellectual functioning of the adolescent influences his behavior and emotions.

According to Piaget (Piaget, 1967; Flavell, 1963), the capacity for formal operations appears in early adolescence. This style of thought allows the youngster for the first time logically to manipulate thought itself. In the preceding phase of concrete operations, the child developed a capacity for logical manipulation

of isolated problems and an understanding of the interrelation-
ships of material objects. The advent of formal operations allows
the construction of general theories of the interrelationship between various facts, problems, and ideas. As the adolescent develops the capacity to think about thought itself, he is able to
manipulate mere possibilities. Piaget states further that the emergence of a new stage in conceptual development is invariably
marked by an increase in the egocentric use of the new cognitive
ability and by a preoccupation with testing and utilizing the recently acquired skill. The adolescent is therefore fascinated with
his shining toy of truly abstract thought, and he plays with it
endlessly.

The adolescent applies this ability for abstract thinking to his
world and overemphasizes its strengths and capacities as a tool
for reshaping the reality around him. Clinically, this tendency
appears as a belief in the omnipotence of thought and a grandiose
overestimation of the adolescent's capacity to alter his world by
merely thinking about it. There is often a sense of impatience
with adults, who seem to be dawdling and needlessly complicating
problems which could easily be solved by a logical approach. In
many youngsters, this development is accompanied by a quickness
and acuity of logical thinking which is truly outstanding. In this
regard, it is of interest to note that many mathematicians and
theoretical scientists, who deal almost entirely in symbolic logic,
make their most important theoretical contributions during late
adolescence and early adulthood.

This development in the cognitive area reinforces the emotional
predisposition to narcissism during adolescence. The omnipotent,
messianic preoccupations in the thought of the adolescent may
be determined not only by his narcissistic withdrawal from the
real world and internal objects, but also by the parallel developments in the unfolding of the cognitive apparatus. It seems
that the adolescent needs and deserves the opportunity to play
with his thoughts and to develop elaborate if unrealistic and fanciful plans to revolutionize social, political, and scientific practice
just as the infant needs to shake his rattle and the latency child

to build his collections as they master and consolidate earlier cognitive development.

A related area in which the adolescent makes use of his newly developed skill in manipulating thought is in the discussion of ideologies. The adolescent is struggling toward a sense of commitment to some life view and therefore spends a great deal of time thinking about and talking about lifestyles and the meaning of existence. This interest in ideology is readily observed in the articulate, studious, middle-class adolescent with his endless dialogue about life goals and values. However, as Shainberg (1966, 1970) has shown, the preoccupation of certain constricted and limited adolescent boys with their automobiles is also an implicit representation of their mechanized sense of self.

The therapist who wishes to treat adolescents must be prepared to listen to extended discussions which he would dismiss as intellectual defensiveness and resistance in adult patients. In fact, he should not only listen, but at appropriate times join the ideological discussion. Some guidelines for dealing with intellectualizing in adolescents are offered later.

THE ADOLESCENT AND SOCIETY

The adolescent's view of adult, organized society contains inherent elements of ambivalence. If the adolescent intends to find a place for himself in society, he naturally will have a strong curiosity about the nature and structure of this organization he plans to join. As noted, however, the adolescent is above all things a deductive thinker. His curiosity about society does not necessarily lead to an active study of its institutions, methods of operation, and reward systems. In addition, he is sadly deficient in knowledge of the behavior of human beings. Since he is utopian in outlook, he can develop only a limited interest in a historical perspective. He is more likely to devote himself to extensive fantasy, speculation, and theorization based on the most superficial and cursory examination of the data.

The adolescent who "drops out" and cannot accept the possibility of amalgamation into the adult world may be more interested in a depth study of society, but the value of his efforts may be decreased by the strong bias which accompanies his work. He is interested only in verifying his opinion, already self-validated, that society is corrupt, unchangeable, and inimical to basic human needs.

Even the adolescent who is more favorably inclined toward the adult world will have some mixed feelings about accepting an apprentice or student's role despite the value of this intermediate step on the path to adulthood. The adult world is, after all, his parents' world. The adolescent is still engaged in the struggle to escape dependent ties to his parents. He is reluctant to place himself in a comparable position with other adults. It is very difficult, especially for the younger adolescent, to accept his limitations comfortably, even those that are simply human. Internal conflicts, as well as shortcomings, tend to be externalized and dealt with as though they were environmental enemy forces. The adolescent cannot be entirely at peace with the world because he is not at peace within.

The capacity to tolerate inner strife is developed only gradually. Often, the adolescent cannot afford to learn the truth about society when that information would interfere with some of his self-protective fictions. This is often most clearly apparent in his dealings with the aspect of adult society closest to him, namely, his parents.

This state of affairs is complicated by adult society's views of the adolescent, which is often as irrational and unconsciously determined as are the adolescent's attitudes. Pearson (1958) has described the unconscious competitive, fearful, erotic, and envious attitudes which parents often harbor unconsciously toward their adolescent children. Brody (1968) has viewed adolescents as a minority group, noting that they are often responded to, as a group, with stereotyped attitudes and expectations that could only be described as prejudiced. He also suggests that this state of affairs plays an important role in the formation of an "adolescent contra-culture" with compensatory claims of superiority to the dominant adult society. One of the authors has tried to describe the effect of these kinds of adult attitudes on the management of adolescent behavior elsewhere (Meeks, 1967).

Adolescents struggle along an unstable interface between their peer culture and adulthood. In even the smoothest adolescence, thee is some mutual shaping and accommodation between the adolescent and his parents. The game is one of negotiation and compromise, no matter how much some adults may wish that a stricter approach would simplify life. Our society eventually guides the adolescent into an acceptable adult role in most instances, but, after all the arguments, threats, cajolery, coercion, and capitulations, we find that the process of molding our youth also has altered our notion of adulthood. Maturity and youth constantly shape one another.

Viewed objectively, the battle of the generations would seem to end in victory for both sides in the yield of a wider and more flexible set of adaptive skills. Subjectively, however, both sides often feel defeated. Too often, the young person feels that he has compromised his ideals whereas the adult suffers a nostalgic longing for a simpler and somehow nobler past, now lost forever.

Unfortunately, as we will discuss in detail later, some adolescents are committed to extending their energy to construct a purely fanciful view of themselves, the world around them, and the intentions of other people. These young people, whose sense of "potential competence" has been severely restricted due to early trauma or constitutional deficiencies, are often trapped by the upsurge of omnipotence and omnipotentiability in adolescence. They are no longer influenced by most life events and, without therapy, may simply continue to be preoccupied with adolescent dreams. Often they live these out with tragic, even fatal results. These are the youngsters who suffer "malignant" emotional disorders.

THE ADOLESCENT AS UNCLE TOM

Several studies have suggested that the much-discussed adolescent rebellion is more myth than fact, especially in adolescent girls (Douvan and Adelson, 1966; Grinker, 1962; Offer, 1969;

Offer and Offer, 1968, 1975; Offer et al., 1970). Offer's (1987) recent work concludes that most nonpatient teenagers are well adjusted and get along with their peers, teachers, and families.

Some authors have expressed concern that American adolescents are actually tame organization men who never battle through a real adolescent rebellion and therefore never achieve full autonomy (Friedenberg, 1959, 1965; Goodman, 1960). These authors feel that the apparent conflict between the generations represents an unimportant skirmish whose main function is to obscure the fact that the important battles are not fought. This view probably represents a failure to understand the nature of the adolescent revolution. The revolt that absorbs the adolescent is primarily internal and is directed more against memories of old attachments to the parents than toward current adult domination and control.

Erikson (1968) has argued well that autonomy and a clear sense of identity are always found in some workable and personally meaningful alliance with dominant cultural themes and available role patterns. Although one may yearn personally for the more individualistic, self-directed, and ethically oriented American character of past generations, such an identity may be poorly adapted to current American culture. A workable personality for twentieth-century America may need to emphasize easy amiability and compromise rather than strict adherence to principle in all matters. Current social conditions may favor a generalized, although possibly superficial, friendliness rather than a pattern of mannered formality counterpointed with passionate involvement with a few intimates. The social conditions of urbanization, easy geographic mobility, corporate business structure, and massive population growth which have fostered these styles of relating are factors to which the adolescent must adapt, not conditions that he has created.

Adolescents, despite their affinity for ideological discussion, are not effective agents of real social change. They are more frequently noisy and highly visible riders on a bandwagon they cannot afford to miss. It seems unfair to expect the adolescent, struggling with internal turmoil and possessing only a superficial

Daniel Offer, M.D., and J. L. Offer (1975) have spent much of their professional lives studying the habits of normal American adolescents. They feel that their data do not support the classic explanation of adolescence, especially the description of adolescents as philosphical, ascetic, and introspective persons. Offer (1987) stated that 80% of nonpatient adolescents are happy with themselves most of the time. He estimated that 20% of adolescents are emotionally disturbed.

understanding of the cultural landscape, to do the adult world's dirty work of social criticism and reconstruction. It is enough that he stand ready to follow intelligent and passionate leadership, carrying the banners of the cause and shouting its slogans. Adolescents, as a group, are well informed and thoughtful consumers of new or at least historically relevant ideologies. They are in no position to assume the responsibility of devising and manufacturing them. It has been suggested that the hope for a solution of our social problems lies with our youth. This may be true, if sensible and knowledgeable adults will provide reasonable blueprints for reconstruction. Our youth will labor untiringly if they are provided a job description that makes sense to them and then are left to their own techniques of implementation. Even an author as favorably impressed by the youth culture of the sixties as Roszak (1969) says of the young person's desire for new ideologies, "The appetite is healthily and daringly omnivorous, but it urgently requires mature minds to feed it."

The adolescent who comes to psychotherapy needs assistance in gaining enough freedom from his internal strictures so that he can voluntarily commit himself to the lifestyle of his own choice. His therapist has no right to select the leaders the adolescent will follow, only the responsibility for assuring a reasonably free election.

ADOLESCENT ADAPTATION

Although the adaptive techniques and ego defenses utilized by adolescents are not unique to this age, some characteristic patterns of emphasis can be observed. These general preferences give adolescent patients a particular style and flavor which distinguish them from adult patients to some degree. An awareness of coping behaviors which are typical for the age group is an essential background that allows the therapist to recognize deviations which may have diagnostic importance.

The friendless adolescent and the adolescent who prefers adult companionship are good examples of patterns which should alert the therapist to probable areas of emotional conflict. The turn toward peers is an almost universal adaptive technique for the adolescent. This hunger to have friends is related to at least four pressures on the adolescent.

1. His internal need for narcissistic support. Friends of the same age group can provide support not only by offering the sense of acceptability inherent in belonging to a group, but also by sharing guilt and thus reducing the shattering impact on self-esteem of a superego outraged by the increase in libidinal and aggressive drives at puberty.

2. The strongly felt need to loosen both dependent and unconscious erotic ties to the parents in preparation for eventual independence and mature love. The companionship of peers offers some substitution for the loss of support entailed in this process of leavetaking.

3. The absence of a comfortable, or even bearable, sense of individual identity. Faced with the anxiety of this internal struggle to define a bearable sense of self, the adolescent often prefers the safety of belonging to a "we" to the terror of becoming an "I" (Deutsch, 1967).

4. To a large extent, group formation is forced on the adolescent by social realities. The process of secondary education and the college experience in a specialized and technological society requires us to place large numbers of adolescents together apart from their families. This spatial contiguity, coupled with the "minority group" status of the adolescent, strongly encourages the formation of intense ties between young people.

Adolescents use their peers to back their demands for greater freedom and to validate their grievances toward their parents and the remainder of the adult world. In unity, there is some strengthening in their vulnerable position.

The use of the group to avoid awareness of anxiety is especially evident in the preoccupation of adolescent groups with "fun" and "action." The complaint "there is nothing to do" is not so much the jaded grumbling of a pleasure-mad sophisticate as the anxious lament of a trembling soul desperate to stay one jump ahead of a pursuing host of internal demons.

THE POWER OF WORDS

At times, the adolescent pauses in his flight to turn and face up to the enemy within. He rarely makes this stand alone. His choice of weapons against the demons requires the company of at least one other person who will be asked to serve as a listener. A listener is essential to the plan of action, since the adolescent seems intent on subduing his inner problems with words. He plans to talk them to death, and the adult listener sometimes wonders who will succumb first, the demons or the listener.

This adolescent chatter often has an incessant, driven quality because it is used in the service of intellectual defense. The content of the verbalizations may be frankly introspective at times. These monologues may contain rather accurate insights into some of the adolescent's conflicts which he is able to face by maintaining some distance from their associated affects. Still, as Blos (1963) has pointed out, the defense of intellectualizing does permit greater tolerance of instincts and is therefore largely a positive emergency measure during adolescence.

More often, the voluble ruminations are not so clearly related to the adolescent's personal feelings, but take the form of philosophic discussion. A very personal concern can usually be discovered underlying the philosophic issue when these weighty pronouncements are carefully attended.

A very unhappy 13-year-old spent her first few therapy hours bitterly accusing the adult world, including her therapist, of hypocrisy. No adult, she proclaimed, was what he pretended to be. This led to long and bitter tirades against religion and against her parents for forcing her to attend a church whose articles of faith she could not in conscience accept.

Shortly thereafter, when a therapeutic relationship was established, she wished to discuss her dangerous sexual provocation of older boys whom she told that she was 16. She noted in a letter to the therapist, "I've been yelling about all those hypocrites. I guess I'm the biggest one of all."

At a deeper level, she seemed to be referring to the incongruity between her rigid infantile superego and the emerging sexual feelings which seemed foreign to her. She had some awareness that her precocious leap into heterosexual behavior was "hypocritical" in the sense that it was defensive and by no means an expression of an actual readiness for heterosexual encounter. In her conflicts over denied dependency on her mother and her overwhelming guilt, she tried to maintain equilibrium by a spurious sexual aggressiveness.

If the adolescent can be garrulous at times, he can also be unbelievably taciturn. Total retreat into a glum and irritable silence is more disturbing to most adults than intellectual prattling. The intuitive feeling, often voiced by parents, that withdrawal is more serious than open conflict is correct. Usually, these silences cover a sense of being overwhelmed. During such times, the adolescent frequently adopts ascetic attitudes which cause him to experience almost unbearable feelings of guilt and shame. No progress in integrating the new instinctual striving is made in this atmosphere of self-suppression. At best, the adolescent can use these self-imposed exiles to lower the amount of external stimulation and to lick his wounds. At worst, he can paint himself into a misanthropic corner that he has too much pride to leave, even when he would like to do so.

MISDIRECTION

Magicians discovered long ago that it was not necessary for the hand to be faster than the eye if the observer could be led to look in the wrong place. To accomplish this, the magician uses large and obvious movements to divert attention from more subtle movements which are essential to the trick. Blackstone used to open his act by producing a live goat on stage. The great fuss he raised with his cape diverted attention from the fact that behind the cape he was carrying the goat under his arm! The technique is known as misdirection.

Adolescents seem to use these diversionary tactics frequently, especially in hiding attitudes and affects which they do not care to face or to have others notice. The method is especially effective when the affect to be hidden is a quieter, more gentle feeling. It is not always easy to detect the sadness and dependent longings a young person is experiencing when one's anxious and irritated attention is commanded by his belligerent and angry rantings.

The defensive technique that I am calling misdirection, then, could be defined as the exaggerated expression of one felt affect in order to hide from the self and others the presence of a concurrent, less acceptable affect. The utilization of this defensive operation explains why the adolescent often seems to go to extremes in the expression of a single feeling, especially of anger. Misdirection gives the adolescent a one-dimensional affective tone when it is employed. He appears at these times to be a real "Johnny-One-Note" on the emotional scale. The stereotyped and unchanging nature of the affective expression can be a clue that other shadowy feelings may be lurking behind the fireworks in the foreground.

This defensive pattern is somewhat related to the "reversal of affect" described by Anna Freud (1937). Reversal of affect refers to the adolescent's attempt to avoid the struggle and anxiety aroused by his positive attachment to his parents by reversing these feelings into a bitter hatred. A less virulent technique of disparagement of the parent has been described as a typical adolescent defense against an actively seductive parent of the opposite sex (Sachs, 1966).

Of course, a similar pattern has a wider defensive value in simplifying and resolving identity conflicts. Erikson (1968) has discussed this as a demand for "totality" when a richer sense of "wholeness" cannot be achieved. The adolescent who grasps at totality amputates not just single affects, but larger portions of his personality in order to achieve a constricted, but comfortable, sense of identity. He sacrifices richness and complexity to obtain a shallow sense of certainty (see also Shainberg, 1970).

APOLLO VERSUS DIONYSUS

Special mention should be made of the adolescent's varied attempts to adapt to his superego conflicts. These behaviors are a frequent source of confusion to the adult observer. Very often, when it comes to the adolescent and his conscience, things are simply not as they seem to be.

Pattie was a 15-year-old whose rebellious behavior and apparent sexual promiscuity became so outrageous that her distraught family in desperation placed her in a psychiatric hospital. On the ward, she paraded her precocious pulchritude in a seductive display which made Sadie Thompson look like an inhibited old-maid schoolteacher. Since the adolescent boys on the ward were all racing about, tongues awag, approaching something which might have been called heterosexual panic, Pattie was seen in emergency daily therapy sessions.

In the first two sessions, she contented herself with systematically dismembering her parents with a cool, detached sophistication. By the third session, however, she was ready to give her therapist the full treatment. She somehow eluded the censoring eye of the nurses and arrived for therapy (barely) clad in a brief miniskirt, topped by a low-cut, skin-molded peasant blouse. She spun around in the office modeling her outfit. Then, hands on hips, she leaned seductively forward and innocently asked her therapist, "Now do you see anything wrong with these clothes?" Her therapist retained his composure and looked at her steadily for a long moment. "I think you secretly feel like a dirty slut," he said. "And I think that must be a lousy way to live. Why don't we talk about why you're doing this to yourself?" Pattie broke into tears. "You stupid ass," she shouted and fled the office.

Her flamboyant exhibitionism lessened over the next few days. During the weekend, she remarked to a ward nurse, "Dr. X (her therapist) is not such a bad shrink. At least you can't fool him."

As her therapy proceeded, it became clear that Pattie's extravagant deliquency was simultaneously an effort to disclaim and escape a rigid superego and an unconsciously calculated effort to force others to control her behavior.

The variety of similar patterns is virtually endless. Many adolescents who appear to exhibit poor ego structure and deficiencies in impulse control are actually thrashing helplessly in the grip of an infantile superego which will not permit the comfortable and orderly expression of impulses. These adolescents can permit gratification only by linking pleasure with self-destructive and self-punitive extremes. They feel that it is okay to sin a little or even a lot if you promise to die tomorrow.

Not all of them are so flamboyantly "going down in flames" as was Pattie. The self-destructive behavior may be quieter and more subtle. The adolescent may merely fail his school work, "rebelliously" refuse to accept honors, or demonstrate a sullen refusal to enjoy anything. The built-in self-punishment evens the tally and therefore allows some expression of pleasure-seeking behavior. The combination often appears to the puzzled, angry (and sometimes envious) adult as a self-indulgent and willful flaunting of social expectations. The typical adult response makes it easy for the adolescent to externalize his superego conflict. The limiting adult is invested with the viciousness, rigidity, and anhedonia which actually reside in the adolescent's own superego.

GHOSTS, GOBLINS, AND THINGS THAT GO BUMP IN THE NIGHT

Many adolescents show an intense interest in the supernatural. Some of their morbid preoccupations and beliefs would be quite pathological if expressed by an adult. Usually, these interests do not seem unpleasant or frightening to the adolescent. In fact, they are usually presented in a playful manner and may be the basis of entertainments such as visiting "haunted houses" in groups. Astrology and other occult sciences also hold great fascination for many adolescents.

Frankie, an intelligent, nonpsychotic 16-year-old girl, bounced cheerfully into a therapy session. Bubbling with enthusiasm she announced, "Now I know how to make myself invisible!"

Frankie had frequently discussed a fantasy wish to be invisible which seemed to have multiple dynamic origins. She now explained, "You get a human head and three black beads. You put one bead in each eye and one in the mouth. Then you draw this design on the head and bury it. You water it with the finest brandy for three days and then. . . ."

"Wait, wait," said the therapist. "I'm still back at the beginning. Where do you get the human head?"

"Oh," said Frankie airily. "That's no problem. You just go out and get one."

Even risking the pun, the gleam in her eye could only be described as devilish.

It is striking that much of the interest in the supernatural seems related to the question of death and immortality. One gains the impression that not only is the fear of death very real to the adolescent but death often seems imminent. In typical adolescent fashion, however, this fear is usually handled in a counterphobic manner.

There seem to be two primary sources of this inclination toward the occult within the adolescent. The first we have already encountered as the adolescent's belief in the omnipotence of thought. Reality ties are loosened and magical thinking is easily accepted. It is a logical short step from a personal alteration of reality to a world peopled by witches, ghosts, and seers.

The second factor is the adolescent's effort to relinquish his parents and many aspects of his childhood self. In a psychological sense, death and mourning are an immediate part of the adolescent experience. Since the adolescent's greatest fear is fear itself, he sometimes happily embraces his demons and, gulping back his fears, takes them out for a romp.

Some youngsters become preoccupied with supernatural and occult topics to a degree that goes beyond curiosity about death and immortality and also goes beyond a rebellious interest in beliefs that most adults do not value. These disturbed youngsters make use of satanism, either individually or with a few like-minded friends, as an embodiment of evil power. The purpose of the preoccupation with and belief in evil power—whether it be satanism or the neoNazi philosophy of skinheads—is to organize and represent the intense, chaotic sexual and aggressive feelings that these adolescents are experiencing. According to King (1988), self-styled satanism is a way for disturbed teenagers to organize a value system that endorses violent and antisocial behavior. He also feels that this preoccupation with evil power is synergistic with serious drug use in teenagers, since each one seems to promote the other. In general, the adolescent interest in the supernatural is reinforced by a generalized awakened interest in the irrational and mystical. This social movement is closely linked with the use of psychedelic drugs and other substances. The potential for destructive interactions in this area is quite frightening.

SUMMARY: IMPLICATIONS FOR PSYCHOTHERAPY

These developmental characteristics of adolescence pose many problems in psychotherapy. Because of the adolescent's style of relating and his preference for peers, it is often difficult to establish a therapeutic relationship. This is true not only because of the adolescent's distrust of the therapist, but because of the countertransference attitudes which this negative approach arouses. In the next chapter, we consider the personality characteristics which may help the therapist to establish a therapeutic alliance with adolescent patients. Later, we will be concerned with the techniques of establishing the therapeutic alliance and with the problems which are encountered by the therapist and the patient even after therapy is well under way and through the time of termination.

CITED AND RECOMMENDED READINGS

Blos, P. 1962. *On Adolescence: A Psychoanalytic Interpretation*. New York: The Free Press of Glencoe.

Blos, P. 1967. The second individuation process of adolescence. *Psychoanalytic Study of the Child*. 22: 162–186.

Blos, P. 1977. When and how does adolescence end: structural criteria for adolescent closure. *Adolescent Psychiatry*. 5: 5–17.

Blos, P. 1979. Modifications in the classical psychoanalytic model of adolescence. *Adolescent Psychiatry*. 7: 6–25.

Blos, P. 1980. Modifications in the traditional psychoanalytic theory of female adolescent development. *Adolescent Psychiatry*. 8: 8–24.

Blos, P. 1983. The contribution of psychoanalysis to the psychotherapy of adolescents. *Adolescent Psychiatry*. 11: 104–124.

Brody, E. B. 1968. *Minority Group Adolescents in the United States*. Baltimore: Williams and Wilkins Company.

Deutsch, H. 1967. *Selected Problems of Adolescence (with special emphasis on group formation)*. New York: International Universities Press.

Douvan, E., and J. Adelson. 1966. *The Adolescent Experience*. New York: John Wiley & Sons.

Erikson, E. H. 1968. *Identity: Youth and Crisis*. New York: W. W. Norton & Company.

Flavell, J. H. 1963. *The Developmental Psychology of Jean Piaget*. New York: D. Van Nostrand.

Freud, A. 1937. *The Ego and the Mechanisms of Defense*. London: Hogart Press. (New York: International Universities Press, 1946).

Freud, A. 1958. Adolescence. *Psychoanalytic Study of the Child*. 13: 255–278.

Friedenberg, E. Z. 1959. *The Vanishing Adolescent*. Boston: Beacon Press. (New York: Dell Publishing Company, 1962).

Friedenberg, E. Z. 1965. *Coming of Age in America*. New York: Random House.

Goodman, P. 1960. *Growing up Absurd*. New York: Random House.

Grinker, R. R. 1962. Mentally healthy young males (homoclites). *Archives of General Psychiatry*. 6: 405–453.

King, P. 1988. *Sex, Drugs & Rock 'n Roll: Healing Today's Troubled Youth*. Bellevue, Washington: Professional Counselor Books.

Meeks, J. E. 1967. Some observations on adolescent group leaders in two contrasting socioeconomic classes. *International Journal of Social Psychiatry*. 3: 278–286.

Offer, D. 1969. *The Psychological World of the Teenager*. New York: Basic Books.

Offer, D. 1987. The mystery of adolescence. *Adolescent Psychiatry*. 14: 7–27.

Offer, D. et al. 1970. A longitudinal study of normal adolescent boys. *American Journal of Psychiatry.* 126: 917–924.

Offer, D., and J. L. Offer. 1968. Profiles of normal adolescent girls. *Archives of General Psychiatry.* 19: 513–522.

Offer, D., and J. L. Offer. 1975. *From Teenage to Young Manhood: A Psychological Study.* New York: Basic Books.

Pearson, G. H. T. 1958. *Adolescence and the Conflict of Generations.* New York: W. W. Norton & Company.

Piaget, J. 1967. *Six Psychological Studies.* New York: Random House.

Roszak, T. 1969. *The Making of a Counter Culture.* New York: Doubleday & Company.

Sachs, L. J. 1966. Disdain as defense against parental seduction. *Journal of the American Academy of Child Psychiatry.* 5: 211–225.

Shainberg, D. 1966. Personality restriction in adolescents. *Psychiatric Quarterly.* 40: 258–270.

Shainberg, D. 1970. "It really blew my mind": a study of adolescent cognition. *Adolescence.* 5: 17–36.

CHAPTER 2
therapist qualifications: an essay

NEVER TRUST ANYONE OVER THIRTY

There is a widespread belief that young adults relate comfortably with adolescents and are accepted as leaders with greater ease than older individuals. Lewis (1969) has suggested that young individuals "may represent good identification models whose cultural values have not ossified, and who share an interest in the legitimate age-appropriate interests of youth." There may be considerable truth to this, in that the very young adult is closer to the cultural changes that produce much of the generation gap. Often, however, this affinity is markedly strained when points of disagreement appear between the adolescent and his slightly older mentor. The young adult's closeness to his own adolescent struggles can tempt him to relive them vicariously through the adolescent or to fight against that temptation with rigid moralistic attitudes of rejection and condemnation. Often, the young adult lacks the security of personal identity which would permit him to view the adolescent's impassioned trials and missteps from a perspective of tolerant understanding.

This is not to say that youth automatically prevents one from doing good psychotherapy with adolescents. The point is that being older does not automatically disqualify one. The adolescent can and will trust someone over 30!

The personality characteristics of the therapist are important, however, regardless of his age. The attitudes that he holds toward himself, toward society, toward the nature of human motivation, and toward young people are the factors which will dictate his effectiveness with adolescent patients.

30

GENERAL CHARACTERISTICS

There are some general characteristics which are probably necessary equipment for all psychotherapists. The first of these relates to the basic way that one views his fellow men and their behaviors. Some people are mystified and dismayed by aberrant behavior. They do not look below the surface of apparently strange and incomprehensible actions to their origins in strivings which are universally human. Needless to say, a nonjudgmental view which considers all behavior as potentially comprehensible within a human framework is essential in psychotherapy. Those who deal with the panorama of human adjustments by conveniently dividing the world into good and bad people will be unable to guide any patient through the moral dilemmas of psychotherapy and will be especially ineffective in work with adolescents. This does not mean that the therapist takes no stance in regard to the adolescent's behavior. Obviously, some actions are self-destructive and symptomatic. Timid avoidance of direct confrontation on these issues is as destructive as prudish condemnation. The important point is that even the most repulsive and self-defeating behaviors are comprehensible. The patient needs to know that we believe deeply that there are good reasons for everything he does, even when what he does is not good for others or for himself. The therapist's main activity is to help the patient discover his real goals and reasons. We hope that this book is pervaded with examples of this attitude as it affects the therapeutic response to many different clinical situations. It is basic to psychotherapy of the adolescent.

The therapist can be more successful in helping the adolescent patient understand his inner motivations if the therapist is not an intrusive person. It may seem paradoxical to speak of respect for the patient's privacy while discussing the goal of inner revelation. In fact, this apparent contradiction is not real. Most of us react with some measure of caution to a listener who seems too eager to know all about us. Too active curiosity may kill the cat of spontaneous self-revelation. The adolescent is especially sensitive to psychological intrusion. Early in therapy, he may react to the most casual question as though it were a third degree. He

This "essay" was written by Dr. Meeks about twenty years ago. It seems unnecessary to try to update this particular chapter with more current references. However, readers of this book will want to become acquainted with *Adolescent Psychiatry*, since recently that journal featured a special section on "Countertransference Responses to Adolescents." Peter Giovacchini (1985) organized the section and contributed an article in which he described, among other material, what it feels like and also what to do when your patient refuses to leave the office at the end of the hour. Natasha Wallace and Marquis Wallace (1985) revealed what it was like to present a patient, who was almost noncommunicative, at a continuing case conference. In another paper Stephen Zaslow (1985) presented three interesting case reports and candidly shared his own feelings and reactions.

needs to understand that we want him to get to know himself. Our need to know about him is justified only by our status as a hired guide. What he does, thinks, or wishes is our business only because it is necessary to our work. Since we can only do as much of this work as he wishes, we should encourage him to reveal only those matters that he is ready to expose for purposes of exploration. In fact, it may be important occasionally to caution the adolescent about excessive candor early in therapy (St. John, 1968).

The adolescent therapist's recognition that human drives, appetites, and wishes are universal does not blind him to the variability of the expression of these urges. As Noshpitz (1969) has said, "The wishes are pretty much the same from person to person, but the disguises—ah, there we have the full panoply of human personality to contend with."

We have discussed in the previous chapter some of the disguises which are especially prevalent during adolescence. We must also recognize that the expression of drives varies within a social context. Prevailing mores influence which disguises are deemed acceptable or even praiseworthy and which are regarded as evil, perverse, or pathological (Lewis et al., 1973; Hughes, 1969).

ULTIMATE VALUES

In our opinion, however, the therapist must not drift into a bleak and apathetic relativism based on cynical reductionalism. Dynamically oriented psychiatrists have occasionally slipped into this kind of arrogant contempt for human achievement. We rather suspect that there is a bit of narcissism involved in the insistence that religious insights, artistic creations, and innovative constructs in the business and scientific worlds are "just" the expression of inhibited libidinal or aggressive drives. The psychological pundit then becomes the only person who is actually dealing with basic truth. He rides high until someone points out that his activity consists of "just" sublimated voyeurism and his speculations of "just" mental masturbation.

This simple-minded reductionalism not only ignores the historical fact that man has always searched for transcendental meaning in life, but ignores the importance of ego synthesis and the boundless potential of human mutuality. Adolescents especially need help in recognizing that man does not live for gratification alone, but also moves toward a sense of coherence and meaning within a value context which includes some explicit or implicit stance toward the needs and values of other people. Dynamic psychology has shed a great deal of light on the nature of the drives which energize man's quest for the "good life." All well-trained therapists may be justifiably proud of their knowledge in this regard. On the other hand, we must humbly recognize that our knowledge of the "fuel sources" does not fully enlighten us regarding the details of overall structure of human personality and, further, that it tells us virtually nothing of the best directions for the human spirit to pursue. We know a lot about psychic gasoline, little about detailed structures of the vehicle, less about road maps, and almost nothing about proper destinations.

One essential derivative of the views of the human condition expressed above is optimism. The therapist works best with a basically hopeful viewpoint, tempered by a realistic recognition of the difficulties involved in psychological maturation and the relatively limited help which one person can offer another in the process of moving toward maturity. All human beings need hope, and psychiatric patients are often critically low in their supply. They look to their therapist for replenishment. The therapist can meet this need without perjuring himself or being unrealistic if he has an optimism based on a realistic faith in the human desire for emotional growth and the healing potential of psychotherapy (Harrison and Carek, 1966).

A sense of trust in the basic goodness and worth of all people, regardless of how repulsive their superficial defensive armoring may be, is indispensable to the establishment of a therapeutic atmosphere. Maurice Levine (1942) has described this inner goodness as the "third layer," which may be obscured by a first layer of hostile or avoidance defenses against interpersonal contact and a second layer of anxiety, narcissism, and irrational infantile needs. At the level of the third layer, however, all men long for a warm and fair interaction with their fellow men.

CHARACTERISTICS SPECIAL TO THE ADOLESCENT THERAPIST

This "basic trust" in others must extend to those caught in the developmental squeeze of adolescence if one intends to work effectively with adolescents. Persons who respond to adolescents with stereotyped negative expectations will have little success in treating them. There are people who cannot overcome a tendency to find adolescents irritating or boring for a variety of personal reasons. Other therapists will find that they can respond positively to some adolescents but not to others. It is best that both groups accept their own limitations and refer the disliked adolescents who happen to come their way to others for psychotherapy.

Of course, it is not necessary to approve totally of every adolescent whom one treats. Fromm-Reichmann (1950) even goes as far as to say, "If a person comes to see the psychiatrist, this implies a need for changes in his personality; and if a psychiatrist accepts a person for treatment, this means that he recognizes that person's need for change and that he hopes to be instrumental in the patient's ultimate attainment of these necessary changes. This being so, the question of whether or not the patient in his present mental condition and with his present personality trends is to the psychiatrist's liking is beside the point." Possibly, this viewpoint expects too much of the therapist and ignores the realities of his vulnerabilities. It may be worthwhile for therapists to aspire toward such an ideal goal, but this aspiration should not blind them to their real limitations. Almost all therapists will occasionally encounter a patient whose first and second layers of personality will produce so much anxiety in the therapist that he will be unable to work effectively with the patient. If the therapist cannot overcome this feeling through introspection or consultation with a colleague, he would be unfair to make the patient a victim of his limitations.

Another personality characteristic important to any therapist is a fine sense of tact. The old adage that you can say anything to a patient if you say it the right way is especially applicable to the adolescent patient. With his exquisite narcissistic vulnerability, the adolescent demands a delicate touch. This is easy to overlook, since the adolescent himself, in his single-minded lunge toward an authentic adulthood, rarely shows great tact in his dealings with the therapist.

Skill in tactful confrontation is essential in the early stages of therapy and comes to have a growing importance in the intensely emotional interchanges which characterize later stages of treatment. The ability to be direct and yet courteous in a tumultuous interaction implies a high level of personal comfort in dealing with feelings stirred by the adolescent. A squeamish avoidance of confrontation and interaction cannot substitute for honest communication which still respects the adolescent's feelings. Tact does not imply an absence of firmness or a failure to face issues.

THE ADOLESCENT THERAPIST AND MORALITY, NEW AND OLD

Since the adolescent is most often threatening in the spheres of morals, ideology, and identity, the individual with marked conflicts in these areas may find it difficult to be comfortable with the adolescent. This is perhaps especially true of the therapist with latent, unexplored problems of this kind, the therapist who long ago settled for "totality" rather than "wholeness" for himself (Erikson, 1968).

The adolescent questions and attacks primarily those values which Veblen called "institutional process values." These are the values which receive their authority from tradition or other forces superordinate to individual men. These include those deriving from religion, status, and the vague coercive strength of the "establishment." They may be contrasted with "instrumental process values" which are more pragmatic and oriented toward problem-solving on a personal human plane. Wheelis (1958) has discussed the role of both processes in cultural change and in the inertia against change.

Obviously, with their basis in tradition and their prospective content, the institutional process values are critically scrutinized by the adolescent both as external representatives of his superego strictures and because of their importance in the development of ideological structures.

The therapist who is unaware of his own inflexible assumptions in this area may find the adolescent's challenge of traditional values quite troubling on a very personal level. His sense of outrage may block any effort to treat the adolescent's productions objectively and therapeutically. On the other hand, the therapist who is still actively seeking his own identity and is still in rebellion against cultural values is probably no better prepared to deal with the adolescent. He may inflame the adolescent's natural tendency toward iconoclasm and overlook the more important civil war within his patient which can only be resolved successfully through compromise and accommodation to psychological reality. The uncertain therapist may go even further in abdicating his responsibility and look to the adolescent patient to provide him with a workable ideology in a changing cultural scene. This unfortunate reversal can only result in chaos, not just in the therapeutic situation, but in the adolescent's life. Problems of this kind are especially likely to arise when therapists have strong utopian wishes which are untempered by a historical perspective on the complexities of social living and some of the inherent paradoxes in human makeup.

The therapist must try to prevent his anxieties (or his enthusiasm) about social revolution from obscuring the adolescent's main purpose in attacking social institutions. Despite historical currents, the individual adolescent's primary goal is to alter his own rigid conscience. It is the therapist's responsibility to assist him in this task with all the honesty and objectivity he can muster. In our experience, when this job is properly managed, the adolescent's politics become quite reasonable, although they do not always agree with ours.

ON ACTING ONE'S AGE

The adolescent therapist needs to be content with his own life and his own age level. This includes a comfortable awareness of the areas of living in which he is disappointed with himself. Arrival at maturity always includes facing up to some ambitions that have not been realized and mourning some fantasies which have never been gratified in reality.

The adolescent patient of the same sex easily becomes a potential vehicle for the accomplishment of frustrated self-expectations. Where the therapist has floundered, his adolescent alterego, benefited by the therapist's sage advice and counsel, may succeed. Once the adolescent's idealized image of the therapist is abused in this manner, it becomes very difficult to reestablish a therapeutic relationship which the patient can trust as totally committed to his best interest. Instead of being helped to become his own person, he has been issued as a new edition of the therapist.

Equally destructive to the adolescent patient is the therapist who feels defensive regarding his own deficiencies. Adults of this kind frequently react to adolescents as a threat and are fearful that the younger person will surpass them. Their response to this anxiety may be a subtle or overt suppression of the adolescent.

The challenging, competitive, depreciating, provocative adolescent can elicit this anxious suppression in adults who are gen-

erally fairly self-assured. Many adolescents are masters at ferret-
ing out the hidden emotional vulnerabilities and tender spots we
all harbor. Some of them can work on these relentlessly in an
attempt to assuage some personal sense of inadequacy or to justify
the avoidance of emotional involvement with the therapist. The
only dependable defense that the therapist can mount against
such an attack is personal comfort with his own peculiar configuration of strengths and shortcomings. Sometimes, it is necessary
to tell some of the more clever, shrewd, and manipulative adolescents honestly that we realize they can probably outsmart us
if they wish, adding that we can only hope that they will decide
to use their talents to help themselves rather than to prove their
superiority. Some of them can eventually understand that beating
the therapist is a hollow victory which brings no worthwhile tro-
phy or prize.

Still, the therapist's self-esteem frequently takes quite a beating.
He cannot depend on adolescent patients for any narcissistic supplies, since the adolescent has little to spare early in treatment,
whereas, later, adulation cannot be accepted without harming the
patient. The therapist must look for his emotional gratification
outside his therapeutic work. His own life must be sufficiently
gratifying so that he does not need to have his emotional needs
met by his patients. There are other rewards in treating adolescents which we describe in the chapter on termination, but the
therapist must not look to them for sustenance. He must be
sustained by other people outside of his work.

This need for sustaining human relationships in one's personal
life is especially felt during the runs of "bad hours" which therapists often encounter. To our knowledge, no one has ever adequately explained the phenomenon, but most therapists have
noted "good weeks" and "bad weeks" with their patients. At
times, it seems as though every patient is getting worse and holding the therapist totally responsible for this plight and hating him
for it. Even the strongest therapist's shoulders begin to bend
under the weight of session after session of depression, discour-
agement, and anger. His free time is interrupted by frantic parental and patient telephone calls which report runaways, suicide

threats, and a variety of demands for instant miracles. At this point, the most dedicated therapist wonders why he did not choose some sane and safe profession, say lion taming. He buys a book on the circus world and begins to read.

Surprisingly, if he maintains some degree of therapeutic objectivity and struggles with the problems, the tide turns. Suddenly, it seems that all his patients are improving and growing. He feels like a veritable genius and even his adolescents cautiously admit that he seems to know what he is doing. He throws away the circus book and wonders whether he should write the definitive work on psychotherapy. At the height of his elation, everything crashes again, and he pulls his circus book out of the wastebasket and tries to find his place.

Of course, this is an exaggeration, but it carries a grain of truth. The swings do disturb therapists, especially those who are experiencing them for the first time and do not yet appreciate their cyclic nature. We have the impression that they are more noticeable with adolescents because of their volatility and tendency to go to extremes. Sometimes, the reasons are apparent. Experienced psychotherapists dread the end of vacations not just because they hate to give up their pleasant regression, but because they expect that their patients will be angry over their absence when they return. Because of the prevalent anger, they expect some difficult hours. Other rough periods may be related to periods of time when the therapist is relatively less effective because of personal problems, fatigue, or minor illness. Still, there are those runs of "bad sessions" which appear inexplicable. These are probably due simply to the chance concurrence of periods of resistance and negative transference in several patients. Of course, such periods are actually evidence that therapy is effective and the patients are involved. A therapy which "runs smooth" is a therapy in which nothing of importance is happening. Still, we are inclined to accept consensual validation. If ten patients in a row tell us that we are not helping them, that we are personally obnoxious, incompetent, and a little stupid, too, it is not easy to retain balance, objectivity, and self-respect. The same thing could be said in reverse about the "good periods" when everyone seems to agree that we are unusually gifted, charming, helpful, and lovable. Through both kinds of excesses, the therapist must try to maintain a sense of professional competence and balanced optimism. 'Tis easier said than done.

The temptation to utilize the adolescent to gratify frustrated libidinal needs is perhaps even more dangerous than the possibility of using them for narcissistic self-enhancement. Although it is probably extremely rare for a therapist actually to act out sexual feelings toward an adolescent, the frequent occurrence of disruptive erotic countertransference and vicarious participation in adolescent sexual behavior is easily detected. It appears, sometimes with disarming honesty, sometimes masquerading as humor or unwarranted prudishness, in the material which younger therapists bring to supervision. It also makes itself known in the fantasies, dreams, and therapeutic blunders of the more seasoned practitioner.

Of course, it is not surprising that the adolescent is capable of stirring forgotten yearnings, especially in America. Not only is the healthy and vigorous adolescent undeniably attractive as a sexual object, our culture, contrary to all reason, assigns him a comfort in instinctual expression far beyond that enjoyed by the mature American. When this mythical image is coupled with the adult's nostalgic mourning for missed opportunities during his own adolescence, the mixture is potentially explosive. In these situations, the adolescent is not a passive victim. Because of his intense need for affection, the adolescent often can be quite seductive toward his therapist. The psychotherapist who would really prefer to be an adolescent, rather than treat an adolescent, is likely to encounter serious problems in the erotic area.

What is needed, of course, is not total freedom from such stirrings, but a comfortable awareness that they are present, and, more importantly, that they are illusory. If the therapist does not have a clear grasp of these realities, he or she can be easily led astray by the adolescent patient. Because of internal difficulties with his own superego, the adolescent must become a master of corruption. Since he practices daily on his own inflexible superego, he is likely to endeavor with equal fervor and subtlety to corrupt the superego of the therapist. In his skilled presentation, sadistic behavior can be disguised as healthy rebellion and movement toward autonomy; a narcissistic exploitation of another individual may be presented as growing sexual freedom and a healthy interest in heterosexuality. If the therapist has difficulty calling a spade a spade in his or her own life, the therapist may wake up at various points in therapy to find that the adolescent has taken him or her on quite a stroll down the primrose path.

THE THERAPIST AND RESPONSIBILITY

All of this touches indirectly on another necessary qualification for treating adolescents. This is the capacity to define one's area of responsibility and then to assume it without excuses or complaints. Adolescent patients frequently raise very confusing issues around the nature of the therapist's responsibility. Because of their dependency conflicts, the adolescents often say verbally that they are totally responsible for their own lives and the therapist need not concern himself. At the same time, they may communicate non-verbally partial or total irresponsibility which invites the therapist to prevent disaster. Obviously, since the goal is to maximize independence and autonomy, the therapist wishes to take as little direct responsibility for the adolescent as is consistent with common sense. Some therapists even say that their only responsibility is to make the adolescent aware of his real motivations and to discuss the likely consequences of any decisions in reality, leaving the final responsibility for his behavior always to the adolescent. This is a tempting posture, but we do not believe that it is consonant with psychological reality or with a realistic view of ethical professional behavior. It breaks down when faced with pathological self-destructive aims and in dealing with excessive aggression toward others. The therapist must recognize that at times the adolescent cannot take responsibility for himself because his "self" is overwhelmed by guilt, rage, or other turbulent emotions. The therapist must serve as an emergency ancillary ego at these times. If he does not accept this responsibility, tragic results such as suicide or homicide may prevent the adolescent from ever having a chance at autonomy and self-direction.

Other adolescents, who we have already described as having malignant problems, can be reached for treatment only if the therapist is willing to take control of their lives. Their omnipotent distortions must be addressed directly and their efforts to live out imaginary lives in illusory worlds must be interrupted. We will discuss these cases more completely later.

The important guiding principle for now is that the therapist takes responsibility for the adolescent's behavior only when it is essential for the youngster's welfare and the continuation of therapy. He relinquishes this responsibility at the earliest safe moment. He also encourages the adolescent to explore his reasons for soliciting the rescue operation in the first place. The therapist's behavior is regulated by the adolescent's cues and direct and indirect requests. Individuals who have a personal need to control or dominate others or to have others dependent on them are poorly suited to function as adolescent psychotherapists. They will tend to assume responsibility for the adolescent's life because they need to do so, not because the adolescent is asking for temporary assistance to prevent the overthrow of his rational decision-making capacity.

We must also consider the question of what the therapist is responsible for providing within the therapy contract. Obviously, the therapist does not offer to provide an active cure to a passive and helpless patient. Clearly, the therapist must teach the patient to share the responsibility for the process and the outcome of psychotherapy. The therapist, however, does have the responsibility for knowing what psychotherapy is all about and how the patient should function in order to derive maximum benefit from the undertaking. He has the further responsibility to convey this information to the patient in a way he can understand. The mechanics of this process are detailed in chapter 4, "The Therapeutic Alliance With the Adolescent," and in chapters 6, 7, and 8.

The therapist has a continuing responsibility to recognize those times when the adolescent is unable to function well as a patient. At these times, it is the therapist's job to notify the adolescent of this state of affairs and to help the adolescent to understand the forces that sidetracked the treatment process. The adolescent must do the important work of therapy. The therapist's primary responsibility is to provide on-the-job training and some tactful quality control. The therapist can never "give" insight. If the therapist knows his job and stays in his proper role, he may help the adolescent to find his own insight by saving him the effort of looking in the wrong places. This does not imply passivity. In the role of expert guide, the therapist must often be quite active in asserting his leadership. On the other hand, he must be as unobtrusive as possible when the adolescent is on the right track.

THERAPY FOR THE THERAPIST

It is probably apparent to the reader that the kind of flexible and objective self-awareness described above can usually be achieved only through the hard-won insights of an intensive personal experience in psychotherapy or psychoanalysis. For most individuals, this is probably true, although one cannot overlook the occasional person who seems to reach a balanced knowledge of himself without the aid of formal therapy. Furthermore, many individuals seem to have a kind of personal integration which some adolescents can utilize as an anchoring and orienting focus even though these adults show little of the flexibility extolled above. These people, who are often referred to as "strong personalities," can offer a great deal to the troubled adolescent if their strength is real so that they have no need to recruit converts to their idiosyncratic view of life. The therapeutic experience such a person can offer the adolescent may be limited in its scope and goals, but it may be sure and valuable within its limitations.

SUMMARY: WHAT PRICE INSIGHT?

In closing these remarks on the optimal personality makeup of the aspiring therapist of the adolescent, we should mention one final "true believer." This is the psychotherapist, usually (but not always) unanalyzed himself, who has perverted an oversimplified psychoanalytic understanding into an institutionalized process value system. Such a therapist holds with a religious fervor to the belief that "real" therapy consists solely of making unconscious conflicts conscious. The inadvisability and occasional danger of such an approach with most adolescents have been pointed out by several authorities in the field. The adolescent is struggling, with already overburdened equipment, to effect a synthesis of conflicting tendencies within his personality. He cannot be assisted by an approach which further accentuates the schisms within him and ignores his desperate need for his defenses.

The effective therapist for the adolescent patient is above all things a pragmatist. His personal value systems, even if committed to such a lofty and irreproachable value as absolute intrapsychic awareness, cannot be allowed to take precedence over the central task of aiding the adolescent to achieve any organization of his warring personality fragments that is reasonably safe for the patient, fairly benign and constructive toward his environment, and yet productive of a personal sense of vigorous direction in living. A sense of pluralism of human behavior and value patterning, an acceptance of the fascinating variety of viable and useful human identities, is useful to any therapist but is of critical importance to those who treat adolescents.

It should go without saying that such a view breeds both respect for one's younger fellow men and a healthy sense of humor in watching oneself and the adolescent patient as both struggle with their roles in the human comedy.

CITED AND RECOMMENDED READINGS

Erikson, E. H. 1968. *Identity: Youth and Crisis.* New York: W. W. Norton & Company.

Fromm-Reichmann, F. 1950. *Principles of Intensive Psychotherapy.* Chicago: University of Chicago Press.

Giovacchini, P. L. 1985. Countertransference and the severely disturbed adolescent. *Adolescent Psychiatry.* 12: 449–467.

Harrison, S. I., and D. J. Carek. 1966. *A Guide to Psychotherapy.* Boston: Little, Brown & Co.

Hughes, H. S. 1969. Emotional disturbance and American social change. *American Journal of Psychiatry.* 126: 21–28.

Levine, M. 1942. *Psychotherapy in Medical Practice.* New York: The Macmillan Company.

Lewis, J. M. 1969. Changing moral concepts. *Southern Medical Journal.* 62: 290–294.

Lewis, J. M., et al. 1973. Development of a protreatment group process among hospitalized adolescents. *Adolescent Psychiatry.* 2: 351–362.

Noshpitz, J. 1969. Drugs and adolescents. Presented at a seminar on childhood and adolescence by the Department of Postgraduate Education, University of Texas Southwestern Medical School at Dallas, April 25–26, 1969.

St. John, R. 1968. Developing a therapeutic working alliance with the adolescent girl. *Journal of the American Academy of Child Psychiatry.* 7: 68–78.

Wallace, N. L., and M. E. Wallace. 1985. Transference/countertransference issues in the treatment of an acting-out adolescent. *Adolescent Psychiatry.* 12: 468–477.

Wheelis, A. 1958. *The Quest for Identity.* New York: W. W. Norton & Company.

Zaslow, S. L. 1985. Countertransference issues in psychotherapy with adolescents. *Adolescent Psychiatry.* 12: 524–534.

CHAPTER 3

the diagnostic evaluation of the adolescent patient

The evaluation process has the goal of understanding the adolescent's problem, accessing the youngster's strengths, and choosing a course of therapy which can utilize the strengths to move the adolescent toward maturity and emotional harmony with self and environment. This does not assume that harmony is necessarily compliant. The adolescent may develop into an effective, constructive critic of his or her world.

Sanchez (1986) was a resident in psychiatry at the time she wrote an award-winning article on the psychiatric diagnosis of adolescents. Sanchez pointed out that the psychiatric evaluation of these youngsters is complicated by the characteristics of adolescence itself, the therapist's conceptual framework, the personality of the therapist, sociocultural factors, and familial factors. She also developed a lengthy bibliography on this subject. According to Blos (1962), the evaluation must consider constitutional and physical givens, important life experiences, inner psychological structure, developmental status, and relationships with important others. These complex issues may be organized as the answers to seven basic questions.

1. *Does the adolescent have constitutional, genetic, or other organic limitations which have significantly affected development and which may now limit the potential for ego growth?*

The presence of mental retardation, brain damage, attention deficit disorder, specific learning disability, and the like are important facts in the comprehensive understanding of any adolescent. These problems color early development, producing

46

some fairly predictable attitudes toward others and the self. They also impact adolescence in a direct way, often interfering with the efforts of the young person to individuate and gain an independent self-confidence.

Severe physical illnesses, particularly if they are chronic and limit activity, may produce an enforced dependency which disrupts adolescent development. The illness may also set the adolescent apart from peers either in a factual way or in the adolescent's view of himself or herself as "different."

One needs to remember, however, that even youngsters with ego impairments can still benefit greatly from properly planned therapy. The judicious use of inpatient placement, medication, remedial education, and social skill training can work near wonders even in youngsters with basic and irreversible ego deficits.

There is also growing evidence that some illnesses have very strong genetic elements. There is convincing evidence that vulnerability to the development of depression (especially bipolar affective disorders), severe alcoholism, and schizophrenia is hereditary. A careful family history may yield very useful diagnostic information.

Major mental illness during adolescence often presents in atypical forms. Feinstein (1982) has pointed out that adolescents with manic-depressive disorder may have dramatic behavioral symptoms, in addition to pathological mood swings. For instance, manic-depressive illness can be manifested by severe adolescent rebellion; exaggerated self-esteem with grandiose conceptions of physical and mental powers; and sexual acting-out. When patients who have presented as behavior problems show intense affects, puzzling symptom pictures, and rapid changes in function, the possibility of major affective or psychotic illness should be carefully explored. A detailed mental status examination and formal psychological testing may help the therapist understand what is happening in the patient's mind.

It is also possible that previously undetected medical or neurological conditions are causing or contributing to the adolescent's psychological and behavioral symptoms. Any suspicious findings, especially when the overall clinical picture is atypical or inconsistent, should lead the clinician to follow up with biological testing and referral to a pediatrician or neurologist. These issues are discussed in chapter 22.

2. *What is the best level of psychological development which the adolescent has achieved?*

This question is complex and difficult to answer for any psychiatric patient. In adolescents, who frequently deal with developmental stress by either regression or an equally confusing premature leap forward, the problem may be bewildering. The distinction between regression and fixation, so important to prognostication, is often very uncertain during the fluidity of the adolescent phase.

Only meticulous attention to a complete developmental history and the capacity to decipher the latent content of the adolescent's behavior and verbalizations can yield the data for even a tentative conclusion on this point.

3. *What kind of object relationships has the adolescent established, especially with his parents?*

Correct assessment of this side of the adolescent's development is obscured by the phase-specific peculiarities of relating which were described earlier. It is particularly hard to derive a realistic view of the adolescent's previous style of relating to the parents in the face of reversal of affect, disparagement, and other defenses calculated to help the adolescent divest himself of dependent ties to the parent.

Again, the history plays a crucial role in arriving at the answer to this question. The adolescent's less guarded description of his relationships with peers may also be of assistance. Particular attention should be given to the covert expectations, hopes, and fears which the adolescent holds in regard to his friends. These frequently reveal a great deal about the strengths and conflicts present in the previous relationships with parents.

4. *Why is the patient ill now?*

In many youngsters brought for therapy during adolescence, the answer is simply that they are ill now because they have always been ill. This is true of youngsters with very severe behavior disorders which result from a basic failure in the socialization process. The parents may be antisocial themselves, overtly or covertly, or simply so rejecting of the child that they have never provided the affection and direction necessary to even rudimentary emotional development and identification with society's rules and goals. These youngsters are brought to psychotherapy in adolescence, not necessarily for the first time, primarily because their increased strength, cleverness, and motility have widened and deepened the impact of their antisocial behavior on their environment.

Other individuals, struggling with adolescence reasonably well, become ill in response to external traumatic events. Although their symptomatology is colored by their developmental phase, the focus of therapy should be on the mastery of the precipitating event.

Still, most adolescent patients are victimized by specific developmental stresses. Their illness is precipitated by the onset of adolescence and the tasks inherent in that period. This is not to say that their conflicts are purely adolescent. Very often, perhaps usually, adolescence merely activates and highlights points of relative weakness in the personality structure. These unsolved growth problems may not have been troublesome in earlier stages, but careful review of the developmental history usually reveals their presence underground prior to their eruption into open view during the volcanic upheaval of adolescence.

For most adolescents, this reactivation of latent conflicts has positive value which outweighs its negative implications. During the "trial run" at adulthood which adolescence permits, the young person has another opportunity to discover, demonstrate, and correct personality flaws without the severe and possibly irreversible consequences which might attend their emergence after commitment to adult goals and responsibilities.

Of course, this holds true only if the adolescent holds some hope of achieving adult competence. If the adolescent despairs inwardly and cannot reach out to others, the upheaval of the adolescent period simply leads to further inner disarray with a resulting increased need to distort reality even more flagrantly in the frantic effort to maintain a fictional sense of safety.

5. *Is the adolescent conflicted?*

This question could be restated in two other ways. Is the adolescent's behavior and adjustment ego-alien? Is the adolescent motivated to change?

The problem in answering these questions is the adolescent's reluctance to admit directly to a sense of conflict. He is much more likely to try to bluff it out and make the best of a bad thing, although there are some exceptions to this rule, especially in older adolescents. His indications that he is unhappy with himself and would welcome assistance are likely to be subtle and carefully hedged. Many experienced therapists think that even the adolescent who asks for psychotherapy is more likely asking for help against his parents than for help for himself.

Many therapists, especially those who are relatively inexperienced, place too great an emphasis on verbalized motivation. All patients who approach therapy honestly are ambivalent about it. Conscious motivation is a straw in the whirlwind of primitive emotions unleashed by exploratory psychotherapy. Most patients weather these storms only because their attachment to the therapist strongly reinforces their rational wishes to improve. Often, it is possible to assess the true nature of the adolescent's motivation only after a trusting involvement with the therapist has developed. Actually, before this stage has arrived, the adolescent himself does not know whether he is "motivated" or not.

6. *Does the adolescent have the capacity to view himself with reasonable objectivity and the willingness to describe his view to the therapist?*

This is, of course, a central question, since in outpatient therapy the therapist will have to rely heavily on the adolescent to report honestly both his behavior and his feelings as a basis for the therapeutic work. One cannot expect too much, however, especially in younger patients. Some defensiveness, distortion, and self-protection are anticipated and do not contraindicate outpatient work. All adolescents can be expected to "play games." One only expects that they will gradually develop a capacity to discuss the rules of the game and the prizes they are trying to win.

In the case of some youngsters with narcissistic and borderline disorders, the initial goal of therapy is to draw their unrealistic game playing into the therapy relationship. This "make believe" relationship is tolerated until the patient is gradually able to see the world and himself or herself more clearly.

7. *Will the adolescent's family permit and help the adolescent to change?*

The answer to this question may depend on the therapist's skill as well as the family psychodynamics. However, in cases of severe family system distortion the acceptance of and even need for psychopathology in the family's children make this question crucial. No adolescent is going to gain and hold psychological growth unless the family supports healthy functioning.

These seven questions are clearly interrelated to one another. One might even say that they are largely different ways of looking at the same basic question: how sound is the basic personality structure in this particular youngster?

The adolescent who has previously functioned in large measure at age-appropriate levels and has achieved fairly gratifying and stable object relationships probably has the capacity, if given proper assistance and if his family can allow it, to utilize the therapist as an ally in productive self-scrutiny. This remains true even if the presenting behavior is chaotic and bizarre. Trying to decide the true nature of the premorbid adjustment in the face of the distortions of the adolescent and his parents is truly a perplexing enigma. A tremendously important therapeutic step will have been accomplished if this problem can be resolved with substantial accuracy.

The remainder of this chapter is devoted to a description of the mechanics of the evaluation procedure followed by a fuller discussion of the diagnostic questions mentioned above and, finally, by the application of the answers to therapeutic planning.

THE EVALUATION PROCESS

There are no set rules stipulating the form which the evaluation of the adolescent patient and his family should take. Procedures must be dictated by the circumstances of the individual case and by the particular preferences and skills of the examiner. Any approach which permits a contact with the adolescent and his family comfortable and extensive enough to allow the collection of sufficient data to answer the diagnostic questions posed above is acceptable. However, experience can offer some guidelines which will apply to most adolescents.

It is often preferable to set up the initial contact directly with the adolescent, especially the older adolescent. Many adolescents are very concerned that the therapist will form an alliance with their parents. Other adolescents may not resent the coalition between parents and therapist, but may be encouraged to take a passive role, hoping that the adults will straighten things out for them. Scheduling the initial interview with the adolescent clarifies the therapist's intention to appeal to that part of the adolescent which is striving for autonomy, self-direction, and responsibility. It also offers the therapist an opportunity to observe how the adolescent responds to this invitation to maturity.

When the adolescent patient is opposed to the consultation, he also gives us the opportunity to observe how effective his parents can be in dealing with him. Many parents will ask how they should present and explain the necessity for the evaluation. This permits the therapist to demonstrate his willingness to help the parents, as well as his expectation that the parents take a significant portion of the responsibility for helping their youngster.

The parents should be advised to be honest with the adolescent not only about the nature of the interview, but also about the parents' reasons for requesting it. The therapist may freely offer advice about appropriate wording, since this is basically an attempt to educate the parents to a psychological view of their youngster's problem.

The father of a 15-year-old boy who was tyrannizing his family and involving himself in minor delinquencies called to discuss therapy for his son. When the therapist suggested an interview with the boy, his father said, "I don't think he'll come. He is already mad at us, especially my wife. He'll think we're trying to say that he's crazy."

"Do you think that he is?" the therapist asked.

"No, but he is acting very strangely. Sometimes he sits and stares at nothing for hours."

"I wonder if he's afraid that he may be going crazy," the therapist said. "Maybe you should discuss your concern with him. Tell him that you are worried about him and that you think he is probably worried about himself."

After further discussion of the appropriate approach to the boy, the father finally asked, "What if he still doesn't want to come, even after all that?"

"From what you tell me, that's very likely the way it will be," the therapist said. "What do you feel you should do as his father if it turns out that way?"

There was a long pause. Then the father emitted a long sigh which seemed a mixture of resignation and resolution.

"He'll be there," the father said.

The therapist simply cannot be a party to any parental plan to skirt the issue by pretending the youngster is coming for a physical checkup, to discuss school planning, or to take some tests for an ill-defined purpose. Such dishonesty would defeat the whole effort to establish an atmosphere of honesty, trust, and open communication. In situations where there is a high level of family conflict, however, it is appropriate for the parent to present the evaluation as a family undertaking. The adolescent may be told, "We have arranged for a series of interviews with Dr. X since we all seem to be having trouble living successfully as a family." Since this is quite true, there can be no disadvantage in emphasizing it to the adolescent. Suggesting this approach also has the advantage of making this point quite clear to the parents.

Some parents will not be able to accomplish the task of bringing their adolescent to his initial interview in a reasonably acceptable frame of mind unless the therapist departs from this usual pattern and provides them with some direct assistance. In these instances, the therapist should honestly admit to the parents that his contact with them may pose some problems later with their youngster.

The parental interviews should focus tactfully on the parents' already demonstrated problem in discharging their appropriate function in family leadership. If their problem cannot be resolved in a few contacts with the therapist, this supplies an early negative answer regarding the parents' capacity to assist the therapy. The therapist must then consider whether therapy for the adolescent would be more appropriately conducted on an inpatient basis or whether an extensive period of therapy for the parents should preceed any effort to work directly with the youngster. It is impossible to treat the adolescent if he is in omnipotent control of his environment or if his parents are determined to destroy him if he remains in their company.

Many therapists do not follow the procedure outlined above. They feel that they can evaluate the adolescent more effectively if they follow a more traditional child psychiatry approach and obtain a full developmental history from the parents prior to the interview with the adolescent.

Both approaches probably have their advantages and pitfalls. It is probably wise to choose the approach which feels most comfortable and then to utilize it consistently. The therapist gradually becomes acquainted with the particular "side effects" of his favored style and develops skill in managing them. As stated earlier, the end result is more important than any rule of procedures.

At some time during the evaluation, however, the therapist has the right and the responsibility to insist on seeing the parents, no matter who is seen first. The occasional adolescent who objects to this reasonable request is actually revealing an aspect of his problem which needs to be carefully explored and acceded to only under the most unusual circumstances. The therapist who agrees to this arrangement usually finds that he is the next victim of his patient's secretive control and that his therapeutic usefulness is nil.

When the adolescent is interviewed, the therapist must decide how many sessions are needed to gain the necessary information for treatment planning. This may vary from one or two interviews with an articulate adolescent who is "ripe" for therapy to four or five or even more if the adolescent is silent or otherwise highly defensive.

Many therapists find that one or more family sessions are useful in the course of a diagnostic evaluation. These may even include other siblings or relatives, such as grandparents, who live in the home. These family sessions not only may reveal patterns of family interaction which might be missed in individual interviews, but may assist the family in defining their problems and understanding what must be accomplished later during therapy.

PARTICULAR PROBLEMS IN THE DIAGNOSTIC INTERVIEW WITH THE ADOLESCENT

Negativism

The initial task in the diagnostic interview with the adolescent patient is to define the purpose of the interview and to help the adolescent to recognize and deal with his reactions to the procedure. Unless some measure of cooperation can be obtained, the diagnostic process cannot proceed. The most common problem with the adolescent patient is an open reluctance or refusal to participate in the interview. Even in dealing with this initial negativism, however, the therapist can gain important diagnostic information. Although the manifest emphasis is on conscious feelings about the present situation, the adolescent will display his usual defensive techniques and reveal some of his conflicts when confronted with the request that he talk openly about himself. The therapist should make note of these responses, but should comment on them only as they relate to the evaluation procedure. This is especially true in the younger adolescent, who may be more frightened by the implications of a psychiatric evaluation than patients of any other age group. These children are old enough to realize some of the implications of psychiatric referral, but are not old enough to have the objectivity of the adult or older youngster. The strong upsurge of instinctual impulses with which they are struggling, as well as their tendency to confuse fantasy with action, makes the discussion of their inner feelings very threatening. In addition, many of them attribute their prob-

lems to their guilty secrets—especially masturbation—and often
live in terror of being revealed. In short, they are already secretly
convinced that they are crazy—a confirmation they certainly do
not need!

Adolescents of any age who are straining to maintain a shaky
adjustment based on omnipotent defenses fight off self-disclosure
for the same reason. They see honesty and exposure of limitations
and vulnerability as threats to any sense of self-worth. Since they
recognize only the extremes of triumphant, all powerful superiority or helpless worthlessness they do not welcome investigation which threatens their public facade.

Early Negotiations

In all adolescents, the decision to consult a psychiatrist, even
when self-initiated, gives rise to intense feelings. If the examiner
does not attend carefully to these reactions and help the patient
to deal with them, he will have great difficulty in obtaining the
information he requires. The reactions which one anticipates are
closely bound to the age of the patient. The early adolescent is
likely to respond to the stress by denying that he has problems
of any kind. The 14- to 16-year-old patient is likely to admit that
there are problems, but then to blame them on his parents. The
older adolescent is better able to appreciate that at least some of
his difficulties are related to his own attitudes and feelings.

Adolescents of all ages, however, are skilled negotiators. Those
who are resistant to the exploration of their problems begin testing the therapist even during the diagnostic process. They are
interested to know whether the therapist will take an authoritarian, parental role with them. The testing may take the form of
direct invitation. After having revealed something of himself in
spontaneous conversation, the adolescent may suddenly ask,
"Wouldn't you like to ask me some questions?" The unwary examiner may accept the invitation and confirm the adolescent's
ambivalent hope and fear that he is faced with still another adult
who wishes to arrange his life. A better response might be to
comment, "I think you are doing very well in telling me about

yourself. Please go on." With the younger adolescent, one might go even further in encouraging responsibility by commenting, "I sometimes ask a lot of questions with younger children, but with guys your age I have found this usually isn't necessary."

The patient may also try directly or indirectly to force the therapist to promise that he will reward the youngster for discussing certain topics or for simply participating in the diagnostic evaluation. This may be presented negatively, "I don't see how talking about all this is going to help me." At other times, the appeal may be more openly dependent. "Mother says if I tell you all about my problems, you can straighten me out."

Can You Help Me?

Of course, the therapist cannot permit himself to be pulled into such an unprofitable contract. The focus must be returned to the obvious fact that diagnostic understanding must precede any reasonable decision about what can be done to help matters. The youngster can be told that he and the therapist can discuss this question when the diagnostic work is completed. Some openly rebellious adolescents would challenge this comment by declaring that they already understand themselves and know that they do not need psychotherapy or help of any kind. The therapist must either ignore or challenge this opinion, since obviously it would dictate an untimely end to the diagnostic process. The manner in which the therapist chooses to respond to this ultimatum will depend on his tentative understanding of the particular adolescent. If anxiety appears to be the predominant obstacle to discussion, the approach would be sympathetic and supportive. The therapist might agree that the youngster has demonstrated ability to solve many of his own problems. The therapist can explain that he has no wish to interfere with that process, but can also comment that perhaps there are some problems which the youngster has not entirely solved as yet and which may be difficult to discuss. It may be wise at that point to add, "At any rate, I'd like to get to know you a bit better." The therapist can then ask a neutral question regarding the youngster's school, hobbies, or plans for the future. This may permit a more natural flow of talk with more subtle introduction of important topics. The youngster may comment, for example, that he is interested in motorcycles, but that his parents will not buy him one. The therapist can then open the discussion of the parent-child relationship in a natural manner by asking, "They're not too interested in motors, eh?"

Youngsters who appear more angry and rebellious may require a more direct approach. The therapist may need to state openly that he feels the patient is simply stating his opposition to the consultation when he says that he does not need any help. Since most rebellious youngsters have not originated the idea of psychiatric referral, this fact may be recalled to him. The therapist can then inquire directly about feelings and wonder whether the attitude toward the diagnostic evaluation is mainly derived from anger. This may allow a discussion of the youngster's feelings about doing things that his parents recommend or demand of him, including his feelings about the evaluation. If he is able to reveal his rebellious attitude toward his parents, he may go on to a more extended discussion of his feelings about rules and authority figures.

Other youngsters are merely being provocative and teasing when they say that they do not need help. They do not expect an answer to their dare, but are testing to see whether the therapist is an anxious and defensive adult who must rise to every bait thrown his way. They are best managed by ignoring the gauntlet and pressing forward with the real business at hand. Others deserve a light, "Frankly, I hope you're right. My schedule is pretty full right now. However, someone thought you needed help and it's my job now to form my opinion. I can't just accept yours. Let's go ahead and see whether you and I agree or disagree."

You Better Not Help Me!

Not infrequently, however, one encounters an adolescent who has successfully erected a defensive facade which depends upon an apparent omnipotent control of the environment. Often, these youngsters are quite successful in manipulating their families. Since they do manage to externalize their illness, they feel quite strongly that they "have it made" and feel absolutely no wish to have their arrangement interfered with. As a rule, such youngsters would not be candidates for outpatient psychotherapy and would have to be either placed in a controlled environment which they could not manipulate or managed quite differently by their parents before they would be amenable to psychotherapy.

If outpatient therapy is undertaken in these cases it is often necessary to utilize special approaches with the adolescent as well as the family. We will consider these youngsters in chapter 5, discussing the reasons for their "malignant" resistances in more detail and exploring techniques which may permit them to utilize therapy.

On Keeping Your Cool

Commonly, the early interviews with an adolescent resemble a verbal fencing match more than a typical psychiatric interview. It is impossible to anticipate the myriad forms which the adolescent's testing behavior may assume during the diagnostic evaluation. The therapist must rely on his basic commitment to an open-minded, objective evaluation to guide his interaction with the adolescent. Since it is difficult, if not impossible, to work a confidence game on a person who is disinterested in larceny, the therapist can usually avoid being drawn into fruitless arguments with the adolescent. Like Sergeant Friday, the therapist should "just want the facts."

Since therapists are human, however, they probably will lose some of their rounds with adolescents. The therapist who wishes to work with adolescents must be able to shrug these off and return to the work at hand. A relaxed humorous comment to the effect that the adolescent won that round can sometimes actually improve the relationship between the patient and the therapist. Adolescents often have great difficulty in laughing at themselves and are therefore very critical of adults who are too stiff and self-important. Perhaps the adolescent, with his own narcissistic problems, intuitively recognizes that he cannot work with an adult who is similarly afflicted. At any rate, a sense of humor and a casual attitude are valuable attributes in interviewing adolescents. They are rivaled in importance only by the trait of honesty.

Tell It Like It Is

Adolescent patients frequently test this characteristic also. The adolescent who is engaging in behavior which is either extremely antisocial or very bizarre often asks the therapist's opinion about the seriousness of the problem. It is important that this question not be dismissed lightly. The therapist can reply that he can see that these are things that would worry anyone and must be a source of great concern to the adolescent. When this concern appears to be lacking, the therapist may well comment on this and wonder why the child is so disinterested in his own welfare. This may include an objective recounting of the personal risk involved in the behavior in question, including its effect on the youngster's opinion of himself.

An intelligent 18-year-old dropped out of college, although his work was at an acceptable level. He readily accepted psychiatric referral, since his parents were extremely distraught and he saw the evaluation as an opportunity to prove to them that his decision was entirely rational.

He was extremely cooperative during the initial interview, but demonstrated a breezy nonchalance about his decision to leave school. He spoke at length about how "up tight" his parents were, laughing at their distress over his withdrawal from school. His own philosophy of life emphasized the pleasures of the moment, and he was good-naturedly critical of the competitive attitude at the college he had been attending. Toward the end of the first interview, the therapist commented that the patient described his situation as though he were recounting a story about a friend. He was told that the incongruity between the importance of his decision to leave school and the absence of any strong feelings in the matter puzzled the therapist.

The young man became grave, but did not reply. On the following day, he called for an appointment, stating that the therapist's words had caused him to do some thinking. He had slept poorly and wanted to discuss some of his thoughts and feelings.

In the next interview, he began to explore his long-standing competitive relationship with his father, although it was much later in therapy before he began to appreciate the origins and extent of his inability to succeed and his true motives for leaving college.

Youngsters who have given up on themselves more completely, such as the seriously delinquent adolescent who has wholeheartedly adopted a negative identity, cannot so readily utilize the invitation to treat themselves more kindly. Still, the invitation must be clearly conveyed and continually repeated. Even the delinquent who actually does harm others pays a great personal price in the bargain. He must be asked why he always seems to express his aggression by drowning others in his own blood.

ONCE THE INTERVIEW GETS GOING

If these gross resistances to the diagnostic process can be managed, the interview with the adolescent can be conducted more or less in the same way as the diagnostic interview with an adult. Although it would be beyond the scope of this book to deal exhaustively with the techniques of psychiatric interviewing, some points of special interest in the initial interview of the adolescent should be mentioned.

The Adolescent and Silence

Silence is an important technique in psychotherapy, but most psychiatrists feel that it should be avoided in initial interviews. There is always the danger that the patient, who as yet has no relationship with the therapist, will interpret silence as disinterest and unresponsiveness. It is even less advisable to permit the adolescent to stew alone in mute discomfort. Silence is likely to accentuate the adolescent's anxiety, his fearful fantasies regarding the therapist, and his difficulty in perceiving the sympathetic and helpful attitude of the therapist. Any discussion, no matter how apparently or actually trivial or unrelated to the purpose of the evaluation, is preferable to an anxious silence. If necessary, the therapist should carry the conversation, periodically inviting the youngster's participation, and gradually assuming a more passive role as the child begins to talk more. As we have noted earlier, careful attention should be given to the youngster's feelings regarding the evaluation itself. Silence often results from anxiety or anger directly related to the evaluation.

The Adolescent and Confidentiality

Confidentiality is a point of great concern to many, perhaps most, adolescents. At times, the fear that the therapist will report their conversation to the parents becomes virtually a paranoid preoccupation. Often, this worry is not verbalized openly, but can be detected through its influence on the course of the interview. The adolescent may suddenly appear anxious after revealing something about himself and even retract the statement. The alert therapist will usually be able to guess when the question of confidentiality is troubling his patient. The problem should be openly discussed, not because this will always settle the issue, but to demonstrate an openness and honesty that may gradually convince the adolescent that he can trust the therapist.

It is usually possible to raise the subject of confidentiality as a natural part of the evaluation process. The youngster usually understands what you are driving at if you bring it up as a concrete issue rather than as an abstract concept. For instance, after interviewing the adolescent and before meeting with the parents, the therapist can ask, "Of all the things we have talked about, what is okay to discuss with your parents and what things do you not want them to know about?" The patient's answer may tell a lot about his relationship with his parents and it also protects the therapist from making some blunder with the parents early in the game. Of course, once the adolescent has given his view of confidentiality, the therapist should explain his own understanding of how it works.

Again, in the question of confidentiality, the therapist is confronted with the need for negotiation and discussion with the adolescent. If one promises complete confidentiality, this may pose serious problems. If the adolescent later confides plans for serious antisocial behavior, preparations for a suicide attempt, or other dangerous actions which require intervention, the therapist will have to break his promise in order to enlist the aid of parents or others. The admission by the adolescent patient that he is using illegal drugs without his parents' knowledge poses a delicate dilemma in this area, which today's adolescent therapist faces with painful regularity. Therapists generally do not promise to withhold knowledge of criminal activity from a minor's parents. In the case of the drugs, the activities are not only felonious, but are potentially quite dangerous to the adolescent. Still, many therapists who would be quite concerned and anxious in the knowledge that a female adolescent patient was engaging in active sexual behavior accept drug usage without blinking an eye! The problem of psychoactive drug usage is complex and is considered in detail later, but it is clear that it is another subject in which the adolescent should not be assured of blanket confidentiality.

What then can the therapist promise? First of all, and probably most reassuring to the adolescent, the promise can be given that the therapist will not convey any information to the parents without informing the adolescent of his intention to do so in advance. The adolescent's greatest fear is of a secret coalition between his parents and his therapist.

Second, the therapist should state clearly that the adolescent's feelings are confidential. Only the adolescent's actions will ever be considered for possible discussion with his parents, and then only if in the therapist's judgment the particular actions represent a danger to the therapeutic process, other people, or the adolescent himself.

ENTER THE PARENTS

Although some therapists suggest that the adolescent should be asked whether he is willing to permit the therapist to talk with his parents, this probably only confuses the youngster and creates an atmosphere of unreality. Parental involvement in their affairs is a fact of life for most adolescents, unless they have already left home. To play along with the adolescent's fantasy that he can solve his conflicts with his parents by wishing the adults out of existence can only block any rational therapy. The adolescent's parents have a right to know, in general terms, what their youngster's problem is, how serious it seems to be, the reasons behind the therapeutic recommendations, and what they can do to assist their youngster. These assertions remain true even when the adolescent's complaints against his parents are well grounded in objective evidence of parental inadequacy. To ask the adolescent's permission to talk with his parents implies that troubling family interactions can be safely ignored. This would not seem to be a very productive premise with which to begin therapy.

It does seem appropriate to offer the adolescent the option of attending the postdiagnostic conference with the parents. Youngsters of this age do have a right to be fully informed of plans which involve them. Conducting the treatment-planning session as a family interview may also be helpful in promoting an atmosphere of objective exploration toward family problems which have previously been the occasion for disruptive anger and mutual recrimination. This is also a good time to spell out the ground rules of psychotherapy (if this is the recommendation), including the rules regarding confidentiality mentioned above. This subject is explored more fully in chapter 9, "The Parents of the Adolescent Patient." Many adolescents, even when offered the opportunity of attending the postdiagnostic conference with their parents, will prefer to have an individual interview at the end of the diagnostic period to discuss the findings and recommendations.

OTHER DIAGNOSTIC PROCEDURES

At times, one needs information about the adolescent which requires referring him for psychological testing, physical examination, or other procedures. These recommendations tend to be resisted by adolescent patients. If the interview situation, which at least resembles typical social interaction, is frightening, the prospect of being tested with instruments that the patient does not understand poses an even greater threat. Adolescents are aware that psychological tests are designed to extract information which the patient may not have intended to reveal. Because of his many secrets, the adolescent certainly does not want his mind read.

It is important to explain honestly to the adolescent why the additional studies are necessary and what information they may reveal. When the adolescent is not given this information and allowed to discuss it fully, he often reacts to the diagnostic studies as though they were devious attempts to "get the goods on him." An electroencephalogram (EEG) may be interpreted as an underhanded effort to find out if he has damaged his brain by masturbating or by taking drugs or, in more disturbed youngsters, as a way of finding out his dirty thoughts.

In the postdiagnostic conference, it is important to report fully the findings of the special procedures and to correlate them with the youngster's life experiences. If, for example, an EEG has been ordered to rule out complex partial seizures in a youngster with episodic rage reactions, the negative findings should be correlated with the absence of postictal phenomena, amnesia, and other clinical data which have already been discussed with the patient. It should be noted briefly that projective tests may give a very misleading picture of the adolescent unless they are administered and interpreted by a psychologist with extensive experience with adolescents. Youngsters in this age group frequently appear much more ill than they actually are if their test productions are judged by adult norms.

Tests which screen for drugs have been much improved in recent years. Most necessary tests can be done with urine samples. When drug use is suspected the tests should be used even if the youngster denies usage. Many of the tests are quantitative and aid in understanding how extensive drug use has been. Adolescent refusal to submit to urine testing usually has the same meaning as a positive test.

Although it hardly needs to be stated, no evaluation of an adolescent is complete without a current thorough physical examination. This should be arranged through the family physician since it is often too confusing to adolescents to have both psychological and physical testing and evaluation by the same person.

DIAGNOSTIC INTERVIEWS WITH PARENTS

Several goals must be kept in mind simultaneously during the diagnostic sessions with the parents of an adolescent patient. The parents' feelings about their child's problems may range from a deep concern, verging on panic, through rage and wishes to reject the child, to subtle enjoyment of the youngster's behavior. Most often, the parents are puzzled and frightened, especially if the adolescent appeared to be adjusting adequately during earlier childhood. Their intense feelings result in a loss of perspective, which causes difficulty in gaining information about past family relationships and events in the youngster's earlier life. The parents must be offered the opportunity to ventilate these feelings, not only to clear the way for consideration of historical data, but because of the importance of such feelings to an understanding of the adolescent's current life situation.

Usually, it is possible to learn a great deal about the parents' conscious and unconscious attitudes toward the adolescent by carefully noting which aspects of the current situation they choose to emphasize in their discussion with the therapist. However, some caution should be exercised in drawing conclusions from observations made during the emotional turmoil which often characterizes initial diagnostic contacts. Defensive reactions both to the family crisis and the prospect of revealing their family problems to an outsider may produce confusing distortions.

The mother of a 14-year-old delinquent girl was referred for therapy by her daughter's therapist. The referring psychiatrist, who had performed the diagnostic evaluation on the family, apologized for the referral, stating, "I don't think there is much you can do. This mother would really just like to pretend that this girl is not her daughter. She's the coldest fish I ever saw."

Actually, the mother wept throughout most of her first therapy hour. She expressed her conviction that her daughter's problems were completely her fault and recognized that she was still struggling with antisocial impulses, especially in the sexual area, herself. When asked why she had not told the referring physician of these concerns, she could only say that she was in a state of shock after the daughter's delinquencies came to light.

"I guess I thought someone was going to come and arrest me," she said.

DEVELOPMENTAL HISTORY

The importance of detailed information about psychological development in children has been challenged in recent years. A number of studies have demonstrated that the accuracy of parental recall is rather poor. It is still worthwhile to spend some time in asking about the adolescent's earlier development even if one cannot accept the parents' statements as literal truth. One can often detect evidence of gross difficulties in psychosocial progression, such as serious maternal depression during infancy, separations from one or both parents, family deaths, and periods of poor adjustment such as difficulty in toilet training. It is also possible to draw some tentative conclusions about the extent of parental investment in the child and the quality of the parent-child relationship in the past. Parental statements in this area must be explored and taken as tentative, since the current family conflict may influence memory selectively and impart a retrospective overemphasis or denial of negative aspects in the parent-child relationships. Often, persistent attention to the history is rewarded with valuable data, such as the parental recollection that their belligerently independent adolescent has shown considerable evidence of excessive dependency on one or both parents in the past.

Even if the information gathered in a developmental history only approximates the actual occurrences, the process of inquiring about longitudinal development helps the parents to refocus their efforts toward understanding their youngster's problems. The very act of exploring the past suggests to the parents that their youngster's problems are comprehensible and possibly soluble. The investigation of the family history may also bring to light any feelings of guilt which the parents harbor about their role in the adolescent's difficulties. When these are openly discussed, the therapist can compliment the parents for their frankness, suggest that emotional problems are rarely so simply understood, and state his intention to discuss frankly with them all factors which may have had importance in creating the family difficulties.

It is also important to do a careful search of the family history for evidence of mental illness or drug abuse which might have hereditary elements. This is valuable not only when it turns up actual evidence of familial diseases but when it merely gives the family the opportunity to ventilate concerns in that area.

"Well, she's just like your wacky Aunt Ruth!"

"Don't be ridiculous, woman. Aunt Ruth's not blood kin to us. She just married Uncle Sam."

"Oh, yeah. I forgot."

And so forth.

In the case of adopted youngsters this data is very important although sometimes difficult to obtain since the adoptive parents may have limited information about the youngster's biological relatives. Certainly the adoptive parents' fantasies and projections in this area may prove very important.

Some therapists prefer to have the parents interviewed by a colleague. This has some disadvantages in that the parents are better able to support the therapy fully if they have had a valuable personal experience with the therapist. For this reason, it seems wise for the adolescent's therapist to spend some time with the parents, even if he is unwilling or unable to conduct the parental diagnostic interviews. The trust which can result will be invaluable during difficult periods in the adolescent's therapy. Even if there are few difficult periods, adolescents who undergo successful psychotherapy will move toward independence from the parents. Many parents find this transition emotionally painful, even if they intellectually recognize that it is necessary. A positive relationship to the therapist may permit the parents to tolerate essential growth without consciously or unconsciously sabotaging the therapy.

DIAGNOSIS IN ADOLESCENCE

There is a danger in assigning a clinical diagnosis to the adolescent. Erikson (1968) has pointed out that the adolescent is very susceptible to the expectations of his society. The adolescent's present and future role is partially defined by the reaction of his culture to him. It is clear that some clinical psychiatric diagnoses, such as schizophrenia and psychopathy, carry powerful implications for future functioning, and are in effect statements that the adolescent's problems are chronic and his prognosis poor. The effect is to decree an identity as a sick individual for the adolescent. Since the troubled adolescent is especially unsure of what and who he is, he may be very sensitive to such definitions of his identity. For this reason, it is important to exercise caution in assigning clinical diagnoses during the fluidity of the adolescent period. Even if the patient and his family are not directly appraised of the diagnosis, it will certainly affect the therapist's attitude toward his patient and will indirectly be perceived by the youngster.

This cautionary statement does not alter the fact, however, that there are adolescents who are doomed to a lifetime of psychiatric disability (Masterson, 1967). In fact, some investigators feel that the early onset of schizophrenic symptoms, coupled with a history of childhood problems of poor academic performance, poor peer relationships, and evidence of "minimal brain dysfunction," strongly suggests a poor prognosis for the schizophrenic (Offord and Cross, 1969). It is unfair to assign the adolescent prematurely to the life pattern of chronic psychiatric illness, but it is equally unfortunate to hold out false hope and to apply extensive and unwarranted treatment approaches to families and youngsters who are already burdened with the crushing problems of coping with process schizophrenia.

The diagnostic classification system offered by the Group for the Advancement of Psychiatry (GAP) (1966) suggests that the diagnostician attempt to differentiate between "acute confusional state of adolescence" and "schizophrenic disorder, adult type." A third category of "other psychoses of adolescence" is included to permit the classification of those symptom pictures which cannot be easily fitted into one of these two categories. This classification system also recommends avoiding terms such as borderline psychosis, prepsychotic states, latent psychoses, or pseudoneurotic psychoses, utilizing instead the appropriate personality disorder category with a notation of severity and a description of the disturbances in ego function drawn from a specially prepared symptom list.

The GAP report has also dropped the diagnostic terms "psychopath" and "sociopath." Instead, they utilize the general category of "tension discharge disorders" with two subcategories, "impulse-ridden personality" and "neurotic personality disorder." Generally, the latter group is more amenable to outpatient psychotherapy. The diagnosis suggests an inner state of conflict which is expressed through symbolic unacceptable behavior. Potential personality strengths exist which may be mobilized by appropriate psychotherapeutic help. Impulse-ridden personalities suffer from more serious deficiencies in personality structure. Treatment must include extensive retraining, external controls on behavior, and gradual correction of early deficiencies in ego development.

The entire GAP report should be carefully reviewed, not only because of its usefulness as a nosological system, but because of its thoughtful discussion of the complex theoretical issues underlying the classification of emotional illness in children.

DSM-III-R also provides the categories of schizophreniform disorder and brief reactive psychosis to permit the clear recognition of psychotic symptomatology without making a full scale diagnosis of schizophrenia when the duration of psychotic symptoms is less than six months but more than two weeks (schizophreniform disorder) or when psychotic behavior follows a severe stress and lasts no longer than two weeks (brief reactive psychosis).

It will be interesting to follow youngsters given these diagnoses to ascertain whether their adult adjustments show a clear outcome pattern.

In general, it would seem preferable for the clinician to make every effort to arrive at the best possible clinical diagnostic category in every adolescent whom he evaluates. This clinical diagnosis may then be viewed as highly tentative, since it is recognized to represent a cross-sectional statement regarding personality structure during a period of life in which longitudinal changes may be quite rapid and very extensive. Masterson's (1967) research indicates that diagnostic categories do have predictive value, however, despite the problems of correct assessment.

THE DIAGNOSTIC SUMMATION

Despite the need to establish a tentative clinical diagnosis, prognostication and treatment planning depend more on an overall assessment of the strengths and weaknesses of the adolescent's personality functioning than on any diagnostic term. The diagnostic data should be reviewed with an eye to the seven questions posed earlier.

1. *Is there clear evidence of biosocial ego deficiencies in the form of a history of learning disability or attention deficit disorder? Have these problems been diagnosed earlier and have the parents provided understanding at home and available remediation and treatment?*

If the youngster's problems have been previously undetected, the years of failure and frustration have often scarred not only the adolescent's self-image but also relationships with other people. Severe narcissistic disorders, delinquency, drug use, and other "malignant" patterns of disability are often the end point by the time adolescence arrives. Treatment must address these defensive positions adequately before remediation is possible but the long-range need to help the youngster achieve success must be kept in mind even while struggling with unpleasant defenses.

Is the youngster suffering from a major mental illness? A strong family history of mental illness or addiction, major disorganization on mental status, and evidence of delusions or hallucinations in the absence of drug ingestion all suggest the possibility of major affective illness or psychosis. Even when the patient's primary symptoms are behavioral, these findings suggest the need for psychological and biological testing to search further for evidence of specific disease entities. This vigilance is especially important now that the pharmacotherapy of the major illnesses is highly effective.

2. *What level of psychosocial development has the adolescent achieved?*

Although the adolescent may be obviously preoccupied with pregenital concerns and behavior at the time of referral, other diagnostic data may lead you to suspect that this represents a regression. A documented history of performance at a better level is one observation which would encourage a better prognosis. In addition, the patient may present dreams, fantasies, or a style of relating during the diagnostic interviews which will belie the primitive psychological picture suggested by the presenting symptoms.

A 16-year-old boy was seen for evaluation because of stealing, destruction of property, and periods of staring vacantly into space. His parents stated that he was uncontrollable and they were concerned that he might become homicidal.

In his interview, he varied between angry silences, anal obscenities, and tight-lipped avowal to "get" his parents for arranging the consultation. Whenever the therapist asked a question or made a comment, the boy would lean forward menacingly and snarl, "What?"

The therapist repeated himself a few times, and then realized what was happening. He commented amiably to the boy, "I get the feeling that you're trying to scare me out of saying anything. You must be pretty worried about what I might say."

"I don't give a shit what you think of me," the boy snapped.

"How about what you think of you?" the therapist asked.

For a moment, the boy lowered his guard and grinned.

"Well, now that might be worth talking about some," he said.

Actually, he was not able to talk about his crippled self-esteem and foundered through the remainder of the interview, angry and suspicious. However, his brief comment did reveal that he was potentially capable of engaging in a human relationship at something other than an anal control level.

It is particularly difficult to assess correctly the best psychosocial level achieved by the adolescent because of the tendency for regressions during this phase of development to be "ego regressions" rather than "libidinal regressions." Anna Freud (1965) has noted that in ego regression primitive impulses are accepted and acted upon, rather than giving rise to internal conflict. The adolescent's ego is relatively weak and is therefore easily drawn into the regressive process. The absence of resistance to the infantile impulses and the lack of conflict can cause the adolescent's immaturity to resemble fixation more than regression. This can lead the therapist to conclude incorrectly that the adolescent is fixated at pregenital levels.

3. *What kind of object relationships did the adolescent have with his parents prior to the onslaught of adolescence?*

Although historical data will be of central importance in answering this question, much can be learned from observing what the adolescent emphasizes in rejecting his relationship to his parents. Generally speaking, those adolescents who have been most dependent on their parents are the most adamant in their demands for independence. Very often, their shrill and uncompromising insistence on total freedom and their denial of any attachment to their parents are accompanied by behavior which is unconsciously calculated to pull their parents into their affairs. The louder the adolescent screams that his parents treat him like a baby, the more likely it is that he is struggling with intense dependency yearnings toward them.

A similar situation exists in some adolescents who are extremely angry with their parents for not being omnipotent. These children have, for a variety of reasons, invested their parents with a fantasied capacity to protect them from all harm and to ensure their success in all endeavors. When this illusion collapses with the onset of adolescence, the youngster feels cheated. Often, the parents are denounced as phonies, hypocrits, or idiots. The tone of disappointment is conveyed by a joke which a teenage girl told her psychotherapist.

A teenage boy approached his father with questions about the conflict in Nicaragua, abortion, government's role in social programs, and the like. He wanted his father to give him clear-cut judgments and answers, but instead the father, after each question, equivocated, noting that the situation was very complex and that there was no simple answer. He ended his comments each time by saying, "You're just going to have to make up your own mind on that, son."

After this happened five times, the son finally said, "Dad, would you rather I wouldn't bother you with all these questions?"

"Gosh, no!" said the father. "You have to ask questions. How else are you going to learn?"

In the joke, it is the father who fails to recognize that there are some things that he cannot teach, but in fact the disillusioned adolescent himself is begging, "Say it ain't so, Pop!"

We have already mentioned the adolescent who utilizes disdain to protect against incestuous feelings. One may also suspect Oedipal conflicts when the adolescent reports and demonstrates a pattern of constant bickering with and withdrawal from the parent of the opposite sex, especially when this is accompanied by accusations of sexual repression and unattractive personal qualities. This follows a general rule of thumb with the adolescent. When he stresses and emphasizes one particular vector of affect, you may get a glimpse of significant problems if you sight backward along the arrow in a reverse direction. Often, the adolescent unknowingly betrays his real feelings when he "doth protest too much."

4. *Why is the patient ill now?*

Generally speaking, adolescent illnesses which are precipitated by clear-cut external events, such as the death of a family member, or which result primarily from the stress of the developmental crisis of adolescence respond well to outpatient psychotherapy. This is true even when the regressive features of illness are quite marked. On the other hand, even deviations which appear relatively minor on the surface may be very difficult to resolve if they reflect long-standing personality patterns. Generally, a chronic situation of this kind suggests a strong family involvement in the behavior pattern. Typically in these instances, the impetus for consultation comes from outside the family group. In these cases, the final three questions will usually be answered in the negative. The adolescent is not conflicted, the family has no real wish to permit or aid in change, and the adolescent will be unable to observe his own feelings objectively as a result of his comfortable immersion in a neurotic family pattern. Some alternate treatment approaches for these youngsters and their families will be discussed later.

It should be noted that adolescents and their families are no more skilled than other psychiatric patients at recognizing the events which precipitate emotional illnesses. Often, the examiner must take the responsibility for noting temporal connections between life occurrences and the onset of symptoms of illness. The examiner can then search for the dynamic connections between the meaning of the particular event, the developmental history of the adolescent, the adolescent's verbal and nonverbal behavior during the diagnostic study, and the course of the illness. Only in this way can the true significance of the traumatic event be fully understood.

5. *Is the adolescent in conflict?*

As stated above, except for some older adolescents, one rarely encounters an adolescent patient who views his symptoms as totally ego-alien, completely originating within himself, and subject to solution by self-understanding. Like the adult patient with a weak ego structure, the adolescent is largely alloplastic, self-justifying, and resistant to any therapy which would require him to face up to himself.

The examiner must content himself with minor clues that the adolescent is dissatisfied with himself. These brief self-disparaging comments, veiled hints of guilt, and half-admitted anxieties are viewed as the surface evidence of the presence of workable discontents below ground which can be tapped later, when the adolescent is comfortable enough to permit exploration.

The examiner should also ask the parents if the adolescent has expressed discontent with himself or with his symptoms. Naturally, their answers must be studied in the full light of their motivations. Angry, rejecting parents may see the most anxious youngster as blissfully unregenerate. On the other hand, indulgent, overinvolved parents may misread deep self-concern in the faint scribblings of manipulative mock remorse.

Only when there is some real evidence of inner conflict, even if faint, should the adolescent be considered for individual outpatient treatment. If the conflicts are only between the adolescent and the outside world, the adolescent will not be motivated to form a therapeutic alliance. These youngsters will require other treatment approaches, at least initially, to produce any hope of success. Often, this question cannot be answered definitely without a trial period of treatment. Many adolescents with neurotic personality disorders appear to be impulse-ridden personalities until the pattern underlying their "senseless" acting out can be appreciated (Sifneos and Nemiah, 1984).

6. *Does the adolescent have the potential capacity to observe his own feelings and behavior and to report them with some degree of objectivity?*

Many aspects of the diagnostic information must be considered in seeking the answer to this question. The presence of at least low average intellectual ability is probably a necessary basis for a therapeutic approach which relies on a verbal readjustment of attitudes and experiences. Youngsters with unchangeable reality problems, including serious impairments in organic brain functioning, may be unable to face themselves honestly without benefit of a specially constructed living situation which could be adjusted to their special needs. Outpatient psychotherapy, with its emphasis on personal responsibility, may place undue demands on the coping mechanisms of these youngsters.

We have already described briefly the adolescent who has adapted neurotically but successfully to a neurotic family situation. If the parents can offer such a youngster sufficient gratification within the family pathological configurations, there may be little impetus for growth and honest evaluation of the skewed contract which the adolescent has accepted. One can often suspect such a state of affairs when the adolescent accepts the absence of satisfactory peer relationships without complaint and without any apparent drive to achieve them. These youngsters are best treated either in conjoint family therapy or on an inpatient basis if their symptoms are severe. Family therapy is discussed in chapter 8.

Other youngsters may reveal chronic impairment of the capacity to put feelings into words or to share their feelings with others. Rather than showing the disguised and distorted feelings which one expects in adolescent patients, these youngsters either seem totally cut off from knowledge of their inner experience or else have never developed the trust in another person which would encourage them to make the effort of trying to explain themselves to someone. The examiner should accept this view of an adolescent patient with great reluctance and only in the face of overwhelming evidence. Many adolescents have temporary problems in recognizing and describing their emotions which would not interfere with the eventual utilization of outpatient psychotherapy. With only a diagnostic evaluation to guide him, the examiner can erroneously assume that these defects are chronic and irremedial, especially if he is angered or frightened by the adolescent's initial inability to cooperate.

Frankly psychotic adolescents are obviously unable to assess their feelings and behavior realistically. These youngsters usually require inpatient treatment until their reality testing becomes more reliable. Many of those with transient psychotic symptoms may then be candidates for outpatient psychotherapy.

A final group of youngsters who cannot objectively observe their own behavior are those who are intoxicated with their control of the environment and are virtually convinced of their own omnipotence. Usually, their conflicts can be studied only when they are prevented from discharging their every anxiety in action. As a rule, this can be accomplished only with the control and leverage offered by an inpatient setting.

7. *Will his family help the adolescent to grow or at least permit him to do so?*

In adolescent patients, this is usually not a serious problem. Most of the youngsters come to therapy after at least having begun to fight for autonomy. The therapist usually will find that, although the parents may be distressed by this turn of events, the family has recognized that the previous homeostatic balance must be altered.

In the older adolescent, this alteration can often be effected without the parents' active assistance. In fact, in the course of successful psychotherapy, the adolescent can learn to recognize and to accept a reasonable degree of parental ambivalence toward his effort to wrench himself away from the family.

In the younger adolescent, however, the parents may need to involve themselves in the therapy. Most parents are sufficiently troubled by the overt family strife to be somewhat more cooperative than many parents of latency-age children are.

Occasionally, one does encounter parents who are desperately committed to maintaining a pathological tie to their child, even in the face of the adolescent's efforts to force a separation. These parents typically seek the therapist's aid in forcing the youngster to remain under their infantilizing control. In such a situation, it is probably not therapeutic to offer psychotherapy for the adolescent until the parents can be brought to a healthier point of view.

A 17-year-old female high school senior was brought for psychiatric evaluation because of her refusal to accept her father's selection of the college she was to attend.

The girl's objections to the college seemed fairly reasonable, since all of her friends were planning to attend a coeducational school in the area, whereas her father insisted that she attend an exclusive girls' college located some distance from her home. The girl was an outstanding student and correctly pointed out that the girls' school was noted more for its social prestige than its academic excellence. It was also obvious that she was attempting to assert her right to make this important decision in her life for herself.

The father, an extremely successful businessman, was an autocrat of the old school who had little interest in friends or intellectual achievement. He was self-made and put great store in his daughter's associating with "the right people." He asserted that his daughter's choice of school was very suspect and might be based on a wish to "run wild."

When the therapist asked about his evidence for this assertion and otherwise demonstrated a wish to explore the disagreement rather than accepting his view without question, he became quite angry. He stated that he certainly knew what was best for his own girl and had only hoped that "a doctor" could help bring his daughter to her senses. When the therapist asked whether the girl should have any decision-making power in regard to her college education, the father replied sarcastically, "Certainly! To the exact same degree that she intends to pay for it!"

In other cases the pathological tie is not limited to the parent. In these cases there are often elements of protectiveness toward the adolescent which are understandable though ill-advised.

A 16-year-old white male was referred for evaluation. There was a long history of erratic functioning and the patient was actively delusional (although one had to ask the right questions to bypass the boy's paranoid caution and elicit them). There was reason for concern about possible homicidal violence. The psychiatrist recommended hospitalization. The mother wept and begged the therapist to treat the boy at home, "even if you have to see him twice a day." When she calmed down and began to accept the recommendation, the mother admitted the boy was concurrently being evaluated by a second psychiatrist. Interestingly, the adolescent had not mentioned the other doctor. Mother sighed, "I'm afraid he's going to say the same thing. We're going to meet with him next week."

He did and the family accepted hospital treatment.

Fortunately very few parents view their adolescent children as chattel property as the first father did or as part of themselves like the mother in the second case. Most of them are anxious or diffident and require support to function with the kind of helpful firmness which their children need. The techniques and problems of involving parents in the therapy of the adolescent are discussed more fully in chapter 9.

THE POSTDIAGNOSTIC FAMILY CONFERENCE

When the diagnostic information appears reasonably complete, it is necessary to arrange for one or more conferences with the parents and the adolescent to discuss the findings and recommendations. As previously stated, many therapists like to invite the adolescent to sit in with the parents during this conference, whereas a few prefer to have separate meetings with the parents and with the adolescent.

As we have described elsewhere (Meeks and Martin, 1969), this conference is difficult to manage due to the intensity of feelings present both in the family members and in the examiner. However, the necessity for such a conference and its crucial role in setting the stage for the entire therapeutic undertaking cannot be ignored. A tremendous hurdle to successful treatment will have been passed if the family can leave this conference with some sense of direction and with the feeling that the therapist respects their individual feelings.

Unfortunately, this goal is easier to state than it is to achieve. The interested reader is referred to McDonald's (1965) excellent paper on the diagnostic process for a clear description of the problems and techniques of conducting this interview.

No matter how skillful the therapist becomes in conducting the postdiagnostic conference, he will not be able to use the skill without a clear diagnostic conception. The family dynamics, clinical diagnosis of the child, and the genetic and dynamic understanding of the adolescent must be carefully thought out prior to the postdiagnostic interview. Without his preparatory work, the therapist cannot hope for the kind of conciseness and clarity which will be necessary for effective communication with the family.

Full consideration of the diagnostic data will often suggest that individual psychotherapy for the adolescent is not the immediate treatment of choice. It is difficult to specify these situations with exactitude, but some general suggestions can be offered. These may be organized around the specific recommendations which might be made.

Hospitalization

The decision to hospitalize the adolescent is not to be taken lightly. The fact that the adolescent frequently views psychiatric hospitalization as a verification of his worst fears about himself is only one of several reasons that inpatient treatment is fraught with danger. The inevitable presence of restrictive structuring in even the most liberal group situation, the loss of contact with normal peer experiences and opportunities, and the invitation to regression and an accentuation of dependency conflicts all militate against a positive result in hospital treatment of the adolescent.

Easson (1969) has stated that only the adolescent who can neither handle his inner drives nor utilize meaningful relationships with other people to help himself needs inpatient psychotherapy. He points out that even the severely narcissistic youngster with good ego strength can manage himself and continue his psychological growth. Youngsters with very weak egos who can form warm relationships with family members and peers can be guided into a successful adjustment through such external support.

There are adolescents, however, who can be treated properly only within a psychiatric hospital. The program for the hospital treatment of the adolescent has to be especially constructed to meet the needs of this age group. Many structures have been devised and utilized with success, ranging from programs which mingle adolescents with adult patients to those with separate adolescent units. Some programs separate the functions of the child's psychotherapist and his administrative psychiatrist, whereas other hospitals insist that these functions be combined in the same individual. Still, most programs develop common features which include a recognition of the adolescent's need for vigorous activity, both physical and mental, some plan to develop group cohesion and a "protherapy" orientation among the adolescents, and a system of limitations and privileges designed to control the adolescent's propensity to live out his problems rather than discuss them (Holmes, 1964; Lewis et al., 1973). The availability of a special school program which is carefully coordinated with the psychiatric treatment team is generally accepted as a basic need. This is less crucial in very brief hospital stays but school is a normalizing and organizing element in any treatment program. Since a high percentage of disturbed adolescents show evidence of academic difficulties as part of their problem, it is advisable to seek a program which at least provides skilled academic testing and evaluation. Generally speaking, individual hospital programs tend to be designed either for brief hospital care, intermediate care, or for prolonged intensive treatment. There are many problems in attempting to combine these three approaches in a single unit.

BRIEF HOSPITALIZATION. The brief care units are valuable for the adolescent who is caught in an acute crisis situation. This may include those who might be diagnosed as showing an "acute confusional state," as well as some adolescents who are reacting to transient stress with suicidal or homicidal impulses. Some adolescents who have "gone wild" as a way of dealing with superego conflicts also may benefit from brief containment. Some youngsters with an acute toxic psychosis also require brief hospitalization for detoxification and evaluation.

For these youngsters, hospitalization is aimed at dealing with the emergency situation, utilizing drug therapy, containment, and support to avert disaster. Usually, the evaluating therapist will wish to manage the youngster's hospital care, hoping to establish a therapeutic relationship during the hospital stay. Outpatient therapy can then be utilized to deal with the chronic personality problems which predispose the youngster to emotional breakdown.

A 16-year-old boy, home from prep school during the Christmas holidays, developed marked suicidal ideation as the time for returning to school approached. A suicidal attempt led to an emergency diagnostic study. Evaluation revealed marked confusion and a strong tendency toward impulsivity. The preoccupation with suicide as a solution to a chronic sense of failure suggested that hospital care was the only reasonable plan.

During the three-week hospitalization, the boy formed an intense tie to the therapist and revealed a good capacity for self-observation and verbalization of feeling. Arrangements were made for the boy to return to school locally and attend outpatient psychotherapy sessions three times a week. Soon, it was possible to reduce the sessions to twice weekly and to explore the youngster's long-standing neurotic conflicts. The therapy continued for two years with no further need for inpatient care.

INTERMEDIATE HOSPITAL CARE. Many adolescents with acute psychosis, massive resistance to treatment, chemical dependency, and other severely disorganizing illnesses which are often accompanied by major family disruption cannot be stabilized in short-term hospital units. Yet, if the family is potentially functional and the youngster's problems are acute, long-term hospital or residential treatment would seem unnecessary or inappropriate. A hospital stay of two to four months, however, if properly designed, can lay the groundwork for successful outpatient therapy.

In order to succeed, the intermediate program needs to accomplish several goals:

1. Contain acting out and provide strong pressure to make pathological defenses ego-alien. This is done through development of a therapeutic milieu, strong family intervention, and utilization of nursing staff as supportive limit-setters. Medication may be important if symptoms result from psychosis.

2. Discover important areas of weakness in adaptive functioning and provide intense remediation to strengthen them. This includes learning problems, deficiencies in social skills, difficulties in identifying and expressing feelings, and other ego functions.

Although a hospitalization of a few months may not allow sufficient time for total correction of these deficiencies, hope can be established and the young person can experience some success in areas where he has become demoralized. This experience of success can lead to higher motivation for treatment and a decrease in the resistance and defensiveness based on hopelessness and lack of trust.

3. Active family therapy is an essential element in these hospital programs. In many of the cases described above, the family has become dysfunctional and is not only not a help to the adolescent patient but may serve to permit or encourage continued maladaptive behavior. It is necessary to gain the family's support and to strengthen their capacity to assist the adolescent. Successful family intervention usually includes combined education and psychotherapy as will be described in more detail in chapter 24, which deals with inpatient therapy.

EXTENDED HOSPITAL TREATMENT. Those adolescents who require long-term hospital treatment comprise a different group. This recommendation should be reserved for those with marked defects in early ego development usually associated with families who are unable or unwilling to correct these deficiencies in the present. These youngsters therefore require a prolonged corrective living experience. For these youngsters, there is no disadvantage in the structured nature of the hospital setting. Structure is essential to fill their need to learn adaptive techniques, control of their impulses, and skills in interpersonal relations. The potential of the inpatient setting to induce regression is not a hindrance to their care, but can rather be turned to the advantage of the adolescent. The enormous dedication and skill necessary to cope successfully with the regressive transference manifestations which appear in the adolescent in residential therapy are well described by Rinsley (1965, 1967).

When this type of therapy is to be recommended, it is often wise to extend the diagnostic period, especially that portion spent with the parents. This precaution allows the development of the closest possible relationship with the parents, which may be utilized to aid them in dealing with their resistance to separation from the patient. In many adolescents who require hospital care, this will be a very difficult job, since the parents have often crippled the adolescent in order to bolster their own defensive structure. The parents will often resist hospitalization in order to protect their personal equilibrium. In the resistance to the separation, grossly irrational fantasies tend to be projected onto the therapist who recommends hospitalization, the institution, and the staff of the hospital. Often, these can be dealt with if the therapist has had sufficient contact with the parents to establish open communication and a sense of trust. At times, a period of unsuccessful outpatient treatment is necessary, both to demonstrate that hospitalization is essential and to gain enough therapeutic ground to permit the parents to accept the recommendation. In the youngsters who truly need this intensive approach, problems are chronic and proper preparation is more important than speed of disposition.

Perhaps the most crucial element in successful referral for hospital care is the diagnostician's conviction that inpatient care is essential. This clarity of conviction must not be allowed to falter in response to patient or parental pleas, promises, or threats. Parents can be reassured to some extent in regard to their fears about social stigma, their child's anger at them for taking the step to hospitalize, the dangers of the youngster mingling "with all those crazy people," and the like, but there are problems in that. There is a social stigma associated with hospital care. The child will likely be angry . . . and so on. The point is that the crucial need for hospital treatment outweighs these concerns and that conviction must be clearly conveyed. In a very real sense, when one is recommended for hospital care, there should be no viable alternative. If there were, the evaluator would be suggesting it!

At this point we are only discussing referral for hospital treatment. The complex process of delivering hospital treatment will be discussed in chapters 23 and 24.

Family Therapy and Group Psychotherapy

The indications for recommending group psychotherapy or family therapy as primary treatment approaches are covered in the chapters dealing with these modalities ("Group Psychotherapy of the Adolescent," chapter 7; "Family Therapy," chapter 8).

Wait and See

In many mild adolescent disturbances, the therapist may attempt to help the parents and the adolescent to define their problems more productively during the diagnostic contact and during the postdiagnostic family conference. This does not differ materially from the crisis-intervention technique described above. If some success is achieved in clarifying the issues, the therapist may wish to recommend that the family attempt to work on the problems for a period of time without outside help. If this recommendation is made, it is important to discuss specifically with the family what will be done during the "wait" and what behaviors and attitudes they should hope to "see." Although time is often helpful in the resolution of adolescent crises, many pathological solutions may be avoided by the constructive use of counsel during the wait.

Waiting for further developments may also be wise in cases which will probably eventually need treatment but where the adolescent or his family shows marked current ambivalence about entering the treatment process. Often continuing or accelerating problems will intensify the discomfort the family feels and help to focus the need for a commitment to therapy.

SUMMARY: FROM UNDERSTANDING TOWARD THERAPY

Some of the issues surrounding the diagnostic evaluation of adolescent patients resist rigid codification. Although certain approaches seem to be regularly useful, flexibility is the keynote in the attempt to obtain useful and reliable diagnostic information.

Our next task is to consider the ways in which dynamic understanding can be translated into effective therapy with the adolescent patient. This task can be undertaken only when a therapeutic alliance is established. The next chapters attempt a description and working definition of the therapeutic alliance, as well as a discussion of how one can effect such a tie with the distrustful, narcissistic, and "fickle" adolescent. First we shall consider the traditional alliance with the basically "neurotic" adolescent. Later we will discuss more difficult cases.

CITED AND RECOMMENDED READINGS

Blos, P. 1962. *On Adolescence: A Psychoanalytic Interpretation.* New York: The Free Press of Glencoe.

Easson, W. M. 1969. *The Severely Disturbed Adolescent.* New York: International Universities Press.

Erikson, E. H. 1968. *Identity: Youth and Crisis.* New York: W. W. Norton & Company.

Feinstein, S. C. 1982. Manic-depressive disorders in children and adolescents. *Adolescent Psychiatry.* 10: 256–272.

Freud, A. 1965. *Normality and Pathology in Childhood.* New York: International Universities Press.

Group for the Advancement of Psychiatry. 1966. *Psychopathological Disorders in Childhood: Theoretical Considerations and a Proposed Classification. Volume VI, Report No. 62.* Publications office: 419 Park Avenue South, New York, NY 10016.

Holmes, D. J. 1964. *The Adolescent in Psychotherapy.* Boston: Little, Brown & Co.

Lewis, J. M., et al. 1973. Development of a protreatment group process among hospitalized adolescents. *Adolescent Psychiatry.* 2: 351–362.

Masterson, J. F., Jr. 1967. *The Psychiatric Dilemma of Adolescence.* Boston: Little, Brown & Co.

McDonald, M. 1965. The psychiatric evaluation of children. *Journal of the American Academy of Child Psychiatry.* 4: 569–612.

Meeks, J. E., and J. Martin. 1969. Teaching the techniques of the post-diagnostic family conference. *Journal of the American Academy of Child Psychiatry.* 8: 306–320.

Offord, D. R., and L. Cross. 1969. Behavioral antecedents of adult schizophrenia. *Archives of General Psychiatry.* 21: 267–283.

Rinsley, D. B. 1965. Intensive psychiatric hospital treatment of adolescents: an object-relations view. *Psychiatry Quarterly.* 39: 405–429.

Rinsley, D. B. 1967. Intensive residential treatment of the adolescent. *Psychiatry Quarterly.* 41: 134–143.

Sanchez, E. 1986. Factors complicating the psychiatric diagnosis of adolescents. *Adolescent Psychiatry.* 13: 100–115.

Sifneos, P. E., and J. C. Nemiah. 1984. Assessing the suitability of patients with character disorders for insight psychotherapy. In *Character Pathology: Theory and Treatment,* edited by M. R. Zales. New York: Brunner/Mazel.

CHAPTER 4

the therapeutic alliance with the adolescent

THE CONCEPT OF THE THERAPEUTIC ALLIANCE

For many years, psychoanalysts have described the need to develop and utilize a conscious, cooperative portion of the patient's personality as an observing ally during the storms of transference feelings which appear during analysis. In Freud's 1912 paper, "The Dynamics of Transference," he pointed out that, paradoxically, transference is both the force which binds the patient to therapy and encourages cooperation, as well as the major resistance to analysis. Balint (1952) has called the binding force the "adult, affectionate and aim inhibited form" of the transference. Bibring presented a paper on the "therapeutic alliance" at the Psychoanalytic Congress in 1936. Fenichel wrote of the "rational transference" in 1941. In his book on analytic technique, Greenson (1967) emphasized the importance of this relationship with the therapist, which he preferred to call the "working alliance."

All of these concepts refer to the necessity for a pact between the analyst and an observing portion of the patient's ego aimed at an honest and uncritical examination of the patient's inner experience.

Recently, it has been recognized that a similar alliance must be found in order to conduct dynamic psychotherapy properly. The psychotherapist allies himself with the healthier, more reality-oriented aspect of the patient's ego for the purpose of observing the maladaptive, neurotically defended, and conflicted portions of the personality. There is general agreement that this alliance is created through the orderly interpretation of affective and de-

88

fensive behavior toward the therapist. In fact, Friedman (1969) has suggested in an excellent review article that this aspect of the therapeutic bond is a result of progress in therapy rather than an initiator of therapeutic change. Certainly, the result of maintaining a therapeutic alliance with the adolescent patient is a strengthening of the observing ego—"the capacity for self-scrutiny without self-judgment and without action" (Long, 1968).

WILL THE REAL OBSERVING EGO PLEASE STAND UP?

In adolescents, the observing ego is something of a paradox. At times, the adolescent seems completely emerged in self-observation. Ruminative preoccupation with inner feelings, interminable musings over real or imagined inadequacies, and detached experimentation with new feelings states and altered states of consciousness all appear to signal the emergence of a capacity to stand aside and observe one's own psychological structure and functioning. This capacity is demonstrably unstable, however, and the adolescent also expends great effort in denying his impulses, affects, and needs. Often, this tendency to disavow his inner life is reinforced by an explosive tendency to act, rather than to think or feel.

A primary reason for this unstable state of affairs is the adolescent's conflict with his superego. The emerging capacity for self-observation can flower only as the harsh and unrelenting superego of early adolescence is gradually modified toward a more flexible and humane code of conduct.

STRENGTHENING THE EGO IDEAL

Blos (1962) has described and Long (1968) has amplified the adolescent's use of a special friendship to accelerate the development of the ego ideal. The special attachment is made to a friend of the same sex, usually somewhat older. "The essential thing is that the older (or bigger) person displays some essential traits that are lacking or that the young adolescent feels are lacking in himself" (Long, 1968). These traits are then idealized to provide the missing perfection of the self so that narcissistic balance is partially restored. This relationship is later internalized as a stabilizing but also liberalizing introject. The friend's values are gradually abstracted and detached from their origin and come to exist completely in their own right in the adolescent's mind. To quote Long again, "Because the boy can now better accept his instinctual drives and control and direct them, he can now look upon himself as more of a man and can be to a significant degree more objective about himself, and eventually also more objective in looking at his parents. That is, the establishment of the ego ideal acts as a supporting plank for the development of an observing ego."

In the process of developing a therapeutic alliance with the adolescent patient, the therapist may find that he has become the youngster's "special friend" in the sense described above (see Adatto, 1966). Even when this does not happen, the therapist's permission to discover and relate to an older friend of this kind may be one of the most important gains in therapy. When the capacity for noncritical self-observation appears, many adolescent patients seem virtually to "cure themselves" with relative rapidity.

It should be emphasized that the primary function of the therapeutic alliance with the adolescent is to assist the youngster in understanding the link between his feelings and his behavior in the present. The adolescent's anxiety about the future and his fear of regression contraindicate extensive focusing on the genetic determinants of his behavior. In psychoanalysis of adults, and to a limited extent even in dynamic psychotherapy with adults, the therapeutic alliance is utilized to promote and regulate a controlled regression. This approach cannot be utilized extensively with the adolescent. Early developmental defects and severe fixations cannot be worked through during early adolescence because the necessary degree of regression would threaten the progressive and synthetic thrust of the developmental period. Brief regressive episodes appear spontaneously and account for the fluctuating transference of adolescent patients. However, only the older adolescent can tolerate the careful study of these ego states. The therapist must usually focus his efforts on helping the adolescent to recover from regressions. As a rule, adolescents respond to a correct and appropriate interpretation by a progressive developmental leap forward rather than by further regression and exploration of genetics. If the therapist tries to interfere with this tendency by encouraging the development of a regressive transference, many adolescents will bolt from therapy. The conscious, rational alliance must be emphasized, not the irrational, infantile bonds to the therapist.

Since the alliance is of central importance yet is often difficult to achieve even with the neurotic adolescent, the techniques and problems associated with this phase of therapy are discussed in some detail.

FOSTERING THE THERAPEUTIC ALLIANCE

The basic technique of establishing the therapeutic alliance is the timely interpretation of affect and defense as stated above. This process can be restated as helping the adolescent to recognize that his behavior is motivated by inner feeling states. Early in the therapeutic situation, these feeling states are commonly impatience, frustration, feelings of helplessness, and a sense of narcissistic impairment over the need to consult a psychotherapist. Some of the typical early defenses against these painful affects include rebelliousness; passive compliance; timidity; disdainful, condescending attitudes toward the therapist; and cool, aloof intellectualizing. Recognizing these defenses and the feeling states which they disguise is the first order of business in psychotherapy. This may be overlooked when the adolescent's primary defense is passive compliance. These adolescents appear to be "good" patients, eager to get right to work on their problems. The therapist should not be deceived into confusing this frightened obsequiousness with a true therapeutic alliance.

More often, the adolescent therapist must proceed to the clarification of the connection between feeling and action by means of a difficult way station, namely, through interrupting the adolescent's propensity to act in order to avoid feeling. When the therapist challenges this pattern, he is quickly cast in the role of a critical parent, a superego figure. It is a difficult but crucial undertaking to convince the adolescent that "Why did you do that?" is a neutral question, rather than a statement of moral disapproval.

SAYING NO THE EGO WAY

Adolescent acting up and acting out must be limited by the therapist. The only rational basis for the authority to direct behavior proceeds from the therapist's knowledge of the conditions required for effective therapy. In short, the adolescent is told that his behavior is none of the therapist's business except that some actions interfere with the therapeutic process and these must be controlled or therapy will not proceed properly. Often, it is also possible to demonstrate that acting out disrupts the youngster's psychological harmony or threatens to harm him. The therapist tries to convey his wish that the adolescent win the developmental war while keeping it clear that it is the youngster's battle and that the therapist cannot fight it for him. This position is more convincing to the adolescent when it becomes apparent that the therapist has the same benevolent, inquiring attitude toward all symptomatic behavior, whether it is "wrong" or not.

Sarah, a 15-year-old in psychotherapy because of promiscuity and poor academic performance, was openly skeptical of the therapist's assertion that his disapproval of this promiscuous behavior was not based on moral indignation. She jeered at the assertion that there were reasons behind her behavior that she did not understand and which could not be explained by her statement that she was "hypersexed." She continued to believe that the therapist was "another square" with "hang-ups about sex" who was trying in typical bluenose fashion to interfere with her fun.

After some positive transference had developed, the girl began to study secretly. Eventually, she brought an excellent report card to a psychotherapy session as a seductive gift to the therapist and as proof of her value. She was at first offended, and then amazed that the therapist did not praise her "good" behavior. Instead, the therapist noted that she did not seem to be enjoying the grades and that this suggested she had worked hard because she felt for some reason that it was expected of her. She talked for a few moments about her motives for improving her academic performance, then said, "You know, I've been telling you what a sex expert I am. Actually, the only reason I was willing to come see you in the first place is that I have never enjoyed sex. Not once. I love the idea of sex, but in practice it's lousy for me. Yet I practice and practice and practice. I know that sounds crazy."

The therapist agreed that this must be a puzzling state of affairs and suggested that he and the patient try to understand it together.

The adolescent is exquisitely sensitive to any manipulative control which threatens his tenuous sense of autonomy. Unless the therapist maintains his neutral, sympathetic but inquiring attitude toward all the adolescent's behavior, he cannot convince the adolescent that his goal is to foster understanding, not to dominate the patient through psychological warfare.

"DON'T KNOCK YOURSELF"

The therapist should be quick to point out tendencies toward judgmental and self-critical attitudes in the adolescent. The adolescent should be encouraged to look for the sources of his behavior, attitudes, and affective states, rather than call himself names. The goal of therapy is to increase self-understanding and inner psychological strength and flexibility, not to suppress annoying behavior. Often, the demonstration of therapeutic neutrality and of the motivational origins of behavior can be made effectively through the office interaction with the patient.

A 16-year-old boy started his first three therapy sessions by slouching in his chair and lighting a cigarette. The therapist's inquiry about the meaning of the behavior made him angry. "You mean I can't even smoke in this crummy office?"

"I didn't say there was a rule against it. I just have noticed that you never talk about smoking, yet you light up the moment you hit that chair."

"So what?"

"So we're here to understand why you do the things you do."

"Because I want to, okay?"

"Well, if you want to go through a session standing on your head and playing a harmonica, I guess that's okay, but I'd probably ask you why you wanted to."

The boy grinned, and then asked carefully, "Are you going to tell my parents I smoke here?"

"We can talk about that in a minute, but I wonder why you're doing something here that you know your parents disapprove of."

The boy hung his head. "Yeah. I know I shouldn't smoke. It would kill my parents if they knew. I don't know why I'm always bad."

"I don't think it's going to help to criticize yourself. Let's try to understand what's really going on here."

"Well, I kinda wanted to see what you'd say about the smoking."

The smoking represented an attempt to corrupt the therapist by implicating him as an accessory in a forbidden behavior. Without a persistent effort to expose the reasons behind the smoking, the therapist would have been either maneuvered into a compromised position or forced into an arbitrary prohibition. In either case, no therapeutic alliance could develop. Later, when the therapist was calmly able to confront the boy with his tendency to manipulate people, the boy said, "Yeah, I like to have my way with them, I guess."

The therapist did not pick up on the sexual implications in the wording, but commented, "I'm sure there are reasons why you can't trust people enough to be honest with them. That's one of the things we might try to understand."

Eventually, the boy was able to talk easily about what he called his "crook tendencies," both in terms of their disadvantage to him and the situations in which they appeared. The capacity to observe himself in action and in feelings was finally achieved.

TOWARD TRUE FREEDOM

The youngster discussed above was finally able to realize that "just wanting" to perform certain actions was actually the end result of many forces within himself. This recognition is extremely important in the treatment of the adolescent. The startling realization that his freedom of choice is being sabotaged by unknown inner forces greatly strengthens the adolescent's motivation for therapy. The young person's wish for freedom and autonomy will then be a support to the therapeutic effort to change rebellion into true freedom and self-direction rather than merely to substitute slavish submission to instinctual drives for earlier submission to the parents.

Several psychological forces within the adolescent interfere with his acceptance of this liberating insight. The typical narcissistic, omnipotent defensive conformation of adolescence, reinforced by the preoccupation with formal operations and the omnipotence of thought, is severely threatened by the idea of unconscious motivation. The adolescent feels a desperate need to see himself as absolute master of his fate. The idea that he is not infinitely malleable but must adapt himself to his own instinctual drives, his own conscience, and external social demands is offensive and frightening. The flip side of total control is total helplessness. When the bubble of his omnipotence is punctured, the adolescent tends to feel completely vulnerable and pitifully weak. The therapist must be extremely supportive and sometimes quite forceful to convince the adolescent that ignoring a fire in the basement or merely trying to "think it away" is an excellent way to get burned. The therapeutic support consists of helping the adolescent to see that his real abilities to devise methods of putting out the fire or confining it to safe areas are much greater than he thought. In short, the therapist supports the adolescent's ego skills to discourage his reliance on magic omnipotence. One of the authors has described some of the techniques for dealing with a similar problem in latency age children who cheat at games. Many of the technical approaches hold with adolescents also (Meeks, 1970).

In dealing with the same technical problem, Holmes (1964) has suggested the interesting technique of having the rebellious adolescent role-play cooperative and friendly behavior for a short period of time. He feels that this device often mobilizes affects which have been absorbed in the egosyntonic symptomatic behavior.

'TIS AN ILL WIND—

It is important not to drift into a pattern of only observing and studying pathological and maladaptive behaviors within the therapeutic alliance. A fair and objective evaluation of the adolescent will always reveal areas of strength and competence, often unrecognized by the patient. These must be included in any total observation of psychological functioning. This is also true of the adaptive value of ego defenses. For example, a distrust of appearances may result in interpersonal touchiness in the adolescent, but it also characterizes the personality of many successful social and scientific innovators. If the adolescent is to learn to trust the objectivity and honesty of the therapist, he must have the opportunity to see the therapist patiently look at all sides of every question. This strengthens the patient's faith in the therapist's position of friendly neutrality. It is a demonstration of the therapist's wish to avoid intruding and his determination to provide the adolescent with as much information as possible so that the youngster is better prepared to reach his own decisions.

ADOLESCENT ATTITUDES TOWARD A THERAPEUTIC ALLIANCE

The wishes and fears with which adolescents face the beginning of therapy have very little congruence with the goals of the therapist. Consciously, the adolescent is fearful of becoming embroiled in another dependency relationship, whereas unconsciously he hopes and fears to find in the therapist the gratification of various irrational and childish wishes. Because of these emotional currents, the adolescent typically utilizes various techniques to avoid the establishment of a therapeutic alliance. He may project negative attributes onto the therapist or externalize his difficulties and invite the therapist to criticize or reject him. Other adolescents attempt to convert the therapeutic situation into a friendly parent-child relationship in which they will be advised and assisted. Others are overwhelmed by massive superego pressure and can only condemn themselves and beg for mercy.

UNHOLY ALLIANCES

The distortions of the therapeutic relationship just described can usually be managed by the patient application of the principles previously enumerated. However, Keith (1968) has described another group of resistances which he appropriately designates as "unholy alliances." These must be recognized and avoided in order to achieve a usable therapeutic alliance. Keith classifies these structurally as unholy alliances 1) with the id, 2) with pathological ego defenses, and 3) with the superego.

Id Alliances and the Swinging Therapist

All of the unholy alliances are dangers with the adolescent patient. Id alliances are especially seductive, since the therapist is often eager to appear more understanding, tolerant, and "hip" than the other adults whom the adolescent criticizes. The therapist who finds himself discussing specifics of sexual behavior, techniques of outwitting parents, or the absurdity of official authority early in therapy may well suspect that he has been drawn into an unholy alliance with the id or with id derivatives. The result of such an alliance is the weakening of the adolescent's controls and an upsurge in impulsive acting-out behavior. The lack of a true alliance may be demonstrated through overt hostility which the adolescent soon directs toward the therapist, probably with the unconscious goal of inviting external control. It is of crucial importance to avoid this alliance with the adolescent because of his tenuous controls and his resultant fear of his strong feelings and impulses. Because of these fears of loss of control, many adolescents will react to an id alliance with intense anxiety which leads to defensiveness, silence, and attempts to avoid the entire therapy process. The therapist is viewed as an actual threat, a tempter who is encouraging them to lose control of themselves and give rein to the worst aspects of their nature.

This pitfall can be avoided by remembering that it is unwise to interpret or discuss aggressive or sexual material until the distinction between thought and action is clearly established and the adolescent understands that the therapist's encouragement of free expression includes only thoughts and feelings. Only a comfortable recognition that the therapist is opposed to impulsive and unwise action can create a proper atmosphere for the open expression of strong feelings and lead to a true therapeutic alliance. To fantasy that one is omnipotent is a dangerous luxury. It is a game of pretense that the therapist must not play even temporarily. Stated differently, the adolescent can never be seduced into a therapeutic alliance, and the therapist who attempts to deal with his uncomfortable patient in this way is likely to end up with an unworkable and unholy alliance with the id.

A 15-year-old girl was referred for psychotherapy after her parents learned that she and her boyfriend were having sexual intercourse regularly. In early sessions, she admitted that she was promiscuous and eagerly volunteered specific information on her sexual fantasies and adventures in seduction. The therapist ignored her racy stories and merely commented repeatedly on the absence of affect in her friendships as well as her cool and distant way of relating to him. Her titillation gradually ceased and she began to describe her feelings of contempt for all her sexual partners and eventually her wish to outsmart the therapist and show him up as "another dumb, horny male."

Over a period of time, it was possible to create a friendly and honest therapeutic alliance which allowed a moderately successful exploration of the girl's serious character problems which had prevented her from forming close emotional ties. Therapeutic results were first apparent when she began to develop satisfying friendships with girls for the first time since early childhood.

Alliances With Pathological Ego Defenses

The primary pathological ego defense which may be utilized in an unholy alliance by the adolescent is intellectualization. The intelligent, psychologically minded adolescent, often well read in popular psychology (or even Freud, Erikson, Fromm, etc.) can discuss fascinating insights for hours on end while remaining totally untouched by therapy. The defense may even be actively used to act out competitive and demeaning attitudes toward the therapist under the guise of enthusiastic cooperation. If the therapist, relieved that he does not have to struggle with one of those belligerent, uncooperative adolescents, joins in an alliance with this defense, a therapeutic alliance will not appear. Instead, therapy will deteriorate into sterile, philosophical discussions gradually producing feelings of boredom and despair in both therapist and patient.

There is a place in the therapy of the adolescent for ideological discussion and even for the defense of intellectualization. However, it is important first to establish a therapeutic alliance strong enough to allow the experiencing and reporting of affect. This can only be accomplished by refraining from extensive discussion of conceptual content early in therapy when affective contact has not been established with the adolescent. The intellectualizing patient should be asked to define all jargon such as "hostility," "ambivalent," "erotic," "incestuous," "really meaningful," "I–Thou relationship," and the like. He is asked what he means by those words and asked to tie them to concrete experiences and his feelings during his involvement in those real-life interactions. The therapist, of course, avoids any technical terms, using instead emotionally laden, everyday words such as "mad," "angry," "burned up," "sexual," and even slang sexual phrases if these do not seem unduly seductive with the specific patient. Generalities are discouraged and specifics are sought. The goal, of course, is to bring real emotion into the session. When affect does appear, either in the description of events outside the psychotherapy session or in direct relationship to the therapist, this is encouraged by a demonstration of interest and acceptance.

An 18-year-old college freshman was seen for psychiatric evaluation when he became psychotic following the ingestion of LSD. Even after the brief overt psychosis cleared, he remained rather grandiose, preoccupied with cosmic issues of good and evil. Psychotherapy with limited goals appeared feasible despite the fragility of the personality structure.

Initially, the general philosophic structure and preoccupation were accepted, although not encouraged. The therapist occasionally interjected the observation that personal feelings were important and seemed absent from the patient's thinking. The patient's objection that he intended to rise above his feelings was received with friendly skepticism. The extremely intelligent young man was reminded of historical examples in which philosophical systems were distorted by the personality quirks of their innovators. At the same time, the patient's infrequent references to "human weaknesses" in himself were applauded as evidence of his desire to know himself and thereby avoid the blind errors of other ideologists. Gradually, a capacity for self-observation was developed, although the therapist had to continually disavow the patient's attempt to cast him in role of maharisha.

The conviction that people did not rise above their feelings was constantly reiterated and was demonstrated to the patient in his own behavior whenever possible. The therapist himself continually insisted that his only area of competence was in understanding emotions and that this skill was the result of special training, rather than any supernatural power or mysterious talent. Gradually, the patient was able to admit that much of his aloof, mystical superiority covered anxiety and feelings of inferiority and that philosophical detachment was often his way of dealing with feelings of frustration and helplessness.

Greater caution was necessary in approaching the intense anger which he covered with a fervent pacifism and masochistic turnings of the other cheek. Only after repeatedly showing him evidence of his capacity to have strong feelings without acting on them was it possible to comment directly on his anger. The intensity of his fear of losing control of his aggressive impulses was illustrated by his delusional projection of a "conspiracy of evil" which he felt was trying to make him "homicidally insane" during his initial psychotic episode.

One of the points which I have tried to make in this case illustration is the need to accept the positive aspects of adolescent intellectualization. Since adolescents place such importance on logical thought and ideological speculation, it would be a gross technical error to dismiss their intellectual efforts in therapy as useless and unacceptable resistances. Instead, one accepts intellectualization but does not support it. The therapist continues to point out that feelings are also important. A patient and persistent effort is made to bring affect into the therapy hours without making a direct critical attack on the defense of intellectualization. The therapist does not ally himself with the pathological ego defense, but neither does he try to force the adolescent to abandon it before he is ready. In behavioral terms, the therapist positively reinforces affective expressions and attempts to extinguish intellectualization by failure to reinforce that behavior.

To a lesser extent, adolescents may attempt to draw the therapist into alliances with other pathological ego defenses, especially denial and reaction formation. In these instances, the therapist maintains his neutrality and encourages greater objectivity without directly assaulting essential defenses. In the emergency states which appear during adolescence, many pathological defenses will be utilized by adolescent patients. The wise therapist approaches them with respect and caution, but it is rarely necessary for the therapist to give his stamp of approval to distortions of inner or outer reality.

The Unholy Alliance With the Superego

It is almost impossible to avoid completely an unholy alliance with the superego in adolescent psychotherapy. It is natural for the adolescent to maneuver to externalize his conscience. This developmental characteristic will be brought into the adolescent's relationship with his therapist, since it is universally present in the adolescent's interactions with all significant adults. This propensity is commonly expressed by the strategy of acting up provocatively to seduce important adults into meting out sadistic punishment. This pattern is described in detail in the section of chapter 1 which discusses the adolescent's interaction with his environment. The therapist, as an important environmental figure, must be constantly alert to the danger of being drawn into this kind of relationship with the adolescent patient. The unavoidable technical requirement to limit defensive acting out automatically places the therapist in a precarious position from which he can all too easily slide into a superego alliance.

A 13-year-old boy's easygoing amiability was successfully interpreted as a resistance against his inner feelings. The boy's father was an angry, harsh, competitive man who frequently struck the youngster whenever he challenged any of the father's rules or statements. The youngster was able to discuss some of his anger in a session during which he was able to recognize that his excessive deference and compliance toward the therapist was a defensive continuation of a pattern that he utilized with his father to cover his inner feelings of rage.

In the next session, however, he was silent and sullen. Near the end of the session, he suddenly stated that he was "going" and headed for the door.

The therapist, rather surprised, tried to keep him in the room, and a mild shoving contest developed. The therapist recognized his error and was not surprised to encounter a very negative youngster in the next session.

He discussed the boy's need to "pick a fight" and indicated his interest in understanding how the boy felt about remaining in the office. The youngster was congratulated on the honesty he was demonstrating in his relationship with the therapist and was assured that his anger could be discussed.

Of course, the adolescent does need to externalize superego issues in order to find ways to modify his harsh conscience while using the external agent as a temporary protection against the unwise expression of impulse. The adolescent therapist can expect to be used in this way and can be helpful by tolerating some distortion of his intentions. An almost daily example occurs around the question of continuing therapy during difficult periods. Some version of the following conversation is a periodic commonplace during the therapy of many adolescents.

Adolescent (in anger): I never did need to come here. I sure as hell don't need you, and I'm not coming back in here for any more of these silly talks.

Therapist: That's not too surprising. We both know you have a tendency to run away from things when they make you too nervous, but you're strong enough to stay and talk about your feelings.

Adolescent: Why should I sit through this? Do I have to come back?

Therapist: You know that you need therapy. That's not the question. What are you really up to with all this quitting talk?

Adolescent: Okay, I'll be here next week. I should have known you wouldn't let me quit.

Therapist: Why do I have to stop you from doing something that wouldn't be good for you?

Adolescent: Aw, forget it. I'm not going to quit your precious therapy.

Therapist: Sorry, I can't forget it. Just not quitting won't cut it. We need to look at how you're trying to set me up.

Adolescent: God! Even my parents aren't this hard to get along with.

Therapist: Maybe they're mainly interested in how you behave—what you do. I'm interested in why you do things and how you feel. Sometimes it's easier to do what you think I want than to look at your feelings. The only reason that it's any of my business whether you quit or not is that it would interfere with your therapy.

Adolescent: Very funny! But you did say that I need to stay in therapy. You are telling me what to do!

Therapist (laughs): Yeah. Simon Legree rides again.

Adolescent: Aha! You admit it!

On it goes as the adolescent forces the therapist into a superego role. Still, the therapist must resist the temptation to criticize the adolescent for his provocation, to threaten him, or otherwise behave in a punitive way. This does not mean that the therapist avoids superego issues. Later, we consider the methods of dealing with material in this area in a way that encourages emotional growth.

The immediate point is that only the observing ego is a dependable ally in therapy with the adolescent. Even when a superego alliance produces a diminution of acting-out behavior, there is little true gain in maturation. The surface improvement tends to be ephemeral in most cases. In other instances, it is maintained through an ascetic constriction of personality which chokes off spontaneity and the capacity for pleasure—a terrible price to pay for superficial socialization. There has been no gain in independence and autonomous control in either case.

RECOGNIZING THE ALLIANCE

If the therapist is able to avoid unholy alliances and to respond with appropriate empathy, tact, and precision to the adolescent's defensive operations, evidence of a therapeutic alliance begins to appear. It is important to recognize and acknowledge this important new skill in the adolescent without implying a paternalistic endorsement of "good" behavior. Perhaps, the most meaningful acceptance of the alliance is a comment which merely recognizes its value in the therapeutic process. Its value is purely "instrumental." It is a tool which permits more effective therapeutic work.

In order to credit the adolescent with his discovery, however, it is necessary to recognize its appearance. The alliance may show itself in various forms, depending on the style and personality of the adolescent patient. One recognizes its presence primarily through a subtle change in the tone of the sessions. The atmosphere is somehow no longer totally adversative. The therapist recognizes intuitively that he can relax somewhat, since his patient has at least become interested in observing and understanding the frightened, wary, guarded, and devious styles of relating which have characterized him in earlier sessions. In short, the therapist no longer feels that he is working totally alone in opposing the patient's resistances.

CHECKPOINTS FOR THE ALLIANCE

This general "feel" for the situation can be checked against some behavioral specifics which usually attest to the development of an alliance.

1. The patient occasionally says, "I'm not sure I know why I did that," or "I think I understand why I got so upset," or "Can you understand what I really was upset about?" In other words, the patient demonstrates a tendency to reflect on his affective experience, or at least a willingness to allow the therapist to suggest an underlying motivation for an intense feeling state. This is particularly meaningful if the affective experience in question directly involves the therapist. "I think the reason your comment made me so angry is—."
2. A switch from threatening actions to discussing thoughts and exploring their origins. Instead of "I'm not coming back here," a change to "When you say things like that, I get so angry at you I feel like quitting."
3. Paradoxically, the development of the therapeutic alliance may also be indicated by a more tolerant attitude toward episodes of loss of impulse control. These episodes are dis-

cussed with moderation and objectivity, rather than withheld, bragged on, or criticized with an air of self-loathing. The attitude is not merely intellectualization, however, since the accompanying affects are not isolated but are discussed. The adolescent can say, "I lost a battle, but overall I feel I'm winning the war."

4. A recognition and discussion of affects appearing during the session. The patient is able to comment, "I don't know why, but this discussion makes me very nervous."

5. A recognition and acceptance of ambivalence as an internal reality. No longer "My parents treat me like a baby," but rather "Sometimes I want to grow up, but at other times it scares me to death."

6. A reflective, curious response to appropriate confrontations and interpretations rather than a defensive, critical reaction.

All of these attitudes may appear as isolated occurrences without signaling the arrival of a therapeutic alliance. They represent merely some specific behaviors which may serve as checkpoints for verification of the general air of cooperation described above. Without the overall sense that the therapist has been accepted as a working partner, these behaviors mean nothing.

MAINTAINING THE ALLIANCE

The therapeutic alliance is a delicate structure which is constantly threatened by the anxiety which results from its operations. The successful functioning of the alliance leads repeatedly to upsurges of aggression and erotic feelings which are threatening to the working coalition, especially since these feelings frequently become directed toward the therapist. The adolescent, with his constant search for real objects, has great difficulty in understanding the meaning and nature of transference. We discuss the overall management of transference in adolescent psychotherapy in the next chapter. It is mentioned in this context merely to note that it is a major force acting against the maintenance of the therapeutic alliance.

The fluctuations which characterize ego functioning during adolescence are themselves a threat to the steady maintenance of a therapeutic alliance. During periods of marked regression, the rational therapeutic alliance may be scuttled along with other reality-oriented ego functions. The adolescent therapist must be flexible and adapt himself to the startling changes in level of functioning and defensive patterning which the adolescent shows from one session to the next. The adolescent patient himself often does not view these "moods" as changeable reflections of aspects of the self. He tends to see each new ego state as the way he "really" feels and the way life "really" is. The therapist must try to utilize the therapeutic alliance to assist his patient in accepting his complexity and variability. Westman (1970) has suggested that when the adolescent seems to ask "Who am I?", the therapist can often be most helpful by replying, "Many people. It depends on circumstances inside you and conditions around you." The therapist assists the adolescent to maintain a sense of "wholeness" and personal continuity despite rapid and puzzling changes in mood and attitude.

EXTERNAL THREATS TO THE ALLIANCE

In addition to internal dangers, the alliance may also be threatened by external events. Parents may unknowingly or consciously sabotage the alliance for a variety of motives. Possessive parents may be threatened by the affectionate tie between the therapist and the child. Controlling, hostile parents may view the therapist as an agent of their control and convey this image to their youngster. Other parents may actually be threatened by the improvement they observe in the adolescent if these changes interfere with family patterns which are important to neurotic stability. Some ideas regarding the management of these problems are presented in chapter 9, dealing with the parents of the adolescent patient.

Other external occurrences may produce such intense affects that the adolescent is forced to erect rigid defenses which cannot be explored for a period of time. These occurrences may be the illness or death of an important person in the adolescent's world or an overwhelming defeat or disappointment in the adolescent's personal struggle for competence and acceptance. During these periods, the adolescent needs to withdraw and mourn. The therapist must recognize the legitimacy of this need and accept a role of passivity and empathic sharing until the adolescent is prepared to work again. More active intervention during such a period may permanently impair the therapeutic relationship.

These instances do permit the therapist to observe the adolescent's style of dealing with loss. He can determine whether the adolescent acts to avoid grief and mourning by total introjection of the object rather than by a gradual identification with the desirable characteristics of the loved one and rejection of those characteristics that do not fit his personality needs and his aspirations (Laufer, 1966; Root, 1957; Rochlin, 1965). When the mourning process goes awry or is avoided by the adolescent, the therapist may act to encourage the appropriate expression of grief and the constructive adaptation to loss. However, when the adolescent's grief and mourning are appropriate, the therapist should remain unobtrusive and grant the necessary time for the work to be completed.

WHAT TO DO UNTIL THE ALLIANCE COMES— AND WHEN IT DOES NOT

The therapeutic alliance may simply never materialize. This can result from the failure to respond accurately or effectively to early defenses or affects in a particular patient. In these instances of therapeutic error, an open discussion of the problem may permit a new start. If this is not possible, transferring the patient to a different therapist may be considered. Before carrying out transfer, however, it is worthwhile for the therapist to examine his decision closely to be sure his plan does not merely represent a rejection of the adolescent based on countertransference. Even when this proves to be the case, a transfer may still be in order. However, the therapist and the adolescent will benefit if the real reason for the transfer is recognized and discussed .

The problems are somewhat different when the patient was simply never a candidate for outpatient psychotherapy. No matter how carefully the diagnostic process is conducted, some errors will occur. When this is recognized, one must present the problem and the new recommendations to the patient and his family without undue embarrassment or apology. This situation is discussed further in the chapter on termination.

WHY DOES THE ADOLESCENT STRIVE FOR THE ALLIANCE?

After surveying all these problems, one might wonder why the therapeutic alliance ever survives the vicissitudes that it meets. These negative forces we have just enumerated are countered by two positive effects which tend to balance them. The first of these is the sense of freedom and release which usually results from increased self-awareness. The adolescent is motivated to persevere because of the sense of mastery which accompanies therapeutic gains. This rational advantage is bolstered by the adolescent's pleasure in the identification with the working therapist. The frequency with which adolescent patients develop the ambition to be a psychotherapist reveals both the identification and, at least very often, the defensive fear of passively losing identity unless they turn passive into active and "go the therapist one better." In my opinion, this defense should not be challenged. Instead, the adolescent should be permitted to regard himself as a junior partner and eventual peer so long as he does not use his psychological insight destructively toward himself or others. After all, when the therapeutic alliance is functioning properly the adolescent is literally functioning as his own therapist much of the time. Even when the adolescent uses his newfound skill destructively, the perversity of such a practice can be interpreted without attacking the identification.

Sarah, the 15-year-old girl with the symptom of promiscuity described earlier, had many preoedipal problems with her mother illustrated by multiple oral-autoerotic behaviors in early childhood.

In the middle course of therapy, she had developed considerable expertise in observing and interpreting her be-

havior and feelings. During this time, she related an interchange with her mother. The mother saw the patient's
kittens, already quite large, nursing the mother cat. She reacted with anger and disgust that such large kittens "would
not leave their mother alone." Sarah interpreted her mother's disapproval of libidinal pleasure and associated to her
mother's negative statements about sexuality. She then told
of accusing her mother of being chronically unhappy because of neurotic self-denial (a correct interpretation, by the
way). She told the mother she really should see a psychiatrist.
The mother became quite angry and criticized Sarah for
needing psychiatric help, since that revealed her lack of
"true Christianity."

Sarah was initially indignant at her mother's reaction
"when I was only trying to help her." The therapist noted
he had been unable to detect much sympathy or understanding in Sarah's comments. Could it be that Sarah was angry
and critical of her mother, simply using her insight as a more
effective weapon of attack?

Sarah was able to accept the interpretation and turn to
an exploration of the origins of her overreaction to her
mother's attitudes toward the cat. She eventually recognized
her identification with the aggressively demanding kittens
and her guilt because her mother acceded to her wishes but
then induced guilt through an air of sadness and martyrdom.

Later in therapy, she came to a sympathetic and affectionate understanding of her mother. She was able to support and encourage the mother to find community activities
in which the mother's dependency needs could be met comfortably and without shame or disgust.

EVIDENCES OF A FAILING ALLIANCE

The recognition that the therapeutic alliance has collapsed usually comes from the same intuitive grasp of the total therapy
situation which was mentioned as the best evidence of the presence of the alliance. One senses a new tendency toward oppo-

sition, not so much toward the therapist but toward the work of therapy. Again, the therapist senses that he is struggling alone in his efforts to utilize the therapeutic session to aid the process of self-understanding. The adolescent is no longer manning one of the oars, and the therapist must paddle upstream without assistance.

Again, there are isolated events which help to confirm the overall impression.

CHECKPOINTS FOR FAILURE OF THE ALLIANCE

1. An absence of any evidence of self-observation and exploration. The adolescent is again immersed in experience and shows little interest either in understanding his role in creating his personal emotional experiences or in dealing effectively with these experiences.
2. Subtle or gross actions directed toward the therapist which are dismissed as unimportant even when they are noted. Examples would include coming late, missing sessions, interrupting the therapist, frequently misunderstanding the therapist's words, and other manifestations of hostility, but also bringing gifts, praising the therapist, and other seductive behaviors.
3. The reappearance of defensive attitudes which were previously interpreted, understood, and discarded. Again, this is accompanied by a bland disregard of the implications of the behavior.
4. A return of manipulative behavior and attitudes toward the therapist. Stated differently, there is a return to neurotic interpersonal interaction with the therapist expressed in action rather than verbalized for exploration.

REESTABLISHING THE ALLIANCE

If the therapist identifies a disruption of the therapeutic alliance, he can then work to repair it. The therapist should recognize that no other work will be useful until the alliance has been reestablished. No matter how much inherent interest the content of the sessions may hold, the therapist should utilize only that portion of the material which may help to rebuild the therapeutic alliance. In the absence of a working alliance, the therapist's intervention will be ineffective or even antitherapeutic.

How, then, can the therapist reestablish the alliance? The first step is the identification of the cause of the disruption. As mentioned above, the most common sources of disruption are the anxiety and uncomfortable affects released through the activity of the therapeutic alliance itself. One very honest 13-year-old, confronted with her resistance, stated the problem succinctly: "The trouble with looking at yourself is that it doesn't feel good."

Of course, this is the very stuff of which therapy is made. The therapist should accept the inevitable fact that properly conducted psychotherapy produces pain and all people try to avoid pain. The adolescent patient has every right to complain about this and to expect his therapist to sympathize. Mankind has always chafed under the painful demands of reality. Surely, we can be sympathetic and supportive when the adolescent frets at these nettles. Of course, the therapist's sympathy is directed at helping the adolescent to bear this realistic fact of life, not toward shielding him from it.

When confronted with a break in the therapeutic alliance, the therapist needs tactfully to acknowledge with his patient the change in their relationship. Often, the therapist will have to explain to the adolescent that his change is not viewed as "goofing off," obstinacy, or rebelliousness. The distinction between resisting the therapist and resisting the therapeutic process often needs extensive clarification if the adolescent is to learn how to observe this interaction objectively and without feeling criticized by the therapist. It is essential to help the adolescent to understand that his interactions with the therapist will be treated in the same objective, curious, nonjudgmental way with which the therapist responds to his other affective experiences.

Tammy, an attractive and petite 17-year-old blonde, requested psychotherapy one night in the midst of a family row over her poor school performance. She told her therapist that her real reason for wishing to be in therapy was a feeling that life was passing her by and that she was unable to form close friendships that were meaningful to her. Over the first few psychotherapy sessions, Tammy formed a warm relationship with the therapist and utilized her capacities for introspection with some success in understanding her relationship to her hard-working, intense, and somewhat driven mother. She was able to recognize that her poor academic record reflected both a repudiation of her mother's anxious way of life and a fear of competing with the mother.

Throughout this time, she periodically complained that she did not seem to be popular. Although she first blamed this unpopularity on her moral standards, which she felt were higher than those of most of the girls at her school, she gradually recognized that she was somehow "turning off" the boys who showed an initial interest in her. As this became a focus in therapy, the therapist commented on the fact that Tammy did not seem to take her femininity seriously and seemed in many respects to treat relationships between boys and girls as though they were a game that did not involve any intense feelings. Tammy's response at the time was to distort the comment somewhat and to state defensively that she has engaged in some necking and that she was not afraid of sexuality.

However, in the next interview Tammy was visibly anxious and found it difficult to talk. She fidgeted in her chair and regularly pulled at her skirt. She tended to avoid the therapist's direct gaze and frequently blushed whenever she would try to speak. After a few minutes of this, she was able to become somewhat comfortable, but seemed to be talking at a very superficial level and showing none of her characteristic curiosity about her own feelings, thoughts, and behaviors.

When the therapist commented that it seemed Tammy had lost a good deal of interest in exploring her feelings, Tammy felt that she was being criticized. After the therapist clarified that this was not the case and suggested that feelings about therapy and the therapist could be openly discussed, Tammy was able to say that she was feeling somewhat annoyed with the therapist when she left the previous session and was aware that she was quite upset. She stated further that she could not remember the topic of discussion from her previous session and volunteered that this was unusual for her, since as a rule it was quite easy to remember her sessions. The therapist supported her honesty in this and encouraged her to continue talking about any reactions that she might have had toward the therapist.

Initially, she spoke with some timidity, but gradually this diminished as Tammy began to complain that the therapist was "finding problems" that she did not know she had. Because of this, she could not be sure whether therapy was helping her or making her worse. She noted that generally she enjoyed a good mood most of the time but that she has been rather depressed for the entire past week. At this point, the therapist reminded her that he had commented that she sometimes treated life as a game and refused to take it seriously and suggested that perhaps she found this necessary because of some tendency toward depression, which she was attempting to avoid. The therapist supported her honesty in facing up to some of these sad feelings and wondered with her which course of action held the greatest promise in the long run.

"Well, if you can stand a blubbering idiot, I guess I can weep my way through it. I suppose I've known this all along myself," Tammy replied.

It seems that Tammy's discomfort was related to sexual feelings toward the therapist which were activated by his direct recognition of Tammy's femininity. However, in the absence of a therapeutic alliance strong enough to deal with this kind of material, the appropriate response was in the direction of dealing with the uncomfortable affects stirred by the therapy process in the interest of reestablishing a therapeutic alliance. The techniques of management of sexual transference in adolescents are discussed in the next chapter.

If the disruption of the alliance arises from some unfortunate event in the adolescent's life, a period of unobtrusive and un-demanding support will need to precede any attempt to reestab-lish a therapeutic alliance. As mentioned above, the therapist must allow the adolescent to take the initiative in indicating an interest in continuing the exploratory work of the treatment unless the grief reaction itself is seriously distorted. More likely than not, the adolescent will indicate his readiness to go back to work by complaining, "We don't seem to be getting much done in here lately!" The complaining adolescent may be quite surprised to see his therapist, somewhat worried during the mourning period, suddenly smile and say, "Man, I can't tell you how relieved I am to hear you say that! Let's get with it."

Parental sabotage of the alliance must be recognized and dif-ferentiated from stresses arising from the therapy itself. Often, parental interference is signaled by comments which disavow pre-vious areas of conflict with the parents. The adolescent, on the contrary, reports "therapeutic sessions" with the parents and may imply that they can help him more than the therapist. Especially if such periods coincide with or follow anxious phone calls from the parents, the suspicion of parental sabotage is justified. These problems are discussed more fully in a later chapter, but it is well to recognize that the problem cannot be handled unilaterally with the adolescent patient once it has reached this level. The parents themselves must be helped either through a collaborative ther-apist or directly by family conferences.

THE ALLIANCE IN PERSPECTIVE

The therapeutic alliance is not only essential to any psycho-therapy; it coincides with an important developmental task of the adolescent period—the emergence of the observing ego. There-fore, the development and maintenance of a therapeutic alliance with the adolescent patient assume a double importance. We have explored some of the particular problems and pitfalls in estab-lishing a therapeutic alliance during this phase of psychosexual development. We have also tried to point out that the maintenance of the alliance is inextricably linked to various other aspects of therapy, especially the transference tendencies of the adolescent and the problems of the adolescent's parents. The capacity to establish a therapeutic alliance is an essential skill for the therapist of the adolescent.

At this time therapists are struggling to treat increasing numbers of adolescents whose problems make it extremely difficult for them to develop a classical therapeutic alliance. Because of severe defects in their sense of self they cannot even grasp the concept of growing through honest self-scrutiny and often cannot understand the therapist's role as a separate and helpful human being. In the next chapter we will try to understand the subjective experience of these youngsters and to explore techniques for helping them.

CITED AND RECOMMENDED READINGS

Adatto, C. P. 1966. On the metamorphosis from adolescence into adulthood. *Journal of the American Psychoanalytic Association*. 14: 485–509.

Balint, M. 1952. *Primary Love and Psycho-analytic Technique*. London: Hogarth Press. (New York: Liveright Publishing Corporation).

Blos. P. 1962. *On Adolescence: A Psychoanalytic Interpretation*. New York: The Free Press of Glencoe.

Freud, S. 1912. The dynamics of transference. *Standard Edition, Volume 12*, pp. 97–108.

Friedman, L. 1969. The therapeutic alliance. *International Journal of Psychoanalysis*. 50: 139–153.

Greenson, R. 1967. *The Technique and Practice of Psychoanalysis, Vol I*. New York: International Universities Press.

Holmes, D. 1964. *The Adolescent in Psychotherapy*. Boston: Little, Brown & Co.

Keith, C. R. 1968. The therapeutic alliance in child psychotherapy. *Journal of the American Academy of Child Psychiatry*. 7: 31–43.

Laufer, M. 1966. Object loss and mourning during adolescence. *Psychoanalytic Study of the Child*. 21: 269–293.

Long, R. 1968. The observing ego and adolescent development. *Rev. Inst. Nac. Neurology*. (Mexico) 2: 8–12.

Meeks, J. 1970. Children who cheat at games. *Journal of the American Academy of Child Psychiatry*. 9: 157–170.

Rochlin, G. 1965. *Griefs and Discontents: The Forces of Change*. Boston: Little, Brown & Co.

Root, N. N. 1957. A neurosis in adolescence. *Psychoanalytic Study of the Child.* 12: 320–334.

Westman, J. 1970. Personal communication.

CHAPTER 5

malignant defenses, malignant resistances, and atypical alliances

Although the model of the therapeutic alliance described in the previous chapter is one that the therapist should always strive for, it cannot always be achieved. In some ways it must be regarded as an ideal since as Adatto (1966) has pointed out, many adolescents in psychotherapy will utilize the therapist as a real object in their psychological development. Some youngsters, particularly psychotic and borderline youngsters, youngsters with severe narcissistic pathology, and youngsters with severe character problems exaggerate the adolescent tendency to force the therapist to play a role in their lives which is quite different from the image of a neutral, objective guide.

It seems evident that many of these adolescents cannot tolerate the degree of distancing and neutrality implied in the traditional therapeutic alliance. Their sense of self is so fragmented and distorted that they cannot develop the degree of relatedness to a real person in a specific role which would allow an even-handed and nonjudgmental discussion of their psychological functioning. From a pragmatic clinical viewpoint, however, it seems that many of these youngsters benefit materially from a psychotherapeutic interaction in spite of the absence of a therapeutic alliance dominated by observing ego functions.

Progress in the absence of an ideal alliance is a psychotherapeutic process which is still poorly understood and relatively unexplored. Many therapists are very uncomfortable when they are pressed into a role in the adolescent's life which seems at variance with their own professional identity as a psychotherapist.

DEVELOPMENTAL FACTORS: THE CONCEPT OF COMPETENCE

The forces that produce a sense of hopelessness in the adolescent include all those which afflict adults including unresolvable internal conflicts, significant losses, major physical illnesses, and the like. The adolescent faces, in addition, major developmental strains which probably account for the high rate of emotional disability during the adolescent years in spite of generally robust health, massive increases in drive energy, and an appropriate future orientation which generally would allow for some discounting of current difficulties and discouragements. The adolescent's problem is that he or she is sufficiently mature and well informed to become acutely aware of a need for self-confidence, problem-solving skills, adequate educational background, interpersonal effectiveness, and a whole range of coping abilities which We will lump together for ease of communication into the word competence. The adolescent knows that these skills are prerequisite for adult success—and knows that he or she does *not* have them. The adolescent simply does not have sufficient maturity and experience to have these skills well honed, especially during early adolescence. These are abilities that will only gradually take shape during the course of adolescent development and will reach their fruition in early adulthood with continuing refinement, if all goes well, until senility or death diminishes capacity.

Since it is very difficult for adolescents to wait, this awareness of inescapable skill requirements compared to current ineptitude produces anxiety for the most normal of adolescents. This anxiety is typically expressed in the erratic adaptational level shown by many young people which includes periods of disavowed dependency and helplessness alternating with periods of unrealistic grandiosity. In the relatively normal adolescent, both of these extremes are subordinate to more extended periods of limited and focused dependent learning relationships coupled with peer and adult support. The entire process is sustained by the optimistic expectation that the goals of adulthood are achievable.

Still there are periods of concern. At times during this adaptation the adolescent will consider anxiously some identities and lifestyles which would lower the complexity and intensity of his anticipated adult adjustment. The very bright and academically capable adolescent may think of living quietly on a farm somewhere, communing only with nature and perhaps the county agricultural extension agent.

Searching criticism of the adult culture is common not only because the adolescent needs to find values and objectives worthy of sacrifice and effort but also because he hopes there might be a lighter load, an easier path.

Fortunately—given the inner strengths developed through childhood and latency, a reasonable degree of support and training from the current adult population, peer friendships, and the major positive developmental thrust provided by nature—most adolescents arrive rather successfully at the same kind of flawed but generally productive and enjoyable adulthood that most of us have achieved.

However, our concern is with the sizable group of adolescents who encounter significant problems in reaching this realistic and highly desirable endpoint. We need a little more discussion about how normal development proceeds in order to orient ourselves to the basic differences in the problems that our adolescent patients encounter.

MORE ON THE CONCEPT OF COMPETENCE

Obviously the development of a sense of competence is a highly complex series of conscious and unconscious mental operations. We would like to artificially simplify that complexity in order to focus the discussion. We suggest that competence—the inner confidence that one can cope successfully with people, learn new skills, and master challenges—grows out of an ongoing interaction between the development of individual personal skills coupled with positive and helpful interactions with other people.

The relationship between personal experimentation and the use of help is most obvious in the young child where the joy of mastery and the widening scope of exploration and experimentation are periodically interrupted by frustration or anxiety which is allayed through temporary supportive contact with a trusted and empathic adult. This sequence of events is at its peak during the final stages of the toddler's effort to gain individuation—that period of life so aptly designated by Mahler (1975) as the period of rapprochement.

During this alteration between adventuresomeness and retreat to psychological home base, we can assume that there are corresponding internal variations in the subjective sense of competence. The toddlers venturing forth to try new things, explore new areas, and test new skills surely must have a sense of positive expectation which can evaporate rapidly if they encounter unexpected setbacks or frightening events. In their tearful rush back toward their mothers one can observe no evidence of their previous self-confidence and hopefulness.

However, as the mother provides appropriate support while encouraging and accepting the movement away from her at the child's own rate, we can observe a gradual increase in the youngster's ability to tolerate greater uncertainty, overcome larger obstacles, and explore ever more unfamiliar terrain and events. We must assume that youngsters in some way build within their own minds a capacity to comfort themselves. There must be an internal prospective image which recognizes a growing ability to comprehend and problem solve and also an expectation of the reliability of help from others when individual effort is not sufficient. In short the toddler gradually develops a competence based on recognition of personal mastery skills coupled with trust that when these skills and abilities are not sufficient alone, appropriate help and support will be provided from a basically kindly and supportive world of others.

Along with these developments there is a simultaneous growth of emotional depth, an ever widening capacity for empathy, and most important, an ability to develop affectionate attachments. These emotional developments allow an increasing openness to intimacy which leads over a lifetime to a degree of self-affirmation and consolidation of identity which carries marked resilience to stress.

Unfortunately in clinical work, therapists are involved primarily with people who have encountered serious problems in successfully developing this sense of competence. Oversimplifying again for the purposes of discussion, there may be advantages to thinking of patients as being from two groups. The first group is made up of those adolescents who have progressed to the point of accepting personal competence as a reasonable goal even though they may doubt their ability to achieve that desirable endpoint. This group was just considered in the chapter on the traditional therapeutic alliance. The second group is constituted of adolescents who do not accept competence as their psychological objective, indeed who cannot even conceive of achieving that status.

Many of the concepts used here are quite similar to the traditional notion that patients may have either genital or pregenital sources of their difficulties. Yet, it is worthwhile to consider the issues from this slightly different perspective for clinical reasons. Conceptualizing the issues in the ways that I will be suggesting may be helpful in planning therapy and particularly in understanding transference reactions and the nature of the therapeutic alliance.

The influences of Kohut (1971), Masterson (1978, 1981), and Kernberg (1975, 1978, 1984) will be obvious although we do not pretend to the careful psychoanalytic theoretical discipline that they bring to their writing. Our comments should be considered purely in a clinical framework.

YOUNGSTERS WITH BENIGN DEFENSES

Let us begin with the group of patients who develop an acceptance of competence as a goal that they desire but despair of achieving. These are individuals who usually have not had major biological or constitutional defects, have enjoyed "good enough" mothering in their earlier years, and who are accepted by their parents as separate, reasonably intact human beings. They develop difficulties in achieving an accurate and positive view of themselves because something about their more or less realistic nature—a view of them closely resembling their actual selves—causes one or both parents excessive fascination or anxiety. In other words the adolescent either "seduces" or threatens one or both parents through characteristics that the child actually or potentially possesses, such as masculinity, femininity, intellectual potential, or the like. In other instances it is not so much that the parents react in this way as it is that external events such as divorce, death of a parent, illness in the parent, illness or injury to the child, or other happenings are interpreted as though they reflected parental displeasure, disappointment, or lack of affection for the developing youngster. Obviously we are talking about the broad range of neurotic adolescent problems and adjustment reactions serious enough to cause the adolescent to be referred for therapy.

Adolescents who come for treatment with a background like this usually see themselves as the problem. They suffer from various fears about themselves, fears which might be characterized as irrational but not unreasonable. They worry, for example, that their thoughts and feelings are bad or shameful or silly or childish. They worry that they themselves are inadequate, too little, too dumb, too ugly, too thin, too fat. Probably most of them do not really believe that the fears are true. These are concerns that they are supposed to believe and that indeed do trouble them. With careful listening, however, one can usually hear an almost playful air of pretense in the neurotic fears. These adolescents are presenting us with a gravely important drama but the tragedy is only tentative; the hero may still save the day. Deep down these adolescents know that they have the capacity for competence. They think in some dim and hidden way that they have been placed under a curse which forbids them to express their abilities and enjoins them from enjoying their capacity to love and be loved.

Such adolescents come to therapy searching for a seer who will understand the truth of their situation, solve the riddle of the Sphinx, and release them from their maledictions. The trials they set us to prove ourselves have been described in the previous chapter. They test our integrity, intelligence, and benevolence with inventive and sometimes frightening challenges to see if we can be trusted to face their inner demons. Understanding these tests and avoiding carefully set traps are the basic skills which add an extra dimension to psychotherapy with adolescents.

Once the bewitched adolescent is satisfied that the therapist is trustworthy, friendly, and reasonably able, therapeutic work tends to unfold in a rewarding and interesting manner within the framework of a therapeutic alliance. Although appropriate family work and reasonable attention to educational and other developmental needs are always a part of treatment, the important and central event is the dyadic re-creation within the transference relationship of those encounters and misunderstandings which led the youngster to believe he or she had been jinxed. Since the therapist has no wish or motive to diminish the youngster's competence and no fear of adolescent attractiveness, vigor, and adequacy, many of the previous distortions can be resolved and the youngster leaves therapy with capacities unleashed.

Because this positive outcome is very frequent for this kind of adolescent patient, we can think of their defenses as benign defenses, and their resistances as benign resistances. This is not to deny that treating them takes skill and sustained effort. There are no easy adolescent patients. The problems of this group are only *relatively* benign.

Before considering the second group of adolescents, it is necessary to talk about family dynamics in a little more detail. As mentioned earlier, the youngsters with benign defenses have encountered a need to distort their true natures because of their interaction with their parents or at least their perception of this interaction. Yet, most of the families of these youngsters retain a strong respect for reality and a capacity to internalize conflict even while they confuse their children regarding their true value and capabilities. These parents do not act out themselves though they have neurotic discomfort. They transmit similar neurotic problems to their children while in most other respects training them well for functioning in the world. They do not use their children directly to satisfy their own needs although they may use them to buttress their defenses. Of course, they still damage the child by projecting their fearful and constricting vision of the child's nature.

There is a second group of families strong enough to fill the developmental needs of the child up to a point of genuine individuation who nonetheless have problems in their own relationship with reality. These parents, though basically neurotic, do transmit to the youngster permission for ego regression and at least for certain specific areas of acting out. This is the concept of the superego lacunae (Johnson, 1965).

Marilyn, 14-years-old, came to residential therapy because of uncontrollable acting out. She was involved in total rebellion against her parents, promiscuity, alcohol and drug abuse, and absolute belligerence toward all adults and all of society's rules. Yet, given a residential staff offering consistent limits, positive attention, and a reflective exploratory attitude toward her behavior, Marilyn quickly demonstrated her basic strengths as well as her neurotic distortions about her sexuality and her capacity to function as an individual. As one might expect the past history gave many clues that Marilyn indeed was healthier than her presenting picture might have suggested. She had had a stable childhood; in fact there was evidence of overattachment and excessive dependency on the mother with some separation problems in early latency. Difficulties began only when secondary sexual characteristics appeared in early adolescence. In this instance a long-term follow-up revealed that Marilyn's mother had been struggling with intense antisocial impulses at the time of Marilyn's early adolescence. These tendencies later erupted in a series of extramarital affairs and an arrest for shoplifting even though the family was quite wealthy.

The point is that not every neurotic adolescent presents with an internalized problem and a positive desire for psychotherapy. On the contrary there is usually at least some effort toward an alloplastic solution. In the case of families where behavioral resolutions are accepted, there may be a considerable overlay of acting out behavior. One must also consider the important distinction between fixation and regression, considering the best level of development achieved by the child and recognizing that, in a panic over failure to move forward, the adolescent often shows both instinctual and ego regression. The degree of regression can be considerable, particularly if drugs are added to the problem mix. These points are usually revealed clearly if the diagnostic process has been methodically followed as described in chapter 3.

MALIGNANT DEFENSES

Many adolescents who present in extreme rebellion against the world, reality, adults, and conventional expectations are not just going through a phase, are not disguised neurotics, and are not benign in their defenses, resistances, or their treatment outcome. The problems are malignant, very destructive to any opportunity for emotional development and very difficult to treat successfully. Unfortunately, they now comprise a large percentage of the caseload of most adolescent psychiatrists.

The early history of these adolescents often reveals evidence of basic defects in the ego apparatus. Many of them have suffered learning disability, attention deficit disorder, neonatal brain damage, or other difficulties which have compromised the basic apparatus for modulation of affective and motor discharge and development of cognitive skills. Often in addition to these disadvantaged emotional beginnings, there is evidence that the nurturing environment was deficient, frequently to a tragically extreme degree. Stories of early neglect and abandonment, child abuse, and sexual molestation are not uncommon. Even when there is not such active ill-use of the child, there is still clear-cut evidence of marked family system pathology. This pathology usually includes severe distortions of generational boundaries, active and direct use of the child to meet parental needs, a bewildering muddle of communication, and a general readiness to distort aspects of reality when these are uncomfortable or inconvenient for family members. The impact of these forces on the developing child is predictable and devastating. To varying degrees in each of these children the effort to gain a sense of competence is undermined by two factors: personal ego skills are deficient and the development of trust in the dependability of helpfulness of surrounding adults is sabotaged.

That success is necessary to encourage and support skill development is obvious to both our common sense and our obser-

vations of children. Youngsters tend to simply stop trying if they
encounter repeated failure. Severe stunting of skill development
will follow since all ego skills require success and practice. The
youngster is reluctant to try new environmental challenges, senses
the environment as a threat, and does not develop an inner conviction of mastery. This can be reversed or at least ameliorated
through careful support and handling by the parents (see Thomas
et al., 1968). If this help is not available, however, the negative
spiral into disordered functioning accelerates.

We have discussed earlier the need for dependable dependency
support to promote a youngster's acceptance of challenge and
to forestall a paralyzing fear of the environment. The absence of
this support, especially when coupled with personal deficiencies
in coping skills, leads to a sense of helplessness, panic, and a
fearful dread of real world challenges. These terrified youngsters
cannot move beyond infantile omnipotence as their primary system for feeling safe in the world. Tentative efforts to cope realistically are doomed to failure since they lack both skill and
persistence, so the child regresses to omnipotent defenses again
and again.

As these youngsters grow older they enhance omnipotent fantasy with both the motor and intellectual skills that develop in
the course of maturation. Ingenious arguments, manipulations,
and distortions obscure the basic irrationality of their world view
to themselves and to others. The families' lack of commitment to
reality further supports this pseudosolution. Indeed, if the particular family system pathology needs an ill or deviant youngster,
the family may directly and indirectly promote, support, and even
require continuation of the unrealistic world view. The therapist
is faced with a conspiracy to confuse the issue, avoid the important
questions of life, and preserve the magical world view.

Since these children do not anticipate successful mastery of
challenges, they avoid those developmental tasks which would
point up their areas of vulnerability. As a result their developmental skills lag steadily further behind their age mates. As their
inner sense of helplessness and incompetence increases, their
need to delude themselves and others grows and their efforts to

Students of psychotherapy will discover a confusing landscape of articles and books which address the theory, the diagnosis, and the treatment of borderline and narcissistic personality disorders. It would be good to have a map to guide the exploration of these territories—and several maps are available. Munich (1986) described manifestations of narcissism in adolescents and speculated how Kohut and Kernberg might handle the same clinical situations. Masterson (1971, 1978, 1981) has critiqued the views of Kohut (1971) and Kernberg (1975) and has advanced his own theory: that the narcissistic personality disorder is fixated before the development of the rapprochement crisis, while the borderline personality disorder is an inability to resolve the rapprochement crisis. Masterson's work applies particularly to adolescents. Meissner (1984, 1988) and Druck (1989) have prepared "atlases" on the diagnosis and treatment of borderline patients. Druck's book is helpful because he explains and contrasts four basic models for understanding borderline psychopathology.

maintain a myth of omnipotent control over themselves, others, and their external world becomes ever more desperate. Because of this series of events, by adolescence their defenses are often malignant and if they come for therapy the resistances they bring are malignant also.

The omnipotent defenses are usually action-based to a degree far beyond the normal alloplastic tendencies of the adolescent. Not only do these youngsters act out, their acting out is energetically directed toward changing the world around them in ways that are clearly unrealistic.

For example, severely delinquent adolescents act as though there is no need to follow rules, as though all needs can be met immediately, and as though the goodwill and support of others is unnecessary. They pretend that everything can be obtained by cunning, intimidation, or simple theft.

It is important to remember that these syndromes are active, coherent adjustment efforts, not simply the chaotic and random breakthrough of impulses. For example, careful observation of any severely antisocial youngster shows that much acting out is done to buoy a flagging sense of omnipotent control rather than because the youngster is upset or out of control. The delinquent youngster needs the "fix" of conning someone, successfully pulling off a caper, or simply intimidating someone in order to maintain a sense of self-esteem. Paradoxically, this need can be intensified by a friendly or supportive interaction or anything else that threatens the defensive stance. If these youngsters looked at themselves objectively, in the real world, they would see a lonely, insecure, unsuccessful child perpetually pursued by anxiety and depression. However, in the gangland fantasy of an all-conquering, daring macho man or gun moll fearlessness, there is a sense of safety and strength. Unfortunately, since the youngster is not omnipotent at all, there is an ever recurrent need to re-project the flickering outline of this fragile mirage (Meeks, 1979).

However, no matter how unsuitable this solution appears to us, it is the only possible solution the adolescent can imagine. It is not possible to learn or to gain in skills without facing areas of inadequacy and vulnerability. You can't learn what you don't know that you don't know. These youngsters are unable to entertain such a frightening vista and must view themselves as all-conquering know-it-alls at all times. Obviously then, these youngsters do not present themselves to a psychotherapist with a sense that they are troubled. They may admit that things are messed up but if so they place the blame outside themselves and complain of unfair teachers, harsh law enforcement personnel, unreliable friends, and, of course, stupid psychotherapists. In other words, what we see as their problems are all that they have going for them. Their pathology is egosyntonic to say the least.

Even at those times when these adolescents cannot maintain this self view, there is still no entree for the therapist. When the omnipotence is shattered and the youngsters recognize their destructiveness to self and others, that awareness causes a massive helpless depression which cannot even conceive of solution and which eventually must lead to suicide or another effort to reinstate the omnipotent defenses. Yochelson and Samenow (1976) have called this the "zero state."

These adolescents do not view their defensive structures as problematic; in fact, they actively look for people who will support these distorted life views. If they cannot find friends who share their view of the world, they will avoid human contact. Anyone who tries to relate closely to them while questioning their unrealistic lifestyle or, heaven forbid, espousing a more realistic approach to life's difficulties, very rapidly becomes an enemy, subject to active attack. Their motto might be, "Love me, love my illness."

Naturally, this presents some difficulties for the prospective psychotherapist. By the very nature of our profession the circumstances which lead to our contact with these adolescents set the stage for a very negative encounter. They wouldn't be in our presence if everything were as wonderful as they want to believe. These adolescents do not approach the therapist with the sense of playful curiosity about themselves that can be developed through a therapeutic alliance with youngsters with benign defenses. The universal initial adolescent negative reaction to therapy tends to continue in these cases of malignant defense. These youngsters are not won over by fairness, objectivity, and benevolence. Indeed as these adolescents see things, these characteristics in the therapist pose a serious threat to maintenance of their only possible emotional safety. They try to cure the therapist of dangerous tendencies such as benevolence, honesty, and objectivity. The patients actively try to corrupt, intimidate, enrage, disgust, or in some other way invalidate the therapist's stance as a friendly and helpful adult. They do not want a kindly and wise seer since they have actively concocted—with a little help from their parents and friends—an illusory self, and truth about this is the last thing in the world they want to hear.

In spite of these difficulties the character pathology in these youngsters is malignant but neither untreatable nor unavoidably psychologically terminal. If these adolescents are not able to let us be involved with them in an intimate dyadic psychologically exploratory relationship, some other approach may permit them to see us as a potentially useful adult.

Perhaps we can begin to explore an approach by considering a metaphor. If the youngsters with benign defenses were in search of a benevolent seer, *these* youngsters are looking for the Wizard of Oz. Aware that they are lacking in heart, brain, or will, these boys and girls hope to find a magician who can grant them their wish for wholeness which they believe will provide a grandiose and omnipotent success. This hope for magic solutions takes them to cults, gurus, and modern day delinquent Mr. Fagans who are always ready to exploit their dreams. How can we, who pride ourselves on being scientific (or at least empiric) and non-exploitive, follow the old therapeutic truism and meet *these* patients where they are?

Obviously we would not suggest that we promise magic solutions since we cannot deliver them. On the other hand we may need to accept these patients' need to distort our function in order to tolerate therapy with us. Also, we may have to become comfortable with the fact that we actively influence patients. We have not always been willing to acknowledge that we utilize our positions of perceived or real power and authority in ways that are subtly or not so subtly coercive. The following clinical vignette illustrates this point. We have chosen Ralph because he is a transitional example, if you will, a somewhat milder, eventually verbal version of malignancy.

Ralph was referred for psychotherapy as a 16-year-old near the middle of his sophomore year in high school. The referral was initiated by Ralph's mother over Ralph's protest and with only lukewarm support from the father. The mother requested to speak with the psychiatrist before Ralph was seen and was given an appointment.

She explained that she had been quite concerned about Ralph for two or three years. She stated that Ralph had never been an outstanding student but had accomplished an acceptable performance in elementary school. She also noted that in the earlier grades Ralph was friendly, socially accepted, cheerful, and "resilient." When Ralph was in the

sixth grade the family moved and Ralph had to enter a different school. The mother felt that this experience was very
hard on the boy although he did make some new friends
and appeared to be adjusting to his new situation. The seventh grade also did not present problems, but in the eighth
grade Ralph began to have significant problems with the
other youngsters. He stated that he was not liked and began
to be more reticent at home. He began to have difficulty
getting to school on time in the mornings, and his grades
began to deteriorate.

Near the end of the eighth grade the parents consulted a
psychologist who stated that he felt too much pressure was
being placed on Ralph. The mother said that much of this
pressure came from her husband, an extremely successful
and aggressive businessman who owned his own company.
The mother stated that Ralph's father was affectionate and
relaxed with their 13-year-old daughter but focused his attention on Ralph entirely around school performance, work
at home, and other achievement goals.

Both parents were quite intelligent and basically cooperative. After the school conference they made an effort to
follow the advice they had been given. The father stopped
complaining to Ralph regarding his poor performance although he continued to voice anger and disappointment to
Ralph's mother regarding the boy.

Near the end of the eighth grade year Ralph's best friend
Danny moved out of the area. At that point Ralph seemed
to completely give up all social contacts. He did make an
effort to keep in touch with Danny by mail but seemed to
always compare himself unfavorably with his lost friend. He
was particularly upset when Danny wrote with the news that
he had a serious girl friend. At that time Ralph told his
mother, "Danny's made it and I haven't."

Ralph's steady slide continued through the ninth grade.
Toward the end of that year the parents took him to a psychiatrist who evaluated Ralph and told the parents that he
had very poor self-esteem and was moderately depressed.

Ralph went to the psychiatrist reluctantly. He had attended only two sessions when school ended and Ralph got a job. He quit therapy telling his parents that he would return to treatment in the fall. However, in the fall he refused to see the psychiatrist again, stating "I've got it all together." The parents insisted that he go back for at least one session. Ralph went late to his appointment and told the psychiatrist, "Don't let my mother make any more appointments." At the beginning of the tenth grade Ralph indicated that he wished to enroll in distributive education which allowed him to attend school a half day and work. His grades continued to be poor although he seemed to be performing acceptably in his job as a gas station attendant. The mother felt that he had gotten rather heavily into pot. She stated that a few weeks before Ralph had told her that he was quitting marijuana.

The mother felt Ralph was worried about his masculinity. A friend of his once told her that Ralph gave up too easily in making friendships with girls. The friend indicated that Ralph had called one girl for a date but when he received a negative reply he withdrew and refused to call any more girls. Ralph said at the time that he would never have a girl friend.

The mother stated that she felt Ralph was extremely depressed. He had recently said to her, "You think life is great and wonderful. I hate it." When the mother wept in response to hearing this despairing comment, Ralph became angry with her and shouted, "Stop that, that's what made me such an old lady." On another occasion he told the mother that when he was 21 he would get a gun and finish all of this. The mother felt that Ralph looked depressed almost all of the time. She was very worried about him and seemed particularly concerned about her relationship with the boy. She and Ralph had had excellent communication until about two years ago. He had told her during the time when they were closer, "You're proud of me, but I'll never make father proud of me." The mother said that she and the father had argued a good deal during Ralph's early life. She admitted that she might be somewhat indulgent and overprotective but felt that the father was unreasonably demanding of precocious independence from Ralph. The father was especially strict regarding table manners and total obedience to rules when Ralph was a young child.

During this interview the therapist asked to speak to Ralph's father. She seemed somewhat hesitant, stating that she felt Ralph's father "had given up on Ralph." The therapist sensed that mother was trying to "sell" Ralph to him. She seemed concerned the father would discourage the therapist from making a treatment effort with her son. When the therapist insisted, however, she agreed and Ralph's father did accept an appointment.

The father was a very handsome man, noticeably younger in appearance than his wife though they were approximately the same age. He was cooperative and stated, "Ralph's having a lot of problems with his own feelings about himself." When asked to expand on that, he replied, "The ones I fasten on depend on my mood. I'm moody and I reflect a lot." In his opinion the family had "normal family frictions" and probably "doesn't communicate too well."

The father focused a great deal on Ralph's performance difficulties, admitting that Ralph's poor school achievement bothered him. It bothered him even more that Ralph was difficult to get up in the mornings and customarily went late to all scheduled activities. The father admitted he was extremely annoyed by Ralph not seeming to care whether he was on time or not. Interestingly the father stated that he felt Ralph had "given up on himself." He noted that Ralph's one ambition was to be a guitarist in a rock group but that in fact Ralph had demonstrated no musical talent. The father stated that the only thing he and Ralph did with mutual pleasure was ice skating.

Both parents indicated that Ralph had told them that a traumatic event occurred during his eighth grade year that he could not discuss with them. This secret, Ralph stated, was the cause of his depression and continuing problems.

An interview with Ralph was scheduled although both parents had some concern that he would not keep the appointment. They asked if there was any point in "forcing" Ralph to come to the interview. The therapist told them that Ralph should come to the appointment if they had to drag him there. In fact, Ralph came reluctantly but voluntarily. He was overweight, unattractive, clearly depressed, and just as clearly sulky and petulant. His long hair was lank and appeared dirty and his dress was somewhat sloppy and disheveled. He spoke reluctantly and there was considerable conscious withholding, but in addition there was genuine psychomotor retardation. Though there was no apparent thought disorder, it did seem that Ralph occasionally became confused and had some difficulty in maintaining his train of thought. He stated rather early in the interview in a somewhat challenging way that he was not going to talk about his real problem. The therapist elected to pursue a friendly cross examination since Ralph's manner somehow suggested that that was what he expected and needed. This interrogation gradually revealed the following points:

1. Someone had let him down in a very serious and painful way but Ralph could not talk about this.
2. Ralph had a secret too embarrassing and painful to disclose.
3. "Half the time" Ralph felt hopeless and thought that his problems were insoluble.
4. The effort to solve his problems was too much trouble anyway.
5. He could not trust the therapist because the therapist might use information against him or simply not understand him or both.

Ralph said that both parents irritated him, especially his mother. She irritated him first of all by being too nice and explaining too much and secondly by singing nursery rhymes and "acting like a kid sometimes." Ralph thought that at times he blamed his parents for his problem. His blaming did not take any definite form, "just the way they are. They raised me." Ralph stated that he had never told his mother that he was angry at her because she was very sensitive and "it would hurt her." When asked how he would know she was hurt, he stated that she would cry. Ralph was unable to say anything specific about how his father irritated him but with some prodding said, "bugging me like waking me up or sometimes treating me like a little kid."

Ralph quickly seemed uncomfortable about these complaints toward his parents and added, "It's probably all just my fault, I don't know." He stated that he did not have any friends but that he would like to have some if they were "the right kind." When asked what sort would be the right kind, he stated, "Someone who doesn't hurt me. Someone I can trust, and someone who is popular."

The therapist formed a diagnostic impression of an extremely narcissistic boy with a severe depressive neurosis. The presence of multiple neurotic traits of compulsive rumination, phobic tendencies, and a suspiciousness which verged on the paranoic suggested poor ego structure and the possibility of a borderline personality organization. Both the parents and Ralph were told that Ralph's problems were extremely serious. When Ralph stated that he still did not wish to have therapy, he was told firmly that he had only two choices, either to come in for individual sessions or to be part of family therapy. He was told that he did not have a right to refuse therapy in view of the pain and concern which his unhappiness was creating in his family. The effect of this comment seemed to be more supportive and face-saving than upsetting to Ralph. He was able to accept individual treatment on this basis.

The first few months of treatment with Ralph were characterized primarily by long silences and an extreme dearth of material. He seemed to be relaxing, however, and occasionally would enter into brief discussions with the therapist. The therapist maintained an extremely active, cheerful, and chatty manner although Ralph's sullen silence and unresponsiveness sometimes caused the one-sided happy chatter to sound a bit like the babblings of a good-natured idiot. After about four months of treatment Ralph announced that he would like to describe the traumatic events which happened to him in junior high but that he was not sure he could. This, of course, represented a significant breakthrough since previously he had stated that he was absolutely unwilling to discuss this matter. The therapist took this as permission to prod, pry, cajole, and actively pursue this material. Three or four sessions later Ralph described the events which happened in the eighth grade. Basically they involved a competitive run-in with a youngster who became his enemy. This youngster had considerable skill at teasing and was able to get groups of youngsters to laugh at Ralph on a few occasions on the school grounds. The ultimate upset occurred when this enemy drew a caricature of Ralph on the school wall with spray paint, particularly emphasizing Ralph's somewhat oversized nose. All the kids laughed and thought the picture was funny. Ralph was humiliated.

Over the next few sessions Ralph continued to discuss the impact of these events on his attitudes and thinking. It became clear that he had developed an almost paranoid attitude toward other youngsters which at times approached "ideas of reference." For example, if Ralph would see two youngsters laughing together he would wonder if perhaps they were talking about him and laughing at him. He also came to feel that school work was not important. He dreaded attending school each morning and could hardly force himself to go, thus accounting for his chronic tardiness. He became more and more seclusive and did not wish to talk with his family since he felt sure they would not understand his problem. He was concerned that his father would criticize him for not dealing more effectively with the situation while his mother would be overly sympathetic and excessively supportive. Specifically he felt that his mother would tell him that he was a handsome and likeable youngster when he felt convinced that he was ugly, obnoxious, and unlikeable.

Several months were spent dealing with Ralph's reaction to these events in early adolescence. The therapist focused particularly on the absence of any memory of overt anger, desire to retaliate, or obvious competitiveness in Ralph's response to his peer problems. Initially Ralph flatly denied having any such feelings but gradually began to recover some memories of anger and competitiveness. These bothered him a great deal and he confessed them with tremendous guilt. At the time of entry into treatment Ralph was an avowed pacifist who stated that he had strong moral opposition to violence in any form. Violence for Ralph included many behaviors normally regarded as appropriately aggressive and competitive. For example, he felt that one should never criticize another person even for constructive reasons since that might inflict pain on the other individual.

At this point in treatment the material shifted slightly and Ralph began to talk about his difficulty with girls and his intense desire to have a girl friend. As he described the relationship he wished for, it became clear that his fantasied goal was a symbiotic union with an adored girl friend against the rest of the world. It was crucial to Ralph that his girl friend be absolutely beautiful not only in his own eyes but in the consensual evaluation of the entire world. He recognized that this was unrealistic but maintained that it was crucial to him. Ralph would initially be reticent and reluctant to describe fantasies of this kind, but once they were voiced he would adopt a stubborn defense of his right to have his emotional wishes met. His attitude was, "I don't care if it's crazy, that's what I want anyway." In connection with the discussion of his sexual development and his attitudes toward himself as a male, Ralph gingerly approached another secret. He was never able to confess it on his own, but when the therapist suggested that he had many guilt feelings about masturbation, Ralph wept and admitted that that was the subject he had been alluding to. Again he adopted the attitude that the only solution to this problem was for the therapist to assist him in giving up this totally unacceptable habit. When the therapist finally told him that he thought that was unlikely until the time that Ralph had a sexual relationship with a girl, Ralph was annoyed and declared that the therapist had thereby "undone all the good we've done here."

Ralph continued to argue that the habit of masturbation could be overcome if only the therapist could help him. Ralph insisted on explanations as to why the therapist would not join him in this effort. He was extremely reluctant to accept the reality of the sexual drive and felt that he should rise above it in much the same way that he insisted he should be able to overcome any feelings of anger or competitiveness.

These complaints were merely specific instances of Ralph's general dismissal of the value of therapy. Although he now attended regularly and without protest, he maintained a sullen grumbling attitude toward the treatment effort, frequently noting that it had not helped him. The therapist's attitude toward all these complaints was to accept them without comment even though the family reported that Ralph's behavior had improved considerably and Ralph himself admitted reluctantly that his report card had improved dramatically during the last reporting period. He assured the therapist that it was because he had easy courses and in any event it was of no importance to him.

At this point in therapy Ralph presented another obsession which he stated was virtually exhausting him. In describing the development of this obsession, Ralph inadvertently revealed that his social contacts had increased considerably. In these interpersonal situations Ralph would predictably become anxious at times and would feel he had to get away and be alone so he could "think about the world." What Ralph meant by "thinking about the world" was devising his own mind solutions to all human problems. He felt that if he could solve racial prejudice, poverty, war, and general human suffering so that everyone in the whole world could be happy, then he himself could be content and happy also. If he failed in these mental gymnastics, happiness would be impossible for him. He was convinced at times that with enough perseverence and time, he could succeed at this grandiose undertaking. At other times he recognized the obsession as "a ridiculous mind game" that was serving a defensive function in containing his interpersonal anxiety and his fear of the new situations occurring in his life.

Shortly after this, Ralph found another solution to his dilemma. He announced to the therapist that he was quite sure that the therapist was somehow contacting the youngsters and teachers in his school to "put in a good word for him." He admitted that this seemed impractical and when pushed said that possibly it was only a feeling or thought that he had, but nonetheless he felt "pretty sure" most of the time that the therapist was actively interceding to cause people to treat him better. The "delusion" was particularly interesting in that it was accompanied by a great increase in Ralph's social activity and his comfort with it. He began to date and his parents reported that he now had several friends who frequently called him and came by to visit. Ralph's attitude toward this benevolent interference in his life was somewhat mixed. He was pleased that the therapist wanted things to go well for him but stated that he felt bad that he could not do it on his own. At no time, however, did he ask the therapist to stop interfering nor did he seem angry or resentful about the fantasied intrusion into his personal life.

This phenomenon persisted for approximately four months and then was abruptly dismissed as "a silly idea." During these four months Ralph solidified his social situation and his academic performance converted to a virtual straight A report without much apparent effort on Ralph's part.

Around this time Ralph stated that he felt he only needed to come in weekly. This decrease in frequency of sessions was accepted by the therapist. Ralph used his weekly appointments primarily to report ups and downs in his fortunes in the dating game. He would periodically repeat his worries that he was ugly and that no girl would ever like him. These self-derogatory ruminations slowly became less and less frequent. Ralph gradually developed a capacity to formulate a psychological understanding of why certain relationships did not work out well. He became much more aggressive in pursuing girls that he liked. Although their physical attractiveness remained extremely important to him, he no longer pursued only the girl he regarded as the most beautiful in the class. He now preferred girls who were very attractive but also of interest to him as human beings. After a few months of weekly meetings Ralph stated that he thought he could handle life on his own. This decision came soon after Ralph established a "steady" relationship with a girl. Ralph talked a good deal about this relationship which sounded basically healthy although the couple did spend a great deal of time alone. There did seem to be considerable mutual dependency in the bond. Still, Ralph and his girl friend did socialize in group situations and both of them retained friendships with other youngsters. Ralph showed the therapist the girl's picture. Needless to say, she was very pretty.

Ralph also began to show considerable self-discipline in his academic endeavors, developed a clear-cut vocational goal, and was looking forward to college with positive anticipation. He left therapy with awkward but sincere appreciation. His mother kept the therapist informed of Ralph's continuing success in college.

One year after termination of the first period of psychotherapy the father in this "perfect" family abruptly announced that he was leaving his wife for a younger woman. At that time the mother entered therapy, dealt with her anger and loss, and emerged a healthier person.

As a postscript, Ralph returned for psychotherapy on a once a week basis two years after graduation from college because of a continuation of his difficulties in intimate heterosexual relationships. However, the remainder of his adjustment was adequate and he did not regard himself as being markedly depressed. He has responded very well to traditional, insight-oriented psychotherapy during this course of treatment.

Ralph's case is more clear cut than many involving youngsters with malignant problems. Ralph's solutions to his conviction that he could never be competent were mental and psychological. Therefore they were closer to the neurotic patients that we understand so well than those defenses encountered in many of the more violently acting out youngsters in this group. Ralph did use drugs and massive withdrawal, but these were never totally embraced. In addition, since Ralph had some capacity for reflection, it is somewhat easier to follow the inner experience of the transference. However, the same kind of absurd idealization and unrealistic expectation of help that Ralph brought to therapy can be observed in the incoherent antisocial youngster who becomes attached to his or her therapist. Overhearing "my therapist can whip your therapist" conversations on a therapy unit for antisocial youngsters can be quite enlightening.

The basic point is simply that Ralph and his more aggressive counterparts will view their therapists differently than the neurotic patient. Our readiness to accept unrealistic and even outrageous temporary roles in these patient's lives is important, particularly early in therapy. Some of these roles may offend our identity as scientifically oriented, democratic, liberal, objective, and realistic permissive helpers. We may at times have to assume active postures, promise results, demonstrate and even remember and recount the patient's progress for them, and finally, gradually accept their demystification and humanization of us.

Kohut (1971) has described a process of normal development characterized by a gradual disillusionment with the narcissisticly invested idealized parental image. This disillusionment occurs without any direct verbal disavowal of omnipotent powers on the part of the adult. The unavoidable frustration of unrealistic hopes regarding the adult leads to gradual relinquishing of unrealistic wishes. In the psychotherapeutic relationship, relinquishing this illusion is, of necessity, telescoped in time and tends to be enormously painful and regularly accompanied by alternating periods of depression and rage directed toward the therapist (Wolf, 1984).

Davy, a 16-year-old boy, was admitted to a psychiatric hospital because of a suicide attempt. In the hospital setting he appeared markedly inhibited, frightened of his age-mates, and often near psychotic in his fearfulness of the environment and in his capacity to drift into long periods of reverie during which he seemed totally disinterested in his surroundings. The developmental history revealed that Davy had always been extraordinarily dependent on his mother who regarded him as an extremely sensitive, intelligent, and a "very special human being." He had never had good peer relationships and had tended to be the scapegoat in his classes throughout his school experience.

In his individual sessions Davy spoke very little to his therapist regarding personal matters. He was quite willing to discuss his hobbies which included sports (though he did not participate personally), literature, and music. In all of these areas Davy was unusually well informed and showed a quick and incisive logic which was quite impressive for his age. When pressed to discuss his personal difficulties including the suicide attempt, he would become evasive. If the pressure was continued, Davy would simply clam up.

In family therapy, however, Davy began to express his concern about being overly dependent on his parents and began to ventilate feelings of frustration and anger when his mother's behavior seemed to him to be infantalizing. He also began to rebel against being the scapegoat in the peer group and twice became involved in physical fights when he felt he was being "pushed around." As his general functioning improved, it was decided that Davy could be discharged from the hospital and followed in outpatient treatment. This decision was maintained even though Davy quickly reverted to his social isolation on his return home. Although he continued to decry his inability to relate to people outside his family, he could not bring himself to make any active efforts to change that state of affairs. In his individual treatment, Davy began to speak more freely about himself and his ideas. At the same time he seemed overly interested in the virtual "honor" of being a patient of his therapist. He was preoccupied with the therapist's national reputation, complimented the therapist on the brilliance and subtlety of his simplest statements, and sang the therapist's praise to his family and anyone else who would listen. During this period he confided a variety of grandiose wishes and fantasies about himself and also recounted some embarrassing and frightening daydreams and wishes. He was particularly concerned about some homicidal fantasies and admitted that his suicide attempt was partially an effort to "rid the world of a potential murderer."

As the months went by, the unqualified admiration of the therapist continued but a new theme of identification with this power and Davy's self-adulation became increasingly clear. For example, Davy would develop complex, imaginative metaphyschological theory systems and present them in detail to the therapist. The manner of presentation suggested that he was attempting to earn the admiration of the therapist through emulation of the therapist's area of interest. Although there were some undercurrents of competitiveness, these seemed much less important than the desire to be praised by a "hero" figure.

Gradually, however, Davy began to look for clay feet. He devised situations, such as refusing to attend school, which created crises in which the therapist was powerless. He also showed a wry humor directed at the exalted image of the therapist which he had created. Usually Davy reacted with open anger and disappointment when the therapist had to cancel appointments. During this period, however, Davy suddenly accepted an absence with cheerful indifference. When asked why he wasn't upset this time, Davy replied, "I've come to accept that it's just part of having a semifamous psychiatrist."

Davy was quite depressed during this period. The disappointment of recognizing the therapist's human limitations and lack of magical power was clearly painful. Davy varied between grief and rage toward the therapist. Only gradually was he able to begin to struggle realistically with his own life. After two and a half years of therapy Davy grudgingly admitted, "I guess I'm a lot less crazy than I was two years ago and I suppose you had something to do with that." For the therapist this was quite a comedown from his previous grandeur in Davy's eyes, but for Davy it was a significant improvement in his ability to recognize the genuine value of another human being.

Kernberg (1968) has described in detail the primitive defenses which the borderline youngster uses. He comments particularly on the defense of splitting which is often employed in varying combinations with the unrealistic idealization just described. It is important that the therapist listen attentively to the negative feelings of rage and frustration expressed toward others during the period when the therapist himself is idolized. It can be safely assumed that this hostility and depreciation will eventually be expressed in the transference also. Other youngsters may begin therapy by presenting the negative side of their tendency to split. These youngsters may continue to idealize their parents or other adults and utilize the therapist as the target of their negative projections. This is particularly likely because of projective identification, commonly utilized by these youngsters, which leads them to fear that the therapist is harboring those destructive impulses which are, in fact, struggling for expression in their own minds.

It is important to remember that these styles of relating are not "defensive" in the usual sense. They are more akin to "acting-in"—a demonstration within the treatment situation of serious deficiencies in their previous relationships with parenting figures. They require a gradual living through of these primitive ways of attaching to another human in order to repair damaged or un-

developed intrapsychic personality structures. The self-object patterns of relating in therapy may take several different forms.

THE THERAPIST AS A CORRECTIVE SUPEREGO FIGURE

Another atypical relationship which frequently proves constructive without actually measuring up to a genuine therapeutic
alliance occurs with some youngsters who present with superego
pathology. Johnson (1965), writing about the treatment of youngsters with superego lacunae, has provided important guidelines
in this area. She feels that a major aspect of the treatment relation
with these youngsters is concerned with the search for an incor-
ruptible adult model. In treating youngsters with superego defects, the therapist must remain comfortably alert to the inevi-
tability of efforts to corrupt his conscience. One can be sure that
the patient will, with varying degrees of subtlety, try to get the
therapist to join him in breaking rules or at least in condoning
the youngster's asocial or antisocial behavior.

One therapist described a situation with a patient who was
being interviewed in the course of a stroll. The adolescent was
drinking a soda and as the therapist and patient passed a fence
with a large sign which said "NO TRESPASSING," the patient
casually tossed his empty bottle over the fence. The therapist was
briefly in a quandary since any action on her part seemed to be
corrupt. If she said nothing, the patient could assume that she
countenanced the littering. If she allowed the patient to climb
the fence in order to retrieve the can, that would involve defying
the clearly posted sign. Fortunately, she had the presence of mind
enough to stop and reflect out loud on the dilemma. She said
that though it was hardly the end of the world, she preferred to
follow rules even in this somewhat trivial matter. She considered
the possibilities open to her and the patient's interpretation of
them. She carefully avoided suggesting that the patient had deliberately put her in this moral bind. Her demeanor made it clear
that she did not intend to move on or continue the discussion
until a solution within the rules could be fashioned. After a few
minutes of this the patient said sarcastically but with an undertone

of respect, "Oh, if you're such a goody two shoes, I'll get you out of this one." He picked up a fallen limb, raked the bottle to the fence, retrieved it, and dropped it into a waste receptacle. The therapist complimented him on his ingenuity and thanked him for solving her dilemma.

Other youngsters' may utilize the therapist more directly to strengthen their reality testing and superego controls as Aichorn (1935) has described. A handsome and muscular 15-year-old boy with a history of multiple juvenile offenses regularly insisted to his therapist that he "didn't give a damn" what the therapist thought of his behavior. In spite of this avowal, he gradually began to describe his planned antisocial behavior in advance during his therapy sessions. For example, he would tell the therapist that he badly needed some material object that he did not have the money to buy. He would then talk about the possibility of stealing the object or of dealing in drugs in order to obtain funds. The patient would then state that he knew the therapist disapproved of such activities but would then challenge the therapist as to how the problem could be solved without getting into trouble. At these times the therapist would offer various alternatives such as doing extra work around the home to obtain funds or saving up his allowance. Inevitably the patient would scoff at the advice, but invariably he would follow it. The patient would then return to the next session to complain that the solution was dumb and that he preferred to do things as he had done them in his anti-social past. In spite of this constant harping and apparent hostility, the patient continued to grow and develop, not only avoiding legal problems but showing steady improvement in school work, family relationships, and socialization.

Another 15-year-old boy with strong delinquent tendencies and a history of almost homicidal rage outbursts and physical fights showed sudden and persistent improvement in his functioning shortly after he was hospitalized in an adolescent psychiatric unit. During group psychotherapy another patient asked the boy why he had stopped fighting with everyone and the patient explained, "My doctor is a champion boxer. I'm not about to tangle with that guy." The patient had learned that the therapist was a boxer from a hospital employee who had known the therapist in high school. In fact, the therapist was 10 pounds lighter than the patient and had not boxed in 20 years. In situations of this kind, the patient creates the therapist in some image which allows emergency control of his frightening impulses. It is important to recognize that although these images may be somewhat primitive and at variance with the self image of benevolent nurturing preferred by the therapist, they may be temporarily important to the patient. For a brief period the patient may need to provide himself with the fantasy of someone strong enough and aggressive enough to counter the tempestuous violence within himself. The image of this helpful authority can be gradually modified as the therapist demonstrates in his direct management of the patient a kinder, warmer, but still reliable style of impulse control.

As noted in the introduction, we are on relatively uncharted ground when we accept or at least do not directly disavow such unrealistic images of ourselves. For one thing, we are much more vulnerable to countertransference errors because we are less guided by our tradition and training. Treatment relationships of this kind approach patterns described in psychodrama and go well beyond Alexander's notion of the corrective emotional experience. Since the therapist at least passively takes a role in the externalized drama created by the adolescent patient, there is considerable danger that the adolescent may be used for self-gratification. For example, if the patient places one in the position of a powerful superego figure, the therapist may unconsciously enjoy exercising this power and authority over another person's life. This gratification may prevent the therapist from helping the adolescent take control of his own destiny.

It is apparent that these special relationships must be regarded as temporary stages in treatment. Aichorn (1935) stated that the therapist who assisted the delinquent youngster by permitting and encouraging narcissistic transferences could not continue the treatment at the point where the patient became more neurotic and thus available for a more intensive and dynamic treatment experience. However, Aichorn actively pursued a transference of this kind and may have thereby limited his availability as an object of other transference tendencies. In some cases it does appear that the patient can come to understand his need for a distorted image of the therapist, work through this need, and proceed to a more traditional alliance with the same individual.

The therapist must take complete responsibility for sorting out the emotional currents in these atypical treatment alliances. In the traditional therapeutic alliance, this responsibility can be shared to a greater extent with the patient. Supervision with peers or with more experienced psychotherapists is an important aid in maintaining objectivity and in preventing countertransference errors. Self-scrutiny is also very important.

In reviewing these somewhat unusual psychotherapeutic encounters, one can utilize the same questions which shed light on transference patterns with any patient.

"How does the patient seem to wish to view me?"

"What does he want from me?"

"What is this role that he is placing me in doing for his psychological functioning?"

The answers to these questions require a careful understanding of the patient's developmental history, his current level of psychological functioning, and his overall life situation. When the questions can be answered with some degree of accuracy, the therapist can consider further questions.

"To what extent is it ethical and comfortable for me to serve this function for the adolescent patient?"

Giovacchini (1974) has described one type of patient who is extremely difficult to tolerate because his transference pattern challenges the basic identity of the therapist as a helping person. Other unrealistic transference needs may be disturbing because of particular unresolved conflicts in the life of the therapist or because of current life problems which may be present in the therapist's personal realm. For example, if the therapist is involved in a legal action or other situation which requires genuine aggression, it may be too uncomfortable to be viewed as a fierce and combative figure by an adolescent patient.

One final question must be asked about the therapeutic relationship.

"Can this style of relating conceivably lead eventually to healthier psychological functioning for the adolescent patient?"

It does seem possible in some cases to assist a troubled adolescent without ever achieving a genuine therapeutic alliance. As implied earlier, perhaps the mechanism of growth is related to the adolescent's use of the therapist as a "real object." In these cases the patient creates in the person of the therapist a particular adult image which can be internalized to complete aspects of development which had not been previously realized. As in the case of Ralph, these notions regarding the therapist may be quietly discarded when the patient no longer requires them. In other situations, as was the case with Davy, the unrealistic expectations of the therapist are relinquished only with great reluctance and pain.

BASIC TECHNIQUES IN YOUNGSTERS WITH MALIGNANT RESISTANCES

The alert reader may be asking, "Aren't you now suggesting the development of unholy alliances? Just a chapter ago you were warning us against them."

True, the therapist *did* accept, even invite, a pathological superego alliance with Ralph. Why is it now an acceptable technique?

1. Probably nothing else would have worked. A previous effort to meet Ralph with a permissive therapeutic approach aborted quickly. Besides, dynamically Ralph was so totally preoccupied with moral ruminations little else interested him.

2. The approach was used knowingly, recognizing that there would be repercussions which would have to be handled. In Ralph's case these appeared as a benign delusion that the therapist was helping him through an omniscient and omnipotent intrusion into his daily life. In short, the relationship developed in this form because that was the level of Ralph's internal psychological organization, perhaps the only level at which Ralph could relate in an integrated, reasonably com-

fortable, sustained manner. The therapist accepted this and let Ralph come to utilize him as an idealized image as a step in integrating a picture of himself as a competent person. Initially Ralph could only believe that his success was the result of the therapist's activity on his behalf, but with this imagined safety, Ralph could experiment even more actively in the world.

There are a few changes in attitude which insight-oriented psychotherapists need to make in order to treat youngsters with malignant defenses.

1. It is usually necessary to assume active control of the youngster's life to some extent. With Ralph the control was merely verbal, but in other cases it may be necessary to use the power of the juvenile court, overt parental pressure, or residential placement. This active stance is almost always necessary in order to interrupt the youngster's effort to maintain omnipotent defensive maneuvers. A creative variant of this active role is the use of a "bogeyman" as described by O'Connor and Horowitz (1984).

   Obviously, many therapists do not enjoy taking direct and coercive action with the patients and need supervision and support in order to tolerate the patient's resulting anger and efforts to intimidate.

2. Related to taking control is the need to function without a traditional alliance. It is difficult to accept the distortions the patient makes of the therapist's true role. This is especially true when the patient acts to discredit the therapist's role as a healer. This is often the case for an extended period. Remember that the patients are threatened by the possibility of disclosure to a much greater extent than are neurotic patients. To exaggerate, the neurotic youngster has an inferiority complex; these youngsters *are* inferior—at least that's the way it feels to them. They aren't just princes under an evil spell, they have never seen or even imagined their kingdom. Since they always feel the therapist is a threat to

their illusions, they do not move toward a more trusting bond until much later in therapy. For a long time the therapist is viewed as an enemy to their basic security.

3. The alliance, even when it is friendly and functional, tends to make the therapist something other than what he or she actually is. The youngster uses the therapist as a "self-object," a replacement part in their own psychic machinery and often this means the child will focus on only a portion of the therapist's personality and attributes.

4. The therapist needs to accept and learn to manipulate a "cast of thousands" rather than the intense dyad which we experience in psychotherapy of the neurotic. The youngster with malignant defenses mobilizes friends to defend important emotional pretentions, populates the world with villains and heroes, and often manages to bring much of this into the therapy in very direct ways. These patients don't just talk of such things. The therapist gets irate phone calls, concerned visits, critical letters, and more. Efforts to collaborate with parents, school officials, probation officers, and even co-therapists turn into frustrating battles as the youngster's splitting and manipulating has each helping individual worried about the competence, motivation, and even intentions of the others.

   This is why team treatment in some form is necessary with these youngsters. As the youngster projects elements of his or her fragmented self onto different team members and then sees them somehow harmonized as the team somehow reaches consensus, there is an opportunity for internalization, integration, and growth in the patient.

5. The therapist must take responsibility for ensuring success experiences for the patient. This includes providing appropriate remediation and academics or social skills, taking an active, even inspirational and exhortive, educational role in treatment, and then serving as the patient's memory and "scorekeeper" so that successes are noted and recalled by the patient.

6. The therapist must accept limited goals even after great efforts. These youngsters do not tend to "get well" in the sense that many neurotic youngsters do. They often improve and show growth as Kohut has described by becoming more creative, wiser, and more able to laugh at themselves and others but without moving beyond a basically narcissistic personality and lifestyle. They also remain vulnerable and often need periodic brief contact with the therapist during periods of stress even after formal therapy has ended.

SUMMARY

Adolescent therapists are encountering many adolescents who do not respond well to traditional psychotherapy. Our challenge is to treat these youngsters with sensitivity to their special needs without being drawn into antitherapeutic pathological interactions based on an unhealthy interaction between our unresolved narcissistic and pregenital personality fragments. In this effort we do not yet have the clear and time-tested guidelines which exist for treatment approaches to the neurotic and therefore we are at greatest risk for countertransference error, especially since, in order to be effective, we often must be more active. Our best protection is always supervision, peer supervision, and personal therapy when necessary. Gradually our skills in using ourselves as instruments to help these "malignantly" disturbed adolescents will improve.

We cannot adequately discuss the various forms these "malignant" action defenses may assume. For example, many youngsters with severe eating disorders including anorexia nervosa and some cases of bulimia probably have similar basic psychopathology. In their case, control of food intake and weight becomes the narrow, artificial world in which they try to exercise an omnipotent control. Many of them clearly have borderline personality organization but their effective treatment is complicated by the nutritional and medical complications generated by the symptom. There is considerable controversy at this point about effective therapeutic approaches and the reader is advised to carefully study a broad range of the recent literature in order to prepare for effective treatment of these difficult young people.

Reasonable satisfaction and contentment in our personal lives are necessary to sustain us when these patients have a desperate need to deny *our* competence and *our* worth as human beings.

Creative activities and efforts to expand our own imaginations may make temporary acceptance and understanding of magical thinking in our patients easier (Brandt, 1983).

CITED AND RECOMMENDED READINGS

Adatto, C. P. 1966. On the metamorphosis from adolescence into adulthood. *Journal of the American Psychoanalytic Association.* 14: 485–509.

Aichorn, A. 1935. *Wayward Youth.* New York: Viking.

Brandt, L. M. 1983. The fairy tale as paradigm of the separation-individuation crisis: implications for treatment of the borderline adolescent. *Adolescent Psychiatry.* 11: 75–91.

Druck, A. 1989. *Four Therapeutic Approaches to the Borderline Patient.* Northvale, N. J.: Jacob Aronson.

Giovacchini, P. L. 1974. The difficult adolescent patient: countertransference problems. *Adolescent Psychiatry.* 3: 271–288.

Johnson, A. M. 1965. Sanctions for super-ego of adolescents. In: *Searchlights on Delinquency,* edited by K. R. Eissler. New York: International Universities Press.

Kernberg, O. F. 1968. The treatment of patients with borderline personality organization. *International Journal of Psychoanalysis.* 49: 600–619.

Kernberg, O. F. 1975. *Borderline Conditions and Pathological Narcissism.* New York: Jason Aronson.

Kernberg, O. F. 1978. The diagnosis of borderline conditions in adolescence. *Adolescent Psychiatry.* 6: 298–319.

Kernberg, O. F. 1984. *Severe Personality Disorders.* New Haven: Yale University Press.

Kohut, H. 1971. *The Analysis of the Self.* New York: International Universities Press.

Mahler, M. S., et al. 1975. *The Psychological Birth of the Human Infant.* New York: Basic Books.

Masterson, J. F. 1972. *Treatment of the Borderline Adolescent: A Developmental Approach.* New York: John Wiley & Sons.

Masterson, J. F. 1978. The borderline adolescent: an object relations view. *Adolescent Psychiatry.* 6: 344–359.

Masterson, J. F. 1981. *The Narcissistic and Borderline Disorders: An Integrated Developmental Approach*. New York: Brunner/Mazel.

Meeks, J. E. 1979. Behavioral and antisocial disorders. In: *Basic Handbook of Child Psychiatry, Volume 2*, edited by J. D. Noshpitz. New York: Basic Books.

Meissner, W. W. 1984. *The Borderline Spectrum: Differential Diagnosis and Developmental Issues*. New York: Jacob Aronson.

Meissner, W. W. 1988. *Treatment of Patients in the Borderline Spectrum*. Northvale, New Jersey: Jacob Aronson.

Munich, R. L. 1986. Some forms of narcissism in adolescents and young adults. *Adolescent Psychiatry*. 13: 85–99.

O'Connor, J. J., and A. N. Horowitz. 1984. The bogeyman cometh: a strategic approach for difficult adolescents. *Family Process*. 23: 237–249.

Thomas, A., et al. 1968. *Temperament and Behavior Disorders in Children*. New York: New York Universities Press.

Wolf, E. S. 1984. Self-object relations disorders. In: *Character Pathology: Theory and Treatment*, edited by M. R. Zales. New York: Brunner/Mazel.

Yochelson, A., and S. E. Samenow. 1976. *The Criminal Personality*. New York: Jacob Aronson.

CHAPTER 6

the problems of ongoing psychotherapy with the adolescent

Most, if not all, psychoanalysts would agree that even the neurotic adolescent patient is not a candidate for a thoroughgoing and complete psychoanalysis (Adatto, 1966; Corday, 1967; Josselyn, 1957). It would be even more foolish to attempt total resolution of the adolescent's conflicts through psychotherapy. The goal, instead, should be to assist the adolescent to achieve an ego synthesis which would permit him a moderate degree of gratification within the limits of social reality (Gitelson, 1942, 1948). This synthesis may include many areas of unresolved conflict managed, bound, and partially neutralized by productive, growth-oriented compromise character formations. After all, the proper concern of adolescence is the construction of a viable and sustaining identity. The further refinement of personality is the task of young adulthood.

TECHNIQUES OF PSYCHOTHERAPY WITH ADOLESCENTS

Bibring (1954) has divided basic therapeutic techniques into the categories of suggestion, abreaction, manipulation, clarification, and interpretation. He has noted that psychoanalysis emphasizes clarification and interpretation, utilizing the other activities only to further the interpretive work. He includes within the meaning of the term *manipulation* all those actual emotional interactions between the patient and his therapist which Alexander might have called "corrective emotional experiences." Bibring says, "Manipulation . . . can be defined as the employment of various emotional systems existing in the patient for the

156

purpose of achieving therapeutic change either in the technical sense of promoting the treatment, or in the curative sense, for manipulative measures too can be employed in a technical as well as a curative way."

Although the term *manipulation* seems a poor one in terms of its other connotations, if it can be taken in the neutral sense which Bibring intends, it can be used to describe the most important technical device utilized in the psychotherapy of the adolescent. If interpretation is the basic key in psychoanalysis, then the adolescent's relationship to the therapist, with the opportunities that this permits for new emotional learning experiences and the more effective utilization of "emotional systems existing in the patient," is the comparable key in adolescent psychotherapy (Gitelson, 1948). It is within this interaction that the adolescent can gradually recognize his emotional needs and learn which of them must be modified and which can be gratified safely in interaction with other human beings.

These comments are even more compellingly true in the cases of youngsters with malignant defenses. Clarification and interpretation can be used with them only in regard to their narcissistic vulnerability for long periods of their treatment. Any other interpretation is felt as an attack.

It is difficult to define precisely the differences between interventions which are appropriate to the goals of psychotherapy with adolescents as opposed to those which would be appropriate in psychoanalysis. Buxbaum (1954) has suggested that psychotherapy should focus on interpreting defenses rather than impulses. Although this is a useful distinction, it gives little practical guidance regarding the proper management of manifestations of impulse when they appear as transference phenomena in the course of psychotherapy. Bibring (1954) suggests that the basic difference between psychoanalysis and other dynamic therapies lies in the degree to which other therapeutic interventions take precedence over interpretation. Certainly, the interpretation of unconscious conflicts plays a relatively minor role in the psychotherapy of the adolescent.

When we attempt to state what is important in adolescent psychotherapy, we are reminded, as Freud stated long ago, that therapy resembles a chess game. Aside from the opening and closing moves, therapy must be learned largely from experience, but it does try to define the goals of the game and to demonstrate some common strategic problems and their management.

UTILIZING THE THERAPEUTIC ALLIANCE

The Therapist as a Trusted Adult Friend

The very existence of a comfortable therapeutic alliance has substantial inherent and immediate value to the adolescent. It permits the adolescent to be dependent without the dangers involved in his dependent ties to his parents. The adolescent needs a trusted adult outside his family group, but may have few opportunities to find such a relationship in a society characterized by isolation of neighborhoods without social cohesion. It is a necessary and valuable function of therapy to provide this kind of relationship.

The therapeutic alliance allows a moderate degree of psychological support, guidance, and reassurance to the adolescent. Most adolescents seek and will utilize advice and opinions from their therapist, especially if the therapist shows no special interest in controlling them or in demonstrating his adult superiority. In many adolescents, marked psychological growth follows merely from the opportunity to speak freely with an adult who quietly demonstrates his interest and respect.

Closely related to the supportive function is the educational role of the therapist. Often, the adolescent longs for an adult who can offer factual answers to troubling questions. Adolescents still worry that they may be sexually abnormal despite the increase in sexual sophistication in our time. The questions are more refined, and often more disguised, since few modern teenagers consciously fear that masturbation will drive them to insanity or cause hair to grow on the palms of their hands. Fear of homosexual impulses, concern about the size and appearance of genitals, worries over sexual attractiveness, concerns about body size or shape, unrealistic self-expectations in the dating game, fears of being hypersexed or hyposexed, and the like are commonly brought to the therapist. Although these questions can rarely be settled by education alone, since they often are partially rooted in unconscious conflicts, the adolescent deserves truthful answers. This at least helps the adolescent to distinguish those concerns which are realistic from those which are related to his personal problems.

A 16-year-old boy finally was able to drop his bravado and confess his feeling that girls did not like him. He felt that he was ugly, even grotesque. He said that this bitter conviction was a major cause of his multiple delinquencies. The therapist asked how he knew that girls did not like him. As the boy discussed his interaction with girls, it became clear that he treated them in a haughty and superior manner to avoid being rejected.

The therapist encouraged him to try being friendlier to a few girls in his class and to report his results. He returned discouraged. He had tried friendliness, but nothing happened. The boy was further encouraged to ask one of the girls for a date. The therapist explained that the boy looked like a regular guy to him. He should take a chance, even though there was always the possibilty that his offer would be rejected. The boy was told that girls expected to be pursued and that he could not expect them to show interest in him if he did not woo them. The therapist even helped plan an evening which a girl would enjoy and appreciate. Along with the practical advice, the youngster was openly encouraged and supported. The invitation was accepted, and the evening proved at least a partial success. The boy began dating fairly actively. His emotional reactions to dating experiences opened the door to exploration of the boy's sexual conflicts. Among other things, it soon became clear that the virtual delusion that he was ugly was related both to his "ugly" (that is, sexual) thoughts about girls and his perception of his mother's view of men and her early reaction to the sight of his penis.

Without the practical help and advice on dating procedures, which barely stopped short of dialing the telephone
for him, the work of therapy could not have continued.

Dating is only one social reality which the adolescent may not
understand. Some have a poor concept of how families, schools,
communities, and governments function. The disillusionment
which often follows the loss of childish belief in the perfection
of hallowed institutions may lead to a bitter cynicism. After some
of this disappointment is worked through, extensive reeducation
regarding many aspects of the social and political facts of life may
aid in the process of maturation. Although the therapist should
not present himself as a fount of wisdom on all subjects, he can
raise questions and cite experiences which broaden the adolescent's view of his world. Since honesty is the cornerstone of the
therapeutic relationship, this implies a willingness to admit that
institutions are considerably less than perfect. As a rule, these
discussions are much more valuable after the adolescent's superego can permit him to admit that he is not perfect either. He
can then use knowledge of society's faults and problems as a guide
to productive adaptation rather than a defensive self-justification.

In the case of the more seriously damaged and deficient youngsters we discussed in chapter 5, the therapy must often be more
actively educational. Often the assistance of expert educators in
special areas is necessary. The adolescent may need remedial education; methodical, detailed social skills training; or organized
and formal help with values clarification. As mentioned earlier,
this introduces the "team" into the therapy experience and often
provides many opportunities for splitting which have to be recognized and utilized constructively. Since these teams have historically functioned mainly in inpatient settings, much of the useful literature on the subject is found in discussions of inpatient
treatment (Zinner, 1978; Schwartz, 1984; Palmer et al., 1983;
O'Connor and Horowitz, 1984).

The Therapist as Guide in the Search for Self-Understanding

These pedagogic and supportive roles, however, are secondary
to the primary therapeutic goal of increasing the adolescent's

insight into his own emotions and their effect on his attitudes and behavior. The therapist tries to teach the interested adolescent everything possible about his physical functioning and the world in which he lives, but this information is less valuable than those things which the adolescent learns about his own wishes, attitudes, and style of relating to other people. Information of this kind, however, cannot be taught at the level of intellectual discourse. It emerges almost as a byproduct of the experiential interaction between the adolescent and the therapist. The adolescent gradually reveals his emotional makeup in the interplay with his therapist. It is through the exploration of this living, vital experience with another individual in the here and now that the adolescent may be helped to know himself.

TALKING WITH THE ADOLESCENT—ON BEING NATURAL

In order to have a relationship of suitable intensity with the adolescent, the therapist must learn to conduct psychotherapy in a reasonably relaxed, conversational style. Most adolescents cannot tolerate a silent, totally passive "blank screen" technique or a stiff and stilted style of therapy, especially not early in the treatment process. For a variety of reasons, including their tender narcissism, their distrust of adults, and the expectation of moral criticism, they usually react to silence and formality with intense anxiety and increased defensiveness. The difficult technical dilemma is to be reasonably talkative and responsive without being directive or intrusive. Once the adolescent gets unwound and comfortable, the therapist's silence is viewed as a positive willingness to listen. This recommendation to "chat" with the adolescent does not imply an awkward attempt to speak "hip talk" or to act like an adolescent. The adolescent is usually "turned off" by an adult who does not conduct himself like a grownup. What is appreciated is an openly friendly, quietly cheerful manner designed to make the adolescent as comfortable in the office as his inner feelings will allow him to be.

LET'S FIGHT IT OUT

Arguing with adult psychotherapy patients is generally discouraged and even recognized as an indication of countertransference. Adolescents, on the other hand, expect to argue. They spend a great deal of their time arguing with parents and friends. In these arguments, they are often learning and changing, although they rarely admit it at the time. Frequently, an adolescent patient ends one session fiercely defending some viewpoint against his therapist and opens the next session by emphatically stating the very opinion he was battling only a few days before. The adolescent usually does not bother to credit the therapist for those ideas and insights which he appropriates. Naturally, the wise therapist leaves well enough alone and does not demand a credit byline. Although the adolescent himself may push an argument to the bitter end, he expects his therapist to be able to admit when he is wrong. The adolescent therapist cannot afford the appearance of arrogant certainty and pompous self-assurance. If he uses his knowledge too forcibly, the therapist may find that he has won an argument but lost a patient. In fact, whenever possible, the therapist should admit areas of ignorance, especially when the adolescent is knowledgeable on the subject. Since adolescents are always being taught by adults, they appreciate the opportunity to demonstrate their knowledge. Usually, it is easy to find areas in which the adolescent knows more than the therapist if the therapist is comfortable enough to accept this reversal of roles. Often, these occasions develop around the discussion of dynamics and motivations. When the adolescent realizes that his opinions and ideas are respected and considered on their merit even when they conflict with a statement made by the therapist, the therapeutic relationship is strengthened. Since many adolescents find it almost impossible to admit it when they are wrong, they admire the adult who can do so without a loss in self-esteem. Since they often feel that they "know it all" while actually fearing that they know nothing, they can relax with an adult who easily admits areas of ignorance and imperfection while demonstrating a comfortable self-respect.

THE ROLE OF CONFRONTATION AND INTERPRETATION IN PSYCHOTHERAPY OF THE ADOLESCENT

Confrontations and clarifications involve showing the patient what he is doing either without knowing it or without recognizing its importance or its connection with other behaviors and attitudes. In interpretation, we address ourselves to why the patient performs certain actions or expresses certain thoughts. Interpretations are often further distinguished as interpretations of defense or resistance and interpretations of content or impulse. These distinctions have some value in organizing a discussion of interventions, but within the reality of the psychotherapy process, they often merge and overlap. In our example of the youngster who smoked in his therapy session, the confrontation (what the youngster was doing) led quickly to a consideration of the why of his behavior. This is the proper sequence of effective interventions, since they must concern observable behaviors or attitudes which are important to the patient in the here and now. This is especially important in adolescent psychotherapy, since the adolescent typically encodes his most important messages in behavior rather than words (Easson, 1969). Effective confrontations which decipher these loaded behaviors often lead to anxiety and the emergence of powerful affects. Often, the impulses behind these affective storms are extremely apparent to anyone who has some understanding of unconscious motivations. The adolescent may reveal rather directly impulses and fantasies which are seen in adults only in states of extreme regression whether these are pathological or deliberately induced through careful psychoanalytic work. These impulses should not be interpreted. Nothing can be gained by pointing out the adolescent's homosexual, incestuous, or homicidal wishes even when these seem virtually conscious.

This kind of awareness is not useful to the adolescent and can only further compromise an already overburdened ego. The therapist instead extends himself to support the adolescent's ego, encouraging healthy defenses and emphasizing the adolescent's control over unacceptable impulses. One of the most important jobs for the adolescent therapist is to recognize those times when the adolescent is fearful of losing control. The therapist then offers help by recognizing the anxiety and by trying to assist the adolescent to find ways in which he can deal with the emerging impulses.

A large, aggressive, 16-year-old borderline youngster was regularly confronted with the fact that much of his behavior suggested a need to intimidate and compete with his therapist. This led to extensive discussion of his father's worship of his athletic prowess which was accompanied by excessive physical affection which verged on homosexual seduction.

In one session, the boy became extremely excited, anxious, and agitated as he compared himself with the therapist. He shouted that he was more intelligent, stronger, and "more of a man" than the therapist. The therapist agreed that he was a fine young man, but also noted that he seemed worried that he would misuse his capacities or only use them to show up other people. The therapist expressed his confidence that the boy would make constructive use of his abilities. The youngster calmed down somewhat and recognized that he had been saying, in effect, that he had a "superpenis." He laughingly asked, "I guess I made it sound like it was long enough to polevault with, eh?"

In the next session, he reported a wild session of joking fantasy with a male friend in which they carried the idea of penile size to more and more ridiculous extremes. They had collapsed in hysterical laughter over the recognition that the man with a "super SUPER penis" would not be able to wear normal clothing or even drive a car for fear of an erection. The homosexual nature of the fantasy was implied as the patient and his friend joked about the insoluble problems which the girl friend of such a man would face.

The therapist accepted the joke and joined in the laughter. Later, he added that the youngster seemed also to be making an important and serious point about manhood, namely, that there was much more to being a man than physical attributes or even intellect. Although positive potentials were important, their constructive utilization was of even greater consequence. This episode seemed to be a turning point, and gradually the youngster was able to apply some of his competitive energy in more productive pursuits.

In short, confrontations are commonly used in the psychotherapy of the adolescent. On the other hand, interpretations of unconscious content are rarely indicated. When such impulses must be mentioned, as in our example above, the emphasis is properly on the fear of their expression. Such interpretations of fear of loss of control are accompanied by acceptance and support of any defense which is adaptive (or even just harmless) that the adolescent can muster to regain his sense of self-mastery. It should be noted that defenses suggested by the therapist are rarely useful to the adolescent. In fact, suggesting specific activities to handle an anxiety and replace acting out behavior usually interferes with the therapeutic alliance. The adolescent reacts as he does to well-meaning adults who counsel, "Instead of running all over town with those weirdo long-haired friends of yours, why don't you stay home and read a good book?" Only the adolescent can really feel his itch, and only he can figure out where to scratch himself.

Although we feel that this basic approach holds generally with adolescent patients, we are indebted to Dr. Merlan DeBolt for reminding us of one important exception to the rule. This occurs with adolescents who are painfully aware of wishes, ideas, or fantasies which they regard as insane and terrifying. These youngsters need open discussion of their fears of homosexuality, incest, or murder to accomplish what DeBolt has suggested might be called a "corrective associational experience" or a "corrective ideational experience." This allows them to learn that these ideas need not lead to action or to psychosis, but may be treated as uncomfortable but harmless thoughts. Confusions of this kind frequently develop in youngsters with limited intellectual ability or borderline ego function.

Mark was an attractive, husky boy of 16 who had a tested full scale IQ of 87. His academic performance was extremely poor in the highly competitive school setting that his ambitious parents forced on him. In addition, he showed an intense and unreasoning contempt for his mother despite all her efforts to show affection and concern for him. This antipathy was pushing Mark toward delinquency.

Gradually, the therapist began to recognize that Mark was terrified of being alone with his mother. Over a period of several months, a therapeutic alliance developed and the therapist felt that he must approach the matter directly with Mark.

"Mark," the therapist said one day, "I get the feeling that your mother scares you."

"Naw," Mark said. "But she is trying to ruin me."

"I'm not sure I understand what you mean by that."

"Well, it ain't something I can tell you, but she's trying to ruin me."

The therapist considered his choices. From a number of things Mark had said, he felt sure that the boy's fears of his mother were generated primarily by incestuous wishes. He also knew that Mark's thinking was extremely concrete and that he would probably misinterpret his mother's hysterical mannerisms. He decided to take the bull by the horns.

"Mark," he said, "have you ever had the feeling that your mother wanted you to fuck her?"

Mark hardly hesitated. He seemed relieved that things were out in the open.

"Yeah. She does want me to. It's not just something I think. She doesn't sleep with my dad. I don't think she ever has. She wants me to screw her."

The therapist knew that since Mark was adopted, it would be impossible to prove to him that his parents, in spite of separate bedrooms, did have intercourse. Instead, he elected to focus on Mark's direct perceptions of family reality.

"When did you first get the idea that she wanted you to have sex with her?"

"When she used to take nude sunbaths outside my window. I'd watch her and get a hard on."

The therapist explained that any teenage boy would react with excitement to the sight of a nude woman whether it was his mother or not. He assured Mark that his feelings were perfectly normal under the circumstances.

The next several sessions were devoted to convincing Mark that if he acted on his idea that his mother was seducing him it would lead to much trouble for him. The therapist patiently explained that some women, including Mark's mother, had a strong need to be admired and loved. They did not know how to meet these needs except by sexually teasing men, even including their own sons. However, they were not really aware of what they were doing and would be horrified and frightened if the men responded to their sexual provocation. Mark was told flatly, "Boys do not screw their mothers, no matter how things may appear."

Following this period of therapy, Mark began to make a few friends outside of the home and even attracted a girl friend. He continued to be somewhat cautious and distant around his mother, but did not constantly criticize her as in the past. He came to refer to his incestuous wishes as "those dumb thoughts I used to have."

GENERAL MANAGEMENT OF TRANSFERENCE
WITH ADOLESCENTS

Younger adolescents feel intensely and use projection with abandon. They often are totally unaware that their picture of another person is constructed within their own mind. Their "transference" feelings usually seem totally real to them. This holds not only in therapy, but in their relationships with other adults and peers. We have discussed the narcissistic needs which give rise to this style of relating in the chapter on the dynamics of adolescence. Because of this characteristic, the primary problem in managing transference in adolescent therapy is simply to convince the adolescent that the projection originates within his mind, not in external reality. This undertaking is, like much of life, easier to describe than to accomplish.

First of all, there is the adolescent's compelling need to be right in his opinion of others. He is struggling to construct a world which makes sense to him and within which he can live. Marked distortions are desperately defended, since to relinquish them would expose him to a confusing external world and to confusion

Practicing psychotherapy seems like a solitary pursuit, in that a therapist does not often have the opportunity to see another therapist at work. Most psychotherapy trainees wonder what other therapists do and say in their sessions with clients. The clinical vignettes in this book are intended to be as specific and concrete as possible. The reader may wish to look up articles in which the authors candidly share their own thoughts and words in case studies. E. James Anthony (1988), an erudite and articulate child analyst, has often shared his experience through detailed case reports. Galatzer-Levy (1985), Williams (1986), and Massie (1988) have published interesting case histories of the treatment of adolescents. Tolchin (1987) presented several clinical examples to show how "telephone psychotherapy" can be an important and useful method with some adolescents.

within himself. He would be left without confidence in himself as one who can see life, including other people, clearly. Part of his desperate defensive structure designed to control his sexual and aggressive drives is founded in this obsessive concern with "being right" and being in control.

For most adolescent patients, considerable educational work must precede any clarification of transference distortions. The aim of this educative effort is to lead the adolescent to put his trust in a groping, gradual objectivity, rather than in an impulsive, intuitive, and subjective global grasp of interpersonal relationships. Later, when his intuitions are less defensive in origin, he can learn to trust them again and to utilize these "hunches" in conjunction with a reasoned, "secondary process" approach to life.

Many techniques may be valuable in accomplishing this goal. Often, it is wise to begin with work on those distortions produced by other people. The adolescent may describe a friend who has changed his attitude radically toward the patient or another person. The patient may be shown how both attitudes were based more on the friend's inner needs than on the characteristics of the object. It can be further pointed out that this is a common tendency in human relationships. The technique of universalization may be extensively utilized in this area. The therapist may wish to offer a benign personal anecdote if one comes to mind.

This educative groundwork will need to be repeated until the adolescent seems to get the idea. When he begins to offer illustrations of his own, concerning himself or others, these are accepted and the adolescent should be given credit for his wisdom. The simple comment, "I think you're right," from the therapist may encourage the adolescent to continue his objective scrutiny of interpersonal judgments.

A 16-year-old girl was panicky about her relationship with a special girl friend. She lived in constant fear of offending the friend. This came to a climax when the friend called and dramatically demanded that the patient bring her drugs for a suicide attempt. When the patient refused, her friend became very angry and accused her of never wanting to help!

The patient was finally able to recognize that her friend was determined to feel rejected by others and had to engineer situations in which this would be unavoidable. Since the patient had similar tendencies both within therapy and with others, it was possible to use this insight productively later in her treatment. Whenever she was angry because the therapist had opposed self-destructive behavior, he would say, "Now you *know* I dislike you, since I won't even help you kill yourself."

THE ADOLESCENT WHO LIVES FOR POWER STRUGGLES

In some patients, there is little opportunity to build a background for acceptance of transference clarifications. These youngsters enter therapy with a flurry of hostile allegations about the therapist. They view the therapist as a computer, already programmed with preconceived ideas and attitudes about them and with very definite plans for their future. Many of these youngsters come from families in which they have been the victims of just this kind of "externalization" (Brody, 1965), or else have grown up in families in which virtually no limitations were set by parents. Instead, the parents have relied on cunning and underhanded techniques for influencing behavior. It is useless to deny the accusations of these youngsters, since experience has taught them that their parents deny their intrusive control while continuing to practice it. "We don't want to tell you what to do; we only want you to be happy. Now here's what you must do in order to be happy." It also does little good to ask what they themselves want to do. Their interest is only in opposing what they imagine to be the therapist's wishes, not in asserting their own. If you insist that you are interested in their wishes, they often reply that their wish is to quit therapy, run away from home, or take some other action which any responsible adult would have to oppose out of concern for their welfare.

It is difficult to relate to youngsters of this kind, since their whole existence is bound up in soliciting control struggles. Strictly speaking, their attitude toward the therapist is not an expression of transference so much as a symptom and a way of life. One can only empathically accept their anger and frustration while sharing in a friendly way the awareness that no therapist could please them, since they are determined to pick a fight. Therapy is designated then as a friendly battle (at least friendly on the therapist's side), and the therapist accepts his adversative role with as much grace and humor as he can manage. It is important to credit the adolescent with his victories in these sallies. As Holmes (1964) has pointed out, these victories will be numerous. Often in these cases, no true therapeutic alliance forms, and the therapist is actually conducting supportive psychotherapy, functioning more as an unaccepted and unsung guardian than a true psychotherapist. However, this role may be literally lifesaving for some of these youngsters. Some of them return, when they are older, with greater capacity to cooperate in therapy.

As mentioned in chapter 5, others form atypical alliances which do permit genuine emotional growth if the therapist can be flexible. The transferences are basically narcissistic with varying degrees of idealization and use of the therapist as a self-object. The patterns observed in adolescents are basically similar to those described by Kohut (1971) and others. The differences are mainly related to the adolescents' greater tendency to act on transference distortions. This tendency toward action requires the therapist to have some genuine external control of the patient's life to avoid potentially hazardous acting out. Usually the family can provide this external support to the treatment effort but in some cases, as mentioned earlier, residential care may be necessary to make treatment possible.

Of course, therapy is undertaken only if there is a clear and compelling need for treatment. Some of these angry, narcissistic adolescents discover productive and safe ways to engage their environment and may mature and mellow considerably without therapy. This sometimes permits the youngster to seek therapy in a more cooperative frame of mind.

GARDEN VARIETY TRANSFERENCES

The more typical outpatient youngster shows transference attitudes which are subtle and related to the material which is emerging in therapy. Although the younger adolescents still tend to have difficulty in recognizing the internal origin of their transference attitudes, they can be prepared educationally to explore this possibility.

It is important to recognize and clarify transference as it appears. Often, the adolescent is reluctant to voice feelings about the therapist, especially if these are negative. It is usually up to the therapist to detect the tendencies implied in behavior and to verbalize them for the youngster at the proper time. For example, the adolescent may reveal a competitive oedipal transference by describing his accomplishments, only to diminish them quickly. The alert therapist notes this and assures the adolescent that he has a right to be proud of real accomplishments, noting that he behaves as though he expected the therapist to criticize either his accomplishment or his pride in it.

As in this example, it is usually necessary with the adolescent to point out his unspoken assumptions while simultaneously clearly disclaiming the projected distortions. Words alone are often not enough. After the transference attitudes are clearly demonstrated, one must actively show by attitude, words, and behavior that they do not accurately reflect the therapist's true characteristics. In short, the therapist tries to neutralize irrational transference distortions as quickly and totally as possible.

A 14-year-old boy was convinced that his therapist felt he was stupid. He was surprised when the therapist asked his advice about which make of automobile to purchase. The therapist asked for specific information which the youngster could easily supply from his extensive reading in this area. The youngster was especially impressed that the therapist actually wrote down the information he gave. Later, the boy expressed his amazement. The therapist said, "What's so strange about it? I know a lot about how people feel and behave. You know a lot about cars. You came to me for help; why shouldn't I ask for your help?"

In a similar way, the transference feeling that the therapist is disinterested may be offset by remembering the details of the patient's comments in a previous session or by actually offering practical help and advice.

Since the goal in adolescent psychotherapy is not to elicit regression and a transference neurosis but to increase ego control, these active interventions are indicated even though they would interfere with classical psychoanalysis. Transference is interpreted to the adolescent only to prevent interference with the therapeutic alliance. The therapist always acts to clarify the irrationality of the transference and to diminish its impact in the therapeutic situation.

This is not to say that transference attitudes are ignored or denied. The adolescent is not encouraged to pretend that his irrational feelings do not exist. These feelings are noted and brought to conscious attention. He is then helped to recognize that they originate in his own mind. Finally the patient is supported in his attempt to deal with them as creatively as possible. Every effort is made to interfere with the adolescent's tendency to deal with the therapist as a real object for libidinal or aggressive drives. It should be recognized that this is a difficult technical problem, since only the older adolescent is capable of maintaining objectivity toward intense transference attitudes. The younger patient needs a healthy dose of reality and early intervention to prevent the development of an explosive and destructive transference.

There are certain types of transference patterns which regularly appear in the treatment of adolescents. All of them interfere with the therapeutic alliance and with ego growth in the adolescent and therefore require early recognition and active management.

The Erotic Transference

Sexual transferences are common in adolescent psychotherapy. They are extremely frightening to the younger adolescent who has developed neither a comfortable acceptance of his sexuality nor the subtle ego techniques for expressing these feelings with any finesse. As a result, open manifestations of sexual transference during the psychotherapy of younger adolescents are often panicky eruptions of a rather crude kind. At other times, the feelings are held in fearful secrecy. They are apparent only in the blushing, agitated confusion of the adolescent's behavior. Often, these youngsters simply cannot tolerate a young therapist of the opposite sex because of the overwhelming intensity of their sexual fantasies.

Even though older adolescents are better prepared to modulate their feelings, they still must face the incestuous implications of their responses much more directly than the adult patient who can partially rationalize his feelings since the therapist is an approximate age peer. The awakening of similar feelings in adolescents places them in the same fearful oedipal situation which they have been attempting to escape in their own family. If these stirrings are not actively managed, the result is often a precipitous flight from the danger represented by the therapy relationship.

A 14-year-old girl squirmed and twisted in her chair while telling her therapist of a fantasied relationship with an older boyfriend. During the recital, she was in an intense state of excitement. Her twisting and turning resulted in extensive exposure of her genital area. Her comments were crudely suggestive and her seductiveness was grossly evident. She seemed in a virtual frenzy of sexual excitement mingled with intense anxiety.

The therapist commented that her mind seemed to be more on fun than on the work of therapy. She agreed, giggling. The therapist stated firmly and gravely that the therapy hour was not a place for fun. She would have opportunities for fun with her friends, but the therapist was interested in understanding her feelings, not in having fun with her. This firm disavowal of interest in her seductive overtures allowed the girl to gain control and returned the emphasis of the session to therapeutic goals.

With great relief, she joked, "Boy, you're really square."

The therapist agreed firmly, "Yes, I am."

With older adolescents, the expression of erotic transference feelings is more subtle and approaches that seen in adults. Still, even the older adolescent can rarely handle sexual transference feelings openly. It would be unwise to focus attention on their origins or to encourage their elaboration. Instead, the therapist emphasizes their value in emotional growth and their defensive function, clearly and tactfully maintaining his unavailability as a real sexual object.

A 17-year-old girl left "gifts" for the therapist session after session. She forgot cigarettes, matches, change, and other small objects. During this time, she became more and more distant and quiet. When the therapist linked these two patterns of behavior, the girl blushed. She admitted to a fear that she might "get a crush" on the therapist. She did not want this to happen, since it would be humiliating and childish to have such a "puppy love."

The therapist assured her that she could feel friendly and emotionally close without necessarily developing a crush. He added that crushes were often expressions of liking and admiration which did not imply that the young person loved the elder in the same sense that she would someday love a person of her own age.

The therapist was attempting to offer himself as a friendly, supportive father figure who would not respond seductively to her.

The Omnipotent Transference

The omnipotent transference is even more seductive than the erotic transference with the adolescent. The expectation that the therapist will have answers to all questions and solutions for all problems bears enough similarity to some ordinary or at least fantasied relationships between the generations to be quite attractive. The therapist expects to offer some realistic advice and help to his adolescent patient in the normal course of conducting psychotherapy. It is easy to drift gradually into a relationship in which the adolecent presents as a helpless, idiotic emotional cripple, repeatedly rescued from disaster only because of the brilliance of the therapist.

As gratifying as such a situation may be to the therapist's narcissism and his own unresolved infantile omnipotence, it is catastrophic to the goals of psychotherapy. When these transference attitudes are challenged, the adolescent usually reacts with irritation or open anger. This occurs because the transference actually covers the adolescent's secret fantasy of personal omnipotence. After all, the adolescent grants the therapist his power! It is also the adolescent who enjoys its benefits. The therapist only serves as a dupe, fronting for the adolescent's defense against his fear of confronting reality without magical powers.

In adolescents with malignant defenses and basic fixation in pregenital, narcissistic psychopathology the issue is different. The transference manifestation of omnipotent expectations is not a relatively benign regressive phenomenon but rather the demonstration within the therapy of the core problem.

A 15-year-old boy who had been sexually and physically abused by his father was being treated in a residential treatment center. His father, out of his life for many years, yet technically retaining custody of the youngster, called and demanded to take the boy out of the center. The boy told his therapist he didn't want to see his father. When the therapist tried to discuss the legal and technical problems involved in keeping a legal parent away from his child, the boy began to scream and threaten the therapist.

"You hate me. You can keep him away if you want to. If you try to kill me, I'll kill you."

He was calmed with great difficulty only after the therapist promised him he would protect him against the parent.

Through the course of several years of therapy the patient only gradually gave up the feeling that his therapist had complete power over the events that affected the patient. This attitude persisted side by side with a fairly realistic recognition of the therapist's lack of omnipotence in other matters.

This kind of omnipotent transference cannot be avoided since it results not from countertransference but from the patient's personality structure. It is resolved only by a gradual process of idealization, carefully dosed disillusion, and gradual recognition of self-worth as outlined in chapter 5.

The Negative Transference

Adolescents, like younger children, can rarely tolerate continuing psychotherapy in the face of a strong negative transference. As indicated above, intense and pervasive negative feelings toward the therapist usually do not represent transference. They express, rather, an intensely negative attitude toward all adults in authority. Negative transference should also be differentiated from the defensive hostility which many adolescents flaunt. This "porcupine" attitude often covers painful feelings of shame, inadequacy, and anxiety. This type of negative attitude often disappears when the adolescent recognizes that the therapist will respect his feelings.

Some younger adolescents are so fearful of therapy that they cannot risk any positive attitudes toward the therapist. In this instance, the negativism represents an attempt to avoid therapy by forcing the therapist to reject them.

True negative transferences may appear early in therapy. This occurs when the therapist happens to resemble a disliked figure from the past. Such occurrences are rare. More frequently, early negativism results when intense ambivalence is split and the therapist is cast into the role of the bad parent. Often, the relationship with the parent improves superficially as a result of the split. If the parents cannot understand what is actually happening, they may consider the adolescent to be cured and withdraw him from therapy prematurely.

SOURCES OF NEGATIVE TRANSFERENCE FEELINGS. Later, in therapy, true negative transference attitudes are usually more subtle and disguised than the global rejection described in the patterns above. The therapist may realize he is being slyly depreciated, pointedly ignored, or craftily maneuvered into ridiculous positions. These situations are marked by the collapse of the therapeutic alliance and disinterest in the therapeutic work.

These vague, unstated negative attitudes must be brought into the open for discussion. From the therapist's point of view, they should be explored objectively to determine their origin. We have already described the normal and ubiquitous angry reaction to those interventions which cause narcissistic injury to the adolescent. Any comment which interferes with a functioning defense, thereby increasing anxiety, naturally arouses some hostile feelings toward the disturbing influence. These angry feelings are not truly transference phenomena. They are affective reactions to the reality of the therapy situation. They are tolerated by the adolescent only because both his positive feelings for the therapist and his growth experience within therapy give him hope that the overall process will be beneficial to him. Because of this positive orientation toward the future, he can accept some pain in the present. Since he has a sense of trust in the therapist's positive attitude, he can forgive some injuries to his pride.

When faced with a hostile patient, the therapist must also consider the possibility that he has actually attacked the patient. Whether the insult has been direct, as in an angry or deprecatory response to provocation by the adolescent, or indirect, as in a subtle betrayal of confidence to the parents, the adolescent may be expected to retaliate angrily. To treat this reaction mistakenly as transference will only compound the therapeutic error.

THE THERAPIST AS FRUSTRATOR. True negative transference reactions occur when situations in therapy reactivate earlier experiences in which negative attitudes toward important loved objects predominated. They appear whenever the therapist, as a representative of reality, is seen as opposing gratification of libidinal (id) drives or appropriate "ego drives." They appear whenever the therapist himself seems to refuse to gratify emotional needs which appear legitimate and important to the patient. They also appear whenever the therapist is viewed as opposing appropriate drives for achievement, independence, and autonomy. Obviously, the feelings cannot be considered as transference if the therapist is in fact antagonistically opposed to his patient's wishes for pleasure and accomplishment. It is the inappropriate and incorrect projection of these attitudes originating from previous introjects which constitutes transference.

The therapist will, of course, unavoidably frustrate the adolescent. Therapy is designed to explore and investigate impulses, not to gratify them. However, the long-range goal of therapy is clearly to aid the patient to maximize gratification and minimize frustration.

The therapist may be seen as a frustrating parent when he questions the relative value of immediate pleasure as opposed to long-range goals. In the terminology of psychoanalysis, the therapist favors the reality principle over the pleasure principle. This stance is often mistaken for a generalized ascetic opposition to gratification. The adolescent has not as yet synthesized his drives with a wider appreciation of his own future survival and well-being. Often, he is willing to sacrifice prudent self-protection for the impulsive gratifiction of an immediate urge. Opposing this tendency frequently gains the therapist a reputation as a wet blanket with his adolescent patient.

Just as frequently the therapist can "spoil the fun" by interpreting the true motive behind certain "pseudolibidinal" activities. Pointing out that a planned seduction seems more hostile than sexual may produce intense resentment in the adolescent patient. Clarifying the destructive motives involved in helping a "friend" get drugs or run away from home can lead to rage at the therapist. In these instances, the therapist is calling attention to the hidden hostile pregenital components which the adolescent is attempting to "bootleg" under the guise of a loving act. It is this hidden hostility which is actually freed for expression toward the therapist. The therapist is accused of puritanical suppression to avoid recognizing that the rage actually belonged to the adolescent all along and was merely disguised, disowned, and projected.

On the other hand, the adolescent's anger because the therapist will not personally gratify his libidinal transferences is, from the adolescent's point of view, a justified response. The therapist is certain to let the adolescent down in this regard. The adolescent will direct many vague wishes and hopes toward his therapist. He may expect the therapist to fill various neurotic expectations magically. He may hope to become omnipotent, free of depressive feelings, or imbued with phallic power. He may hope for symbiotic nurture or libidinal gratification. Since the therapist cannot meet these needs, the adolescent will inevitably feel disappointed and even cheated. This, of course, produces feelings of anger toward the therapist, who may be viewed as spitefully withholding gratification.

"YOU DO NOT WANT ME TO SUCCEED." The adolescent patient who suspects the therapist of thwarting his ambitions is often struggling with strong destructive competitive urges. These may be oedipal or more primitive wishes to dominate or destroy the therapist completely. These urges cause guilt which may lead to fears of retaliation or to projection of the unacceptable impulses onto the therapist. These defensive maneuvers help to justify the hostile competitive feelings toward the therapist and partially relieve guilt and anxiety.

Management of the Negative Transference

In all instances of negative transference, there are basic rules which may help to restore the therapeutic alliance. First, the neg-

ative feelings must be accepted objectively as additional experiential data for therapeutic exploration. Objective acceptance implies not only the avoidance of counter-attack, but also a quiet
yet firm refusal to accept unrealistic blame. Occasionally, therapists, in a well-intentioned eagerness to appear fair and open-
minded, will accept excessive criticism and hostility from the adolescent without pointing out that the anger is irrational. This
attempt to help the adolescent express his "true feelings" can
interfere with the therapeutic process by implying that the feelings are justified by the therapist's personality or behavior. This
obscures their intrapsychic and unconscious origin and confuses
the patient. In addition, as Fromm-Reichmann (1950) has pointed
out, inviting the patient to express his hostility actually serves to
prevent the genuine expression of hostility and to protect the
therapist from hearing honest anger from his patients.

As the adolescent is encouraged to explore the causes of his
anger (or annoyance or irritation, if the adolescent prefers to
soften his terms) in the same way that he has learned to study his
other feelings in therapy, some clues usually emerge which help
to clarify the general origin of the anger. The therapist can begin
to guess whether he is being seen as a "spoilsport," a selfish
withholding parent, or a competitive bully. These transference
attitudes can then be countered by the therapist's words and
actions as described above in the general section on management
of transference. The question of how far the transference feelings
should be allowed to develop before they are actively neutralized
can only be decided by clinical judgment. Older, healthier adolescents can tolerate longer and more thorough exploration of
negative transferences, whereas younger and more disturbed
youngsters need quick and active aid in reality testing in order
to sustain the therapeutic relationship.

A successful intervention which dissolves the negative transference reaction is often followed by a period of regression and
depressive affect in the adolescent. In some instances, this depression may be obscured for a period of time by a defensive elation.
The depression results from some degree of awareness of the
personal origin of the frustrated wishes and a dawning recogni-

tion that the wishes are incompatible with reality and must be abandoned. It is always sad to realize, even dimly, that a gratification must be relinquished. During this period, the therapist must steer a close course between excessive sympathy and cold, unfeeling objectivity. When the adolescent is mourning a lost illusion, he needs both empathic understanding of his sense of loss and help in remembering that what was lost was, after all, always only an illusion. The pleasures of reality, although sometimes dimmed by complexity and responsibility, at least have the advantage of actually existing. The therapist gently encourages the adolescent to recognize that, with all its faults, reality is the only dependable source of pleasure.

The Therapist as Superego

Patients of all ages frequently see their therapists as superego figures. This tendency is especially marked in the adolescent patient. Indeed, the success of adolescent psychotherapy frequently hinges primarily on the skill with which superego conflicts are managed. These conflicts are strongly reflected in the therapeutic relationship and produce countless complex dilemmas. It is quite difficult to guide an adolescent toward a self-respecting sense of firm impulse control while also assisting him to relax the rigid, relatively passive, and asexual superego of latency.

Within the therapeutic relationship, the adolescent frequently sidesteps this developmental task by projecting his superego onto the therapist, as we have previously noted. All of the therapist's interventions tend to be experienced as superego sanctions. Because of his moral preoccupation, it is difficult for the adolescent to understand other rationales for foregoing the gratification of any impulse.

WHAT DOES YOUR CONSCIENCE SAY? The initial phase of the work with the adolescent's superego conflicts consists of recognizing and clarifying the pattern of his internalized moral prohibitions. It is crucial to demonstrate that these are the adolescent's own taboos, which he is attempting to ignore, externalize, or otherwise escape. The therapist insists, on the other hand, that the route

to real freedom demands open and honest confrontation with
these internal policemen. They can be altered only through conflict, not avoidance.

The techniques of confronting the adolescent with his own
superego vary with the particular personality structures which are
encountered. The most common pattern is the adolescent who
rebels against his own conscience and then reveals his guilt
through self-destructive behaviors. If the connection is repeatedly
brought to the youngster's attention, he can gradually become
aware of his sense of guilt and of the unconscious interdiction
that he is violating.

Other superego restrictions produce only inhibitions and personality constrictions. These may reveal themselves in therapy as
overcontrol of certain impulses or conversely as a defiant over-
emphasis on some aspect of life. For example, both the shy, inhibited adolescent and the brassy, insolently bawdy youngster may
be revealing strong unconscious guilt feelings around sexuality.

Some youngsters present their superego problems more
openly, clearly cognizant that their feelings of excessive guilt are
irrational. Other adolescents expect to be relieved of guilt feelings
while continuing to do things which are self-centered, exploita-
tive, and destructive to others. There are also adolescents with
defects in superego structure who require active confrontation.
This is also necessary at times with youngsters who are attempting
to escape superego pressures with various bribes and rationali-
zations.

A 17-year-old boy professed extremely high moral standards and was extremely critical of middle-class hypocrisy.
At the same time, he did not hesitate virtually to blackmail
his wealthy mother for money, utilizing the most flagrant
and often dishonest manipulations to extort the cash that
he wanted. This dishonesty was motivated by spiteful oral
rage and rationalized on the basis that he had no respect
for his mother and should get from her what he could. This
behavior allowed the youngster to maintain a fantasy of symbiotic sustenance secretly while disavowing any sense of dependency. It gradually became clear that his secret delin-

quency was one source of the boy's nagging sense of inferiority.

He came to therapy one day nonchalantly planning the purchase of a new automobile. The therapist asked where he got the money, since the youngster had been complaining of being broke. The boy explained that he had told his mother that he had learned he had a terrific "inferiority complex" which might be ameliorated by driving a flashy car.

"You implied that you learned that from therapy?" the therapist asked.

"No, but if she wants to think that, it's sure okay with me. It's not my fault she's stupid."

"It isn't okay with me. I don't want to be part of your con game. Besides, you are throwing away your chances in therapy for a bunch of chrome and steel. I can't go along with that."

"What do you mean?"

"Do you have any idea of how much that lousy car is really costing you? If you want to live the life of a con artist, that's your business, but let's at least be honest about what you're doing when you come here."

THE THERAPIST'S VALUES. It should be obvious that the therapist cannot remain completely neutral in moral questions. By the very nature of his work and his technical operations, the psychotherapist conveys a value system. Emotional honesty, self-awareness, fairness in interpersonal relationships, and reasonable control of impulse, coupled with a tolerance of unacceptable fantasy and a preference for reality gratifications over neurotic gratifications, are values which are revealed by the therapist's general approach to the adolescent. Whether these values are derived from a scientific knowledge of the nature of man or merely represent a personal credo which characterizes most people who become psychotherapists is a debatable point. The therapist should be aware of the moral assumptions that he holds, regardless of their origins. London's (1964) book, *The Modes and Morals of Psychotherapy*,

provides a thorough and enlightening discussion of many pertinent issues in this regard.

Since the adolescent therapist is even more of a pedagogue
than his adult therapist counterpart, he should not hesitate to
admit his moral biases frankly and to defend them energetically.
Since the younger adolescent tends toward a "black or white,"
right or wrong view of morality based primarily on institutional
sanctions, it is useful to him to discuss some of the more rational
and informed foundations for moral conduct. Some degree of
sexual restraint has more to recommend it than a puritanical fear
of sin or a terror of the social stigma of illegitimate pregnancy.
The dangers of exploiting others or of being exploited and the
difficulties involved in accepting emotional responsibility for the
sexual partner are only two of the issues which would recommend
some degree of caution in sexual expression. It should be kept
in mind, however, that the honest expression of one's own moral
stance does not mean attempting to impose that morality on the
adolescent patient. The youngster must reach his own definition
of righteousness and live by that.

The adolescent is not only involved in a dramatic unconscious
moral upheaval; he is also learning to think out his value system.
The therapist must provide not only professional help in understanding the internal struggle, but a model as a rational adult
with considered opinions regarding the proper conduct and
meaning of life. He does not force these views on his young
patient, but neither does he attempt to avoid his responsibility
as an adult to offer his ethical conclusions based on a long period
of considered experience and observation of human interaction.
Such openness in discussion also encourages the adolescent to
think about his own assumptions and to use his own powers of
logic to the best possible advantage. Obviously, this kind of teaching should never deteriorate into self-righteous moralizing. The
adolescent quickly loses interest when he feels that he is listening
to a sermon. As Long (1968) has said, "In my own mind I think
of therapy with adolescents as follows: The adolescent is alone
and driving a car down the highway at 50 miles per hour, but
has never driven before, has only watched others. I am in another

car trying to shout advice to him. If he can make use of the advice he will, but he has to bring the car under control by himself. And I must first get across to him that I am not the 'fuzz.' "

Even more important than what the therapist says is what the therapist does and reports doing. Adolescents are accustomed to encountering adults who espouse high standards while not actually living them. They expect a similar corruptibility in therapists and search for it.

A 15-year-old, rather delinquent youngster who didn't work in therapy told his therapist, "Look, Doc, this is a drag for both of us. I'm only coming because the old man says I have to. I ain't never gonna talk to you. So . . . what do you say I don't come and you bill the old man anyhow. I'll never tell and we can split the dough."

Unfortunately for us very human and imperfect therapists, the invitation to corruption is not always so blatant and recognizable. When we do perceive the invitation we need to reject it firmly but matter-of-factly. Adolescents often interpret extreme prudishness and self-righteousness as indirect evidence of temptation.

SPECIAL TECHNICAL PROBLEMS

A few special technical problems which are regularly encountered in the psychotherapy of adolescents deserve brief comment.

Embarrassment Over Being in Therapy

Adolescents frequently feel intensely ashamed of their need for psychotherapy. This reaction is most common in the early stages of treatment, but may recur throughout the therapeutic encounter. The patient may complain either of a personal feeling of shame or of concern about what friends or others will think.

As we noted above, the adolescent is extremely ashamed of his dependency wishes. This developmental fact explains a large part of his discomfort in the therapy relationship. An exclusive emphasis on the normative aspect of this attitude, however, can obscure the specific meaning of the shame in particular patients.

Obviously, those adolescents who have the most intense dependency needs will tend to have the strongest feelings of shame. It is important to help them to see the wish for care which is hidden behind their fear of accepting help. This can be approached in the same way that other hidden wishes are gradually revealed, if the therapist is alert to its presence. What is important is the recognition that those adolescents who do not have marked dependency needs accept this part of therapy without undue fuss.

Some adolescents who express embarrassment are speaking for their parents. Although the social stigma associated with therapy has lessened in recent years, it has not disappeared. In addition to this cultural factor, many parents view the need for therapy as a negative reflection on their parenthood. The attitude is conveyed to the adolescent, who feels that his need for psychotherapy shames his family. Unless the parents can be helped to view the situation more objectively, therapy may be seriously compromised.

Finally, the adolescent who has marked feelings of social anxiety and inferiority may focus these on the therapy process. The youngster then blames psychotherapy for his lack of social success. One can only encourage these adolescents to persevere while gently refusing to accept total blame for their discomfort. The question of whether they should tell their friends that they are in treatment should be explored dynamically in the therapy rather than defensively answered.

Bringing Friends

Some adolescents, far from hiding their involvement in therapy, announce it widely in their peer group. This may represent, in addition to an expression of exhibitionism, an attempt to avoid serious involvement in therapy. Instead of a private and important relationship, therapy and the therapist become subjects of social chatter. However, there is some value in this sharing of the therapy experience. Often, the peer group can be helpful in lowering anxiety and the discussion may be a learning experience. In any case, as Easson (1969) has pointed out, it is pointless to forbid the behavior, since the therapist cannot enforce such a rule.

Other youngsters occasionally appear at sessions with friends whom they wish to bring into the treatment room. The motivations for such behavior vary widely, but, in my opinion, the action should be viewed as a transference behavior. If this is true, it should be treated as a communication to be examined and understood.

A 16-year-old boy appeared for his therapy session with a friend in tow. He asked if the friend could accompany him to the therapy hour. The therapist replied that the time was his and he could use it as he wished.

The two boys joked uncomfortably while the therapist watched quietly, occasionally commenting on the vaguely hostile tone of their conversation.

The patient finally asked his friend to wait for him in the reception area. When he was alone with the therapist, he asked, "Well, what do you think of my friend? My parents don't want me to run around with him."

"I don't really know him. What do you think of him?"

"I think he's fine."

"If you're sure of that, I wonder why you brought him here to get my opinion?"

The patient began cautiously to explore his feelings about his friend. He admitted reluctantly that the boy was immature, self-centered, and hostile to adults. He also began to look at similar traits in his own personality which caused him to be defensive when his friend was criticized.

In this instance, a friend was brought to therapy as a proxy. If the therapist criticized the friend, it would mean that it would not be safe to reveal certain unacceptable personal traits and attitudes in therapy.

The wish to refer a friend to the therapist, although often reflecting a positive attitude toward the treatment experience, may also express a wish for a smokescreen to divert attention from the original patient. Generally, it is wise to insist on exploring the motives behind the referral rather than to accept the new patient. If the friend clearly needs help and desires it, the patient may be directed to a competent colleague. Later in therapy, the referral of a friend may be an indication that the patient is ready to consider termination.

Requests for Special Attentions

Some adolescent patients develop intense dependency ties to the therapist. They may request extra appointments, telephone the therapist, or request extra therapeutic contacts of various kinds. When this type of behavior develops late in therapy, it often resembles the behaviors described by Balint (1968) in *The Basic Fault*. As Balint points out, there is little advantage to be gained by attempting to meet these primitive needs for nurture. What the patient does need is a quiet, undemanding therapist who can patiently allow the regressed patient to come to peace with his inner feeling of emptiness and deprivation. (For the genetic origins of this sense of inner emptiness and futility, see Winnicott, 1958.)

In adolescents, this sense of deprivation, of having lost something central to life, often leads to delinquent behavior. The adolescent feels that he has been gypped by life and demands to be recompensed. If the therapist can avoid being caught up in the flamboyant protest toward current conditions and can focus his attention on the inner state of incompleteness, the delinquencies often stop. The therapist must avoid, however, holding out a false promise of total gratification. As we have noted earlier, adolescence is not the time for extensive remediation of early fixation points. The therapist merely accepts the deprived adolescent's complaints and anger as emotionally legitimate while quietly encouraging the adolescent to confront the problems of maturity despite his feelings of emptiness and incompleteness.

Silence

Brief silences may represent productive and creative periods in psychotherapy with adolescents. In fact, the capacity to sustain a period of silence without excessive anxiety often marks a significant growth in self-confidence and acceptance of inner feelings for the adolescent. The therapist should not be quick to fill these silences.

More often, however, silences in adolescent psychotherapy are defensive. They serve to avoid the discovery and expression of angry fantasies which might appear if the adolescent spoke freely. The management of these defensive gaps in communication is extremely difficult with adolescents. It is almost impossible for an adolescent to tolerate the tension involved in remaining silent while confined in an office under observation. This tension is blamed on the therapist, thus increasing the hostile affect and further blocking communication.

In the older adolescent, silence can often be managed within the therapeutic alliance by interpreting the patient's fear of his angry impulses. In younger or more disturbed adolescents, it may be wiser to "let them off the hook" by talking to them or suggesting some activity after mentioning that they feel too upset to talk. This obviously means sacrificing some potential depth of therapy in order to salvage a tolerable therapy relationship.

In some adolescents, silence does not represent a transference phenomenon, but rather a character defense of inhibition and withdrawal. Some of these youngsters have never learned to view emotional communication in a positive way. These youngsters require skillfull and tactful education in the value and techniques of conversation. During this period, the therapist must be prepared to carry the major burden of responsibility for the therapeutic dialogue.

Utilizing Dreams and Artistic Creations

Although the focus of adolescent psychotherapy is on ego functioning, this does not rule out the appropriate utilization of symbolic productions such as dreams, stories, poems, and paintings. The adolescent often is quite creative and we can learn a great deal from the study of his productions. This need not interfere with the emphasis on reality functioning if the therapist confines his comments about the symbolic materials to their relevance in the adolescent's attempt to achieve ego synthesis.

Litowitz and Gundlach (1987) described how adolescents use written material as a semiotic system, to represent their ideas and feelings to others and to themselves. Their writings—plays, letters, journals, diaries—contain echoes of the voices of family members, friends, and other people who inhabit the internalized world of the adolescent writer. These authors point out that adolescents use writing to sort out familial and other identifications, to explore levels of intimacy and self-revelation in interpersonal relationships, and to try out various roles and voices. Sosin (1983) studied the diaries of several adolescent girls and expressed the concept of diary writing as a transitional object. That is, diary writing seemed to have a self-mirroring and self-soothing function for these girls. They also used the diary to inhibit acting out and to contain volatile affects.

It is true that adolescents often offer their creative products to the therapist as a substitute for themselves. The unwary therapist may be drawn into a dispassionate intellectual discussion of the "ideas" contained in the art work as though these ideas were totally unrelated to the adolescent's life. Needless to say, adolescents should not be encouraged to retreat into autistic daydreams. However, dreams and creative fiction often reveal valuable information about the adolescent's real concerns even when he is attempting to avoid them.

Jimmy was a 16-year-old youngster with marked problems in adjustment. He abused drugs, totally rejected parental guidance, had dropped out of school, and showed little interest in the future or in any sublimated interests in the present. His conscious attitude was one of nonchalant disinterest in his plight. He said that the goals of adult life meant very little to him and that he intended to live merely for his immediate pleasure.

In the tenth therapy session, he reported the following dream:

"Our whole family was flying somewhere. My parents each had their own small private plane, but I was flying a B-17. I landed it on the first fueling stop, but then I became frightened. I knew that only one man had ever landed the B-17 alone, without a copilot or crew. I was afraid to take off again."

Discussion of the dream content yielded the information that Jimmy had taken a few flying lessons in the past, but had been frightened by some near accidents on landing. His instructor had to take over the controls to complete the landings. Jimmy felt scared and ashamed. He admitted that he had been questioning the importance of learning to fly. He easily accepted the suggestion that his loss of interest in flying was related to his anxiety about his ability to handle the plane. The therapist commented that people often convince themselves that they do not really want to do the things they are afraid they cannot do. Jimmy admitted that he really wanted very much to learn to fly.

"By the way," the therapist asked casually, "what was the name of your plane?"

"B-17," Jimmy replied.

"When is it that you'll be 17?" the therapist asked pointedly.

"Why, next month," Jimmy replied.

Then, the light dawned. "You mean you think the dream was about being scared to grow up, to be 17?"

"The prospect has been known to scare guys, especially if they feel they have to manage it completely alone," the therapist replied.

Then, he added with a grin, "Sometimes, they get so worried about it, they have to pretend they don't care at all."

Although Jimmy was somewhat skeptical, his own dream and associations were difficult to dismiss completely. Gradually, his derogatory attitude toward the goals of maturity diminished. He began to discuss plans to return to school with appropriate concern about his ability to handle age-appropriate tasks.

The therapist did not comment on the family fragmentation or the possible sexual implications in the dream, since these were not relevant to the current phase of therapy.

Similar therapeutic work may be accomplished by using the artistic creations of adolescents.

David was a brilliant and creative boy of 17. His considerable talents were severely dulled by obsessive rumination, intellectualization, and isolation of affect. He entered therapy because of chronic depression and gnawing fears of masculine inadequacy.

Although he forced the issue of psychotherapy by threatening suicide, he was initially extremely resistant to all attempts to link his behavior and feelings to his actual life situation. He was particularly opposed to any discussion of his feelings for his mother and father. He assured the therapist haughtily that he was in no real sense their offspring and that they no longer mattered to him in the least.

A few sessions later, David timidly brought a poem to his therapy session. It was an excellent literary effort. (The poem was so excellent that it was later published under the author's real name. Therefore, it cannot be reproduced here without compromising confidentiality.) The therapist told David frankly that the poem was good. David did not like the poem, however. He dismissed it as "egocentric adolescent raving."

The therapist asked David what the poem was intended to convey. After a supercilious lecture on the bourgeois mentality that sought a moral message in every work of art, David condescended to comment on a few of the "thematic images" suggested in the poem. He said that the poem "obviously" had to do with the complete solitude of the individual and his "terrifying isolation in the infinity of existential vacuity."

The therapist said that he saw a different theme. He read the poem slowly aloud, verbally underlining the numerous words and phrases in the poem that seemed to refer to birth symbols and to man's origin from his fellows rather than his isolation. The therapist stated calmly that the poet may have intended to emphasize man's separation from his fellows, but the poem seemed to say that no man sprang full formed, alone, and self-sufficient from emptiness.

David listened quietly, and then asked softly, "So I am my father's son?"

"What do you think?"

"I think that I am asserting through negation."

"Can you put that simply for me?"

"You know what I mean. He must really have a hold on me if I have to pretend I don't even know him."

The therapist's goal was not so much to call attention to the father-son relationship, but to help David move beyond his sterile autistic isolation and into affectively meaningful material. Once again, the adolescent's own words, written in a sense in spite of himself, were the agents of change.

A Little Help From Some Friends

Individual therapy isn't always the treatment of choice. At times group therapy is useful instead of the individual approach or in addition to individual therapy. The next chapter focuses on some of the problems of using that approach and some methods of making group psychotherapy successful.

CITED AND RECOMMENDED READINGS

Adatto, C. P. 1966. On the metamorphosis from adolescence into adulthood. *Journal of the American Psychoanalytic Association.* 14: 485–509.

Anthony, E. J. 1988. The creative therapeutic encounter at adolescence. *Adolescent Psychiatry.* 15: 194–216.

Balint, M. 1968. *The Basic Fault: Therapeutic Aspects of Regression.* London: Tavistock Publications.

Bibring, E. 1954. Psychoanalysis and the dynamic psychotherapies. *Journal of the American Psychoanalytic Association.* 2: 745–770.

Brody, W. M. 1965. On the dynamics of narcissism: I. externalization and early ego development. *Psychoanalytic Study of the Child.* 20: 165–193.

Buxbaum, E. 1954. Technique of child therapy: a critical evaluation. *Psychoanalytic Study of the Child.* 9: 297–333.

Corday, R. J. 1967. Limitations of therapy in adolescence. *Journal of the American Academy of Child Psychiatry.* 6: 526–538.

Easson, W. M. 1969. *The Severely Disturbed Adolescent.* New York: International Universities Press.

Fromm-Reichmann, F. 1950. *Principles of Intensive Psychotherapy*. Chicago: University of Chicago Press.

Galatzer-Levy, R. M. 1985. The analysis of an adolescent boy. *Adolescent Psychiatry*. 12: 336–360.

Gitelson, M. 1942. Direct psychotherapy of the adolescent (1941 symposium). *American Journal of Orthopsychiatry*. 12: 1–41.

Gitelson, M. 1948. Character synthesis: the psychotherapeutic problem of adolescence. *American Journal of Orthopsychiatry*. 18: 422–431.

Holmes, D. J. 1964. *The Adolescent in Psychotherapy*. Boston: Little, Brown.

Josselyn, I. M. 1957. Psychotherapy of adolescents at the level of private practice. In: *Psychotherapy of the Adolescent*, edited by B. H. Balser. New York: International Universities Press.

Kohut, H. 1971. *The Analysis of the Self*. New York: International Universities Press.

Litowitz, B. E., and R. A. Gundlach. 1987. When adolescents write: semiotic and social dimensions of adolescents' personal writing. *Adolescent Psychiatry*. 14: 82–111.

London, P. 1964. *The Modes and Morals of Psychotherapy*. New York: Holt, Rinehart & Winston.

Long, R. 1968. The observing ego and adolescent development. *Rev. Inst. Nac. Neurol.* (Mexico) 2: 8–21.

Massie, H. N. 1988. Intensive psychodynamically oriented treatment of two cases of adolescent psychosis. *Adolescent Psychiatry*. 15: 487–504.

O'Connor, J. J., and A. N. Horowitz. 1984. The bogeyman cometh: a strategic approach for difficult adolescents. *Family Process*. 23: 237–249.

Palmer, A. J., et al. 1983. The "adoption process" in the inpatient treatment of children and adolescents. *Journal of the American Academy of Child Psychiatry*. 22: 286–293.

Schwartz, R. S. 1984. Confidentiality and secret-keeping on an inpatient unit. *Psychiatry*. 47: 279–284.

Sosin, D. A. 1983. The diary as a transitional object in female adolescent development. *Adolescent Psychiatry*. 11: 92–103.

Tolchin, J. 1987. Telephone psychotherapy with adolescents. *Adolescent Psychiatry*. 14: 332–341.

Williams, Frank S. 1986. The psychoanalyst as both parent and interpreter for adolescent patients. *Adolescent Psychiatry*. 13: 164–177.

Winnicott, D. D. 1958. Primary maternal preoccupation. *Collected Papers: through Paediatrics to Psycho-analysis*. London: Tavistock Publications. (New York: Basic Books.)

Zinner, J. 1978. Combined individual and family therapy of borderline adolescents: rationale and management of the early phase. *Adolescent Psychiatry*. 6: 420–447.

CHAPTER 7

group psychotherapy of the adolescent

There is something inherently seductive about the idea of treating disturbed adolescents in a group. The age group has a spontaneous interest in getting together and the conditions of current social reality require adolescents to spend most of their waking hours interacting within formal and informal peer groups. Developmental pressures cause these groups to hold great fascination and importance for the young person (Buxbaum, 1945).

It has been reasoned that group therapy would take full advantage of this natural grouping in the adolescent period, converting a distraction from individual therapy into a powerful therapeutic alternative. The troublesome dependency-independency-authority conflict with adults would be diluted by the presence of other young people in the treatment setting. Prompted by friendship and mutual concern, group members would recognize and confront maladaptive behavior in one another, including self-destructive pathological clashes with authority figures. These interventions would have great impact since they could not be dismissed as "uptight adult hassling." Theoretically, group psychotherapy should lead to effortless success.

Unfortunately in practice group psychotherapy with adolescents often does not unfold in that way. Group members do not settle into a friendly acceptance of one another. Instead they approach each other with silence, suspicion, and defensive affectations. They may not approach at all. Many groups disintegrate after a meeting or two.

If the group survives, perhaps because of external pressure to attend, the authority conflict is not diluted. In fact, instead of struggling with a single snarling youngster, the therapist is confronted with an angry and disruptive mob. Therapists have been known to disband groups out of fear for their own safety or at least their reputation in their clinic or private office building. Naturally, this extreme is unusual, but there are plenty of frightening war stories around to alarm the uninitiated.

Some therapists have succeeded in corralling their group, only to find that their reasonable, cooperative patients expect them to do all the work. The therapist is clearly accepted as a powerful leader and is beseiged with requests for advice, practical help, and infantile support.

These unfortunate experiences (and others even worse) follow from a failure to consider all aspects of adolescent development, psychopathology, and the dynamics of group formation during adolescence as they affect the formation and function of therapy groups.

There are many youngsters who need psychotherapy who will either fail to respond to the group approach or who may even be damaged by this technique. These youngsters may easily be screened through careful evaluation prior to group placement. If diagnostic study suggests that the presenting complaint results from ego depletion with panic and disorganization barely contained, the youngster is not a candidate for outpatient group therapy (Josselyn, 1972), at least not before a period of individual therapy. In individual work, youngsters of this kind can utilize an extremely dependent transference to gradually strengthen and widen their defensive skills and to partially resolve the primitive conflicts which are dangerously near eruption. At that point they have the potential to utilize interaction with peers constructively. Earlier they would have merely experienced a lively, challenging group as another stress to an already overburdened coping system. Sugar (1972) has described the utilization of self-selected peer groups in cases of this kind. Many very disturbed adolescents of this type need group therapy in a protected inpatient setting.

A second category of youngster who cannot benefit from group therapy is fixated at a level of development which does not value the opinion or support of peers. Such adolescents often present with psychosomatic or self-destructive behavior which seems clearly motivated by a need to coerce nurture from adults. They require an infantile feeding relationship with a caring adult to maintain marginal functioning.

Ann, a thin, tense, 14-year-old, had been in psychotherapy with three different therapists since age eight when her multiple neurotic symptoms of school phobia, abdominal pains, vomiting episodes, and multiple phobias first became evident. Her mother was a narcissistic, infantile, and extremely unhappy woman who had been in psychoanalysis for eight years. She made no secret of the fact she experienced Ann as an unlovable burden. Her father was distant and rigid, confining his family interactions to occasional outbursts at his daughter when she interfered with any of his plans and criticism of his wife for not coping better with the children's management and control. Ann's problems had been variously diagnosed as an anxiety neurosis, borderline psychosis, and childhood schizophrenia. Psychotic diagnoses had been considered because of Ann's general disorganization and because some of her phobic concerns were quite bizarre. For example, she feared she might wet herself at school but responded to this common worry by wearing four to six layers of undergarments. She also was periodically fearful that her hair was falling out, that she had cancer, or that she had performed acts that she had only thought about. Reality testing clearly was shaky.

After a year and a half of therapy with her latest therapist she had stabilized markedly and was symptom free. She began to move toward adolescent concerns and behaviors, but complained chronically that she had no friends at school. The therapist tried to explore her role in this state of affairs with very little success. Motivated more than a little by countertransference annoyance, he pushed her to join an adolescent group where her ways of relating to agemates could be directly observed. She agreed reluctantly, insisting on continuing individual sessions concurrently (though she complained constantly that they were valueless).

In the group she was paralyzed with anxiety, developed a blind hatred for the female cotherapist, and alienated the

other group members with her childish and demanding behavior. In one active session while being confronted by another group member, her eyes rolled back in her head and
her neck muscles went into spasm so that she literally could
not "see what was being said." She had to leave the meeting.
The support of extra individual sessions allowed her to recover quickly and, after some ambivalence, she decided to
return to the group where by subduing herself, she was able
to attain a degree of acceptance. However, it was the therapist's opinion that she had only survived the group experience, not that it had benefited her. She remained in individual therapy after the group was terminated, and
maintained her symptomless but constricted adjustment
even as the frequency of appointments was gradually reduced to one a month.

Similar failures, more dangerous to the group than to the patient, may occur with unsocialized acting-out youngsters. Of
course, many adolescents who present with antisocial behavior
are basically well socialized and are handling neurotic or developmental problems in an alloplastic manner. They work out quite
well in group therapy. However, those youngsters who have never
shown evidence of adequate object relations and the capacity for
affectionate attachment will not respond to group pressure and
cannot adapt to group expectations.

Fortunately, most youngsters who should not be in group have
some awareness of this fact. They, like Ann, resist the plan for
psychotherapy. Although some youngsters who do well in group
resist the idea initially, strong reservations should lead the therapist to review his diagnostic thinking carefully before pressuring
the youngster to enter group psychotherapy. As a rule, the appropriate group candidate is anxious about the prospect of group

work but is also fascinated and intrigued by his fantasies of what
may happen.

WHY ADOLESCENTS WANT TO BELONG

Some consideration must also be given to the nature of spontaneous adolescent groups. The developmental pressures which

drive the adolescent toward his peers and the emotional needs which he hopes to satisfy in peer groups strongly affect the readiness with which adolescents will relate to one another in a therapy setting and the style of communication which will tend to occur. These developmental factors also influence the reception the therapist can expect as the therapy group's leader.

In early adolescence the youngster turns toward peers under the pressure of his need to emancipate himself from his family. It is more of a panicked flight than a positive quest. As the parents are rejected and devalued, their utility as sources of narcissistic support is weakened or lost. The youngster does not yet have a suitable substitute internal mechanism for maintaining his sense of worth. The peer group provides a temporary emergency support system. This means, however, that the adolescent's friends must be people he can view as equals or superiors and that they must offer him a primarily positive reflection of himself. Naturally, he is willing to conform slavishly to group norms in order to obtain this acceptance. The adolescent is very particular in choosing his associates. His ties are somewhat fickle, since he will drop any friend who falls from favor with the remainder of his gang. It is the rare 14-year-old who will maintain an open friendship with a youngster whom "everyone else" regards as "weird" or "queer."

As the youngster grows older, the peer group increasingly becomes important as a support system in the task of modifying the superego. The group shares guilty secrets with bravado and even encourages previously unacceptable behavior, particularly actions which defy adult authority. However, group members are not merely "partners in crime," they also offer one another limits based on the human rights of other members of the group. They may also persuade individuals not to "go too far" because certain behaviors may be dangerous to the individual or may threaten the continued existence of the group. Therefore the group serves both to loosen the constraints of the latency conscience and to provide an alternative, reality-based system of controls.

As these developmental tasks are mastered, the adolescent becomes increasingly interested in his peers as real people. Relationships become less narcissistic and attachments are based on positive attraction rather than flight from the family of origin. Bonds are still somewhat tentative and there is considerable role playing, but relationships are warm and enduring over relatively extended periods of time. Even friction and controversy are accepted as necessary and valuable aspects of a rounded experience in the group.

This progression is often interrupted or uneven in the troubled adolescent. Many patients, even in late adolescence, are still more invested in the search for "psychic bandaids" than in learning from an honest give-and-take relationship. This fact creates two kinds of problems in the early stages of adolescent group psychotherapy.

First of all, the troubled adolescent is reluctant to accept his fellow group members. It is difficult for the patient to idealize people who are gathered with him because they too "have problems." He is frightened by the prospect of losing self-esteem through accepting membership in a group of "misfits." If some group members have strikingly different defenses, social styles, or socioeconomic backgrounds, the patient's certainty that he is in the wrong place grows exponentially. Some patients are often lost to the group at this point. As those who remain begin to find some group members who seem acceptable as "friends," there is a strong tendency for the group to fragment and develop cliques and scapegoats. It is a trying time for the therapist whose goal is to promote total group cohesion.

A second problem is created by the narcissistic vulnerability of the adolescent. Because of the need to use peer relationships for narcissistic confirmation, the adolescent tends to hide his problems and to cooperate fully with the same defensive strategy as it is utilized by the other group members. The patients want to avoid criticism and are understandably reluctant to throw the first stone. Each patient pretends to offer what he hopes to receive— total acceptance and admiration. Any confrontations that occur tend to be directed toward scapegoats and are hostile and distancing. It is easy for the therapist to become the only one in the group who "hassles the kids who are okay." He must be careful also to avoid being the only one who "takes up for the dopey ones."

The adolescent's use of peers to assist in the modification of his conscience also carries a threat to the successful formation of a therapeutic group. Most groups will test the therapist in this area. In more subdued groups, the discussions of forbidden thoughts and actions will be carried on initially before and after the therapist enters the group. Sooner or later, however, some group member will be either brave or nervous enough to broach the topics in the therapist's presence. Other groups are much more bold. In either case the group must know the therapist's stance. Will the therapist encourage acting out or will he come across as a parental-superego figure? Will he be corruptible, seducible, and manipulatable or repressive and rigid? Of course, the opportunity of therapeutic exploration is lost if the therapist is drawn into an unholy alliance with either the id or the superego. This problem has been considered earlier in regard to the development of the therapeutic alliance in individual psychotherapy and the principles of management are the same in groups. However, the countertransference pressures of facing a group involved in externalizing superego issues are greater than those encountered with individual patients, particularly when the group seems in danger of transforming itself into a vicious, salacious street gang before one's eyes. Skilled group therapists have managed to navigate this risky period spontaneously, but many problems may be avoided by utilizing some of the technical structuring patterns suggested later in this chapter.

This brief discussion of developmental issues which influence the achievement of group cohesion underlines the fact that the natural tendency of adolescents is indeed to form groups, but not groups that are inclined to explore the meaning of behavior (Meeks, 1973). Of course, groups can be helpful, even therapeutic in the broad sense, without investigating the meaning of behavior. One successful strategy of group therapy with adolescents is to simply accept the basically narcissistic, supportive patterns of spontaneous groups and to harness these forces for constructive goals. This technique does not encourage introspection and will be described briefly. A second approach which utilizes structural techniques intended to encourage introspection, investigation of motives, and scrutiny of the emotions which underlie interpersonal transactions will be discussed in greater detail. Many groups actually develop some characteristics of both types of group structure.

THE OPEN-ENDED SUPPORTIVE GROUP

Therapeutic groups which focus on changing self-destructive behavior by embracing and manipulating natural patterns of adolescent behavior in groups have been rather successful in a variety of settings (Sadock and Gould, 1964; Franklin and Nottage, 1969; Kraft, 1968). These groups have certain characteristics in common although there is considerable variation in their membership, specific procedures, and goals. Initial membership is often compulsory and enforced by outside agencies such as probation agencies or the officials of a residential treatment institution. The groups are open-ended and, in fact, often define the addition and successful assimilation of new members as their primary function. Members are selected primarily on the basis of their symptom or because of their presence in a particular institution. The group, then, is rather homogeneous, either for symptom (drug usage, delinquency, etc.) or through common experience in daily living circumstances. The work of the group is oriented toward fairly circumscribed goals, usually either altering the common symptom behavior or improving the adaptation to the common living situation.

The basic force for change in these groups is a core of committed "old members" who have been converted from a prior involvement in the symptomatic behavior to an alternative lifestyle. They credit the group and its leader for their success in changing. They are familiar with the gratifications and temptations of the negative behavior and recognize immediately the common defensive patterns and attitudes that insulate the new group member from awareness of the destructiveness of his maladaptive symptoms. Since they have decided that the symptomatic behavior is unwise and self-destructive, they are quite willing to confront the new member. Their self-esteem now depends on maintaining the wisdom of their decision so the new member's defense of the rejected behaviors represents a personal threat and is vigorously attacked. Since they have also "been there," however, the old members tend to temper their assault with empathy, support, and open confession of their own shortcomings.

The technical devices utilized by leaders in these groups are primarily inspirational, supportive, and directive although group members may actively pursue hidden motivations. Exploration is primarily directed toward subtle manipulations of the group and its leader by the unrepentant new member. Interpretations and confrontations are mainly aimed at unmasking the new member, helping him to "shape up" and stop "playing games." On the other hand, extended discussion of personal genetic and dynamic material tends to be viewed with suspicion since such material may be used as a justification for the unacceptable behavior, an excuse to avoid essential change, a "cop-out."

In many ways the leader of these groups serves primarily as a consultant and support to the old members who carry the main thrust of the rehabilititative work. The leader is there to help if the old members become discouraged or if they are manipulated into an unnecessarily punitive or overly permissive position in relation to a particularly difficult new member. The leader assists the group in maintaining focus on its tasks and values. Usually he or she does this without commenting on the motives or problems of the older members. The leader points out that the old members may temporarily lose sight of the purpose and correct procedures of the group because their task is difficult. Leaders avoid criticism or discussion of the old members' psychopathology since this might weaken their loyalty to the group and lessen their influence on the new members.

The narcissistic values of being "right" and "cool" are usually sufficient reward for the old members' work in the group, especially as these values are continually reinforced by the successful conversion of new members to the group ethic. The group provides an opportunity to obtain admiration from a peer group which is acceptable (i.e., the members are streetwise, tough, know the drug scene) without engaging in behaviors which are dangerous and self-destructive. The group also provides a reasonable new superego model divorced from childhood and the parents. The almost evangelical drive to help other youngsters provides an important sense of worth and mission which can substitute for the need to prove one's self in daring and illegal actions.

Although these groups are powerful agents for change, there are many limits to their application. It may be that some environments are so brutally unfair and destructive that adolescents subjected to their viciousness are unreachable. However, skilled workers with honest commitment can ameliorate some of the damage in the worst environments (Stebbins, 1972). The difficulty of finding therapists with sufficient empathy, skill, toughness, and concern to activate the group and form the original pro-therapy core of "old members" is an important limitation. Many are called, but few succeed and persevere. Yet, when these groups function well they can be heaven sent to many of the youngsters with "malignant defenses" discussed earlier. The narcissistic support of a well-functioning group can make it possible for the youngster to give up destructive omnipotent defenses and learn human and constructive alternatives. The amazing treatment record of Alcoholics Anonymous and other similar group treatment organizations can teach us a great deal about the value and power of this approach.

Still, some youngsters cannot respond to any form of group therapy. Those so socially immature as to be immune to group pressure and group rewards cannot respond to a therapy based on these factors. Open-ended support groups are also relatively ineffective in correcting symptomatic behavior which is grounded in severe neurotic conflict, particularly when the behavior is part of a generally masochistic pattern.

Even with an appropriate leader and members who fit, there are potential problems. Failure to influence one or more new members is demoralizing and can erode collective self-esteem. Trusted old members can relapse in response to increased stresses in their lives with an even greater disruptive impact on the group.

Charismatic new members may tempt the entire group to return to old value systems. In short, the group ties are basically narcissistic and therefore somewhat unreliable when pressures mount. The group leader's own charisma, flexibility, and clinical wisdom will be severely tried as he attempts to maintain a positively functioning group entity over time.

THE CLOSED, EXPLORATORY THERAPY GROUP

The developmental impediments to adolescent group work may also be circumvented by altering the structural characteristics to encourage the development of a group ethic of emotional openness and exploration. The model described here does permit the addition of occasional new patients at infrequent intervals, but is basically designed for a group with constant membership and a reasonably prolonged existence. It is basically designed for outpatients. Under these circumstances, further modifications are necessary to ensure continuing parental cooperation in the group work.

The open-ended group described above can afford to neglect parental involvement since the group basically substitutes for the family and discourages extensive discussion of family relationships. In contrast, the dynamically oriented group is virtually certain to consider in detail the impact of family problems on the attitudes, feelings, and interpersonal quirks of its members. These discussions will tend to activate latent family conflicts and may lead the parents to sabotage treatment or even terminate the adolescent's group membership. The needs of the parents must be considered if the group structure is to be successful. This parental involvement in the group will rarely substitute for specific therapy directed toward their marital or personal problems. Although some parents benefit personally, the primary goal is to enlist their enlightened support for the work of the adolescent group.

We can now turn to a description of the model. As in the remainder of the book, the procedures will be described explicitly with the clear recognition that other therapists have utilized other techniques successfully. Models must be altered to fit treatment conditions and personal preferences.

Members must be chosen carefully for outpatient dynamic group psychotherapy with an eye to both the needs of the individual youngster and the overall composition of the group.

The criteria of group selection are hardly scientific, but some principles seem clinically sound. We have already mentioned some youngsters who should be excluded from groups. Additional criteria should be mentioned. It seems important for the prospective member to have parental permission and, preferably, parental encouragement to join the group. Good group work produces anxiety and resistance. If the parent is poised to support flight from the experience, it is unlikely that most adolescents will be able to resist this invitation to escape immediate pain in the interest of long-term benefits.

The youngster himself should have at least a modicum of positive motivation for the group experience, perhaps limited initially to a mixture of interest and anxiety with an agreement to try the group for a month or two. The youngster's motivation will be evaluated in more depth during the evolution of individual treatment contracts, a process which will be described later.

Some attention should be given to choosing a group population which will be socially compatible within broad limits. Early impressions of other group members are important and adolescents are often harsh in their judgment of superficial characteristics. For example, a psychotic youngster with the same style, vocabulary, dress, and social experience would probably be less threatening to an adolescent group than a healthier youngster with a disfiguring physical defect or a background and lifestyle which seemed "weird" to the other members.

An adolescent group jelled with surprising rapidity except for Bill, a 17-year-old who remained withdrawn and uncomfortable through the first four meetings. He requested an individual interview where he told the therapist the group

wasn't helping him. The other kids seemed strange and unfriendly and he intended to quit. When pressed about his
discontent his complaints were vague. The therapist commented on Bill's uncharacteristic silence in the group meetings and wondered if he could really assess the other members' friendliness without being more open. Bill responded
with angry tears.

"I can't."

"Why not?"

"You're stupid. Why did you put me in a rich kids' group?"

Though the therapist hadn't realized it, every member of
the group except Bill came from very affluent families. They
spoke casually of their cars, going out to dinner, and attending concerts. Bill's father was a university professor who
couldn't afford such luxuries.

In this case, Bill's educational and social background was
actually quite similar to those of the other group members.
They were quite prepared to accept him although he felt
very "different" from them.

Bill was able to resolve his discomfort and work successfully in the group. His reaction is described merely to illustrate the adolescent's exquisite sensitivity to superficial social
differences.

Some attention must also be given to the "balance" of the
group. Passive and silent members must be offset with some "talk-
ers." Youngsters inclined toward "acting out" solutions to conflict should be placed in groups which include some youngsters
who reflect or even ruminate on their feelings before acting.
Mostly one must depend on an intuitive sense of how the group
will fit together. This sense is never infallible, but the chances for
success are increased by knowing the individual youngsters reasonably well. This kind of knowledge can only be obtained
through fairly prolonged pre-group individual evaluation.

PRE-GROUP EVALUATION

The diagnostic advantages of pre-group evaluation have been
mentioned but these sessions are central to group success in other

ways as well. The early stages of group therapy are extremely
anxiety producing for many adolescents so it is important for
each group member to have a stable, trusting relationship with
the therapist prior to the first group meeting. Many youngsters
should be started in group only after a period of individual psychotherapy with the therapist. Others may be referred by therapists who do not do group work themselves but believe the patient would be helped by a group experience. If the colleague's
assessment is correct, these youngsters may require only a few
individual sessions to get acquainted with the therapist and learn
something of the pattern of group work he follows. Of course,
the group therapist also uses these meetings to assure himself
that the youngster is ready to function constructively in the group.
If he does not think so, the patient can be referred back to the
original therapist for further individual work.

If the group will have cotherapists, they can divide the evalu-
ative work between them. This has practical advantages since most
therapists do not have group evaluation time in their normal
schedule and are somewhat overburdened by the extra work involved in preparing to begin a group. The procedure does produce some technical problems since group members may resist
group involvement and cling to their individual relationship to
the cotherapist who evaluated them. However, this problem is
preferable to the risk of early group dissolution. In any event,
this excessive attachment to the therapist quickly diminishes as
the group members become acquainted and form attachments to
one another.

Pre-group meetings also allow patients to elaborate their anxieties and fantasies about group therapy. The therapist can correct frightening misconceptions and explain the goals and procedures of the group. The ground rules of the group such as
prohibitions against physical contact, the desirability and limitations of confidentiality, the need for regular attendance, the procedure for quitting the group, and the expectation that each
group member will formulate a treatment contract for the group
can be discussed fully. The youngster has the opportunity to consider his treatment goals and to solicit the therapist's help in

shaping a treatment contract which he would be comfortable in sharing with the group. This is important since many youngsters wish to discuss very sensitive topics in the group, but would be understandably reluctant to disclose these fully in an initial meeting of the group. For example, the 15-year-old boy who has never had a date and is terrified of girls may need permission to limit his first treatment contract to "I would like to improve the way I get along with girls." At the other extreme from youngsters who might say too much are those who require pressure and assistance to come up with any personal treatment goals. The pre-group individual sessions provide an opportunity to explain that comments like "I'm only here because my parents sent me" or "I was just curious about what happens in groups" will not suffice.

Pre-group meetings also permit the therapist to clarify his expectations about how the group will proceed. Comments such as "when a group really gets going, you get pretty involved with the other people" both explain the importance of regular attendance and set the expectation that group members should comment on each others' absences, consistent lateness, or precipitous desire to quit the group. The therapist has defined these behaviors as evidences of concern rather than meddling in someone else's business. Similar double duty is accomplished by predicting some of the problems the youngster may expect in the course of the group experience. "If this group really works like others I've had, there will be pretty open talking about how people feel about one another. Sometimes you may not like what people say about how you're coming across." "You know, there may be things about people in the group that annoy you. Now at school you might just avoid that person, but in a group it's important to talk about how you really feel even if you're afraid the other person may get mad or have their feelings hurt. Do you think you can do that?" Of course, these comments are tailored to the dynamics and relating style of the individual youngster. The diagnostic evaluation often allows a fairly accurate prediction of the types of group interaction which a given youngster will find most uncomfortable. Naturally these structuring comments do not guarantee that the group will actually move toward confrontation, emotional openness, and exploration of interpersonal processes, but it begins that process by presenting the possibility for such interactions and implying that the therapist expects these possibilities to occur.

Once the therapist has determined that the youngster seems appropriate for the group that is being formed, the therapist may want some form of commitment that the patient is truly interested and will actually show up for the first meeting. Also, these youngsters are usually quite curious about who are the other prospective members and what is wrong with them. "Are they nerds or retards or geeks?" is implied, if not stated directly. It is usually possible to be reassuring by mentioning some of the psychosocial strengths of the other group members, while acknowledging that they all have problems of one kind or another: "One guy in the group used to play football until he broke his leg. There's a girl who did a solo in her school musical." Another technique is starting a sign-up sheet, a formality familiar to every high school student:

Group Therapy Sign-up Sheet

I want to be in the therapy group that will be on Thursdays, 4:00 to 5:15, starting October 15.

Name   Grade   School

What this sign-up sheet does is communicate to the prospective group member that there are other real kids who are going to be in the group. It tells a minimal amount of information about the other patients and the information that it does tell has been volunteered by the youngsters involved, since they know that the sign-up sheet is going to be seen by other patients who are interested in being in the group. The process also creates a sense of commitment on the part of the patients who do sign up on the sheet.

The therapist predicts the patient will be emotionally accepted in the group and also states a rule when he explains, "the reason we make a fuss about someone stopping is because a lot of times the group wonders why someone quits, maybe even blames themselves. If you decided to leave the group—let's say you got your problem worked out—it would be important to explain that. The rest of the members would probably hate to see you go and they might wonder if it happened because of something they said or maybe they weren't interesting or good enough. So we ask anyone who thinks about quitting to bring that up at the start of a meeting and to tell why they're thinking of leaving the group. The other good thing about this is for you, the person who's thinking of quitting, it gives you a chance to hear what the other people think about your reasons for quitting and gives you a chance to think it over. And that's good, because stopping the group is a pretty important decision and you'd want to think about it pretty seriously."

OBJECTION! Your Honor, the doctor is leading the patient. You bet your sweet id.

And that's only the beginning.

THERAPIST ACTIVITY

The leader of an adolescent group must work actively at promoting spontaneity and intimacy (Anderson, 1972). The therapist's activities include structuring group tasks and procedures and the usual group leader's activity of conceptualizing and verbalizing the group experience (group process) as it unfolds, but these professional activities are not enough. The therapist must also be active as a person, alive and involved in the group. He needs to share his own feeling responses to the meaningful emotional interactions which develop between group members.

Obviously this activity poses potential dangers of encouraging excessive dependency in group members. The therapist may be seen as a guru, a teacher, a good parent. These developments need not be unhealthy if they are recognized and discussed openly. If the therapist is alert and free of excessive needs for power or status, there will be plenty of chances to support emerging leadership in the group. The therapist's overt and explicit interventions can often decrease as the group's momentum grows, but he must remain an actively interested and emotionally invested observer.

In the seventh session of an adolescent group the therapist confessed his discomfort.

"I don't know. It seems like I'm talking too much in here. I don't think I'm giving other people enough chance to talk and that's really bad, because I'm not even getting to know you guys well enough to know whether I'm saying the right things."

Mike, a previously silent 16-year-old, said, "You're not. I'm sorry, but we need to get the kids talking. Me too, I guess. I haven't said much myself. I think we ought to interview each other, like take turns being the patient. Everyone could ask three questions—course if you don't think. . . ."

"Sounds great to me, but maybe you'd better ask the other kids."

"Okay, but Mike has to go first." Everyone chimes their agreement that Mike had to be the first "patient."

Everyone has their own style of activity. The important point is that passive, detached, dispassionate scrutiny may have great value in some scientific settings. The adolescent psychotherapy group is not one of them.

THE GROUP CONTRACT

The group contract or the group rules of the group are nothing more than a set of conditions which group members agree to follow in order to achieve treatment results they desire. This quality of informed consent and mutual commitment needs to be emphasized to offset any fantasy that group contracts are made in heaven or in the therapist's head. The anticipation of possible control problems in adolescent groups may lead the therapist to focus on a long list of prohibitions as the primary content of the group contract. The adolescents correctly perceive this as a frightened insistence on a superego alliance and respond according to their particular pathology. Overly inhibited youngsters slavishly obey the rules and youngsters in rebellion fight them. Neither group becomes involved in treatment.

The fundamentals of the group contract have already been discussed with each youngster during his pre-group individual sessions. Each therapist must decide the basic working conditions under which he or she can conduct meaningful group therapy. Many would consider most of the following rules important for the reasons given.

1. No hitting in the group. The therapist explains the obvious fact that people cannot speak honestly with one another unless they are assured that the therapist and the group will neither permit them to hit or be hit. Some therapists extend this rule to "no physical contact" to rule out physical expression of positive feelings (kissing, sitting on laps, etc.) along with the expression of aggression. This may be questioned on the grounds that it introduces some confusion by including "hittin' and huggin' "in the same category as though they were somehow interchangeable or related to the same emotional origin. Secondly, the vagueness of the general rule suggests that the therapist is reluctant to confront adolescent sexuality directly. Finally, from a practical viewpoint, some physical contact (i.e., embracing a crying fellow member) may be decidedly constructive.

   In inpatient group therapy, however, stricter rules are wise. First of all, the patients live together night and day so that feelings become very intense. They should not be further fueled by physical contact, even if it is innocent. We will discuss inpatient treatment more thoroughly in a later chapter. This chapter is meant to focus on outpatient group therapy.

2. Regular attendance is expected. If it is totally impossible to attend a session, it is the patient's responsibility to contact the therapist and explain why the absence is unavoidable.

The therapist explains that the members need to get to know one another very well in order for the group to be helpful. This requires very regular attendance. In addition, the unexplained absence of a member wastes valuable group time as the present members speculate on the reasons for the absence. Some members may even inhibit their group participation out of concern that some interaction with the absent member drove him away.

3. Any member who considers leaving the group should announce his intention at the beginning of a group session and permit full discussion of the decision. The reasons for this rule have already been discussed. Some therapists require a group notification of two sessions or more. Theoretically this makes sense; however it may invite passive aggression if some group members perceive the rule as a disguised attempt to force members to remain in the group when they have definitely decided to quit.

4. Each group member will be expected to make an individual treatment contract. This expectation will be discussed further in this chapter.

5. The group is told that the group will function best if there is no discussion of the group proceedings with others. Some therapists feel that this rule is impossible to enforce and add, "If you must discuss something that occurs in here with your parents or anyone else, at least don't use names."

6. The therapist or cotherapists may also wish to explain their position regarding confidentiality, namely that they will not discuss things that occur in the group or information revealed there unless, in their judgment, a group member is in danger of harming himself or others. Some therapists also reserve the right to answer parental questions regarding treatment progress. Most adolescents seem to accept their parents' right to know if the youngster is utilizing treatment appropriately, but some therapists feel uncomfortable with "sending home report cards."

7. The group is told that any contact between members outside the group sessions should be reported in the next group

meeting. It is explained that important group issues may be missed if group members have discussions which exclude the remainder of the group.

8. Some therapists forbid outside contact, but there are serious difficulties in taking this position. It is a rule that cannot be enforced, seems artificial, and invites rebellion. Also, many therapists have observed that much extra-group contact is supportive, pro-therapy, and conducive to the development of group cohesion.

These conditions are not presented as a list of dogmatic regulations. They are discussed with the group as important issues which require resolution. This does not mean they are totally or even primarily negotiable. For example, few therapists would consider working with a group that could not agree to refrain from striking one another. The therapist must press for the conditions he needs, attempting to convince the group of the therapeutic necessity of each rule. There is no reason to avoid "sales talk." The resulting contract is designed to benefit everyone, especially the group members.

THE INDIVIDUAL TREATMENT CONTRACT

The practice of requiring each group member to formulate a personal treatment goal and to verbalize the goal to the group has several advantages. It is not an unreasonable expectation when the adolescent receives assistance with the difficult job of thinking through his contract in the pre-group individual sessions. It is probably true that any youngster who is suitable for out-patient group work is able to make this degree of commitment. However, the therapist must be willing to permit some face-saving reservations. For example, it is probably acceptable for the adolescent to say, "Well, the *real* reason I'm coming to the group is because my father says I have to, but since I'm here, I might be interested in learning more about how boys should treat girls." The group presentation of individual treatment contracts is taken up as soon as the group completes consideration and acceptance of the group contract, often in the first session. The therapist introduces the topic by saying, "Okay, since we've agreed to those things, let's get on to people's individual contracts. Remember we said everyone would tell the group why they're coming here and what they hope to accomplish in the group. Who wants to go first and get it over with?"

Usually someone will volunteer, but if not, the therapist can ask a member to begin. Each contract is open to discussion by the group and the therapist and may be accepted or rejected as inappropriate. Generally speaking, any serious goal which seems neither destructive or foolishly grandiose is accepted. One does not expect or need psychologically sophisticated contracts at this stage in adolescent group work.

The two primary purposes of requiring contracts in the initial sessions are to open problem areas for group discussion and to provide the therapist with legitimate, neutral instrumental authority. Since each member has asked for help with a specific problem, the "mutual protection pact" of denial which often characterizes adolescent groups during their formative period is less likely to develop. The open admission of difficulty and the request for help give both a focus and permission to the other group members as they consider commenting on a fellow member's verbal or nonverbal behavior in the group. For example, if a youngster has stated that he is coming to the group because he wishes to learn how to make friends, the group feels more free to confront him with his silence, sarcasm, or egocentricity without feeling they are intruding or merely being hostile. "Maybe the reason you have trouble making friends is that you're always cutting people down. At least you do here."

The therapist is also in a better position to avoid the unholy alliances with either id or superego. The process of making individual treatment contracts defines him as a consultant to the group. He becomes an expert given the responsibility for guiding the group toward behaviors which will permit the individual members to accomplish their chosen goals. If it becomes necessary to set limits on group behavior, the therapist does this as a leader exercising his duty to help the group accomplish its aims, not as an offended uptight parent figure. His function is executive and oriented toward promoting better ego functioning with the group.

Any contract which is sincere will accomplish these two purposes. As the group work continues, contracts may be altered and refined. The therapist may suggest changes, or new definitions of the problem may be offered by the patient or other group members. For example, the therapist may comment to a patient, "I would like to suggest a change in your contract now that I know you better. I don't think you exactly have a problem in making friends. I think you should consider working on your tendency to expect too much of friends and the way that causes you to be disappointed in people and overly critical." Later yet the contract may evolve to, "Trying to stop setting people up to prove they don't like me and that I'm better than they are."

The treatment contract is only a tool so its value will depend on the skill with which it is used to further the group work. Some therapists are worried that adolescent patients will not accept this condition of group work. They might consider the possibility that a group so resistant to the treatment process is unlikely to be successful in any case. Perhaps it is better to dissolve an unworkable group early in its course so that more suitable treatment approaches can be attempted. In actual practice, most adolescent groups will accept this condition of treatment. Naturally some of the more resistant members will hold back, but as more and more group members commit themselves to a treatment contract, the pressure to "get aboard" grows. The contracted members point out that it is only fair that all members reveal their problems and aspirations to the group.

THE PARENTS

Many patterns of parental involvement have been utilized in group work with adolescents. Some therapists conduct concurrent treatment groups for the parents or arrange for such groups to be conducted by a colleague. Attendance at these groups may be required as a condition for accepting the adolescent in the group. These groups are sometimes quite difficult and unsatisfactory because the parents are unmotivated and do not recognize a need for treatment. However, a skillful therapist can often make these groups effective by permitting the parents to focus on their youngsters initially, gradually using common themes and problems to build group cohesion and a capacity for personal therapy work.

Another successful approach involves periodic family meetings, basically an adolescent group meeting with the parents invited. The adolescents may also be seen individually with their families. These approaches are effective and are well received by the parents. The only potential disadvantage is that family work closely linked to the group may dilute the intensity of the attachments formed within the group. If the aim is to maximize group intimacy so that the group can serve as a microcosm of emotional life, this may be a disadvantage too serious to accept.

Another alternative is to approach the parents as collaborators in the group process, leaving any direct therapy they may require outside of the group involvement. A parents' meeting is called just prior to beginning the adolescent group. The therapist or cotherapists present the aims and methods of the group didactically, explaining all aspects of the group procedure in detail. The parents are told that their youngsters' individual problems will be approached indirectly through the creation of a human relationships laboratory experience in the group setting. The parents are offered examples to demonstrate how this experience serves to develop the capacity for self-awareness and skill in relating to other people in a fair and honest way.

The parents are told of the problems and disadvantages of this approach. The therapist admits that this kind of work creates considerable anxiety which may cause their youngster to express desires to leave the group. They are warned that youngsters often attempt to manipulate their parents to support their flight from the group by suddenly claiming all problems have been solved, being amazingly cooperative in the home, expressing concern about the morality and mental health of other group members, or trying to imply that the therapist is hostile toward the parents.

The parents are assured that they are not expected to force their youngster to remain in group. The desire to quit may be appropriate. The therapist merely wants their support in asking the youngster to discuss his decision and the reasons for it in the group setting. The parents are asked to refer any complaints their adolescent may have about the group or the therapist to a group meeting, encouraging the open expression of negative feelings in the group setting so that the youngster's emotional experience within the group can be as complete as possible. The parents are told that if they have any questions about the group or the therapist's behavior, these should be discussed directly with the therapist.

The importance of confidentiality is discussed so that the parents can understand why the therapist cannot fully disclose the happenings of the group to them. The therapist also explains why he needs their permission to talk openly with their youngsters about any contracts the parents and therapist may have. Parents are encouraged to call the therapist with any questions or information but to inform their youngster that they are calling. They should also tell their adolescent the general content of what they intend to say.

Group fees and policies about absences are discussed along with an explanation of the importance of regular attendance.

The parents are encouraged to ask questions and to be sure they understand and agree with the plans for the group. The therapist tries to discourage intensive discussion of individual problems except when these lend themselves to illustration of general group concerns and techniques. Some questions may be referred to the other parents and some worries, such as fears that a particular youngster may not speak in group, may be generalized. The therapist can then talk in a general way about the way the problem will be handled in the group.

Similar meetings may be held periodically during the life of the group. They are always announced in advance to the adolescents. The parents develop considerable comaraderie and an atmosphere of mutual support for the adolescents' group work as these meetings continue. Some group interaction often develops among the parents. Frequently this is of both diagnostic and therapeutic value. In all meetings the therapist maintains the confidentiality of the group, but permits the parents to share information they may have regarding the progress and behavior of group members including their own youngster.

THE WORK OF THE GROUP

Once the tasks of developing cohesion and open communication are achieved in an adolescent group, the observed interactions are very similar to those seen in adult groups. The words and issues differ, of course, but the work of recognizing, confronting, and resolving interpersonal blocks to group progress is technically similar to adult work. The therapist gradually becomes less of an active structuring agent and moves toward a more reflective, interpretive stance in the group.

There are two rather common patterns in adolescent group work which do differ somewhat from the typical adult group. The first concerns the frequency and intensity of direct competition with the therapist. Of course, similar interactions occur in adult groups, but the adult patient is usually less frightened by his effrontery than is the adolescent. Often the adolescent can express his new strength only in the context of totally discounting the therapist's importance to him. Frequently he announces his desire to leave the group. The persistence of occurrences of this kind in adolescent groups is related to the adolescent's need to utilize adults as identification figures. With the support of the group, the adolescent goes through a cycle of testing the therapist, accepting (or even idealizing) him, challenging the therapist and testing him again at a less dependent level, and then accepting a new relationship on this more egalitarian basis. No special group techniques are necessary in the management of this pattern of behavior. The cycle merely needs to be recognized as a natural growth experience which is basically constructive for the adolescent involved. If the group therapist can comfortably accept the challenge and support new strength in the member, the remainder of the group can usually remind the challenger of remaining problems and prevent his precipitous departure from the group.

The second problem results from the adolescent's relative lack of conceptual skill with which to describe the subtle and intricate nuances of interpersonal transactions. This deficiency can usually be countered verbally if the therapist can develop the capacity to describe complex social phenomena in words and images familiar to the adolescent. This kind of translation is sometimes insufficient or unconvincing. In these situations, judicious use of psychodrama and gestalt techniques to make the impasse tangible may be indicated. These experiments often permit the group to comprehend the emotional factors beneath surface behavior and to feel the power of hidden forces operating in the group.

Pat, age 15, was silly and disruptive in a group that had decided to work seriously. He fended off efforts of group members to engage him in serious talk with clowning and flippant remarks. The group was angry and wanted Pat ejected since he was "just goofing off."

Pat had made an individual treatment contract but had described considerable anxiety about joining the group during pre-group individual sessions. The therapist was sure that the clowning reflected this anxiety rather than lack of motivation, but comments to this effect did not decrease the group's anger at Pat or change his defensive style.

The therapist proposed a "psychological exercise" which he said "might help the group members to understand one another better." One member (a popular boy) was blindfolded. He was asked to choose someone to lead him around the room. Without hesitation he chose one of the attractive girls in the group. After they had traversed the room without incident, they were asked to describe their feelings. The boy laughed and said it was fun—"A good excuse to hold hands with Cathy." The girl said she'd worried a little that he was walking too fast. Once or twice she thought he might bump into things and blame her.

"Okay, we'll talk some more about how you reacted later. Right now let's try someone else. How about you, Pat?"

"No siree, you're not gonna put that snot-rag on my face. Germs. Germs!"

"Yes, come on Pat."

Pat ambled up slowly, rolling his eyes in mock terror.

"Stop clowning, Pat," a member said.

Pat ran his hand over his face as though to wipe off a smile and pulled a solemn expression. The handkerchief was tied in place and he was asked who he wanted to lead him. He named the female cotherapist. She declined and told him he had to ask a group member. Pat began to look tense and worried beneath the blindfold as the silence lengthened.

"Come on, Pat, who do you pick? Hurry up."

Pat abruptly tore off the blindfold and rushed to his seat, clearly troubled and upset.

"You look scared," the therapist commented.

"They'd run me over something. They hate me anyway." Pat was obviously serious.

"God, he's really scared," a member said.

"Yeah, he doesn't trust anyone but the doctor."

Pat continued to have problems in the group, but the members were more sympathetic and were able to sense and explore his very real fear of people his own age.

ADOLESCENT GROUP THERAPY IN PERSPECTIVE

There is a good deal of literature available on both theoretical and practical aspects of group therapy with adolescents. Berkovitz (1972), Brandes (1973), Rachman (1975), Sugar (1975), Slavson and Schiffer (1975), Schiffer (1984), and Azima and Richmond (1989) have all published books on this subject. In addition to discussing the general principles of group therapy with adolescents, some of these authors (such as Berkovitz and Azima and Richmond) have chapters that address specific issues and populations, such as group therapy with minority teenagers, group therapy with delinquents, or group therapy with alcohol and drug addicted youngsters. In addition, Berkovitz (1975, 1987) has written extensively on the use of group therapy in high schools. The history of adolescent group psychotherapy has been chronicled by Rachman and Raubolt (1984). Bernet (1982) described the technique of verbal games, which is useful in group therapy with younger adolescents. Oldfield (1986) has pioneered a specialized style of group therapy called The Journey. Oldfield employs a rich variety of technique, including guided imagery, role playing, and mask making. In The Journey, teenagers recapitulate the steps through adolescence, which have been captured over the centuries in myths, legends, and folktales.

It seems that therapists are increasingly eclectic in their choice of treatment techniques. This would appear to be a reasonable development in a field where no single treatment approach has been demonstrated to have clear superiority. One benefit of this eclecticism is that it permits various combinations of treatment approaches tailored to the individual needs of a specific adolescent and his family. The combination and integration of individual and group therapy with the same therapist as described by Kaplan and Sadock (1971) for adults is gaining deserved popularity among adolescent therapists. The two forms of treatment appear to catalyze movement in each.

Group work may also be combined with family therapy or utilized to assist in dealing with a specific problem in ongoing therapy. For example, a group experience may provide a transition between a successful but extremely dependent individual therapy relationship and termination. Placement in a group may help an adolescent who is excessively enmeshed in his family to emancipate during the course of family therapy.

In short, group psychotherapy is a technique which can be helpful or disastrous to the troubled adolescent. Careful initial and continuing diagnostic evaluation should dictate when it is used and decide which other techniques need to be combined with it for maximum benefit.

The method of beginning and conducting group therapy described here is only a skeleton. It is useless, even dangerous, without training and experience both in group therapy and work with individual adolescents. There is no substitute for supervised experience in a live encounter with real adolescents.

TERMINATION

The issues involved in termination of group psychotherapy differ from individual work because group members are at various points in their development, yet the group must stop at one moment in time. In practice, termination of group therapy can occur because of clinical progress for the individual, but entire groups are usually terminated because of external events. Many therapists designate the life of the group at its very outset. A common pattern is to start groups in September and terminate them in June since many adolescents are unavailable in the summers. Individual decisions are made at termination as to whether a youngster should return for another group in the fall, continue in individual work, or leave treatment entirely.

Regardless of how this practical issue is handled, it does seem important for the group to have a clear and definite point of cessation. If the group is permitted to merely drift apart, the therapist deprives the members of the opportunity to face and learn from their idiosyncratic responses to separation. There is also considerable value in the process of reviewing the group's progress and assessing its benefits to each member. This can be organized around the individual treatment contracts of each member. The opportunity to address both the triumphs and failures of the members and the therapist offers both a chance for consolidating gains and for identifying areas that require further attention, in or out of formal therapy.

ONGOING THERAPY AND THE ADOLESCENT'S PARENTS

Psychotherapy with the adolescent has an additional complexity which so far we have mentioned only briefly. Even when the therapist has a clear grasp of the therapeutic alliance, considerable skill at conversing with adolescents, and the ability to recognize transference and handle it therapeutically, he may still run into difficulties related to the adolescent's family. We turn now to two chapters which address the technical problems raised by the complex interrelationship of the adolescent and his parents.

CITED AND RECOMMENDED READINGS

Anderson, R. L. 1972. The importance of an actively involved therapist. In: *Adolescents Grow in Groups*, edited by I. H. Berkovitz. New York: Brunner/Mazel.

Azima, F. J. C., and L. H. Richmond. 1989. *Adolescent Group Psychotherapy*. New York: International Universities Press.

Berkovitz, I. H. 1972. *Adolescents Grow in Groups*. New York: Brunner/Mazel.

Berkovitz, I. H., editor. 1975. *When Schools Care: Creative Use of Groups in Secondary Schools*. New York: Brunner/Mazel.

Berkovitz, I. H. 1987. Value of group counseling in secondary schools. *Adolescent Psychiatry*. 14: 522–545.

Bernet, W. 1982. The technique of verbal games in group therapy with early adolescents. *Journal of the American Academy of Child Psychiatry*. 21: 496–501.

Brandes, N. S., and M. L. Gardner. 1973. *Group Therapy for the Adolescent*. New York: Jason Aronson.

Buxbaum, E. 1945. Transference and group formation in children and adolescents. *Psychoanalytic Study of the Child*. 1: 351–365.

Franklin, G., and W. Nottage. 1969. Psychoanalytic treatment of severely disturbed juvenile delinquents in a therapy group. *International Journal of Group Psychotherapy*. 19: 165–175.

Josselyn, I. M. 1972. Adolescent group therapy: why, when and a caution. In: *Adolescents Grow in Groups*, edited by I. H. Berkovitz. New York: Brunner/Mazel.

Kaplan, H. I., and B. J. Sadock. 1971. Structured interactional group psychotherapy. In: *Comprehensive Group Psychotherapy*, edited by H. I. Kaplan and B. J. Sadock. Baltimore: Williams and Wilkins.

Kraft, I. A. 1968. An overview of group therapy with adolescents. *International Journal of Group Psychotherapy*. 18: 461–480.

Meeks, J. E. 1973. Structuring the early phase of group psychotherapy with adolescents. *International Journal of Child Psychotherapy*. 2: 391–405.

Meeks, J. E. 1974. Adolescent development and group cohesion. *Adolescent Psychiatry*. 3: 289–297.

Oldfield, D. 1986. The adolescent crisis: a hero's journey. *The Early Adolescent Magazine*. 1(2): 20–27.

Rachman, A. W. 1975. *Identity Group Psychotherapy with Adolescents*. Springfield, Ill.: C. C. Thomas.

Rachman, A. W., and R. R. Raubolt. 1984. The pioneers of adolescent group psychotherapy. *International Journal of Group Psychotherapy*. 34: 387–413.

Sadock, E., and R. E. Gould. 1964. A preliminary report on short-term group psychotherapy on an acute adolescent male service. *International Journal of Group Psychotherapy*. 14: 465–473.

Schiffer, M. 1984. *Children's Group Therapy: Methods and Case Histories.* New York: Free Press.

Slavson, S. R., and M. Schiffer. 1975. *Group Psychotherapies of Children: A Textbook.* New York: International Universities Press.

Stebbins, D. B. 1972. "Playing it by ear," answering the needs of a group of black teen-agers. In: *Adolescents Grow in Groups*, edited by I. H. Berkovitz. New York: Brunner/Mazel.

Sugar, M. 1972. Psychotherapy with the adolescent in self-selected peer groups. In: *Adolescents Grow in Groups*, edited by I. H. Berkovitz. New York: Brunner/Mazel.

Sugar. M. 1975. *The Adolescent in Group and Family Therapy.* New York: Brunner/Mazel.

CHAPTER 8
family therapy

INTRODUCTION

Family therapy has come of age as an important treatment modality in the management of troubled adolescents during the past two decades. An early neglect of the developmental and intrapsychic aspects of family therapy has been rectified by the involvement of many child psychiatrists and analysts in family work. The intricate play of developmental pressures, family structure, and family communication patterns has added both theoretical and clinical richness to our understanding of personality development (Minuchin et al., 1967). An early emphasis on the form of family therapy (for example, narrow insistence on having every family member present in every session) has matured to a recognition that the essence of the family therapy approach is a clear conceptualization of emotional disorders within their family context. The most effective family intervention at a given point in therapy may consist of an individual interview with an adolescent child or that youngster's placement in group psychotherapy. Frequently it may be separate interviews with the parents to strengthen the husband-wife relationship.

The family therapist appreciates the fact that these direct therapy contacts with individuals or subgroups of the family have great effects on the entire family structure. For example, the therapist makes a strong statement supporting the importance and legitimacy of the husband-wife relationship apart from the couple's parenting function merely by scheduling an interview which will focus exclusively on this subgroup and role relationship within the family. This message will reverberate throughout the family, influencing or perhaps threatening previous configurations of family priorities, alliances, and status distributions. The family-oriented therapist attempts to anticipate these repercussions, arranging those interventions which will accomplish the family alterations which further family growth, flexibility, and effective communication.

This brief introductory comment is intended to convey a sense of the increasing clarity of therapeutic conceptualization in family therapy. The first practical step, however, is diagnostic. There are two very different types of families who need family therapy and it is very important to make this distinction. The first type is a family whose family member is indeed suffering from a catastrophic mental illness or is adjusting to a catastrophic life event such as terminal illness, rape, or loss of a loved object. In these families family therapy is performed to enable the family to look at the catastrophic event, to educate them about its effect on all family members, and to mobilize the strengths of the family to recover. A combination of crisis intervention, psychoeducational and supportive problem-solving approaches will be utilized (Lantz and Thorward, 1985).

For example, parents who have just discovered that their handsome bright 17-year-old son is manic-depressive or schizophrenic must have help to mourn the loss of the healthy son, education regarding the illness, and help to plan effectively for his future needs. In most instances the parents should assume no responsibility for the development or maintenance of a primarily organic illness. Parent/family advocacy support groups such as the Alliance for the Mentally Ill are of great assistance to these families. These experienced self-help groups object strenuously to the mental health profession's tendency to reframe the illness to include the family in the pathology.

In the second type of family the identified patient's psychopathology is interwoven with the psychopathology of the family. This chapter will focus on this type of family in which the identified patient suffers from a symptom that is, in fact, affected by and perpetuated by the behavior and attitudes of other family members. These families are emphasized because they often are the most difficult and confusing families encountered by the beginning family therapist. Special problems are also raised by special family constellations such as single parent families and "step-families." These situations will be addressed in chapter 19.

The treatment of the pathologically intertwined family has become fairly well defined. The therapist proceeds methodically through several steps in his approach to the family. First he works to obtain acceptance as a temporary and yet important member of the family group. Minuchin (1974) has referred to this crucial step as "joining." Its successful accomplishment is necessary to the next step of redefining the "emotional illness" in an individual family member as instead a family problem, a problem in family functioning which is partly manifested through the symptomatic behavior of the designated patient. This step is quite difficult in some families. Certainly it is rarely accomplished by mere theoretical insistence. The family must be shown, not told, that the family system, not the symptomatic member, is in need of help and change. As Rabiner et al. (1962) have noted, even the scheduling of family therapy tends to increase the guilt and defensiveness in the family members.

Once these two steps are accomplished, the therapist is able to use his special role in relation to the family to block maladaptive patterns of relating within the family and to encourage exploration and experimentation with the styles of interaction which may be more satisfactory. In this effort he may utilize the entire range of psychiatric interventions, perhaps emphasizing interviews with the entire family, but certainly not restricting himself to this format. The choice of interventions is guided by a tentative diagnosis of the family patterns and pathology. This conceptual framework is constantly revised and refined to include the data which are revealed by the family's response to those interventions which the therapist attempts.

This process is quite complex. In many ways it is a more difficult skill to master than is individual therapy, since it requires greater activity on the part of the therapist and is therefore more prone to induce errors, both because of countertransference and the ease with which subtle verbal and nonverbal cues can be missed in the turmoil of an active family session. The family therapist is truly a participant observer and very busy at both jobs. These

There are at least three general forms of family therapy—
which means that the serious student can investigate the
different theories and techniques and develop a style that
suits himself the best.

Strategic family therapy is exemplified by Jay Haley (1971,
1980). He thought that the symptoms of the individual patient were manifestations of dysfunction within the family
and concluded that the individual could not change unless
the entire family changes. Haley would not be helping the
family achieve insight through therapy, but would give the
family explicit instructions about how to change their behavior. Sometimes the instructions are intended to manipulate or even trick the family members into more healthy
ways of relating to each other.

Structural family therapy can be represented by Salvador
Minuchin (1967, 1974). His approach is to join the family
in searching for the patterns or structures which are the
foundation for the patient's or the family's symptoms. In a
therapy session, Minuchin would actively teach the family
how to engage each other more constructively.

Analytic family therapy or object relations family therapy
has been described by David Scharff and Jill Savege Scharff
(1987). This method uses psychoanalytic methods such as
helping the family members recognize unconscious material,
interpreting, developing insight, and making use of transference and countertransference phenomena. They would
assume a more neutral stance in the therapy and would not
try actively to shape or manipulate or instruct the family.

statements should not be construed as a warning against the dangers of doing great damage through family therapy. As Wynne
(1965) has noted, family systems are very resilient and, in fact,
hard to change. Still, effective work in the area requires careful
study and supervised experience. One of the best introductory
texts is *Families and Family Therapy* (Minuchin, 1974) which is
clear and concise and highly sophisticated.

The purpose of this brief chapter is merely to whet the appetite of those adolescent therapists who have not considered the positive applications which family therapy offers in adolescent psychotherapy. Family therapy as a formal approach has some particular indications which will be considered now, followed by a more complete explication of the steps in family therapy mentioned earlier.

INDICATIONS FOR FAMILY THERAPY

Conjoint family therapy with the entire family seems to be the treatment of choice in certain situations and for certain kinds of emotional disorders.

Crisis situations in adolescence, including runaways, suicide attempts, and illegitimate pregnancies, often are best approached through family interviews. These sessions are of value in encouraging the family to find more adaptive ways of responding to the immediate problem and, in addition, may reveal the chronic family problems which resulted in the eruption of symptomatic behavior in the adolescent. In many of these families the underlying excessive closeness of the adolescent to one or more family members may be the cause of a runaway or delinquent action which represents an ill-advised attempt at emancipation. Unfortunately, many families do not seem motivated to continue in therapy once the immediate crisis is resolved (Morrison and Collier, 1969).

PROBLEMS OF ENMESHMENT

Even in the absence of crisis, the adolescent whose difficulties seem primarily related to problems in separating from his parents is probably best treated in conjoint family therapy. These youngsters may present with clear developmental immaturities including social anxiety, academic difficulties, and overt clinging, childish behavior. They may disguise their excessive dependence, with the family's collusion, as psychosomatic illness and complaints of illness. Of course, this family pattern may be precipitated and potentiated by the presence of actual physical disease, particularly chronic illness, in the child. As mentioned earlier, these families may come to therapy only at the time the adolescent tries to extricate himself from the excessively close family bonds. Occasionally the family is pressured into therapy by external agencies such as the school who detect the adolescent's social immaturity.

The basic problem in many of these families is an unsatisfactory marital relationship leading to inappropriate utilization of the adolescent to satisfy parental affectional needs or to provide a buffer between the parents. Therapy efforts are directed to strengthening the husband-wife subgroup if possible. If this seems impractical, the dissatisfactions can be rendered more explicit and the parents can be assisted to meet their needs outside the family while the adolescent's desire to separate is strengthened and supported. The therapist needs honest empathy for the "holding-on" parent in these families in order to keep the families in treatment and permit the eventual release of the adolescent. It is very easy for therapists with a special interest in adolescents to overidentify with the youngster. Merely blaming the parent and lecturing about the adolescent's right to a life of his own will only increase anxiety and perpetuate the frightened clinging pattern in the family. Many of these parents know at some level what they are "doing wrong." They need help in discovering alternatives.

The first step in altering excessively close bonds in a disturbed family is to understand the origin of the enmeshment. Very often the explanation is to be found mainly in the emotional history and needs of the parent. In other instances, however, the origin of the overattachment is mainly in the child. For example, children who are especially vulnerable due to constitutional or organic deficits in ego apparatus may subtley pull their parents into initially appropriate protective relationships which only gradually deteriorate into destructive bonds. Another example is the pathological bonds which develop in the families of chemically dependent patients as a result of the addictive process. We will discuss that specific problem in chapter 21, but the point is that we need to carefully evaluate situations of family enmeshment since each has its own history and family function. In addition it is wise to remember that all families faced with serious emotional problems tend to regress and this may exaggerate the apparent degree of excessive dependency and enmeshment actually present in the ongoing family system. Family interaction is just that—*inter*action—and there is often hidden complexity and more wisdom than we suspect at first glance even in families with serious problems.

EXTERNALIZING FAMILIES

Another group of adolescents who may be assisted through family therapy are those who live in families who externalize problems. In these families each member is preoccupied with the shortcomings of various other family members, and tends to feel that whatever unhappiness and adjustment problems he is having actually result from shortcomings of another family member. If individual sessions are held they are dominated by complaints directed against other members of the family. If the therapist sees two family members separately and discusses a recent upset with each, he is often left wondering if the two people were actually involved in the same event. There is virtually no introspection and the capacity for self-observation seems as limited as the skill in finding faults in other family members is hypertrophied.

Diagnostically, adolescents from these families often present as behavior disorders or personality disorders. Usually the pathology is relatively ego-syntonic and the adolescent rejects designation as a patient. However, since he clearly sees the pathology in other family members, he may accept family therapy as necessary.

Family therapy in these cases is difficult and trying for the therapist who is constantly being sought as an ally against other family members. With patience and dogged perseverance, however, it is possible to gradually require these families to communicate in ways that diminish the need for cycles of recrimination and blame. For example, the therapist, after assuring himself that he has effectively "joined" the family, may prohibit critical statements between family members. All communications must be translated into personal requests and statements of per-

sonal need. For example, if the father wishes to complain that
his wife is not affectionate, he must say, "I feel lonely and I need
affection. Is there any way I can help you show me more warmth?"
In previous family discussions he probably would have said, "Our
trouble is that you're a frigid bitch." The therapist may also require the parents to sit together and even request that they hold
hands. The purpose of these maneuvers is not to forcibly graft
these new behaviors on the family. The goal is merely to block
previous stereotyped interactions which serve to avoid awareness
of internal feelings by displacing them on other family members.
Of course, many other techniques will be utilized in the tedious
and prolonged effort to change destructive relationship patterns.
The examples offered are merely illustrative of the way in which
the therapist actively moves to alter family tradition.

FAMILIES WITH A SCAPEGOAT

Another adolescent who may be best treated through family
interviews is the youngster whose pathology is required to maintain a neurotic family homeostasis. This includes youngsters with
"superego lacunae" but also a variety of other situations in which
the adolescent is made into a scapegoat by his family. In some
of these cases it is necessary to provide a period of individual
therapy to the scapegoat, in order to raise his status in the family
group and to discover and activate personal goals which lie outside the scapegoat role. Without this special assistance, the scapegoat is often unmotivated to give up his central role in the family.
Like the man who has been ridden out of town on a rail, he feels
the procedure is uncomfortable but more of an honor than
merely walking like everyone else.

FAMILIES WHO ABUSE YOUNGSTERS

Family therapy with families who have been involved in actual
physical or sexual abuse of children is a special and difficult undertaking (Galdston, 1971; Isaacs, 1972). Treatment must often
include careful measures to ensure the safety of the child but
must also sensitively address the family attachments which survive

even this threat to family affections (Lutz and Medway, 1984). Keep in mind that there is a range of input in incestuous activity from the sometimes almost innocuous sibling contacts through stepparent-child contacts to the parent-child contacts which have the most serious consequences (Scharff, 1982).

FAMILY DIAGNOSIS

The family therapist is interested in assessing family functioning in a number of interlocking dimensions. The first of these considers the family boundaries. The therapist tries to determine if there are clear generational boundaries, boundaries between individuals in the family, clear boundaries between the family and the surrounding society, and clear sex role boundaries. Pathology may result from excessively rigid boundary definitions or from boundaries which are vague or capriciously changeable.

The second structural feature of the family which is observed is the nature of the subgroups within the larger family. For example, a common dysfunctional subgrouping consists of mother and children allied against the father. The result is that the father is rendered ineffective in the parenting role and is lost to the wife as a gratifying husband. In normal families subgrouping occurs in a variety of patterns determined by the emotional or practical issues which occupy the family at the moment. There is flexibility and alliance patterns shift without strong family efforts to resist the changes.

The therapist also studies the family patterns of communication, noting both the conceptual clarity and the affective range. Normal families have relatively open communication which tends to be clear and determined by present needs rather than defensive maintenance of family myths or the need to deny particular affective states. Some disturbed families cannot permit the expression of angry feelings. When these threaten to emerge, communication may be blocked by irrelevant expressions of mutual concern or warmth. Other families block expressions of tender feelings. In very disturbed families communication may be unintelligible—a "mystification of logic" (Stierlin, 1974).

During the diagnostic period of family therapy the parenting skills and styles of the family are also delineated. Do the parents provide appropriate nurture? Are they able to set limits? Can they provide information in a form which is usable and accurate? Can they deal openly with husband-wife conflict or do they utilize the parenting function to fight one another? Have they relegated parenting, particularly the emotional components of the parenting role (Stierlin, 1974), partially or wholly to one of the children? These and many other questions must be answered if one is to plan an effective treatment approach for the specific family. Another whole arena of investigation is opened by studying the family "missions" which adolescent children may be assigned by parents or even grandparents or other powerful members of the extended family (Stierlin, 1977).

Finally the therapist observes the family's style of problem solving. He is interested in seeing whether the family permits wide involvement in reaching decisions and planning actions or depends on one autocratic leader. If there is a single leader, is he or she supported or is there implied rebellion and contempt behind the apparent passivity of other family members? The therapist will encounter other families who seem incapable of reaching a decision. In these families there is no leadership or the process of problem solving is so contaminated by raging affective conflicts that it becomes chaotic and inconclusive.

A model for normal functioning in families is needed in order to understand problem patterns. A very useful discussion and evaluation system is provided in *No Single Thread* (Lewis et al., 1976).

FAMILY TREATMENT

After diagnostic evaluation it is possible to arrive at treatment goals for a specific family. These goals may have levels of priority although the therapist considers the entire picture in all his interactions with the family. For example, the therapist may decide that a family's confusing style of communication is a basic problem which must be actively confronted early in treatment. At the same time, however, he may be aware that one purpose of the disjointed communication is to disguise the fact that the overtly respected father is actually powerless in the family. He may choose then to focus on the communication problem by utilizing the father as his ally, thus simultaneously attempting to improve the father's status and to reveal the family's use of confusion to block the father's competence.

As the therapist intervenes to change the family, his approach must constantly respond to the countermeasures the family mobilizes to prevent change. The process is not static but interactive.

Throughout the treatment contact, the therapist focuses primarily on family strengths and skills. Even behavior which must change is usually relabeled positively even while it is questioned and blocked. An intrusive, domineering mother may be told that she is taking too much responsibility and pressure in the family. Her husband may be asked to take over some of the work, "to give your overburdened wife a little rest from all her worries." A general expectation that family members will help one another is regularly voiced by the therapist. The value position that mutual support is the function of the family is clearly enunciated, even when the needed support is a limit. "Johnny has a problem in that rules sometimes make him angry. Now you need to help him with that by making rules clear and not arguing about them or trying to explain them when he's angry. It might really be a help to him to know that he can talk with you about the rules later, when he's calmed down."

Needless to say, the focus in family therapy is on the present, although the content of sessions may have many references to past events. When the family begins to recount past history they sometimes do so in order to refocus on the individual designated patient as the "real" problem in the family. Talk of the past is sometimes, therefore, defensive—a countermeasure aimed at neutralizing therapeutic activity. There are at least three exceptions to this general rule. Occasionally, the family will bring up the past in order to reveal a family secret to the therapist. Of course, this is not defensive, but a step in opening the family interactions to the work of therapy. The clear difference from defensive use of the past is that these past occurrences continue to have a strong impact on the entire family in the present and knowledge of them helps to clarify current issues and conflicts.

A second exception tends to occur late in family therapy when an individual family member has dropped his defensiveness and has accepted personal responsibility for his role in the family problems. At that time, a member may focus on experiences from his past which serve to distort appropriate responses to present family reality. It may be useful at this point to refer the family member for individual therapy.

The third exception relates to those situations in which the patient is reenacting important past events. These may include family secrets, family myths, or turning passive into active as when a victim becomes the victimizer. A common example, of course, is the multigenerational recurrence of child abuse.

Since it is impossible to even mention the endless variety of problems and techniques which may mark the course of family therapy in this brief consideration of the approach, the reader will merely be offered a brief summary and a list of some of the important writings on the subject.

SUMMARY

Family therapy offers much as the primary therapy in certain kinds of adolescent problems and may be useful as a temporary adjunct to other treatment methods in many other cases.

It differs somewhat from other intensive therapy approaches in that it depends less on introspection and insight to achieve lasting change than does either individual or group psychotherapy. The family therapist, in his direct interactions with the family, is more of an orchestra conductor and participant than an interpreter of events. He does not aim merely to help the family understand itself. He acts to change the family so that it no longer blocks the understanding and growth of its members. Understanding—true, deep emotional understanding—often accompanies these changes as an important byproduct.

Therapeutic activity, however, is not random or dictated by countertransference. It is carefully planned following a careful diagnostic study of family pathology. Family therapy is not anti-intellectual and intuitive in its conception. Although the therapist may reveal more of himself than is customary in more reflective therapies, this revelation is directed only partly by his subjective experience of involvement in the family. This spontaneity must be tempered by a precise understanding of the purposes for which he is utilizing himself as a living instrument. Arriving at this understanding will require the best intellectual and professional skills one can command along with a painstaking multigenerational assessment of the many dimensions and capabilities of each family member as created and revealed in their history together (Boszormenyi-Nagy and Spark, 1973). Achieving the goals of family therapy will require a combination of activity and restraint which equals the most challenging demands of any form of psychotherapy.

CITED AND RECOMMENDED READINGS

Ackerman, N. W. 1958. Toward an integrative therapy in the family. *American Journal of Psychiatry*. 114: 727–733.

Ackerman, N. W. 1982. *The Strength of Family Therapy: Selected Papers of Nathan W. Ackerman*, edited by D. Bloch and R. Simon. New York: Brunner/Mazel.

Bell, J. E. 1963. Recent advances in family group therapy. In: *Group Psychotherapy and Group Function*, edited by M. Rosenbaum and M. Berger. New York: Basic Books.

Boszormenyi-Nagy, I., and G. Spark. 1973. *Invisible Loyalties*. New York: Harper and Row.

Bowen, M. 1978. *Family Theory in Clinical Practice*. New York: Jason Aronson.

Galdston, R. 1971. Violence begins at home: the Parents' Center project for the study and prevention of child abuse. *Journal of the American Academy of Child Psychiatry*. 10: 336–350.

Haley, J. 1971. *Changing Families: A Family Therapy Reader*. New York: Grune and Stratton.

Haley, J. 1980. *Leaving Home: The Therapy of Disturbed Young People*. New York: McGraw-Hill.

Isaacs, S. 1972. Emotional problems in childhood and adolescence: neglect, cruelty and battering. *British Medical Journal*. 2: 224–226.

Lantz, J. E., and S. R. Thorward. 1985. Inpatient family therapy approaches. *Psychiatric Hospital*. 16: 85–89.

Lewis, J. H., et al. 1976. *No Single Thread*. New York: Brunner/Mazel.

Lutz, S. E., and J. P. Medway. 1984. Contextual family therapy with the victims of incest. *Journal of Adolescence*. 7: 319–327.

Minuchin, S. 1974. *Families and Family Therapy*. Cambridge, Mass.: Harvard University Press.

Minuchin, S., et al. 1967. *Families of the Slums*. New York: Basic Books.

Morrison, G. C., and J. G. Collier. 1969. Family treatment approaches to suicidal children and adolescents. *Journal of the American Academy of Child Psychiatry*. 8: 140–153.

Rabiner, E. L., et al. 1962. Conjoint family therapy in the inpatient setting. *American Journal of Psychotherapy*. 16: 618–631.

Satir, V. 1964. *Conjoint Family Therapy: A Guide to Theory and Technique*. Palo Alto, Calif.: Science and Behavior Books.

Scharff, D. E. 1982. *The Sexual Relationship: An Object Relations View of Sex and the Family*. Boston: Routledge and Kegan Paul.

Scharff, D. E., and J. S. Scharff. 1987. *Object Relations Family Therapy*. Northvale, N.J.: Jason Aronson.

Spiegel, J. P. 1957. The resolution of the role conflict within the family. *Psychiatry*. 20: 1–16.

Stierlin, H. 1974. *Separating Parents and Adolescents: A Perspective on Running Away, Schizophrenia and Waywardness*. New York Times Book Company.

Stierlin, H. 1977. *Psychoanalysis and Family Therapy*. New York: Jason Aronson, Inc.

Watzlawick, P., et al. 1967. *Pragmatics of Human Communication*. New York: W. W. Norton.

Wynne, L. C. 1965. Some indications and contraindications for exploratory family therapy. In: *Intensive Family Therapy*, edited by I. Boszormenyi-Nagy and J. L. Framo. New York: Hoeber Medical Division, Harper and Row.

CHAPTER 9

the parents of the adolescent patient

THE PARENT–CHILD RELATIONSHIP DURING ADOLESCENCE

Many parents would agree that adolescence is the most trying period in the experience of rearing a child. For the parents of the disturbed adolescent, this phase of growth may be virtually unbearable. Problems which have been latent become menacingly overt. Dependency problems blossom into pitched battles as the adolescent invites parental involvement and help by his maladaptive behavior, and then vilifies the parents for babying him and trying to live his life for him. Competition becomes vicious as the adolescent's overdependence on intellectualization and grand sweeping generalities lead him to view the parents as narrow, dull, and ineffective. Superego externalization causes the parents to be viewed as harsh and joyless on some occasions, as immoral and self-indulgent on another day. Any parental defensiveness, self-justification, or counterattack provokes a vengeful rage and a sullen sense of martyrdom.

There are basic elements of duplicity in both generations during this developmental phase. The adolescent is actually struggling against intensified dependent and sexual ties to his parents. At the same time, he wishes to gain autonomy and independence. This combination of increased emotional investment coupled with the urgency to escape the family is hardly conducive to openness and honesty in the adolescent's interactions with his parents.

On the other hand, many parents of disturbed adolescents are dishonest in their relationships with their children. Although consciously claiming to desire independence and maturity for their youngsters, they unconsciously undermine growth because of their neurotic needs. They act to prevent separation, heterosexual maturity, or self-sufficiency in their child when these would

241

threaten their own tenuous adjustment or result in an unbearable sense of loss to them. The degree of tenacity with which the parent clings to the adolescent varies with many factors including the extent of parental psychopathology and the realistic sources of substitute gratification available to the parent. The widowed mother, living alone on meager funds, obviously faces greater problems in relinquishing her last son than a happily married woman in comfortable financial and social circumstances, although both must deal with some sense of loss. Both the adolescent and his parents have reasons for obfuscating the terms of the unwritten contracts which regulate their interchange.

The tendency for the family to regress if the adolescent has serious emotional conflicts adds to the problem for the adolescent psychotherapist. Parents often present with their "worse foot forward" because of the pain they feel over frustrated efforts to help the adolescent. Often they treat the therapist as the child treats them, making unrealistic demands, rejecting help, and being unduly critical. This can lead the therapist to exaggerate the parental pathology and, sometimes, to identify with the adolescent and minimize the youngster's contribution to the family distress.

ENTER THE THERAPIST

The therapist who ventures into this devious and supercharged intrigue as a catalyst to emotional growth can expect to become embroiled with both parties. In order to work successfully with adolescent patients, one has to accept this involvement with the parents. Even when the parents are referred to a colleague for therapy, they will usually still insert themselves directly or indirectly into the adolescent's therapy. This involvement should be expected and utilized. Attempts to avoid it or deny its occurrence are at best futile, at worst tragic. The probabilities of a successful treatment are increased by planning a constructive reaction to the welter of emotions between parent and child. Ignoring the certainty that these forces will be expressed in the therapy can only leave the therapist blindly reacting to the manipulations of both his patient and the patient's parents. Although the technical approach may be individual psychotherapy of the adolescent, the therapist must remember that the entire family is the real patient.

This does not mean that the therapist adopts a tough and pugnacious determination never to be "sucked in" by neurotic family patterns. It does mean that the therapist is alert to the multiple determinants and implications of the communications which he receives from the parents or from the child about the parents. It means that this awareness is utilized to promote growth and independence and to protect the vulnerable and crucial therapeutic alliance with the adolescent. If this bond is sacrificed in order to pacify immediate strains in the parent–child relationship, the therapist has lost the effective foothold necessary to help the family. All attempts to influence and manipulate the therapist, whether they originate from the adolescent or his parents, must be received with the same respectful, objective, exploring attitude which is accorded all other relevant material. This analysis of underlying meaning determines whether the therapist reacts to the manipulation with interpretation, firm limit setting, or temporary acquiescence. The therapist tries to choose the response which offers greatest promise of promoting the long-range goals of the therapy.

THE PARENTS AND THE THERAPEUTIC CONTRACT

The effort to develop a workable therapy contract with the parents of the adolescent begins in the postdiagnostic family conference. The most common roadblock at this early stage is the therapist's failure to insist on the necessary conditions for an effective psychotherapy. This reluctance to "drive a hard bargain" may often be a response to parental ambivalence about the proposed psychotherapy. Their conscious or unconscious fears that the family homeostasis may be jeopardized lead parents to threaten, offer deals, or otherwise attempt to influence the conditions of therapy. These efforts will not be difficult to manage if the therapist keeps the minimum requirements of outpatient psychotherapy clearly in mind.

Basic Conditions of Outpatient Individual Psychotherapy

1. *The patient must have a real choice about beginning and continuing therapy after clearly understanding its nature and purpose.*
   Of course, several interviews may go by before the adolescent has finished testing the therapist, sending up trial balloons, and generally "casing the joint." Only then does he have any real understanding of the nature and purpose of therapy. Simply telling him what therapy is all about accomplishes very little. It is sometimes useful to offer a negative adolescent a definite number of interviews in which to decide whether he wants to involve himself in therapy. Even if his decision is positive, his willingness to accept and to continue therapy may be evidenced only by his appearance at his sessions. If he comes without being threatened, bribed, or physically coerced, this may be accepted as prima facie evidence of an interest in the treatment process even if he grumbles constantly and regularly questions the need for therapy. On the other hand, if he must actually be forced to attend the sessions, it is unlikely that progress is possible. Some modicum of responsibility for his own treatment must be assumed by even the very young patient. If a youngster is unwilling to accept this degree of responsibility for his behavior and his difficulties, it is likely either that the family is strongly invested in his problems, that his problems do not give him enough serious difficulty to justify therapy, or that he is so immature, irresponsible, and unable to accept guidance that his problems could best be managed in an inpatient setting.

2. *The adolescent must be allowed to come to therapy for* his *problems.*
   A psychotherapy program explicitly or even implicitly undertaken to shape adolescents to some parental expectation or to persuade or dissuade them in regard to a particular action is doomed before it begins. Adolescents must be in therapy for themselves. Their reasons for coming must be accepted and therapy must begin with their concerns. Of course, in the long run, successful therapy may produce some or all of the results which would please the parents, but this happy circumstance must only be a fortunate byproduct of

autonomous choices made by the emotionally maturing adolescent.

The adolescent must separate and individuate. His goals must be his own, neither arising from passive compliance to parental wishes or based on blind rebellion against those wishes.

3. *The patient's communication with the therapist must be confidential unless or until the therapist feels that a clear danger to the patient or others exist.* The parents can expect to be told whether therapy is progressing satisfactorily, but not the feelings, fantasies, and concerns which the adolescent voices in treatment. They have a right to know "how things are in treatment," but not "what is going on in treatment."

4. *The therapist and the patient must have an honest relationship.* The therapist cannot agree to lie to the patient. Although he will not "tell all" to the parents, he must feel free to inform the patient of the occurrence of each contact with the parents and the content of these interactions at any time that this information seems therapeutically relevant or at any time that the adolescent wants to know. The therapist will "keep secrets" from the parents, but will, if it seems indicated, feel free to "tell all" to the patient.

5. *In matters which pertain directly to the treatment process, there can only be one therapist.* If the adolescent verbalizes feelings about the therapist at home, these should not be evaluated by the parent, but should be referred back to the next therapy session. If the adolescent expresses uncertainty about continuing therapy, he should be told to discuss this concern with the therapist as he would discuss any other idea or feeling. If the adolescent asks parental opinions of a comment or a procedure employed by the therapist, the parents should ask the adolescent what he thinks and whether this has been discussed with the therapist directly. If the parent feels the therapist has behaved inappropriately, the parent should discuss this feeling directly with the therapist.

These requirements may sound autocratic, stringent, and unrealistic. Many parents react to them as if they were just that way.

They feel that the therapist is intruding into the sanctity of their home to dictate their management of their own child. As a matter of fact, this is precisely what the therapist is doing. However, it must be recalled that the therapist is assuming this authority at the request of the family. The therapist has been hired to lead the family members in their effort to improve family functioning. This position as therapeutic leader is untenable unless the parents grant authority in matters pertaining directly to the psychotherapy.

If the therapist is so passive, nondirective, or timid that he fails to explain the role that must be played, the therapist is in no position to confront the parents when they trespass into the expert's area. If he does not assume firm therapeutic leadership, he may soon find himself being utilized as the family scapegoat. The family members may handle their hostilities, anxieties, and depressions by turning them on the therapist. That poor mortal may soon feel like the bystander who tried to break up a marital argument and ended up being attacked by the husband and wife, now comfortably united in their rage at the outsider.

Even more frequently, the adolescent will attempt to avoid limits and feelings of guilt by playing the parents against the therapist. The parents can avoid being drawn into such manipulations if they have a clear conception and acceptance of the therapist's temporary leadership role.

The parents are likely to become angry when the therapist sets limits on them, just as the adolescent reacts with anger when his acting out is questioned and opposed. This should not deter the therapist from doing the job. If the family is treatable, the parents will come to respect the therapist for courage and determination to assume responsibilities. If they intended all along to employ the therapist only so long as he did not really interfere with the status quo, it is better to get that fact out into the open.

Of course, it is not necessary for the therapist to be belligerent or combative. The therapist must remember that he serves purely at the family's pleasure. He is never in a position of telling the family what they must do, only what must be done if therapy is to succeed. Even in this, one must humbly remember that even therapists may be wrong! However, it has been said that wisdom consists of acting on the basis of incomplete information. The therapist must be a decisive leader even though he cannot claim absolute certainty. If there is good reason to believe that a request for a vacation, a schedule change, or a family discussion about the therapist interferes with therapy or represents resistance, it is the therapist's duty to convey this opinion frankly and with conviction. If parental behavior continually interferes with therapy, it is his duty to explain that treatment will be impossible unless the parents are able to understand and change their disruptive actions.

Function of the Treatment Contract

The contractual terms discussed are intended as a guide for the therapist in making arrangements with the parents for treatment. A rigid demand for absolute compliance with these conditions would stifle the parents' interaction in the treatment process. The list of conditions is not presented as a binding package deal during the postdiagnostic family conference. Generally, only those points which are raised directly or indirectly by the family need to be emphasized. The others are merely mentioned in a brief, matter-of-fact manner. Even though parents agree to this contract, they are likely to break one or more clauses under the pressure of emotions stirred in the course of treatment. The previous explicit or tacit agreement, however, allows the therapist to highlight the motives involved in the breach, since the parent cannot claim simple ignorance of the proper helpful role in regard to the treatment process. The parent who cannot accept the contract, as well as the parent who accepts and then complains that the agreement is unfair, also reveals his family-bound pathology directly to the searchlight of therapeutic curiosity. It must be emphasized, however, that parents do deserve education regarding the goals and methods of psychotherapy. If they do not understand these goals and methods and their own proper role in facilitating their achievement, they may interfere with the therapeutic undertaking out of simple ignorance, which may be misunderstood as neurotic meddling.

The real importance of guidelines is to help the therapist to avoid falling unknowingly into unsatisfactory agreements. By holding firm ideas of the working conditions that he needs, the therapist is alerted to recognize those parental anxieties which lead to unwillingness to allow their youngster every possible advantage in the treatment situation. When parents begin to negotiate for unworkable contracts, the therapist has an alarm system that warns him not to defeat himself in his therapeutic efforts before he even gets underway.

Enforcing the Terms of the Contract

Actually, the therapist has no power to enforce any of the clauses of the therapeutic contract with the parents. Their cooperation depends on their understanding of the reasons that the therapist makes certain requests and the extent of their trust in his professional competence and his benevolence toward the entire family.

In a very real sense, the therapist not only must maintain a shaky therapeutic alliance with the adolescent, but also must maintain one which may be even more tricky with the parents. The alliance with the parents is partially cemented by their mature wishes for their youngster to improve and attain self-sufficiency. Therapy cannot be conducted if the parents are totally devoid of this healthy desire. Fortunately, this bleak condition rarely exists in parents who seek treatment for their adolescent. Usually, this hope for successful maturation is present, but is opposed by a variety of anxieties, neurotic ties, and cultural expectancies. The therapist must appeal to the best in the parents in an attempt to strengthen the healthy portion of the parental tie with the adolescent.

Mr. and Mrs. Jones brought Janet, their 13-year-old daughter, for psychiatric evaluation because of poor school performance, a dawdling, passive refusal to perform household chores, and general "emotional immaturity." Mrs. Jones particularly complained of Janet's clinging, demanding attitude toward her.

A most cursory evaluation of the family relationships revealed serious strains and blatantly neurotic accommodations to many hidden conflicts between family members. Mr. Jones was an extremely successful television executive. Because of the pressures of his job and a poorly defined "heart condition," he expected and received remarkably solicitous treatment from all family members. Nothing was expected from him in the home. Janet and her sister understood that they must remain absolutely quiet when he was in the house. Mr. Jones's heart condition was especially sensitive to any angry sounds. The mother threatened the children with the responsibility for their father's death whenever they argued or fought while he was within earshot. Even if the mother became annoyed with them and shouted, she blamed them for this threat to the father's health.

In fact, the mother nagged the children and especially Janet, the older, constantly. She hovered over their every move and was preoccupied with the fear that they might be kidnapped due to her husband's prominence.

Janet was a timorous, anxious child. Her manner was obsequious and pollyannish to a degree which suggested conscious caricature of her mother's expectations. She spent her diagnostic interview explaining her many academic and social problems, besieging the therapist with demands for advice and instant help.

After diagnostic study, the therapist told the parents that Janet needed psychotherapy. The parents' role in the problem was approached warily and counseling was recommended for them. Mrs. Jones spoke for them and stated that she did not wish to have treatment. She explained that a friend of hers had become overly dependent on a therapist and that she felt therapy might "ruin" her. She also felt that therapy might be upsetting and "too much for Mr. Jones's delicate health." The therapist wondered if the couple had similar fears about Janet's therapy. Mrs. Jones admitted that she did, but expressed confidence in the therapist, whom she felt "seemed to understand what Janet needed."

Somewhat reluctantly, the therapist decided to try to work with Janet. His diagnostic hunch that Janet had considerable hidden strength proved correct. She moved rapidly into an active therapeutic alliance and made remarkable strides toward an increased maturity.

The parents were very pleased with Janet's initial changes, since they discerned a new openness and sense of responsibility at home coupled with considerable improvement in her schoolwork.

However, when Janet suddenly made friends with Dolores, a mildly rebellious and sexually aware girl, the mother's attitude toward therapy underwent a rapid and drastic change! She telephoned the therapist to tell him coldly and firmly that she thought Janet no longer needed treatment and, in fact, was afraid treatment was making Janet worse. With some difficulty, the therapist convinced her to come to his office to discuss the reasons for her change in attitude.

Mrs. Jones had calmed down by the time she arrived for her appointment. She said she recognized that it had been silly for her to say Janet should quit treatment. If she had stopped to think, she would have realized that Janet was mistaken in her notions that the therapist approved of the friendship with Dolores! Mrs. Jones was sure the therapist would clarify the matter and show Janet how harmful the friendship was to her.

The therapist agreed that this was one possible course of action. He wondered, however, what Janet's reaction might be if the parents and the therapist took over the responsibility of choosing appropriate friends for her. Would she perhaps be tempted to return to her old pattern of irresponsibility and total dependence on adults? Might it be better to permit her some freedom in this area, maintaining safeguards by structuring the time which Janet and Dolores spent together in a wholesome manner? The therapist admitted that this approach represented a calculated risk. Dolores might have a negative influence on Janet; however, if the parents and the therapist maintained a friendly relationship and showed respect for Janet's good judgment, she might discuss her interactions with Dolores openly and allow them to help her utilize the relationship constructively. The therapist empathized with Mrs. Jones's wish to help Janet avoid danger. He pointed out that he and Mrs. Jones were in total agreement on this point and need only discuss the best techniques for achieving this goal without causing excessive dependence. He also told Mrs. Jones quite frankly that he understood that it frightened her when she did not know exactly what Janet was thinking and doing.

Mrs. Jones began to cry. She confessed that she knew the therapist was correct. In fact, she knew all along that he would suggest this approach and that it was the proper one. She recognized that she had wanted to remove Janet from therapy to avoid discussing the emotions and family problems which caused her to want to "treat Janet like a two-year-old." Then, she said, "I realize I'm going to need to study that whole mess. Oh, well, I knew if I came here today, I'd leave with a psychiatrist's name in my hands."

Mrs. Jones meant that she had finally decided to accept referral for psychotherapy.

Preserving the therapeutic alliance with the parents frequently requires both encouraging the healthier aspects of the parent-child relationship and sympathetic acceptance of parental anxieties and needs. This combination of factors must also be utilized in helping the parents to involve themselves in collaborative therapy or counseling.

REFERRING PARENTS FOR TREATMENT AND COUNSELING

A purist might argue that all troubled adolescents come from troubled families and that therefore all parents should have personal therapy in conjunction with their child's treatment. In practice, however, many parents do not consciously recognize any relationship between family problems and the symptoms of their disturbed adolescent. A fierce resistance is the only result if these parents are arbitrarily forced into a treatment relationship.

The most important factor to be considered in deciding whether to refer parents for psychotherapy or casework is whether such a step is really necessary.

Do the Parents Need Treatment?

The presence of a clear relationship between parental attitudes or marital patterns and the psychopathology of the adolescent does not necessarily mean that it is crucial for the parents to have treatment. Some parental problems are the result, not the cause, of adolescent difficulties. It is hard to grow up, and there are enormous variations in the adaptive equipment which each child receives through the accidents of heredity, prenatal and neonatal illnesses, and uncontrollable environmental experiences.

Over and above these considerations is the fact that parents often grow over the years, whereas their children may carry some precipitates of earlier difficulties in the form of character defenses or symptoms. The father who was anxious and unsure of his competence at age 24 may be a much more relaxed and accepting father at age 36. His 16-year-old son may still need therapy because of defensive patterns which he developed at age four in order to deal with his father's excessive oedipal rivalry. Treating the father in the present would not necessarily assist the adolescent to resolve his (now internalized) problems with male authority.

Some adolescents may even be encouraged to evade responsibility for their own problems if the parents' need for treatment is overemphasized. It is obvious that many young people manage a satisfactory adjustment despite fairly marked psychopathology in their parents. Since effective psychotherapy with parents may well require two to three years and extend beyond the adolescence of the young patient, the therapist certainly cannot demand complete parental mental health as a prerequisite to the successful treatment of his young patient. Generally, it is wise to encourage the adolescent patient to accept his parents as "givens" and then to assume the responsibility for managing his own life productively. If the parents become healthier, with or without therapy, so much the better.

When Parents Must Have Help

Still, there are family situations which are incompatible with psychotherapy of the adolescent. The youngster who lives in a family which maintains itself by encouraging the adolescent to assume a role inappropriate to his age (such as an infantile or, conversely, an adult role), an inappropriate sex role, or a role which is clearly destructive (such as a criminal or "stupid" role) can rarely utilize a therapeutic approach which permanently excludes the parents. Curiously, these youngsters are often surprised by the recommendation that their parents receive therapy; in fact, they often oppose treatment for the parents. This observation may be useful in diagnosis and planning. The adolescent who shrieks, "Why don't you treat my parents? They're the ones who need it," may not be the youngster whose parents have drawn him into a comfortable neurotic impasse.

Those parents who do need treatment must often be brought gradually to a recognition of their need by their child's therapist. Careful preparation is often necessary if the parents are to utilize a therapeutic experience constructively. Therapy which is undertaken without a felt need is rarely successful. Some parents arrive for the diagnostic evaluation with a vague recognition of the family's involvement in the adolescent's problems. Others readily come to such an awareness during the diagnostic process in the postdiagnostic family conference. Still others, like Mrs. Jones in our earlier example, can recognize their enmeshment only after improvement in their child disturbs the family homeostasis. Because of this third group, it is often necessary to plan treatments which begin with only the child in treatment, but with clear knowledge that eventually the parents will need direct help. This help is offered when the parents are ready to use it. They are led to recognize their need through their contact with the child's therapist. These early contacts are discussed more fully below.

It should be noted that a valid recognition of involvement in a youngster's problems must be differentiated from the defensive offer to "do anything that will help our child." This passive offer to be "worked on" does not imply any usable awareness of the family pathology. The current sophisticated, "I know we must be doing something to cause all this," may also mask an unspoken blithe attitude of, "But I don't have the slightest idea of what it could be, nor do I really care to know!"

Needless to say, the task is far from completed when a successful referral for therapy is accomplished. The skillful cooperation of two therapists in a collaborative treatment arrangement is a complex topic in itself. The therapists must depend on mutual respect, open communication, and emotional honesty to avoid being manipulated into overidentification with their respective patients to the extreme detriment of the overall goals of therapy. When a collaborative therapist treats the parents, the interactions with the parents described below are kept between the parents and their own therapist whenever possible. In the following section, these interactions are presented primarily as they occur when the adolescent's therapist is working alone.

THE PARENTS AND THE ONGOING THERAPY
OF THE ADOLESCENT

The Telephone Contact

During the therapeutic work with the adolescent, some continuing contact with the parents is necessary to ensure their cooperation and support. The telephone is a useful instrument for much of this contact. The parents may be instructed to call if they have information or questions. They are told that they should let their adolescent know when they call and the general topic of discussion. Experience shows that most parents do not abuse this opportunity to contact the therapist ad libitum. Early in the therapeutic contact, the calls may be frequent; however, these calls usually decline fairly rapidly. If the therapist reserves a specific period in his day for returning phone calls, the arrangement need not be burdensome. The parents who do call with extreme frequency make up one group of parents who require direct treatment. In the course of these telephone contacts, along with occasional interviews, the therapist has the opportunity to create a trusting and understanding relationship with the parents. This will allow him to make referral for personal treatment a positive and meaningful recommendation. The parents often come to recognize their need for help through their relationship with the therapist and are more accepting and motivated for treatment. Although some difficulties may arise around transferring their therapeutic relationship, this gap can usually be bridged through the cooperative efforts of the two therapists. The parents' therapist must accept the early allegiance to the adolescent's therapist and avoid competitive responses and professional jealousy. The adolescent's therapist must respect the parents' therapist and assist the smooth transfer, tactfully resisting the parents' efforts to cling to the original therapist. Joint sessions involving the parents and both therapists may help to convey the mutual respect of the team and aid the parents to accept a team concept and approach.

Parents Who Never "Bother" You

It was mentioned that anxious, uncertain, or controlling parents, who tend to telephone frequently, make up a portion of those who need referral for treatment. Without this assistance, they find it difficult to provide the living area of maximum freedom and personal responsibility safely surrounded by firm boundary lines of acceptable behavior which the adolescent needs if he is to reap the benefits of psychotherapy.

Those parents who never call the therapist may need help even more. Most of them are so frightened of "doing the wrong thing" that they exclude themselves from their child's life. Some of them are merely displaying a lack of interest in the youngster or outright rejection of the child. Some of the parents have brought their adolescent for psychotherapy only as social insurance so that no one can ever accuse them of not "doing everything possible to help the child." Involving these parents is difficult, if not impossible. Even if the attempt is unsuccessful, it helps the adolescent to see and accept the reality of his family situation. It is difficult enough to grow up in a rejecting home without the additional burden of being deluded about the facts of the matter. Telephone contact with the parents, then, has both therapeutic and diagnostic value. In utilizing this and other contacts with parents, it is worthwhile to keep Irene Josselyn's (1957) perceptive words in mind. "If anxious parents are not always equated with meddling parents and parents who remain remote from the situation until or unless the therapist appeals to them are not always seen as rejecting parents, if instead the parental attitude toward treatment is incorporated in the overall evaluation of the case, the relationship between the adolescent, his parents, and the therapist will have greater likelihood of success."

If the contacts between the therapist and the parents are handled openly with the adolescent, these contacts should not interfere with the therapeutic alliance between the therapist and the child. It is possible, of course, to create problems through the inappropriate management of the relationship with the parents. Parents usually call for advice on the management of adolescent behavior, for recommendations for dealing with family crises, or in order to seduce the therapist into an alignment with them in the neurotic family conflict. The motives for contact must be evaluated, not only with each family but in each individual instance, in order to respond appropriately.

The Value of Advice and Education

Often, the appropriate response is to provide the advice or information which is requested. Many parents have only the vaguest notion of what behavior to expect from an adolescent. They may be deeply concerned over one piece of behavior which is age-appropriate while blandly accepting other behavior which evidences severe distortion of normal development. The therapist should provide the parents with information regarding the developmental phase. This can be done directly and also by suggesting reading sources which may assist the parent. Our recognition of the central role of emotional factors in shaping parent-child relationships often leads to an excessive depreciation of the value of the intellect. In past generations, knowledge of normative child behavior was disseminated informally through the extended family and the cohesive wider community. Since this effective casual instruction is largely unavailable under current social conditions, it must be replaced by more formal educative efforts. Parents need models of family interaction and child behavior, not to adopt blindly, but to utilize as guidelines.

It is helpful for the therapist to have a firm grasp of normal adolescent development in order to be comfortable in educating parents. The young therapist, who is recently out of graduate school or medical school, may feel intimidated that an average set of middle-aged parents may know a lot more about day-to-day life with teenagers than he does. The beginning therapist usually knows more about normal adolescence than he realizes, but he needs a way to organize and articulate his wisdom. In addition to learning from teachers and from textbooks and other professional sources, the beginning therapist can draw on his own life experience. He also might have the opportunity to get in touch with his own ambivalent and otherwise complex feelings about adolescent issues through his personal therapy or psychoanalysis.

Therapists can learn about normal adolescent development through professional literature as well as reading handbooks that are intended primarily for parents. The modern literature on normal adolescent development probably started with Stanley Hall (1916) and continued through classic authors such as Gesell and Ilg (1942) and Inhelder and Piaget (1958) and, of course, Erikson (1963). More contemporary books on this subject include works by Coleman (1971), Dourvan and Adelson (1966), Konopka (1976), and Offer (1969). Some textbooks have chapters on normal adolescent development, such as Malmquist (1979), Petersen and Offer (1979), and Schechter et al. (1972).

Many books on parenting are available, some of which are listed in the separate "Bibliography for Parents" at the end of this chapter. These books deal with emotional interactions within the family, the importance of communication, discipline, fostering self-esteem, and timely issues such as alcohol and drug abuse. The therapist should read carefully any book which he recommends to parents—for his own edification and also to be sure he agrees with its general philosophy. A complete knowledge of the book's contents will also allow the therapist to spot any parental distortions and discuss them with the parents.

The therapist also advises freely about matters which directly concern the psychotherapy. He is the expert on the subject and should not expect the parents to know whether the child can safely miss sessions, reduce their frequency, change therapists, or terminate. In these matters, he needs the observations and opinions of the parents to assist him, but the final decisions are his.

Advice to Avoid

There are traps to avoid in advising parents directly. These mistakes may be generally described as any intervention which accepts the "cookbook theory" of child rearing, that is, the over-emphasis on parental behavior rather than parental feelings and attitudes. Specifically, this problem frequently arises around requests for advice on "discipline." The parents who need support in this area often are unable to use it wisely. If they are extremely unsure of their prerogatives, they may counter their youngster's angry reaction to limits by announcing that the limit was recommended by the therapist. This appeal to "expert opinion" has the effect not only of completely negating the adolescent's respect for his parents, but also of interfering with the nonauthoritarian therapeutic alliance. This devious exercise of authority merely causes both parent and therapist to appear frightened of direct communication with the adolescent. If the therapist must assume a limit-setting function with his patient, he should do so in a direct, person-to-person manner.

Other parents who ask advice regarding discipline merely want the therapist to join them in their effort to dominate the adolescent. Dispensing explicit advice on techniques of controlling the child is rarely in harmony with the therapist's goal of increasing the adolescent's autonomy and independence, regardless of the motive which drives the parents. It is wiser to explore the goals and aims of parental discipline, leaving the methods completely up to the parents.

Many parents do need help in understanding the purposes of limit setting. Fuller knowledge allows them to evaluate the complex reactions of their adolescent to family rules and to use these reactions as information which will help them to understand the teenager's real needs. They should be assisted to see the plea for control and structure which may be hidden in flagrant rebellion. Some of them can understand the ways in which their youngster may utilize "crime and punishment" to deal with his guilt. They are also helped to see that their anxiety about granting reasonable freedom to an adequately functioning youngster may represent envy of his vitality or fear of being deserted. As we have suggested elsewhere (Meeks, 1967), the management of limits is a delicate barometer of the emotional climate between adults and adolescents. It should be fully utilized in the therapeutic effort, not closed off by rigid directions from the therapist.

Parent Support Groups

Some parents are extremely isolated from other families in the community—perhaps because they have frequently moved and have not had time to establish new friendships or because of a perverse family tradition of aloofness or because both parents work and there is little time for socializing in the neighborhood. Single parents may be so busy working and raising their children that they don't save time to stay in touch with their own peers. In any case, parents find themselves dealing with their teenagers in a social vacuum and winging it from one crisis to the next.

Parents benefit tremendously from neighborhood networking, which basically means that they stay in touch with the parents of their own children's friends. Since teenagers spend much of their day checking with each other on how to beat the system in one way or another, it makes sense for those teenagers' parents to have some form of informal but regular communication. Parents can be a tremendous support to each other and can learn from each other's experiences. Parent support groups are organized through local high schools, perhaps as part of the antidrug program at the school; by community mental health centers; by social service agencies; and by organizations such as Tough Love. In addition to parent support groups, some agencies offer parenting education. One example of organized parenting education is called Parent Effectiveness Training.

Probably the most effective parent support group is the kind that arises spontaneously out of a felt need within a neighborhood:

> Mr. Collins was a single parent who unexpectedly came to have custody of his 14-year-old son. The boy's mother had died, so he suddenly came to live with the father in a way that was difficult for everybody. Mr. Collins felt overwhelmed by the magnitude of his situation, suddenly having to deal with school arrangements, suspicions of drug and alcohol abuse, discipline, medical care, and all the other details of full-time parenthood. Mr. Collins sought help from a therapist because of his own feelings of confusion and panic and he took the opportunity to get some tips on how to raise a young adolescent. The therapist gave some suggestions on how to address some immediate issues regarding the son and he gave Mr. Collins another appointment in two weeks.
>
> At the second appointment Mr. Collins announced that he had the situation under control. In the meantime, he had organized a meeting of four or five sets of parents in his neighborhood, who all had sons of about the same age. The parents found it extremely helpful to compare the "policies and procedures" which they had in their own households. They decided to establish a few rules that would be consistent through the neighborhood, such as no phone calls before 8 a.m. or after 9 p.m. They also agreed *not* to agree on other issues, such as whether to allow their sons to wear earrings! The therapist congratulated Mr. Collins on being both innovative and industrious in assuming his role as a new parent.

Helping Parents to Manage Crisis

Any therapist who accepts the responsibility of treating adolescent patients must expect parental telephone calls announcing crises within the family. Parental anxiety is high, not only because of the adult's tendency to project and expect the worst from the adolescent, but because of the adolescent tendency, based on impulsivity, to deliver the worst. Many emergency calls from parents are disguised requests for support, muted complaints about the course of therapy, or subtle attempts to lure the therapist into a family intrigue. These can generally be recognized for what they are by the obvious disparity between the level of parental anxiety and the magnitude of the behavioral problem described. The therapist, of course, insists on a leisurely exploration of the questions raised; if necessary, he schedules a full interview for this purpose.

Mrs. Smith called her son's therapist in the evening. She apologized for bothering him, but rushed ahead breathlessly.

"I don't know what I can do with Jeff! He refuses to study for his midterm. I know I should let him handle this, but you can't just stand aside and watch them ruin their lives! What should I do? Should I force him to study?"

"How would you do that?" the therapist inquired.

"That's why I called you. What can I do?"

"I'm not sure you need to do anything. Jeff's been doing pretty well in his work lately, hasn't he?"

"Yes, but he's going to ruin it all. You must tell me some way to get him to work."

"What does your husband think?"

"Oh, he isn't here. He's out of town this week. I'm so mad at him! He's never here when I need him."

"Have you been feeling pretty alone?" the therapist asked.

"Yes," said the mother, crying. "I sure have. And now Jeff won't even let me help him with his work. He ordered me out of the room and said he'd study like he wanted to. I only wanted to help him!"

"I know that, Mrs. Smith. I guess some company would be nice for you, too. I think your loneliness and need for company when your husband is away are things you ought to discuss in your next therapy session."

"What about Jeff?"

"I believe it would be best to respect his wish to work alone. After all, you and your husband have just put a lot of work into helping him to take responsibility for his own work—sink or swim."

"Well . . . I guess you're right. I may just call up a friend and visit a while to relax myself."

"That sounds like a pretty good idea to me. I do think this is something you ought to explore pretty carefully with Miss Jones (her therapist) next time you see her."

There are some situations, however, that do constitute bona fide crises. Most of these are discussed in Part Two of the book which deals with special problems in adolescent psychotherapy. Suggestions for dealing with the parents involved in such emergency situations are offered there.

When confronted with crises of any kind, the therapist often feels that he is walking a thin line between overinvolvement in the situation and a failure to assume appropriate helpful responsibility. It is obvious that a realistic emergency situation such as a suicide attempt or a runaway cannot be met with excessive therapeutic aloofness and cold objectivity. At such a time, parents need very direct emotional support and explicit advice on handling the problem. At the same time, the therapist must be careful not to be stampeded into an antitherapeutic action by parental anxiety and manipulation. It is wise to ask for full information before taking action. One does not wish to advise that the police be called in order to protect a runaway when the actual situation is merely one of the adolescent being out of the home for three or four hours without notifying the parents of his whereabouts.

The therapist also attempts to avoid usurping parental responsibility or permitting the parents to dump a trying situation entirely into his lap. An example might be the therapist's personal participation in a search for a runaway. Only in extremely rare and unusual situations would such a departure from the therapeutic role into direct care for the adolescent be appropriate.

This wavy and indistinct border between directing the therapy and directing the adolescent's daily life is the line of demarcation between parental responsibility and therapist's responsibility in all matters pertaining to the adolescent. The adolescent patient himself should assume as much responsibility as he can on both sides of the line. When he is not able to take care of himself, the parents assume responsibility temporarily until he is able to handle the job again. When the lapse in responsibility directly affects his psychotherapy, the parents should defer to the therapist and be guided by him.

The therapist should never permit himself to be maneuvered into taking greater responsibility than he can realistically discharge. If the patient is suicidal, homicidal, or otherwise in real-life danger, the therapist must inform the parents and insist that they assume ultimate responsibility for their child. Of course, the therapist offers all possible assistance to them in this undertaking. Some explicit approaches to managing these situations are suggested in Part Two of the book.

TALKING WITH THE ADOLESCENT PATIENT ABOUT HIS PARENTS

Just as the parents of the adolescent need help in understanding and assisting their youngster through this turbulent phase, the adolescent needs direct assistance in dealing with his parents. The typical adolescent has many complaints about his parents which may be presented so convincingly that the beginning therapist is tempted to identify with the apparently victimized youngster, viewing all his difficulties as understandable reactions to parental unfairness. With greater sophistication, the therapist comes to realize that many of these complaints are unjustified in reality and represent primarily projected adolescent pathology. This focus, true as far as it goes, overlooks the interactional nature of family pathology. Although the adolescent may be entirely incorrect in his accusations, his basic sense that his parents are actively contributing to his psychopathology may be entirely accurate. Parents do have emotional needs and emotional conflicts and these are often inappropriately expressed in the parent-adolescent interaction. Sooner or later, this portion of the adolescent's problem must be faced in his psychotherapy. It is unrealistic to ask the adolescent to face and accept painful realities about himself, his society, and his friends while protecting the parents from similar honest appraisal. In his role as guide, the therapist will be drawn into this exploration of parental personality and motivation. Often, he will have to accept or reject interpretive comments offered by the adolescent, and at times he will need to share his own impressions of unconscious family pathology.

It should be obvious that the therapist is on dangerous ground whenever he deals with any material which cannot be directly verified with his own patient. With the adolescent and his parents, the therapist runs the additional risk of being manipulated into taking sides in a neurotic power struggle. The adolescent may use therapeutic comments as ammunition to attack his parents. This misuse of information is more common early in therapy before the adolescent is able to face his personal responsibility for his problem, his conflicts, and the course of his life. The therapist should be sure of the therapeutic alliance and confident of his patient's growing maturity before verifying parental psychopathology to the adolescent. Even then, the adolescent must be helped to see that the existence of psychopathology in his parents does not excuse him from responsibility for managing his own life. To blame his parents for his failure and unhappiness may merely allow the adolescent to continue being miserable. To understand why his parents may have had some problems in parenthood may permit the adolescent to forgive them and concentrate on making the most of his own assets and liabilities.

The greatest hazard to the successful resolution of the adolescent's resentment toward his parents is the countertransference of the adolescent's therapist. There are some therapists who relate well to adolescents but who fail therapeutically with them because of their own unresolved (and often unrecognized) resentment of their own parents. These therapists are still locked in a chronic state of adolescent rebellion themselves. They often overtly or covertly encourage their adolescent patients to wallow in their refractory rage toward their family. The therapist and the adolescent may then avoid facing the inevitable need to accept the burdens of maturity. Unfortunately, they also forego maturity's gratifications and pleasures.

Perhaps, the core dynamic behind such prolonged spite is the stubborn refusal to accept the bitter fact that no one is omnipotent and that each human being must face the struggles of existence without a magic ally. As long as one can mesmerize oneself with complaints about "how it could have been if only my parents had been different," one can hold onto a dream of a nirvana that might have been.

Of course, there are other factors which may interfere with this therapeutic step. The therapist may overidentify with his patient, especially if the parents are hostile, rejecting, or irresponsible in their behavior toward the adolescent. It is helpful to remember, however, that these parental attitudes are shaped by the parents' endowments and experiences. If the therapist adopts a deterministic, causal view toward his adolescent patient's psychopathology, he should allow the parents a similar objective acceptance. All parents are doing their best with their children. There are no bad parents, only some who are unequal to the demands of parenthood. The therapist may need to offer firm restraint on some of the parents' destructive floundering, but he cannot permit himself the luxury of casting them in the villain role. His adolescent patient settles for this easy way out on pain of perpetual psychological invalidism. Some parents make it quite difficult for their adolescent to grow up, but this does not change the nature of reality. The adolescent must grow up anyway, or live with the misery of a lifetime of emotional infantilism. The therapist must help the adolescent to accept this difficult fact. He can be very gentle in this confrontation, but he must also be very firm. A widespread reluctance to force this issue is suggested by Masterson (1967) as one possible reason for poor long-range therapeutic results in his study of treated adolescents.

Rebellion Versus Freedom

The adolescent also needs help in seeing that his perception of himself as a younger child and his wishes to enjoy a more dependent relationship with his parents frequently lead him to overreact to their expectations and wishes for him. Even when

the parents are controlling and push the youngster toward preconceived goals, the adolescent must learn to be free to reject
or (even more difficult) accept these goals according to his own
needs and abilities. Often, the adolescent mistakes rebelliousness
for freedom. He cannot choose any goals which happen to coincide with parental desires, even when the goals are identical
with the adolescent's own ambitions. Obviously, under these circumstances he is not free to do what he wishes. The adolescent
can sometimes grasp this through an allegory: "It seems to me
that if you were ravenously hungry and your parents commanded
you to eat a beautiful and delicious meal, you would refuse!"

The adolescent also needs help in recognizing that the parental
tendency to "treat him like a child" does not actually make him
childish. He is only in danger from his own childish wishes. The
immature adolescent takes umbrage if his parents dare to remind
him to drive carefully. The mature adolescent recognizes the concern and anxiety for his well-being implied in the warning and
responds reassuringly to the parents. Even if he suspects that the
overconcern has roots in suppressed hostility toward him, he still
realizes that the hostility is not expressed because the parents
also love him and are fearful that their anger will harm him. He
is aware that he is a separate person with ambivalences and defenses of his own. This complex understanding is eloquently expressed in his simple explanation, "Aw, they're good parents.
They're just worrywarts. Hell, I'm not perfect myself."

"If Only I Could Get Away From Them"

Frequently, adolescents express the desire to leave home. This
wish is part of the fantasy that they could be mature if only they
did not have to live with their parents. In some cases, there is a
degree of truth in this idea. There are parents who undercut
healthy adolescent independence. However, even in these families, geographical distance will not resolve the adolescent's ambivalence. Sooner or later, the adolescent must be willing to give
up the regressive gratifications that the family offers in favor of
maturity and independence. In other words, the adolescent's

most dangerous opponent in his struggle for independence is his own wish for dependency. Some adolescents can understand the clarification, "Could it be that you want to run away from home quickly to avoid thinking about really growing up and leaving home?" This paradox can be expanded by pointing out that a poorly considered, precipitious departure from home may actually be designed to ensure failure, a parental rescue, and continued dependency. As Blos (1967) has commented, these youngsters are "doing the wrong things for the right reasons." In these adolescents, this conflict is often reactivated with the therapist as termination approaches. They are tempted to "quit" treatment prematurely to avoid openly facing the pain of separation which would appear during a planned termination.

SUMMARY

In many respects, the management of the complex relationships between the youngster and his parents and between the parents and the youngster's therapist is the most important and delicate task of psychotherapy during adolescence. The therapist must obtain and keep the trust and cooperation of the parents without compromising the adolescent's movement toward independence from the family. The parents must be mobilized to accept and support the eventual goal of the young person's emancipation. Often, they will need the support of their child's therapist, if not personal therapy, to bear the pain of releasing the adolescent and reestablishing family homeostasis without him.

In some cases the only treatment approach likely to yield positive results is conjoint family therapy. The indications for this approach and a brief overview of the treatment techniques involved are discussed in chapter 8.

After the qualified therapist has performed an adequate diagnostic study, chosen an appropriate candidate for outpatient psychotherapy, formed a therapeutic alliance with parents and child, and effectively responded to the ongoing problems of psychotherapy, he still faces one final crucial task. He must effect a termination at the correct time and in a constructive manner.

Some of the issues and techniques involved in this phase of the therapy are considered in the next chapter.

BIBLIOGRAPHY FOR PARENTS

There is no individual book that will be suitable for all parents. Among other issues, the choice would depend of the treatment style of the therapist; the strengths, weaknesses, and values of the parents; and the particular situation within that family. These books do not all say the same thing—in fact, they flatly disagree on some aspects of raising teenagers.

Dr. Alan M. Cohen. *Kids Out of Control.* Summit, N.J.: The PIA Press, 1989. Written by an adolescent psychiatrist for the general public, this book describes the difference between normal teenagers and antisocial teenagers. Dr. Cohen explains what parents can do on their own and also how to use professional help.

Dr. Don Dinkmeyer and Dr. Gary McKay. *The Parent's Guide.* Circle Pines, Minnesota: American Guidance Service, 1983. This is a text book for a parenting course called Systematic Training for Effective Parenting of Teens. It has ten chapters which should be studied and applied in sequence, one step at a time.

Dr. James Dobson. *The Strong-Willed Child: Birth through Adolescence.* Wheaton, Illinois: Tyndale House, 1978. Dr. Dobson is a psychologist with a Christian orientation. His message has been expounded on a radio show and several videos, that parents should have deep love and affection for their children, but should also exercise their authority through appropriate discipline.

Dr. Don Fleming. *How to Stop the Battle with Your Teenager.* New York: Prentiss Hall, 1989. Dr. Fleming is a psychologist, who believes in "firm discipline coupled with caring." The book is organized in a directive, cookbook approach, which includes precise, step-by-step solutions to a large range of adolescent issues.

Dr. Richard Gardner. *Understanding Children: A Parent's Guide to Child Rearing.* Cresskill, N.J.: Creative Therapeutics, 1983. Dr. Gardner is a child psychiatrist who is also a prolific author. He has written books about hyperactivity and divorce and other topics for children, for parents, and for professionals.

Dr. Haim Ginott. *Between Parent and Teenager*. New York: Macmillan Company, 1969. Dr. Ginott died several years ago, but his books are still popular. They have a warm, supportive style.

Dr. Thomas Gordon. *Parent Effectiveness Training: The Tested New Way to Raise Responsible Children*. New York: New American Library, 1970. Dr. Gordon is a clinical psychologist who developed the P.E.T. system, an educational program for parents that has been taught in thousands of cities in every state. The book describes the technique of "active listening" and the use of negotiation to arrive at solutions that meet the needs of the youngster and the parents.

Dr. Robert Kolodny et al. *How to Survive Your Adolescent's Adolescence*. Boston: Little, Brown and Co., 1984. This is a large, comprehensive book which was put together by a physician, a social worker, a psychologist, and a writer. It does not give detailed advice about parenting, but covers many aspects of normal and deviant adolescent development.

Dr. John E. Meeks. *High Times/Low Times: How to Cope with Teenage Depression*. New York: Berkley Books, 1989. This book is intended for parents and teachers and other nonclinicians who may deal with depressed adolescents. It illustrates the many manifestations of depression in adolescents and also explains how therapy and medication are helpful.

Dr. Philip Osborne. *Parenting for the '90s*. Intercourse, Pennsylvania: Good Books, 1989. Dr. Osborne is a psychologist who has an eclectic approach, in that he takes part of the Dobson approach and part of the Gordon approach and part behavior modification. He emphasizes the importance of the "No Problem Area," the times "when parent and child are together and neither one is upset."

Rev. Paul Swets. *How to Talk So Your Teenager Will Listen*. Waco, Texas: Word Books, 1988. Rev. Swets is a Presbyterian minister who was assisted in writing this book by his son Judson, a high school senior. It is an upbeat book which focuses on the details of effective communication, such as the interplay of the personality traits of the parent with the temperament of the teenager.

Phyllis and David York and Ted Wachtel. *Toughlove*. New York: Bantam Books, 1982. Toughlove is a national movement, with the basic principles that parents should assert themselves to stand up to their unruly adolescents and that they can derive support from parent groups within their community. Toughlove is intended for "young people whose outrageous behavior requires unorthodox responses."

CITED AND RECOMMENDED READINGS

Blos, P. 1967. The second individuation process of adolescence. *Psychoanalytic Study of the Child*. 22: 162–186.

Coleman, J. 1971. *The Adolescent Society*. New York: Free Press.

Dourvan, E., and J. Adelson. 1966. *The Adolescent Experience*. New York: John Wiley.

Gesell, A., and F. L. Ilg. 1943. *Infant and Child in the Culture of Today*. New York: Harper.

Hall, G. S. 1916. *Adolescence*. New York: Appleton.

Inhelder, B., and J. Piaget. 1958. *The Growth of Logical Thinking from Childhood to Adolescence*. New York: Basic Books.

Josselyn, I. M. 1957. Psychotherapy of adolescents at the level of private practice. In: *Psychotherapy of the Adolescent*, edited by B. H. Balser. New York: International Universities Press.

Konopka, G. 1976. *Young Girls: A Portrait of Adolescence*. Englewood Cliffs, N.J.: Prentice-Hall.

Malmquist, C. P. 1979. Development from thirteen to sixteen years. In: *Basic Handbook of Child Psychiatry*, edited by J. D. Noshpitz. New York: Basic Books.

Masterson, J. F. 1967. *The Psychiatric Dilemma of Adolescence*. Boston: Little, Brown.

Meeks, J. E. 1967. Some observations on adolescent group leaders in two contrasting socioeconomic classes. *International Journal of Social Psychiatry*. 13: 278–286.

Offer, D. 1969. *The Psychological World of the Teenager*. New York: Basic Books.

Petersen, A. C., and D. Offer. 1979. Adolescent development: sixteen to nineteen years. In: *Basic Handbook of Child Psychiatry*, edited by J. D. Noshpitz. New York: Basic Books.

Schechter, M. D., et al. 1972. Normal development in adolescence. In: *Manual of Child Psychopathology*. New York: McGraw-Hill.

CHAPTER 10

termination of psychotherapy with the adolescent

I TERMINATION OF THERAPY AND
THE ADOLESCENT PHASE OF DEVELOPMENT

In an earlier chapter, we suggested that the technically necessary process of forming a therapeutic alliance with the adolescent has the additional beneficial effect of strengthening the adolescent's observing ego. This therapeutic instrument, therefore,
has a curative value of its own because it promotes a developmentally crucial task. The proper management of the termination
of adolescent psychotherapy is perhaps even more important,
since the basic function of all adolescent development is to complete a "second individuation" (Blos, 1967). The separation from
the therapist, both physically and psychologically, is an integral
part of the entire psychotherapeutic process. Many of the earlier
gains of psychotherapy may be lost through unskilled management of the issues and technical problems raised in the termination phase. It is equally true that this part of therapy offers
the opportunity for observing and partially resolving many adolescent dilemmas which may remain latent until the adolescent
is confronted with termination. The series of decisions concerning
the methods of ending an important personal relationship arouses
important developmental conflicts. Often, the actual leave-taking
in therapy comes to symbolize the process of loosening the bonds
to internalized parental images and giving up the magical omnipotent and passive expectations which go with them. When the
termination of psychotherapy becomes the microcosmic representation of this accommodation to young adulthood, it is indeed
a momentous event in the adolescent's life. This is often the case

271

in the treatment of youngsters in middle and late adolescence, especially the latter.

One may expect a wide gamut of defensive and regressive maneuvers as the adolescent attempts to deal with the anxieties which accompany the important psychic restructuring related to termination. Emotional upheavals, symptom recurrences, and episodes of self-destructive fantasies and even behavior (often calculated to provoke rescue and reinstatement of dependency) may alternate with wishes to flee prematurely or deny the importance of therapy and the therapist, to "run away from home to avoid leaving."

Youngsters with "malignant" defenses and major fixations in pregenital positions will experience the greatest difficulty in terminating. In a sense they are actually not ready for termination even after fairly successful treatment. Often, even late in treatment, they still need the therapist to test reality, support their self-worth, and focus their psychic energy. We will discuss these youngsters, including those who cannot be terminated, later in this chapter.

It follows from these developmental considerations that the termination of psychotherapy with the adolescent must be correctly timed, sensitively related to his particular needs, flexibly managed, and conducted with maximum alertness to complicating countertransference issues.

DECIDING TO TERMINATE THERAPY

In our opinion, successful psychotherapy contracts with adolescents tend to be unnecessarily prolonged. This may result in a blunting of the developmental thrust toward independence, which partially nullifies the positive impact of the therapy. Individuation, the goal of adolescent development, is best served by assisting the adolescent toward a workable character synthesis and then quickly moving aside so that the adolescent's new strengths propel him toward real and available objects outside of the sheltered therapy office. The problem of course is to have reasonable confidence that the synthesis is stable enough to permit continuing individuation in the real world rather than pseudoadult "shadow playing" of old and outmoded childhood relationships (Blos, 1967). It is our impression that the therapist frequently withholds this confidence too long from youngsters who have clearly found the right path to maturity out of an anxious desire to walk along and guard the adolescent all the way to the goal. Actually, much growth can occur once the previous "vicious circle" is converted into a "virtuous circle" (see Wender, 1968). There are other motives for unduly delaying termination which are discussed below. Even if the therapist acepts the premise of early termination, he still has to establish some guidelines for deciding when to consider its initiation.

General Patterns Which Suggest that Termination Should Be Considered

Both Menninger (1958) and Fromm-Reichmann (1950) have offered excellent descriptions of the general changes in a patient which suggest that termination is near. Hiatt (1965) has elaborated these and offers explicit and useful guidelines for terminating psychotherapy. Even though these authors were dealing with adult patients, many of the basic ideas contained in their discussions of the problem of termination can be extrapolated to adolescent psychotherapy.

In the adolescent, as in the adult, one looks for symptomatic improvement, a heightened capacity for nondestructive pleasure (especially in interpersonal relationships), greater comfort with the acknowledgement and appropriate expression of a wide range of emotions in himself and others, a capacity to laugh at himself, and other quasi-objective phenomena which Hiatt (1965) has listed in detail. In addition, one expects a more objective attitude toward the therapist. Intensive transference reactions leading to expansive overevaluation of the therapist's skills, capacity to nurture, or wisdom, as well as hostile devaluation and belittling of his abilities, should be minimal and should be recognized as distortions by the adolescent patient when they do occur.

NORMAL COMPARED TO WHAT?—THE NEED FOR DEVELOPMENTAL NORMS

The problem of deciding when termination should be considered is complicated in the adolescent by the need to measure the characteristics mentioned in the above section against a scale of developmental norms. For example, some tendency to mild depressive episodes, interpersonal touchiness, and a slightly shy and coquettish treatment of the therapist are expected behavioral characteristics of the 13-year-old adolescent girl. They do not indicate a need for further therapy. Older adolescents gradually approximate the young adult model and consequently signal a readiness for termination with general behavioral patterns which resemble those described for adults. Reasonable levels of expectation for adolescents of various ages may be developed by observing the behavior of normal adolescents (every therapist should make the effort to become acquainted with some), reading descriptive studies of normal adolescent behavior, and to some extent by recalling one's own adolescent behavior and feelings.

If you want to be a little obsessive in comparing your adolescent patient with a group of normal teenagers, try informally assessing him with the "Autonomous Functioning Checklist." This instrument, described by Sigafoos et al. (1988), is usually completed by parents to measure behavioral autonomous functioning in adolescents. It is divided into subscales. including routine personal care and family-oriented functions, the extent to which the adolescent handles his interaction with the environment, the ways in which the adolescent chooses to use free time, and social involvement and pursuit of vocational directions.

There is another point which is obvious, but which may be forgotten in the heat of therapeutic ambition. It is impossible, even with the most skillful psychotherapy, to resolve emotional conflicts which are related to developmental tasks beyond the youngster's years. The 13-year-old girl described above cannot be expected to achieve final resolution of her oedipal attachments, since this maturational step normally occurs later in life, often not until young adulthood. She would be ready for termination when she could show a dawning appropriate interest in boys her own age (or slightly older), a budding capacity to identify with her mother's positive female traits without total fear of a homosexual bond, and a capacity to move in and out of regressive pregenital positions with relative comfort. The absence of paralyzing rigidities and inhibitions or defensive pseudoadult behaviors would indicate that she had "gotten back on the developmental track." Some writers on therapy of adolescents have not sufficiently emphasized this point (for example, see Corday, 1967). One does not try to accompany the adolescent on his entire developmental journey, only to guide him off sidetracks and back to his age-appropriate station on the main trunk of the developmental line.

At times, the therapist must point out the limitations of therapy to the adolescent patient himself. Despite the inner thrust toward independence, the youngster may find a comfortable therapeutic alliance hard to relinquish. The patient recognizes that the collaborative work with the therapist has helped him to free himself from many inner terrors. He naturally hopes that the same device can help him resolve other dilemmas, even when these are desirable "growing pains." The therapist must gently and firmly prevent the adolescent patient from using psychotherapy as a magic talisman to ward off or delay necessary developmental struggles.

Naturally, not all adolescent patients will be able to reach ideal goals even when these are corrected for developmental variation. Adolescents who have severe ego defects on the basis of constitutional or organic pathology, severe emotional deprivation, or grossly disturbed family relationships will always show some distortions in personality functioning related to these basic defects.

Treatment in the above cases aims at establishing a workable synthesis which will probably include defensive patterns which are partially crippling. One attempts to work to a point where personality functioning provides some pleasure and sense of identity to the adolescent without seriously infringing on the rights of other people. If the underpinnings of the adolescent's personality have been crushed in early life, he will probably always move with a psychological limp. The therapist only hopes that he can help him learn to get around and take care of himself despite the disability.

Some Checkpoints For Termination

The only reliable basis for a decision to terminate therapy is a careful consideration of general behavior (in and out of the therapist's office) in comparison with developmental norms. When this global and partially intuitive assessment suggests that the adolescent is ready for termination, this impression can be checked against some specific behaviors which often appear in conjunction with an inner readiness for greater independence. The hunch that termination is near is reinforced when:

1. A growing appropriate involvement with peers results in a friendly and nonprovocative decrease in interest in therapy. The genuine gentleness and warmth toward the therapist which accompany this "drifting away" clearly differentiate it from the defensive avoidance of dependency relationships which one often sees early in therapy.

2. The adolescent wants to discuss the "hang-ups" of a friend without relating these to himself—that is, these problems are discussed without contrasting them with his own problems in an attempt to minimize his difficulties, divert attention from himself, or show his own plight as more serious or deserving of sympathy. In short, the adolescent appears to have the necessary emotional energy and comfort with his own identity to concern himself about another person with reasonable objectivity and clarity of ego boundaries.

3. The adolescent suggests that the therapist could help this friend. When the expectation of what the therapist could offer the friend is reasonable, this often signals a willingness to share the therapist. Often, we suspect, it is also an unconscious attempt to deal with guilt feelings engendered by the wish to "abandon" the therapist by offering a replacement.

4. The adolescent shows a capacity for more objective evaluation of his parents, considering both their assets and their

liabilities as human beings. He is able to accept their strong points as identification models while rejecting some of their weaknesses.

5. The adolescent uses fewer superlatives. Hiatt (1965) has noted this change in adults, and it seems to hold for adolescents. However, it should be remembered that the normal adolescent may use more superlatives than the sick adult. In adolescents, one expects not a total avoidance of superlatives but a greater capacity for moderation than noted earlier in treatment.

6. The adolescent rarely acts out in regard to the therapy. He comes on time, does not battle over scheduling hours, does not haggle over stopping on time, and rarely needs to "play games" by teasingly withholding information, feelings, and ideas. There is a sense of simple forthrightness which is age-appropriate.

7. The adolescent inquires about the possibility of termination in a frank and comfortable manner. This is an especially good indicator of approaching readiness for termination if it is accompanied by appropriately mixed feelings delivered with typical adolescent sentimentality. "I really think I'm about ready to split this scene. Damn trouble is, I'm so used to you nagging me to look at why I draw every breath, I'm gonna miss you. Man, I never thought I'd say that!"

8. The adolescent's use of alloplastic defense mechanisms is less frantic and more realistic and shows greater consideration for the complexities of human needs and motivations. It would be neither reasonable nor desirable for the adolescent to give up his efforts to change himself or his environment (see Keniston, 1970). It would be detrimental to our development as a society and a personal dereliction for the adolescent to accept the social status quo with all its defects calmly. Efforts to change malevolent social conditions, even if the efforts are disruptive and unpleasant, do not necessarily suggest that the adolescent is emotionally ill.

The healthy adolescent may even remain somewhat utopian and naive in his plans for social change. It is the single-minded demand that the environment accommodate completely to the idio-syncrasies of the adolescent that suggests a defensive utilization of social activism or cultural philosophy. A reasonably mature compromise in the choice between internal modification and al-teration of outer reality is an acceptable point for termination. It is especially encouraging if the adolescent shows some recog-nition of both his capacity to change things and his limitations as an agent of social change, succumbing neither to grandiosity nor apathetic withdrawal.

THE THERAPIST'S PROBLEMS WITH TERMINATION

On "Letting Go"

Pearson (1958) has pointed out that adults have many motives for emphasizing the inadequacies of adolescents. Pumpian-Min-dlin (1965) has described still other unconscious sources of envy which may lead to underevaluation of adolescent abilities. These generational factors, which may include protective and compet-itive elements in varying degrees, contribute to the therapist's reluctance to let his young patients handle things on their own. Of course, the adolescent patient can also lead the therapist to kick him out angrily and prematurely with an open or veiled prophecy that his attempted independence will fail and he will come crawling back. This, of course, is not really "letting go."

In addition to these generational distortions at the time of termination, the therapist faces the discomfort which every hu-man being feels when he relinquishes a valued relationship. At the ending of a successful psychotherapy with an attractive ad-olescent, the honest therapist must often admit to a "forgotten parent" element in his complex of feelings. This aspect of his reaction might be stated as, "Now he wants to leave me, just when I get him grownup enough to be useful and enjoyable to have around." The frequency of this countertransference attitude may be part of the reason that many adolescents seem slightly guilty and apologetic about their appropriate wish to terminate and handle their own affairs.

The therapist's problem in letting go probably explains the frequency with which final sessions are taken up with Polonius-like lectures and advice. Fortunately, the now-healthy adolescent is usually indulgent and forgiving of the therapist's lapse into pomposity. If the adolescent were not, the therapist might undo much of his good work in ego building by this effort to reassure himself of his importance to the adolescent.

Of course, there is one very practical reason that the therapist has some reluctance to terminate successfully treated cases. Since the therapeutic alliance with these youngsters is firmly established, he anticipates their sessions with comfort and even pleasure. When they are terminated, who will take their place?—probably an angry, devious, defended, difficult youngster who will carry little of the load of the therapeutic work for some time to come. Small wonder that the therapist is tempted to hold onto his comfortable and cooperative youngster past the time when the adolescent really needs him.

On "Kicking Out"

I have emphasized the factors which tend to prolong therapy unnecessarily. Countertransference problems may also lead to errors in the other direction. Hostile feelings toward an adolescent, especially if these feelings are unconscious, can lead the therapist to exaggerate the patient's progress in order to rationalize an angry rejection as an appropriate termination. A narcissistic or omnipotent need to achieve quick results may tempt the therapist to skip over important and necessary therapeutic work. Parental pressure based on realistic financial problems or emotional needs may hurry the insecure therapist. Fear of erotic urges stirred by closeness to the patient can cause a panicked wish to withdraw and terminate in the interest of self-protection.

On both sides, the therapist must rely on his intellectual and emotional honesty, accepting the fact that he will invariably err in both directions on occasion.

TECHNIQUES OF TERMINATION

The key word in termination of the adolescent is flexibility. Rarely can the adolescent terminate smoothly and with finality in one try. The "open door" policy recommended by Buxbaum (1950) for analytic patients is almost mandatory for the adolescent patient. No matter how carefully one approaches the emotional reactions which termination stirs in the adolescent, it is usually necessary for the patient actually to experiment with physically leaving therapy, returning briefly, and going away again. One reason for this is the expected continuation of developmental storms which may trigger temporary regressive episodes that the adolescent knows the therapist can help to clarify and resolve. More often, however, it seems that the adolescent merely needs to visit home briefly. The purpose of these visits is considered below.

Introducing The Idea Of Termination

Often, the adolescent will verbalize an appropriate interest in termination. When he does, Menninger's (1958) suggested reply, "I think you could finish up soon," is useful. It introduces the issue of termination in a definitive way without committing the patient or the therapist to any set time. The answer also implies that the adolescent and the therapist have further work to do within a finite time limit. It also maintains the focus on the adolescent's responsibility for finishing the job.

Many adolescents will not suggest termination in a direct manner. Many of them are too comfortable in a helpful dependency relationship, which is not inappropriate to their stage of life. Normally functioning adolescents still need understanding adult friends, adult listeners, and adult advisors. When all these characteristics are combined in a trusted adult who has stood by them through many very difficult periods, it is easy to see why they are not eager to give him up.

Although it is important to avoid the appearance of kicking the adolescent out of therapy or shaming him for his dependency wishes, it is also important to introduce the topic of termination as soon as the adolescent is emotionally ready. This need not be done abruptly or tactlessly. The patient will present numerous opportunities for the therapist to introduce the idea of termination in a positive light. The therapist's attitude should imply the calm assumption that he and the adolescent share a pleasant anticipation of a healthy, warm, and constructive parting of the ways, although both may have some mixed feelings about it.

The patient's pride in his independent functioning and his constructive use of object relationships which he has developed on his own are supported and approved as they begin to appear in the course of therapy. More and more, the adolescent says, in one way or another, "And here's another thing I handled well without your help." The therapist replies, in one way or another, "That doesn't surprise me or hurt my feelings. You're a rather competent person and I'm glad of it."

Very gradually, the adolescent is encouraged to rely on his own resources with less help from the therapist. It is often useful to introduce brief discussions of one's own limitations and dilemmas in therapy hours. This does not imply a discussion of deeply personal problems or conflicts the therapist may encounter, since the adolescent is unprepared to face and deal with the full impact of adult problems in living. The goal is merely to help the adolescent realize that the strengths of maturity derive from skill at problem solving and the acceptance of reasonable personal goals. The therapist must be careful not to overwhelm the adolescent or to suggest that the therapist himself finds life too difficult.

Terminations of this kind may be rather prolonged. The therapist should not succumb to pressures or temptations to rush things.

Sarah, the 15-year-old with problems of promiscuity, academic difficulty, drug use, and poor interpersonal relationships who has been mentioned previously, had a long and difficult termination phase.

Strong dependency yearnings which were violently denied early in therapy came to be centered on the therapist. It became necessary to point out repeatedly Sarah's tendency to play at helplessness in order to elicit a supportive helping response from the therapist. When Sarah was able to see this clearly, she joked, "You know if you told me I could solve a problem by holding my breath five minutes, I'd try it, turn blue, and swear it worked!"

Although she gradually came to utilize therapeutic help more realistically, she showed little indication that she regarded her arrangement with the therapist as anything less than lifelong.

Around the end of the second year of treatment, Sarah was symptom-free and enjoying moderately good social relationships in and out of her family. Her first indication of an awareness that therapy would have an end came when she reported angrily that her father had asked her when therapy would be over. She regarded this as evidence that he wished to undermine her treatment (actually this had been a problem early in therapy). The therapist wondered if her father's present comment might be seen rather as a compliment, an indication that she seemed well to him. Sarah asked if the therapist thought she was ready to stop treatment. The therapist replied that he had not thought too much about it before, but, since she had brought it up, she had been handling things very well and if she continued to work hard, the idea certainly would not seem totally unreasonable within the near future.

Sarah didn't say anything more about it in that session, but came to the next interview loaded with problems to discuss. "Everything," she declared, "is falling apart. I'm all strung out!" She then recounted a series of concerns that sounded rather trumped up. The therapist commented that perhaps she was feeling a need to work out all of her problems in a hurry, since the idea of termination had come up in the last hour. He added that he really suspected that Sarah herself was quite capable of dealing with most of the problems she had mentioned.

Over the next few months, Sarah vacillated between feeling that she was ready to "quit" and a panicked feeling that she could not deal with life without the therapist's help. The therapist confronted her with her tendency to confuse herself and tied this to her invariable use of the word "quit" to describe termination. He suggested that perhaps it was difficult for her to imagine two people parting in a friendly way. She seemed to have a need to "go away mad" or to imagine that the other person was angry with her, which tended to interfere with her comfort in functioning independently.

This interchange led to a more direct expression of a variety of ambivalent fantasies about termination. At times, Sarah accused the therapist of being tired of her and disgusted with her inability to handle her own life. At other times, she was sure that the therapist would not let her "quit—I mean stop. Oh, dammit, why do I always say 'quit'?"

Even the issue of the fee was raised again, although Sarah was able to decide she was glad the therapist was paid to see her. "I guess it keeps it all straight and on the up and up."

Again and again, the therapist discussed the concept of voluntary separation based on a mutual agreement that it was time for new kinds of relationships. Often, it was possible to universalize about the adolescent's wish to leave home, not because he hated his parents or they hated him, but because he was ready for another phase of life. The distortions and conflicts around this issue in Sarah's real family were discussed rather fully during this time.

A full six months after termination was first mentioned, Sarah took LSD again for the first time in over a year. She came to her next session a bit sheepishly, but approached the exploration of the "slip-up" (as she called it) with a determined air. She mentioned that she realized she had no real desire to "trip." The experience was unpleasant and she felt annoyed with herself under the drug and could not achieve the state of pleasant "boundlessness" which she had previously experienced with the drug.

"I kept thinking, 'I'm only doing this for X's (her therapist's last name) benefit.' It was pretty lousy. I'd really feel silly except I know I'm trying to figure out how to stop coming here without being mad about it."

She continued to explore her behavior objectively and with skill for several minutes, and then said angrily, "Well, aren't you going to say anything?"

Genuinely surprised, the therapist spontaneously replied, "Gee, I'd be glad to, but you were doing so well yourself!"

Somehow, this seemed to reach Sarah more than the voluminous explanations the therapist had offered earlier. She shook her head in wonderment.

"That's all there is to it, isn't it? You really don't mind helping me. You really believe I don't need it any more."

"Yeah. That's it exactly. Wish I could have told you sooner."

"Oh, that's okay. I think you did. I just listen slow."

She paused for a moment, and then said softly, with tears in her eyes, "I'm ready to stop seeing you now, but don't expect me not to miss you."

Needless to say, the therapist did not escape the session dry-eyed either.

Sarah terminated in four more sessions, utilizing them primarily to talk of her feelings of sadness which were accompanied by a quiet sense of excitement. She was especially looking forward to leaving home for college and talked a good deal of her plans.

In the ensuing three months of high school and the summer vacation, Sarah did not contact the therapist. She wrote from college after three months to report that things were going well and that she had many friends. She said that she also liked her dormitory "mother" and occasionally liked to talk with her.

". . . but," she added, "I don't lean on people totally any more. I can always use help, but mostly I lean on me."

The therapist returned a brief note congratulating her on being happy and stating that he enjoyed hearing from her. She did not write again.

Sarah's case illustrates many of the issues which tend to appear around termination of therapy. These include anxiety over separation, fears of rejection, anger over relinquishing omnipotent expectations of the therapist, and a desperate struggle toward personality integration. In adolescents who have needed a less intense attachment, the conflicts are often briefer and more easily resolved. Some of these conflicts may be fleeting and hardly visible. They are all usually there in some form, however. In adolescents with a less sound therapeutic alliance, more may be acted out. Instead of talking about "quitting" as Sarah did, these youngsters may actually quit, with a need to return later and deal with the issues more directly when they learn that the therapist will neither condemn them for bolting nor pursue and rescue them from their impulsive folly. Some adolescents also show a greater need to "return home" in order to relinquish lingering hopes that the therapist is omnipotent, the perfectly desirable sexual partner, or the source of unlimited gratification.

Mike was a 16-year-old who handled termination by denying his dependency and feelings of loss. He insisted on leaving therapy only two sessions after the therapist had agreed with his assertion that he had "pretty well worked out his problems."

Two months later, he called, insisting on an interview on that very day. The therapist said that he would be glad to see him, but did not have an opening for two days. Mike angrily accepted the appointment. He used the session to express his sad feelings over breaking up with a girl friend he had been dating for six months. The therapist agreed that partings were sad, but indicated that he felt Mike was handling his feelings quite well. He added that he saw Mike's capacity to cry and feel sad about the breakup as evidence of emotional health and a necessary and appropriate preparation for dating again.

Mike seemed relieved. He expressed thanks for the help which the therapist had given him during treatment. When he left, he shook hands with the therapist, smiled with some wistfulness, and said, "Thanks again. You're really okay." He seemed somewhat sad and left the office rather slowly.

Therapy—Interminable

Some adolescents cannot be totally terminated. Despite the best therapeutic efforts, they are unable to manage their dependency needs without indefinite support from the therapist. This may be due to an inability to see the therapist's insistence on separation as anything other than a rejection. These patients are so convinced that they are unlovable that any attempt to terminate them is seen as a wish to be rid of them. They cannot believe any explanation of termination as a vote of confidence for them and as a bittersweet separation experience for the therapist. Dewald (1965) described the catastrophic reaction of a patient to his announcement that he was terminating her because of a move to a different city. The amazing thing was that his only contact with her in quite some time had consisted of intermittent brief telephone calls designed to monitor her medication! It is also interesting to note that the patient was able to accept the termination and to reconstitute psychologically after an interview in which she expressed her intense feelings about being left.

Schizophrenic patients, many borderline and narcissistic patients, suicidal adolescents, and other adolescents who actually have no dependable family seem especially likely to prolong therapy indefinitely. Many of these youngsters fall into the pattern we have described earlier as patients with "malignant defenses."

Ekstein (1983) has written metaphorically that to tolerate the separation involved in termination the adolescent needs a transitional object—a "teddy bear of adolescence." The more severely disturbed adolescents, Ekstein says, have unstable identifications which must be periodically restored. " . . . Whenever the teddy bear is lost, it has to be established through another phase of treatment."

The therapist may elect to reduce the frequency of therapy sessions gradually with these potentially interminable patients without pressing the issue of finalizing termination. If holding the therapist in reserve, as it were, allows the patient to make a more successful adaptation, there is no compelling need to withhold this support. It is a relatively inexpensive and harmless addiction. However, it would seem wise to reevaluate the overall situation periodically. If the patient's life situation or ego strengths improve sufficiently, it may be possible to bring him back into more frequent therapy sessions for a brief period in order to effect a true termination. Wiener's (1959) description of the results of forced termination on several chronic patients suggests we may occasionally classify patients as interminable when termination is actually possible. Pumpian-Mindlin (1958) has stated a similar opinion. Especially in the adolescent, we should make every possible effort to complete emancipation.

Unfortunate Endings

There are two situations in which termination cannot be handled as constructively as one might wish. These are the termination of unsuccessful attempts at treatment and those terminations which are caused by external events.

TERMINATION OF UNSUCCESSFUL ATTEMPTS AT THERAPY. In the termination of unsuccessful treatment contracts, those in which it has been impossible to establish a therapeutic alliance, one attempts to salvage as much as possible. Hopefully, these terminations will not be abrupt or come as a surprise to the adolescent patient. The honest therapist will have commented on the absence of a true alliance periodically during his contacts with the youngster. As we have seen earlier, the formation of the alliance is a necessary condition for dealing with other material. The therapist should avoid "going through the motions" of the therapeutic work before completing this essential task.

The patient's inability to form a therapeutic alliance should be approached sympathetically and in a spirit of benevolent inquiry, but the therapist should still make it clear that no useful work can occur without this alliance. If the patient's mistrust of others, defensive structure, or living situation makes an alliance impossible, it is preferable to admit that and suggest termination. Often, the adolescent is as frustrated as the therapist and has mentioned interruption of treatment several times himself. One can only try to make the dissolution of the therapy effort as constructive as possible. If a different treatment arrangement such as inpatient care appears indicated, this recommendation may be made to the adolescent and his parents. If the youngster's problems are less serious, it may be more advisable to part as amicably as possible, hoping that the youngster will be able to return later in a more accepting frame of mind.

Martha was referred for psychotherapy against her will when she was 13 because of poor school performance, lack of friends, and passive-aggressive behavior toward all authority figures expressed by forgetting, procrastinating, and other techniques which tormented her energetic, domineering, and compulsive parents.

Martha was the family scapegoat. Her mother persisted in efforts to organize Martha's life completely despite her inability to counter Martha's passive opposition effectively. Martha's father was openly contemptuous of her and either avoided her or slashed at her verbally. Martha preferred this treatment to her mother's worried nagging.

Martha was impossible to involve in any meaningful therapeutic alliance. She seemed terrified that she would be controlled by the therapist and defended herself by denying that she had any inner motivations and feelings. She was, she said, "a very simple person." She made fun of the therapist's comments by caricaturing them into ridiculous pseudo-Freudian nonsense. If the therapist asked about an episode of forgetting, Martha would say, "Oh, yeah. I forgot my glasses because I detest glasses. You see, I was frightened by a pair of glasses when I was a little child."

In spite of this attitude toward the work of treatment, Martha seemed to like the therapist personally and rather enjoyed her hostile bantering with him. During the few months that she was in treatment, she made some improvements in her social relationships and in getting along with her parents. Martha herself tended to deny that things had changed, and when she could not deny the changes, she made it very clear that she did not feel they were related to her contact with the therapist. Martha continually protested that she did not need treatment. The therapist finally decided that it would be wiser to accept the symptomatic improvement and stop therapy. This was done with the statement that the therapist felt Martha still had unsolved problems.

Almost three years later, the therapist was called to see Martha because of an impulsive suicide attempt. Martha had ingested poison and was in real medical danger for several days. During this time, the therapist visited her regularly in the hospital. He noted that Martha seemed less frightened of him, more relaxed, and able to be genuinely appreciative of his attention during this trying period.

Psychotherapy was reinstituted at Martha's request. Although she remained rigidly defensive, she showed some interest in understanding her emotions and was less condescending toward the therapist. Some useful therapeutic work was possible under these circumstances.

Other adolescents return to therapy much less dramatically than Martha. Often, it appears that the therapist's willingness to release them allows these youngsters to return of their own volition.

Of course, some do not return. Sometimes, one hears that they found another therapist with whom they can work more comfortably. Sometimes, one hears that they have been through several therapists without success. This may happen when the parents remain too involved in dictating the goals of therapy. It also happens when the youngster has insufficient trust and interest in other people to allow the development of any enduring human relationship.

FORCED TERMINATION. At times, therapy must be terminated because of the therapist's illness, death, or change of location. Adult patients' reactions to these losses have been well described in the literature (Ross, 1968; Dewald, 1965). The reactions of adolescents appear similar, from my observations. The response is one of grief. Anger is expressed toward any new therapist until the feelings toward the lost therapist are accepted and resolved. The patient works through his ambivalence toward the old therapist gradually and only then is able to form an attachment and a therapeutic alliance in his new treatment relationship.

SOME FINAL COMMENTS ABOUT TERMINATION

Do Not Expect A Rose

Adatto (1966) has described the narcissistic investment of the adolescent which prevents total analysis of transference during the adolescent period. From his patients who returned for analysis as adults, he also learned that he had been introjected to a surprising degree and had served as an important internal figure in the intervening years. "Analytic associations in the adult phase indicate that I not only became an object of transference but was also introjected as a new object who acted as a transition between the old and the future, growing 'organically' from the past, and actively used in restructuring and synthesizing the psychic apparatus."

I feel there is a valuable lesson for adolescent therapists in Adatto's observations. The therapist often helps his adolescent patients toward health without knowing it and certainly without their explicit acknowledgment. He is often much more important to them than they can let him know!

The adolescent does not wish to admit dependency. Still, he often takes the therapist's comments, reflective stance, and noncritical, exploratory attitude home with him. He may ignore, kid, and even deride the therapist in the office, but at home he secretly mulls everything over. He would rather, in the words of a popular television commercial, "do it himself." The therapist should be prepared to allow him that face-saving maneuver, so long as "it" gets done.

When the therapist is able to see the growth and development that may continue even after psychotherapy has officially ended, he is amply repaid for his efforts.

At Last!—The Payoff For The Therapist

As valuable byproducts of his therapeutic efforts with adolescents, the therapist may collect a broadening sense of involvement in social conflict and social change as well as a more wholesome grasp of the mutual interdependence of the generations. The need to recognize and retain the enduring human bonds which transcend cultural change and social upheaval challenges the therapist's wisdom as the searching adolescent forces him into the problems of the immediate present. Ossification and ivory tower isolation are at least delayed, if not prevented. Treating adolescents may not keep one young, but it tends to discourage the worst features of aging—the impoverishment of thought and constriction of viewpoint.

As the therapist reflects on what the adolescent has given him, perhaps he will even be able to find the strength, enthusiasm, and faith to prepare himself for the next adolescent patient. And who will replace his departing young friend? As noted earlier, the new patient will probably be an angry, devious, defended, difficult youngster who will carry little of the load of treatment for some time to come. In short, in many respects and for everyone concerned, termination is always a new beginning. The adolescent begins again, more completely self-reliant. The therapist begins again, not only with a new patient but with a new impetus to the development of his own "ego integrity" (Erikson, 1950). As he moves toward this goal, he avoids despair and the fear of death. To the extent that he succeeds, he may be able to help his adolescent patients to avoid the fear of life.

CITED AND RECOMMENDED READINGS

Adatto, C. P. 1966. On the metamorphosis from adolescence into adulthood. *Journal of the American Psychoanalytic Association.* 14: 485–509.

Blos, P. 1967. The second individuation process of adolescence. *Psychoanalytic Study of the Child.* 22: 162–186.

Buxbaum, E. 1950. Technique of terminating analysis. *Journal of Psychoanalysis.* 31: 184–190.

Corday, R. J. 1967. Limitations of therapy in adolescence. *Journal of the American Academy of Child Psychiatry.* 6: 526–538.

Dewald, P. A. 1965. Reactions to the forced termination of therapy. *Psychiatric Quarterly.* 39: 102–126.

Edelson, M. 1963. *The Termination of Intensive Psychotherapy.* Springfield, Ill.: Charles C. Thomas.

Ekstein, R. 1983. The adolescent self during the process of termination of treatment: termination, interruption, or intermission? *Adolescent Psychiatry.* 11: 125–146.

Erikson, E. H. 1950. *Childhood and Society*. New York: W. W. Norton.

Fromm-Reichmann, F. 1950. *Principles of Intensive Psychotherapy*. Chicago: University of Chicago Press.

Hiatt, H. 1965. The problem of termination of psychotherapy. *American Journal of Psychotherapy*. 19: 607–615.

Keniston, K. 1970. We have much to learn from youth. *American Journal of Psychiatry*. 126: 1767–1768.

Menninger, K. 1958. *Theory of Psychoanalytic Technique*. New York: Basic Books.

Pearson, G. H. J. 1958. *Adolescence and the Conflict of Generations*. New York: W. W. Norton.

Pumpian-Mindlin, E. 1958. Comments on techniques of termination and transfer in a clinic setting. *American Journal of Psychotherapy*. 12: 455–464.

Pumpian-Mindlin, E. 1965. Omnipotentiality, youth and commitment. *Journal of the American Academy of Child Psychiatry*. 4: 1–18.

Ross, W. D. 1968. Persisting transference after interrupted psychoanalyses and other therapeutic relationships. *Comprehensive Psychiatry*. 9: 327–343.

Sigafoos, A. D., et al. 1988. The measurement of behavioral autonomy in adolescence: the autonomous functioning checklist. *Adolescent Psychiatry*. 15: 432–462.

Wender, P. H. 1968. Vicious and virtuous circles: the role of deviation amplifying feedback (DAF) in the origin and perpetuation of behavior. *Psychiatry*. 31: 309–324.

Part
Two

introduction

This section of the book deals with special problems which may be encountered in the psychotherapy of adolescents. These topics are discussed separately to allow elaboration of the technical complications introduced by extreme behavior patterns. The suicidal adolescent, for example, requires particular precautions and introduces unique countertransference issues. These were largely omitted in Part One in order to avoid tangential excursions which might have detracted from the continuity of the presentation. Despite the separation of syndromes in Part Two, the basic techniques described earlier apply in these special cases as well as in the more "average" case.

Many of the topics discussed in Part Two are more controversial than the general treatment approaches described in Part One. Where disagreement does exist, we have tried to mention the points of controversy and to include bibliography references which may be consulted for more thorough explication. We have generally tried to offer a more complete bibliography on the specialized topics, since the experience of any one therapist with these cases is usually limited. One must rely heavily on the reported experiences of colleagues.

Part Two is intended primarily as a beginning reference source for the therapist when he is confronted with a case involving one of the symptom complexes which are covered here. The chapters are self-contained and may be read in isolation from one another.

As in Part One, we have generally recommended one specific approach as the best method of dealing with each clinical situation. In treating these difficult and complicated problems, suggesting that one technical method is best is even more risky than in the discussion of general techniques. As in Part One, the suggested "right" approach should be viewed as an orienting statement. Each therapist must think out his own philosophy and technique, utilizing only that portion of the approach described here which seems comfortable and useful in his own work. If our "orientation" serves to catalyze this thinking process in the individual therapist, it will have served its intended purpose.

CHAPTER 11

the adolescent at school

School, with all of its academic, behavioral, and social ramifications, is the adolescent's work world. For better or for worse, his life at school is the single most important parameter that defines the youngster's intellectual ability, physical skills, social competence, his ability to separate from parents, and his finesse in coping with rules and adult authority. The adolescent's sense of self-esteem depends on his success at school and the things related to school, such as sports and activities with peers. The school experience is so encompassing that it touches on countless facets of the adolescent in psychotherapy. We are addressing a few of these, focusing on school performance evaluation as a diagnostic tool; school refusal; learning disabilities; and attention-deficit hyperactivity disorder in adolescence.

SCHOOL AS MICROCOSM

It is easy to start an evaluation of an adolescent by asking him about school—his grade; his schedule; his teachers; extra-curricular activities; athletic accomplishments. What does he consider his best subject and why is it the best and what are they studying right now in that subject? What does he consider his worst subject and why is it the worst and what are they studying now in that subject? Is there a drug problem in his school? How does he get to school? Whom does he sit with on the bus?

School is a good topic with which to initiate the evaluation process for several reasons. First, the youngster sees this as a natural line of questioning. Since school is such a big part of his life, the examiner seems like a normal person to want to get that information first. Maybe, the youngster thinks, shrinks aren't so weird after all!

Second, most adolescents find these questions to be easy to deal with. Even if school happens to be an area of great difficulty, it is still relatively easy for a teenager to answer matter-of-fact questions about his daily schedule and his likes and dislikes about high school.

The third reason that school is a good initial topic is the most important: a discussion about high school can be an extended in vivo projective test. The examiner can learn a lot from what the adolescent says about his fellow students, since he may project his own opinions and feelings onto them. When he describes his teachers or the school's administrative staff, he may be displacing feelings about his parents. When he tells you how he reacts to the frustrations of plane geometry, he is revealing a little piece of his world-view and his style of responding to challenge.

Another approach is to talk about a movie about school. For instance, *The Breakfast Club* was a popular movie about five stereotypical adolescents who had to show up on Saturday morning for detention. Almost every American teenager was willing to identify with one or another of these characters and could address in some detail the social relationships among the students in the movie.

It is easy to guide the initial interview from the topic of school to almost any other subject. With a little imagination the therapist can find a transition from some aspect of school to a discussion of drugs and alcohol, sexuality, depression, family issues, or whatever. The therapist may want to come back to the subject of school and education toward the close of the interview. At that point it may be good to inquire about the future, what the patient is going to be doing after graduation, what his aspirations may be for employment or for college. This is not only a nice way to tie up an evaluation interview and to move on from the immediate imbroglio to thinking about the promise that the future holds, it also gives valuable information about your patient. Does she have a vocational ambition? Can he imagine himself as an adult? . . . as a husband? . . . as a parent?

This chapter addresses several clinical aspects of the adolescent's life at school. We will discuss school refusal. We will consider the adolescent who has a learning disability or attention-deficit hyperactivity disorder. We will discuss the role of alternative schools and will refer to the relationship between the therapist and school personnel.

SCHOOL REFUSAL

"School refusal" is simply a phrase that indicates a particular piece of behavior, i.e., nonattendance at school. It is not a diagnosis and it is not a syndrome. It is a symptom that warrants a diagnostic evaluation and it turns out that there are several possible causes. Although we generalize reluctantly, the underlying explanation or the dynamics of the school refusal are frequently related to the developmental level of the child:

—Young children in elementary school have trouble going to school because of separation anxiety, which has been called school phobia. They are afraid of the insecurity associated with being away from the parents.

—Early adolescence is approximately the years of junior high school, the seventh and eighth grades. These youngsters stay home from school because they are afraid of what will or what they fantasize will happen at school. They are usually afraid of the challenges of peer relations that arise in early adolescence. They usually have expanded mundane early adolescent concerns into major problems: that other kids won't like them, that they will be picked on, that something is wrong with their bodies, that they will be exposed as mentally and physically incompetent.

—Middle adolescence is approximately the years of high school, especially the ninth to the eleventh grades. When these youngsters refuse to go to school, it may be necessary to sort out whether the school refusal is simply truancy, which has a delinquent bent to it, or is phobic in nature. The truant adolescent avoids both school and home and is usually out in the neighborhood with friends. The phobic adolescent avoids going to school and stays home by himself. Truancy often comes as a surprise to parents, while they are usually well aware of their youngster's fears and phobic concerns.

Phobias and Fears

While "school refusal" usually implies only a piece of behavior, the term "school phobia" refers to a particular syndrome with its own pattern of symptoms, individual dynamics, and family pathology. Coolidge (1960, 1974, 1979) and his colleagues at the Judge Baker Guidance Center in Boston studied many children and adolescents with school phobia. They felt that the fundamental dynamics in all the age groups were basically the same. That is, the children and adolescents were comfortable when close to the parents, especially the mother, and they were reluctant to give up their dependence in order to advance along the line of separation and psychological autonomy. This symptom in a younger child was frequently an acute impasse and yielded to active treatment. In fact, the long-term outcome was related more to the depth of the counseling with the mother than it was to the nature or duration of the treatment of the child. However, Coolidge found that the occurrence of school phobia in an adolescent was more ominous because these patients had more fixed personality traits and were resistant to treatment. In the case of adolescents, the patient and the parent may conspire for years to avoid true emotional separation, but this pathological collusion may not be recognized until overt symptomatology occurs in adolescence.

Mogul (1969) used the symptom of school refusal to show that a particular piece of behavior may have been determined by completely opposite dynamics. He presented four adolescent boys, all of whom avoided school or refused to attend school. "Yet in two of the four cases, this behavior signified the failure to relinquish infantile object ties resulting in failure of further growth or in regression. In the other two cases, the same overt behavior had just the opposite significance: it was directly in the service of freeing these adolescents from early object ties and dependence to create an identity as an independent adult." For instance, one of the boys avoided going to school and stayed home with his mother and played with his younger brother. On the other hand, another youngster refused to continue school in a college preparatory program because he wanted to move on with his own nonacademic ambition of becoming a forester or a farmer. Mogul pointed out that it would not make sense to provide the same therapy for both of these adolescents. In the case of the first boy, who had the traditional form of school phobia, the goals of therapy would be to help him achieve psychological independence and also to stay in school. In the case of the second youngster, who was in the process of achieving psychological independence, the goal of therapy would be to help the parents accept that their son might not be going to college.

The person with a phobia is afraid of something in his mind; the person with a fear is afraid of something in the real world. In addition to being phobic, there are other reasons why an adolescent may manifest school refusal. He may simply be afraid of real bullies who control the day-to-day life at that particular high school. He may have an unrecognized learning disability, which has convinced him over the years that school is a perpetually frustrating and disheartening experience. He may be experiencing prepsychotic confusion and is protecting his fragile ego from any stimulation he can avoid.

Outpatient Treatment of School Phobia

The treatment of school refusal first requires the therapist to consider some or all of the possible patterns described and to make a specific diagnosis. The treatments for drug abuse, conduct disorder, psychosis, and other causes of school avoidance are discussed elsewhere in this book. In this chapter we will focus on the treatment of the dependent adolescent who is overly anxious about dealing with the tasks of adolescence and fearfully over-attached to home and parents.

The ideal therapy regimen for these youngsters includes family therapy, individual therapy, and an adolescent therapy group. The family meetings allow the therapist to observe first hand what happens among the family members and also provide an opportunity to make sure that everybody understands the priorities in the treatment process. It may be helpful to use the family meetings to discuss changes in the parents' roles. For instance, suppose the patient's mother is easily manipulated or easily swayed by the adolescent's demands for dependency. It might work for the father to be more involved with the youngster's school attendance. That is, it could be the father who drops the patient off at school in the morning and it could be the father who takes the calls from the school nurse when the patient feels ill.

In individual therapy, the youngster and the therapist can explore the details of the student's ambivalence about growing up. Participation in a well-functioning therapy group can be very helpful. The group members can give the school-phobic youngster a good deal of support and helpful advice about how to cope with the real-life difficulties of high school life as well as a model for more independent functioning. In the process, the school-phobic patient may use the group to learn how to develop sincere and mutually satisfying peer relationships.

The therapist will need to consider other aspects of treating the school phobic adolescent. It is almost always important to maintain a dialogue with the high school guidance counselor. The counselor will be delighted to hear from you and will be able to give you some valuable information. For example, if the teenager has been telling you that her third period French teacher is an intolerant and sadistic person, the counselor may be able to give you a second opinion. Also, it may be helpful to work out a "back-to-school" program for the phobic adolescent in which it is clear that the patient absolutely must go to school every day, but at the beginning will only go to two periods of class. After a week or so, the expectation would be to attend three periods, and so on. At the beginning it may work better if the adolescent is told that all she has to do is show up and sit in the classroom and that the teacher will not have any expectation of her to perform. As the youngster accommodates, the expectations are raised. In order for any kind of program like this to work, it is important to have a clear understanding between the guidance counselor, the teachers, the student, the parents, and the therapist.

Many phobic patients and their parents ask that the student be put on home-bound teaching, in which the city or county school department sends a teacher to the student's house for several hours each week and the student is thereby excused from attending school. That is usually not a good idea, since it simply makes it easier to avoid addressing and resolving the underlying issues. Some schools do arrange for "home-bound instruction," but that means that the student is tutored individually in a separate room at the school itself and not really at home.

Some school phobic youngsters become extremely anxious, to the point of having the symptoms of a panic attack. They are certainly unhappy and frequently chronically depressed. The depression is derived from realizing that they are not functioning to the level that they should and also that they are being asked to give up the comfortable and comforting tie to the mother. Both the panic attacks and the depression may respond to anti-depressant medication.

The therapist should have a sense for timing and for setting priorities in treating school phobic adolescents. In the initial phase of therapy it is desirable to try a crisis intervention approach. That is, convey at the outset that it is important for the youngster to be back in school. It is his "job" to be in school every day and it is important to keep up with the assignments, whether or not he is attending class. Point out that it will be good for his sense of self-esteem and will give him a feeling of mastery if he overcomes his fears and stays in school. In a later phase of therapy, while the patient is attending school at least part of the time, you can explore what makes it so hard to be at school and the underlying reasons for the anxiety.

Alternatives to Outpatient Treatment

Other treatment interventions should be considered, if there is no progress with outpatient therapy or if the clinical situation is especially difficult:

—inpatient treatment on an adolescent psychiatry unit that has a good school program, if the youngster has been out of school for several weeks and is resistant to outpatient therapy.

—a psychiatric day treatment program, if both the parents and the patient are motivated for treatment, but the youngster is too disabled to continue at his regular school.

—transfer to another high school or a private school or an alternative school, if it seems clear that the school refusal was caused by the students or the teachers or the circumstances of the original school. Students who refuse school may say that all they need is a fresh start in a new school, and sometimes they are right.

—referral to a residential treatment center, if further evaluation reveals that the youngster will need prolonged physical separation from home in order to accomplish true psychological separation.

School Refusal in Other Syndromes

The behavior of school refusal may not represent school phobia at all, but may be the top of a totally different iceberg. For instance, it may be learned through clinical evaluation that the school refusal is a manifestation of incipient psychosis. In that case the therapist would not be encouraging the youngster to return to school immediately, but would be considering psychotropic medication and perhaps hospitalization. If the school avoidance is a result of continuing drug and alcohol abuse, the therapist should consider referral to an adolescent chemical dependency program. If the problem is chronic truancy and the parents are unsuccessful at disciplining their child, the therapist should think about involving the legal system, in the guise of a probation officer.

ADOLESCENTS WITH LEARNING DISABILITIES

Concern for children and adolescents with learning disabilities is one of those issues that has touched many professional disciplines. The first person to describe these syndromes in a systematic manner was a neuropsychiatrist, Samuel Orton (1937). Another prominent individual in this field has been a pediatrician, Melvin Levine, who spent a career studying learning disabilities and educating the public about them. Levine (1987, 1989) has organized a comprehensive and elegant summary of the neurodevelopmental functions which need to interact effectively for a child to learn. A child psychiatrist, Larry Silver (1979, 1989), has insisted that professionals must think holistically in order to understand fully clients with learning disabilities. He states that it is necessary to consider many variables, such as "the constitutional and neurological substrate; intrapsychic and interpersonal dynamics; learned behaviors; and family and other significant system interactions." In other words, the basic neurological problem alone cannot explain the entire symptom picture in these youngsters and treatment may need to be multifaceted.

DSM-III-R uses the following categories for specific developmental disorders, which is the official terminology for learning disabilities:

—Academic skills disorders
    Developmental arithmetic disorder
    Developmental expressive writing disorder
    Developmental reading disorder
—Language and speech disorders
    Developmental articulation disorder
    Developmental expressive language disorder
    Developmental receptive language disorder
—Motor skills disorder
    Developmental coordination disorder

In general, the first criterion in *DSM-III-R* is that the achievement level, as measured by a standardized, individually administered test, is markedly below the expected level, given the person's schooling and intellectual capacity. The second criterion cited in *DSM-III-R* is that the disturbance or defect significantly interferes with the person's functioning in that specific area.

Learning disabilities may also be classified according to the nature of the dysfunction. These include perceptual problems (that is, an impairment in the processing of sensory inputs), cognitive problems (an impairment in the integration of these inputs), memory problems, language problems, and motor problems. Some major texts on this subject have been edited or written by Benton (1978), Gaddes (1985), Hund (1983), Mosse (1982), and Myklebust (1971). Silver (1984) published a book which is primarily intended for the parents of learning-disabled children and adolescents. It summarized the laws that pertain to educational placement. Certo (1984) published a book primarily for educators, which advocates that handicapped youngsters should be in the same setting as nonhandicapped students.

Case Example

Learning disabilities are usually first noticed in elementary school, because the child's academic achievement is below what would be expected from his overall intelligence. School personnel do screening tests to see if the child's actual achievement is at least two years below his expected level. As appropriate, more detailed tests are performed to determine if a specific learning disability is handicapping the child. It is unusual for a learning-disabled youngster to reach adolescence before his condition has been evaluated, but sometimes it happens. One problem is that special education teachers are trained to work with younger children and some may not know what to do with the learning disabled teenager.

Jeff was a 14-year-old ninth grade student who was underachieving and was very unhappy. His parents were very frustrated because of what they perceived to be chronic, willful disobedience. The father was a businessman who was transferred frequently, so the family traveled and Jeff had been in several schools, including two that were overseas. He was never in any school long enough to be both noticed and evaluated.

Jeff was brought for psychiatric evaluation because his extreme passive-aggressive behavior was interfering with his school work. Jeff would sit quietly in class, but would flatly refuse to respond to the teacher's questions or do any written work. Some days he would spend his time in class reading quietly to himself—not magazines or comic books, but novels. He occasionally did homework, but would not turn it in.

Jeff also refused to participate in the psychiatric evaluation. After his mother parked the car, Jeff bolted from the parking lot. He did agree to be in an adolescent therapy group, which he perceived as less threatening, and he later became willing to see the therapist individually to complete the evaluation. Although Jeff was friendly and tried to be cooperative, he frequently withdrew into passivity. When he spoke, he had trouble expressing himself in a smooth, fluent manner. He enjoyed reading and listening, but it was hard for Jeff to communicate verbally, whether orally or in writing.

The psychiatrist referred Jeff and the parents to a tutor who specialized in evaluating and teaching children with learning disabilities. The tutor's evaluation clearly demonstrated Jeff's handicap in expressive language. The tutor continued to work with Jeff and she became the first person to really understand how to communicate with him. In a sense, the psychotherapy became adjunctive to the educational therapy.

What the Therapist Can Do

The therapist can begin helping the youngster with a learning disability in several ways by helping him understand his cognitive strengths and weaknesses. One way to do this is to obtain a copy of the educational testing and go over it with the patient in some detail. This can start the process of helping the adolescent to accept and understand how his own style of perceiving, organizing, and expressing information is different from the way other people do it. It is hard for a teenager to understand a deficit, when he never experienced the function in the first place. Once understood, it may also be hard to accept. Denial can be very powerful. For example, one adolescent who was color blind refused to believe that there really were other colors until he was informed that he could not enter naval pilot school because he could not read the numbers on the Ishihara cards.

Once there is an alliance, you can help the youngster find ways to compensate for his areas of weakness. When you get down to details of designing an educational strategy, this needs to be done by an educator who understands learning disabilities. But it is

The Association for Children and Adults with Learning Disabilities (ACLD) is a national, nonprofit organization with almost a thousand local chapters. Its purpose is to advance the education and general well-being of children and adults with learning disabilities and attention disorders. It is useful to refer patients and parents to this organization, if they want more information or the support of individuals with similar concerns. The address of the national office of ACLD is 4156 Library Road, Pittsburgh, PA 15234.

within the realm of the psychotherapist to make some suggestions: that the youngster who has impossible handwriting might save up for a typewriter, preferably one that automatically checks the spelling; that the youngster with poor memory should always write his assignments in a notebook. You might also help the adolescent plan for his future in terms of his strengths, rather than his weak areas. A person with really poor fine motor coordination should think about becoming a psychiatrist rather than a dentist.

Therapy with youngsters who are learning disabled usually is supportive and somewhat didactic. These adolescents need extra help to learn information that other teenagers come by automatically. For instance, these boys and girls have a tendency to be out of touch in many ways, including their awareness of sexuality. They tend to be naive and do not pick up incidental information the way most teenagers do. These youngsters need extra help in learning social skills—how to act, talk, and dress. The learning disabled adolescent may become lonely and depressed because he is uncertain about these matters.

The therapist plays a crucial role in helping the adolescent work through the narcissistic injury inherent in accepting anything other than perfection. This is aided by finding ways to enhance self-esteem, which usually takes the form of identifying and then capitalizing on the youngster's God-given abilities. In the case of Jeff, the boy with the severe impairment in expressive language, it came to the therapist's attention that he was within three merit badges of becoming an Eagle Scout. He obviously had some sense of ambition and perseverance which needed to be encouraged.

Another way to give a youngster permission to think positively about himself is to mention important or popular people who have also had learning problems. We don't know if Albert Einstein had a learning disability—but he did fail to receive his diploma from secondary school because he did so poorly in history, geography, and languages. Some contemporary examples of individuals who have done very well, despite having some form of learning disability, are Cher, Tom Cruise, and Magic Johnson.

ATTENTION-DEFICIT HYPERACTIVITY DISORDER

What becomes of hyperactive children? What happens to all the children with attention-deficit hyperactivity disorder when they grow up? Some of those hyperactive children were treated with medication and with other interventions, such as behavior modification approaches, and did well. As they matured physically, the attention deficits seemed less of a problem and they were able to continue into adolescence without any further treatment. On the other hand, many hyperactive children grow into problematic adolescents and eventually into irritable, irascible adults.

It is important for therapists who work with adolescents to appreciate the long-term course of attention-deficit hyperactivity disorder. In order to understand why we say that, think of yourself seeing an adolescent for an initial assessment who is impulsive and who is not goal-directed and who is unhappy with his accomplishments. It is one thing if those symptoms have developed over the last few months because of some external stressor. It is altogether something different if the adolescent has been distractible and impulsive since early childhood. If that is the case, he has come to believe that he is not able to be as successful as other teenagers.

The natural history of attention-deficit hyperactivity disorder has been studied by Gabrielle Weiss and her colleagues (Hoy, 1978; Hechtman, 1982; Weiss, 1985). These three references

Gabrielle Weiss, M.D., is professor of psychiatry at McGill University and also director the Department of Psychiatry at The Montreal Children's Hospital. She had the foresight in the 1960s to undertake a prospective study of hyperactive children. Weiss (1985) and her collaborators (Hoy, 1978; Hechtman, 1982) evaluated this group of patients and the matched controls when originally referred prior to puberty, during mid-adolescence, during late adolescence, and as adults. They were able to document the natural course of attention-deficit hyperactivity disorder.

represent three stages of the same longitudinal study. That is, a group of hyperactive children were re-evaluated at early adolescence, during late adolescence, and at young adulthood. The first follow-up occurred when the cohort of hyperactive patients had reached a mean age of 14. At that point they were still having many difficulties. Although they were less hyperactive than previously, they continued to be more restless than controls, distractible, emotionally immature, unable to maintain goals, and had developed poor self-esteem. Compared to matched controls, the hyperactive youngsters had failed more grades and had lower ratings in all subjects on report cards. The hyperactive teenagers continued to be impulsive rather than reflective. About 25% were involved in antisocial behavior, which was higher than matched controls.

The second follow-up occurred when the cohort of hyperactive children had reached a mean age of 19. At that point the research team found that there were three categories of outcomes. Roughly 30-40% of the research subjects had a fairly normal outcome, in that they were working or in school full-time; they had an acceptable work history; enjoyed stable friendships; and did not feel unusually lonely or isolated. Another 40-50% of the subjects had significant social, emotional, and impulsive problems. This group reported an unstable work history; disagreements with peers or supervisors; frequent moves, which were often sudden and impulsive; and they lacked long-standing, close relationships with either sex. About 10% of the original subjects were seriously disturbed at this follow-up during late adolescence. Their disturbance was manifested by either psychiatric disturbance or antisocial behavior. They reported much unemployment; jail terms; admission to psychiatric hospitals; a lack of intimate friends and sometimes even a lack of acquaintances; and serious depressions with suicide attempts.

Wender (1987) and Crabtree (1981) also described their work with adolescents with hyperactivity and minimal brain dysfunction. Crabtree pointed out that it is important to diagnose the condition, because it helps the therapist understand the patient and to empathize with the unique experience of the self as damaged, defective, and helpless to control the forces and interferences within. The therapist should recognize the patient's need for structure and for explanations that are concrete and expressed in relatively simple terms.

The use of medication such as Ritalin (methylphenidate) or Cylert (pemoline) should be considered on an individual basis. Some adolescents and also adults with attention-deficit hyperactivity disorder continue to respond to these medications. Care should be taken because of the possibility that an adolescent patient or his friends might abuse these medications. Medication should not be prescribed unless the therapist believes that the patient will use it responsibly and will accurately report its effects.

Paul was a 16-year-old high school junior who came for psychiatric evaluation because of academic underachievement. He was failing several courses. Although he claimed to study hard, he just couldn't perform well enough to please his parents, especially his father. Paul's father was a successful business executive who expected his family members to operate in a timely and efficient manner. There was a continuing battle between Paul and his father. In fact, this family dynamic was so striking that the therapist concluded that Paul was asserting himself and rebelling in the safest way available, by pretending to study but by not accomplishing anything.

The therapist developed this formulation and explained his observations and interpretations to Paul, who listened politely but remained doubtful. The therapist held family meetings in order to help Paul and his father understand each other better and to collaborate in finding a solution to the problem of Paul's underachievement. In the course of these family meetings Paul tried to explain his subjective experience when he was in class and when he tried to study at home. He described how he simply couldn't stay on the task, that extraneous details would intrude on his concentration. It eventually dawned on the therapist that Paul was describing one form of attention-deficit hyperactivity disorder.

The possibility of a trial of medication was discussed with Paul and his father. They both were intrigued by the notion that the psychiatrist might be on to something and they agreed. Ritalin was prescribed and the result was dramatically positive. Paul found that he could concentrate and began to enjoy reading and assimilating the material that he had been studying so hard. His grades improved significantly and continued at a satisfactory level through his junior and senior year. Paul's achievement in chemistry went up so suddenly that his teacher thought he was cheating.

The ongoing battle between Paul and his father was the result, rather than the cause, of his underachievement. As they stopped arguing about his poor grades, Paul and his father became able to respect each other and enjoy their relationship.

ALTERNATIVE SCHOOL PLACEMENTS

There is no easy way to predict exactly which students are going to do well in different school programs. In this chapter we will express some general guidelines, but in practice it becomes necessary to talk to school personnel and to know something about their educational goals and philosophies. Some therapists are good at matching up a specific client with an appropriate educational program, especially if the therapist has taken the time to visit and become familiar with the schools available in her community.

Public Schools

City and county school departments are responsible for providing an appropriate education for all students in their jurisdictions, including the handicapped children. The United States law defining that responsibility is Public Law 94-142. It is the basis for the rules and regulations which the various states have established. The selection of the special education services for a particular child depends on the nature and severity of the problem. For instance, an adolescent with a relatively minor learning disability might be placed in a resource room for one or two of his class periods each day, where he will receive individualized help with basic skills and with homework assignments. A youngster with a more profound learning disability will spend less time in the mainstream classes and more time in a self-contained program for students with similar disabilities.

Likewise, a student with a serious emotional problem may be placed in a self-contained program for children with emotional disorders. Since learning disorders and emotional disorders frequently occur in the same group of students, some school departments have large special education programs which deal with both learning problems and emotional problems. In any case, school personnel are responsible for identifying the students who need a special program, for evaluating these students, and for placing them in appropriate educational settings. Most school personnel are happy to receive any input that the youngster's therapist may wish to offer regarding this decision.

Private Schools

Sometimes parents wonder if their child would do better in a private school or a parochial school. There are many reasons why a family might want to choose a private school, most of which do not have anything to do with emotional or psychological issues.

The parents may feel that their child will have a more rigorous education at a private school and then move on to a better college. They may feel that it would be less likely that their child would be exposed to drugs and violence and sex at a private school. The parents may be motivated by social reasons or geographic convenience or by family tradition.

Some private schools have features which are particularly helpful for adolescents with certain psychological needs. For instance, a youngster who is quite timid might do better in a school which is small and where virtually every student is automatically included in recreational and social events. A student who is on the lackadaisical or even irresponsible side might do well in a school with small classes where the teachers are able to keep on his case. A student with a learning disability, but not severe enough for the public school system to notice, might do better in a private school where faculty members are interested in disabled students and have a reputation for creative teaching.

Boarding Schools

In a similar vein, there are a number of reasons why normal parents might want to send their normal children to boarding school. Most commonly, they feel that there are academic and social advantages. Also, many boarding schools offer a sense of discipline and mission and comradeship which may be hard to find in the local community high school.

There are also clinical situations where the best treatment is to go to a good boarding school. For instance, consider a youngster in an enmeshed family who is not addressing any of the issues and tasks of adolescence, because he is so tied up in a hostile and dependent relationship with his parents. In his heart, that boy is going to want to stay home and argue with his mother and will be able to come up with numerous reasons why home is best for him. In his head, however, the same patient will be able to understand on an intellectual level that he needs to find some way to grow up. The therapist may want to promote the patient's psychological growth by recommending a good boarding school.

It might be possible to continue seeing the patient during vacations, to monitor and encourage the process of separation and individuation.

Another reason to consider a boarding school is to get the youngster out of a contentious, inflammatory situation at home. That is what happened with Tyrone:

> Tyrone was a 16-year-old tenth grader, whose mother dragged him in for a psychiatric evaluation. Tyrone was almost out of control. He was furious at his mother and verbally abused her. Some of his anger had a paranoid quality to it. He refused to follow any form of reasonable discipline. He was accomplishing nothing at school.
>
> Tyrone's parents had separated and were in the midst of an extremely angry divorce. The parents made endless accusations against each other. The father came in to participate in the evaluation. He was a dogmatic, opinionated, and physically overwhelming man. He expressed the opinion that he could successfully supervise and discipline Tyrone if he were just given a chance. Tyrone insisted on living with his mother and told the therapist that he had plans to run away to another state, if he had to live with his father.
>
> The psychiatrist recommended intensive therapy for Tyrone and counseling for the parents, in order to help the parents leave the boy out of their battle. The psychiatrist advised the family that hospitalization would be necessary if Tyrone were not able to control himself. At that point the parents precipitously and unexpectedly agreed on one thing, that Tyrone should go to a boarding school. Tyrone seemed relieved at the prospect of getting out of the war zone. The psychiatrist was skeptical about that plan, because he doubted that the boy's anger and mental disorganization would be cured by a simple change of environment.
>
> Several months later Tyrone was home for Christmas vacation and saw the psychiatrist. Tyrone was doing fine. He described the rigid, no-nonsense school in glowing terms. His mother confirmed that the staff at the school were quite complimentary about Tyrone's behavior and school work.

Tyrone spoke most highly of his track coach, whom he idolized. Tyrone was introduced to long-distance running and he had become a fanatical runner. He became the best cross-country runner in his school and he competed successfully in regional and state events. He suggested that the psychiatrist take up running as a way to get a healthy, nonchemical high.

Tyrone was lucky. His "referral" to boarding school allowed him to get out of an extremely stressful situation. The school provided good role models and a chance to sublimate his major emotional conflicts.

For an adolescent, school can make you or break you. School can be the best part of your life or the worst part. The therapist can take a school history as one indicator of the student's success at the basic tasks of adolescence. The therapist should make sure that the treatment plan includes helping the adolescent be successful at school and at work. Succeeding in a good school can help the adolescent compensate for losses or defects in other parts of his life.

CITED AND RECOMMENDED READINGS

Benton, A. L., and D. Pearl. 1978. *Dyslexia: An Appraisal of Current Knowledge.* New York: Oxford University Press.

Certo, N., et al., editors. 1984. *Public School Integration of Severely Handicapped Students.* Baltimore: Paul H. Brookes Publishing.

Coolidge, J. C., et al. 1960. School phobia in adolescence: a manifestation of severe character disturbance. *American Journal of Orthopsychiatry.* 30: 599–607.

Coolidge, J. C. 1974. Observations of mothers of 49 school-phobic children evaluated in a 10-year follow-up study. *Journal of the American Academy of Child Psychiatry.* 13: 275–285.

Coolidge, J. C. 1979. School phobia. In: *Basic Handbook of Child Psychiatry, Volume Two,* edited by J. D. Noshpitz. New York: Basic Books.

Crabtree, L. H. 1981. Minimal brain dysfunction in adolescents and young adults: diagnostic and therapeutic perspectives. *Adolescent Psychiatry.* 9: 307–320.

Gaddes, W. H. 1985. *Learning Disabilities and Brain Function: A Neuropsychological Approach,* second edition. New York: Springer-Verlag New York, Inc.

Hechtman, L., et al. 1981. Hyperactives as young adults: various clinical outcomes. *Adolescent Psychiatry*. 9: 295–306.

Hoy, E., et al. 1978. The hyperactive child at adolescence: emotional and social functioning. *Journal of Abnormal Child Psychology*. 6: 311–324.

Hynd, G., and M. Cohen. 1983. *Dyslexia: Neuropsychological Theory, Research, and Clinical Differentiation*. New York: Grune & Stratton.

Levine, M. D. 1987. *Developmental Variation and Learning Disorders*. Cambridge, Massachusetts: Educators Publishing Service.

Levine, M. D. 1989. Learning disabilities at twenty-five: the early adulthood of a maturing concept. *Learning Disabilities: A Multidisciplinary Journal*. 1: 1–11.

Mogul, S. L. 1969. Clinical assessment of adolescent development. *Seminars in Psychiatry*. 1: 24–31.

Mosse, L. 1982. *The Complete Handbook of Children's Reading Disorders: A Critical Evaluation of Their Clinical, Educational, and Social Dimensions*. New York: Human Sciences Press.

Myklebust, H. R., editor. 1971. *Progress in Learning Disabilities*. New York: Grune & Stratton.

Orton, S. T. 1937. *Reading, Writing and Speech Problems in Children*. New York: W. W. Norton & Co.

Silver, L. B. 1979. Children with perceptual and other learning problems. *Basic Handbook of Child Psychiatry, Volume Three*, edited by J. D. Noshpitz. New York: Basic Books.

Silver, L. B. 1984. *The Misunderstood Child*. New York: McGraw-Hill.

Silver, L. B. 1989. Psychological and family problems associated with learning disabilities: assessment and intervention. *Journal of the American Academy of Child and Adolescent Psychiatry*. 28: 319–325.

Sugar, M. 1987. Diagnostic aspects of underachievement in adolescents. *Adolescent Psychiatry*. 14: 427–440.

Weiss, G., et al. 1985. Psychiatric status of hyperactives as adults: a controlled prospective 15-year follow-up of 63 hyperactive children. *Journal of the American Academy of Child Psychiatry*. 24: 211–220.

Wender, P. 1987. *The Hyperactive Child, Adolescent and Adult: Attention Deficit Disorder through the Lifespan*. New York: Oxford University Press.

CHAPTER 12

depression, suicidal threats, and suicidal behavior

Suicide is an important cause of death during adolescent years even without counting those "deaths due to accidental cause" which may be consciously or unconsciously suicidal. A case in point is the mortality rate compiled by motorcyclists. Nicholi (1970) has explored the dynamics involved in this particular self-destructive behavior.

The suicide rate among adolescents, especially white male adolescents, has increased markedly over the last thirty years. During the 1950's about 4 out of every 100,000 adolescents (ages 15 through 24) committed suicide each year. During the 1980's the incidence of suicide among adolescents had risen to more than 12 per 100,000. The rate among white adolescents and young adults is even higher, over 20 per 100,000. Some groups of Native American adolescents also have a disproportionately high rate of suicide. It is upsetting to note that these figures begin to approach the rate for elderly white males (over 40 per 100,000 population).

A number of theories have been advanced to explain the increase in adolescent suicides but none has been definitely proven. The most commonly mentioned factors include the demographic increase in numbers of adolescents; the general emotional state of the culture; the increase in drug and alcohol abuse among adolescents; and factors such as greater mobility and divorce, which interrupt effective family functioning and therefore the nurture of the adolescent. The population cohort of the baby boom generation has generally shown an increased incidence of depression and suicide (Klerman, 1989), not merely an increase in absolute numbers. Using a demographic model, Holinger

318

(1982, 1989) predicted that the suicide rate among adolescents and also the juvenile crime rates would level off or fall during the 1980s and 1990s.

FACTORS WHICH AMELIORATE SUICIDE POTENTIAL IN DEPRESSED ADOLESCENTS

It is perhaps surprising that the rate of suicide attempts and successful suicides is as low as is estimated. The threat of object loss and punitive superego pressures, two important dynamic factors in suicidal behavior, are virtually endemic to adolescence. Suicidal ideation and fantasies of glorious death are probably extremely common among young people. Possibly, many adolescents are protected from their self-destructive impulses by a combination of felt parental concern and the relative ease with which new relationships can be formed during the period.

Another factor, to which we alluded in an earlier chapter, is the adolescent's alloplastic avoidance of depressive affect. The tendency toward depression is probably basic to many of the emotional disorders observed during adolescence. Certainly, it plays a major role in many delinquent behavior disorders, drug abuse, the runaway, and learning problems. This depression is related primarily to the state of object deficiency which accompanies the necessary decathexis of parental introjects. Often, the delinquent behaviors which serve as defenses against depression are clearly self-destructive "little suicides." Very frequently, they are accompanied by a conscious sense of self-loathing. The adolescent says, "I don't care what happens to me," but his behavior suggests that the unspoken conclusion of the statement is, "but I hope it's something terrible."

Morrison and Collier (1969) have pointed out the multiplicity of symptoms in adolescents who were referred to their emergency service because of suicide attempts. The authors regarded "school refusal and truancy; sexual promiscuity, occasionally associated with pregnancy; boredom and withdrawal, a variety of physical symptoms; compulsive hyperactivity; threats of physical assault; runaway; and the use of drugs or alcohol" as "associated symptoms of depression" in their cases. Interestingly, suicide attempts were the most frequent reason for referral to their emergency service, a finding which was duplicated in a similar program in Cleveland (Mattsson et al., 1969). Both studies emphasized the role of family disruption in precipitating the suicidal behavior.

It is important to remember, however, that not all acting out is "masked" depression. Depressed youngsters may show their discomfort by acting out but other youngsters act out for different reasons. In any case, even youngsters who present primarily with behavioral symptoms have clear cut depressive symptomatology which can be discovered by appropriate evaluation when depression is actually the basic problem (Carlson, 1981).

MOTIVATIONS FOR SUICIDAL BEHAVIOR

Toolan (1962) has stressed the "call for help"—an attempt to manipulate parents which motivates both the runaway and the youngster who attempts suicide. In many cases, however, the secondary gains sought through suicidal behavior seem less important than its relationship to primitive internal conflicts.

Some combination of factors, usually including a chronic history of dependency deprivation, reversal of child-parent roles, and threatened abandonment, gives rise to a sense of hopelessness, helplessness, and worthlessness. The suicidal attempt then serves as a "trial by ordeal" or "gamble with fate" whose positive verdict is (at least temporarily) accepted. Since fate (the primitive superego) allows life to continue, the youngster is reprieved (Weiss, 1957, 1966). Both aspects of the suicide attempt are essentially "magical acts" (Wahl, 1957) aimed at attaining irrational goals.

The above pattern has a tendency to repeat itself so that recurrences of suicidal behavior are not unusual, especially if the response of important loved ones is not supportive. King (1969) has underlined the importance of the therapist's concern in response to a suicide attempt. Sabbath (1969), speaking of family relationships in the suicidal adolescent, speculates that suicidal behavior appears when the child perceives himself as "expendable" because the family unconsciously wishes that he would disappear or "drop dead."

Some authors have suggested that suicidal behavior in adolescents is related to genital conflicts. These do appear in the history as unsuccessful romances, conflict over incestuous feelings toward parents, and the like. In our experience, closer investigation usually shows that the romance failed because of overpossessive, demanding behavior and that the incestuous ties interfered with a previously satisfactory dependency relationship. The block to moving comfortably into heterosexual roles in the depressive adolescent is the unresolved primitive tie to the mother.

It is important to remember in evaluating any suicide attempt or suicide gesture that the suicidal behavior seems to the adolescent to be a solution. Although we may regard suicidal behavior as a problem, our young patients often view it as the only possible solution to a variety of chronic and immediate problems in their lives (Teicher, 1979). Suicidal ideation and suicidal activity are ego states which are often felt as somewhat pleasurable by the distressed adolescent. This is true in varieties of depressive disorders where the suicidal behavior promises relief from the psychic pain but it is also true in situations where there are major manipulative elements in the suicidal behavior as may occur in behaviorally disordered adolescents. Shame or anticipated shame can also lead the adolescent patient to see suicide as the only honorable response (Schneer and Brozovsky, 1961).

MANAGEMENT OF THE SUICIDAL ADOLESCENT

The management of suicidal behavior depends on the evaluation of a complex set of factors. One must first consider the seriousness of the suicidal behavior. If the youngster utilized an extremely lethal method (shooting, hanging), it may be that the attempt aborted by purest chance. If the attempt was planned without provision for discovery, it is clearly more malignant than an attempt carried out with built-in arrangements for being rescued. The clinical diagnosis is also important, since some studies suggest that successful suicide may be related to the nature of the psychiatric disorder (Weiss, 1966; Pfeffer, 1988). Balser and

Masterson (1959) described a higher incidence of successful suicide in schizophrenic adolescents and in those who have lost a loved parent through death. The latter youngsters often seem driven to "join the loved one."

Most adolescents who survive suicidal behavior fall clearly into the "suicide attempt" category, as opposed to the "aborted successful suicide" category. Still, there are marked variations in the extent to which the adolescent must stack the cards against himself in his gamble with fate. He may need to make his odds so poor that a completed suicide is virtually a certainty.

In addition to assessing the adolescent's inner drive to self-destruction, the therapist must consider the extent of environmental stress, especially family disintegration. The possibility of family compliance or even encouragement of suicidal behavior should be investigated. Finally, the adolescent's wider social environment should be evaluated. Social isolation, poor school performance, parental loss (Greer, 1964), and disruption of important friendships and romantic alliances increase the likelihood of repeated suicidal attempts (Barter et al., 1968; Stanley and Barter, 1970).

Children and adolescents learn from somewhere that people leave letters before they kill themselves and even before they threaten to kill themselves. Parents and teachers sometimes find these notes and ask therapists to assess their significance. Of course, such a note could give the therapist valuable insight into the youngster's sense of desperation and depression. Ordinarily the therapist would want to discuss the note with the patient himself. Any suicide note by an adolescent is a very important signal and should be taken very seriously. We are not aware that this issue has ever been researched systematically, but perhaps it is possible to characterize some suicide notes as statements of true suicidal intentions while others are "merely" cries for help. The two notes reproduced in this chapter illustrate this point. One note was written by a boy who was quite depressed, but did not commit suicide—it has an angry, complaining, demanding quality to it. The second note was written by a girl who immediately afterwards walked in front of a train—this message is ex-

NOTE BY A DEPRESSED PATIENT,
WHO DID NOT ATTEMPT SUICIDE

This note was written by a 15-year-old boy, who then left it in his room where his mother was sure to find it. He clearly was requesting and even demanding help from his parents. This note, like all the clinical information in this book, has been modified and disguised.

Would someone please help me? I'm so lost. I want so badly for my life to end. No one understands my problems. No one, except Hanna. My one and only true friend. Can't someone bring Hanna and have her straighten me out? I want to talk to her. I need help badly. Bring her to me. Let her talk to me. I want to talk to her. You people don't give a damn if I kill myself, but she does. No one loves or even cares for me. Hanna is the only one in the world who listens to me. Please—for one time—listen to me before it's too late.

J.S.—class of '89

tremely sad and has an apologetic tone. We are not suggesting that these are hard and fast criteria that determine suicide potential, but the content and tone of the suicide note are data that should be considered.

After weighing the multiple factors involved, the therapist must make a decision regarding the advisability of hospitalization. Often, this decision must be taken on very incomplete data distorted by the chaotic and charged emotional atmosphere which surrounds suicidal behavior.

Hospitalization Of The Suicidal Adolescent

Certainly, the therapist cannot afford to take undue risks with the life of his young patient. Although some authors suggest an almost laissez-faire attitude toward the possibility of patient suicide (see as an example Bosescu, 1965), most therapists feel much more responsible for the protection of their patients. Litman's (1965) study of therapists who had lost a patient through suicide

NOTE WRITTEN BY A GIRL WHO COMMITTED SUICIDE

This note appeared in an article in the *Washington Post* several years ago. Melissa was 14. After she wrote it, Melissa stepped in front of a train and was killed.

To my dear Mom,

You always ask me if there's anything wrong. I said, "No, I'm OK." Mom, I wasn't telling the truth. I was never OK. I was very depressed. I ran away from all of my problems. I am taking the easy way out. I am admitting to myself that I am a weak person not able to handle the weight of life.

I am very sorry to put you all through the troubles. I think everything I have to do is done. I drank some wine and took some pills. But before I did all that I prayed to my father God in heaven. I asked him to forgive me but he won't. I don't blame him for that. Please pray that I don't be sent to hell, because then I won't be able to come back and watch over you and help you. I want to do that.

Mom, please don't have a nervous breakdown and be crying all the time. I don't want you to. I want you to live forever and ever, the way you want to and I will always love you very much. Please try and forgive me.

I love you always and always.

Love,
Melissa

demonstrated that the event had a stunning impact on the practitioner. We return to this issue during the discussion of countertransference problems with the suicidal adolescent.

In any event, most therapists agree that, if the patient appears to be actively suicidal, he must be protected through immediate hospitalization. However, one must remember that hospitalization itself is not free of risk. The therapist must consider not only the routine risk involved in hospitalizing any adolescent, but the particular problems associated with the suicidal patient (Slaby and Kramer, 1984). It has been observed that there is an extremely high risk of suicide during the period immediately following discharge from the hospital (Moss and Hamilton, 1955).

In spite of these realistic warnings, hospital treatment is frequently essential at least in the early stages of therapy of the actively suicidal adolescent. The growing recognition over the last few years of the frequency with which major affective illnesses have their onset during adolescence requires careful diagnostic evaluation of any youngster presenting with depressive or suicidal symptoms.

Diagnostic evaluation includes a careful history of behavior and symptoms with particular attention to cyclic swings in mood and level of activity, the family history of affective disorder, the question of whether symptoms and aberrant thoughts fit the patient's mood, the presence or absence of drug abuse, and the presence or absence of overt evidences of primary depression such as crying spells, sleep disturbances, and disturbances in energy level or food intake. Of course, it is very important to interview adolescents carefully regarding their moods. One needs to keep in mind that adolescents will sometimes minimize the degree of depressive symptomatology they are feeling, particularly if they are using drugs or delinquent behavior in an effort to avoid a depressive collapse. Observing the youngster over time and inquiring about mood again after a trusting relationship is developed may be necessary in order to discover even fairly major dysphoric moods (Cytryn, McKnew, and Bunney, 1980; Davis, 1979).

The value of biological testing for endogenous depression is controversial. However, there is evidence that the tests, particularly the dexamethasone suppression test, does have value in confirming biological depression particularly if the cortisol assay is standardized to local norm, the test is not used in the presence of other conditions which would give false positives, and if the diagnostician attends mainly to clearly high test scores rather than those in the borderline range of normal (Carroll, 1985; Livingston et al., 1984; Khan, 1987).

Hospitalization is also necessary for almost all patients who need antidepressant medication or lithium therapy for severe depression and suicidal behavior. Starting these medications on an outpatient basis is a risky procedure since there is a considerable delay in onset of effectiveness which may be very discour-

aging to a deeply depressed youngster. The medications themselves are quite toxic and have become one of the major agents
utilized for suicidal drug overdoses. Although it is not possible
to state categorically which patients require drug treatment, it
should be considered for a patient who has a history of recurrent
episodes or a family history of manic-depressive illness.

The purpose of the inpatient phase of treatment of the suicidal
adolescent is to stabilize the clinical picture, find the appropriate
drug treatment and proper dosage, and support the patient's
transition into ongoing outpatient psychotherapy for underlying
personality and emotional problems.

Outpatient Treatment Of The Suicidal Adolescent

If the suicidal risk is not considered to be seriously imminent,
treatment of the suicidal patient can sometimes be initiated in an
outpatient setting. Even when inpatient treatment has been necessary, it is usually important to follow that treatment with ongoing outpatient psychotherapy. This home management of the
suicidal patient requires attention to three areas. These are: 1)
"sterilizing" the physical home environment, 2) parental therapy,
3) direct therapy with the adolescent.

STERILIZING THE HOME. Although people may point out that a
determinedly suicidal patient can always find a way to kill himself,
there are many advantages in clearing the home of all easily available lethal materials. The parents and the adolescent are told,
separately or in joint session, that suicidal feelings come and go.
Confidence is expressed that eventually the adolescent will be
glad that he is alive. Because of this, he will be offered all possible
protection to allow him the opportunity to reach this attitude
toward himself. The therapist explains the necessity of making
the home as safe as possible to decrease the possibility of impulsive suicidal behavior. All potentially lethal medications, poi-
sons, firearms, and razor blades (electric razors are quite satisfactory) should be removed from the home. The suicidal
adolescent patient should be restricted from driving automobiles
or motorbikes alone until the therapist feels it is safe. Although

the adolescent may protest these measures, they represent tangible proof that his parents and his therapist want him to live. This reassurance may play a larger role in the preventive value of the "sterilization" than the relative absence of the means for suicide (Mintz, 1966). If the parents do not cooperate in this effort, the therapist may be sure of their unconscious or conscious participation in the suicidal behavior. Placement outside the home may be necessary under these circumstances.

It is wise to advise against prolonged parental absences during the early phases of therapy with the suicidal adolescent. Youngsters who are struggling with suicidal thoughts should not be burdened with excessive solitude. In addition, separations from the parents are potent precipitants of suicidal ideation and behavior in these vulnerable adolescents (Levi et al., 1966; Margolin and Teicher, 1968). Anecdotally, one is surprised at the frequency with which suicide attempts occur shortly before parents leave on a planned trip. Perhaps more surprising, the parents often ask the therapist if they should go ahead with their plans!

PARENTAL THERAPY. Many parents of suicidal adolescents are themselves extremely depressed, even suicidal (Margolin and Teicher, 1968). Many are overtly or covertly rejecting of their child (Sabbath, 1969; Schrut, 1964). These problems are often associated with and intensified by severe marital conflict (Stanley and Barter, 1970). Suicidal behavior has been found to be a response to unconscious dynamic issues within some families (Shapiro, 1987). Even when the parents do not appear seriously disturbed, they need extensive support and help because of the intense anxiety engendered by the suicidal attempt and the difficulties of parenting a potentially suicidal child.

The treatment approach for parents of suicidal adolescents is basically supportive, since unmet dependency needs are common determinants of the rejecting attitudes toward their own child. In those who are clinically depressed, antidepressant medication may be a valuable adjunct. This medication should never be dispensed to the parent in a suicidal dose. As with the adolescent, hospitalization may be necessary to initiate treatment.

Often, it is wise to provide these parents with a therapist of their own. Despite themselves, they may tend to feel envious and rivalrous of their youngster if all share the same therapist. If collaborative therapy is arranged, the adolescent's therapist must remain alert to any evidences that the family is withdrawing from his patient. This suspicion must be quickly conveyed to the parent's therapist, whose active steps to reestablish family reintegration and at least minimal support of the adolescent may be literally lifesaving.

Both Morrison and Collier (1969) and Mattsson et al. (1969) have pointed out that many families with suicidal children can accept help only during the immediate crisis and lose interest quickly. Of Morrison and Collier's 30 cases, only 8 came for further interviews and only 2 were in treatment one year after the suicidal attempt. In the Cleveland study, 15 of 75 families failed to effect any further study or treatment after the crisis contact, although it was recommended. It does appear that a crisis-intervention approach involving the entire family may often be effective therapy for these disorganized families (Schrut, 1968).

It is sometimes helpful to provide informational material to parents. Not only is it educational, but it also helps the parents sense that there are many other families that are in the same boat. Meeks (1988) has written a book for parents and other adults who are interested in adolescent depression. The National Institute of Mental Health (Sargent, 1986) and the American Psychiatric Association (1988) have distributed educational material for the public, including pamphlets on depression and on adolescent suicide.

DIRECT THERAPY OF THE SUICIDAL ADOLESCENT. We have discussed the pharmacologic therapy of depressive illness in adolescents in only the most superficial way. This treatment approach is not only of great importance, it is also changing quite rapidly. The adolescent therapist needs to read the current literature and remain updated on appropriate treatment approaches as new data is gathered. Medication is important not only for the treatment of the immediate episode but plays a major role in the prevention of recurrences (Prien et al., 1984).

Whether or not drugs are needed, the real key to the long run success of therapy in the suicidal adolescent is the provision of understanding, acceptable dependency gratification, and a gradual opportunity for emotional growth within the therapeutic relationship. In a world which the adolescent views as chaotic, unreliable, and uncaring, the therapist must offer the youngster a consistent, corrective therapeutic relationship (Easson, 1969; Meeks and Schwartzbeck, 1979; McCarthy, 1987). Even in cases of clinical bipolar affective disease, psychotherapy is necessary to assure acceptance of the illness and the need for drug treatment.

The initial task in the psychotherapy of the suicidal adolescent is to establish a dependency relationship which the adolescent can accept without "losing face." Many of these youngsters are extremely threatened by their intense dependency wishes. The therapist must often utilize humor, extreme tact, and vigorous support of independent behavior to help the adolescent tolerate being helped. The techniques of treating a special patient of this general group, the "wrist slasher," have been described by Grunebaum and Klerman (1967) and expanded by Doctors (1981).

When the dependency relationship is established with the adolescent, the problem becomes one of gradually assisting the youngster to become more self-sufficient without stirring fears of abandonment. The pace of therapy is characteristically slow, and the intense needs of these patients exert a drain on the therapist. A study of suicidal behavior during psychotherapy has suggested that attempts often follow a perceived rejection or negative prognostic comment from the therapist (Wheat, 1960). The therapist must be alert to countertransference hostility toward the demanding suicidal patient. It is imperative that the youngster not become "expendable" again.

There are a number of reasons why therapists may tire of the suicidal adolescent. This youngster has little capacity to assume responsibility for himself and often indulges in a great deal of whining and complaining. He continually sees other people, including the therapist, as withholding and unfair. No matter how giving the therapist may be, it is never enough. The therapist often begins to feel that he is trying to fill a bottomless pit. At other times, he begins to blame himself for his inability to meet the patient's insatiable demands. Some suicidal adolescents add to the countertransference problems by continuing periodically to threaten or attempt suicide. Often, they use the veiled or direct threat of suicide to extract special considerations from the therapist such as dramatic late-night phone calls or extra appointments. The therapist senses that if necessary many of these youngsters would play their trump card—a real suicide.

The combination of sympathy for the patient's real despair and emptiness, competing with frustration and anger over the youngster's emotional blackmail, makes for a turbulent and uncomfortable countertransference. The therapist is in fact walking a tightrope in many cases. If he capitulates totally in the "suicide game" and guarantees to meet the adolescent's unrealistic, non-negotiable conditions for continuing to live, he can actually drive the adolescent to suicide. On the other hand, if he refuses to negotiate at all, insisting that the adolescent must decide whether to live or die himself, his patient may commit suicide in pique and dejection over losing the game.

The therapist must remember that these youngsters manipulate and demand because they are unable to meet their needs in any other way. They are convinced that no one will give them anything freely. They also believe that without "gifts" they are nothing. They feel that all good things come from others and that they are hollow and bad. They must blackmail, threaten, and coerce others. For them, this manipulation is literally a matter of life or death. Only gradually can they come to see themselves as possessing any inherent strength and worth.

In the management of crisis periods with suicidal youngsters, consultation with a colleague is of inestimable value. The objectivity of an uninvolved fellow therapist helps to prevent any mismanagement of the case which might result from the primary therapist's emotional discomfort. Decisions of whether to hospitalize the patient, how to respond to one of the "life-and-death" deals which these patients often propose, and whether to allow the patient to take a trip or go away to college are better shared than made alone. The practical advantage of consultation in medicolegal terms is also readily apparent. There is an obvious additional dividend for the patient if consultation allows the therapist to be comfortable about his legal liability and his ethical responsibility.

In the later stages of psychotherapy, after the development of a reasonably stable therapeutic alliance, it may be possible to deal more directly with the patient's dependency needs and masochistic defenses. Premature interpretation of the adolescent's active role in creating his own misery tends to be felt by these patients as criticism, "Rather than giving me the understanding and sympathy that I need, you too say that it is all my fault." Feeling abandoned, the patient may again become suicidal. Some of these depressed and empty youngsters require almost indefinite support with the frequency of supportive sessions only slowly and cautiously diminished (Easson, 1969). As mentioned in the chapter on termination (see the section "Therapy—Interminable"), this arrangement should be periodically reviewed with an eye to the possibility of actually completing the work.

—And If You Lose

Sadly, even the most skillful therapy cannot always prevent the suicidal adolescent from killing himself. The therapist is then faced with the task of dealing with his feelings of grief, guilt, and inadequacy. Litman (1965) has noted that therapist responses in this situation range from defensive denial and rationalization to virtual refusal to accept a suicidal patient ever again. From Litman's observations, it appeared that the therapists who succeeded in mastering their feelings generally did so by presenting the case to professional colleagues with an attitude of trying to learn something about preventing a similar occurrence in the future.

PREVENTION AND POSTVENTION OF SUICIDE

When the incidence of adolescent suicide increased in recent years, many professionals became alarmed and sought to create programs for the prevention of these deaths. Shaffer et al. (1988) developed an elaborate and scholarly assessment of these programs. He criticized the didactic school-based suicide prevention programs for following a "low risk strategy." That is, "given the low base rate of teen suicide, very few of the adolescents receiving the programs are likely to attempt or commit suicide." It may be, however, that some of the youngsters who participate in these programs do identify themselves as being emotionally troubled and desiring further counseling or professional help. Many communities have established suicide hot lines, but it is not known whether these efforts have actually affected the incidence of adolescent suicide. Shaffer pointed out that it would make sense to focus one's efforts at prevention at the population of adolescents who are known to be at the highest risk. If that were done, professionals and school personnel would direct most of their interventions to teenage boys who have made a previous attempt or who are depressed.

Rosenberg (1989) made recommendations regarding adolescent suicide prevention after surveying 29 professionals who had many years of experience in this field. After considering a number of possible interventions to prevent adolescent suicide, the ones that were thought to be most effective in reducing adolescent suicide was finding ways to restrict the access of adolescents to firearms and the identification of high-risk youths.

In some communities the media, especially television news and newspapers, have made a very big deal out of an adolescent suicide. In some cases reporters have attempted to interview family members, friends, and classmates of the youngster who has died. Television cameramen have been known to use telephoto lenses to shoot through school windows at the survivors of a deceased student and to enter a church and attempt to film the funeral. News reports tend to glamorize the suicidal behavior—the mere fact of putting it on the front page makes suicidal behavior seem exciting, extremely special, and attractive in some strange way. It certainly would make parents and professionals wonder if their own children and patients might try to copy the suicidal behavior that has been idealized and romanticized. One would also wonder whether the suicide clusters that have occurred in some communities have been facilitated by local news reports.

Attempts have been made to study systematically the effect of newspaper stories on suicide rates (Blumenthal, 1973; Phillips, 1974); the effect of television news stories about suicide on the adolescent suicide rate (Phillips, 1986); and the effect of television movies on adolescent suicide (Gould, 1986; Phillips, 1987). Some studies and anecdotal accounts suggest that some adolescents are influenced to commit suicide by what they see on television and read in newspapers. Other studies do not support that conclusion. Even if there were a relationship, it would mean that only a small number, perhaps 5 or 10%, of adolescent suicides occur because of the influence of the media. The vast majority of adolescent suicide is a result of other causes mentioned in this chapter, such as severe depression, profound disappointments, serious family problems, and substance abuse. But even if the effect of television and newspapers on the adolescent suicide rate is slight, it would still behoove the editors to maintain both good taste and ethical principles. For instance, it would seem proper that a newspaper would not emphasize or highlight an adolescent suicide; would not glorify or romanticize the behavior; and probably would not mention the specific method that was used.

Postvention refers to the steps that are taken following a suicide, to support the survivors and to reduce the possibility that another person will follow the example and also commit suicide. It would seem that group and individual meetings with family members, close friends, classmates, and certain other acquaintances can be very helpful. It gives the survivors a chance to share their grief, to address their guilt at not preventing the suicide, and to ventilate their anger and frustration at the deceased. It also gives the professionals involved an opportunity to identify other youngsters who are at greater risk for committing suicide and following up with them on a more individualized basis. If this is done in a thorough and sensitive manner, it hopefully would interrupt the tendency for further suicides to cluster around the first one.

Some school systems have gone overboard and created extremely elaborate suicide prevention and postvention programs. It would seem a better balance to include suicide awareness as part of a broader health curriculum, which also includes drug awareness, sexuality awareness, AIDS awareness, etc. Following a suicide in a high school, we do not think it is useful or appropriate for the principal to get on the intercom and announce to the entire school that one of the students killed himself. Nor do we think it necessary for the entire school to divide up into discussion groups to meet with visiting mental health professionals or for half the school to go home for the rest of the day because they are too upset. What does make sense is to hold discussion groups for adolescents who are at greater risk, such as friends and acquaintances of the deceased student; adolescents who have previously threatened or attempted suicide; and young people with serious emotional problems or substance abuse problems. The school staff could also let it be known that anybody else is also welcome to attend these meetings. It also seems healthy and generous for the parents of the suicide victim to include the youngster's friends and classmates in the funeral activities. Finally, the school might want to channel the intense feelings of the surviving students into something positive, like planting a tree or creating some other kind of memorial.

SUMMARY

It is a frightful responsibility to become involved with a youngster who is struggling with the question "to be or not to be." The drama and finality of suicide conspire with the personality traits of suicidal youngsters to make treating the suicidal adolescent one of the psychotherapist's most exacting experiences. The wise therapist will recognize his limitations and refuse to treat more of these youngsters than he can manage. Most therapists find that two or three potentially suicidal adolescents are the upper limit that they can effectively treat. Therapists with depressive tendencies of their own may find it best to avoid working with any youngsters of this kind.

CITED AND RECOMMENDED READINGS

American Psychiatric Association. 1988. *Let's Talk Facts About Teen Suicide*. Washington, D.C.: American Psychiatric Association.

Balser, B., and J. F. Masterson. 1959. Suicide in adolescents. *American Journal of Psychiatry*. 116: 400–404.

Barter, J. T., et al. 1968. Adolescent suicide attempts. *Archives of General Psychiatry*. 19: 523–527.

Basescu, S. 1965. The threat of suicide in psychotherapy. *American Journal of Psychotherapy*. 19: 99–105.

Blumenthal, S., and L. Bergner. 1973. Suicide and newspapers: a replicated study. *American Journal of Psychiatry*. 130: 468–471.

Carlson, G. A. 1971. The phenomenology of adolescent depression. *Adolescent Psychiatry*. 9: 411–421.

Carroll, B. J. 1985. Dexamethasone suppression test: a review of contemporary confusion. *Journal of Clinical Psychiatry*. 46: 13–24.

Crumley, F. E. 1981. Adolescent suicide attempts and borderline personality disorder: clinical features. *Southern Medical Journal*. 74: 546–549.

Cytryn, L., et al. 1980. Diagnosis of childhood depression: a reassessment. *American Journal of Psychiatry*. 137: 22–25.

Davis, R. E. 1979. Manic-depressive variant syndrome of childhood. *American Journal of Psychiatry*. 136: 702–706.

Doctors, S. 1981. The symptom of delicate self-cutting in adolescent females: a developmental view. *Adolescent Psychiatry*. 9: 443–460.

Easson, W. M. 1969. *The Severely Disturbed Adolescent*. New York: International Universities Press.

Garfinkel, B. D., et al. 1982. Suicide attempts in children and adolescents. *American Journal of Psychiatry*. 139: 1257–1261.

Gould, M. S., and D. Shaffer. 1986. The impact of suicide in television movies. Evidence of imitation. *New England Journal of Medicine*. 315: 690–694.

Greer, S. 1964. The relationship between parental loss and attempted suicide: a control study. *British Journal of Psychiatry*. 110: 698–705.

Grunebaum, H. U., and G. L. Klerman. 1967. Wrist slashing. *American Journal of Psychiatry*. 124: 527–534.

Holinger, P. C., 1989. Epidemiologic issues in youth suicide. In: *Suicide Among Youth: Perspectives on Risk and Prevention*, edited by C. R. Pfeffer. Washington, D.C.: American Psychiatric Press.

Holinger, P. C., and D. Offer. 1982. Prediction of adolescent suicide: a population model. *American Journal of Psychiatry*. 139: 302–307.

Jacobziner, H. 1965. Attempted suicides in adolescence. *Journal of the American Medical Association*. 191: 7–11.

Khan, A. U. 1987. Biochemical profile of depressed adolescents. *Journal of the American Academy of Child and Adolescent Psychiatry.* 26: 873–878.

King, J. W. 1969. Depression and suicide in children and adolescents. *General Practice.* 36: 95–104.

Klerman, G. L. 1989. Suicide, depression, and related problems among the baby boom cohort. In: *Suicide Among Youth: Perspectives on Risk and Prevention,* edited by C. R. Pfeffer. Washington, D.C.: American Psychiatric Press.

Levi, L. D., et al. 1966. Separation and attempted suicide. *Archives of General Psychiatry.* 15: 158–164.

Litman, R. E. 1965. When patients commit suicide. *American Journal of Psychotherapy.* 19: 570–576.

Livingston, R., et al. 1984. Abnormal dexamethasone suppression test results in depressed and nondepressed children. *American Journal of Psychiatry.* 141: 106–108.

Margolin, N. L., and J. D. Teicher. 1968. Thirteen adolescent male suicide attempts: dynamic considerations. *Journal of the American Academy of Child Psychiatry.* 7: 296–315.

Mattsson, A., et al. 1969. Suicidal behavior as a child psychiatry emergency. *Archives of General Psychiatry.* 20: 100–109.

McCartney, J. R. 1987. Adolescent depression: a growth and development perspective. *Adolescent Psychiatry.* 14: 208–217.

Meeks, J. E. 1988. *High Times/Low Times: The Many Faces of Teenage Depression.* Washington, D.C.: PIA Press.

Meeks, J. E., and C. Schwartzbeck. 1979. Management of depression in adolescents and young adults. *Journal of Current Adolescent Medicine.* 1: 22–31.

Mintz, R. S. 1966. Some practical procedures in the management of suicidal persons. *American Journal of Orthopsychiatry.* 36: 896–903.

Morrison, G. C., and J. G. Collier. 1969. Family treatment approaches to suicidal children and adolescents. *Journal of the American Academy of Child Psychiatry.* 8: 140–153.

Moss, L. M., and D. M. Hamilton. 1955. Psychotherapy of the suicidal patient. *American Journal of Psychiatry.* 112: 814–820.

Nicholi, A. M. 1970. The motorcycle syndrome. *American Journal of Psychiatry.* 126: 1588–1595.

Pfeffer, C. R. 1988. Clinical dilemmas in the prevention of adolescent suicidal behavior. *Adolescent Psychiatry.* 15: 407–421.

Pfeffer, C. R. 1989. *Suicide Among Youth: Perspectives on Risk and Prevention.* Washington, D.C.: American Psychiatric Press.

Phillips, D. P. 1974. The influence of suggestion on suicide: substantive and theoretical implications of the Werther effect. *American Sociological Review.* 39: 340–354.

Phillips, D. P., and L. L. Carstensen. 1986. Clustering of teenage suicides after television news stories about suicide. *New England Journal of Medicine*. 315: 685–689.

Phillips, D. P., and D. J. Paight. 1987. The impact of televised movies about suicide: a replicative study. *New England Journal of Medicine*. 317: 809–811.

Phillips, D. P., et al. 1989. Effects of mass media news stories on suicide, with new evidence on the role of story content. In: *Suicide among Youth: Perspectives on Risk and Prevention*, edited by C. R. Pfeffer. Washington, D.C.: American Psychiatric Press.

Prien, R. F., et al. 1984. Drug therapy in the prevention of recurrences in unipolar and bipolar affective disorders. *Archives of General Psychiatry*. 41: 1096–1104.

Robbins, D. R., and N. E. Alessi. 1985. Depressive symptoms and suicidal behavior in adolescents. *American Journal of Psychiatry*. 142: 588–592.

Rosenberg, M. L. 1989. Developing strategies to prevent youth suicide. In: *Suicide Among Youth: Perspectives on Risk and Prevention*, edited by C. R. Pfeffer. Washington, D.C.: American Psychiatric Press.

Ross, M. 1969. Suicide among college students. *American Journal of Psychiatry*. 126: 220–225.

Sabbath, J. C. 1969. The suicidal adolescent—the expendable child. *Journal of the American Academy of Child Psychiatry*. 8: 272–289.

Sargent, M. 1986. *Depressive Disorders: Treatments Bring New Hope*. Rockville, Maryland: National Institute of Mental Health.

Schneer, H. I., et al. 1961. Events and conscious ideation leading to suicidal behavior in adolescence. *Psychiatry Quarterly*. 35: 507–515.

Schrut, A. 1964. Suicidal adolescents and children. *Journal of the American Medical Association*. 188: 1103–1107.

Schrut, A. 1968. Some typical patterns in the behavior and background of adolescent girls who attempt suicide. *American Journal of Psychiatry*. 125: 69–74.

Shaffer, D., et al. 1988. Preventing teenage suicide: a critical review. *Journal of the American Academy of Child and Adolescent Psychiatry*. 27: 675–687.

Shapiro, E. R., and J. Freedman. 1987. Family dynamics of adolescent suicide. *Adolescent Psychiatry*. 14: 191–207.

Slaby, A. E., and P. D. Kramer. 1985. Evaluating and managing self-destructive potential and behavior in a hospital setting. *The Psychiatric Hospital*. 16: 33–39.

Stanley, E. J., and J. T. Barter. 1970. Adolescent suicidal behavior. *American Journal of Orthopsychiatry*. 40: 87–96.

Teicher, J. D. 1979. Suicide and suicide attempts. In: *Basic Handbook of Child Psychiatry, Volume 2*, edited by J. D. Noshpitz. New York: Basic Books.

Teicher, J. D., and J. Jacobs. 1966. Adolescents who attempt suicide. *American Journal of Psychiatry*. 122: 1248–1257.

Toolan, J. M. 1962. Suicide and suicidal attempts in children and adolescents. *American Journal of Psychiatry*. 118: 719–724.

Wahl, C. W. 1957. Suicide as a magical act. In: *Clues to Suicide*, edited by E. S. Shneidman and N. C. Farberow. New York: McGraw-Hill.

Weiss, J. M. A. 1957. Gamble with death in attempted suicide. *Psychiatry*. 20: 17–25.

Weiss, J. M. A. 1966. The suicidal patient. In: *American Handbook of Psychiatry, Volume III*, edited by S. Arieti. New York: Basic Books.

Wheat, W. D. 1960. Motivational aspects of suicide in patients during and after psychiatric treatment. *Southern Medical Journal*. 53: 273–278.

CHAPTER 13

the runaway

Running away from home is a time-honored American tradition. Few people reach adulthood without having angrily marched out from their home (often at age five or six) with the intention of making their way in the world. Many teenagers of past generations chose this abrupt emancipation from home and made it stick. Americans, with their emphasis on early independence and self-sufficiency, have an amused respect for the plucky youngster who grimly sets out to make his fortune. We have all loved Huck Finn and a long list of other picaresque heroes.

In recent years, runaways have become much more common, and much less amusing. Almost every large city has large numbers of preteens and teens who have fled from their homes and families.

Some of these older youngsters are merely liberating themselves from objectively cruel and unbearable living situations. Indeed one should always consider the possibility of incest or sexual abuse in any runaway of an adolescent girl. For other adolescents, running away is almost purely a symbolic expression of unconscious conflict, a true neurotic symptom. Most often, the runaway child is signaling a family disturbance which involves both himself and his parents. The running away in this case serves both to discharge family tensions temporarily and to symbolize the conscious or unconscious wish of one or both parents to desert their family responsibility—to "walk off and leave it all." According to Jenkins (1969), "The home background of the chronic runaway child is typically one of parental rejection from birth or before birth and one of parental severity and inconsistency."

Most runaways are managed by various social agencies in the community. Occasionally, however, a runaway is the initiating

339

event in a psychiatric referral or occurs in the course of evaluation or therapy with an adolescent referred for other reasons.

The personal dynamics of the youngster who feels compelled to run away from home usually centers around a dependency–independency conflict. Typically, the youngster is confronted with strong feelings of helplessness and wishes for dependency in a context which makes these feelings appear shameful, dangerous, or incapable of fulfillment. The resulting sense of panic leads to a desire to escape the painful situation, to prove self-sufficiency, and yet secretly to seek out a benevolent helper. The runaway is both running from something (a disappointing object) and toward something (a fantasied gratifying object). The similarity between the dynamics of runaways and depression has been noted in referring to the act of running away as a "depressive equivalent" (Chwast, 1967; Morrison and Collier, 1969; Glaser, 1967; Toolan, 1962).

Jane, a rather well-behaved girl of 15, impulsively ran away from home, leaving with a boy she knew only as a "guy with a pretty bad reputation." She convinced herself that she loved him and accepted "speed" and sexual advances, stating that these experiences were "beautiful." She maintained this view even after the boy deposited her on a street corner and failed to return for her. She was then picked up by a "nice guy" who convinced her to return home.

Jane felt that she had run away from home because she could no longer "talk to her father." She said that he treated her "like a baby." She felt that he was very unfriendly to boys who visited the home to call on her. She also complained that he was contemptuous of her opinions.

The parents admitted that the home was very unhappy for all family members. Both parents had frequent, strong conscious wishes to escape from a situation in which they felt trapped.

In a family session, Jane wept and asked her father, "Why can't it be like it used to be?"

When asked how long things had been going badly, she indicated a time which corresponded to her pubertal development.

Jane's mother was preoccupied with Jane's brother. The father had been a major source of dependency support until the biological changes of puberty forced awareness of the sexual components within the relationship.

Parents react to runaways with varying mixtures of anger, guilt, and shame. They cannot entirely ignore the runaway's dramatic denunciation of them as parents even when they have little honest affection for the child. The intense emotional reactions to the accusations contained in the act make it difficult for parents to respond rationally to the practical problems raised by a runaway. Some parents may also unconsciously prefer to rid themselves of the responsibility for the youngster's care. They are guilty over the runaway, but not entirely displeased.

The following classification of runaway behavior is offered as an aid to diagnostic treatment planning. Naturally the various types of runaway behavior overlap. One should not substitute labels for careful evaluation of the individual runaway youngster.

TYPES OF RUNAWAY BEHAVIOR

1. *The Adventurer.*

A great many youngsters who run away from home for a short period of time during mid-adolescence are basically emotionally healthy. They seem to be seeking an opportunity to prove that they are self-sufficient and that they can survive without the support of their parents.

Although it is obvious that many of the dynamics of separation and individuation are exaggerated in these young people, the actual runaway behavior seems to result primarily from cultural factors. Most of these adventurous youngsters come from suburban affluent families in which they have been sheltered, perhaps excessively. Often they are taught directly or indirectly that the larger urban world is extremely dangerous. The desire of such youngsters to venture forth into this "urban jungle" may represent little more than a self-prescribed rite of passage designed to overcome fears of independence. Although many of these youngsters describe minor difficulties with their parents or with

school authorities, these difficulties do not sound serious. Often
the complaints contain a predominant theme of being underestimated and overly directed. On direct psychiatric examination
these youngsters do not show evidence of severe psychopathology. Their families seem equally free of severe disturbance and
the social history does not reveal evidence of earlier trauma or
serious impairment of the developmental process.

Most of these youngsters do not show a repetitive runaway
pattern. They return home feeling older and wiser and resume
their previous pattern of adjustment, often maintaining that the
runaway experience was a valuable and important part of their
development. In many cases, the runaway experience leads to
subtle or obvious changes in family dynamics. The adolescent may
be treated with greater respect, given more psychological distance, and more clearly recognized as an individual agent (Howell
et al., 1973).

2. *The Hedonist.*

These youngsters may superficially resemble the Adventurer
described above since they too run without any evidence of severe
conflict with family members or with other important adults. The
frictions which have been presented in their lives tend to center
around issues of freedom and controversy over rules. Superficially the fights sound similar to those "normal" runaways. However, closer investigation reveals that these complaints have much
less substance and that the Hedonist feels irritated and constricted by even the most reasonable restraints on their absolute
freedom to do as they wish. These youngsters may not appear
calloused or angry; their affability depends on the adult's willingness to give them their way on all matters that affect their
immediate pleasure.

Although the families in this category appear to have genuine
affection for their youngsters, a careful history often shows that
limit setting has always been cursory and ineffective. The parents
tend to fear the youngster's anger and displeasure and have a
long history of indulging and entertaining the child. This approach worked satisfactorily in the earlier years of development,
but when the youngster's appetites became more adult, conflict

appears as the parents attempt to curb the youngster's pleasure seeking for the first time. Frequently this effort to set limits is instigated by external social pressure emanating from the adolescent's school or some other agency of the larger society. Family dynamics often reveal a reason for psychological overevaluation of the child by one or both parents. This excessive narcissistic investment is the source of the hedonistic collusion which interferes with appropriate discipline.

The origins of parental indulgence in some of these cases may be more complex. Reaction formations to rejecting feelings or parental narcissistic preoccupation may lead to "pampering" of the child in order to avoid genuine interaction and emotional investment. This pattern is sometimes seen in families of the wealthy or powerful in those cases where parenting is an activity with low priority compared to the glamour and excitement of the adults' lives. The adolescents, in any case, come to see immediate pleasure as the only reasonable goal of life.

These pleasure-oriented youngsters tend to run away to situations where they can find other youngsters who share their philosophy of life. As a rule they do not go to adult-organized shelters for the runaway, since their motive for running is not to find assistance in dealing with family problems, but to engage in activities which have come to be forbidden in the family and in the community where they reside.

In a psychiatric interview these young people do not present as severely disturbed. They often admit freely that they enjoy the freedoms that they have found away from their home setting. At times their basically infantile viewpoint leads them to illnesses caused by overindulgence in drugs, the uninterrupted and sleepless pursuit of pleasure, and sexual promiscuity. Although the negative effects of their pleasure seeking may lead to superficial promises to reform, they are difficult to treat successfully in an outpatient setting even when the parents are cooperative and involved. Having tasted the joys of unfettered license, they tend to run periodically when temptations are particularly attractive. These youngsters may gradually mature as they are faced over the years by the demands of reality. This maturation is particularly likely to occur if the parents can be helped to deal more realistically with the youngster's self-indulgence. In some cases, hospital or residential treatment may be necessary in order to assist the youngster in accepting the requirements of living within the constraints of the reality principle.

Some of the problems of engaging these youngsters in treatment are addressed in chapter 5. Their narcissistic and grandiose belief in the possibility of continuous pleasure without personal effort can be interrupted only if the parents can become more effective limit setters or if the youngster's hedonistic extremes lead to legal difficulties, or if drug use leads to addiction and a clear need for treatment. In other words, something or someone must interrupt the patient's headlong pursuit of pleasure before therapy has any chance of success.

3. *The Loner.*

The next three categories of runaway behavior are basically drawn from Stierlin's (1973) classification of runaway youngsters based on family psychopathological patterns. His general classification is based on the conceptualization that there are three types of families which produce in the adolescent a desire to run away. The first of these he describes as the excessively binding family. These families tend to hold their youngsters too close either through excessive gratification of dependency wishes or through a process of "mystification" which prevents the youngster from becoming aware of his own wishes and desires. As the youngster reaches adolescence, he finds his emerging sexual and aggressive drives cannot be contained within the family and experiences the desire to emancipate himself.

However, since his knowledge of the external world and his capacity to relate to peers are extremely deficient, his skill in adapting to the world outside the home is markedly impaired. If he does attempt to run away, the absence is brief since he is unable to find, attract, or utilize alternative sources of gratification. His loneliness and extraordinary dependency forces a quick return to the family, but the adjustment there is also unsatisfactory so that the wish to run again occurs sooner or later.

Family therapy in these cases is essential but is difficult to arrange. Inpatient therapy is almost always needed but difficult to maintain. The parents of these youngsters are extremely threatened when their child is removed from the family. They are driven by their desparate need to maintain their unwholesome bond with the child to disrupt and undermine treatment. Often they become hostile toward the residential staff and are prone to sign the youngster out of the hospital against medical advice.

The therapist who hopes to succeed with these families must be patient and persistent. Often therapy must be interrupted and started many times before successful treatment can proceed. This degree of effort is indicated, however, since the situation is malignant. The family situation is extremely unstable and dangerous since the youngster's inability to find satisfaction within or outside the family may lead to severe depression and impulsive suicidal behavior.

4. *The Hood.*

This runaway youngster is produced by a family configuration diametrically opposed to the family which produces the lonely runaway. Stierlin describes this family as one with an expelling mode. The child is experienced by his parents as an unwanted encumbrance to their own desires and pleasures. He is rejected and neglected and forced to fend for himself and meet his own needs at the earliest possible age and in any way that does not require the parents' time and attention.

Such a youngster runs away from home basically because there is nothing at home for him. The long background of deprivation and emotional coldness have their anticipated result and the child tends to be emotionally cold, predatory, and unscrupulous. He does not trust emotional ties of any kind and is well prepared to maintain himself and to succeed among the criminal element on the street. In short, he tends to be a successful runaway but a hazard to conventional society. Naturally, it is extremely difficult to interrupt the adjustment mode by means of any currently known psychotherapeutic approach. Some techniques described in chapter 5 may engage some of these emotionally stunted young people. Residential therapy is often essential.

5. *The Emissary.*

Stierlin's third family type does not bind or expel the child, but sends the youngster on a "mission." The youngsters from these families are subtly encouraged to leave the home for a period of time to engage in activities which indirectly benefit one or both of the parents. Often these children act out id impulses which the parents' superegos forbid them to express directly.

The dynamics are those originally described by Johnson and Szurak (1952) in their classic paper on "superego lacunae." Other family missions may be more related to the vicarious testing of ego possibilities as in one of Stierlin's cases in which a father who was frightened of changing jobs and moving to a new community seemed to utilize his youngster's runaway as proof to himself that the change was not as dangerous as he feared.

Diagnostically one may be alerted to this type of runaway when a youngster's behavior during an absence from home is clearly marked by extensive involvement in a specific activity which the family mission requires. For example, the daughter who is being utilized to act out mother's inhibited sexuality may concentrate on active sexual behavior during her runaway. Another clue may be the parents' preoccupation with a specific behavior. Most of these "Emissary" youngsters maintain some contact with the home and often report on their behavior by telephone or on their return home. Often one is amazed to learn that the parents have rather complete knowledge of the youngster's location and activities throughout the runaway period. This information is especially surprising in view of parental inactivity in retrieving the youngster.

Actually, this particular pattern of runaway behavior is unlikely to change without extensive alteration of the family dynamics achieved by direct treatment of the parents or through family therapy. Inpatient treatment accompanied by intensive family work may be necessary in order to help the dynamics become conscious.

FIRST YOU MUST FIND THE CHILD—

The therapist's task falls into two phases. The first is to assist the parents to focus on the concrete situation. The parents' attention should be turned to seeking the child actively, since the likelihood that the youngster will engage in dangerous behaviors is quite high. The adolescent's denial of panic and dependency often results in a defensive sense of omnipotence. Under the spell of this sense of magical power, the adolescent may attempt extremely daring and hazardous activities such as stealing, sexual excesses, or drug experiments. It is wise therefore to attempt to locate the runaway as quickly as possible. This is especially important in the case of the preadolescent and younger adolescent in whom immaturity and poor judgment increase the probability of hazardous behavior.

In recent years, some youth communities have organized themselves to provide care for the runaway. In many cities, these groups actually encourage the disgruntled youngster to leave home with the promise of satisfactory alternative living arrangements. In spite of the destructive effects of such Pied Pipers, the current social arrangements have some advantages. An experienced policewoman comments, "There was a time when almost every girl who ran away would end up pregnant by the time we found her. This isn't true anymore. The kids tell us they don't have to take up with men now to earn their way, that they can go to the hippie communes and there they all live like brothers and sisters" (Birdwell, 1970).

Twenty years after this quote, there are fewer hippie compounds and there is more danger on the streets but many runaways do manage to find relatively benign supports. This is not something a parent should count on, however. The risks are very high indeed.

Parents should be encouraged to contact the police as soon as they are sure that a runaway has occurred, with instructions to bring the youngster home when he is located. In addition, the adolescent's friends should be contacted, since adolescents rarely run away alone. Often, these friends have no intention of revealing the whereabouts of the missing adolescent. Their statements should be taken with a grain of salt, since they usually are actually trying to mislead the parent to cover the runaway's tracks. Still, instances do occur where the friend is not sure his friend's decision to run away was wise. He may be willing to help if he feels that it is in his friend's best interest. Needless to say, if the parent's call is angry and threatening, the friend is likely to conclude that any sensible person would run away from such a mean person and keep going. The parents should also contact those agencies located in the areas of the city where runaways are known to congregate.

None of these approaches would have any chance for success except that most runaways want to be found. They expect to be searched out and need to save face by making some effort to avoid detection and return to the home. They want to come home only if the parents really want them back and will show it. Once this assurance has been convincingly demonstrated, they often return quite easily after putting up enough resistance to maintain the respect of their friends.

The parents also need explicit advice on how to treat the adolescent when he is found. They may also require help for their own feelings in order to carry out the advice. Since the goal is to deal with the runaway event in a therapeutic way, the parents are asked to adopt an attitude of trying to understand why running away was necessary. The parents should avoid angry, accusative, and punitive attitudes as well as apologetic, self-accusatory, guilty comments. The therapist should offer an early appointment, preferably within 24 hours, for the family to consider together the reasons for this particular attempted solution of the family's conflicts. The therapist should convey to the parents an open-minded desire to understand, neither assigning blame nor permitting the parents to finalize unchallenged any premature and oversimplified explanations which merely cast blame on the child or on themselves.

—THEN YOU MUST TREAT THE FAMILY

When the family arrives for the emergency family conference, the second phase of the therapist's job begins. This phase includes both diagnostic and treatment-planning tasks. The therapist attempts to evaluate the factors involved in the runaway. To what extent is the child responding realistically to impossible family circumstances, struggling with a neurotic conflict, or scapegoating himself to accommodate a family conflict? The answers to these questions suggest the type of help which should be recommended. The chronologic and psychologic immaturity of the adolescent also plays a role in deciding on the best approach in a given case.

In many instances, it is wise to arrange placement for the child whose home is realistically unsuited to adolescent needs. Confinement accompanied with active psychotherapy may be necessary for youngsters whose ego resources are limited. These youngsters will need external controls to avoid running away again when they feel stressed. Usually, the parents require concomitant therapy during the child's placement so that the youngster does not return to the same psychological setting which produced the problems originally.

A few runaways can be managed as outpatients. This group includes those who see their running away as an ego-alien symptom—an inner compulsion they would prefer to overcome. Some of the cases which closely approximate the "family neurosis" model may also be included, with a collaborative or a family psychotherapy approach. However, it should be recognized that symptoms rarely disappear magically at the initiation of a therapy program. One can predict to the parents that in outpatient therapy (or even inpatient care, for that matter) some repetition of the act of running away is a very real possibility. When it does occur, most therapists as well as parents have intense affective responses to this callous abandonment and indictment by the adolescent. Predicting the possibility of such an occurrence in advance may be helpful in attempting to maintain a therapeutic attitude.

CITED AND RECOMMENDED READINGS

Birdwell, R. 1970. Quoted in "Runaway Problem Growing," feature article by M. Schwartz. *Dallas Morning News*. Sunday, June 7.
Chwast, J. 1967. Depressive reactions as manifested among adolescent delinquents. *American Journal of Psychotherapy*. 21: 575–584.

Glaser, K. 1967. Masked depression in children and adolescents. *American Journal of Psychotherapy*. 21: 565–574.

Howell, M. C., et al. 1973. Reminiscences of runaway adolescents. *American Journal of Orthopsychiatry*. 43: 840–853.

Jenkins, R. L. 1969. Classifications of behavior problems in children. *American Journal of Psychiatry*. 125: 1032–1039.

Johnson, A. M., and S. A. Szurek. 1952. The genesis of anti-social acting out in children and adults. *Psychoanalytic Quarterly*. 21: 323–343.

Morrison, G. C., and J. G. Collier. 1969. Family treatment approaches to suicidal children and adolescents. *Journal of the American Academy of Child Psychiatry*. 8: 140–153.

Stierlin, H. 1973. A family prspective on adolescent runaways. *Archives of General Psychiatry*. 29: 56–62.

Toolan, J. M. 1962. Depression in children and adolescents. *American Journal of Orthopsychiatry*. 32: 404–415.

CHAPTER 14

the violent adolescent

Vehement theoretical arguments flourish around the question of whether or not there is such a thing as an aggressive drive. The basic question is whether aggression is a learned reaction arising from frustration or whether it originates in an inborn instinctual drive. Waelder (1960) offers a detailed marshaling of the evidence which bears on the debate, but no definite answer seems possible. Currently, because of the recent flood of highly publicized violent acts, the proponents of the inherent drive theory seem to have the upper hand. There have been several popular books which have propounded this concept with varying degrees of scientific support (Ardrey, 1961; Lorenz, 1966; Morris, 1967). Golding's (1955) *Lord of the Flies*, a fictional account of the natural viciousness of a group of young boys isolated on a remote island, has had tremendous popularity among college students of the last decade, suggesting that there is ready acceptance of this view of human nature.

Actually, most research data suggest that aggressive behavior arises primarily in response to specific stimuli in the environment (Bandura and Walters, 1959; Dollard et al., 1963). Case studies of severely aggressive individuals usually contain much evidence both of severe frustration and of clear models of violence during the formative years (see Capote, 1966). Obviously, this does not settle the question, since it is clearly much easier to manipulate and research variables in the environment than to establish or disprove the presence of an innate biological drive. Some observations of the relationship between destructive behavior and the achievement of object relationships suggests that aggression is an inherent human tendency which must be socialized within the matrix of a loving and nurturing human relationship if it is to be

351

channeled into benevolent uses (Hartmann et al., 1949; A. Freud, 1949; A. Freud and Dann, 1951).

It may be that the most fruitful view of the basic nature of human aggression would regard aggression as a universal potential in human beings, yet almost infinitely variable in its expression. If appropriate growth conditions are provided for the young child, the potential for aggression is detectable primarily as an anlage of constructive capacities for active pleasure seeking and problem solving within the personality. Under less perfect developmental conditions, the potential may unfold in twisted and malevolent forms destructive toward the self and others.

The psychiatric literature contains many excellent discussions of violence as an instinctual behavior and the political meanings of violent behavior. There are many reviews of the frequency of violence occurring in the psychiatric population (Kalogerakis, 1971; Kaufman, 1962; Madden, 1977; Sosowsky, 1978; Zitrin et al., 1976). Hollander (1985) and Lewis and her colleagues (1976, 1979, 1982) have studied violent, incarcerated juveniles and have shown that the behavior of these youngsters can be understood through the complex interaction of environmental, psychiatric, and neurological factors. The use of medication to calm the acutely disturbed patient and the techniques through which staff can be trained to deal with threatening behavior in the psychiatric hospital have also been addressed (Kinzel, 1970; Nadelson, 1977; Penningroth, 1975; Shevitz, 1978; Stine et al., 1982; Wilson, 1976; Yudofsky, 1989).

Perhaps the reason for so few comprehensive discussions regarding the management of the violent patient is related to the behavior itself. First of all, it is clear that violence occurs in patients covering the entire diagnostic spectrum. Psychotic, brain damaged, intoxicated, and even severely anxious patients (McDonald, 1938) occasionally erupt into violence. In addition, the behavior itself is episodic rather than constant so that in a very real sense the question is not really how we should treat violence in the inpatient setting but how we should prevent it and modify its origins for the future.

Dorothy Otnow Lewis, M.D., (1976, 1979, 1980, 1982) is a faculty member of the Yale University Child Study Center. She collaborated with Jonathan Pincus, M.D., a neurologist, in studying the relationship between delinquency and psychiatric disorders and neurological abnormalities. Lewis, Pincus, and their colleagues studied youngsters referred by a court clinic and also juveniles who had already been incarcerated. The cursory assessment of these youngsters may have revealed simply a conduct disorder. Lewis found that a careful examination and a more thorough history turned up significant psychological and neurological pathology, such as paranoia, hallucinations, and seizures. The more violent children were also more likely to have experienced or witnessed extreme physical abuse.

Clinicians are faced with an episodic event and one that we predict very inaccurately. For one thing there are too many causes. First is the entire range of contributing organic factors which, even if one excludes temperament, includes overt brain damage resulting from perinatal cerebral insults, infection, or injury (Eliot, 1978; Karniski et al., 1982; Lewis et al., 1982). In addition, in most studies the overall thrust of research findings suggests strongly that more subtle defects in cognitive functioning, such as learning disorders, also predispose to violent delinquency (Karniski et al., 1982). Drug intoxication, particularly with alcohol, PCP, and secobarbital, strongly increase the possibility of violent outbursts (Rinklenberg and Stillmen, 1970; Simons and Kashani, 1978; Tinklenberg et al., 1981). Withdrawal reactions from these drugs and particularly the amphetamines may also include violent behavior as a component.

To further extend our already long list of important factors, we must now look to the life experiences of the adolescent. There is extensive data to indicate that youngsters who have been the victims of violent physical abuse themselves are more likely to show violent behavior later. Even if the violence in the home has not been directed personally toward the child, merely observing the habitual utilization of violence as a problem-solving technique encourages the adolescent to adopt this behavior as part of the coping armamentarium.

Stubblefield (1967) and Meeks (1979) have written summaries of the relevant issues in the assessment of antisocial behavior. This entire group of antisocial patients deserves very careful attention. Robins (1966) has clearly documented the appalling adulthood which generally awaits the youngster with serious antisocial behavior problems.

Adolescents Who Fear That They May Become Violent

Some adolescents may be much more threatened by their angry thoughts than those adolescents just discussed. Youngsters with borderline psychoses or severe personality disorders are frightened not just by the imaginary power of their thoughts, but by concern that they may be unable to stop themselves from carrying their thoughts into action. These youngsters require a sensitive and supportive recognition of their fear of losing control. They are terrified of the damage that they might do and of the retribution which would follow. Some of them can be reassured by the symbolic promise of external assistance, whereas others need concrete evidence that they will not be permitted to run amuck. In both cases, the youngster's capacity and responsibility for self-control are underlined as necessities. The working defenses against hostile discharge should be respected and supported.

The therapeutic emphasis should be placed on recognizing and discussing the fear of loss of control rather than on the anger itself. The efforts which the patient makes to contain himself are accepted even if they are pathologic, illogical, or even emotionally crippling. These defenses should not be interfered with until it is clear that the adolescent is completely safe from the dangers of overt expression of destructive physical aggressiveness. The therapist never focuses therapeutic attention directly on the rage until he feels reasonably confident that the violent impulses can be vented and considered at a verbal and symbolic level.

Those youngsters who cannot feel safe without concrete evidence of external control may need inpatient treatment. Often, it is difficult to decide if this is necessary without a period of trial therapy.

Mark was a 16-year-old of sturdy build. He out-weighed his therapist by 20 pounds and was in outstanding physical condition, since his fears of inner feminine and dependent strivings drove him to a herculean program of physical culture. He was referred for psychotherapy because of multiple minor delinquencies and a belligerent attitude toward parental discipline. On several occasions, the parents felt that Mark was forcibly restraining himself from striking them. His mother admitted to extreme fear that Mark might hurt her. However, Mark had never lost control.

Mark accepted treatment because of his concern over his inability to go to sleep without nightly calisthenics carried on until he dropped from exhaustion long after midnight. He worried about this symptom, since he recognized that it "wasn't good for health."

In an early session, Mark became very angry when the therapist commented that he seemed afraid to look at some of his frightening feelings. Mark took this as an insinuation of cowardice and immediately challenged the therapist.

"Can you admit that you're afraid of me?"

"Should I be afraid of you?"

"Don't give me that crap. What would you do if I came over there and knocked the shit out of you?" Mark said. He dramatized the comment by clenching his fist and half rising from his chair.

"Frankly, I think you are strong enough to keep from hitting me even when you're angry with me. I guess if I were wrong and it looked like you couldn't keep from coming after me, I'd holler for all the help I could get. I don't see that hitting me would help you. I'd try to get enough people here to keep you from hurting me or getting hurt yourself."

Mark relaxed visibly as the therapist spoke, but still seemed tense. The therapist continued, "Do you think I should get

someone to sit in with us until you are sure that you can
talk about being mad without throwing your fists?"

Mark looked at the therapist to be sure he was serious.
When he was convinced, he relaxed.

"Naw, I'm not gonna hit you. You sure make me mad,
though."

"Mark, I know it seems to you that I'm picking on you.
That's not my aim. It's just that we've got to take an honest
look at your hangups if we're going to get anywhere here."

"Go ahead, Doc. I'll try to behave myself."

3   THE HOMICIDAL ADOLESCENT

For most adolescents, violence is a feared thought or a frightening potential. Unfortunately, for others it is a very real possibility and a substantial risk. If these youngsters can be recognized prior to the eruption of homicidal behavior, tragedy may
be averted.

There are some clues, gleaned from the study of youngsters
who have committed extreme acts of violence, which may alert
the therapist to the possibility that homicidal behavior could occur.

Most authors who have studied youngsters who commit acts of
murderous aggression have described a family in which open violence is a commonplace (Easson and Steinhilber, 1961; Kaufman, 1962; Bender, 1959). Often, the child himself has been a
target of physical abuse. If not, he has commonly witnessed brutal
fights between the parents. Flagrantly seductive behavior, alternating with brutality, toward the child has been noted in many
cases. Often, the child is encouraged to be violent. His aggressive
assaults are not firmly limited. The parents may predict that he
will eventually injure or kill someone. In several cases (Easson
and Steinhilber, 1961), the parents permitted the youngster to
keep and add to a collection of dangerous weapons even after
he had shown assaultive behavior. Often, there is a history of
dangerous aggressiveness toward family members or pets. According to Kaufman (1962), the violent acts are followed by calm-
ness and a lack of remorse in the violent schizophrenic adolescent.

Many homicidal youngsters are willing to discuss their plans or fears of violent behavior if they are asked about them. The therapist should explore violent fantasies carefully. Does the adolescent have a particular person whom he wishes to hurt or fears that he may hurt? Has he thought of particular times when he might act or the weapons that he might use? Has he obtained these weapons? Has he practiced with them? Through a series of questions, it is possible to assess the current level of homicidal intent. The history helps to clarify the danger of an impulsive and unpremeditated homicidal act by illuminating the success that the youngster has had in controlling strong feelings and delaying action. Solomon (1967) feels that evidence of "poor rapport with the examiner" and "evasiveness" also indicates a more serious possibility of violence, possibly because this suggests paranoid tendencies. Scherl and Mack (1966) pointed out the active role of the victim in a study of adolescent matricide. The presence of a person who seems to be "asking for it" in the adolescent's environment increases the possibilities for homicide.

MANAGEMENT OF THE VIOLENT ADOLESCENT

The dangerously homicidal adolescent obviously needs immediate hospitalization. The family must be informed clearly of the seriousness of the adolescent's danger to others. Confidentiality does not hold when it appears likely that the adolescent will be unable to restrain himself from injuring others. The therapist should arrange for hospitalization under circumstances which assure his own safety as well as the safety of those who will be with the adolescent during the process of hospitalization. The quiet presence of several people reassures the adolescent struggling for control that he will be prevented from hurting anyone. The adolescent should be told that the therapist is hopeful that he can control himself without help. It is important to be honest and open with the potentially violent adolescent, especially if he has paranoid tendencies. He should be told directly and firmly that the therapist feels that any eruption of violence would be terribly damaging to the adolescent himself as well as unfair to others.

The adolescent should be assured that the therapist will take all possible precautions to prevent this from occurring. Of course, it is only with the extremely precarious adolescent that such elaborate cautions are necessary. In most instances, the firm statement that hospitalization is necessary will be sufficient to calm the adolescent, since it promises the early availability of external support and control. Needless to say, it is important to avoid any provocation, physical competitiveness, or unkindness toward a youngster who is on the verge of an aggressive outburst. Any individuals who are brought in to help are there to strengthen restraint and control, not to offer counter-aggression.

The acute treatment of the violent actions of a patient is basically limited to efforts to contain that behavior in the safest way possible utilizing humane restraint and/or a variety of medications. When the youngster is physically out of control, medications are important for sedation, lowering general excitement, clearing confusion, and for short-term chemical restraint. Physical restraint is essential since violent adolescents are paradoxically frightened by their own potential loss of control and yet it is usually not therapeutic to sedate them so completely that all aggressive tendencies are suppressed. When this is done, one usually also loses the degree of alertness necessary for genuine involvement in treatment. Still, disturbed adolescents need reassurance that the environment will control them safely and without excessive counterforce.

As a rule, the violent adolescent should not be treated as an outpatient until the threat of violence has abated. The failure of his defensive mechanisms and his fear of his own destructiveness make it difficult for him to explore his feelings without the structure and safety of an inpatient setting. For a description of the philosophical issues of patient control and practical procedures utilized in one college mental health service, the reader is referred to Halleck's excellent paper (1967).

Some violent adolescents meet the *DSM-III-R* criteria for intermittent explosive disorder or organic personality syndrome, explosive type. Yudofsky (1989) has discussed how medication can be used with these patients on a continuing basis to reduce the frequency or intensity of future violent episodes. He said that antipsychotic medication has been misused. Yudofsky recommended that antipsychotic medication be used "only for the management of aggression stemming from psychotic ideation or for the intermittent management of brief aggressive events related to organic aggressive syndrome." Likewise, sedatives and minor tranquilizers may be helpful in managing acute situations, but not the chronically aggressive individual. Although lithium carbonate has been suggested for the treatment of violent patients, Yudofsky stated that he did not find lithium useful for these patients unless the violence and agitation actually were a result of manic affects. He did agree that carbamazepine has been helpful in treating patients with aggressive disorders. He also reported that beta blockers, such as propanolol, have been helpful in controlling rage outbursts which are the result of some form of brain damage.

5   DIRECT TREATMENT OF THE VIOLENT ADOLESCENT

One common thread which unites all of the causative factors which we have described earlier is their impact in the individual's adaptive skills. Generally speaking, all of the etiological elements which we have discussed act to impair ego functioning and the successful development of secondary narcissism. In various ways these conditions or events interfere with either the structures which determine coping skills or with the necessary learning experiences which would encourage their proper development.

It is a commonplace observation that delinquent adolescents as well as adolescents with intermittent explosive disorder and most youngsters with paranoid problems demonstrate low self-esteem and generally feel helpless and driven by the winds of fate. They do not believe that they possess the ability to control their own lives. Clinical evaluation of their capacities often confirms a deficient level of skills in interpersonal relationships, study and learning habits, and techniques of problem solving.

Given this state of affairs, the tendency to develop Erikson's negative identity patterns and to embrace life styles which permit achievement of a "pseudo-competence" is very understandable. Pseudo-competence is gained for example, through that spurious sense of mastery which results from drug use with its artificial sense of well-being. Pseudo-competence may also be gained by joining subcultures with value systems which confer prestige and a sense of accomplishment to those who cannot gain such prizes in the more conventional world. For example, in the deliquent subculture impulsive daring and short-sighted bravado as well as physical violence may gain one a reputation for bravery and leadership. Rebellion against standard measures of success such as academic performance in this subculture would be applauded rather than condemned. In that world a prudent measuring of risk and consequence may be viewed simply as "chicken."

Violence plays a very important role in the world of pseudo-solutions. Violent acts are clear cut and simple as well as rapid and easily seen. To make the point through an oversimplification, a latency child in the playroom can spend frustrating extended periods of time attempting to build a tower from blocks. If he has some problems with coordination or in his capacity for visual conception, the effort may be attended by a variety of failures as blocks tumble down or refuse to rise in the directions of the little child's dreams. Even when the task is successfully completed, the structure may or may not please the youngster or he may fear that it is not good enough for others. He will worry about what others think since construction is always at least partially done to please, impress, and reward others. On the other hand, with a single, decisive, powerful swipe of the hand the largest tower of blocks can be reduced to instant shambles. The resulting sense of mastery, total control, and strength is highly satisfying. Often it is accompanied by a sense of triumph over the play therapist and a gleam in the child's eye that says he is happy to be relieved of the burden of trying to please. This satisfying piece of violence toward an inanimate object carries a sense of finality which makes one feel that a problem has been *solved*. No more fumbling around! The destructive action also provides a sense of self-sufficiency and independence of others which we have called pseudo-competency and which can be at least temporarily very reassuring.

Trying to build a tower can be slow and frustrating if your skills are poor or if you are subjected to harsh criticism or expect to be, based on your previous experience. In the effort one feels weak, ineffective, oppressed by the demands of others and discouraged and frustrated. In contrast, knocking the tower across the room is quick, makes one feel strong, and sweeps away the demands of others in one carefree and triumphant moment. Pseudo-competence is the silver lining of self-doubt and servitude.

The leap from our simple example to the complex topic of violent behavior is a large one and we will lose something in the translation. However, if we expand our definition to include not only violence toward other people but extreme outbursts of violence toward property and if we keep in mind that the complexity of the topic will always defeat any efforts toward excessive generalization, we may gain from applying some of these ideas to two well-documented examples reported outside of the clinical literature.

In the first example a nomadic young adult, attempting to stabilize what has reportedly been a somewhat turbulent youth, was employed by a farmer. The drifter formed a warm relationship with the farmer's family, especially his latency age son, and reportedly was content in his new position. However, the farmer faced a number of economic difficulties, many of which clearly resulted from unfair business tactics perpetrated by a major competitor whose goals for development in the area were quite different from those held by the farmer. As a result of his employment by the farmer, the drifter also experienced considerable harassment and even humiliation at the hands of the outside competitor. Eventually the tactics engaged in by the villainous competition became so reprehensible and threatening that the drifter, apparently in a fit of white rage, armed himself, went into the home territory of the competitor, and in the course of a gunfight killed the competitor and his associates.

A second example involved a washed-up ex-boxer (probably with some degree of brain damage secondary to that experience) who became gradually convinced that the union with which he and his relatives and friends were involved was wicked and grossly oppressive. Ignoring all realistic caution and using only his bare fists, he eventually erupted into violence against that group of individuals.

Both of these examples illustrate some of the common characteristics of the violent person. According to Halleck (1980), two of the common motives for engaging in violent activity are to escape oppression and to increase self-esteem. In our examples both of these motives seem predominant. Some of you may have recognized our first example as the behavior of the character Shane from the movie of the same name and our second example as the character played by Marlon Brando in the famous movie *On the Waterfront*. In these two films one is gradually led to identify with a sympathetic character who encounters escalating frustration at the hands of villainous and violent opponents. Gradually both the character and the viewer are forced to conclude that the only solution is a violent one. I think it is safe to say that almost everyone who sees these movies experiences the final scene of violence as justified, satisfying, and very logical. Shane and Brando were heroes, their violence heroic.

Halleck (1980) also notes three other common motives for violent behavior: 1) to gain power or control over others; 2) to gain territory or wealth previously held by others; and 3) to gratify emotional needs such as sadism or revenge. If the motives we described for Shane, namely to escape oppression and to increase self-esteem or at least to avoid humiliation, are heroic motives for violence, then the three we've just named might be considered to be the villain's motives for resorting to violence.

Now with our oversimplified model let's look at the nature of violent behavior in adolescents. Are they villains or are they heroes? To some extent the answers to this question depends on one's perspective. Inpatient treatment staffs often feel that the adolescent patient is threatening violence or engaging in violent behavior in order to gain power and control over them and to satisfy an unhealthy desire to feel triumphant over staff and staff rules. In the case of some adolescent patients the staff believes that the youngster gains a pathological emotional thrill from intimidation and violent behavior. Villains for sure! These staff opinions are often inaccurate or at least distorted and exaggerated. However, the attitudes are understandable countertransference reactions to the threat of violence. In fact, it may be incorrect to refer to these staff attitudes as countertransference. They may be simply human reactions to real intimidation and a very rational fear of violence.

One needs to also recognize that a number of antisocial youngsters regularly utilize violent action to gain power and control over others. They use force to secure and maintain their drug dealing territories; they use violence and threats in outright extortion for financial gain. Some of them embrace a villainous self-image with considerable comfort and enjoy thinking of themselves as tough, streetwise "enforcers." It is difficult not to see these youngsters as intentionally "villainous" in the framework we have been describing.

The point is, for the most part these youngsters are not violent in a treatment setting. Since they are basically entrepreneurs who somewhat voluntarily and consciously utilize violence to gain fairly rational ends, they are more similar to the individuals in organized crime or the professional "hit men" who utilize violence not out of passion but from a conscious decision that it will gain them certain objectives. Their "malignant" defenses work relatively well, usually have considerable external support, and can be altered only with great effort and under circumstances that permit extensive control of them.

In residential settings these genuine villains recognize quickly that there is little to be gained by open shows of force since they are unlikely to emerge victorious. They may secretly engage in a variety of intimidating activities in order to gain special privileges among the patient group as well as to enjoy the sense of power that may come from being feared. However, when directly challenged they rarely explode into violence toward the staff but engage instead in negotiation, subterfuge, conning, and other techniques which are more likely to be successful. Villainous adolescents may frighten and intimidate residential staff but in fact rarely erupt directly into violent activity at least as long as the overall milieu remains constructive. These individuals can become quite dangerous under riot conditions as reports from a number of riots on adolescent units have confirmed. However, in the normal course of events almost all treatment problems with violence comes not from villains but directly from heroes.

Let us tell you about Bobby T.

Bobby was 17 years old when he was admitted to the hospital because of uncontrolled polydrug use, inability to accept any limits from his mother, disinterest in getting a job or pursuing any occupational goals, and an increasingly dangerous tendency to become involved in violent physical fights. In the three months prior to admission Bobby had been involved in numerous fights, two of which were very serious. In the first one he had received a massive laceration of his face and head which had already required one episode of plastic surgery and appeared to need a second intervention to avoid serious scarring. He emerged from the second fight with two broken fingers and an injured leg. In addition Bobby had been in trouble with the law, having been arrested once for breaking and entering and on another occasion for possession of a switchblade knife. Bobby was opposed to the hospitalization and insisted that he had no serious drug problems. He did admit, however, that he had been feeling depressed quite a bit since his graduation from high school and was concerned that he did not seem able to develop any interest in his future. He agreed somewhat ambivalently to give the hospital a chance.

Over the first few weeks of hospitalization, psychotherapy sessions with Bobby were characterized by a steady diet of opposition, negativism, and disputation. He questioned the basic therapeutic philosophy of the hospital program which he regarded as pollyannish and unrealistic. He was afraid we would turn him into, as he put it, "a pussy." It should be noted that Bobby engaged in these argumentative activities with considerable skill. Unlike many youngsters with malignant defenses, Bobby had no evidence of brain damage or other organic deficit aside from one febrile seizure in early childhood. He had no learning problems and his IQ was a sparkling 135. He was a worthy opponent on the fields of verbal battle.

Bobby particularly objected to the efforts of the staff and the psychiatrist to convince him that his involvement in violent fighting was part of his difficulty. In fact, even after he began to recognize that drugs presented more of a problem for him than he originally admitted and that they did play a major role in his chronic depression, he still argued for the necessity of frequent violent response in his environment. It should be noted that Bobby was not a ghetto child but in fact lived in a lower middle class to middle class neighborhood which was not characterized by massive social disorder nor ridden with crime. Bobby's predilection for fisticuffs was socially deviant in his environment.

Bobby did not claim that his violent behavior was purely self-defense. He saw it instead as directed toward assuring social justice and maintaining his own good name and self-esteem. Gradually Bobby described his peer interactions and the role that fighting played in them. In his depressive view of himself Bobby did not really expect to be liked. In some ways his situation with peers was a reenactment of his place in his family. Bobby's mother had been twice divorced. In her opinion neither man had been particularly fond of Bobby. Bobby's younger brother had a congenital heart defect and was overprotected and doted upon by mother and the maternal grandparents. Bobby's older brother was adored by the grandparents who rationalized his cruel physical domination of Bobby. Bobby's mother worked all day so that Bobby was often left at the mercy of his big brother who had taunted and beat on him regularly throughout much of his early childhood. When mother would come home she would feel sorry for Bobby and take up for him but this seemed only to increase his brother's anger at him. This annoyance tended to be expressed on the following day when mother was no longer around to provide protection. Bobby soon learned not to complain about his brother and instead gradually became more effective at fighting back. By the time adolescence came around the older brother's intimidation was greatly reduced because Bobby could hold his own in a fight. However, the two brothers occasionally still got into it and had to be separated to prevent the possibility of bodily harm to one or the other.

In any case, Bobby's friends encouraged Bobby to see himself as unusually brave and tough. They called on him as a bodyguard whenever any of them were bothered by other youngsters around the school or the community who were regarded as bullies. When they had a problem they would sic Bobby onto the offender. Bobby would taunt and chastise the enemy until he either engaged in a fight or backed down publicly and promised not to bother Bobby's friends again. Naturally, this position in the peer group marked Bobby as the modern equivalent of a gunslinger so those who wished to make a name would periodically "call him out" since if they were able to whip Bobby they would prove their mettle. Bobby was quite paranoid about the possibility of being hurt in this way and was very worried that the hospitalization might lower his physical skills which he kept carefully honed by working out regularly in a community gymnasium. Bobby was also willing to consider giving up drugs because he recognized that on several occasions he had lost fights and indeed, as mentioned before, had been badly hurt because some of his enemies simply waited until he was sufficiently under the influence of drugs so that he would not be effective in combat. On the other hand, Bobby was convinced that a moderate amount of alcohol greatly increased his effectiveness in battle since it lowered his pain threshold, removed anxiety, and raised his enthusiasm for the fight.

Naturally in the small society of the psychiatric treatment unit Bobby was tempted to utilize his skills as a fighter. There was absolutely no doubt that he saw himself as a hero. His near fights occurred when he defended the honor of some of the girls on the unit, stood up for a youngster whom he saw as oppressed and unfairly treated, and of course most often when he felt the yolk of oppression was settling on his own neck. There were some near scrapes with the staff around the highly structured and somewhat strict controls of the unit. As noted earlier, Bobby was not accustomed to rules and generally ignored those placed on him by his mother. He experienced the inpatient restrictions as demeaning and frequently saw the staff as simply trying to, as he put it once, "prove they had the keys."

Bobby's management in treatment was extremely complex and proceeded on a number of fronts. Family therapy was quite active and had to include his brothers. Since his mother had received a diagnosis of bipolar affective illness, Bobby was carefully tested for any biological evidence of endogenous depression. These tests were negative. There were lots of other issues too. However, it may be more truthful than poetic to say that most of Bobby's treatment centered around two goals. The first was to help Bobby see that he had the basic equipment and many basic attributes of genuine heroism while the second was redefining his previous behavior and his natural inclinations toward violence as less heroic than he previously had thought. We tried to convince Bobby that he could be competent. He didn't need pseudo-competence.

First of all the entire staff worked to understand Bobby's view of the world. They decided together to avoid power struggles with him as much as possible by carefully orienting him to all of the rules before he was in a position of conflict with any of them and by offering him options and choices whenever possible. They made the decision to accept and indeed to praise verbal opposition, labeling it as honesty and independence of thinking. This acceptance was always accompanied by a reminder that behavioral compliance with the rules and expectations of the unit would still be required even when Bobby disagreed with them. Every effort was made to encourage Bobby to become active in the student government and to learn the acceptable approaches to changing rules and practices on the unit. The staff learned early that like many potentially violent people Bobby required a good deal of physical distance. Bobby seemed to experience people standing close to him and particularly people touching him as an invasive provocation. He even avoided extended eye contact not apparently out of embarrassment but out of a fear of being controlled or dominated—as though he thought everyone had the power of the evil eye.

While accommodating some of Bobby's defenses, it was decided that his fear of backing down would be addressed as a weakness—an understandable weakness, but a weakness nonetheless. Every possible example of times when it took courage to avoid a fight or provocative comment were noted and underlined to him. His tendency to be used by others to fight their battles was pointed out sympathetically as an understandable insecurity rather than as a noble knight errant mission. This was first addressed around his interactions with the youngsters on the unit who used him to gain their ends but was gradually expanded to help him look at his peer interactions at home.

Bobby never agreed verbally with any of these new versions of reality which were presented to him. In fact, he continued to argue, verbally defend the underdog, and to describe his plans to wreak physical havoc on almost everyone that made him angry. However, his actual behavior changed in many ways both overt and subtle. Bobby became pleasant to be around. He smiled and relaxed and in obvious ways sought out the company of the male staff that he admired, with only the expected transparent adolescent denial of dependency and desire of approval. More important, when the chips were down around important treatment issues with other patients, Bobby almost invariably came through with good advice, human supportiveness, and sensible compromises. He was clearly a constructive leader and was elected representative to the student government from his treatment team. Finally he was discharged to outpatient treatment, still verbally promising nothing and indeed suggesting that he might well continue extensive contact with his old friends and with drugs but at the same time demonstrating entirely different interactional patterns within his family and with the treatment team which he left with appropriate affectionate regret.

Bobby illustrates the assertion that the successful treatment of the violent adolescent is largely a matter of the modification of a hero. It also suggests that treatment may require an inpatient setting. In addition to some of the individualized elements which we described in the case of Bobby, there are general approaches which are also important. First of all there needs to be a clear statement that violence will not be permitted in the treatment program accompanied by a clear explanation for the necessity of this posture. It must be made clear to each patient that although the staff does not wish to be hurt, that concern is not the only reason why violence is forbidden in the treatment setting. The treatment process is defined as an effort to learn to deal with one's feelings and with other people in such a way that there can be a satisfaction with life, no disabling symptoms, and sufficient comfort and happiness to avoid the temptations of omnipotent solutions such as drugs or violence. To gain these goals the patient will need to learn to deal with intensely angry feelings as well as many secret feelings of shame and inadequacy which cause him or her to feel highly vulnerable when they are exposed. It is obvious that it would be impossible to create an atmosphere where anger could be discussed openly, where differences between people could be addressed honestly and directly, and where people would feel safe to reveal uncomfortable secrets about themselves if the environment included the possibility of physical violence. In other words, violence is not permitted because violence would destroy the very hope that brought these youngsters to treatment, namely the hope that they can be treated and will be able to help themselves gain a more satisfactory life.

There are some unstated assumptions in this discussion. Clearly we are looking at things entirely from the patient's subjective perspective. We know, however, that the sense of oppression felt righteously by many of our patients is seen as very unrealistic by the rest of the world. A treatment program tries to make the patient feel more rationally powerful, therefore less vulnerable to oppression. Treatment also tries to redefine malice and oppression. For example, limits and controls are shown to be beneficial organizers of life rather than arbitrary attacks on autonomy. If paranoia distorts benign intentions or if drug detoxification produces pathological sensitivity, these issues are addressed with medication, explanation, and any other intervention that may help to constructively redefine the situation. Phantom enemies can be dispelled.

However, the entire sense of reality of the youngster cannot be challenged.

The legitimacy of the angry feelings and even desires for violence which the patient feels must be accepted and legitimate alternatives must be presented. These alternatives include such things as assertiveness training, symbolic outlets such as art therapy, opportunities for supervised confrontation of conflict between patients and between patients and staff, and a willingness to understand the origins of the anger and to assist the patient in resolving any internal chronic hostility which may be troubling them. Finally, as I think we could see in the treatment of Bobby, the treatment program needs to espouse convincingly a value system that insists that it is more heroic to avoid violence than to inflict it on even the most deserving villains. This may not be a universal truth but, at least in the treatment milieu, the adolescent can learn that it is possible to find solutions without violence and for many of them perhaps more importantly to gain honor and respect through building competence in positive interactions with others. Even if the lesson does not hold in all situations throughout all time, it is still worth learning that there is more genuine satisfaction in the laborious and intricate task of building a tower than in the illusory triumph of destroying one.

CITED AND RECOMMENDED READINGS

Ardrey, R. 1961. *African Genesis*. New York: Atheneum.
Bandura, A., and R. H. Walters. 1959. *Adolescent Aggression*. New York: Ronald Press.

Bender, L. 1959. Children and adolescents who have killed. *American Journal of Psychiatry*. 116: 510–513.

Capote, T. 1966. *In Cold Blood*. New York: Random House.

Dollard, J., et al. 1963. *Frustration and Aggression*. New Haven: Yale University Press.

Easson, W. M., and R. M. Steinhilber. 1961. Murderous aggression by children and adolescents. *Archives of General Psychiatry*. 4: 1–9.

Elliot, F. A. 1978. Neurological factors in violent behavior. In: *Violence and Responsibility*, edited by R. Sadoff. New York: Halsted Press.

Freud, A. 1949. Aggression in relation to emotional development: normal and pathological. *Psychoanalytic Study of the Child*. 3: 37–42.

Freud, A., and S. Dann. 1951. An experiment in group upbringing. *Psychoanalytic Study of the Child*. 6: 127–168.

Golding. W. 1955. *Lord of the Flies*. London: Faber.

Halleck, S. L. 1967. Psychiatric management of dangerous behavior on a university campus. *American Journal of Psychiatry*. 124: 303–310.

Halleck, S. L. 1980. Social violence and aggression. In: *Comprehensive Textbook of Psychiatry*, edited by H. I. Kaplan, et al. Baltimore: Williams and Wilkins.

Hartmann, H., et al. 1949. Notes on the theory of aggression. *Psychoanalytic Study of the Child*. 3: 9–36.

Hollander, H. E., and F. D. Turner. 1985. Characteristics of incarcerated delinquents: relationship between development disorders, environmental and family factors, and patterns of offense and recidivism. *Journal of the American Academy of Child Psychiatry*. 24: 221–226.

Kalogerakis, M. G. 1971. The assaultive psychiatric patient. *Psychiatric Quarterly*. 45: 372–381.

Karniski, W. M., et al. 1982. A study of neurodevelopmental findings in early adolescent delinquents. *Journal of Adolescent Health Care*. 3: 151–159.

Kaufman, I. 1962. Crimes of violence and delinquency in schizophrenic children. *Journal of the American Academy of Child Psychiatry*. 1: 269–283.

Kinzel, A. F. 1970. Body-buffer zone in volent prisoners. *American Journal of Psychiatry*. 127: 59–64.

Lewis, D. O. 1980. Diagnostic evaluation of the delinquent child: psychiatric, psychological, neurological and educational components. In: *Child Psychiatry and the Law*, edited by D. H. Schetky and E. P. Benedek. New York: Brunner/Mazel.

Lewis, D. O., and D. A. Balla. 1976. *Delinquency and Psychopathology*. New York: Grune and Stratton.

Lewis, D. O., et al. 1979. Violent juvenile delinquents: psychiatric, neurological, psychological, and abuse factors. *Journal of American Academy of Child Psychiatry*. 18: 307–319.

Lewis, D. O., et al. 1982. The medical assessment of seriously delinquent boys: a comparison of pediatric, psychiatric, neurological and hospital record data. *Journal of Adolescent Health Care*. 3: 160–164.

Lorenz, K. 1966. *On Aggression*. New York: Harcourt, Brace and World.

Madden, D. J. 1977. Voluntary and involuntary treatment of aggressive patients. *American Journal of Psychiatry*. 134: 553–555.

McDonald, M. W. 1938. Criminally aggressive behavior in passive effeminate boys. *American Journal of Orthopsychiatry*. 8: 70–78.

Meeks, J. E. 1979. Behavioral and antisocial disorders. In: *Basic Handbook of Child Psychiatry*, edited by J. D. Noshpitz. New York: Basic Books.

Morris, D. 1967. *The Naked Ape*. New York: McGraw-Hill.

Nadelson, T. 1977. Borderline rage and the therapist's response. *American Journal of Psychiatry*. 134: 748–751.

Penningroth, P. E. 1975. Control of violence in a mental health setting. *American Journal of Nursing*. 75: 606–609.

Rinklenberg, A., and W. Stillmen. 1970. Drug use and violence. In: *Violence and the Struggle for Existence*, edited by D. Daniels, et al. Boston: Little, Brown.

Robins, L. N. 1966. *Deviant Children Grow Up*. Baltimore: Williams and Wilkins.

Scherl, D. J., and J. E. Mack. 1966. A study of adolescent matricide. *Journal of the American Academy of Child Psychiatry*. 5: 569–593.

Shevitz, S. 1978. Emergency management of the agitated patient. *Primary Care*. 5: 625–634.

Simons, J. F., and J. Kashani. 1979. Drug abuse and criminal behavior in delinquent boys committed to a training school. *American Journal of Psychiatry*. 136: 1444–1448.

Solomon, P. 1967. The burden of responsibility in suicide and homicide. *Journal of the American Medical Association*. 199: 321–324.

Sosowsky, L. 1978. Crime and violence among mental patients reconsidered. *American Journal of Psychiatry*. 135: 33–42.

Stine, L. J., et al. 1982. What is the role of violence in the therapeutic community? *International Journal of the Addictions*. 17: 377–392.

Stubblefield, R. L. 1967. Antisocial and dyssocial reactions. In: *Comprehensive Textbook of Psychiatry*, edited by A. M. Freedman and H. I. Kaplan. Baltimore: Williams and Wilkins.

Tinklenberg, J. R., et al. 1981. Drugs and criminal assaults by adolescents: a Republican study. *Journal of Psychoactive Drugs*. 13: 277–287.

Waelder, R. 1960. *Basic Theory of Psychoanalysis*. New York: International Universities Press.

Wilson, J. G. 1976. A program for the prevention and management of disturbed behavior. *Hospital & Community Psychiatry*. 27: 724–727.

Yudofsky, S. C. 1989. Organic personality disorder, explosive type. In: *Treatments of Psychiatric Disorders, Volume 2,* by American Psychiatric Association Task Force. Washington, D.C.: American Psychiatric Association.

Zitrin, A., et al. 1976. Crime and violence among mental patients. *American Journal of Psychiatry.* 133: 142–149.

CHAPTER 15
the adolescent in legal difficulty

The problem of delinquency is much too complex for thorough discussion here (see Stubblefield, 1967). Some authors (Offer and Sabshin, 1963; Offer et al., 1965; Grinker, 1962) have found that a relatively high percentage of "normal" adolescents have committed one or more delinquent acts. Other authors (Masterson, 1967; Douvan and Adelson, 1966) have not found such a high incidence of "acting out" in their adolescent groups. In disturbed adolescents, however, overt antisocial acts are common. These illegal activities appear in youngsters with a variety of diagnostic pictures. They may accompany psychoses and personality disorders of various types. Even basically neurotic youngsters may on rare occasions behave in a delinquent manner (Marohn and Ostrov, 1979; Meeks, 1979). Because of this propensity for alloplastic expression of conflict, the adolescent therapist is frequently faced with the family crisis produced when an adolescent is arrested and threatened with possible legal action.

The therapist is often expected to assume the role of the omnipotent protector who will rescue the adolescent from the throes of the legal process. Since the legal position in regard to the adolescent offender is somewhat ambiguous, the therapist is sometimes actually offered this power by well-meaning legal authorities. Judges, probation officers, and others involved in juvenile correction are well aware of the role which family and individual psychopathology plays in many cases of juvenile delinquency. If a qualified and respected psychotherapist makes a strong plea that a particular child be managed medically rather than legally, charges are frequently dropped and the youngster is simply released from any legal responsibility for his delinquent behavior.

In the case of some basically normal and neurotic youngsters whose delinquency represents an isolated symbolic act, dropping of legal charges in favor of medical management may be an appropriate action. Unfortunately, the youngster who is struggling with a general problem of impulse control or the specific defects associated with superego lacunae is poorly served by such a failure in legal process. His pathologic sense of infantile omnipotence is strengthened. Society seems to be too frightened, just as his parents have been, to oppose his destructive impulses firmly. The adolescent feels this timidity as hostility and secretly believes that he is being given more rope with which to hang himself. The result is often a frightened repetition or intensification of testing behavior.

Youngsters with problems of impulse control need the external limits and structure which the legal apparatus may provide. An example of effective cooperation between probation officers and psychotherapists has been described by Kimsey (1969). Although the psychotherapist should never encourage or support vengeful, punitive approaches to the antisocial adolescent, he must recognize the value of the law and its official representatives in helping the adolescent master his impulses. Parents must be assisted to accept a similar attitude.

Parents will often be tempted to alleviate their feelings of guilt (which may be quite justified) by interfering with the process of law. Such ill-considered "help" may prevent the adolescent from recognizing his responsibility for his own behavior. It is hard for the adolescent to come to grips with himself if the parents tell him that their past mistakes "caused" his current legal problems. It is more productive for the parents to explore carefully their past and present contribution to their child's problems with rules, accepting and dealing with any guilt in an adult and mature manner. Confessing their "failure" to the child and begging his forgiveness can only compound previous errors and problems in the parent-child relationship.

Adolescents in trouble do need sympathy and help. However, the sympathy should be for the personal problems which tempt or force these youngsters into behavior that leads to loss of freedom and a lowering of self-respect. Help should be directed at encouraging personal growth and protecting both the adolescent and society realistically until a safe level of maturity and self-control is obtained.

Often, the therapist will not have the opportunity to deal with the adolescent or his parents until after an unrealistic "rescue" has been accomplished. In this case, the implications of corruption should be actively pursued in the therapy of both the adolescent and his parents. If such subtle encouragement of acting-out behavior is allowed to continue, the eventual results are always therapeutically disappointing and often literally tragic (Johnson, 1965; Millar, 1968; Leventhal and Sills, 1963).

THE DIFFICULTIES OF THE PROFESSIONAL

Parents and legal authorities are not the only people who have great trouble in dealing constructively with delinquent youngsters. The history of professional interest in delinquency suggests that we have had great difficulty in understanding and treating youngsters who act out. Eissler (1949) has suggested that the many confusing statements made regarding delinquency result from the fact that alloplastic expressions of psychopathology are very similar to normal behavior in that in both cases action is utilized to alter reality. He also notes that while neurotic and psychotic patients show clear evidence of discomfort, the "delinquent" appears to be having a very good time with his disability. Although most modern psychiatrists would agree with a theoretical position which stated that delinquency was the result of psychopathology, there does not seem to be any comparable eagerness to treat this particular pathological condition. For example, Robins's (1966) study of youngsters evaluated in the St. Louis Child Guidance Clinic revealed that those youngsters with severe behavior problems were less likely to receive extensive treatment. The followup study also demonstrated that this group of youngsters was at a high risk for the development of psychiatric disorder in later life. Careful psychiatric evaluation of delinquent youngsters by Lewis and Balla (1976) and by McManus et al. (1984)

has demonstrated that many youngsters in legal trouble are in fact seriously psychiatrically ill. It is also true, however, that many people are reluctant to recognize the presence of genuine psychopathology in youngsters who commit antisocial acts.

The relative neglect of this significant group of disturbed youngsters has many roots. It is more difficult to engage these children and their families in meaningful therapeutic work and they are often quite unpleasant to work with. In addition, the behaviors which characterize delinquent adolescents stir strong and uncomfortable feelings in the professional. The temptation to respond with punitive attitudes if not punitive actions is merely human. The view that the delinquent youngster is willfully bad (and enjoying it at that) is the historically traditional way of understanding delinquency. In fact it is only in very recent years that problem youngsters have been viewed in any other way. Prior to the twentieth century, antisocial youngsters were viewed as criminal and their misbehaviors were severely punished.

Of course mental health professionals rarely think about human behavior in this way, or certainly become uncomfortable if they realize that they do. It is possible that some notable tendencies to deny the reality and seriousness of antisocial personality problems may be partially the result of reaction formation against punitive attitudes such as those described above.

THE ADOLESCENT AT COURT

There are several ways in which an adolescent and his parents could find themselves at court. These experiences range from minor encounters to extremely serious situations, with the possibility of conviction on felony charges and incarceration for many years. Teenagers who do have significant emotional problems may well come to the attention of mental health professionals through a referral from court personnel, instead of being recognized by a school guidance counselor or a pediatrician. That is not to say that every adolescent at juvenile court has an identifiable and treatable psychiatric condition, but many of them do.

In some communities parents use the local police and the intake workers of juvenile court as the "heavies" who will give their child a good talking to, perhaps scare him a little in the process, and generally set him straight. This may all be done on an informal basis, without any charges being established or filed. For instance, the police may pick up an adolescent for shop-lifting. Even if the store does not press charges, the police might take the adolescent down to the station and then call his parents to come and pick him up. When the call comes, the parents might say that it will take them a few hours to get to the station and the police may want to talk a little harsh to him in the meantime.

The most common way for adolescents to participate in the court process is to be charged with a status offense. The term "status offense" refers to behaviors which are serious enough to involve a minor in juvenile court, but which are not crimes when committed by an adult. For instance, adolescents can be taken into custody for behaviors such as truancy, disobedience to school authorities, running away, and sexual promiscuity. Each case will be reviewed by a magistrate or other court official and, if appropriate, will be found to be in need of supervision or intervention. Thus, the acronym of PINS or CHINS or MINS for Person/Child/Minor in Need of Supervision. There is some controversy as to whether the whole concept of status offenses serves the needs of either adolescents or the rest of us. The history of the concept and the arguments pro and con have been summarized by Sacks (1980).

An adolescent who commits a crime may be arrested and eventually tried as a juvenile in a juvenile court or as an adult in the criminal court. In general, an adolescent is more likely to be tried in juvenile court if the crime was nonviolent, if he is relatively young, and if he is thought to be suitable for rehabilitation. An adolescent is more likely to be transferred or waived to adult court if he was closer to age 18 at the time the crime was committed, if the crime was violent and he is considered dangerous to the public, and if he does not seem amenable to rehabilitation. For instance, a 15-year-old who is a first offender and stole a car is likely to be tried in juvenile court. On the other hand, the prosecutor of a 17-year-old charged with rape is going to ask the judge to waive the case to adult criminal court. Psychiatrists and other mental health professionals may become involved in this process, since the court may be interested in clinical data in order to determine whether the youngster is dangerous and whether he is treatable (Barnum, 1987; Benedek, 1985). This has become an extremely important decision, since adult courts hand out adult-sized sentences—a court in Texas recently gave a group of suburban teenagers, most of them prominent members of the high school football team, sentences of up to twenty years for participating in a string of robberies. In another case, the Supreme Court held that it is not unconstitutional for a man to receive the death penalty, although he was a juvenile at the time he committed the offense.

Whether he is tried in juvenile court or an adult criminal court, the adolescent has more rights than he used to. Prior to the landmark decision by the Supreme Court of *In re Gault* (1967), it was assumed that the juvenile court judge would be looking after the interests of the juvenile offender. Prior to *Gault*, juvenile proceedings were conducted in a relaxed, nonadversarial manner without the need for formal fact-finding and defense attorneys. In *Gault*, the Supreme Court held that juveniles are entitled to most of the due process rights afforded adults, such as the right to notice of charges, the right to an attorney, the privilege to avoid self-incrimination, and the right to call and confront witnesses.

EVALUATION AND TREATMENT

In order to effectively treat the delinquent, we must recognize his serious ego defects. Superficially this defect in ego functioning seems primarily related to a "weakness" which interferes with impulse control. However, it may be more useful to see the eruption of impulses in the delinquent as a final desperate effort to compensate for other ego deficiencies.

The ego of the antisocial youngster is highly dependent on external agents for a variety of functions including management of stimulation levels, directing and maintaining attention, modulating affects, and a whole range of subtle operations related to the regulation of interpersonal relationships, particularly those that are emotionally important. Of course, these are the skills which enable one to master the environment and to maintain secondary narcissism and a sense of adequate selflhood.

It may be that the deficiency in these skills, whether it results from temperamental characteristics, constitutional or organic defects in the ego apparatus, or deficient parenting, is the core disorder in delinquent youngsters. Clinical experience often leads one to feel that the differences between the impulse-ridden youngster and the so-called neurotic disorder is quantitative rather than qualitative. Even a youngster who expresses an internalized conflict through antisocial behavior is revealing a failure in internalization and socialization. Followup of hyperactive children shows that many develop antisocial personality disorders as adults (Weiss et al, 1985).

If we assume a basic defect in mastery skills in delinquent youngsters, we can expect that there would be efforts to compensate for such a basic deficiency (Thomas and Chess, 1984). Some compensatory mechanism can be observed in the superego pathology of these youngsters, in their persistent efforts to alter reality, and perhaps in some aspects of their relationships within their families. Lacking a capacity for mastery, they must attempt to maintain a sense of omnipotence.

The clinical evidence for superego defects in antisocial youngsters is obvious. There is often a lack of remorse and conscious guilt regarding actions which are clearly harmful or unfair to other people. There is also research evidence that delinquents show a lower capacity for self-critical guilt than do controlled adolescents.

Other youngsters who act out appear to have indirect evidence of harsh and punitive superegos. The basically self-destructive quality of much of their behavior, their frequent tendency to apparently arrange detection and punishment, and their vulnerability to periods of self-hatred and depression suggest that some delinquents expend a great deal of energy in attempting to avoid strong feelings of guilt. One is also impressed by the extreme lengths to which these youngsters will go in order to maintain a sense of grievance against the world in order to justify their hostile and destructive behavior. Redl (1951) has been particularly articulate in describing the almost delusional quality of the delinquent youngster's sense of unjust treatment and the reluctance he demonstrates to relinquish this interpretation of the motives and actions of others. The youngster will insist he is being mistreated even in the face of repeated demonstrations of trustworthiness, friendliness, and kindness. This kind of behavior suggests that the youngster is attempting to avoid an internal sense of guilt regarding his antisocial behavior.

This is not to suggest that delinquent youngsters have normal superego function. It is obvious that they do not. However, it may be that much of the superego distortion observable in antisocial youngsters may be secondary to a basic defect in coping skills rather than the proximate cause of the antisocial behavior.

The limited adaptive skills of behaviorally disordered youngsters are also reflected in their attitudes toward reality. Superficially, delinquent youngsters are clever, shrewd, and manipulative. They are often quite effective in forcing other people to accommodate to them. Delinquents often appear willful and controlling, determined to have things their own way. For example, the normal youngster is willing, perhaps after a bit of grumbling, to adjust to his teacher's assignment of the difficult project, while the youngster with a behavior disorder may expend considerable energy avoiding the task or convincing the teacher that his expectations are too high. Many times the problem youngster may avoid the task and may be viewed as someone who gets away with things while other youngsters are forced to produce. What is often overlooked in this analysis of the situation is that the healthier youngster's superior coping mechanisms allow him the luxury of accepting the teacher's demand while the behaviorally disordered youngster is forced by desperation to persist in his efforts to avoid a task that he feels he cannot master. The delinquent youngster fears change, novelty, and being overwhelmed. He develops one aspect of his coping skills, those that relate to adapting reality to his limited skills, to a fine art. Unfortunately, this emphasis on controlling others actually leads to a continuing and growing atrophy of other skills.

It is well known that most delinquent youngsters tend to view themselves as helpless and out of control. They feel that they are the victims of fate and bad luck. They have very little sense that they can control their own destiny. Frenzied efforts to control individuals, events, and situations may be recognized primarily as efforts to gain some illusory sense of impact and personal importance.

From the psychological point of view, the antisocial youngster's assessment of his place in the world is correct. In fact, he is not master of his fate because of the previously mentioned ego defects. Although he misunderstands the reason for his lack of self-direction, his compensatory effects to prove that he is running the show (of his own life) are as understandable as they are ineffective in improving his situation.

Finally, it should be recognized that many delinquent youngsters use their parents as ancillary ego agents while denying that their parents' interventions are desired or helpful in any way. Many delinquent youngsters are masters of techniques for eliciting an unusual degree of parental support, direction, and even intervention in the youngster's interaction with his environment. At times this help is requested or demanded openly but more commonly delinquents provide an indirect invitation for assistance through constant failure in adaptation and apparent lack of concern regarding their dangerous situation. Obviously, the parents feel that they must step in and save the youngster.

Often the delinquent youngster can gain a measure of success with the direct assistance of his parents, but there are other defensive advantages in involving them in his affairs in any case. If the youngster continues to fail in spite of parental aid, he can define that aid as interference, babying, or domination, all of which may then be utilized as explanations for the failure.

Specific treatment techniques may be individual, group, or family. The selection of a treatment approach or combination of approaches will depend on the specific case and the nature of the motivation for change. Regardless of the approach, however, one needs to keep in mind the basic coping defects at the core of the problem and the primary defenses that the delinquent youngster utilizes in order to avoid facing this hidden deficiency. This defensive structure will surely lead the delinquent patient to act out again, to attempt to involve the therapist in a direct power struggle of some kind, and in efforts to corrupt the therapist. If one is able to patiently avoid becoming enmeshed in these defensive operations while continuing to provide affectionate acceptance coupled with reasonable limit setting, the delinquent youngster is provided with an atmosphere in which he can once again resume emotional and psychological growth.

Some delinquent adolescents do not respond to outpatient treatment, no matter how sensitive or brilliant the therapist may be. Many court-involved youngsters are referred to specialized day treatment programs and a variety of residential programs. The residential programs include traditional residential treatment centers, training schools, group homes, and wilderness programs such as Outward Bound. Some of these alternative treatment programs have been reviewed by Sarri (1985). Perhaps the most unusual "residential" program for delinquent youth actually traveled from place to place in the form of a wagon train. Some antisocial youngsters do seem to respond to long-term placement in a wilderness-type program. When confronted by the long, cold winter ahead and the need to build their own log shelter, some of these narcissistic adolescents lose their sense of omnipotence and entitlement. Not all delinquent youth respond to psychotherapeutic approaches and residential programs, but many do. Some future generation of therapists will probably be able to predict more accurately which interventions will succeed with particular adolescents.

CITED AND RECOMMENDED READINGS

Barnum, R. 1987. Clinical evaluation of juvenile delinquents facing transfer to adult court. *Journal of the American Academy of Child and Adolescent Psychiatry.* 26: 922–925.

Benedek, E. P. 1985. Waiver of juveniles to adult court. In: *Emerging Issues in Child Psychiatry and the Law,* edited by D. H. Schetky and E. P. Benedek. New York: Brunner/Mazel.

Douvan, E., and J. Adelson. 1966. *The Adolescent Experience*. New York: John Wiley & Sons.

Eissler, K. R. 1949. Some problems of delinquency. In: *Searchlights on Delinquency*, edited by K. R. Eissler. New York: International Universities Press.

Grinker. R. R., Sr. 1962. "Mentally healthy" young males (homoclites). *Archives of General Psychiatry*. 6: 405–453.

Guyer, M. J. 1985. Commentary: the juvenile justice system. In: *Emerging Issues in Child Psychiatry and the Law*, edited by D. H. Schetky and E. P. Benedek. New York: Brunner/Mazel.

In re Gault. 1967. 387 U.S. 1.

Johnson, A. M. 1966. Sanctions for superego lacunae of adolescents. In: *Searchlights on Delinquency*, edited by K. R. Eissler. New York: International Universities Press.

Kimsey, L. R. 1969. Out-patient group psychotherapy with juvenile delinquents. *Disorders of the Nervous System*. 30: 472–477.

Leventhal, T., and M. Sills. 1963. The issue of control in therapy with character problem adolescents. *Psychiatry*. 26: 149–167.

Lewis, D. O., and D. A. Balla. 1976. *Delinquency and Psychopathology*. New York: Grune and Stratton.

Marohn, R. C., and E. Ostrov. 1979. *The Psychological World of the Juvenile Delinquent*. New York: Basic Books.

Masterson, J. F. 1967. *The Psychiatric Dilemma of Adolescence*. Boston: Little, Brown.

McManus, M., et al. 1984. Psychiatric disturbance in serious delinquents. *Journal of the American Academy of Child Psychiatry*. 23: 602–615.

Meeks, J. E. 1979. Behavioral and antisocial disorders. In: *Basic Handbook of Child Psychiatry, Volume 2*, edited by J. D. Noshpitz. New York: Basic Books.

Millar, T. P. 1968. Limit setting and psychological maturation. *Archives of General Psychiatry*. 18: 214–221.

Offer, D., and M. Sabshin. 1963. The psychiatrist and the normal adolescent. *Archives of General Psychiatry*. 9: 427–432.

Offer, D., et al. 1965. Clinical evaluation of normal adolescents. *American Journal of Psychiatry*. 121: 864–872.

Redl, F., and D. Wineman. 1951. *Children Who Hate*. Glencoe, Ill.: Free Press.

Robins, L. N. 1966. *Deviant Children Grow Up*. Baltimore: Williams and Wilkins.

Sacks, H. S., and H. L. Sacks. 1980. Status offenders: emerging issues and new approaches. In: *Child Psychiatry and the Law*, edited by D. H. Schetky and E. P. Benedek. New York: Brunner/Mazel.

Sarri, R. C. 1985. Treatment alternatives in juvenile justice programs: a selected review. In: *Emerging Issues in Child Psychiatry and the Law*, edited by D. H. Schetky and E. P. Benedek. New York: Brunner/Mazel.

Stubblefield, R. L. 1967. Antisocial and dyssocial reactions. In: *Comprehensive Textbook of Psychiatry*, edited by A. M. Freedman. Baltimore: Williams and Wilkins.

Thomas, A., and S. Chess. 1984. Genesis and evolution of behavioral disorders: from infancy to early adult life. *American Journal of Psychiatry*. 141: 1–9.

Weiss, G., et al. 1985. Psychiatric status of hyperactives as adults: a controlled prospective 15-year follow-up of 63 hyperactive children. *Journal of the American Academy of Child Psychiatry*. 24: 211–220.

CHAPTER 16

the sexually active adolescent

THE HETEROSEXUALLY ACTIVE ADOLESCENT: A RELUCTANT LIBERTINE

Many young adolescents have sexual experiences. Even more youngsters would like their friends (often including their therapist) to imagine that they have an active sex life. The virile pursuit of girls is a socially sanctioned part of male adolescence. In recent years, in conjunction with the "sexual revolution," a similar readiness for experimentation of an overt kind has come to be expected of girls, at least in some cultural settings.

Without doubt, this social expectation is strongly reinforced by puberty's biological thrust toward sexual maturity. Observation suggests however that personal anxiety about adequacy and peer group pressure institute premature sexual behavior with greater frequency than any inner surge of lusty passion. Usually, early adolescent sexual drives are fairly well balanced by interpersonal anxiety and intrapsychic guilt, unless the anxiety is offset by a greater fear of being branded, by self or others, a sissy, chicken, wienie, nerd, or queer. Many of the adolescent boys who are seen in psychotherapy are either consciously plagued by doubts about their masculinity or driven to aggressive sexual exploitation to ward off the emergence of these doubts from the unconscious.

Some girls turn toward frantic sexuality during early adolescence to combat the regressive homosexual tie to the mother (Blos, 1963). They show more interest in scandalizing their mother and manifesting their complete scorn for her rules of behavior than in the boys that they pursue. They are not interested in any emotional relationships with the boys that they seduce. Often, they are more masculine than feminine in their aggressive conquest of males. They show virtually no tenderness toward the boys and often prefer to have many boyfriends on the string. Many of these girls engage in group sex with a number of boys, the "gang bang." In all of their sexual behavior, they exhibit a swaggering, triumphant, and spiteful attitude, both toward their mother and their sexual partners. When they become comfortable in therapy, they readily admit that intercourse itself gives them little or no pleasure. They do, however, enjoy shocking people with the prodigal sexuality. They also take pride in recounting their "track record," the number of boys that they have seduced. Particular pride may be shown over success in seducing a boy who was generally considered shy, innocent, or morally upright. One gets the uncomfortable feeling that they are displaying their collection of scalps when they list their sexual conquests. Any kind words are reserved for boys who treat them with indifference and contempt. "He don't give a shit about anything" is a highly complimentary description of a male companion.

Youngsters "on the drug scene" are often engaged in exploitive, affectionless, and promiscuous sexual behavior. The frantic search for new pleasures with denial of long-term consequences is part of the general push for a sense of omnipotent superiority to any rules of behavior or need for temperance. The syndrome will be addressed more completely in chapter 21 "Chemical Dependency in Adolescents."

Other adolescents, male and female, utilize sexual behavior self-destructively in the service of a punitive superego. In these instances, the sexual behavior may serve more to prevent true pleasure in sexuality from emerging than to move toward its attainment. The goal of these youngsters is to solicit external control and condemnation. This censure reinforces the faltering primitive superego and reinstates its domination over the instinctual life. The overt sexual behavior of these adolescents is marked by exhibitionistic display and subtle contrivance to be caught. Often, they blame their sexual partners for "leading them astray." It is not unusual to see this pattern repeat itself in a cyclic fashion with periods of prudery alternating with episodes of complete license.

In short, there is considerable counterfeit sexuality in word and deed during early adolescence.

In therapy, heterosexually active youngsters may attempt to maneuver the therapist into a stand against their sexual behavior on moral grounds. If the therapist opposes their sexual involvement because they are "too young" or because they are unmarried, the youngsters are usually satisfied to argue, relieved that they do not have to face their real problems. There are few adolescents who would not prefer to see themselves as precocious, daring, and immoral rather than frightened, childlike, or hamstrung by a rigid conscience.

Even the late adolescent, the college student, may use sexual behavior more as a defense against anxiety than as an expression of mature, responsible affection. This topic is discussed more fully in the Group for the Advancement of Psychiatry report on "Sex and the College Student" (1965).

Not all adolescents are sexually active. One study (Ostrow, 1985) reported that by their seventeenth birthdays 37% of the girls and 53% of the boys had sexual intercourse. This was in a suburban middle-class environment. There are many factors which seem correlated with being sexually active: youngsters who do not live with their natural parents are more likely to be sexually active; so are youngsters who are performing below average in school; black adolescents are more sexually active than white youngsters. Some youngsters are inhibited by religious prohibitions, are intimidated by strict parents, or are cautious because of concern about AIDS and other sexually transmitted diseases. It may be just as important to inquire why a patient is not sexually active as to study why he is.

PSYCHOTHERAPEUTIC MANAGEMENT
OF THE HETEROSEXUALLY ACTIVE ADOLESCENT

It is very easy for the psychotherapist to be drawn into a subjective response to the adolescent patient's report of sexual activity. He may view the adolescent boy's flight into hostile "making out" as a healthy move toward masculinity, ignoring its defensive, sadistic, pregenital nature. Conversely, unconscious envy and competitiveness may lead to an excessively suppressive attitude toward a budding comfort with male assertiveness of an appropriate kind. With adolescent girls, the therapist may panic over the possibility of pregnancy or may slip into a subtle seductiveness. Powerful myths surround the subject of adolescent sexual behavior, and these influence the adolescent psychotherapist along with the remainder of society. When these social forces act in synergy with serious unresolved adolescent conflicts within the therapist, the result can be either an explosive unconscious sanctioning of destructive sexual acting out or, equally harmful, a stiff moralism which merely suppresses sexual strivings and stunts the adolescent's emotional growth.

On Being an Old Fogy

There seems to be general agreement that a "sexual revolution" has occurred, although there is considerable disagreement concerning its exact nature and its desirability (Shainess, 1968; Halleck, 1967; Lief, 1968). More than ever, the adolescent patient will be disposed to view his psychotherapist as morally old-fashioned. The therapist usually cannot avoid revealing his values regarding sexual behavior even if he tries to remain scrupulously objective. It is probably unwise to remain morally "faceless" with an adolescent. At the appropriate point in treatment, it can be very helpful for the therapist to discuss his moral views frankly with his young patient. This is especially valuable if the therapist will differentiate between those views which have some support in experience and those which "just feel right to me."

Most psychiatrists value honesty and genuineness in human relationships, responsibility for one's behavior, avoidance of exploitation of others, and the relative superiority of long-term intense emotional commitments over casual, hedonistic attachments. Halleck (1969) has pointed out that youth often value style, "coolness," and nonpossessive relationships with a limited emotional commitment. Obviously there are some points of congruence and some diversions when the two lists of values are compared. As a rule, the points of congruence offer a "value

agreement base" solid enough to support psychotherapy. Our
young people do not advocate exploitation of others, interpersonal dishonesty, or self-deception. This common ground is usually sufficient for the exploration of symptomatic, pseudosexual
behavior in psychotherapy. This is possibly as far as the psychotherapist should venture in evaluating and assessing the sexual
behavior of our youth. If there is a detectable note of resignation
in this position, it is due to our personal belief that Deutsch (1967)
is correct in stating, "It has been my observation that an adolescent who invests his entire libido in genital gratification, for an
over-long and energy-consuming period, suffers with regard to
his capacity for sublimation, which may not fully recover during
the process of maturation." Unfortunately, at this point in our
history, American society offers little assurance of the value and
desirability of extensive sublimations. In many communities, it
seems almost quixotic to expect our young patients, already anxious and vulnerable, to delay gratifications which are virtually
pressed on them by prevailing social mores in order to achieve
a kind of personality richness and subtlety which seems of ques-
tionable adaptive value in their surroundings. At any rate, we may
have to relax our pursuit of the ideal sufficiently to accomplish
the possible—again, the exploration and treatment of neurotic
distortions of sexual behavior.

If we accept this limitation and agree that it is not the function
of the adolescent therapist to dictate or enforce moral codes,
sexual behavior may be evaluated as any other interpersonal trans-
action. A few of the questions which must be asked in the attempt
to evaluate the authenticity of any sexual activity are offered in
the next section.

Evaluating The Meaning of Sexual Behavior

Do the stated goals of the behavior match the adolescent's
actual management of the situation, or does the adolescent appear to be deceiving himself? Does he desire sexual gratification
or punishment for sexual behavior? Is he demanding an adult
prerogative verbally while clinging to childish irresponsibility and

dependency? To what extent does the sexual behavior serve the defense of "misdirection?"—that is, does the emphasis on sexuality hide a depression or a hostile, aggressive attitude toward other people? Does the sexual behavior appear relaxed and integrated in the personality or forced and counterphobic? Is the adolescent leaping into sexual behavior to avoid anxiety-producing sexual fantasies? To what extent are these frightening sexual fantasies related to oedipal involvements at home or with the therapist? How closely does the adolescent's relationship to his sexual partner approximate a mature, realistic human sharing? How much is the relationship still colored by identification with the partner, projection, idealization, narcissism, and other factors which diminish the humanness and autonomy of his lover?

These questions are complex and difficult to answer. They are offered only to concretize some of the issues implied by the truism that sexual behavior is an expression of the entire personality, not an isolated phenomenon which is to be viewed only from biological and moral perspectives. A broad view of the total developmental position of the adolescent permits the therapist to respond appropriately to the relevant growth problems of the adolescent without falling into futile efforts to dictate "proper" behavior.

Usually, however, it is necessary to set limits on sexual behavior in order to deal effectively with the real concerns which are being defended and disguised in the sexual acting out. For those adolescents who are deeply regressed or flagrantly self-destructive, it may be necessary to provide temporary or prolonged external control through hospitalization. In many cases, however, it is possible to establish a therapeutic alliance which is strong enough to manage the behavior. Interdictions are then based on technical considerations and are accepted because of the adolescent's wish to cooperate in a therapeutic process which already promises to provide greater benefits than those conferred by the conflicted sexual activity. The technique of limit setting is more fully discussed in chapter 4.

The therapist must trouble himself with one further question. Does the sexual acting out, even though it contains elements of neuroticism and immaturity, represent a progressive movement in development? The adolescent must experiment in real life. Often, he must learn by making his own mistakes, even in a potentially dangerous area such as sexuality. If the adolescent seems to be honestly evaluating his experiences and profiting by his errors, it may be unwise to emphasize prohibition. When the adolescent can decide for himself that a style of behavior is unsuited for him, he has accomplished a greater strengthening of ego functioning than when he merely desists to "please" the therapist.

It is usually possible to distinguish between acting out for purposes of learning and acting out which is defensive and regressive, although the distinction may not be easy in many cases. Usually, the therapist can sense whether the prevailing tone of therapy is exploratory or evasive. The therapeutic alliance is a useful barometer to watch during episodes of sexual activity. Its fluctuations often gauge the extent to which the flurry of activity represents a turbulent storm of change and growth, or merely more hot air.

The reader is referred to Rexford's (1963) thoughtful paper, "A Developmental Concept of the Problems of Acting Out," for a thorough exploration of the importance of acting out in psychosexual maturation.

ILLEGITIMATE PREGNANCY

Teenage pregnancy out of wedlock is a growing social problem despite improved methods of birth control and the ready availability of abortion (McAnarney and Hendee, 1989; Moore, 1987; Wright, 1966). The personal embarrassment and shame which illegitimate pregnancy causes in some families is commonly resolved by frequently ill-advised marriages (Gebhard, 1958). The divorce rate is extremely high in adolescent marriage (Osofsky et al., 1967; Semmens and Lamers, 1968); thus the original problem is often further complicated by the trauma of divorce.

Although the majority of reported illegitimate pregnancies occur in youngsters from economically and socially deprived backgrounds (Wright, 1966), teenage illegitimate pregnancies are quite frequent in other social classes. In the upper social classes, they are usually handled secretly, through precipitous marriage, abortion, or private arrangements for leaving the community during pregnancy and delivery.

The management of teenage illegitimate pregnancy is complex and involves the cooperative efforts of several professionals. A few programs have been instituted which attempt a comprehensive approach including quality obstetrical care, social work planning, and psychiatric counseling (Wright, 1966; Kaufman and Deutsch, 1967; Osofsky et al., 1967). In many communities, however, the psychotherapist will be called on to manage the crisis of illegitimate pregnancy. Certainly, when the pregnancy occurs in the course of psychotherapy, the therapist will need to be intensely involved in planning and managing for his patient.

The etiology of teenage pregnancy is complex, involving social, cognitive, and family forces as well as unconscious motivational forces within the adolescent girl (Young 1954; Vincent, 1964). Semmens and Lamers (1968) have described and illustrated three categories of teenage pregnancy according to the degree of conscious participation by the girl: 1) the intentional, 2) the accidental, and 3) the unknowing. The unknowing class involves primarily youngsters who either have not been exposed to information regarding conception or have inadequate intellectual ability to understand the consequences of sexual behavior. The psychotherapist will have occasion to deal primarily with youngsters in the first two categories.

The conscious, intentional teenage pregnancy is usually manipulative. The usual goals are either to escape or drastically to change an unacceptable family living situation. Pregnancy may be used to force parental agreement to a marriage which is regarded as unsuitable. Other youngsters use pregnancy as a conscious and deliberate spiteful attack on the parents. Even in these adolescents, other motives may be active at an unconscious level, although obscured by the conscious design. Of course, these unconscious motives are of central importance in the cases which belong in the "accidental" category.

Blos (1963) has described the pseudoheterosexual adolescent girl who utilizes heterosexual behavior to combat a regressive, homosexual attachment to the mother. There is evidence that illegitimate pregnancy occurs in girls who have serious ambivalent dependency conflicts with their mothers and absent or weak fathers (Young, 1954; Barglow et al., 1968; Cattel, 1954; Olson and Worobey, 1984). These dependency needs are often displaced onto the unborn child who is fantasied as "someone who will love me as I have never been loved." This dynamic constellation often interferes with plans for adoptive placement of the baby (Meyer et al., 1956; Barglow et al., 1968). As Barglow stated, "The depersonalized, unsatisfactory quality of the sexual experience and the immediate termination of sexual relations after pregnancy are consistent with a pregenital sexuality."

At times, one feels that the illegitimate pregnancy serves as a device to "get the parents off the hook." The adolescent girl seems to be living out her assigned family role as the scapegoated "bad" child. The fulfillment of the prophecy that she "would come to no good end" retroactively justifies the mother's long-standing neglect and hostility toward her. In these cases, the pregnancy may actually lead to apparent improvement in family relationships. The mother, fully exonerated, may relax her efforts to force the child into actions which define her as unlovable.

One final factor which must be considered in evaluating illegitimate pregnancy is the role of resurgent infantile omnipotence in the adolescent years. This force in mental life leads the adolescent to scorn reproductive reality by taking unwarranted chances, and its collapse is a major factor in the depressions which are seen in pregnant adolescents. The fact of pregnancy is often denied for a varying period (Semmens and Lamers, 1968; Barglow et al., 1968), but eventually it must be faced. The acceptance of the pregnancy completely shatters the adolescent's faith in her personal omnipotence and the omnipotence of her thought processes. This collapse adds to the adolescent's despair and heightens her sense of total helplessness. This is an obvious setting for a suicidal "ordeal" aimed at reestablishing a magical sense of unity with powerful inner and outer forces.

ANOTHER POINT OF VIEW

Aug and Bright (1970) have challenged many of the traditional views of unwed motherhood. These authors conducted a study of 24 unmarried adolescent mothers and 22 married adolescent mothers to determine their degree of psychopathology and their attitude toward motherhood. After studying them in detail, Aug and Bright divided the patients into four groups as follows.

Group I consisted of married girls who gave a history of family stability, warmth of interpersonal relationships, clear-cut family role patterns, and a constant relationship to surrounding social and cultural norms. Familial and religious sanctions against sexual activity were marked and there had been rare premarital intercourse. These young mothers showed a high regard for their infants and a substantial amount of positive affective interchange among family members. They described the father in terms of being a provider, but also a person who evidenced love for wife and offspring.

Group II consisted of unwed girls who seemed well adjusted with reference to their particular environments. It was common for these girls to have sisters and friends with an illegitimate child and a few of these girls were consciously trying to become pregnant. None of them were using contraceptives. These girls did not report a desire to marry the putative father. Even if the putative father was pictured as kind and generous with gifts and money for the mother's expenses, he was not a serious candidate for marriage, at least at that point in time. These girls had close personal relationships with their own mothers. All of these girls kept their babies and they were pleased to have a new baby in the family. In a recent study (Ralph et al., 1984) these findings were replicated in a low income group of Texas adolescents.

Group III included both wed and unwed individuals who showed pronounced disturbance of interpersonal relationships. They presented a picture of deprivation of financial resources and also of practically any positive affective cues in their environment. The parents of these girls were often openly abusive verbally, physically, and occasionally sexually, toward each other and the children. The putative fathers in this group were often heavy drinkers. They were unemployed or passed rapidly from job to job and had histories of a variety of antisocial behavior. These girls were ambivalent or openly negative toward their offspring. They often expressed intense need to have children, but at the same time conveyed thinly veiled hostility toward them.

Group IV was comprised of married black girls, who also exhibited marked disturbance of interpersonal relationships. All of these girls were illegitimate children and were very sensitive about having illegitimate offspring themselves. They all married at the time when they were four to seven months pregnant with their first child. The dominant theme in these people was that of very keen social conflict. They were quite conscious of middle class values which conflicted with the mores of the environment in which they were reared. These girls came from families which were unstable and splintered rather than extended family groups.

In light of their observations, Aug and Bright criticized some of the generalizations that had previously been made regarding out-of-wedlock pregnancy. For instance, one generalization held "out-of-wedlock pregnancy to be the signal of a life gone awry. Without intervention such a girl is doomed to a 'downhill spiral' of failure. In its mildest form this attitude sees all out-of-wedlock pregnancy as pathologic, or at least symptomatic of serious disturbances" (Herzog, 1969). Aug and Bright also criticized the generalization that the population of pregnant teenagers is homogeneous and that the majority of problems are found in the unwed mothers and not in their wed counterparts. Instead of these generalizations, Aug and Bright proposed a sociological and developmental evaluation of the meanings which illegitimate pregnancy may carry for various subcultures.

> "In Group III, unwed motherhood does indeed seem an expression of psychopathology at both an individual and family level. But in Group II, unwed motherhood seems to be a manifestation of an intermediate stage of psychosocial development which, although not yet mature, is quite normal for the subculture in which it occurs. In both of the subcultures which we have described (white Appalachian and urban Negro Bluegrass) the unwed mother may belong to a

closely-knit 'extended family' which consists of her mother and a number of her sisters, plus their illegitimate offspring. The mother role is shared, and the children are 'communal' to some extent. Younger sisters get considerable experience at helping to 'mother' these children, prior to conceiving their 'own'. Such mothering by the younger girls is not at the expense of their own emotional supplies, and is not done in an atmosphere of deprivation.

"Furthermore, in these two subcultures there is a marked dichotomy between the role of mother and the role of mate (sexual partner and helpmate). The notion of mother is quite important, definite, and extensively elaborated, even in the minds of 14-year-olds; but the role of mate is not definite, not elaborated. The male is merely a 'pollinator' who may also contribute some financial support. Although these girls usually had a 'better' relationship with the putative father than the girls of Group III (less conflict, more continuity), nevertheless the girls of Group II did not relate in depth to the putative fathers as mate, and would typically decline an offer to marriage, as irrelevant, as interfering with plans for school or work.

"Thus we have the puzzling phenomenon of girls who have become mothers, and who accept their mothering role and responsibility and do a reasonably good job of it, ... while not yet having mastered certain developmental tasks of adolescence and young adulthood which we ordinarily assume must be mastered before the individual is ready for the psychosocial role of parent. Examples of such developmental tasks which have not been mastered (by Group II girls) are:

1. The attainment of separation and independence from parents (followed by a partial return to the parents is a new relationship based on a relative equality).
2. A capacity for intimacy (in Erikson's sense) with a mate.
3. A commitment to work.
4. A commitment to an ideology; and the development of one's own personal moral values instead of merely incorporating the parent's values.

"On the other hand these girls have progressed on the important developmental tasks of being able to give considerable nurturance as well as simply receiving it. They are still nurtured by their own mothers, but are much more capable of giving sustained genuine nurturance to their infants than are the mothers of Group III. Incidentally, this capacity to continue accepting nurturance from their own mothers stands in sharp contrast to the situation from most middle- and upper-class urban unwed mothers, namely that the latter patients have intense conflict over their dependent ties (in fact all pregenital ties) to their own mothers, and usually are desperate to deny such ties and needs, e.g., by running away, defiance, etc.

"This idea of a normal developmental sequence in which motherhood occurs when other aspects of development are still incomplete is not a new concept. Therese Benedek (1959) discussed the further development which an individual undergoes as a result of the experience of being a parent: development which can proceed along either normal or pathological lines.

"Benedek's formulation of the sources of this further development was largely in terms of libido theory. We might add an additional source, namely that the bearing of a child (in a subculture that places great emphasis and value on the infant) by, say, an unwed 14-year-old girl confers a meaningful positive status within the family, for Group II girls. This is a situation in marked contrast to upper- and middle-class (and some lower-class) families. The multiple supports of such positive social feedback from this meaningful status would seem to aid immeasurably in sustaining a healthy psychological balance.

"Previously, out-of-wedlock pregnancy was often studied from a 'middle-class' viewpoint. This may have been appropriate since many studies involved middle-class populations. Since in the middle class illegitimacy seems to be a problem, however, studies with the above point of view tend to see out-of-wedlock pregnancy in general as a form of sexual delinquence. At the outset of such works there seems to be the assumption that out-of-wedlock pregnancy is a 'deviation' from the 'normal' pattern of development. The data which we have presented seems to indicate that for certain people, out-of-wedlock pregnancy is an accepted (by the subculture) and entirely 'normal' part of 'growing up'. The importance of illegitimacy, therefore, may vary greatly between individuals. One has to look at the individual existentially, as a person, as a family member, and as a member of a particular subculture group. . . ."

It would seem clear that our understanding of the implications of illegitimate pregnancy would be greatly expanded by further objective studies of this kind. It would be particularly useful to the adolescent therapist to have comparable data on the varieties of illegitimacy encountered in girls from middle-class families.

MANAGEMENT OF ILLEGITIMATE PREGNANCY IN ADOLESCENT PATIENTS

Emotionally disturbed adolescent girls (such as those in Aug and Bright's Group III and the neurotic variety described earlier) are frequently reluctant to inform their parents of an illegitimate pregnancy. One strong motivation for seeking abortion is to avoid the dreaded confrontation with enraged or wounded parents. The therapist should not only encourage the adolescent to tell the parents of the pregnancy as early as possible, but should offer his assistance in breaking the news if the adolescent needs and wants it. Some adolescents prefer to have the therapist tell their parents. Others want the therapist in attendance when they convey the information.

Once the fact of pregnancy is known to the family, the therapist needs to provide assistance in dealing with the parents' emotional reactions as well as making practical plans for the girl. The parents can be permitted and encouraged to ventilate their feelings of anger, shame, rejection, and guilt. The therapist must serve as a representative of reality and of the needs of the adolescent without condemning the parents. The parents must be gradually assisted to accept the reality of the pregnancy as well as the fact that their daughter has the ultimate responsibility in decisions concerning the pregnancy. Their role is to provide support, information, and counsel. Since many families in which a teenage pregnancy occurs have never functioned in this constructive and helpful way, extensive parental counseling is often necessary. In addition to this psychological help, both the parents and the adolescent will need factual information which may be best provided by referring them to professionals who devote themselves to the management of illegitimate pregnancy.

Abortion

The first decision which the adolescent girl and her family must face is whether to abort the pregnancy. Naturally, the adolescent therapist should be familiar with the laws and customs of medical practice regarding abortion in his locality. He must also consider his own attitudes toward abortion and convey these honestly to the adolescent and her family (Peck, 1968). Medical opinion is divided in regard to the psychiatric sequelae of abortion. Some authors (Muller, 1966; Kummer, 1963; Simon and Senturia, 1966) have suggested that serious disturbances may follow the procedure. Other investigators have been unable to demonstrate serious psychiatric complications in aborted women (Anderson, 1966; Peck and Marcus, 1966; Ekblad, 1955; Marder, 1970). Most evidence appears to support the statement by Heller and Whittington (1968) regarding one of their cases: "Forcing the young lady to go off, bear the child, and give it up for adoption, we are strongly of the opinion, may be more traumatic by far than abortion is likely to be." In recent years the intense media and political attention to the moral issues in abortion have intensified the potential conflicts of the adolescent girl.

Marriage as the Answer

If abortion is unwanted, the possibility of marriage to the baby's father is often considered. It is obvious that a forced marriage, undertaken only to avoid the shame of unwed motherhood, is rarely indicated. Usually, such a decision merely expands the problem. Of course, in some older adolescents marriage is desired by the couple. Often, the pregnancy was deliberately sought to force parental consent or to overcome rational misgivings within the couple themselves, such as economic considerations. The therapist can serve only as a supportive counselor, helping the adolescent and her family to avoid a foolish decision based primarily on a panicky overconcern with public opinion.

Placement

If neither abortion nor marriage is planned, the adolescent must decide whether to place the baby for adoption or to keep the child and care for it herself. This question may be settled by circumstances outside the adolescent's control as in the disadvantaged minority groups where few prospective adoptive parents are available. When a true option exists, the facts usually favor placement. By placing the baby, the adolescent girl is free to continue her education and maturation until she is truly prepared to accept the responsibilities of parenthood. As a rule, the baby is benefited, since most adoptive parents desire the child with less ambivalence than may exist in the unwed adolescent mother and her family.

Despite the above practical considerations, many adolescent mothers are reluctant to part with their baby. The need to keep the child may be based on a projective identification with the unborn baby in which the adolescent fantasies that the infant will feel abandoned and rejected, as she has. Guilt feelings about the sexual behavior which led to pregnancy may cause the adolescent to feel she should "take her medicine" by accepting the responsibility of child care. She is often strongly reinforced in this opinion by the generally punitive attitude of society toward the unwed mother. Other complex emotional patterns may make it difficult for the unwed mother to accept adoptive placement (Eisenberg, 1956; Schmideberg, 1951; Meyer et al., 1956). The therapist's job is to deal with these feelings with the same exploratory objectivity that he brings to all other issues in psychotherapy. The adolescent has the right to make the final decisions regarding her child, since she must bear the emotional and practical consequences of the choice. The therapist should make it clear that he will continue to offer his therapeutic aid no matter what the girl decides to do. Psychotherapy must continue following delivery, since there are difficult adjustments regardless of which plans are followed. The unwed mother and her parents need continued treatment, since there is a high probability of further pregnancies among girls who have one illegitimate birth.

CITED AND RECOMMENDED READINGS

Anderson, E. W. 1966. Psychiatric indications for the termination of pregnancy. *World Medical Journal.* 13: 81–83.

Aug, R. G., and T. P. Bright. 1970. A study of wed and unwed motherhood in adolescents and young adults. *Journal of the American Academy of Child Psychiatry.* 9: 577–594.

Barglow, P., et al. 1968. Some psychiatric aspects of illegitimate pregnancy in early adolescence. *American Journal of Orthopsychiatry.* 38: 672–687.

Benedek, T. 1959. Parenthood as a developmental phase. *Journal of the American Psychoanalytic Association.* 7: 389–417.

Blos, P. 1962. *On Adolescence: A Psychoanalytic Interpretation.* New York: Free Press of Glencoe.

Cattel, J. 1954. Psychodynamic and clinical observations in a group of unmarried mothers. *American Journal of Orthopsychiatry.* 11: 337–341.

Deutsch, H. 1967. *Selected Problems of Adolescence (with Special Emphasis on Group Formation).* New York: International Universities Press, Inc.

Eisenberg, M. S. 1954. Psychodynamic aspects of casework with the unmarried mother. In: *Casework Papers.* New York: Family Service Association of America.

Ekblad, M. 1955. Induced abortion on psychiatric grounds. *ACTA Psychiatrica Scandinavica (Supplement).* 99: 1–238.

Gebhard, P. 1958. *Pregnancy, Birth and Abortion.* New York: Harper and Bros.

Group for the Advancement of Psychiatry. 1965. *Sex and the College Student.* Vol. VI, Report No. 60. Formulated by the Committee on the College Student. New York.

Group for the Advancement of Psychiatry. 1969. *The Right to Abortion: A Psychiatric View.* Vol. VII, Report No. 75. Formulated by the Committee on Psychiatry and Law. New York.

Halleck, S. L. 1967. Sex and mental health on the campus. *The Journal of the American Medical Association.* 200: 684–690.

Halleck, S. L. 1969. Address to student health personnel. Southern Methodist University, Dallas, Texas.

Heller, A., and H. G. Wittington. 1968. The Colorado story: Denver General Hospital experience with the change in the law on therapeutic abortion. *American Journal of Psychiatry.* 125: 809–816.

Herzog, E. 1969. Families out of wedlock. In: *Family Dynamics and Female Sexual Delinquency,* edited by O. Pollak and A. S. Friedman. Palo Alto: Science & Behavior Books, Inc.

Kaufmann, P. N., and A. L. Deutsch. 1967. Group therapy for pregnant unwed adolescents in the prenatal clinic for a general hospital. *International Journal of Group Psychotherapy.* 17: 309–320.

Kummer, J. H. 1963. Post-abortion psychiatric illness—a myth? *American Journal of Psychiatry.* 119: 980–983.

Lief, H. I. 1968. Discussion of Shainess article. (See below.) *American Journal of Psychiatry.* 124: 1081–1084.

Marder, L. 1970. Psychiatric experience with a liberalized therapeutic abortion law. *American Journal of Psychiatry.* 126: 1230–1236.

McAnarney, E. R., and W. R. Hendee. 1989. Adolescent pregnancy and its consequences. *Journal of the American Medical Association.* 262: 74–77.

Meyer, H.J., et al. 1956. The decision by unwed mothers to keep or surrender their baby. *Social Work.* 1: 103–109.

Moore, K. A., et al. 1987. Statistical appendix: trends in adolescent sexual and fertility behavior. In: *Risking the Future,* edited by S. L. Hofferth and C. D. Hayes. Washington, D.C.: National Academy Press.

Muller, C. 1966. The dangers of abortion. *World Medical Journal.* 13: 78–80.

Olson, C. F., and J. Worobey. 1984. Perceived mother-daughter relations in a pregnant and non-pregnant adolescent sample. *Adolescence.* 19: 781–794.

Osofsky, J. J., et al. 1967. Problems of the pregnant schoolgirl: an attempted solution. *New York State Journal of Medicine.* 67: 2332–2343.

Ostrow, E., et al. 1985. Adolescent sexual behavior. *Medical Aspects of Human Sexuality.* 19: 28–43.

Peck, A. 1968. Therapeutic abortion: patients, doctors and society. *American Journal of Psychiatry.* 125: 797–804.

Peck, A., and H. Marcus. 1966. Psychiatric sequelae of therapeutic interruption of pregnancy. *Journal of Nervous & Mental Disease.* 143: 417–425.

Ralph, N., et al. 1984. Psychosocial characteristics of pregnant and nulliparous adolescents. *Adolescence.* 19: 283–294.

Rexford, E. 1963. A developmental concept of the problems of acting out. *Journal of the American Academy of Child Psychiatry.* 2: 6–21.

Schmideberg, M. 1951. Psychiatric-social factors in young unmarried mothers. *Social Casework.* 32: 3–7.

Semmens, J. P., and W. M. Lamers. 1968. *Teenage Pregnancy.* Springfield, Illinois: Charles C. Thomas, Publisher.

Shainess, N. 1968. The problem of sex today. *American Journal of Psychiatry.* 124: 1076–1081.

Simon, N. M., and A. G. Senturia. 1966. Psychiatric sequelae of abortion: review of the literature, 1935–1964. *Archives of General Psychiatry.* 15: 378–389.

Vincent, C. E. 1961. *Unmarried Mothers.* New York: Free Press of Glencoe.

Wright, M. K. 1966. Comprehensive services for adolescent unwed mothers. *Children.* 13: 171–176.

Young, L. R. 1954. *Out of Wedlock.* New York: McGraw-Hill Book Company.

CHAPTER 17

homosexuality and other sexual issues

This chapter pertains to several loosely related topics which involve adolescent sexual behavior and concerns. These include homosexual fantasies and behaviors, sexual offenses, AIDS, and paraphilias. These topics pertain primarily to male adolescents, although not exclusively. The adolescent or his family may be concerned about his behavior and want to determine whether treatment is needed. A teenager may need help in developing his masculine self-image or in exploring his choice of a homosexual or bisexual orientation. Adolescent sex offenders may need an approach aimed at impulse control. While the topics and treatment approaches considered in this chapter vary, a common thread is the concern experienced by the adolescent or his family about his sexual behavior and the implications this may have for his future.

HOMOSEXUALITY IN ADOLESCENCE

Little data exist regarding either the nature or treatment of adolescent homosexuality in the psychiatric literature. This is somewhat surprising, since homosexual behavior is fairly frequent in the adolescent population. It is well known that many adolescent boys fear passive wishes within themselves which they interpret as "homosexual tendencies." As we have noted, a similar fear often provokes inappropriate heterosexual behavior in the girl. Although the vast majority of adolescents remain terrified of the prospect of sexual inversion, homosexuality appears to be more easily accepted among some subcultures of older adolescents than it has been in the past. The acceptance of homosexuality among older adolescents and young adults is apparent in the Gay Pride marches that occur in many cities each year. There are public figures and political leaders who are openly homosexual and some professional organizations have gay caucuses.

The Pseudohomosexual Adolescent

In adolescence, most "homosexual" feelings actually resemble "pseudohomosexuality" as described by Ovesey (1955). The adolescent boy is uncertain of his masculinity and tends to react to any personal setback as a castration which diminishes his security as a male. These defeats also increase dependency feelings, which are especially likely to be directed toward strong masculine figures. This combination of factors is often interpreted by the adolescent male as evidence of homosexuality. The resulting anxiety often precipitates a further cycle of failure → sense of castration → dependency yearnings → greater fears of homosexuality. Obviously, the boy who is caught up in this sequence finds it very difficult to approach girls with the necessary degree of self-assertion, masculine pride, and self-confidence to attract them. His lack of success in dating perpetuates the vicious cycle of masculine failure. Youngsters caught in such a pattern may develop straightforward symptoms of depression and anxiety or may attempt to disguise their concerns from themselves and others by hyperaggressive acting out. It is important to distinguish "delinquent" behavior of this kind from that which results from basic defects in socialization.

TREATMENT OF THE PSEUDOHOMOSEXUAL ADOLESCENT. If the adolescent presents with a facade of acting out, this must be managed first through the techniques described in chapter 4 (in the sections on developing the therapeutic alliance). When the fears of homosexuality are openly expressed, the therapist can begin to deal with them as outlined in the present section.

The origins of pseudohomosexuality in the adolescent male may include family constellation (such as the absence of an adequate male model), family dynamics (such as a mother or father who is frightened by normal masculine assertiveness), accidental traumas (physical disabilities or homosexual seduction by an older male), or temperamental inclinations toward passivity. It is important for the therapist to understand the beginnings of the heightened sensitivity to failures in masculine functioning. These may be useful later in therapy as the adolescent begins to define and synthesize his own style of male functioning. In this undertaking, he will need to assimilate his personal experiences with maleness in all its idiosyncratic richness.

Early in therapy, however, excessive dynamic exploration should be avoided. It will not help the adolescent if he interprets a genetic reconstruction as an explanation of how he came to be homosexual. The immediate goal is to reassure the adolescent that he is *not* homosexual.

It is important for the therapist to provide a model of active, assertive, and effective masculine functioning from the onset of therapy. Although we have some skepticism regarding the overriding importance of the sex of the therapist in adolescent psychotherapy, pseudohomosexual youngsters probably do need a concrete model of sex-role functioning. The pseudohomosexual boy often responds to this by forming an immediate (pseudohomosexual) dependent, positive, passive transference. This bond may then be utilized to redefine the adolescent's problem as masculine self-doubt rather than incipient homosexuality.

If the timing is correct, the adolescent's revulsion toward his homosexual thoughts and his frustrated yearnings for success with girls may be used to prove his heterosexual orientation to his satisfaction. In addition, the "powerful" therapist should not hesitate to use his status as an expert to state flatly and with conviction that the adolescent is a worried heterosexual and in no way homosexual.

After the therapist convinces the adolescent that he is heterosexual, it is safe to explore the misconceptions which the youngster harbors both about himself and the nature of masculinity. Many of these young men have been rejected by fathers who have defined masculinity in narrow and sometimes unattractively cruel, cold, and combative terms. A corrective redefinition within the treatment relationship can often literally free the adolescent to be "his own man."

The play *Tea and Sympathy* provides a sensitive portrayal of such a young man, although the treatment approach employed by the heroine cannot be generally recommended. She is the wife of the hypermasculine coach—one of the men who disparages the hero's masculinity. She finally offers herself as a sexual partner to the hero in a desperate and successful effort to prove his adequacy once and for all. The story clearly states the unconscious fantasy of the passive male who wins the oedipal contest through gentleness and passive suffering.

Usually, therapy must include active encouragement of appropriate heterosexual behaviors. Often, it is necessary to be quite active in teaching basic dating and conversational skills as well as supporting worth and attractiveness. The occasional misgivings that the boy may be performing heterosexual behavior because of his homosexual attachment to the therapist are usually dispelled rapidly when the youngster begins to have some success with girls.

While supporting masculine assertiveness in the "outside" world, the therapist gradually becomes less active in the therapy. With as much subtlety as possible, the therapist allows and encourages the adolescent to become more assertive and aggressive during therapy sessions. If the boy is able to disagree with a comment, the therapist may allow himself to be convinced, if the comment is not essential to the goals of therapy. Occasionally, the therapist casually defers to an area of expertise which the adolescent possesses. In many small ways, he demonstrates his respect for the younger man's masculinity. The therapist is not pretending that his masculine competence is inferior to the adolescent's. The goal is merely to show the adolescent, as the famous teacher of psychiatry Dr. Maurice Levine was fond of saying, that there can be two men in the same room.

Since many of these young men have secret wishes to be powerful and to dominate other men, it is important for the therapist to insist on his own worth. The therapist has a further opportunity in this phase of treatment to correct the distorted picture of masculinity which these young men harbor. They need to learn that men can be self-respecting, assertive, and competent without being cruel, overbearing, or domineering. In the therapeutic relationship, neither individual dominates or is dominated.

A note of caution should be added. The therapist will find it fruitless to tell the adolescent directly to "be more aggressive" (or "be less passive") toward him. Such a request is a double bind, since by definition autonomous activity cannot be required by another person. Pseudoassertion, which is actually a phony and involuted form of passive compliance, is the only possible result of such a request. The adolescent's self-assertion must germinate and grow spontaneously from his own inner strengths. The therapist can only provide climate control, protection, and applause for the first tender buds.

The Overtly Homosexual Adolescent

The psychiatric literature offers very few accounts of psychotherapy of the overt homosexual during the adolescent period. This may be due to a reluctance to define the adolescent as a homosexual. This caution is reasonable, since overt homosexual behavior during adolescence does not necessarily eventuate in a homosexual life pattern. Identity is fluid during adolescence and experimentation does occur (Freud, 1965). It does not follow, however, that overt homosexual relations during adolescence should be taken lightly. Such relationships, especially if repeated with any regularity, do interfere with the development of an adequate sex-role identity. They are indicative of an unusual degree of anxiety about heterosexual behavior and suggest serious underlying developmental deviation.

ETIOLOGY OF HOMOSEXUALITY. The days are over for thinking that a person's sexual orientation can have a single or simple cause. It is clear that we can no longer satisfy ourselves with simplistic theories of "family configuration" to account for the development of homosexual behavior. (See Kremer and Rifkin, 1969.) It is now thought that every person's sexual orientation is influenced by genetic, hormonal, psychological, and social factors. On the hormonal level, it may be that circulating androgen during the prenatal period may need to reach a particular level in order to cause the fetal hypothalamus to organize in a way that will later facilitate heterosexual development (Dorner, 1976). The interested reader is directed to the extensive publications of Money (1988) and Stoller (1967, 1975, 1985) for new developments in this fascinating research area.

On the psychological level, some investigators of homosexual behavior felt that the basic disorder is a phobic avoidance of the female genitalia (Ovesey and Gaylin, 1965; Socarides, 1960). Early life experiences appear to be of crucial importance (Stoller and Herdt, 1985). Psychoanalytic studies have proposed that homosexuality occurs when boys with overintimate mothers and distant or hostile fathers become fearful of heterosexual impulses (Bieber, 1962). Socarides's (1978) classification of homosexuality included the preoedipal form and the oedipal form. In the former, the child experienced an "inability to traverse the separation-individuation phase . . . and develop a separate and independent identity from the mother. . . ." In the oedipal form, homosexuality is caused by a failure to resolve the oedipus complex and adoption of a negative oedipal position and a partial regression to anal and oral conflicts.

Some mental health professionals would say that homosexuality does not have any etiology at all, because inquiring about etiology implies that there is some pathological process involved. According to Martin (1982), for example, "homosexuality is a normal variation in both sexual orientation and sexual behavior." He would point out that many of the symptoms that gay adolescents experience are a result of prejudice, isolation, and stigmatization, and not derived from the original condition of being homosexual. Isay (1989) has also developed the thesis that homosexuality is a normal outcome of sexual development.

HELPING YOUNGSTERS WHO WANT TO BE STRAIGHT. Most successful therapeutic approaches to homosexuality appear to contain major elements of behavioral modification, alone or in conjunction with an exploration of emotional factors (Bentler, 1968; Thorpe, 1963). Although we have a great deal still to learn, the most promising approaches appear to utilize an early phase of conventional exploratory therapy followed by an active effort to

John Money, Ph.D., has been director of the Psychohormonal Research Unit, The Johns Hopkins University, Baltimore, Maryland. He wrote *Gay, Straight, and In-Between* (Money, 1988). Robert Stoller, M.D., is Professor of Psychiatry at the University of California at Los Angeles School of Medicine. He wrote *Sex and Gender* (Stoller, 1968) and *Perversion* (Stoller, 1975). These men have elucidated the difference between *sex*, which is a biological quality having to do with maleness and femaleness, and *gender*, a psychological state related to masculinity and femininity.

encourage appropriate heterosexual behavior and to extinguish the learned pattern of homosexual arousal (Ovesey and Gaylin, 1965; Fox and DiScipio, 1968). Hatterer (1970) described a comprehensive approach to the treatment of male homosexuality that involved identifying the trigger mechanisms that provoke homosexual feelings; actively encouraging heterosexual identifications; and providing the patient with a "tape capsule," an audiotape made for that specific patient for him to review between therapy sessions. Hatterer found his treatment successful for patients who were motivated to change.

As with the pseudohomosexual youngster, the therapist should make every reasonable effort to discourage the overtly homosexual adolescent from viewing himself as finally and irrevocably homosexual. This crystallization of sexual identity may be tempting to many adolescents who are deeply troubled by guilts and anxieties about heterosexuality. Even if the self-definition of homosexuality may be somewhat repugnant, it may at least offer the relief of a deliberately chosen defeat and retreat.

As always, the therapist can only offer as much help as the adolescent wants. Confusion arises because the adolescent's "wants" are often ambivalent and disguised. It is impossible to evaluate sexual preference origins with an adolescent who is predominantly satisfied with homosexuality, no matter how upset his family and others may be regarding his choice. It is often quite possible to explore this area with an adolescent who says initially that he is satisfied with homosexuality. The therapist decides whether a trial of therapy is indicated after evaluating the adolescent's personality development and functioning, basing his decisions on both verbal and nonverbal communication from his young patient.

A 17-year-old boy managed to convince his parents to arrange psychotherapy for him by telling them that he was worried about possible academic failure.

He quickly told the therapist that his real concern was related to homosexual behavior, which he had engaged in for the past two years. He carefully explained that he enjoyed this behavior and had no intention of giving it up. When confronted gently with the apparent contradiction between his stated attitude and his request for psychotherapy, he explained that he wanted to know more about why he had homosexual feelings. He knew that he would face the possibility of military service soon. He wanted to be sure he understood himself sufficiently to suspend homosexual activities temporarily during this period in order to avoid "dishonorable discharge" and "scandal." The therapist accepted this "contract" with the provision that it would be regarded as a tentative starting point.

In actuality, therapy soon revealed that homosexuality was ego-alien to the youngster. The patient formed a therapeutic alliance quickly and actively explored his inner feelings. Later, he cooperated fully in efforts to direct him into a heterosexual adjustment.

The boy's initial assertion of commitment to homosexuality appeared in retrospect to serve the functions of protecting him from both the fear of change and doubts that he would be able to find other satisfactions. It was easily relinquished when the therapeutic relationship was solidly established.

Certainly, at this point we must approach the therapy of homosexual with an attitude of open-minded inquiry. Clinical research regarding both etiology and effective therapeutic approaches is urgently needed.

HELPING YOUNGSTERS WHO WANT TO BE GAY. Some youngsters are convinced that homosexuality feels right for them. They can describe having exclusively homosexual fantasies from several years prior to puberty to the time that their parents bring them in for medical and psychological evaluation. The youngster may agree to complete the evaluation and even pursue a short trial of therapy, all in the interest of understanding himself more completely and with the idea of exploring both homosexual and heterosexual options. These patients—at least the ones from urban and suburban areas—usually know that after high school they will be able to shape whatever lifestyle they may desire. They may even know that the American Psychiatric Association no longer considers homosexuality an illness. The therapist may wish to encourage the gay adolescent to keep his options open, but in the end the patient will have to establish his own sexual preference.

Of course, many overtly homosexual adolescents who have no intention of considering a heterosexual adjustment may still need psychotherapy. Homosexuals have a variety of psychological problems which may be relatively unrelated to their sexual preference. Homosexual youngsters may also need help in dealing with society's reaction to their lifestyle. Although there have been many gains in social acceptance, many areas of mistreatment and unfairness remain. In addition, many parents have strong negative reactions to their homosexual children. Both parents and children need support and understanding to encourage family re-integration.

Anderson (1987) described a support group for gay adolescents. It was organized "to provide a place where youth who defined themselves as gay could meet and share their experiences with other gay adolescents." About 25% of the participants were girls. In working with these nonpatient youngsters, Anderson found that most of these gay adolescents wished that their parents would be more accepting and supportive of their sexual orientation. He described how families deal with the announcement when gay adolescents "come out" to their parents—the healthier families went through the stages of shock, denial, anger, guilt, and eventually acceptance and acknowledgement.

REALISTIC EXPECTATIONS. The research by Alfred C. Kinsey (1948) included the sexual histories of 12,000 men. He emphasized the continuity of the gradations between exclusively heterosexual and exclusively homosexual histories. That is, some men described "sociosexual contacts and responses" which were exclusively with individuals of the opposite sex. At the other end of the scale were men who were exclusively homosexual in behavior and in fantasy. There were many men in between, which represented various gradations of bisexuality.

It is unlikely that exclusively homosexual men are amenable to changing their orientation through any form of therapy. At least, it would be just as hard as trying to change the orientation of a fundamentally heterosexual individual. Bisexual patients who are highly motivated may be able to modify their lifestyles and sexual behavior. After therapy, however, they still experience homosexual fantasies and dreams.

The therapist of a bisexual adolescent may have reason to be more optimistic. The fluidity of this stage of development creates opportunities. Although the therapist may need to recognize the role of inheritance and prenatal hormones and parental influences, the adolescent will also have the chance to shape his own sense of identity.

ADOLESCENTS AND AIDS

The information that today's teenagers learn about sex and sexuality is quite different from what their parents learned. The content of the "curriculum" is different and the "faculty" is different for these two generations. The current generation of parents learned general information about sex from a parent—usually the parent of the same gender—and went on to get the nitty-gritty details from peers and through their own adventures. The course content mainly pertained to the anatomical aspects of sexual functioning, with a brief reference to the dangers of pregnancy, syphilis, and gonorrhea. The current generation of teen-agers learns a great deal about sex at school. Today's adolescents have already been taught in elementary school the rudiments of the anatomy and physiology of sex. In some areas school per-sonnel provide information about masturbation, homosexuality, contraception, and abortion. It is hard to say very much about any of those topics without conveying something about your sys-tem of values. Most parents want the public schools to promote good values in their children, but disagree about what the specific values should be.

AIDS is a low-incidence, highly lethal, highly publicized, pre-ventable disease, so in the 1980s many school systems rapidly introduced AIDS-education programs for their students. As a result of these public health measures, many high school students learned more about AIDS than their parents. They learned the difference between being infected with HIV (human immuno-deficiency virus); having AIDS (acquired immunodeficiency syn-drome); and having the AIDS-related complex. The typical ap-proach to teaching about AIDS involves traditional classroom instruction and dramatic audiovisual material. Sometimes the vi-deotapes include poignant interviews with patients who are dying from AIDS. The patients are diverse enough to allow every stu-dent to identify with at least one of them. They may be white, black, homosexual, heterosexual, users of IV drugs, or simply recipients of blood transfusions. At the end of the videotape, a caption may tell the viewers which patients have already died, between the time of the taping and the time it was edited and released.

In order to systematically provide fiscal and technical assistance to states and communities that require HIV education programs, the Centers for Disease Control (1988) have surveyed high school students to see what they already know about AIDS and HIV. The great majority, about 90%, of the students knew that HIV infection can occur through IV-drug use and through sexual in-tercourse. However, these youngsters had many misconceptions about HIV infection. About half of the high school students sur-veyed thought that HIV transmission could occur through giving blood, insect bites, using public toilets, and having a blood test. These data have implications for the prevention of HIV transmission among adolescents. Teenagers are going to be much more successful in avoiding infection if they focus their own preventative measures where it really matters (using drugs intravenously, having sex without condoms, and having multiple sex partners) than in avoiding behaviors that do not matter at all (giving blood, having blood tests, etc.).

Belfer (1988) has discussed the implications of AIDS in working with children and adolescents and he pointed out that the illness will have an increasing impact on the psychological lives of both infected and noninfected individuals. He pointed out that public health measures should address adolescents because many teenagers engage in behaviors which increase their risk of infection: multiple sex partners without any form of protection against infection; homosexual behavior; and intravenous drug use. Belfer suggested that interventions should be adapted to specific subgroups of adolescents. For instance, therapists could help educate peer counselors, who would then present AIDS education in youth-conducted rap or discussion groups. Such programs should occur not just in schools, but in runaway shelters and juvenile detention centers and other likely places of contact. He suggested that youngsters who are admitted to hospital treatment programs should routinely receive AIDS preventive education. The subgroup of homosexual adolescents is very hard to reach in a specific manner because this is largely a secret population. In your everyday public high school it would be very hard to conduct a rap session for the homosexual students to talk about AIDS prevention. However, if a community had an ongoing support group for homosexual youth, AIDS would obviously be a good topic for the meeting.

Very few adolescents actually have AIDS—so far. Because of the long incubation period, adolescents may engage in risky activities and become infected with HIV, but not develop the illness itself until adulthood. Almost all the patients with AIDS are adults (who may have become infected as adolescents) and younger children (who were infected during pregnancy or delivery by their infected mothers). However, it is likely that the number of adolescent victims will increase greatly in the next few years. This crisis will involve both boys and girls, since it will be transmitted through heterosexual intercourse.

Fear of AIDS can be an issue in understanding adolescent behavior. For instance, a youngster who had been exposed to HIV infection may become scared to death, and then propel himself into counterphobic sexual behavior in order to prove to himself that no little virus is going to hurt him or kill him.

ADOLESCENT SEX OFFENDERS

A good clinical definition (Ryan, 1987) of the adolescent sex offender is a youth, from puberty to legal age of majority, who commits any sexual act with a person of any age, against the victim's will, without consent or in an aggressive or threatening manner. This definition includes both hands-on offenses, such as child molestation and rape, and hands-off offenses, such as exhibitionism, voyeurism, and obscene phone calls. The vast majority of adolescent sex offenders are males. It is useful to cite examples to clarify the difference between sex offenders, adolescents with sexual disorders, and normal sexual behavior:

—A 13-year-old boy who threatened three younger boys with a screwdriver and then exposed himself to them was a sex offender.

—A 15-year-old boy who stole female underwear and then masturbated with it was not a sex offender, but had a sexual disorder or a paraphilia of fetishism.

—Two 14-year-old boys were wrestling and then fondled each other on one occasion. They were not sex offenders and did not have a sexual disorder, but were doing what some normal teenagers, although not necessarily the majority, happen to do.

In recent years there has been a tremendous increase in psychiatric programs and other specialized programs that treat adolescent sex offenders. According to Murphy (1989), this explosion in treatment programs has been spurred by three interrelated factors: crime statistics, which show that adolescents are responsible for a significant proportion of sexual offenses; a realization that many identified adult sexual offenders began their offending in adolescence; and a feeling that intervention early would be preventive and therefore reduce the number of future victims. Fehrenbach (1986) estimated that as many as 30% of rapes and 56% of child molestations are committed by sexual perpetrators under the age of 18.

Characteristics of Adolescent Sex Offenders

In a review article, Davis (1987) summarized the incidence of adolescent sex offenses, the characteristics of the victims, and the characteristics of the offenders. He pointed out that although there are many theories about the etiology of adolescent sexual offending, there has been very little sound empirical research. For instance, many of the so-called characteristics of adolescent sex offenders are shared with the population of delinquent adolescents who are not sex offenders and even with the general population of all adolescents.

But at the risk of being anecdotal, it is possible to state some factors that seem important in the etiology of adolescent sex offending. For instance, some studies have indicated that an unstable family background and a history of witnessing family violence or being physically abused plays a contributing role in the life histories of adolescent sex offenders. Some studies show that many adolescent offenders had been sexually victimized themselves. It has also been noted that these youngsters have little skill in establishing and maintaining close friendships. They frequently described serious social isolation. These youngsters have also been described as having low self-esteem, poor sense of masculine adequacy, fear of intimacy, gender-identity confusion, poor impulse control, and lack of moral development. The group of adolescent sex offenders overlaps, to some extent, the group of pseudohomosexual youngsters discussed earlier in this chapter.

Sex offenders employ the mental defense mechanism of cognitive distortion. Cognitive distortion is a form of rationalization which the offender uses to justify his behavior. For example, a

16-year-old boy who described a 3-year-old girl as being seductive and enjoying the abuse. Another example of cognitive distortion would be the statement by an adolescent who raped a peer at knife point, that "she asked for it."

The psychiatric diagnoses which are applied to adolescent sex offenders may relate either to the offense itself or to other kinds of emotional or behavioral problems. Regarding the actual sex offense, the patient may meet the *DSM-III-R* criteria for exhibitionism, frotteurism (touching or rubbing against a nonconsenting person), pedophilia, sexual sadism, or other nonspecified paraphilias. Kavoussi (1988) evaluated a group of outpatient male adolescent sex offenders. The most common psychiatric symptoms which Kavoussi identified—in addition to the paraphilia—were consistent with conduct disorder and attention deficit disorder. A smaller percentage of offenders reported symptoms such as social phobia, depression, and obsessions. Some described marijuana abuse and alcohol abuse.

Assessment and Treatment

A question that the practicing therapist must address, in evaluating an adolescent sex offender, is whether to recommend outpatient or inpatient treatment. It is necessary to take into consideration the psychosocial strengths and weaknesses of the individual patient, the amount of structure and emotional support provided by the family, and the need to protect the community. The amount of denial is important to assess. If both the youngster and the family deny that there is a problem, despite findings of juvenile court to the contrary, it is more likely that inpatient treatment is indicated. An adolescent who committed offenses which were violent or which were compulsive should usually have inpatient treatment. Youngsters who were already in outpatient treatment and who reoffended should usually be referred for inpatient treatment.

The assessment and the treatment of adolescent sex offenders has been described by Murphy (1989). In addition to the usual psychosocial and family histories, the evaluator should explore

Fred S. Berlin, M.D., Ph.D., (1989) has been a pioneer in the evaluation and treatment of male sex offenders. Dr. Berlin is director of the Sexual Disorders Clinic, The Johns Hopkins Hospital, Baltimore, Maryland. William Murphy, Ph.D., has evaluated, treated, and researched hundreds of adult and adolescent sex offenders. He has described both the psychological and the physiological evaluation of these individuals (1989a). He has written about the application of cognitive behavioral techniques to the adolescent sexual offender (1989b). Dr. Murphy works at the University of Tennessee and at The MidSouth Hospital, Memphis, Tennessee.

where the offender learned about sex; the possibility of physical and sexual abuse; deviant or paraphiliac sexual experiences; masturbatory history and the fantasies during masturbation; and empathy toward victims. Some treatment centers are equipped to measure the psychophysiological response of sexual arousal. That is, the client looks at pictures or listens to audiotapes that depict sexual relations among men, women, and children in various combinations. At the same time his degree of penile erection is measured with an electronic device. In some cases it is possible to determine exactly what sexual stimuli are arousing and what are not—information which may be useful in confronting the patient's denial and also in designing the treatment plan.

In treating the adolescent sex offender, the therapist will need to communicate with the parents, court officials such as probation officers, and possibly personnel from child protective services. Whether it is inpatient or outpatient, the treatment should specifically and explicitly address the sexual offending behavior. Since sexual offending is a crime, most therapists feel that the offender should be held accountable for his behavior. It usually is helpful to combine individual and group psychotherapy. The group may be particularly powerful in confronting the patient's denial and providing an opportunity for learning basic social skills. The group can also tease out and confront the cognitive distortions which sex offenders practice, which become apparent when they describe in detail their offenses.

A fundamental philosophical belief for most therapists is that sex offenders cannot be cured, but the purpose of treatment is to help the youngster learn how to control his behavior. In that respect, the "recovering sex offender" is similar to the recovering alcoholic. That is not to infer that sex offending is an addiction, but that it is a chronic behavioral disorder that requires the life-long use of compensatory coping skills.

Clinical Illustrations

Parents have their own way of responding, when it is their teenager who has been caught in some sexual activity with a younger child. Some parents have heard about it or seen it so often that they simply do not allow adolescent boys to baby-sit. Some parents overreact to situations like this. Some parents do not react at all. In any case, therapists are frequently asked to evaluate adolescent boys who have been identified by younger children as perpetrators of some kind of sexual misconduct.

Paul, age 13, was brought for evaluation because he had been baby-sitting two young boys and he asked them to take off their pants. Paul had been asked to look after the boys for two hours during the afternoon and it was his first experience as a babysitter. He was considered a responsible boy, but was somewhat immature socially. In an attempt to entertain his charges, he apparently invented a game in which the loser was supposed to pull down his pants for just a second. As the game progressed, Paul decided that the loser should take his pants off altogether. The little boys thought this was a lot of fun and they told their mother about it when she came home.

In the evaluation interview, Paul was embarrassed but was able to relate what had happened while he had been baby-sitting. He agreed that he had gotten very silly with the boys and that he should have acted more grown-up when taking on such a responsibility. He claimed that he did not have any intention of touching or hurting the little boys in any way. When asked about other sexual issues, he had an average amount of facts, curiosity, and misinformation for a 13-year-old. Paul's parents were also interviewed and they were not aware of any other sexual behavior that seemed inappropriate or aggressive. To be thorough, the therapist also arranged for a battery of projective psychological tests, which were normal.

Paul was seen for a few outpatient individual therapy appointments. He had the opportunity to discuss early adolescent sexual concerns with the therapist. The therapist provided some straightforward answers to Paul's questions, but also pointed out that in the future Paul could get information from his parents and also by hanging around kids his own age. The therapist told the parents that Paul had certainly exercised some transitory bad judgment, but reassured them that he did not appear to be a future child molester. To be on the safe side and to satisfy the therapist's own curiosity about Paul's development, a follow-up appointment was scheduled in one year.

This case vignette and the one that follows illustrate one extreme and then another. The behavior by Paul would probably constitute a sex offense, since the "victims" were much younger and under the authority of the perpetrator, but it was certainly a mild form. The second case is a more serious and blatant example of adolescent sex offending.

Jimmy was a 14-year-old white male admitted to an inpatient sex offender program on an emergency basis after it was discovered that he was abusing two stepbrothers and a stepsister while in outpatient treatment. During the evaluation he reported that he had begun sexually abusing at age 12 when he abused a 4-year-old half-sister. He described subsequently abusing five males and one other female. The abuse was quite intrusive—it included his being fellated by the children; performing fellatio and cunnilingus on the victims; and performing vaginal and anal intercourse on the victims. He also reported a history of obscene phone calls at age 11 and window peeping at age 13. He admitted to being sexually abused by an uncle and also described one consenting sexual experience at age 10 with a stepsister who was approximately the same age.

Jimmy had experienced an unusual degree of family trauma. Four years prior to admission a natural sister had died after a lengthy illness. About two years prior to admission his mother died, at which point he came to live with his father and stepmother. His behavior reportedly had changed after his sister's death and became even more problematic after his mother's death. At the time of admission he was shy, avoidant, and socially withdrawn. He was extremely anxious and had difficulty expressing feelings. He had very poor social skills and did not participate appropriately in group activities.

During the course of inpatient treatment further family secrets began to emerge. He acknowledged that he had been abused by his stepfather during his mother's illness. He also admitted that his stepfather had sexually abused his sister, the one who later died. She had told Jimmy of the abuse and the boy subsequently blamed himself for her death.

This case represents a contrast to the earlier story of Paul. Jimmy had a history that indicated the development of a set paraphiliac pattern. He had been sexually abused, had very poor social skills, repeatedly abused children, and had engaged in other paraphiliac behaviors. Adolescents with clinical profiles such as Jimmy's need treatment which is intensive and long-term.

Adolescent sex offenses cover a lot of territory. As these youngsters become more visible and are referred more often for evaluation and treatment, clinicians should be thorough in asking pertinent questions and also reasonably comfortable in pursuing topics that might be distressful or distasteful.

PARAPHILIAS

A paraphilia is a psychiatric disorder in which a patient persistently experiences an abnormal sexual fantasy or abnormal sexual behavior. *DSM-III-R* lists fifteen different paraphilias. What they all have in common is that they involve recurrent intense sexual urges and sexually arousing fantasies which most of us would consider abnormal. What is abnormal is that the person feels sexually aroused by objects which are not human or by people who are not consenting partners.

Paraphilias which may occur in adolescents include:

—pedophilia, which consists of recurrent, intense sexual urges and sexually arousing fantasies involving sexual activity with a prepubescent child. This has already been discussed in the section on the adolescent sex offender in this chapter.

—frotteurism, which is the recurrent urge to touch and rub against a nonconsenting person. It is the touching, not the coercive nature of the act, that is sexually exciting. Frotteurism is usually accomplished in crowded circumstances such as subway trains.

—exhibitionism, which is the recurrent urge to expose one's genitals to an unsuspecting stranger. The stereotypical exhibitionist is the man in the raincoat who "flashes." Another method used by an adolescent exhibitionist was to drive around in his car with his pants pulled down. When he saw a young girl he would pull over and ask for directions. After the girl saw his penis, he would drive off.

—voyeurism, which is the recurrent urge to observe an unsuspecting person who is naked, in the process of disrobing, or engaging in sexual activity. Voyeurism is usually what Peeping Toms are up to. What the adolescent patient would describe is a strong sexual urge which can only be satisfied by peeping. Although he knows it is wrong and is dangerous, he goes out after dark and wanders the neighborhood, hoping to find the opportunity to watch or listen to people having sexual intercourse. He tries to combine peeping with masturbating, and then he feels satisfied until the next night. Sometimes the neighbors catch on and have been known to capture and even shoot at the local voyeur.

—telephone scatologia, which is the *DSM-III-R* terminology for obscene phone calls. This is a fairly common activity of preadolescent and early adolescent boys. In most instances it is self-limited and ends after the thrill wears off. Other boys and men persist in this behavior and also move on to more serious forms of sex offending. Perhaps this behavior will become less common now that the telephone companies have the technology to easily trace all incoming calls.

—fetishism, which is a recurrent intense sexual urge and sexually arousing fantasy that involves a nonliving object, such as female undergarments. This behavior will be discussed in greater detail below, as we attempt to show that a specific piece of sexual behavior could have a number of possible etiologies.

The practical clinical issue regarding fetishism comes up when a youngster is brought for evaluation because it has been discovered that he has been getting into his mother's or sister's underwear. It is good for the evaluator not to jump to any conclusions, since there are several possible explanations for this behavior, which range from the almost normal to the seriously pathological. The evaluator should collect enough information to determine which of the following explanations seems most likely:

An adolescent boy may be quite curious about the things that women usually keep quite private, such as their bras, panties, and tampons. A youngster who is a loner and schizoid may not be able to satisfying his curiosity by the interpersonal methods that most boys use, i.e., comparing notes with his buddies. So he resorts to rummaging around in his mother's drawers to find out what he can.

One of the purposes of adolescent masturbation is to create a bridge between childhood autoeroticism and adult heterosexuality. That is, the adolescent boy may masturbate and fantasize about girls or a particular girl. That is a step in the right direction, in that the masturbation is in the service of moving toward a healthy sexual relationship with another person. The masturbation may involve looking at *Playboy*-type magazines or fondling female underwear. If that is the function that the underwear serves, it is within the range of normal behavior and is not a fetish.

It is important to distinguish between a fetish for female underwear and normal variations of sexual behavior (Becker, 1988). Some males find that heterosexual pleasure is enhanced by involving some inanimate object in the process. For instance, it may increase the man's excitement if the woman wears a particular piece of lingerie. That is not an example of a fetish, but is simply an instance of variety being the spice of life.

A true fetish for female underwear implies that the underwear is not simply an added bonus, but is a prerequisite for achieving sexual excitement and orgasm. In the case of an adolescent, it would mean that the youngster has repeatedly taken underwear from family members and from stores and that he requires the underwear in order to masturbate successfully or to accomplish sexual intercourse.

In taking the history of a youngster suspected of having the paraphilia of fetishism, it is important to ask about other sexual urges and activities, such as homosexuality, exhibitionism, peeping, and obscene phone calls. As we have mentioned several times, patients often have multiple paraphilias. In evaluating an adolescent, it would be useful to explain to him why you are asking him questions about a variety of sexual fantasies and behaviors. It is not that you necessarily think he has engaged in all these activities, but that you are simply trying to get a full understanding of what has been happening.

It would be good to find out what the youngster is actually doing with his mother's underwear. It is not so significant if he is simply masturbating with the underwear. It would seem more ominous if he is actually putting the undergarments on and even wearing them under his regular clothes. Using the underwear for cross-dressing could indicate a serious disorder of gender identity (Green, 1974). It is also ominous if he describes any form of bondage associated with the underwear. See the next section on the adolescent sexual asphyxia syndrome.

Finally, it is important to keep in mind that the adolescent boy who takes his mother's underwear might not have any kind of sexual disorder at all. It is possible that the behavior is simply poor judgment in a youngster who is mentally retarded. The behavior could conceivably be the symptom of a completely different disorder, such as schizophrenia.

ADOLESCENT SEXUAL ASPHYXIA SYNDROME

The sexual asphyxia syndrome is an unusual cause of death among male adolescents. It is estimated that about 250 persons, who are mostly white male adolescents, die each year. Although death usually occurs by hanging, these youngsters are not trying to commit suicide. It is thought that they are intending to enhance the degree of sexual arousal, which they do by inducing cerebral hypoxia by tightening a rope around the neck or by placing a plastic bag over the head. Although they are trying to increase sexual arousal, they sometimes hang themselves or asphyxiate themselves by accident. Thus the name, sexual asphyxia syndrome, which is also called autoerotic death.

It is likely that most of the practitioners of sexual asphyxia learn about it through their own experimentation, although some may hear about it from friends or through sexually oriented magazines. What is surprising is how similar the behavior must be. Judging from the reports in the literature (Rosenblum, 1979; Sheehan, 1988) and from descriptions by medical examiners, the death scenes of these cases have a stereotypical regularity to them. The victims are usually found naked or partially clothed, hanging or with a plastic bag over the head. It is usually apparent that the person had been masturbating and there is often bondage of the hands or feet. Pornographic materials and women's underwear may be present.

Considering the number of male adolescents who are known to die from this practice, there must be many others who try it out and survive. However, it is very unusual to evaluate an adolescent who acknowledges this kind of paraphiliac behavior. But these cases may come to the attention of inpatient therapists. When Sheehan (1988) studied a number of male adolescent suicides, he found that sexual asphyxia accounted for 31% of all the deaths by hanging. It is possible that an adolescent would be discovered practicing sexual asphyxia and would become an inpatient because he was thought to be suicidal. The youngster may endorse that assessment, since it is less embarrassing to be suicidal than to be masturbating under such strange circumstances.

Rosenblum (1979) described the evaluation and treatment of a 15-year-old boy who had been practicing sexual asphyxia for more than two years. It was remarkable in that case that the boy's mother reinforced his behavior in that she knew about it, but never confronted him; she listened at his door, but did not intervene during the act; and she washed the female clothing he used and returned it to his room. The patient was probably relieved that his behavior had finally been discovered and he readily agreed to a contract to stop it altogether.

CITED AND RECOMMENDED READINGS

Anderson, D. 1987. Family and peer relations of gay adolescents. *Adolescent Psychiatry*. 14: 162–178.

Becker, J. V., and R. J. Kavoussi. 1988. Sexual disorders. In: *Textbook of Psychiatry*, edited by J. A. Talbott, et al. Washington, D.C.: American Psychiatric Press.

Belfer, M. L., et al. 1988. AIDS in children and adolescents. *Journal of the American Academy of Child and Adolescent Psychiatry*. 27: 147–151.

Bentler, P. M. 1968. A note on the treatment of adolescent sex problems. *Journal of Child Psychology and Psychiatry*. 9: 125–129.

Berlin, F. S. 1989. Special considerations in the psychiatric evaluation of sexual offenders against minors. In: *Juvenile Psychiatry and the Law*, edited by R. Rosner and H. I. Schwartz. New York: Plenum.

Bieber, I, et al. 1962. *Homosexuality: A Psychoanalytic Study of Male Homosexuals*. New York: Basic Books.

Centers for Disease Control. 1988. HIV-related beliefs, knowledge, and behaviors among high school students. *Journal of the American Medical Association*. 260: 3567–3570.

Davis, G. E., and H. Leitenberg. 1987. Adolescent sex offenders. *Psychological Bulletin*. 101: 417–427.

Dorner, G. 1976. *Hormones and Brain Differentiation*. New York: Elsevier-North Holland.

Fehrenbach, P. A., et al. 1986. Adolescent sex offenders: offender and offense characteristics. *American Journal of Orthopsychiatry*. 56: 225–233.

Fox, B., and W. J. DiScipio. 1968. An exploratory study in the treatment of homosexuality by combining principles from psychoanalytic theory and conditioning: theoretical and methodological considerations. *British Journal of Medical Psychology.* 41: 273–282.

Freud, A. 1965. *Normality and Pathology in Childhood.* New York: International Universities Press, Inc.

Green, R. 1974. *Sexual Identity Conflicts in Children and Adults.* Baltimore: Penguin.

Green, R., and J. Money. 1966. Stage-acting, role-taking, and effeminate impersonation during boyhood. *Archives of General Psychiatry.* 15: 535–538.

Hatterer, L. 1970. *Changing Homosexuality in the Male.* New York: McGraw-Hill.

Isay, R. A. 1989. *Being Homosexual: Gay Men and Their Development.* New York: Farrar, Straus & Giroux.

Kavoussi, R. J., et al. 1988. Psychiatric diagnoses in adolescent sex offenders. *Journal of the American Academy of Child and Adolescent Psychiatry.* 27: 241–243.

Kinsey, A. C., et al. 1948. *Sexual Behavior in the Human Male.* Philadelphia: W. B. Saunders.

Kremer, M. W., and A. H. Rifkin. 1969. The early development of homosexuality: a study of adolescent lesbians. *American Journal of Psychiatry.* 126: 91–96.

Martin. A. D. 1982. Learning to hide: the socialization of the gay adolescent. *Adolescent Psychiatry.* 10: 52–65.

Money, J. 1988. *Gay, Straight, and In-Between: The Sexology of Erotic Orientation.* New York: Oxford University Press.

Murphy, W. D., et al. 1989a. Adolescent sex offenders. In: *The Sexual Abuse of Children: Theory, Research and Therapy,* edited by W. O'Donohue and J. H. Geer. Hillsdale, N. J.: Lawrence Erlbaum.

Murphy, W. D. 1989b. Assessment and modifications of cognitive distortons in sex offenders. In: *Sexual Assault: Issues, Theories, and Treatment of the Offender,* edited by W. L. Marshall et al. New York: Plenum.

Nichols, S. E. 1983. Psychiatric aspects of AIDS. *Psychosomatics.* 24: 1083–1089.

Ostrow, E. et al. 1985. Adolescent sexual behavior. *Medical Aspects of Human Sexuality.* 19(5): 28–43.

Ovesey, L. 1955. The pseudohomosexual anxiety. *Psychiatry.* 18: 17–25.

Ovesey, L., and W. Gaylin. 1965. Psychotherapy of male homosexuality. *American Journal of Psychotherapy.* 19: 382–396.

Rosenblum, S., and M. M. Faber. 1979. The adolescent sexual asphyxia syndrome. *Journal of American Academy of Child Psychiatry.* 18: 546–558.

Ryan, G., et al. 1987. Juvenile sex offenders: development and correction. *Child Abuse and Neglect*. 11: 385–395.

Sheehan, W., and B. D. Garfinkel. 1988. Adolescent autoerotic deaths. *Journal of Child and Adolescent Psychiatry*. 27: 367–370.

Socarides, C. W. 1960. Theoretical and clinical aspects of overt male homosexuality. *Journal of the American Psychoanalytic Association*. 8: 552–566.

Socarides, C. W. 1978. *Homosexuality*. New York: Jason Aronson.

Stoller, R. J. 1967. Gender identity and a biological force. *Psychoanalytic Forum*. 2: 317–325.

Stoller, R. J. 1968. *Sex and Gender*. New York: Science House.

Stoller, R. J. 1975. *Perversion*. New York: Pantheon.

Stoller, R. J., and G. H. Herdt. 1985. Theories of origins of male homosexuality. A cross cultural look. *Archives of General Psychiatry*. 42: 399–404.

Thorpe, J. G., et al. 1963. A comparision of positive and negative (aversive) conditioning in the treatment of homosexuality. *Behaviour Research and Therapy*. 1: 357–362.

CHAPTER 18

the adolescent victim

Adolescence can be a tough time, even in the best of circumstances. It is easy to see how a significant physical or psychological trauma could sidetrack a youngster from his developmental tasks, or even derail him altogether. In every adolescent's environment is an awesome array of potential traumas—ranging from small tragedies (moving away during senior year; hepatitis epidemic that disables the entire football team) to devastating events (suicide by one's best friend; violent death of a parent; incest).

This chapter explores the way adolescents may react to several kinds of trauma. The quality and usefulness of the youngster's coping devices depend on a number of factors, including his psychosocial strengths prior to the trauma; his level of psychological development; the nature of the trauma itself; the youngster's proximity to the disaster or traumatic event; and the availability of support systems in the family and community.

For example,

—an adolescent girl who was raped by her uncle on one occasion and whose family responds promptly and appropriately to this emergency may be able to deal with the anger and embarrassment and sense of violation, and move on with her life.

—an adolescent girl who had been molested by her father on a regular basis for several years has already modified her cognitive style and her manner of relating to other people, in a desperate attempt to have the world make sense to her.

—a boy who was mugged and severely beaten, but did not sustain permanent injuries, may be able to elicit support from his friends and convince himself that he could have clobbered those other guys if there had not been so many of them.

431

—a boy who was beaten and lost the vision in one eye may take a long time to regain his self-confidence and to sleep without having nightmares.

It is ironic that victims of violence get blamed for the horrible things that happened to them. Not only do family members and peers suggest that the victim could have avoided the trouble or the disaster if only he had somehow behaved differently, but the victim may go out of his way to blame himself. For instance, the youngster who was beaten up by local teenage thugs might hear his friends say something to the effect, "If only you had enough sense not to hassle those guys. . . ." Or his dad might remark, "You've got to learn to defend yourself. . . ." Even without these comments from others, the boy is very likely to conclude that there is something wrong with the way he walks or talks or fights, that caused him to become a victim. The adolescent victim may feel quite surprised and relieved when the therapist tells him, perhaps several times, "You are not to blame. It was not your fault that you were mugged."

This chapter uses several forms of trauma to illustrate the variety of coping mechanisms which are available to adolescents. The traumatic forces we will consider are quite different. The Holocaust was a unique experience for our civilization, but it teaches us something about the ability of children and adolescents to survive overwhelming disaster. Another form of trauma discussed in this chapter is incest, since sexual abuse is reported with a frequency that is disheartening. A third topic will be the way adolescents might cope with a serious physical injury. Another form of trauma is discussed in chapter 19, which is the way adolescents deal with parental separation and divorce.

As you consider this material and the clinical vignettes, you should be wondering about the treatment of these clients. Should every trauma victim undergo counseling? Should it be intensive individual therapy or would a support group at a victims' assistance program be just as helpful? If the great majority of untreated rape victims reach a plateau of "recovery" by twelve months after the attack, do they require treatment in the first place? Is it better to let the victim repress the horrible experience or to encourage ventilation of feelings and exploration of fantasies? If the patient has sustained a serious disability and then employs a good deal of denial to avoid facing his handicap, is it the best therapy to leave the patient alone and let him maintain both his relative ignorance and his relative bliss?

It would be nice if all these questions had clear-cut answers. We will be offering guidelines in this chapter for making decisions regarding therapy. In some situations, however, the therapist will have to develop his or her own philosophy about what seems to make sense—whether to take a supportive approach that encourages repression or to actively help the patient discover and experience and express and eventually integrate his feelings. If the latter course is taken, one would hope that the cure is not worse than the illness. Furthermore, it is usually possible to discuss this issue with the patient himself and for the therapist and the patient to decide together on how the treatment is going to proceed. A patient may want to return figuratively to the scene of the trauma, as long as he knows he can trust the therapist to help him bear the pain that he will find there.

POST-TRAUMATIC STRESS DISORDER

Some of the youngsters who sustain a severe trauma develop the syndrome of post-traumatic stress disorder (PTSD). It is certainly not required for the patient to have that particular condition. Some adolescents may respond to an acute distressing situation with symptoms which are less serious. The appropriate diagnoses, if the symptoms are briefer and less disabling, may be one of the adjustment disorders, such as adjustment disorder with anxious mood or adjustment disorder with mixed disturbance of emotions and conduct. If the symptoms become more chronic, the diagnosis might be generalized anxiety disorder or dysthymia.

DSM-III-R indicates specific criteria that should be met for the diagnosis of post-traumatic stress disorder:

—that the person has experienced an event that is outside the range of usual human experience and that would be markedly distressing to almost anyone.

—that the traumatic event is persistently reexperienced in at least one of the following ways: recurrent and intrusive distressing recollections of the event; recurrent distressing dreams of the event; sudden acting or feeling as if the traumatic event were recurring; or intense psychological distress at exposure to events that symbolize or resemble an aspect of the traumatic event.

—persistent avoidance of stimuli associated with the trauma or numbing of general responsiveness, as indicated by at least three of the following: efforts to avoid thoughts or feelings associated with the trauma; efforts to avoid activities that arouse recollections; inability to recall an important aspect of the trauma; markedly diminished interest in significant activities; feeling of detachment or estrangement from others; restricted range of affect; and the sense of a foreshortened future.

—persistent symptoms of increased arousal, as indicated by at least two of the following: difficulty falling or staying asleep; irritability or outbursts of anger; difficulty concentrating; hypervigilance; exaggerated startle response; and physiologic reactivity upon exposure to events that symbolize or resemble an aspect of the traumatic event.

—duration of the disturbance of at least one month.

PTSD is probably the manifestation of both psychological and physiological processes. It may be that the occurrence of PTSD and its severity may depend in part on the life experiences and the personality traits that the individual had prior to the trauma. In addition, however, Kolb (1987) has proposed that the symptoms of PTSD have a neurological basis. He suggested that excessive emotional stimulation stresses and perhaps damages neuronal synaptic structures in the temporal-amygdaloid complex of the brain. His idea is that the symptoms such as affective blunting, startle reaction, hyperalertness, intrusive thinking, repetitive nightmares, etc., are caused by neurophysiological changes.

GROUP EXPERIENCES

Natural disasters and man-made brutalities occur which affect groups of people or entire populations—such as floods, earthquakes, hijackings, and wartime experiences. In some cases it has been possible to study the child and adolescent victims. The purpose of this research has been to document the effect of the trauma on these youngsters; whether there is a particular pattern that emerges; and whether some children are more vulnerable and others seem to be protected from the trauma. Clinicians have also attempted to determine whether any particular treatment helps the victims cope with the trauma more effectively.

A tornado occurred in Vicksburg, Mississippi, in 1953. Block et al. (1956) studied the child and adolescent victims of that disaster. In 1972 the valley of Buffalo Creek in West Virginia was suddenly flooded when a large slag dam broke open. Several small towns were destroyed and 125 people were killed. A team of mental health professionals had the opportunity to interview the survivors and were able to describe the communities and the individuals that were affected. Newman (1976) said that the adolescents were profoundly affected by "the almost total community destruction." In terms of their reactions, "they often had to choose between rebellious predelinquent behavior or compliant social withdrawal. They suffered deeply but privately when their parents broke down under stress."

Mt. St. Helens erupted in 1980. Adams and Adams (1984) studied the community of Othello, Washington, and showed that manifestations of stress in the population persisted for months following the eruption. Shore et al. (1986) also studied the community affected by Mt. St. Helens and found something that was both expectable and interesting. They divided the research subjects into three groups—high exposure to trauma, low exposure, and control—and found a dose-response relationship when these groups were surveyed for psychiatric symptomatology. That is, the high exposure group had a greater degree of anxiety disorder, depression, and PTSD following Mt. St. Helens.

Also, some authors have proposed ways of prevention, to immunize children against some future traumatic experience. For example, children and adolescents who live in areas prone to earthquakes can be educated ahead of time regarding the causes and phenomena of earthquakes. Schools can hold periodic earthquake drills. If you are dealing with a situation that allows for orderly evacuation ahead of time, such as a hurricane, it is known that children do better when families are kept together. Terr (1987) has summarized her own experiences and reviewed the work of others in the area of prevention.

Chowchilla Victims, as Children

A systematic, prospective study that pertains particularly to adolescents was Terr's (1979, 1981, 1983) work in evaluating the victims of the Chowchilla school bus kidnapping. The kidnapping occurred in 1976, when 26 children were taken from a school bus by three masked men at gunpoint. The children were missing for 27 hours. During most of that time they had been buried underground in a truck-trailer. They survived because they rescued themselves—that is, two of the boys dug them out of the hole.

At the time of the kidnapping the victims were age 5 to 14. When they were evaluated during the following year (Terr, 1981), every one of the children manifested significant psychiatric symptoms, which followed particular patterns. During and immediately following the trauma the children experienced fears of further trauma and disturbances in cognitive functions, such as perception and sense of time. Several of the children identified "omens," in that they thought back to the events prior to the kidnapping and they identified specific happenings which they then associated with the trauma. There were many examples of repetitive phenomena, such as recurring dreams, post-traumatic play which repeated the kidnapping experience, and instances of the children reenacting fragments of the kidnapping.

Chowchilla Victims, as Adolescents

What is more pertinent to this chapter was the four-year follow-up (Terr, 1983), when most of the victims had become adolescents. Terr found that every child in the study still exhibited post-traumatic effects. She felt that the severity of each youngster's symptoms was related to the child's prior vulnerabilities, family

Lenore Cagen Terr, M.D., (1979, 1981, 1983, 1987) is clinical professor of psychiatry at the University of California, San Francisco, School of Medicine. Dr. Terr had an interest in research on psychic trauma before the children of Chowchilla had ever been kidnapped. Several months after the kidnapping she learned through a colleague that the families were concerned about the children's emotional reactions and were eager for help. Dr. Terr quickly offered a plan to study these children and adolescents in a systematic manner and also to provide short-term therapy to the victims. She achieved an unusual degree of cooperation, in that she was able to interview every one of the child victims and most of their parents. She was able to turn this unfortunate event into an important learning experience.

pathology, and community bonding. She made the observation that the brief treatment that these children received during the year following the kidnapping did not prevent signs of illness and subjective symptoms four years later.

What were these youngsters' symptoms after four years? At times they could still experience the intense anxiety that had accompanied the original trauma. This even occurred in the group's hero, the teenager who had dug them out of the hole where they were buried. These young victims also described a feeling of profound embarrassment regarding their victimization. That is, they did not like for people to know about or find out about their experience, because it was like announcing how vulnerable they had been during the kidnapping. As you would expect, these young victims were fearful of the possibility of another kidnapping, of strangers, and of particular kinds of vehicles that reminded them of the initial experience. Some of them overcame their earlier fears by repeatedly exposing themselves to the feared objects (such as signal vehicles) or situations (such as being alone).

In the four-year follow-up study, Terr also found that these youngsters did not manifest repression, in that each one could still give a detailed account of the experience. However, they did employ conscious suppression of thoughts and feelings, because they knew they would be uncomfortable in reviving those memories. In spite of their efforts to suppress the memories, some of these children daydreamed so much about the events that their school work suffered. These youngsters still manifested misperceptions and distortions in time sense. Terr described how almost all of these youngsters showed "severe philosophical pessimism," in that they expected a short life or some future disaster. Even after four years the victims described recurrent post-traumatic nightmares and other repetitive phenomena. One would conclude from this study that adolescents who experience severe, acute psychological trauma are likely to have symptoms for a very long time.

THE HOLOCAUST

It may seem strange to discuss the events of the Holocaust in a chapter on the psychological trauma among adolescents, since the events of 1941-1948 are so far removed from the circumstances of today's teenagers. But we will learn something about the coping abilities that adolescents may have in dealing with extraordinary stress. Is it possible that extremely difficult life experiences may shape young people into very hardy and successful adults?

It is hard to imagine the cruelty that the children and adolescents of the Holocaust experienced. Since the Nazi government intended to exterminate Jews forever, it was necessary for them to kill children as well as adults. Children and young adolescents could serve no useful purpose to the government, so the Nazi troops threw them into trucks from rooftops, buried them alive, burned them alive, and allowed them to freeze and starve to death. It is said that children were handed over to German soldiers to use as target practice. Some teenagers survived by escaping and living in forests for several years or walking hundreds or thousands of miles to safety.

Moskovitz (1983) described 24 children who survived the Holocaust and their adaptation as adults. These were the children who came to England after World War II and lived at the Linge-field orphanage and were studied by Alice Goldberger and Anna Freud. Most of them seemed surprisingly healthy and happy as adults—Moscovitz (1985) noted "the wide range of adaptation where there was theoretically no reason to expect to see anything positive."

Two Jewish teenagers of the Holocaust later became famous—one died, one lived. Anne Frank (1953) was age 13 to 15 during the two years that she and her family were in hiding in the ware-house of her father's business. Her diary chronicled her concerns about mundane adolescent issues, as well as her impressive al-truism. Perhaps its most quoted statement was, "In spite of every-thing I still believe that people are really good at heart." Anne's family were sent to Auschwitz. She later was transferred to Ber-gen-Belsen and died there of typhus. Elie Wiesel (1965) was age 14 when he was interred by the Nazis. He survived, came to the United States, raised a family, and spent a lifetime as an author documenting the Holocaust experience and its aftermath.

Another source of information comes from two adolescents who were victims of the Holocaust and who later became psy-chiatrists. Krell (1985) and Rotenberg (1985) were willing to write about their experiences and observations about themselves and other victims.

Rotenberg (1985) was a victim of the Holocaust from 1941 until 1948. He and his family were marched from the ghetto of Czernowitz, Roumania, to an abandoned village in the Ukraine during mid-winter. After his parents and brother died of typhus, Rotenberg and his sisters survived by finding scraps of food and eating grass and leaves. As the war ended in Eastern Europe, Rotenberg lived in orphanages in several countries until he even-tually immigrated to Canada in 1948, when he was 13.

So, how did this experience affect his adolescence, his ability to relate to others, his ability to enjoy life? Rotenberg's experience as an adolescent was "to put as much distance as possible between myself and my past." As a teenager in Canada he actively became part of his new culture. He learned how to get along. He over-compensated tremendously—he learned a new language rapidly and graduated from high school with the highest grades ever achieved in English in his province. He described how he found substitute parents, "to whom I could become attached and who would form some attachment to me."

What makes a person into a survivor? Rotenberg thought that he survived psychologically because he had already experienced the unequivocal warmth and affection of his family, especially his relationship with his father, before the Holocaust took away his parents and every aspect of physical comfort and safety.

Krell (1985) was also a child survivor of the Holocaust who later became a psychiatrist. He was separated from his parents and was in hiding during the Holocaust. He has contacted other child and adolescent survivors and has helped in documentation projects, to secure on tape eyewitness accounts of that time. He found that the child and adolescent survivors found little pride or dignity in survivorhood, unlike their adult counterparts. As adolescents and young adults, what they wanted was to be normal, to have stability in their lives, to create a new solid family unit. To illustrate the adaptibility and resilience of this group, these youngsters caught up on many years of interrupted schooling, in two years or less, in a foreign language. Many of them became university-educated, goal oriented, and successful.

Does this sound familiar? In our own time thousands of children and adolescents from Vietnam and Cambodia have come to this country, having survived a devastating war, deaths of family members, perilous journeys, and years in resettlement camps. Many of them worked hard at becoming part of their new culture and became more successful than their fellow American teen-agers.

We do not completely understand why some adolescents become survivors and others become victims. At least one factor is that family and community values and loyalty and support can help a youngster get through some extremely bad times. That is one conclusion that can be drawn from examples as disparate at the children of Chowchilla and the children of the Holocaust. But when the family is the source of the trauma, it is much harder for the adolescent to emerge as an intact and successful survivor.

The children and adolescents who are victims of incest start out with two strikes against them. Not only have they been severely victimized, but they don't have a strong family or community to fall back on. Their families became the perpetrators and the enablers of their victimization.

INCEST

Incest is not rare. It is estimated that one out of ten children and adolescents has been sexually molested by a trusted family member. In citing that statistic we are including abuse by step-parents and other members of the extended family, not just by parents and siblings. Also, we are not just talking about sexual intercourse, but including fondling, exhibitionistic behavior, and taking photographs for sexual purposes.

Our society's recognition that children are abused and sexually molested by family members has been a long time coming. We seem to have the ability to ignore the ugly side of life. If there is reason to think that something too horrible to contemplate is happening, well, we just don't contemplate it. The history of this issue over the last hundred years has been something like peeling back the layers of a rotten onion. The deeper we looked into the problem, the uglier the damage.

The discoveries of child abuse have followed a pattern. Usually our society as a whole has been complacent. Then one person or a few people point out that something bad is happening to our children. Initially we say, "Oh no, that hardly ever happens." Or that just happens among uneducated people or poor people. Then more and more individuals in the community start noticing and we accept awareness that we really do have a problem of child abuse. Then we become incensed and pass laws. Then we worry whether some of the victims are abused more by the system than by the original perpetrator.

A Short History of Abuse and Incest

In the nineteenth century there were laws which prohibited cruelty to animals. Some of the early cases of child abuse were tried under those laws, since state legislatures had not yet passed laws which prohibited cruelty to children. Up until the 1950s it was thought that physical abuse of children was rare—partly because physical discipline of children was generally more acceptable and partly because most of us did not want to notice the fact that adults in our midst were burning children and breaking their bones. The most important breakthrough in the "discovery" and recognition of child abuse was not accomplished by a psychiatrist or social worker or pediatrician or minister, but by a radiologist in a hospital emergency room. Caffey (1957) noticed a syndrome of children with multiple old and fresh skeletal injuries. He published his discovery and suddenly it was recognized that many children brought to emergency rooms had been physically abused by caretakers.

The recognition of sexual abuse of children was similar. It was known that incest occurred, but most people thought that it must be very unusual and that it happens among very deviant families, usually hillbillies. Students and trainees were learning how Freud's analytic patients had described how their fathers had sexually molested them, but Freud eventually decided that they must have been talking about sexual fantasies rather than real events. Our current understanding is that sexual abuse actually happens, all too often.

There was one more step. Professionals became willing to accept that children, both boys and girls, could be sexually abused. It was harder to accept that adolescents could be molested, since they certainly would be able to fight back or protest or tell on the perpetrator. Not so, since many adolescents have found themselves in situations in which they had to submit to the aggression of a parent or sibling. It happens every which way, with mothers molesting both sons and daughters and fathers molesting both sons and daughters. The most common form of incest is father-daughter incest. It may have happened only once and in a reasonably benign form: an intoxicated father exposed himself to his teenaged daughter. It may have happened many times: a father forced his daughter to have vaginal and anal intercourse from her puberty until she left home to marry at age 17.

The early research on incest started with the tip of the iceberg. That is, Weinberg (1955) studied more than 200 individuals who had been arrested, found guilty, and incarcerated for incestuous activities. He described two types of incestuous families: the in-grown family whose members find it difficult to cultivate relationships outside the family and relate primarily to each other; and the promiscuous family where sexual attitudes are poorly defined and sexuality is permitted with few limits.

In the late 1970s and 1980s there was an explosion of openness about incest. Many women came out of their closets to acknowledge that their fathers or uncles or grandfathers had repeatedly molested them. Forward (1988), Goodwin (1982), and Mrasak (1981) have described the victims of incest and the families of these sexually abused children. Burgess (1979) and Kempe (1984) discussed both incest and also extrafamilial sexual abuse.

It is known that hospitalized psychiatric patients as well as other seriously disturbed individuals, such as violent adolescents, show a high incidence of sexual abuse history. This is true of both sexes, but girls more than boys. What this means in practice is that the clinician should maintain a high index of suspicion of the possibility of sexual abuse and should develop a comfortable technique of inquiring about these experiences as a routine part of the history of the adolescent patient.

Burgess (1974) popularized the term, "rape trauma syndrome," and created a framework for understanding the sequelae of sexual victimization. She described how the psychological damage may be produced in three ways: ethically, in terms of instilling false standards regarding what constitutes usual sexual behavior between adults and children; emotionally, in terms of instilling fear, shame, and guilt; and physically, in terms of anatomic harm. Several authors (Herman, 1986; Renshaw, 1987) have described the acute and long-term psychological symptoms that can occur. Depending on the severity of the attacks and other circumstances, the clinical diagnoses may include adjustment disorder with mixed emotional features, post-traumatic stress disorder, major depression, and many other possibilities. The whole range of anxiety disorders, panic disorders, and phobias may be present.

Two Clinical Examples

One of the most important issues in the clinical outcome during treatment is whether the youngster's family, especially her mother, provide both psychological and physical support. Sally's case shows how the prognosis is more bleak when the victim does not receive the support she needs.

Sally was a 15-year-old girl who was referred for inpatient treatment after a serious suicide attempt which included slashing both her wrists. Sally had been found on the bathroom floor by her mother after she called the mother to say goodbye. After admission to the hospital, Sally revealed in individual therapy that she had been sexually abused by her stepfather from age 8 to 15. The abuse began with occasional fondling and increased in frequency until the stepfather forced Sally to have intercourse at age 11.

The incident which precipitated the suicide attempt included being impregnated by the stepfather and his pressuring her to have an abortion. At the time of hospitalization, the mother and stepfather were still living together.

Sally's treatment included having her confront the mother regarding the incest. The mother was extremely angry and denied all her daughter's allegations. This issue was processed with the mother over many weeks, and still the mother continued to deny and invalidate the patient. When the patient was stronger, it was agreed that both the mother and stepfather would attend a family meeting. Both parents denied and invalidated the patient. They also psychologically blackmailed her by saying that if she withdrew her "outrageous" allegations, they could all "be a family again."

This clinical example is indicative of a difficult prognosis for the patient because of lack of validation for the abuse and unwillingness of the mother and stepfather to take responsibility for the abuse and betrayal of the patient. It was decided that Sally would live with an aunt. She continued to have bouts of depression and acting out.

On the other hand, the adolescent incest victim is much more likely to benefit if the family is able to support the treatment.

That's what happened in the case of Madeline.

Madeline was a 12-year-old girl who was brought for out-patient treatment by her mother and father. Madeline had recently revealed an incident of incest which included forced intercourse by a 16-year-old cousin. Madeline was quite depressed but was willing to discuss the trauma in individual therapy and in family meetings wither her mother and father. The parents were very supportive. In addition, Madeline's mother was able to press charges against the boy who was her nephew. The duration of treatment—weekly individual and family meetings—was about six months. Madeline was able to work through the trauma because of family support and validation.

Treatment of Incest

Many adolescent incest victims benefit from a combination of individual, group, and family therapy. It may be very helpful for the therapist to guide the patient in bringing information from one treatment modality to another. This usually involves rehearsing in one meeting what is going to happen in the next. For instance, the therapist may use an individual therapy meeting to discuss with the patient what she is going to say at the next group meeting. At the group, the therapist may arrange for the members to role play and for the patient to practice how she will confront her parents in the family meeting. Of course, the therapist can meet with the parents and advise them what to do when the confrontation occurs.

Working with the families of these youngsters requires both confrontation and diplomacy. At the initial stages, the parents may react very negatively to the revelation that their child has been abused, especially if the abuser is a close family member. The parents' negative reactions may include denial and a persistent belief that the child is lying. For instance, the parents may wish to organize a "coverup"—but the therapist will need to explain that a report to protective services may be legally and clinically required. The family may accept the fact of abuse but blame

Susan Forward, MSW, Ph.D., (1988) was a therapist in California when she came to believe that there was an epidemic of incest in our country. When she started to talk about her concerns, she was called the "Joe McCarthy of incest" and was accused of conducting her own private witch hunt. A turning point occurred in 1980 when she was on the Merv Griffin show and the entire program was related to incest. Dr. Forward said that the response to that one show was overwhelming, that *thousands* of people called her offices wanting information and help. In addition to treating many victims herself, Dr. Forward has taught therapists throughout the country how to treat victims and their families.

the child. This is especially true in father-daughter incest. The daughter's affectionate and flirtatious behavior toward the father may lead the mother to justify his overt sexual response. The family may accept the truth of the event and feel sympathy for the child but feel embarrassed and uncomfortable. Strong emotions of guilt, shame and fear may overwhelm the family's ability to be helpful to the victim. At times this may take the form of a narrow preoccupation with punishing the abuser, which ignores the needs of the victim. Finally, the family may be ready and emotionally able to help and yet lack sufficient understanding of the expected reactions to sexual abuse and knowledge of what they can do to help.

Forward (1988) has made a number of useful suggestions for the treatment of incest victims. Her style as a therapist is to be active, but also warm and supportive. She has found that incest victims do well in group therapy because they can see that other youngsters have had similar experiences and because they can benefit from the enormous support that can be evoked. However, many of her ideas can also be employed in individual therapy. Forward does not leave the therapy agenda up to the group, since she has definite ideas about what the therapist should be accomplishing. The first step is for the therapist to help the patient deal with her rage at the perpetrator and also at other family members, such as the mother who allowed or perhaps even endorsed the incest. She suggests that group members help each other by taking roles in a form of psychodrama, so that the victim can feel that she is having a dialogue with these people. Forward also encourages the patients to confront their assailants, through writing letters or in family therapy sessions. These confrontations can be extremely cathartic experiences and she structures them so that they are constructive and not simply a violent display of anger. After dealing with her rage, the patient needs guidance to cope with the ensuing depression and to build the foundation for a more healthy sense of identity and self-esteem in the future. In her experience Forward found these patients to be extremely treatable—but the therapist must be assertive enough to make the diagnosis and to guide the patient through her inevitable resistances.

As mentioned previously, adolescent incest victims may develop a range of psychiatric symptoms and syndromes, such as generalized anxiety, chronic depression, and the post-traumatic stress disorder. It is possible with incest victims to see hysterical phenomena such as conversion symptoms, depersonalization, dissociation, and fugue states. Hysterical seizures have been described (Goodwin, 1979; Gross, 1979). Sometimes the dissociative states become organized into multiple personalities. Working backward in conducting an evaluation, it is extremely common in patients with multiple personality disorder to find a history of incest. Bowman (1985) described his work with a 14-year-old girl who developed multiple personality disorder after incestual experiences. He treated her with individual therapy and was able to reconstruct the origin of the personalities and could explain the steps in therapy which allowed the personalities to fuse. Bowman said that the original personality is usually a shy, introverted, bland personality who is unable to experience anger, depression, fear, or sexual excitement. The secondary personalities function to take on the roles that the original personality cannot handle. So, they can be the exact opposite of the original. The dissociations act as a defense mechanism of the ego against painful experiences or memories. Each personality may serve some purpose. One may hold the memories of the painful experiences. One may contain the anger. One may hold memories of enjoying the experience. Although not all therapists would agree with this view, it is an interesting form of speculation.

GETTING MUGGED

Every morning after breakfast the mother of every teenager feels like announcing what the sergeant of *Hill Street Blues* used to say: "Be careful out there!" It is hard to accept that violence is prevalent in our country and that your own child is just as vulnerable as the next one. This section describes some of the psychological sequelae to getting mugged. We are not talking about the feelings that a youngster might have after participating in a street brawl or a gang fight. In those situations the fellow has gotten involved in the fracas voluntarily and also it was an experience of group comraderie, so the injuries wouldn't hurt so much. We are addressing here the experience of being a victim, where the adolescent was not asking for trouble, but got beaten up anyway.

The physical injuries sustained in a mugging can range from minor to life-threatening. The psychological aftermath covers the gamut. The youngster's rage at being victimized might be expressed or might be suppressed, in which case the therapist may need to help the patient recognize and verbalize his anger. The youngster may describe anxiety, panic attacks, and symptoms of post-traumatic stress disorder. He may feel humiliated, ashamed, and move into a state of chronic depression. He may resent how even his friends seem to blame him for what happened. That is, peers of the victim may not want to think about their own vulnerability, so they assume that these misfortunes only happen to fellows who have messed up in some way: "Couldn't you see the guy coming?" The adolescent victim may prefer anonymity and be tired of people asking him about the traumatic event, since it reminds him of being helpless and vulnerable.

In evaluating and treating a patient who has been injured in this way, it is important to sort out the psychological from the neurological complications. If the youngster had sustained a head injury—especially if associated with loss of consciousness, a period of confusion or obtundation, skull fracture, or seizure—there may be emotional symptoms which have an organic basis to them. What looks like an appropriate expression of anger may actually be the irritability, lability, and explosiveness seen in a person with organic personality disorder. What looks like depression may actually be apathy and mental blunting as a result of brain damage.

Silver (1987) has reviewed the psychological manifestations of brain injury. The following case illustrates some of these issues:

A psychiatrist happened to read in the newspaper that a 10th grade student at a private school was placed in juvenile detention after he attacked another boy with a pipe. The student, Barney, had hidden behind a pillar and hit an 11th grader named Roger on the back and head as he went by. Barney was tried as an adult for aggravated assault, but was found not guilty. Barney's defense was that he was a wimpy kid who had been teased by older boys who were basketball players, so his swinging with the pipe was construed as self-defense and justifiable retaliation.

Several months later a neurologist referred the victim of the attack, Roger, to the same psychiatrist for evaluation. Roger had sustained a depressed skull fracture, which had been treated without further complications. Fortunately, there was no apparent neurological damage. However, Roger had become apathetic, socially isolated, and had slipped academically from the honor roll to barely passing.

In the evaluation Roger was a polite, well-mannered boy. He had a soft, low-key style and it was easy to see how his fundamental personality traits could easily turn into chronic passivity and depression. Roger was a strong, sturdy youngster who had been a successful athlete and was on the basketball team, but he said that he had not actually been one of the mean basketball players who had been picking on Barney. It sounded like Barney had picked out Roger to be

his victim because Roger was the most mild mannered basketball player he could find. Roger also knew that the school
administrators knew that Barney had made threats and had
emotional problems, but had not taken any steps to control
him.

Roger was treated in individual therapy, an adolescent
therapy group, and in family meetings. The group members
asked enough questions to help Roger express his anger and
frustration at what had happened. He was able to describe
how the criminal trial of Barney left him feeling helpless all
over again. He put himself on the line by testifying, but was
not vindicated by the outcome of the trial. The ventilation
of these feelings also helped him make an important decision, which was whether to sue his own school for damages.
He felt loyalty to the school and the principal, but he also
thought that the school had put its needs above his own.
The family meetings were notable in two ways. It was important to help the parents avoid compensating by becoming
unnecessarily protective of Roger. Also, they were extremely
uncommunicative with each other. The therapist helped
them express both supportive and other feelings, so that
they could be useful to each other and could also make use
of the support available in the community.

Roger's case is a good example of a youngster who was injured
in a mugging, although not severely. He had psychological complications, was motivated in treatment, and did well.

Denial in the Service of Recovery

The last vignette is this chapter is quite different. Harold was
very seriously injured and he "treated himself" with the use of
denial. Harold's denial helped him get through his day-to-day
routine and it also seemed to energize him to make plans for the
future. As you read this case history, think about whether you
would want to use psychotherapy to remove Harold's denial and
to force him to face the reality of his disability.

Harold was 16 when he was seriously injured playing football. He and a friend got involved in an informal game at a

playground, where he had never been before. He was the youngest and smallest person in the game. But it turned out that this was not your ordinary pick-up football game—it had a closer likeness to assault and battery. On the initial kick return Harold was running with the ball and the other players tried to take him down. Several of them pulled him down and then a whole pile of people were on his back. At first he thought he had just hurt his head, but then noticed that he could not feel anything below his neck. He told everybody to get off of him and told them to roll him over real slow. Somebody called Harold's mother and called an ambulance, but then everybody scattered, except for the friend he had started out with.

Harold had sustained a compression fracture of one of his cervical vertebrae, which caused an incomplete paraplegia. He was treated at a hospital that deals with serious trauma and was also at a rehabilitation center for almost a year. He was able to return home and live with his mother. Although Harold was generally confined to a wheelchair, he was able to walk for short distances. He had limited use of his left arm, with which he was able to feed himself, shave, answer the telephone, open doors, play cards, and take care of his urinary and bowel functions. Even before his injury he had not been an enthusiastic student, but Harold was able to return to high school and he graduated a year after his original class.

This boy's emotional reaction to his injury was understandable and almost predictable. He became discouraged and moody and sometimes had crying spells. He was able to express his anger at the men who had injured him in the first place and at the city for not supervising the playground better and at the doctors for not completely fixing him up. He was frightened by noises and loud sounds, because he felt he could not protect himself if he were attacked by somebody.

Harold also employed the unconscious defense mechanism of denial. When he was at the rehabilitation center the staff noted that Harold's expectations for recovery seemed much higher than what one might realistically expect. His high expectations appeared to win out over his periods of depression. When he was seen for psychiatric evaluation after he had returned home and after he had graduated from high school, Harold still seemed unrealistically optimistic about the future. He was making plans to apply to a local junior college, with the idea that he would later go on to a state university and pursue a career in medicine or in law.

The psychiatrist felt that supportive counseling should be incorporated into Harold's overall physical and educational rehabilitation program. He did not need therapy to get in touch with his anger, which was apparent and was motivating Harold to make something of himself. It did not seem to make sense to treat his occasional crying spells with anti-depressant medication. The question for the therapist was whether to challenge Harold's unrealistic expectations. The therapist chose not to tell Harold to forget about medical school or law school. He did encourage Harold to try to get into junior college and to think about several professions that might be possible for him, such as radio broadcasting or working in an office.

It is easy to find examples of adolescents who feel good about themselves and who succeed, despite a serious physical handicap. Sometimes a child or adolescent requires an amputation of a leg because of bone cancer. These youngsters still learn to dance, run, and ski beyond the beginner slopes. One boy whose leg was amputated was on his high school wrestling team and scored better than many of his peers.

GUIDELINES FOR TREATMENT

Here are some ideas to keep in mind when treating adolescents who have been psychologically traumatized. These are intended as suggestions which each therapist needs to edit and adapt, since it is not possible to organize this material like a cookbook.

1. "If it ain't broke, don't fix it." In your practice you will probably see youngsters who are brought for assessment because

their parents are concerned about some traumatic event that has occurred. You may find that the incident that occurred was fleeting in duration and low in intensity. The patient is able to describe what happened in an appropriate manner and with appropriate affect. The parents seem like reasonable people and are not trying to ignore the event or to blow the incident out of proportion. You will take a thorough history and find that there is no dysfunction at all associated with this traumatic event. What to do? We suggest that you see this as an opportunity for crisis intervention. That means that you see the patient and the parents two or three times, explore the situation, allow for ventilation of feelings, make sure that the family members are supporting each other, and educate the family about the nature of psychological trauma and signs to watch for. Then you wish them well. You may also want to set up another appointment in about three months to see how everybody is doing.

2. If the traumatic event was serious and has resulted in psychological symptoms, recommend treatment. It is usually helpful for the therapist to say up front, "It wasn't your fault." As a general rule it is important for the therapist to help the victim get in touch with the painful feelings associated with the trauma. That usually means fearfulness, feelings of helplessness and vulnerability, rage, and sadness. However, it is not therapeutic in itself to leave your client feeling miserable, so you need to go on to the next step.

3. The therapist should actively find ways to develop and promote a sense of mastery in the victim. That may take the form of confronting the aggressor, through letters or through orchestrated family meetings. It may take the form of the victim testifying at the perpetrator's trial. It may take the form of enrolling in a self-defense class and becoming the local expert in taekwondo. It may take the form of going public and teaching other teenagers how to avoid becoming future victims.

4. Consider group therapy or a support group. Victims find solace in learning that they are not alone. That is, they are not alone in being victims and also they are not alone in having intense and frightening feelings afterwards. Don't expect your average

victim to find the right support group on his own. The therapist may need to get on the phone, find the group, locate the coordinator, and tell the patient how to get to the meeting. Sometimes the local court or mental health center has an organized victim assistance program, which might know about support groups.

5. Make sure that the patient's family and community are being supportive. That usually means that the family should be reasonably sympathetic, should be available to discuss the trauma and the circumstances surrounding it, but should not dwell endlessly on that subject. Perhaps the family should be a little watchful and solicitous, but should not become overprotective. The therapist should inquire how the patient's peers are dealing with the patient's trauma. Sometimes an adolescent victim is injured even more because his former friends shun him, not knowing what to say or do in his company. For instance, a teenager whose father was murdered was afraid to return to school. His fantasy was that his friends would be so squeamish about the subject that they would avoid hanging around with him. This boy was not looking for sympathy or for any special treatment, but just wanted his old friends to include him the way they always did. If this issue seems to be a problem, the therapist could suggest that the patient invite two or three friends to a therapy session. The therapist and the patient should discuss ahead of time the agenda for the meeting and what they would like to accomplish with it.

6. Don't forget that the mind lives in the brain. If the victim you are treating sustained a head injury, the mental symptoms you notice may have a neurological rather than an emotional etiology. If this is a serious consideration, you should consult with a neurologist who is interested in the subtleties of closed head injuries. You may also wish to arrange for neuropsychological testing, which would help you and the client understand his cognitive strengths and weaknesses.

7. Medication may be helpful for some of the symptoms, such as intense anxiety and sleeplessness and severe depression. However, don't expect medication to solve the issues that need to be worked out in therapy.

8. Keep an open mind. Be creative. Depending on the clinical situation you may want to consider hypnosis (to help a client recollect important experiences), relaxation training (for chronic anxiety), in vivo desensitization (for severe phobias), and community networking (when the trauma extends through several families).

The moral of this chapter is that adolescents who have been victimized are able to overcome a tremendous amount of adversity. Sometimes they do it on their own, through conscious strategies or through unconscious mechanisms; sometimes they persevere through the active support of their families and their communities; sometimes they benefit from the relationship and the direction offered by a skillful therapist. It would be nice to know how to plan ahead and raise children to be survivors, but so far nobody knows exactly how to do that.

CITED AND RECOMMENDED READINGS

Adams, P., and G. Adams. 1984. Mount Saint Helens's ashfall: evidence for a disaster stress reaction. *American Psychologist*. 39: 252–260.

Block, D., et al. 1956. Some factors in the emotional reaction of children to disaster. *American Journal of Psychiatry*. 113: 416–422.

Bowman, E. S., et al. 1985. Multiple personality in adolescence: relationship to incestual experiences. *Journal of the American Academy of Child Psychiatry*. 24: 109–114.

Burgess, A. and L. Holmstrom. 1974. Rape trauma syndrome. *American Journal of Psychiatry*. 131: 981–986.

Caffey, J. 1957. Some traumatic lesions in growing bones other than fractures and dislocations. *British Journal of Radiology*. 30: 225–238.

Forward, S. 1988. *Betrayal of Innocence: Incest and Its Devastation*. New York: Penguin Books.

Frank, A. 1953. *The Diary of a Young Girl*. New York: Pocket Books.

Goodwin, J. 1982. *Sexual Abuse: Incest Victims and Their Families*. Boston: John Wright.

Goodwin, J., et al. 1979. Hysterical seizures: a sequel to incest. *American Journal of Orthopsychiatry*. 49: 698–703.

Gross, M. 1979. Incestuous rape, a cause of hysterical seizures in four adolescent girls. *American Journal of Orthopsychiatry*. 49: 704–708.

Kempe, R., and C. Kempe. 1984. *The Common Secret: Sexual Abuse of Children and Adolescents*. New York: Freeman.

Kolb, L. C. 1987. A neuropsychological hypothesis explaining post-traumatic stress disorders. *American Journal of Psychiatry.* 144: 989–995.

Krell, R. 1985. Therapeutic value of documenting child survivors. *Journal of the American Academy of Child Psychiatry.* 24: 397–400.

Moskovitz, S. 1983. *Love Despite Hate: Child Survivors of the Holocaust and their Adult Lives.* New York: Schocken.

Moskovitz, S. 1985. Longitudinal follow-up of child survivors of the Holocaust. *Journal of the American Academy of Child Psychiatry.* 24: 401–407.

Mrazak, P., and C. Kempe. 1981. *Sexually Abused Children and their Families.* New York: Pergamon.

Newman, C. J. 1976. Disaster at Buffalo Creek. Children of disaster: clinical observations at Buffalo Creek. *American Journal of Psychiatry.* 133: 306–312.

Rotenberg, L. 1985. A child survivor/psychiatrist's personal adaptation. *Journal of the American Academy of Child Psychiatry.* 24: 385–389.

Shore, J., et al. 1986. Psychiatric reactions to disaster: the Mount St. Helens experience. *American Journal of Psychiatry.* 143: 590–595.

Silver, J. M., et al. 1987. Neuropsychiatric aspects of traumatic brain injury. In: *American Psychiatric Press Textbook of Neuropsychiatry*, edited by R. E. Hales and S. C. Yudofsky. Washington, D.C.: American Psychiatric Press.

Terr, L. C. 1979. Children of Chowchilla: a study of psychic trauma. *Psychoanalytic Study of the Child.* 34: 547–623.

Terr, L. C. 1981. Psychic trauma in children: observations following the Chowchilla school-bus kidnapping. *American Journal of Psychiatry.* 138: 14–19.

Terr, L. C. 1983. Chowchilla revisited: the effects of psychic trauma four years after a school-bus kidnapping. *American Journal of Psychiatry.* 140: 1543–1550.

Terr, L. C. 1987. Treatment of psychic trauma in children. In: *Basic Handbook of Child Psychiatry, Volume Five*, edited by J. D. Noshpitz. New York: Basic Books.

Weinberg, S. 1955. *Incest Behavior.* New York: Citadel Press.

Wiesel. E. 1972. *One Generation After.* New York: Avon Books.

CHAPTER 19

adolescents in divorced and remarried families

INTRODUCTION

Since about one-half of marriages in the United States end in divorce, there are many children and adolescents whose parents are separated, divorced, and perhaps remarried. Therapists who see adolescents will become involved in this issue in a number of ways:

—by treating adolescents whose parents divorced many years earlier, during their childhood, but whose emotional wounds are still tender;

—by seeing adolescents whose parents are currently divorcing and trying to deal somehow with the needs of the patient, the mother, and the father;

—by being roped into legal disputes regarding custody and visitation, such as being subpoenaed to testify about where the child "really wants to live";

—by seeing blended families and other complex combinations of parents, stepparents, half-siblings, and step-siblings.

When the frequency of divorce increased during the 1960s and 1970s, clinicians rapidly became aware of how seriously younger children were affected by parental divorce. It was thought that the sadness and other psychological effects lasted about a year and then the child would get over it and be back to his usual self. These earlier notions have been corrected. It is now generally accepted that adolescents as well as younger children may also be profoundly hurt by parental divorce. It is also understood that the injury may affect their development and especially their interpersonal relationships for many years.

457

Perhaps the most significant research to document the phenomenon and effects of divorce on children and adolescents has been the work of Wallerstein (1980, 1985, 1989). She identified "three broad, overlapping stages" of divorce. The first stage is the time when the parents' marriage becomes increasingly unhappy and culminates with the decision to divorce and the departure of one of the parents from the household. During this time the children are caught up in a family process that may be violent, extremely unhappy, and disorganized. During the second stage the family members "make efforts to solve problems and experiment with new lifestyles in new settings." The family members may become involved with new partners, new careers, and move to new communities. Life may be unstable and unsettled for several years. The third stage, which may occur several years after the divorce, is marked by a "renewed sense of stability." New patterns and new relationships become established and the family feels more secure. Of course, it is possible that this fragile sense of stability may be threatened by a subsequent parental divorce or other stresses. Wallerstein does not think of these stages as following mechanically one after another. Divorcing families may follow many variations and experience recurrent advances and regressions.

Parental divorce is not always a catastrophe for the adolescent. Sometimes the youngster realizes that divorce is better than the alternative. Sometimes parents manage to go their separate ways in an unusually civilized manner, with respect for themselves and also for the needs of their children. Whether the divorce becomes a gigantic problem or just a medium problem depends on a number of factors—such as the availability of supportive friends and relatives; the adolescent's ability to remain invested in his own issues and tasks, rather than in his parents'; and whether the divorce leads to further displacement, such as a move to a different school or neighborhood. However, the factor that really causes a divorce to be traumatic is how much the parents fight with each other and how much they involve the children in the fighting. What really hurts an adolescent the most is not that his parents now live in different homes or that he lives part-time in

Judith S. Wallerstein, Ph.D., (1980, 1985, 1989) and Joan B. Kelly (1988) designed and published a major longitudinal study of the responses of normal, psychologically healthy children and their parents to divorce. Dr. Wallerstein was the principal investigator of the research, which was known as the California Children of Divorce Study. The children and adolescents and their parents were studied intensively at the time of marital separation and subsequently at eighteen months post-separation and at five years post-separation. The findings of Wallerstein and Kelly (1980) were reported in *Surviving the Break-up: How Children and Parents Cope with Divorce.* As the children reached adulthood, they were examined again ten years following the separation of their parents. The follow-up study was described by Wallerstein and Blakeslee (1989) in *Second Chances: Men, Women & Children a Decade after Divorce.*

at least two households or that he has to accommodate to one or perhaps two stepparents. What really hurts is how much his parents fought with each other and chose to fight over him or through him.

IMPLICATIONS FOR PSYCHOTHERAPY

When helping the adolescent deal with parental divorce the therapist may find it helpful to be more directive than usual. For instance, the adolescent may find himself being sucked into the parental conflict. He may find himself actively allying himself with one parent and rejecting the other. He may feel it is his job to negotiate both big and little issues between the parents. Since the divorce makes his parents miserable, he may think it is up to him to make them happy. It usually is good advice for the teenager to stay out of the fighting and to try to be reasonably neutral. That may be hard to do since the parents may be campaigning for the youngster's vote and affection.

Therapists may see youngsters whose parents divorced many years earlier and who are now referred for a completely separate reason. In such a case the adolescent may appear open and non-defensive about the details and the circumstances of his parents' divorce. He is likely to say some form of: "it really doesn't bother me . . . it was a long time ago . . . it doesn't matter anyway, since there's nothing I can do about it . . . ." The therapist who pursues this matter patiently will probably find that the divorce really does matter in many ways. The youngster is likely to feel resentment that most of his childhood and adolescence has been affected by his parents' agendas. He has repeatedly had to accommodate his schedule to theirs, to move from one household and community to another, to maintain a fragile relationship with the noncus-todial parent through visitation, to adapt to stepparents, to give up the closeness and simplicity of an intact nuclear family, and so on.

Another issue for the therapist to keep in mind is that it seems to be extremely common for adolescents to recapitulate their parents' behavior when they get involved in serious dating rela-tionships. This occurs in a general way, since adolescents and young adults whose parents divorced are more likely to think that they might divorce their own mates at some future time. The phenomenon of recapitulation may also occur in a very specific manner, such as a girl choosing a boyfriend who is similar to her father, the man her mother divorced.

Sally and her mother and stepfather moved from Los An-geles to Boston for two reasons. The explanation offered to the general public was that the stepfather was able to take advantage of an attractive job opportunity in Boston. Pri-vately, they all agreed that the real reason was to get away from Sally's father in L.A. The father was described as an offensive alcoholic who had been physically abusive to the mother and who continued to harass her long after their divorce. The father reportedly was a showy, flamboyant man who worked on the fringes of the motion picture industry.

Sally had been referred for evaluation because of school refusal and academic underachievement. She readily brought up an additional concern of her own—whether she should continue the relationship with her current boyfriend in Boston. It sounded like the bass guitarist of a rock band had selected Sally to be his girl. He dominated the relationship and took advantage of her both physically and psychologically. When they dated Sally had to drive because his license had been suspended after driving while intoxicated. Sally said that she enjoyed being the girlfriend of a local rock star, but she disliked the boyfriend's drinking and his behavior and his control over her.

Sally asked the therapist what she should do about the boyfriend. The therapist sidestepped the opportunity to play parent and said that the decision was up to her, although he was perfectly happy to discuss the situation with her. He did comment a couple of times how curious it seemed that her relationship with the boyfriend was so similar to her mother's relationship with her father. Over the weeks Sally gave the boyfriend an ultimatum to stop drinking, broke up with him, got back together again, and eventually broke up for good. She thought that she had learned something from her mother's experience. In the meantime Sally started dating a boy from her high school who was polite, kind, good looking, and rich. He seemed too good to be true. At that point the therapist started wondering to himself how much the new boyfriend would come to resemble the stepfather.

The issue for Sally, like so many children of divorce, was to remove herself psychologically from the drama that had enveloped her parents. It was important for her to realize that she did not have to act out the roles that had been assigned by her parents, nor did she have to recapitulate her parents' relationship. Sally used an expression which is not unusual for an adolescent girl who lives with her mother, in that she referred to "*our* divorce from Dad." When she used that phrase, the therapist took the opportunity to explore exactly what she meant by "our divorce." The therapist pointed out the obvious—that it may have been the mother's divorce, but it wasn't Sally's divorce at all.

COUNSELING FOR DIVORCED PARENTS

In some cases it is better to intervene by working with the parents rather than with the adolescent. For instance, the therapist may meet with the divorced parents together on a regular basis, such as once a month. The purpose of these meetings is to discuss how the two divorced parents can raise their child in a cooperative and reasonable manner. The most important aspect of this kind of counseling is simply establishing good communication between the parents. For instance, the therapist would be the moderator for discussions on topics such as: clarifying exactly what the visitation schedule is going to be over Christmas vacation this year; figuring out how the youngster can be on his high school basketball team when he is living in two households; and comparing notes on Christmas presents, so that both parents do not get the son exactly the same 10-speed bicycle. In working with divorced parents, it is necessary for the therapist to structure the meetings and keep the parents on task. That is, it does not do anybody much good if the meeting degenerates into a session for digging up old grievences and of angry backbiting.

It is well known that most custody and visitation disputes involve trying to take custody away from the other parent or trying to limit the other parent's visitation. In working with the divorced parents of adolescents, the therapist may find each parent trying to push more visitation and more responsibility off onto the other parent. Sometimes this phenomenon of the parents' trying to unload the responsibility for the adolescent is apparent to all. It's like O. Henry's famous story, "The Ransom of Red Chief." In other cases the process is more subtle, as in the following example.

Two parents, who were both successful professionals, consulted a psychologist who was experienced in custody and visitation evaluations. The parents were in the process of divorcing and said that they both wanted to do what was best for their two daughters, Merrie and Melodie. Merrie was 16 and Melodie was 12. They both expressed the lofty view that they did not want to take the other parent to court and have a big custody battle, but they wanted to work out what was best for the girls in a rational and cooperative manner. They both were concerned that the girls were already distraught over the divorce and were manifesting symptoms. That is, Merrie was acting out sexually and Melodie was depressed and alluding to suicidal ideation.

The parents explained the plan that they had already worked out between themselves. Both of them had important careers and both wanted to continue to work full time. They had agreed on a schedule in which both daughters would alternate between the mother's household and the father's household on a weekly basis. They had agreed on joint custody, so that each parent would be fully responsible for the girls when they were with that parent.

The psychologist interviewed Merrie and Melodie separately and also together. They both were angry and miserable. They strongly resented the arrangement in which they had to live in two different households. The girls did not seem distressed about the divorce itself. They had strong attachments to both parents and were perfectly willing to live with either their mother or father. What they resented was having to live half the time in each household. They had figured out that the parents were putting their own desires above the needs of the girls.

The psychologist met again with the parents and determined the basic issue in the case, that neither parent was willing to take charge of the situation and to provide a full-time home for their daughters. Both parents really wanted the other parent to take full custody of Merrie and Melodie. The psychologist explained his assessment of the girls, that their symptoms were related to feeling rejected and being constantly displaced on a week-to-week basis. The psychologist was able to propose some other options for the parents to consider. One possibility was the traditional arrangement of one parent working only part-time and being able to raise the children. The parent who continued to work full-time would, of course, provide child support. A second possibility was for the girls to alternate on a much longer cycle, such as every six months or once a year. A third possibility was for each parent to be the primary parent for one child. That is, Merrie could live with the father and visit the mother; Melodie could live with the mother and visit the father.

What is instructive in this case is the disguise. The parents had colluded in a way to look like they were only concerned about the girls' welfare, i.e., for the girls to have a continuing relationship with both mother and father. In fact, what the parents really had in mind was to avoid providing what the girls really needed, a consistent household.

MORE SERIOUS REACTIONS TO DIVORCE

Virtually every adolescent whose parents are divorced is affected emotionally, although the impact may range from the subtle to the profoundly tragic. The saddest situations involve a youngster whose entire life has been shaped and distorted by the angry warfare between his parents. For these patients, the experience of divorce was comparable to the sudden loss of both parents by death. Then the "dead" parents come back to brutally browbeat the child, by cajoling and demanding the greater share of the youngster's love and devotion. Then the child falls into the impersonal and seemingly arbitrary machinery of the legal processes. When it seems like the warfare is subsiding, some fresh battle breaks out on a new front. At times, the momentum of this process is so strong that even the most skillful or sensitive therapist is helpless. What good is a brilliant interpretation when the patient's life is picked over by a courtful of determined parents, stepparents, grandparents, attorneys, and judges?

Howie was a 14-year-old boy who was referred to a social worker because of his depression. School personnel had encouraged the father to seek professional help. Howie had been living with his father ever since his parents divorced when he was 8. The father had received custody because the mother had serious psychiatric problems.

On examination, Howie was a slender, anemic-looking boy who was extremely polite and deferential. His speech was remarkable, in that he consistently expressed himself in a soft whisper. When asked to try speaking as loud as he could, he would move up to a loud whisper. He explained in a cooperative manner that his entire day-to-day life consisted of two activities: school work and talking to his mother on the telephone. Although he was not particularly smart, Howie was extremely studious. He was well behaved and conscientious in the small rural school which he attended. His afternoons, evenings, and weekends were spent diligently attending to the details of his homework. The only departure from homework occurred each evening when he spoke to his mother for about an hour on the phone. Although one could say that he was unhappy and depressed, the best way to capture Howie's personality is to say that he was extremely inhibited and constricted emotionally. Although Howie's father was supportive and well intentioned, he could do little to interrupt the mother's intrusive, pathological, and almost symbiotic relationship with her son.

The social worker initiated individual therapy and also had monthly meetings with Howie and his father together. After a while, the therapist arranged for Howie to attend an adolescent therapy group. The social worker spoke to Howie's mother occasionally by phone. As more information was collected, it seemed that Howie had been a pretty normal youngster until his parents divorced. When the mother lost custody, she reacted by becoming much more intrusive and controlling of Howie. Howie came under his mother's control and he did not see any reason why he should stand up for himself or be more assertive with his mother or with anyone else.

This story has a sad ending. Perhaps Howie's mother felt threatened by the idea that the youngster might become more independent. In any case, she went back to court and once again sought custody. She thought that the therapist's notes would be useful to her case, so she subpoenaed them. The indignant social worker resisted the subpoena, since she felt the mother's intrusiveness should not reach into the confidential progress notes of Howie's therapy. But the therapist was not to prevail, since both the mother's attorney and the father's attorney had agreed that the progress notes should be released to the parents for their perusal. The point is that this youngster was victimized by his parents' psychopathology; by the warfare of divorce; and by the legal processes that presumably should be acting in his interests.

In some situations a mere therapist is able to advise and counsel the patient, but is not able to make a dent in the enormous environmental factors that are causing or perpetuating the youngster's problems. In such circumstances, it may be appropriate to recommend that the adolescent attend a boarding school or live with relatives for a while, in order to remove him from the environment. The therapist may be limited to providing a supportive relationship, hoping that time will pass and that eventually the adolescent will be able to separate both geographically and psychologically from the destructive parents.

STEPFAMILIES AND BLENDED FAMILIES

Stepfamilies or remarried families come about in three ways. Nowadays, the most common stepfamily history is that two parents got divorced and then one or both of them remarried. Each time one of the parents remarries, a stepfamily is created. It does not matter whether the child is actually living with that particular parent. Regardless of where he lives, the child of divorced and remarried parents is part of two stepfamilies: his first family is his mother, stepfather, and himself; his second stepfamily is his father, stepmother, and himself. Stepfamilies also occur when a parent has died and the surviving parent remarried. A third possibility is that an unmarried mother might later marry a man other than the child's father, so you end up with a mother, stepfather, and child. In any case, stepfamilies have certain characteristics: the family members have experienced an important loss (of the former parent), whether through divorce or death; there is a new person in the household (the stepparent), who does not necessarily fit in perfectly well; from the child's point of view, there is a "missing" biological parent who is somewhere else; and the child frequently belongs to two different households.

A blended family is a kind of stepfamily which is more complicated. For instance, two divorced parents may marry, both of whom already have children. You end up with both of the adults being a parent (to his own child) and a stepparent (to the spouse's child). Another way to create a blended family is for the parents of a stepfamily to have another child together. In that case, one child in the family still has a stepparent, while the other child has two biological parents in the same family. To add to the confusion, some people use inconsistent terminology and mix up stepfamilies with adoptive families and foster families.

Taking a family history may require a good deal of patience, in order to get all the relationships straight. At a bare minimum, it is important in evaluating an adolescent to get straight who are the people who live in the mother's household and who lives in the father's household. It may help to draw a family tree together.

> During an evaluation interview, the therapist asked an early adolescent how many brothers and sisters he had. The youngster thought for a moment and said "eight." The therapist wanted to make a list of their names and asked the patient to tell something about each sibling, from the oldest down to the youngest, who was the patient himself. The boy was agreeable to this and rather painstakingly created this list. It turned out, however, that the patient only had two brothers and one sister. In his mind, he had also included two sisters-in-law; one brother-in-law; a stepbrother who lived in another household; and a half-brother whom he had never seen, who lived in a distant state with his mother's second husband.

Dr. Emily Visher and Dr. John Visher (1979) have collected a good deal of information about stepfamilies, which has been based on their own personal experience, their clinical experience as a psychologist and a psychiatrist, and their study of available research. The Vishers have pointed out a number of special issues that are confronted by adolescent stepchildren. For instance, adolescence is a time of separating from the nuclear family and establishing an independent role. But if both parents have remarried, "separating from two stepfamily households can be more difficult than separating from one, and confusion over role models can lead to added tension for an adolescent." The Vishers explained that there may be conflict between what is important for the new stepfamily (such as establishing a sense of family cohesiveness) and what is important for the adolescent (such as the loosening of emotional ties with the family). The Vishers suggest that a collision course "can only be averted if the adults in the teenager's life will allow the young person considerable personal space and distance from the family." Another issue for adolescent stepchildren is the sexual relationship between the newly married couple. In intact families children tend to be more oblivious to their parents' sexual behavior, while "in remarriages the adolescents are forced to recognize sexuality as a part of the adult relationship."

The psychotherapy of adolescents within the remarried family has been described by Sager (1983). He has taken the various tasks of adolescence and compared how that task would be addressed in a nuclear family and in a remarried family. We'll take one of these tasks as an example, the task of discerning and integrating those aspects of the parents' personalities that will be helpful to the youth as an adult. In an intact family, "the environment usually lends itself to have the adolescent express various aspects of the parents' personalities." In a remarried family, the adolescent is in a loyalty bind. That is, "when the adolescent expresses a positive connection to one parent, the other parent feels betrayed. In order to survive with this parent . . . , the adolescent may need to reject . . . all aspects of the other parent." And what about the role of the stepparent as a source of identification for the adolescent? Sager said that the youth's relationship with the stepparent may be a positive influence (in that "multiple identifications can offer the adolescent a variety of extended options") or a negative influence (in that "multiple identification can lead to identity confusion, especially if parental figures operate counter to each other and thrust different values and points of view on the adolescent").

Regarding this specific task of helping the adolescent identify with aspects of his various parents and stepparents, Sager offered some good advice for therapists. Basically, the youngster needs "to integrate a realistic picture of both parents, a picture that considers each parent's strengths and weaknesses." What that means in practice is for both parents to encourage the youngster to have a good relationship with both his mother and father. That is an optimistic goal and in some cases is unreachable. Sometimes the youngster has permanently foreclosed his relationship with one of the parents, usually the noncustodial parent.

THE PSYCHOTHERAPIST AND THE COURT

The work of therapy with adolescents in divorced and remarried families can be a complex process and a nerve-wracking experience. These situations become even more problematic when it looks like the parties, i.e., the parents, are heading for a trial at court. The purpose of the trial may be to address the terms of the divorce agreement, such as the division of property or the custody of the children. Even after the divorce, the parties may return to court if there is disagreement about the way visitation is being handled or if the noncustodial parent feels that there has been a change in circumstances that would justify a change in the child's custody. Whatever the reason, a long and angry trial becomes an experience which is at a minimum very difficult and at its worst quite devastating.

The child of the disputing parents is, of course, caught in the middle. Although parents and attorneys and court officials make some attempt to protect younger children from the inevitable loyalty conflicts, adolescents are more likely to be considered fair game. That is, one or both parents may freely discuss the legal issues and strategies with an adolescent child; may expect the youngster's total commitment to that parent's position; and may ask the adolescent to spy on or steal documents from the other parent. When attorneys get involved, they usually leave younger children alone and sometimes never even meet them. However, an adolescent who is involved in a custody dispute is likely to be interviewed by one or both attorneys and asked to come up with very derogatory facts and opinions about his parents. The judge may allow or perhaps expect an adolescent to testify about his relationship with his parents in an open courtroom. Of course, none of this does much for the ideal that adolescents of divorced families should have a good relationship with both parents.

In general, there are two different roles that a mental health professional may have in the context of a custody dispute. One possibility is that the psychiatrist or social worker or psychologist has been asked to perform an independent custody evaluation. Such an evaluation usually consists of an assessment of the youngster and of both parents and recommendations which are intended to be in the best interests of the child. The second possible role is that the professional has already been involved as the therapist of the child or of one of the parents. In these situations a professional may choose *either* to be the evaluator *or* to be the therapist, but it rarely works to try to do both at the same time. When a new client is referred for evaluation, it is helpful to clarify from the outset whether one's role is to conduct an evaluation for the use of the court or to conduct a clinical evaluation and provide therapy.

When Asked to Conduct a Custody Evaluation

Custody disputes are more likely to involve younger children, since most children are still young when the parents' divorce occurs. Another reason why adolescents are less likely to be fought over in court is that adolescents have a much greater say as to where they want to live. That is, a judge is probably going to listen to an adolescent who has a clear and rational preference to live with one parent rather than the other. Since the parents and the attorneys know that the adolescent's own choice is going to be the determining factor, they do not bother to take the matter to court. Many state laws instruct the court to take the adolescent's opinion into consideration, although it is still up to the judge to make the final decision.

Although infrequent, there are custody disputes that involve adolescents. The general method of conducting a custody evaluation has been described by Benedek (1980), Gardner (1982),

Hodges (1986), and Weiner (1985). The American Psychiatric Association (1982) has published both clinical and ethical guidelines for these evaluations. Haller (1981) has discussed some aspects of the custody evaluation as they apply specifically to adolescents.

When an adolescent custody dispute does occur, the noncustodial parent may be alleging that the custodial parent has chronically and habitually influenced the youngster to become emotionally alienated from the noncustodial parent. In evaluating such a case, it is obviously important to keep an open mind. If information is collected in a thorough and unbiased manner, the evaluator should be able to determine how the relationship between the teenager and the parents has evolved over a period of several years. You will find that there is no set or predictable answer to these cases. The teenager's alienation from the noncustodial parent may have been instigated by the custodial parent; may have resulted from the unpleasant or unkind behavior of the complaining noncustodial parent; or may have derived from the youngster's own mental defense mechanisms, completely independent of what the two parents may have done.

Tom, Dick, and Harry were three brothers who had lived with their mother since their parents divorced six years previously. During that time they had continued to see their father, but had grown more and more distant from him. A psychiatrist was asked to evaluate the family because the father was seeking custody of the younger boys, Dick and Harry. Tom was already 19 years old and was away at college. Dick was a junior in high school and Harry was in the 8th grade. The father felt that he should have custody because he could be a good role model for his adolescent sons. Also, he contended that the mother had actively indoctrinated the boys to dislike him.

The evaluation consisted of meeting with each of the parents individually for several hours, in order to obtain a detailed history. The meetings were also used to assess each parent's psychological strengths and weaknesses and each parent's attitudes toward the boys. The evaluator also met with Dick and Harry individually on two occasions, once when they were brought to the appointment by the mother and once when they were brought by the father. The boys gave a consistent and reasonable account of their feelings for both parents. They felt that they had a secure, comfortable relationship with their mother. They were willing to spend time with their father, but they found him to be overbearing, somewhat pompous, and unnecessarily controlling and dogmatic. They could not think of any reason at all to live with the father on a continuing basis. Dick and Harry had apparently arrived at their opinions on their own, without any help from their mother. Furthermore, the father's personality style and behavior with the evaluator was similar to what the boys described. To give one example of the father's desire to control, he had purchased a video camera and instructed the boys to videotape themselves and some friends at the father's household, in order to demonstrate that Dick and Harry were having a good time there.

In this case, the evaluator recommended that the family maintain the status quo, that the boys would continue in the mother's custody and that they should also continue their regular visitation with the father.

Visitation disputes that involve adolescents are also uncommon. Judges realize that it does not make too much sense to tell a teenager exactly how often he or she should visit the noncustodial parent. Adolescent visitation disputes seem to happen more often when the two parents live in distant states and the issue is whether the adolescent is required to visit the noncustodial parent at all. The typical story is that the youngster, with the approval of the custodial parent, does not want to visit the noncustodial parent at all over the summer and other vacations. The noncustodial parent would go to court and ask the judge to order the custodial parent to put the teenager on the plane and send him for the visitation. In situations like this, the court may seek an evaluation from a neutral mental health professional in order to determine whether visitation is truly in the youngster's best interests, whether or not he actually wants to go.

Being the Therapist During the Custody Dispute

It is not unusual to have an adolescent who is already in therapy at the point when the parents embark on a full-fledged custody dispute. It almost always happens that the custodial parent, who was the parent who brought the youngster for therapy in the first place, and the custodial parent's attorney ask the therapist to become actively involved in the custody dispute. That usually means for the therapist to write a report that recommends that the patient stay with the custodial parent and perhaps testify at a deposition or at court. All of this raises the question, What should be the role of the adolescent's therapist when one of the parents has initiated a custody dispute and the court is intending to determine the patient's placement? It is our opinion that a therapist who is already involved in a therapeutic relationship should emphasize his role of helping the adolescent express his feelings, explore his fantasies, and deal with the events that are occurring in his life. In most situations it will be preferable for the therapist to emphasize the importance of his work with the child and to decline the invitation to become actively involved in the custody dispute. That is, the therapist should confine himself to helping the adolescent deal with the process and outcome of the custody dispute and should not try to influence the outcome of the dispute by sending written reports and testifying (Bernet, 1983).

The parent and the attorney usually feel very strongly that the therapist is the ideal person to testify, since the therapist has come to understand that adolescent patient so well and since the therapist can be considered an expert in these matters. The therapist should take care not to succumb to the flattery. Although it looks superficially like the adolescent's therapist is the perfect person to testify in a custody dispute, he really isn't appropriate. For one thing, the therapist is almost certainly biased in favor of the custodial parent, even though he may try very hard to feel neutral. His biases make his testimony almost worthless. Furthermore, there are risks involved in testifying. For instance, the confidential nature of the therapy will almost certainly be violated if the therapist testifies. Also, the therapist's testimony may adversely affect any future therapy with his client. The therapist's active role in influencing the outcome of the custody dispute is going to change the therapeutic alliance with the patient and will also change the relationship with the patient's parents.

Even when the therapist's opinion is adopted by the court, the effect on the therapy itself can be damaging, as illustrated in the following example.

> A woman had custody of her 14-year-old daughter who had anorexia nervosa. There appeared to be a symbiotic relationship between mother and daughter and both of them felt it was important for the girl to be as perfect a child as possible. The girl was in therapy with a child psychiatrist, who was also seeing the girl, the mother, and stepfather in family therapy.
>
> The father sought custody of the girl and the case went to court. The child psychiatrist agreed to testify and recommended that custody remain with the mother and stepfather. The court upheld this recommendation. The mother took the psychiatrist's testimony as unequivocal endorsement of her values and her parenting skills, so she discontinued therapy. After all, a highly credentialed child psychiatrist had stated under oath that she was a good mother. The anorexic girl later required both medical and psychiatric hospitalizations, but the mother steadfastly maintained that her family had received the official stamp of approval.

Although it is usually best for the therapist to avoid active participation in these disputes, the therapist may wish to become involved indirectly by sharing verbal information with the independent mental health professional who is performing the custody evaluation. When the therapist is invited by a parent, an attorney, or a judge to participate actively and make recommendations regarding custody, the therapist can use the opportunity to explain the possible disadvantages of his taking that role. For instance, the attorney will probably have a better case if an independent psychiatrist supports his position rather than the potentially biased therapist.

CITED AND RECOMMENDED READINGS

American Psychiatric Association. 1982. *Child Custody Consultation.* Washington, D.C.: American Psychiatric Association.

Benedek, R. S., and E. P. Benedek. 1980. Participating in Child Custody Cases. In: *Child Psychiatry and the Law,* edited by D. H. Schetky & E. P. Benedek. New York: Brunner/Mazel.

Bernet, W. 1983. The therapist's role in child custody disputes. *Journal of the American Academy of Child Psychiatry.* 22: 180–183.

Gardner, R. A. 1982. *Family Evaluation in Child Custody Litigation.* Cresskill, N.J.: Creative Therapeutics.

Haller, L. H. 1981. Before the judge: the child-custody evaluation. *Adolescent Psychiatry.* 9: 142–164.

Hetherington, E. M., et al. 1985. Long-term effects of divorce and remarriage on the adjustment of children. *Journal of the American Academy of Child Psychiatry.* 24: 518–530.

Hodges, W. F. 1986. *Interventions for Children of Divorce.* New York: John Wiley & Sons.

Kalter, N., et al. 1985. Implications of parental divorce for female development. *Journal of the American Academy of Child Psychiatry.* 24: 538–544.

Kelly, J. B. 1988. Longer-term adjustment in children of divorce: converging findings and implications for practice. *Journal of Family Psychology.* 2: 119–140.

Sager, C. J., et al. 1983. *Treating the Remarried Family.* New York: Brunner/Mazel.

Schwartzberg, A. Z. 1987. The adolescent in the remarriage family. *Adolescent Psychiatry.* 14: 259–270.

Textor, M. R., editor. 1989. *The Divorce and Divorce Therapy Handbook.* Northvale, N.J.: Jason Aronson.

Visher, E. B., and J. S. Visher. 1979. *Stepfamilies: A Guide to Working with Stepparents and Stepchildren.* New York: Brunner/Mazel.

Wallerstein, J. S., and J. B. Kelly. 1980. *Surviving the Breakup: How Children and Parents Cope with Divorce.* New York: Basic Books.

Wallerstein, J. S. 1985. Children of divorce: preliminary report of a ten-year follow-up of older children and adolescents. *Journal of the American Academy of Child Psychiatry.* 24: 545–553.

Wallerstein, J. S., and S. Blakeslee. 1989. *Second Chances: Men, Women, and Children a Decade after Divorce.* New York: Ticknor and Fields.

Weiner, B. A. 1985. The Child Custody Dispute. In: *Emerging Issues in Child Psychiatry and the Law,* edited by D. H. Schetky & E. P. Benedek. New York: Brunner/Mazel.

CHAPTER 20

acute psychotic episodes

Acute psychotic episodes in the adolescent often present serious diagnostic and treatment problems to the clinician. They are also very dangerous to the adolescent patient since the confusion and personality disorganization of the psychosis impacts on a personality which is still immature, largely bound to an immediate time perspective, and prone to impetuous action. The diagnostic process is further complicated by the patient's difficulty in communicating clearly and frequently by an inability or unwillingness to cooperate.

The key issues in management of the acute psychosis in adolescent patients are proper diagnosis, use of appropriate psychopharmacological agents, utilization of inpatient care, and long-term followup care including family treatment.

DIAGNOSIS OF THE PSYCHOTIC STATE

The major conditions which present as acute psychosis during adolescence include schizophrenia, the manic phase of bipolar affective illness, toxic psychoses, and other acute and brief confusional states which do not appear directly related to the major psychoses.

The schizophrenias are perhaps the best known psychotic illnesses of adolescents. It seems clear after years of clinical observation that there is no unitary schizophrenic process but rather a range of schizophrenias. This group of illnesses is complex and includes both "positive" and "negative" symptoms. The positive symptoms include confusion, delusions, hallucinations, and sometimes disorders of motor function such as catatonic excitement

476

or retardation. The negative symptoms are related more to social withdrawal, poverty of emotional life, affective blunting, and general withdrawal from social interaction. As a rule of thumb, positive symptoms often develop with rapidity and in an emotional atmosphere of anxiety and acute distress. On the other hand, negative symptoms are often insidious in onset, develop over an extended period of time, and often seem to cause little distress to the patient. As a general rule, the positive symptoms are more responsive to treatment, are not incompatible with a reasonable long-term outcome, and frequently develop in youngsters whose premorbid adjustment had a number of positive elements. The insidious development of negative symptoms more often signals a chronic and somewhat unresponsive course of the illness.

Schizophrenia in adolescents may be difficult to recognize and diagnose because of the particular style with which the adolescent often presents regardless of the source of his discomfort (Masterson, 1967; Bender, 1959; Sands, 1956).

A 16-year-old boy was being interviewed by a medical student.

Medical student: "Why are you in the hospital?"

Patient: "It's my parents, they're mad because I smoke a little dope and like to hang around with my friends."

Medical student: "Tell me about your friends. Who would you say is your best friend?"

Patient: "God is my best friend."

Medical student: "No, I mean regular friends like people that you have conversations with."

Patient: "I have conversations with God."

Even this flagrantly delusional adolescent tried to present himself as typical and his difficulties as entirely developmental. In long-term followups of adolescent patients with apparently delinquent or behavioral problems one usually encounters a significant percentage who eventually prove to be classically schizophrenic (Gosset et al., 1983; Hartmann et al., 1984; Robins, 1966).

Schizophrenic adolescents may also be misdiagnosed because of the reluctance to recognize and admit that the young person has such a grave and potentially chronic illness. For example, Masterson (1967) found that most adolescents diagnosed as "adolescent turmoil" later proved to be suffering from serious and profound emotional disabilities. It is important for the clinician to look honestly at the patient's condition so that prescribed treatment and long-term planning can be realistic and helpful.

The most important differential diagnoses to be considered are the manic phase of bipolar illness, toxic psychoses (especially those induced by hallucinogens), and the temporary decompensation of the borderline adolescent.

Perhaps the most important alternative diagnosis to consider is that of manic stage of the bipolar affective illness. Many manic adolescents may present as behaviorally disordered or disorganized and psychotic. In the early stages of a manic episode when the patient is still relatively euphoric and well organized, it may be difficult to differentiate the manic state from adolescent rebellion, delinquent behavior, and impulsive acting out. According to one long-term followup study, the diagnoses of mania may be more likely if one can observe or obtain a history of episodes of extensive and excited behavior alternating with other periods of lethargy (Gosset, 1983). In the later stages of a manic episode the patient may be fatigued, frustrated, and increasingly disorganized. Paranoid thinking which borders on or is even frankly delusional is a relatively common occurrence. In addition, grandiose delusions may be utilized in an effort to maintain and justify the previously enjoyed euphoria. Thinking and communication may be disrupted so that the patient may appear blocked, tangential, and irrational.

Some assistance in making the differential diagnosis between manic episodes and acute schizophrenic psychoses can be gained simply by sticking very closely to *DSM-III-R* criteria and maintaining a high index of suspicion regarding the possibility that the illness is manic. A careful mental status with attention to the question of whether or not any delusions or hallucinations are congruent with the patient's mood can be helpful. A careful family history searching for evidence of bipolar illness in close relatives may also be helpful.

The differential diagnosis between schizophrenic psychoses and toxic psychoses induced by drugs is not as easy as one might think. The history of drug ingestion may be difficult to get and may be very inaccurate. Often family members are relatively unaware of the patient's drug use since this is rarely shared openly with parents. The patients themselves may distort their drug use consciously but more often may simply not remember accurately due to the disruption of their perceptions of reality. The psychotic conditions themselves may have many features in common and at times may be basically indistinguishable. The paranoid psychoses which are experienced by some heavy amphetamine users are said to be identical to paranoic schizophrenia. The psychoses caused by phencyclidine (PCP) may also mimic schizophrenic reactions although the degree of frenetic excitement, undirected hostility, and failure to respond to environmental situations may give the accurate diagnoses. Insensitivity to pain and apparent demonstrations of unusual strength may be related to the strong analgesic effect of PCP. The psychotic episode may persist for several days.

LSD psychoses are also very similar to schizophrenia although the occurrence of delusions is less frequent in the toxic LSD psychoses. Visual illusions especially emphasizing color and light, are common. LSD psychoses normally do not last for more than a few hours.

There is some confusion regarding the basic psychological state and long-term prognosis for patients who have drug induced psychoses. One study (Bowers, 1977) suggested that vulnerability to prolonged psychotic reactions following psychotomimetic drug use was related to illnesses in the manic-depressive-schizoaffective spectrum. Another study (Vardy and Kay, 1983) suggested a close relationship to schizophrenia. In either case, a high percentage of youngsters with toxic psychosis from hallucinogen intake seem to have predisposing tendencies toward psychotic disorganization.

DSM-III-R requires a duration of schizophrenic symptomatology for six months to justify the diagnosis of schizophrenia. If the condition has lasted longer than two weeks but not as long as six months the proper diagnosis is schizophreniform psychoses. The *DSM-III-R* also provides for a diagnosis of "brief reactive psychoses" when the psychotic decompensation follows clear external stress and lasts less than one month. Some of these brief psychoses may represent temporary decompensations of patients with borderline personality. It will be instructive to follow these patients over time in an effort to elucidate more clearly their basic psychopathology.

ANCILLARY TESTING IN PSYCHOTIC CONDITIONS

The biological tests for psychiatric disorders have received a good deal of attention over the past few years. One of the most common laboratory tests performed in the country is the drug urine screen. Since the drug urine screen is associated so automatically with evaluating patients for substance abuse, it might not occur to a clinician to request a drug urine screen when seeing a psychotic patient. It is advisable, however, to arrange for a drug urine screen when evaluating an acutely psychotic adolescent in an outpatient setting, in an emergency room, or in the hospital. A variety of psychotic states can be caused by or enhanced by marijuana, hallucinogens, amphetamines, and cocaine.

The use of laboratory and radiological tests has been reviewed thoroughly by Rosse and Morihisa (1988). Biological testing has included the dexamethasone suppression test (DST) and the thyrotropin-releasing hormone stimulation test (TRHST) (Carroll, 1985) as two of the most promising. Although there has been considerable controversy, the dexamethasone suppression test does seem to show promise in the diagnosis of serious depressive disorders when properly applied (Livingstone et al., 1984).

At this time neurobiological testing seems primarily useful as a confirming datum. It cannot substitute for a careful psychiatric evaluation, social history, and family history. False positives with the DST can be created by starvation, drug use, and other metabolic conditions. In the absence of these conditions, a markedly positive DST should be considered as a very strong element of evidence for a biological depression.

On rare occasions mental changes, including psychosis, can be caused by neurological conditions such as tumors. For instance, some patients with temporal lobe pathology have auditory hallucinations, but are not otherwise psychotic. When clinically indicated, the evaluator should consider an electroencephalogram (EEG); brain electrical activity mapping (BEAM), which is an EEG analyzed by computer; computed tomographic scanning (CT scan), which is an X-ray analyzed by computer; and perhaps magnetic resonance imaging (MRI).

Psychological testing can be extremely useful in confirming the diagnosis of psychoses. Careful psychological testing can also discover evidences of organic toxicity or drug effects in youngsters with possible psychoses. It is important that testing be accomplished by a skilled clinician with broad experience in testing adolescents. Adolescent norms are different from those of the adult population.

DRUG TREATMENT OF PSYCHOTIC EPISODES

The pharmacologic and psychologic treatment of severely disturbed adolescents is a very complex topic which has not received the careful attention it deserves. This chapter can only mention some basic points and encourage the reader to a more intensive study of the current literature.

There are many antipsychotic drugs on the market. Current consensus suggests that all of this group of drugs produce beneficial effects by reducing the activity of the CNS neurotransmitter, dopamine. They are equally applicable to psychotic symptoms occurring in a variety of contexts: schizophrenia, mania, or organic psychosis of any etiology. Therefore, the average practitioner would be well advised to be thoroughly familiar with only two or three of them. Properly utilized, these few medications should be effective in the vast majority of adolescent psychotic patients. In complicated cases the practitioner may need to do additional studies, obtain consultation from a colleague who is especially experienced in this area, or transfer the patient to a psychopharmacology specialist. From a practical viewpoint antipsychotic medications are often divided into two categories. The high potency drugs are characterized by low sedation effect (in some cases even an alerting effect) and strong extrapyramidal side effect potential. An example of a high potency agent commonly used is haloperidol. Low potency drugs produce less extrapyramidal effects but tend to produce a higher level of sedation and may have a greater anti-anxiety, anti-agitation effect on patients. The most widely used high potency drugs are given in relatively low dosages and the low potency drugs require a larger milligram dosage to produce comparable antipsychotic effects.

Some people feel that agitated patients may respond better to the low potency, sedating, antipsychotic agents, while patients with more negative symptoms of withdrawal and poverty of thought are benefited by high potency drugs which have more of an alerting effect. The concept has the stamp of common sense but is unproven in controlled studies. In fact, most of the symptoms of schizophrenia that reliably respond to medication are active symptoms such as hallucinations, paranoid delusions, agitation, and the like. Apathy, withdrawal, vague thinking, and impaired judgment are less likely to respond to any antipsychotic regimen.

Treatment is usually initiated with divided dosage of the chosen drug administered every six hours. If the patient is extremely agitated, oral liquid concentrate or intramuscular administration may speed response. If the intramuscular administration route is utilized, the dosage is approximately half the appropriate oral dosage for most agents. With the intramuscular route, greater care must be taken to avoid complications of hypotension. Appropriate dosage ranges can be obtained from FDA recommendations although it should be noted that acutely psychotic adolescents often require the upper range of recommended dosages. As a rule, drug response in adolescence is somewhat more unpredictable than in an adult counterpart. Once an appropriate dosage is achieved, medication is usually given once daily at bedtime since this increases patient compliance, avoids some discomfort from side effects, and improves sleep.

After the patient is well stabilized, maintenance medication is recommended since research data suggest that this greatly reduces the likelihood of relapse. Maintenance dosage of medication usually ranges from a third to a half of the original therapeutically effective dose.

Some patients will require the addition of an antiparkinsonian drug to combat extrapyramidal symptoms which may appear as side effects of the drug therapy. There is a division of opinion about proper administration of the antiparkinsonian drugs. Since these drugs increase the anticholinergic side effects of the antipsychotic drug, have abuse potential, and may produce toxic symptoms, many practitioners do not prescribe them unless the parkinsonian side effects become quite clear and marked. Others have suggested that they be used prophylacticly during the first few weeks of high potency antipsychotic drug therapy because the rate of side effects is high. The drugs can then be withdrawn since studies have shown that 60 to 90 percent of patients will not have a recurrence of parkinsonian symptoms if the antiparkinsonian drugs are withdrawn after three months.

It is generally agreed that drug treatment is most effective when it is accompanied by supportive psychotherapy, particularly well-structured milieu treatment and group therapy which focus on reality issues and improving social interaction. The forms of this treatment are discussed more fully in Part Three of the book.

DRUG TREATMENT OF MANIC EXCITEMENT

When the diagnosis of mania can be established, the treatment of choice is lithium carbonate. Brief use of combination therapy using lithium with the antipsychotic agents may be useful to control extreme agitation until the lithium is able to bring the condition under control since lithium may require two weeks or so in order to produce its full symptomatic improvement. Combination therapy is also often useful in the mixed pictures (sometimes diagnosed as schizoaffective disorder) which are rather common in adolescents.

Prior to instituting lithium treatment it is important to conduct a thorough evaluation of the patient's physical condition with particular attention to the cardiovascular, thyroid, and renal function. As a minimum this should include a determination of serum blood urea nitrogen (BUN) and creatinine as well as checking cardiac function with an electrocardiogram. If the patient's physical condition is good, lithium carbonate is administered orally in small doses which are raised daily until blood levels reach a desired therapeutic range of 1 to 1.2 mEq/l. The lithium level is monitored at least biweekly since it is very important to stabilize the dosage level and to avoid lithium levels above 2.0 mEq/l. When the acute psychotic condition is stabilized it is often possible to lower the lithium level to a range of 0.6 to 1 mEq/l during maintenance treatment.

Lithium therapy should be viewed as a relatively long-term undertaking. If the lithium is withdrawn early in the course of treatment, there is typically a recurrence of the illness. After an extended period of treatment with clear stabilization of lifestyle and adjustment patterns, a cautious reduction in dosage may be considered since lifelong administration of the drug does carry some risk and is, of course, an inconvenience for the patient. Even after stabilization of the maintenance dose, periodic checks of lithium levels on a routine basis are indicated. Of course, if there is any evidence of toxicity such as tremor, weakness, drowsiness, ataxia, slurred speech, or persistent nausea, blood levels should be checked immediately. Lithium toxicity almost always occurs at levels above 2 mEq/l but in some patients it may occur at a lower blood level. It should be remembered that lithium toxicity is potentially fatal and treatment should be aggressive, focusing on maintenance of electrolyte balance, support of vital functions and efforts to increase lithium excretion. This excretion is aided by fluid loading, urine alkalinization (with sodium bicarbonate), and the use of theophylline and/or urea to induce diuresis. Obviously, the treatment of lithium toxicity is a hospital emergency. The patient must be observed carefully for two or three days since the mobilization of lithium from tissue may again raise the blood level to a dangerous degree after an apparent initial success in treatment.

Lithium appears to have been useful with some other atypical adolescent psychotic episodes particularly if they are associated with excitement or expansive thinking. The presence of cycles of mood or cycles of impulsive or agitated behavior may also suggest that a trial of lithium therapy should be considered.

SIDE EFFECTS OF DRUG THERAPY

The psychopharmacological treatment of the adolescent should not be undertaken lightly and it should be continued only as long as it is absolutely necessary. All of the useful agents carry significant potential for side effects. The antipsychotic drugs have a variety of side effects, the most serious being tardive dyskinesia and a variety of sensitivity responses which include blood dyscrasias.

Lithium, as mentioned earlier, has potential for toxicity and has some long-range potential for disruption of thyroid and renal function although renal side effects do not appear likely if the lithium levels are carefully monitored.

THE ROLE OF HOSPITAL CARE IN THE TREATMENT OF THE ACUTELY PSYCHOTIC ADOLESCENT

As a rule acute psychotic reactions in adolescents require hospital treatment. The security, structure, and careful supervision of 24-hour inpatient care are usually necessary in order to deal with the patient's overwhelming anxiety. The adolescent who is undergoing a psychotic disorganization experiences extreme terror regarding the loss of the sense of self, the loss of control over his actions, and a general loss of the sense of meaning. The structure and safety of an inpatient setting are reassuring. Although it may be possible at times to manage acute psychotic reactions through psychotolysis or rapid tranquilization, this procedure is not recommended on an outpatient basis except as an emergency alternative when hospital care is not available.

Hospital care is useful not only for initial and severe episodes of disorganization but as a brief intervention to avoid recurrences and relapses in more chronic cases. Many adolescents with relatively chronic psychotic illnesses can be managed on an outpatient basis if hospital care is quickly available at times of stress or regression.

Adolescents with psychotic reactions can respond positively to a wide range of hospital settings. As a rule they should be hospitalized in a psychiatric unit if at all possible, since the bizarreness of their behavior and their potential for agitation may be disruptive to an adult or adolescent medical unit. As a corollary, it is best for the psychotic adolescent to be treated in a center where staff are experienced in dealing with this type of patient and are calm and confident in their approach. There may be some advantages to treating youngsters of this kind in a mixed adult and adolescent psychiatric population since adults are often more tolerant of the psychotic adolescent's severe regression and inability to function effectively in a group. Psychiatric units which are specialized for adolescents with a broad range of psychiatric difficulties may deal effectively with psychotic adolescents except at those times when their population is heavily weighed toward behaviorally disordered adolescents. Antisocial adolescents may be very critical of psychotic youngsters. In some cases they make scapegoats of the more disturbed youngsters and may treat them in ways that can be quite harsh.

The phenomenon of post-psychotic depression which has been described in adult patients is quite marked in the adolescent population. Although no one knows for sure whether this is primarily a psychological reaction to the experience of the psychotic episode, simply another stage in the psychotic process, or partially related to medication response, it does present additional treatment problems. Antidepressant medication seems to be relatively ineffective and the patient's response to any treatment approach is slow. Based on personal clinical experience, the key elements seem to be patience, understanding the frightening impact of having lived through a psychotic episode, and a tactful acceptance of the patient's reluctance to get involved in life again for fear of "rocking the boat." Gentle but firm and persistent encouragement toward greater activity is necessary over an extended period of rehabilitation.

The literature suggests that a mid-range hospital stay of six to twelve weeks is sufficient time for effective treatment in most adolescent psychotic episodes. This allows for stabilization of the medication regime, followup planning, and the development of a treatment alliance with the family.

AFTERCARE

Most adolescents who have psychotic episodes need extensive aftercare treatment. According to Gosset et al. (1983) continuation in psychotherapy following hospitalization was positively correlated with good outcome at long-term followup.

It is surprisingly difficult to obtain cooperation with aftercare plans in spite of the seriousness of the illness, possibly because both the family and the patient would like to put this frightening episode behind them and are reluctant to be reminded of the painful period by continuing in psychiatric treatment. In addition, psychotherapy often includes concomitant psychopharmacological treatment and compliance with medication regimes is notoriously poor.

FAMILY TREATMENT

Family psychotherapy is crucial to the care of the psychotic adolescent. During the hospital stay the parents' cooperation and understanding of the treatment regime are essential to ensure their support of the treatment program. Since the psychotic adolescent often has great difficulty in making proper choices for himself, the family's understanding and cooperation become essential to the hospital.

Parental cooperation is more likely to be gained by recognizing the tremendous stress involved in caring for the psychotic adolescent than if parents are viewed as basically etiological in the development of the illness. Even if distortions of the family process are important in the creation or maintenance of the psychotic adjustment, these issues are better addressed after the psychotic episode is stabilized. As discussed in chapter 8, "Family Therapy," judgmental assumptions regarding family function are usually counterproductive.

Families often require long-term treatment to support them in the continuing effort to take care of a severely disturbed adolescent. The parents of a psychotic adolescent have a very complex and confusing task thrust upon them. On the one hand, at times they may have to closely supervise and manage the behavior of a highly disturbed person losing contact with reality. On the other hand, they often need to pursue developmental tasks of adolescence, encouraging their child to take a more independent and responsible role. These developmental tasks are usually particularly difficult for adolescents who have sustained psychosis. Often their confidence and security are undermined and residual chronic symptoms impair judgment, impulse control, and social skills. The parents need to learn to evaluate these complex factors in cooperation with the therapist and to seek the delicate balance between overprotection and inadequate supervision and support.

Supportive therapy, specific therapy for an individual parent, or marital therapy may be indicated on a prescriptive basis. Education is usually important. Referral to network support groups such as the Alliance for the Mentally Ill may be tremendously helpful in supplying both emotional support and practical suggestions regarding techniques for coping with this highly stressful family challenge. With tolerance, patience, and sustained educative efforts on the therapist's part, parents can sometimes gradually develop important skills which minimize the disability imposed by psychotic illnesses on maturing adolescents.

CITED AND RECOMMENDED READINGS

Bender, L. 1959. The concept of pseudopsychopathic schizophrenia in adolescents. *American Journal of Orthopsychiatry.* 29: 491–512.

Bowers, M. B. 1977. Psychoses precipitated by psychotomimetic drugs: a follow-up study. *Archives of General Psychiatry.* 34: 832–835.

Cain, A. 1964. On the meaning of "playing crazy" in borderline children. *Psychiatry.* 27: 278–289.

Carroll, B. J. 1985. Dexamethasone suppression test: a review of contemporary confusion. *Journal of Clinical Psychiatry.* 46: 13–24.

Dunn, C. G. 1984. Schizophrenic and other nonaffective psychotic disorders. *Textbook of Contemporary Psychiatry*, edited by C. G. Dunn. Lexington, Mass.: The Collamore Press.

Easson, W. M. 1969. *The Severely Disturbed Adolescent*. New York: International Universities Press.

Gossett, J. T., et al. 1983. *To Find a Way: The Outcome of Hospital Treatment of Disturbed Adolescents*. New York: Brunner/Mazel.

Hartmann, E., et al. 1984. Vulnerability to schizophrenia. Prediction of adult schizophrenia using childhood information. *Archives of General Psychiatry*. 41: 1050–1056.

Kestenbaum, C. J. 1985. Putting it all together: a multidimensional assessment of psychotic potential in adolescence. *Adolescent Psychiatry*. 12: 5–16.

Livingston, R., et al. 1984. Abnormal dexamethasone suppression test results in depressed and nondepressed children. *American Journal of Psychiatry*. 141: 106–108.

Masterson, J. F. 1967. *The Psychiatric Dilemma of Adolescence*. Boston: Little, Brown.

Robins, L. N. 1966. *Deviant Children Grown Up*. Baltimore: Williams and Wilkins.

Rosse, R. B., and J. M. Morihisa. 1988. Laboratory and other diagnostic tests in psychiatry. *American Psychiatric Press Textbook of Psychiatry*, edited by J. A. Talbott et al. Washington, D.C.: American Psychiatric Press.

Sands, D. E. 1956. The psychoses of adolescence. *Journal of Mental Science* (London). 102: 308–318.

Vardy, M. M., and S. R. Kay. 1983. LSD psychosis or LSD-induced schizophrenia? *Archives of General Psychiatry*. 40: 877–883.

CHAPTER 21

chemical dependency in adolescents

INTRODUCTION

The widespread use of psychoactive drugs exploded on the American social scene about thirty years ago. Many aspects of the pattern of drug use have shown changes and shifts; however, there is a surprising stability in the overall frequency of drug use. For example, a survey in 1969 revealed that one third of high school students were experimenting with illegal drugs. According to data accumulated by the National Institutes on Drug Abuse as of 1980, 34 percent of high school seniors had used marijuana within the last month and 9 percent of these seniors used marijuana daily.

In the 1960s the prevalence of drug usage was linked directly to social discontent. Many social critics decried what they saw as America's colorless and crushing preoccupation with cognitive skills at the expense of human passion and spontaneity (Keniston, 1965; Roszak, 1969). Members of the "establishment" were viewed by the '60s youth movement as soulless robots who had sacrificed their humanity for efficiency and technological competence, accepting the bauble of material affluence as a tinseled consolation prize. This negative judgment on "technocracy" led to a questioning of the sufficiency of reasoning and rationality as bases for planning human life (Leary, 1968; Cox 1970; for a more balanced view, see Hartmann, 1964). For a period of time particularly on the West Coast the "hippie" movement was viewed as quasi-religious phenomena in which psychedelic drugs served a central ritualistic and sacramental role (West and Allen, 1968; Brickman, 1968).

During the '60s a life pattern which included psychedelic drugs was often presented as a more enlightened approach to life. The drug user claimed a "revealed" comprehension of the meaning of life which was hidden from "straight" people. Other observers even at the time recognized the constrictive influence involved in such polarism (Mamlet, 1967). Over the next decade it became clear that much of the evangelical drug movement was largely another edition of the romantic tradition of dandyism. The pattern was perhaps best described by Camus (1956). "The Dandy, therefore, is always compelled to astonish. Singularity is his vocation, excess his weight of perfection. Perpetually incomplete, always on the fringe of things, he compels others to create him while denying their values. He plays at life because he is unable to live it."

Of course, most of the young people involved in this lifestyle have now chosen to live life in some form. Some of their choices are so ironic as to be comical. One could understand a metamorphosis to politican, but stock broker—? Perhaps more important than esoteric social issues is the simple fact that American culture has traditionally been very accepting of the state of intoxication. Not only has popular fiction, especially in movies and television, depicted alcohol use as highly normative behavior, it has tended to depict sobriety as dull or even worthy of suspicion. Often the inhibited hero or heroine finds meaningful emotional experiences, romance, and the joy of life only when drunk or high on marijuana. It is encouraging that some recent popular media fiction has featured recovering alcoholics in positive roles.

In any case, substance abuse is endemic in America and this heavy usage certainly extends to adolescents and even latency age children.

DEFINITION OF CHEMICAL DEPENDENCY

It is obvious that many adolescents use drugs, even fairly heavily, without apparent long-term negative consequences. This has led to an effort to define some drug use as social or recreational, some drug use as experimental, and only a portion of drug use as psychiatrically problematic. The difficulty, of course, is that there is no clear line between these categories of drug use.

The accepted definition of addiction in the past has been the occurrence of withdrawal symptoms on cessation of drug intake.

This is a limiting and clinically inadequate guide, especially in the adolescent population. Adolescents are reluctant to describe unpleasant subjective feelings, prone to transmit them into action and explain them on the basis of their current surroundings, and certainly reluctant to admit that their uncomfortable feelings are related to the drug use which they maintain to be harmless. In addition, they are physically highly resilient, having been using drugs for a relatively short time compared to adult addicts, and therefore probably do not have as intense physical reactions as are seen in the older population. Therefore an adolescent may be seriously drug dependent without showing clear withdrawal symptoms.

From a practical point of view the adolescent may be considered to be chemically dependent when drugs become more important to him than human interactions. or when his emotional interactions with others show clear evidence of a loss of sensitivity and empathy. This deterioration in human relationships will be even more clear when we discuss the psychology of chemical dependency. Serious chemical dependency is the likely result whenever an individual finds intoxication to be a superior substitute for human interactions in maintaining emotional stability and psychological comfort.

The preference for chemicals over human contacts may be obscured to some extent by an apparent friendliness with a wide range of other people. Indeed, the adolescent's investment in being with "friends" may be so strong as to almost parody normal adolescent group membership. Unfortunately, these groups are primarily organized around the group experience of drug use. They emphasize a shared secretiveness, preoccupation with maintenance of drug supplies, a spurious sense of superiority to the "straight world," and unfortunately, frequent personal and sexual exploitation of group members.

Obviously, as the pattern of chemical dependency becomes more chronic and severe, more obvious symptoms of psychological deterioration appear including a loss of interest in previous constructive activities, academic difficulties, grossly irresponsible behavior, and even self-neglect or physical symptoms related to excessive drug use.

It is important to remember that the chemically dependent adolescent's move away from people and toward drugs is initially subtle and difficult to detect. It may first appear as a slight loss of sensitivity and empathy in relationships with family and straight friends. Later it becomes more obvious as the adolescent steals from the family to obtain money to purchase drugs and treats family members as enemies if they oppose drug use in even mild terms. It is only when the illness is advanced that the adolescent may reach that desperate and chilling situation in which the youngster will use anyone in order to ensure an uninterrupted supply of a favorite drug. This progression almost always includes a pattern of growing alienation from parents and other family members which is often accompanied by intense hostility, intimidation, and cold rejection. To some extent these attitudes arise from the inner feelings of guilt which the adolescent is attempting to externalize as he provokes the parents and family members to treat him harshly, thus justifying some of their destructive behavior. However, these attitudes of hostility and disinterest also represent to some extent the psychological truth that the adolescent no longer needs the parent since the drugs and drug companions have become the most important source of comfort, solace, and pleasure. The parents are enemies with potential power to interfere with the adolescent's crucial sources of emotional supplies.

ETIOLOGY OF CHEMICAL DEPENDENCY

The etiology of drug use seems to have both biological and psychological elements. There is convincing evidence of a major hereditary element in the vulnerability to addiction, especially clear in the case of severe alcoholism.

The evidence for this hereditary tendency is not merely from statistical research but is confirmed by the everyday experience of clinicians who note a very high frequency of chemical dependency in the family tree of adolescents with serious drug problems. No one knows for sure how much this outcome is related to learned behavior based on the children's observation of parental drug use and how much is a purely genetic vulnerability. However, there is convincing evidence based on studies of children of alcoholics who were adopted at birth into nondrinking families which supports the likelihood that there is a pure biological element (Cardoret et al., 1980; Goodwin et al., 1973; Cloninger, 1981).

Other elements of family dynamics seem important in the genesis of substance abuse in adolescents. Families in which parental drug use disrupts basic family rituals seem more likely to produce a chemically dependent offspring (Wolin et al., 1980). It has also been noted that a history of sexual and/or physical abuse in childhood occurs with great frequency in populations of youngsters with chemical dependency (Wurmser and Zients, 1982). Obviously, neither of these family patterns are independent of parental substance abuse since heavy drug use would impair a parent's ability to maintain family rituals and is also a factor in increasing the likelihood of child abuse.

From a psychological perspective a number of hypotheses have been advanced over the years to account for heavy drug use. Early theories tended to focus on instinct theory and related drug use to need satisfaction. In recent years these formulations have largely given way to concepts that relate the ingestion of drugs to an artificial effort to stimulate normal ego functioning. Wieder and Kaplan (1969) offered the hypothesis that specific pharmacological properties of each drug may serve as a psychodynamic-pharmacogenic "prosthesis." They stated "when an individual finds an agent that chemically facilitates his pre-existing preferential mode of conflict solution, it becomes his drug of choice."

Other authors have noted the use of drugs to modulate affect in individuals who are unable to maintain this function (Sugarman and Kurash, 1982; Marohn, 1983) while others have emphasized the use of the drugs to maintain a sense of omnipotent control and avoidance of primitive superego pressures (Wurmser and Zients, 1982). One does encounter youngsters with borderline or psychotic personality structures who seem to take hallucinogens in order to deliberately distort their perception of reality. Cottle (1969) has described this technique as deliberately throwing away what was already lost. Although this maneuver may appear irrationally pointless, it does bestow a spurious sense of self-control and self-direction. This feels better to the frightened adolescent than being helplessly dominated by dark, inner forces. As one actively schizophrenic boy of 16 explained, "I trip because I need some good hallucinations, at least part of the time." We could add that perhaps he was also comforted by knowing when the hallucinations would appear and knowing that he willed their appearance. In any case, it is interesting that many studies (Hensala et al., 1967; Frosch et al., 1965; Blumfield and Glickman, 1967; Vardy and Ray, 1983; Bowers, 1977) have found that many youngsters who present with "bad trips" have underlying major psychopathology in either the manic-depressive or schizophrenic area.

All of these factors are related primarily to pathological states of chemical usage. It is obvious to most adolescent practitioners that many elements of the adolescent developmental phase may tend to encourage drug experimentation and even passing serious interest in drug usage. The adolescent's dependency needs coupled with his shame about dependence on others make the self-controlled gratifications of drugs and the capacity for self-comforting (Marohn, 1983) very appealing. In addition, the adolescent's turn toward a peer culture, deliberately defined as deviant from adult norms, is also a factor in encouraging drug use. In a very literal sense, the adolescent "sins" to test the penalities and to diminish his terror before his internal inquisitor. Classic adolescent rebelliousness which is actually directed against the internal parental images in the form of the primitive superego may paradoxically increase interest in drug use. Deliberately breaking the law serves to externalize internal states of guilt, focusing the adolescent's concern on real life authority representatives such as parents and policemen whom the adolescent hopes to elude. Even if he is caught, the punishment has some limits, unlike the formless dread provoked by the primitive superego.

It is also important to remember that not all drug-using adolescents are alike by any stretch of the imagination. Some drug-using adolescents seem primarily depressed, lonely, and inhibited. Drugs for them seem to be a vehicle for acceptance, lessening of inhibition, and amelioration of painful social anxiety. Another large group of substance-abusing adolescents seem more sociopathic, grandiose, and arrogant. They use drugs to maintain their sense of excitement, euphoria, and power over themselves and others. A final group of adolescents seem merely dedicated to self-destruction. They use drugs in such a massive, random, and nondiscriminating manner as to regularly threaten their very existence without showing any concern for their own survival, much less their well-being. It seems obvious that we are dealing with a complex interaction of genetic vulnerability, life experience, social expectation, and individual biological responses to specific doses and frequencies of the various chemical agents readily available to adolescents these days. Each case must be carefully evaluated in order to understand the specific youngster's vulnerability to chemical dependency so that gradually we may better understand the basic patterns in this serious illness.

Obviously, many of the youngsters who are heavy drug users fall within the group of youngsters described earlier as those with "malignant" defenses related to severe impairment of their sense of competence. After their chemical dependency and addictive behavior are treated directly, their evaluation and treatment often resembles that described in chapter 5.

THE PROGRESSION OF CHEMICAL DEPENDENCY

Chemical agents will never provide satisfactory answers for the problems that young people experience because of two inherent characteristics of psychoactive drugs. First of all, all drugs have a number of effects on the body. Those that are desired are seen as the drug's pharmacological action while those which are undesired are classified as side effects. Some of these side effects are merely unpleasant while others may actually damage the body.

The second problem with drug use is that the body gradually develops tolerance to the desired effects of any drug. Ever larger doses are required to produce the same effect if the drug is taken with any frequency. Consequently the higher dosage produces more and more of the unwanted effects, many of which are un-affected by tolerance, including those that are harmful. Even the most dedicated drug users have to eventually recognize, if only briefly and sporadically, that the drugs they are taking are pro-ducing negative effects. For example, any adolescent who uses large amounts of marijuana and alcohol will eventually begin to recognize that memory and capacity for concentration are im-paired. The adolescent who uses cocaine regularly will eventually experience some withdrawal depression, damage of the nasal mu-cosa, or simply severe personal and practical problems occasioned by the escalating costs of the habit.

The negative side effects are not merely biological. Regular drug use also impairs the development of ego skills by lowering signal anxiety, obscuring the consequences of behavior, and by producing an illusory sense of well-being without any need for achievement. Interestingly enough, it is not simply "serious" skills that are adversely affected. Adolescents who use drugs regularly and in large amounts blunt their ability to have fun and to find pleasure in everyday activities. The drug dependent adolescent often has few interests or hobbies and indeed is unaccustomed to engaging in any leisure activity except in the intoxicated state. The common final pathway for all of these negative psychological effects is a state of chronic boredom which is only imperfectly relieved by periodic intoxication.

Human relationships, particularly with adults, are severely im-paired by heavy drug use. Partly because of guilt over their be-havior and partly because of the actual opposition of caring adults, these adolescents come to view most concerned adults as enemies since they might potentially interfere with access to the desired chemical. The adolescents' relationships with others be-come increasingly dishonest, manipulative, and hostile so that the need for the drug is actually increased since there is diminished opportunity for meeting needs through interpersonal relation-ships.

The factors just outlined explain why drug dependency is almost always a progressive illness characterized by an increasingly blind and desperate dependency on drugs with a narrowing and ever more intense preoccupation with drug issues. In a curious kind of way, these adolescents have recreated the infantile dependency that they so feared and so desperately were trying to avoid. Rather than becoming omnipotent and self-sufficient, they become increasingly helplessly dependent on the availability of the needed drug and also on people who will supply the agents to them. At this point in the illness there is an astonishing degree of denial. Although the most casual objective observer would see the person's life as massively impacted by blind dependency on the drug, the patient maintains that this is totally untrue. Often the patient will stop using the drugs for a period of time to demonstrate that he can "take them or leave them," but, of course, he always returns to the same pattern of heavy drug use in a relatively brief period. This classical pattern of denial probably represents an emergency measure designed to defend the person against the recognition of the true state of affairs. An honest viewing of the actual situation would be simply too devastating. These adolescents would have to recognize that rather than being omnipotent they have become helplessly dependent on someone else. Of course, they would also have to recognize that they would have to give up drugs to change this state of affairs. That is an unacceptable idea because at this point they regard the drugs as their only practical source of support, pleasure, and self-esteem.

CHARACTERISTICS OF ABUSED SUBSTANCES

The popularity of specific drugs may vary over time. In addition to the process by which a particular individual selects his own drug of choice, broader sociological and economic factors may affect a drug's availability and popularity. These factors include issues such as the supply of a drug in a particular community; the influence of adolescent role models; and the "marketing" of new drug products, such as designer drugs and crack cocaine.

Some of the information in this section has been provided by the American Psychiatric Association (1988).

Caffeine and Nicotine

These substances are mentioned because they are the most extensively used drugs in our country. It is also notable how unpredictable adults are regarding a common issue such as adolescent smoking. Lawmakers and school boards come down on this issue along a very long continuum from very permissive to very restrictive. Some high schools have designated smoking lounges for students; many schools don't encourage smoking, but just look the other way; some schools go to the trouble to actively discourage smoking by teenagers; and in some communities it is illegal for minors to have tobacco in their possession on school property and teenagers are routinely arrested and charged.

Alcohol

Alcoholism is a progressive disease that can start at any age. It clusters in families and most likely has a biological, inherited predisposition. Although it takes five to fifteen years for an adult to become an alcoholic, an adolescent can become an alcoholic in six to eighteen months of heavy drinking. Adolescent alcoholics obviously have greatly impaired social and academic functioning. The physical effects of chronic heavy drinking (such as dementia, delirium tremens, cirrhosis, impotence, and so on) will catch up with them in later life.

Cannabis

Marijuana is the most widely used illegal drug. Among adolescents, its use is associated with tobacco use. That is, adolescents who smoke cigarettes are five times more likely to also use marijuana. In addition to the desired effect of euphoria, marijuana has side effects of impairing short-term memory, concentration, and fine motor skills. It is very dangerous to smoke pot and drive. The "amotivational syndrome" has been hashed over many times, so to speak. There are two schools of thought: one, that chronic marijuana use leads to apathy and loss of ambition; the second, that apathetic individuals with low ambition are the people who are likely to become chronic marijuana users.

Cocaine

Many people feel that cocaine use is the most important issue facing our government today. Even people who consider themselves jaded to the media have been impressed by drug busts netting several tons of cocaine at one location; the epidemic of drug-related murders in many cities; and other evidence of an illegal billion dollar industry. Our adolescent patients have been swept into this calamity in several ways—as users, as family members of addicted individuals, and as drug dealers.

Cocaine is a white powder extracted from the leaves of a common tropical plant, *Erythroxylon coca*. In addition to being a local anesthetic, it is a very strong stimulant which gives a very strong illusion of limitless power and energy. That's why they say, "cocaine lies." Up until recently, cocaine was almost always used by snorting the white powder through the nose or by dissolving it and injecting it with a needle.

Crack cocaine is made by mixing ordinary cocaine with a solution of baking soda in water. A chemical reaction occurs in which cocaine is changed from a salt into a freebase crystalline alkaloid. The result is that crack can be smoked and it is absorbed through the lungs as a vapor, which means that it has an immediate powerful effect. Both regular cocaine and crack cocaine are highly addictive. Not only does it make the user feel extremely good, the rebound effect as the drug wears off makes the user feel extremely bad. The only way to keep feeling good is to keep using. In addition to making the user feel bad, "cocaine kills" by causing heart attacks and heart failure.

Opiates

Opiates or narcotics are a class of drugs which are used legitimately for pain-reduction and cough-suppression. Naturally occurring opiates such as morphine and heroin come from the Asian poppy plant. Other narcotics, such as Demerol, have been synthesized and are used medically as analgesics. Opiate addiction is more likely to occur in adults than in adolescents.

Hallucinogens

The classic hallucinogen was lysergic acid diethylamine (LSD). It causes visual hallucinations and other perceptual distortions, which some people find frightening and other people find pleasurable. Phencyclidine (PCP) is also considered a hallucinogen, although it usually causes agitation and paranoia rather than pretty hallucinations. Clinicians were very concerned about these drugs in the 1960s and 1970s, but they are used less frequently now by adolescents. Hallucinogens used to be considered quite trendy among teenagers, but now they are mentioned by youngsters who are socially out of the mainstream. It is good to be aware, however, that LSD and PCP can be manufactured with simple equipment and chemicals which are fairly easy to obtain, so sometimes they are manufactured and sold locally.

Inhalants

Inhalants are breathable chemicals that produce mind-altering vapors. Most of the inhalants that are abused are actually manufactured for some other purpose, such as gasoline, glue, paint thinners, nail polish remover, cleaning fluid, hair spray, and White-Out. Some inhalants, such as amyl nitrate and butyl nitrate, are packaged in small breakable capsules or bottles that are intended to be broken and the contents inhaled. Inhalants are much more popular among children and adolescents than among adults. While small amounts cause a sense of lightheadedness and stimulation, high doses cause unconsciousness and sudden death.

Sedatives

Sedatives, hypnotics, or "downers" include tranquilizers and sleeping pills, that is, barbiturates (such as Seconal), benzodiazepines (such as Valium), methaqualone (Quaalude), chloral hydrate (Noctec). Sedatives are dangerous because they cause both physical and psychological dependence. Larger doses cause unconsciousness, respiratory depression, and death. It is particularly dangerous to combine sedatives with alcohol.

Amphetamines

Dexedrine and other forms of "speed" can also be abused. Symptoms include anxiety, agitation, and paranoia. Dexedrine and Ritalin are sometimes prescribed for adolescents with attention-deficit hyperactivity disorder. It is extremely unlikely that an adolescent would become dependent on these medications if they are taken in low to moderate doses for the purpose of relieving an attention deficit. It would be dangerous, however, for an adolescent to take high doses for the purpose of getting a buzz.

THE DIAGNOSIS OF CHEMICAL DEPENDENCY IN ADOLESCENTS

The primary factors interfering with the diagnosis of chemical dependency in adolescents are the patient's denial, the tendency of the family to deny the illness, and the chemically dependent adolescent's suspiciousness and animosity toward adults. The result of all these factors is that adolescents typically minimize their drug use or even lie about the role that it plays in their life. At the same time the adolescents usually give indirect evidence of the problem to therapists and other caring adults since they are basically concerned about themselves and retain some hope that someone will be able to help them. They may broach the subject of drugs indirectly through discussion of friends who use drugs or through theoretical discussions about the hypocrisy and overreaction of the adult world to adolescent drug use or in some of the other ingenious ways that adolescents introduce topics into discussion. At other times their approach is more direct—they come to therapy sessions drunk or high on marijuana.

The denial of parents is almost as striking as that of the patients. This pattern of denial is based on a complex family adaptation to the chemical dependency pattern—a pattern of behaviors known in the chemical dependency treatment field as "enabling" (Wegscheider, 1981) .

Enabling behavior on the part of the family refers to those methods of approaching the chemically dependent adolescent which permit or even encourage continued drug use. They include not only denying the existence of the problem in the face of rather obvious evidence of serious drug involvement but also rescuing the youngster from consequences of the drug dependent behavior and in other ways subtly accepting the youngster's self-identification as an addict. The dynamics behind this pattern are complex and may include some elements of family system pathology which require deviant behavior in the child in order to maintain family homeostasis. In other cases the pattern of enabling appears to be a self-protective response to the stress created by the presence in a family of an addicted individual since chemically dependent people often behave with callous disregard for the rights of others and coldness toward other family members. Enabling, in these cases, is designed to simply pretend that this heartbreaking behavior isn't happening. As one mother put it, "I was a happy little blind lady." In any case, one cannot totally count on families to recognize and identify adolescents who need treatment for the chemical dependency problems.

Diagnosis is fairly obvious in the full pattern of advanced chemical dependency which includes a change in associates, deterioration of adaptive functioning in school and at home, and wide variations in mood, communicativeness, and level of consciousness. When these are accompanied by recurrent obvious episodes of intoxication the diagnosis of chemical dependency alone or in combination with other psychiatric problems needs to be made even if the adolescent and the family minimize or attempt to deny the importance of these occurrences.

Diagnosis can be more difficult in other cases where the youngster manages to avoid some of the more clear-cut external manifestations of the problem behavior and instead functions as a "closet addict." In these instances one's suspicion should be roused by more subtle signs such as a loss of interest in previous constructive activities such as academics or extracurricular activities and organizations. These changes are usually rationalized as a simple change in interest patterns, but if they are not replaced by other constructive activities, this explanation should be viewed with some skepticism. Intense degrees of felt and expressed anger toward parents in the face of relatively benign behavior on the part of the parents should also be a warning sign of the possible presence of drug involvement. As mentioned earlier it is sometimes possible to pick up subtle evidence of heavy drug use from the nature of the adolescent's response to the psychotherapeutic process itself.

If suspicion is aroused, the issue can be addressed as any other resistance or problem in the therapeutic process. That is, the question can be raised as to whether appropriate progress can be made in treatment in the face of regular drug use on the part of the patient. Since the patient, due to denial, is likely to be unaware of the negative impact of the drug usage, it may be necessary to apply considerable pressure utilizing the leverage of the treatment contract and one's expert status as a psychotherapist. It is wise to avoid a parental or superego approach to the issue and it is unwise to issue ultimatums unless the parents are in total agreement and everyone is prepared to back up the ultimatums with firm insistence on hospitalization or residential treatment if the youngster continues to use drugs. Instead, it may be useful to suggest to the patient that a period of one month of abstinence would be a useful way to determine whether the concerns about drug use are justified. Obviously if the patient is unable to stay away from drugs for even one month this might demonstrate to him the intensity of his attachment. On the other hand, when youngsters do completely give up drugs for a month there are often changes in their ability to concentrate, plan for their future, modulate affect, and be aware of their own feelings which are obvious to them. This trial period gives a good basis for continuing careful attention to this issue as the psychotherapy goes on.

ISSUES IN THE TREATMENT OF THE ALCOHOLIC AND SUBSTANCE ABUSING ADOLESCENT

The outpatient treatment of these youngsters is complicated by their difficulty in forming a strong attachment to the therapist.

As described above they are, in a sense, more attached to their drugs of choice than human beings when chemical dependency reaches advanced stages. This almost phobic resistance to dependent attachments will certainly extend to the therapist. In the emotional life of the severely chemically dependent adolescent a therapist is merely a means to an end and manipulation and exploitation of the therapist is the common event.

> An intelligent 17-year-old boy hospitalized after a near fatal accidental drug overdose had been in psychotherapy for over a year on an outpatient basis. Early in his hospital treatment he bragged of convincing his outpatient therapist to prevail on his parents to allow him access to the area of the city where he obtained his drugs. He felt no remorse for this and held an attitude of amused contempt toward the therapist whom he felt he had outsmarted.

The therapist who treats a youngster with a serious drug problem needs to recall that these youngsters have found human dependency extremely uncomfortable and unrewarding. They avoid their anxiety about dependent relationships by constantly trying to prove that they are smarter than adults and that they have no need for their help. As a rule, abstinence must be a requirement for successful treatment of these youngsters. If abstinence can be obtained, underlying feelings of depression, yearnings for support, and feelings of anxiety may come to the fore for psychotherapeutic management. However, it is usually not possible for the therapist to compete with the instant and complete solutions to these problems which the drugs provided, at least in the early and middle phases of usage. One must expect to be compared unfavorably with the drug life. This is particularly true as the youngsters regain some of the benefits of abstinence. As their physical and emotional vigor returns, they tend to forget the negative effects of drug use and may idealize the pleasant and gratifying aspects of intoxication. Patients in treatment for severe chemical dependency will periodically be tempted to use drugs. These temptations come from both yearnings for remembered gratifications and urges to self-medicate in the face of some of the emotional discomfort created by life or indeed by the psychotherapeutic process itself (Hartman, 1969; Esman, 1967).

In outpatient therapy it usually is necessary to provide some external support to assist in maintaining abstinence in the face of these temptations. Regular random monitoring of drug urines and membership in support groups such as Alcoholics Anonymous (AA) and Narcotics Anonymous (NA) that encourage continuing abstinence and remind members of the dangers of drug use are useful and perhaps necessary adjuncts to outpatient psychotherapy. Family support and resolution of enabling behaviors in the family system are also crucial.

INPATIENT TREATMENT

Obviously, there are many seriously drug involved youngsters who cannot maintain abstinence on an outpatient basis even with the support of family and treatment procedures such as those described above. For these youngsters, treatment must be started in a controlled, drug free environment where a period of abstinence can be ensured while they gain at least beginning control over their compulsive drug use.

There are several ways to organize an inpatient treatment program for adolescents who abuse drugs and alcohol. Two approaches that are quite different from each other are the medical psychiatric treatment approach and the recovering-community treatment model. The medical psychiatric treatment approach started as an attempt to treat adolescents who abuse substances on units which are actually intended for youngsters with psychiatric conditions. The recovering-community treatment approach for adolescents is derived from the adult-oriented "Twelve Step" Alcoholics Anonymous program. These two models have different philosophies and therapeutic practices. For instance, the traditional psychiatric approach would involve dealing with the anxiety that is created as the youngster gradually gives up his denial of his condition; in the recovering-community model, the patient may be confronted vigorously about his denial. A traditional medical psychiatric program is more likely to include individual therapy and medication; the recovering-community model emphasizes the power of group therapy and a highly structured educational component. The staff in a traditional psychiatric program are more likely to allow a greater degree of freedom of expression, while recovering-community staff may insist on a very strict dress code and rules about hairstyle. In both models family therapy is considered very important.

It is likely that the best treatment approach for adolescent substance abusers is neither of these models, in their original pure form. King and Meeks (1988) described two inpatient programs where they attempted "to merge the expertise of the recovering community with the psychological and developmental insights of adolescent psychiatry. . . ." The treatment included components of a traditional psychiatric inpatient treatment program (daily formal group psychotherapy, prescribed individual therapy, special education, and a variety of activity therapies) and also components of the recovering-community treatment approach (the Twelve Step program and didactic and process-oriented meetings with substance abuse counselors). The family involvement was intensive.

In both outpatient and inpatient treatment the trained drug counselors, particularly those who have previously been addicted themselves, are an invaluable aid to the treatment process. They provide both an empathic understanding of the joys and horrors of chemical dependency and a seismographic awareness of the manipulations and self-delusions which characterize the illness. They do not usually need to see gross evidence of a return to drug use in addicted adolescents because they recognize the very subtle evidences of the mind set which usually precedes or accompanies a relapse. Their comfort in confronting the adolescent drug addict is usually higher than therapists who have not been drug addicted, both because they have the sense of having "been there" but also because they usually have a conviction of the correctness of their assessment which "straight" therapists find very difficult to maintain in the face of blatant denial.

FAMILY THERAPY AND INDIVIDUAL THERAPY

The role of family therapy has already been mentioned. Obviously, intensive family therapy focusing on enabling patterns is very important if the adolescent is to be strongly encouraged to find the strength to persist in new lifestyle patterns. If the family continues to encourage and permit chemical dependency, the adolescent's own temptations to return to drug use will find ready support and likely expression. Adequate therapy for parents of this kind includes major educational efforts to be sure that they understand the nature of chemical dependency, peer support (especially from other families who have successfully dealt with the problem), and appropriate therapy for family system psychopathology which might lead to a need for a scapegoated child.

If these special parameters of therapy are carefully attended to, the chemically dependent youngsters will gradually turn away from compulsive drug use. As a rule, as they give up drug use and abandon the fantasy that drug use in the future will solve their problems, the basic underlying psychopathology will tend to become more obvious and more available to traditional psychotherapy. This change is accompanied by the development of a genuine transference relationship and a strong human attachment to the therapist. At this point in treatment the patients' motivation to maintain this relationship and explore it becomes a very important element in avoiding drug use. Since the therapist is now more important than the chemical substance, the balance has shifted and traditional psychotherapy becomes possible.

However, it should be remembered that a youngster who has been chemically dependent may continue to find the prospect of chemical solutions attractive in the face of unusual stresses, especially those that relate directly to therapy. The time of termination, for example, may be fraught with risk for these youngsters as they deal with the major loss of giving up the therapist. Vacation times and periods of disillusionment with the therapist also raise the spectre of relapse as a treatment complication. This reality should be recognized by the therapist and also conveyed to the parents so that these episodes of return to drug use can be seen for what they are rather than being misdiagnosed as a simple continuation of the drug pattern in which the therapist has just been conned for a longer period than usual.

CITED AND RECOMMENDED READINGS

Abel, E. L. 1975. Marijuana, learning, and memory. *International Review of Neurobiology*. 18: 329–356.

American Medical Association Committee on Alcoholism and Addiction. 1965. *Reports on Dependency on Amphetamines and Barbiturates*. 193: 673.

American Psychiatric Association. 1988. *Let's Talk Facts about Substance Abuse*. Washington, D.C.: American Psychiatric Press.

Blumfield, M., and L. Glickman. 1967. Ten months experience with LSD users admitted to county psychiatric receiving hospital. *New York State Journal of Medicine*. 67: 1849–1853.

Bowers, M. B. 1977. Psychoses precipitated by psychotomimetic drugs: a followup study. *Archives of General Psychiatry*. 34: 832–835.

Brickman, H. R. 1968. The psychedelic "hip scene": return of the death instinct. *American Journal of Psychiatry*. 125: 766–772.

Brook, J. S., et al., editors. 1985. *Alcohol and Substance Abuse in Adolescence*. New York: Haworth Press.

Cadoret, R. J., et al. 1980. Development of alcoholism in adoptees raised apart from alcoholic biologic relatives. *Archives of General Psychiatry*. 37: 561–563.

Cameron, D. C. 1968. Youth and drugs, a world view. *The Journal of the American Medical Association*. 206: 1267–1271.

Camus, A. 1956. *The Rebel*. New York: Vintage Books.

Carson, D. I., and J. M. Lewis. 1970. Factors influencing drug abuse in young people. *Texas Medicine*. 66: 50–57.

Cloninger, C. R. 1981. Inheritance of alcohol abuse. *Archives of General Psychiatry*. 38: 861–868.

Cohen, S. 1964. *The Beyond Within: The LSD Story*. New York: Atheneum Publishers.

Cottle, T. J. 1969. Parent and child—the hazards of equality. *Saturday Review*. 52: No. 5, 16–48.

Cox, H. 1970. *The Feast of Fools: A Theological Essay on Festivity and Fantasy*. Cambridge: Harvard University Press.

De Leon, G. 1988. The therapeutic community perspective and approach for adolescent substance abusers. *Adolescent Psychiatry*. 15: 535–556.

Dimijian, G. G. 1970. Clinical evaluation of the drug user: current concepts. *Texas Medicine*. 66: 42–49.

Esman, A. H. 1967. Drug use by adolescents: some valuative and technical implications. *Psychoanalytic Forum*. 2: 340–346.

Evans, J. L. 1970. The college student in the psychiatric clinic: syndromes and subcultural sanctions. *American Journal of Psychiatry*. 126: 1736–1742.

Frosch, W., et al. 1965. Untoward reactions to LSD resulting in hospitalization. *New England Journal of Medicine.* 273: 1235–1239.

Goodwin, D. W., et al. 1973. Alcohol problems in adoptees raised apart from alcoholic biologic parents. *Archives of General Psychiatry.* 28: 238–243.

Hartmann, D. 1969. A study of drug taking adolescents. *Psychoanalytic Study of the Child.* 24: 384–398.

Hartmann, H. 1964. On rational and irrational action. *Essays on Ego Psychology.* New York: International Universities Press.

Hartocollis, P. 1982. Personality characteristics in adolescent problem drinkers: a comparative study. *Journal of the American Academy of Child Psychiatry.* 21: 348–353.

Hensala, J., et al. 1967. LSD and psychiatric inpatients. *Archives of General Psychiatry.* 16: 554–559.

Johnston, L. D., et al. 1980. *Student Drug Use in America. (1975–1980).* Rockville, Maryland: National Institutes on Drug Abuse, Division of Research.

Keniston, K. 1965. *The Uncommitted: Alienated Youth in American Society.* New York: Harcourt, Brace & World.

King, J. W., and J. E. Meeks. 1988 Hospital programs for psychiatrically disturbed, drug-abusing adolescents. *Adolescent Psychiatry.* 15: 522–534.

Leary, T. 1968. *The Politics of Ecstasy.* New York: G. P. Putnam's Sons.

Lewis, J. M. 1970. *Report of the Ad Hoc Committee on Drug Abuse.* Dallas, Texas: Dallas Independent School District Report.

Louria, D. 1966. *Nightmare Drugs.* New York: Pocket Books.

Louria, D. B. 1968. Some aspects of the current drug scene with emphasis on drugs in use by adolescents. *Pediatrics.* 42: 904–911.

Mamlet, L. N. 1967. "Consciousness-limiting" side effects of "consciousness-expanding" drugs. *American Journal of Orthopsychiatry.* 37: 296–297.

Marohn, R. C. 1983. Adolescent substance abuse: a problem of self-soothing. *Clinical Update in Adolescent Psychiatry.* New Canaan, Conn.: Nassau Publications.

Meeks, J. D. 1982. Some clinical comments on chronic marijuana use in adolescent psychiatric patients. Washington, DC: National Institute on Drug Abuse. DHHS Publication # (ADM) 82–1186.

Pearson, M. M., and R. B. Little. 1969. The addictive process in unusual addictions: a further elaboration of etiology. *American Journal of Psychiatry.* 125: 1166–1171.

Report by the Council on Mental Health and the Committee on Alcoholism and Drug Dependence of the American Medical Association and the Committee on Problems of Drug Dependence of the National Research Council. National Academy of Science. Reprints available from: AMA Council on Mental Health, 535 North Dearborn, Chicago, IL 60610.

Report of the American Academy of Pediatrics, Committee on Youth. 1969. Drug abuse in adolescence. *Pediatrics.* 44: 131–141.

Riefe, P. 1968. *The Triumph of the Therapeutic.* New York: Harper and Row.

Roszak, T. 1969. *The Making of a Counter Culture.* New York: Doubleday.

Stone, M. H. 1973. Drug-related schizophrenic syndromes. *International Journal of Psychiatry.* 11: 391–437.

Sugarman, A., and C. Kurash. 1982. Marijuana abuse, transitional experience, and the borderline adolescent. In: *Adolescent Addiction: Varieties and Vicissitudes,* edited by S. Smith. Hillside, N.J.: The Analytic Press.

Treffert, D. A. 1978. Marijuana use in schizophrenia: a clear hazard. *American Journal of Psychiatry.* 135: 1213–1215.

Ungerleider, J. T., and D. D. Fisher. 1967. The problems of LSD and emotional disorder. *California Medicine.* 106: 49–55.

Ungerleider, J. T., et al. 1968. The "bad trip"—the etiology of the adverse LSD reaction. *American Journal of Psychiatry.* 124: 1483–1490.

Vardy, M. M., and S. R. Ray. 1983. LSD psychosis or LSD-induced schizophrenia? *Archives of General Psychiatry.* 40: 877–883.

Walters, P. A. 1967. Therapist bias and student use of illegal drugs. *Journal of the American College Health Associations.* 16: 30–34.

Washton, A. M. 1989. *Cocaine Addiction: Treatment, Recovery, and Relapse Prevention.* New York: W. W. Norton.

Wegscheider, S. 1981. *Another Chance.* Palo Alto, California: Science and Behavior Books.

West, L. J., and J. R. Allen. 1968. Flight from violence: hippies and the green rebellion. *American Journal of Psychiatry.* 125: 120–126.

Wieder, H., and E. H. Kaplan. 1969. Drug use in adolescents: psychodynamic meaning and pharmacogenic effect. *Psychoanalytic Study of the Child.* 24: 399–431.

Wolin, S. J., et al. 1980. Disrupted family rituals: a factor in the intergenerational transmission of alcoholism. *Journal of Studies on Alcoholism.* 41: 199–214.

Wurmser, L., and A. Zients. 1982. The return of the denied superego. In: *Adolescent Addiction: Varieties and Vicissitudes,* edited by S. Smith. Hillside, N.J.: The Analytic Press.

CHAPTER 22

medical and neurological issues

Therapists who work with adolescents frequently have the opportunity to use medical consultation as well as their own understanding of biology in evaluating and treating their patients. It is easy to find many interfaces between the emotional, physical, and medical lives of these youngsters. These issues don't end after you take the medical history and wrap up the evaluation, since many of the adolescent's concerns in therapy may be expressed in physical or medical terms. Treating adolescents is work that requires assessing and integrating and taking seriously much medical and neurological data.

How many ways can there be for medical topics to come up with adolescents?

On a developmental level, every adolescent is intrigued with and concerned about the physical changes that occur during and after puberty. Many times the teenagers who end up in therapy have not been able to ask the right questions and get the right answers through the usual channels that most adolescents use to get information about sexuality and physical development—such as peers and parents and family doctors. These inhibited and conflicted youngsters may be able to get basic information from a therapist, as long as the therapist is not inhibited and conflicted himself.

Actually, adolescents are curious about many parts of their bodies in addition to the parts related to sex. A youngster who has a serious learning disability may find it both educational and reassuring to have somebody explain how his brain works. It may be that a teacher or psychologist tried to do that when the disability was documented back at age 7, but it may not be until age 14 that the patient has the mental and conceptual ability to follow a simple explanation. An adolescent may find herself very interested in learning about her genetics, as in inheritance. As her own sense of identity unfolds, she may become very interested in sorting out what parts of her personality may have been inherited and what parts were learned and what parts she created on her own. Although the main task for the adolescent therapist is not to teach a biology class, he may frequently find his own professional education a valuable resource in communicating with these youngsters.

A therapist can learn a lot about a youngster by the way the patient deals with both acute and chronic illness. An acute condition may simply be an opportunity to get some mileage out of one's courage and daring. That is probably the dynamic that has perpetuated the nickname of "the kissing fever" for several generations of mononucleosis-prone adolescents. A teenager who has broken a leg being tackled or on a ski trip usually looks pretty happy when his or her buddies visit in the hospital, especially when they bring pizza. On the other hand, a chronic and debilitating condition may be the basis for a good deal of resentment, anger, depression, and social withdrawal.

Many neurological and medical conditions have prominent emotional and behavioral symptoms. Maybe it is true that "anybody who sees a psychiatrist should have his head examined." The adolescent therapist should at least be wondering whether his patient's psychological symptoms have some kind of neurological basis. Neurological conditions that should be kept in mind range from the common (complex partial seizures or temporal lobe epilepsy) to the unusual (Tourette's disorder) to the rare (frontal lobe cyst) to the downright scarce (Klein-Levin syndrome). These diagnoses are mentioned just to make the point and the list is not meant to be comprehensive. Some of these conditions will be discussed later in the chapter.

To mention another way that medical topics come up in therapy with young people, the therapist needs to know the physiological effects of alcohol and abused drugs and other substances that adolescents put in their bodies. If your patient is a self-proclaimed expert on cannabis, it is good to know enough about the topic to judge whether the patient really knows what he is talking about. When the patient is taking psychiatric or other medication, the therapist has an important role in educating the patient about both therapeutic effects and side effects. For instance, it may be important to ask a young man who is taking antidepressant or antipsychotic medication whether there has been a change in his ability to have an erection or ejaculate. He might be very concerned about it and it probably would not occur to him that this change in his potency is related to the medication that is supposed to make him feel better.

The adolescent therapist will find many ways that psychological and physical phenomena interact. Perhaps the most important are hysterical conditions (in which unconscious conflicts cause the loss of or alteration of physical functioning, but without permanent physical changes in any organ) and psychosomatic conditions, such as asthma and peptic ulcer disease (in which psychological factors are related to the initiation of exacerbation of demonstrable organic pathology). Anorexia nervosa is also a good example of an illness in which both the physical and the mental aspects must be given equal attention, so we will use it later in this chapter to illustrate our message.

PSYCHOSOMATIC ILLNESS

DSM-III-R does not actually use the term psychosomatic disorders, but uses the cumbersome phrase, "psychological factors affecting physical condition." Since we think that the future editors of *DSM-IV* are not going to be using a five-word phrase when they can get by with one or two words, for the time being we are going to stick with the old-fashioned terminology of psychosomatic disorders.

The classic psychosomatic disorders described by Franz Alexander (1950) included hypertension, asthma, ulcerative colitis, peptic ulcer, neurodermatitis, rheumatoid arthritis, and hyperthyroidism. The conditions that are most likely to occur in adolescents are respiratory disorders, such as hyperventilation syndrome and asthma; gastrointestinal disorders, such as irritable bowel syndrome, peptic ulcer, regional ileitis, and ulcerative colitis; obesity; and chronic pain, especially abdominal pain.

Contemporary reviews of this subject have been prepared by Kavanaugh and Mattsson (1979) and Thompson (1988). Thompson indicated three factors which must be present simultaneously for a person to develop a psychosomatic disorder: the person must have a biological predisposition to the particular disorder, which could be genetic or secondary to trauma or environmental insults; the individual must have a pesonality vulnerability; and the individual must experience a significant psychosocial stress in his susceptible personality area.

There is not a consensus among psychotherapists regarding the treatment of psychosomatic disorders. Thompson (1988) advocates an integration of medical and psychological treatments. For the treatment of peptic ulcer, for instance, he would endorse the use of medication to block the production of gastric acid and also the use of psychotherapy to address psychological conflicts and maladaptive defenses, if those conflicts are obviously present in that particular client. Other authors (Wilson and Mintz, 1988) emphasize psychoanalytic treatment of the underlying personality disorder. They claim that the premature removal of psychosomatic symptoms could lead to another substituted psychosomatic symptom, addictive disorder, or other psychological symptoms.

The adolescent with a psychosomatic disorder may resist seeing a therapist or a counselor because he thinks that somebody is trying to tell him that his illness is all in his head. He has been experiencing very real epigastric pain and has even seen a very real peptic ulcer after his upper GI series, so nobody is going to get off easy by saying that he has some kind of emotional problem. During the course of the initial evaluation these youngsters usually appreciate a straightforward explanation of how psychosomatic symptoms occur. It may be as simple as something like this: "Your ulcer is caused partly by physical factors and partly by psychological factors. You may have been born with some kind of predisposition for this kind of illness. Your smoking two packs of cigarettes a day may be aggravating it. We also know that you have put yourself under a great deal of stress recently, since you have the idea that you need to get straight A's in order to become valedictorian of your graduating class. And the fact that your parents got divorced last year hasn't helped. We need to take all of these factors into consideration in order to help your duodenum heal up and stay healed. We need to work together—your pediatrician will be prescribing some medication; I am going to help you figure out how to avoid putting yourself under so much pressure; and you can help yourself by not smoking so much.''

The following case illustrates how the recognition of the underlying conflict can help in the resolution of a psychosomatic illness.

Sandra was a 17-year-old high school senior who was referred by the social worker attached to the medical clinic of a large private hospital. The girl had several episodes of low abdominal pain which interfered with her attendance at school and at times was severe enough to cause her to collapse to the ground. A comprehensive medical and gynecological evaluation had been completely normal. The gynecologist considered scheduling the patient for endoscopy, because he thought that the pain could be caused by endometriosis. He decided to postpone that procedure and recommended instead that the patient have psychiatric evaluation and treatment.

During the early part of treatment it became apparent to the therapist and to the youngster that she was a dedicated, extremely responsible, and overly conscientious person who identified greatly with her father. Sandra was the best student in her school in her particular area of interest, which involved math and science; the father was an engineer who was tops in his field, to the point where he occasionally had testified before Congressional committees. It was hard for her to reconcile her wish to be dutiful and another wish to have a good time, like other high school students. Furthermore, the more she identified with her father, the more arrogant she became at school and the more she distanced herself from peers. She set extremely high standards for female peers and for boy friends, which few kids were willing to put up with.

The low abdominal, vaguely gynecological pain appeared to have several psychological determinants. It probably started with the patient's awareness of ordinary menstrual cramps. Sandra was a very intense and driven youngster who seemed to exaggerate the pain in the same way that she exaggerated other emotions and attitudes. The intense pain and the episodes of collapsing seemed to occur at times when some important event was about to occur, which could either turn out to be a great success for Sandra or else what she perceived as an utter failure. Finally, the pain seemed to protect her from becoming physically involved with her boy friend.

Sandra's treatment was a combination of individual, group, and family meetings. The therapist's observations helped Sandra understand that these pains could have a number of interesting explanations and that it would be worthwhile for her to figure out which ones might apply to herself. She learned that it is really nice to have fun some of the time and that a person does not have to be successful in absolutely everything. Finally, she needed permission to identify with some aspects of her father's personality, without being obligated to become a reproduction of him. It also seemed to help for Sandra to graduate from high school and to move on in her life. When she was seen after a semester of college, she was much happier and was not having abdominal pains.

ANOREXIA NERVOSA

The eating disorders which occur in adolescence include anorexia nervosa, bulimia nervosa, and obesity. Both anorexia and bulimia have occurred more often in recent years. The increasing incidence may be related to cultural factors, such as the general popularity of fitness and thinness. Perhaps more of our children

The *Textbook of Psychiatry* published by The American Psychiatric Press has a good chapter on eating disorders by Katherine A. Halmi, M.D., (1988), a professor of psychiatry at Cornell University Medical College. Dr. Halmi's chapter explains the physiology of eating and then discusses the etiology and the treatment of anorexia nervosa, bulimia nervosa, and obesity. Halmi (1989) was also the editor of the section on eating disorders in the American Psychiatric Association's *Treatments of Psychiatric Disorders.*

Derek Miller (1985) has presented "the biopsychosocial etiology and differential diagnosis of syndromes which present themselves with a symptomatic picture that is called anorexia nervosa." He described the typical dynamics of anorexia, which are related to issues of control, helplessness, sexual identity, and generalized identity confusion. Dr. Miller also explained how severely disturbed youngsters can be treated in an inpatient program.

become preoccupied with food because our society enjoys an abundance and an unusual variety of food. Anorexia occurs more often in the middle and upper classes, which are the people who patronize gourmet supermarkets and are barraged with advertising and commentary on nutrition, good food, bad food, and dieting. A child growing up in this culture is going to get the idea that there is something very important about food and what you do with it.

Anorexia and bulimia have been portrayed many times in television shows, movies, and in printed media. As a result, adolescents are much more aware of these conditions. It used to be that an adolescent female would have to discover completely on her own that self-starvation can provide enough primary gain and secondary gain to make it worthwhile. Now all she has to do is read a few magazines or watch popular television shows to learn that anorexia and bulimia are options to be considered.

DSM-III-R requires four criteria for the diagnosis of anorexia nervosa:

1. Refusal to maintain body weight over a minimal normal weight for age and height. That is taken to mean keeping one's weight at least 15% below what would be expected.
2. Intense fear of gaining weight or becoming fat, even though underweight.
3. Disturbance in the way in which one's body weight, size, or shape is experienced. For instance, the person may feel that one area of the body is "too fat" even when obviously underweight.
4. In females, absence of at least three consecutive menstrual cycles when otherwise expected to occur. This may be either primary or secondary amenorrhea.

There are other symptoms which commonly occur in youngsters with anorexia. Usually the illness starts with a period of purposeful dieting, which may be undertaken in order to be more attractive or to be more fit or to be a more competitive ballet dancer or wrestler. During the course of dieting the patient may become preoccupied with issues related to food, such as calories and the size of portions and she may achieve a detailed but flawed knowledge of nutrition. She may start exercising in order to lose even more weight, which can take the form of getting up early in the morning to complete a regimen of calesthenics or jogging.

The most striking psychological symptom is the way the patient distorts her image of herself. Although her cachexia is obvious to family members and her entire physical education class, the patient will insist that she is still a little too chubby in certain places. High school students are aware of this aspect of anorexia nervosa and they sometimes make the diagnosis. In one case, a physical education class sat on the floor and refused to play any more volleyball until the teacher and the school nurse agreed to refer an anorexic student for a professional evaluation.

Patients with anorexia nervosa have characteristic personality traits. These youngsters frequently have been obedient, compliant, and overly conscientious. They have often been hard working in school with good academic records. They were popular with parents and teachers and other adults, but did not succeed at the important adolescent task of forming peer friendships. In general the anorexic adolescent seems to prefer the role of an asexual, dependent, younger child with intense ties to parents, rather than forging ahead into adolescence. In some ways the condition of anorexia nervosa occurs in conjunction with other neurotic, psychotic, or personality disorders.

Anorexia and bulimia have been studied extensively from both a physiological and a psychiatric point of view. The etiology of anorexia nervosa probably starts with a genetic predisposition. A simple but dramatic study of twins (Holland et al. 1984) showed that the concordance rate for monozygotic twins was much greater than the condordance for dizygotic twins. It has been suggested (Gold 1986) that there is an abnormality in the hypothalamus of anorexics, such that an increased production of corticotropin releasing factor leads to higher circulating levels of cortisol. There may also be dysregulation of neurotransmitters, such as serotonin, norepinephrine, and dopamine.

It is possible, of course, to conceptualize this illness in psychological and psychodynamic terms. Bruch (1973) organized the psychological aspects of anorexia and concluded that three criteria should be fulfilled to establish the diagnosis. First, there must be a convincing disturbance of body image, to the point of being delusional. Secondly, there is a distortion in the accuracy of bodily sensations. For instance, these youngsters do not interpret accurately feelings of hunger, fatigue, discomfort, and sexuality. Thirdly, these patients are concerned with being in control, so they find elaborate ways to accomplish that goal. Minuchin (1978) described the families of anorexic patients and his method of treating them.

For the practicing clinician it usually does not matter whether the physiological or the psychological pathology occurred first, since you still need to address both aspects of the illness. It is most useful to collaborate with the youngster's pediatrician. If outpatient treatment is indicated, the pediatrician or her nurse can meet weekly with the patient to monitor her weight and to give advice about how to select a healthy diet. The therapist can provide the individual and family therapy and can consider using psychotropic medication. If the pediatrician and the therapist communicate periodically, the patient will experience a truly coordinated and holistic approach to this complex illness.

In evaluating a patient with anorexia nervosa the therapist must consider the treatment options that are available and make recommendations to the youngster and her family. Hospitalization should be considered for youngsters who are more seriously disturbed, as indicated by an unusually great loss of weight; by severely abnormal electrolytes; by the patient's lack of insight and denial of the seriousness of her fasting; by her lack of willingness to gain weight; and by the lack of family support.

If it appears that outpatient treatment should be tried, the therapist then needs to choose between seeing the patient himself and referring the patient to an outpatient treatment program intended specifically for anorexics. A youngster who has persistent distortions of body image and who does not appreciate the seriousness of her condition may do better in an eating disorders treatment program, since the other group members and the educational component of the program will tune her into the gravity of her illness. However, youngsters who have a "mild" case of anorexia nervosa can be treated in a general outpatient practice. For instance, these patients do well in a heterogeneous adolescent therapy group, in which the patients are dealing with common adolescent issues. It seems to help these patients see that they are struggling with some of the same feelings and conflicts as other teenagers.

One way to approach the outpatient treatment of a patient with anorexia nervosa is to combine the modalities of individual psychotherapy, group therapy, and family therapy. For instance, the patient could have two appointments a week. On one day each week she could come to an adolescent group. The second appointment could alternate between an individual therapy session and a family meeting. It is usually helpful to address the issue of weight on a regular basis, but then spend most of the therapy on other issues.

It may also be helpful to develop a contract that includes the patient, the parents, the pediatrician, and the therapist. For instance, suppose the girl's usual weight should be 120 pounds, but she has been fluctuating between 90 and 95. The parents and the doctors could decide that the absolutely minimal acceptable weight will be 105. It is arranged for the patient to be officially weighed at the pediatrician's office once a week, perhaps on the way to the individual therapy appointment. If her weight is 105 or above, it is agreed that for the following week she herself will be in control of what she eats and her activity level. If her weight is less than 105, for the following week the parents will take over control, by selecting the menu, dishing up her plate, monitoring her consumption, and regulating her level of exercise.

That may seem like a simple behavioral contract, but it should be done in a way to communicate important messages. For one thing, the patient and her parents are not supposed to argue about her eating and her weight all week long. If the family is cooperative, the patient's weight is discussed only once a week. Secondly, the therapist may need to explain that it is a worthy ambition to find ways to get your parents off your case and out of your hair. This contract expresses in a concrete manner that the anorexic patient can be more grown up and more self-sufficient by simply reaching a weight of 105, in which case her parents will leave her alone for a week.

The reader will immediately point out that the typical patient with anorexia nervosa may simply want to be an immature, dependent child rather than an adolescent striving for independence. That's the whole point! The patient will be insisting that she is willing and ready to take responsibility for herself, but then she'll let her weight slip below 105, which will cause the parental infantry to assemble. The discrepency between her words and her actions will give you something to talk about in therapy.

EPILEPSY AND RELATED SYNDROMES

In patients with epilepsy it can be a challenge to sort out the psychiatric phenomena from the neurologic phenomena. In some cases it may not be possible at all. There are several ways that psychiatric and neurologic symptoms can be related and can be confused with each other:

—adolescents with epilepsy can have the same feelings as other patients with a chronic illness, such as secondary depression, apathy, and resentment;

—for some reason, suicide attempts and actual suicide occur more often in epileptics than in the general population;

—whatever caused the epilepsy could be causing other neuropsychiatric symptoms, such as attention-deficit hyperactivity disorder;

—some forms of seizure activity, such as complex partial seizures or temporal lobe epilepsy, may be manifested by prominent mental and behavioral symptoms;

—even when the seizure itself is not occurring, during the interictal period, epileptics may have characteristic personality traits and mental symptoms which could be mistaken for psychiatric conditions;

—some patients may have pseudoseizures, either purposefully or through unconscious mechanisms, which may look a whole lot like real seizures;

—and the chronic use of some anticonvulsant medications, especially barbiturates, may create symptoms such as mental dulling.

Temporal Lobe Epilepsy

Of all the epileptic disorders, temporal lobe epilepsy has interested and intrigued psychiatrists the most. Temporal lobe seizures have also been called psychomotor seizures or limbic seizures. Neurologists frequently use the terminology proposed by the International League Against Epilepsy—in that nomenclature temporal lobe seizures are called complex partial seizures if loss of consciousness is involved and simple partial seizures if consciousness is maintained. Temporal lobe epilepsy has its peak onset at the time of sexual maturation.

A typical temporal lobe seizure begins with an aura; the subsequent ictal episode is usually marked by unconsciousness and a variety of automatisms; and the postictal period follows. If the patient is unconscious during the seizure, he will be amnesic for

Dietrich P. Blumer (1982, 1984) is Professor of Psychiatry at the University of Tennessee, Memphis, College of Medicine. He has extensively studied the psychiatric manifestations of neurological conditions, especially of epilepsy. The book which he edited for the American Psychiatric Press, *Psychiatric Aspects of Epilepsy*, is an excellent map of the boundary between psychiatry and neurology.

what he may do during that time. The patient usually manifests automatisms, which are repetitive, stereotyped movements, such as lip-smacking or scratching or fingering a button or a utensil. Both the aura and the not-remembered part of the seizure tend to be brief, highly stereotyped, and unique for a given patient. The first observable event tends to be the interruption of ongoing activity. But if the seizure discharge is only slight, the patient may continue doing what he was doing and yet have no memory. He may look "conscious" to the casual observer because he is still sitting or standing or walking about. One patient continued to ride a bicycle during a temporal lobe seizure.

Dramatic mental symptoms can occur during the aura and the postictal period associated with temporal lobe seizures. The patient may spontaneously experience strong emotions, including a sense of doom or intense anxiety or, for that matter, intense happiness. As the seizure activity spreads through the association areas of the temporal cortex, the patient may experience visual or auditory hallucinations. General mental confusion, tiredness, and a feeling of depression usually mark the postictal period.

The Interictal State

It is easy to understand the occurrence of mental symptoms as the electrical discharge starts at the epileptic focus and moves through other parts of the brain. What is more interesting and more pertinent to psychiatry is that patients with temporal lobe epilepsy have characteristic mental experiences and personality traits during the interictal state, when they are not having a seizure at all. David Bear (1977, 1982, 1984) and other authors have described an epileptic personality that occurs in patients with temporal lobe seizures, which is characterized by hyperreligiousity, hyposexuality, circumstantiality, and hypergraphia. The idea is that these personality traits are caused by the seizure focus. That is, during the interictal state the seizure focus is not strong enough to precipitate a full seizure, but it is strong enough to influence and mold nearby parts of the brain. Fyodor Dostoyevsky was a famous epileptic who illustrates Bear's syndrome. Dostoyevsky certainly was preoccupied with religious and philosophical issues; what the neurologist would call hypergraphia, other folks call great literature.

While the personality and behavior changes may be subtle in nature, the mood changes may be more striking and more serious. Overall the patients tend to be hyperemotional and intense. Hyperactivity and catastrophic rages have been described in children and adolescents with temporal lobe epilepsy. Episodic outbursts of anger or rage, which contrast with an otherwise goodnatured and affectionate disposition, may occur. Parents may comment on the "Jekyll and Hyde" nature of the youngter's behavior. The anger is often mixed with a depressive mood, and such dysphoric episodes and even prolonged depressions may be the most disturbing symptoms. Treatment with carbamazepine can be helpful and the addition of a modest amount of tricyclic antidepressant or lithium may be very effective.

Other psychiatric syndromes occur in patients with epilepsy, especially temporal lobe epilepsy (Ferguson, 1984). Epileptic patients have presented with a schizophrenia-like syndrome and a bipolar-like syndrome. It is important for the adolescent therapist to realize that these syndromes are part of the epilepsy and not a separate illness. It is hard enough for the teenager and his family to cope with the burden of a chronic illness such as epilepsy. It would be an unnecessary hardship to lay on them the conclusion that the youngster has two serious illness, that is, epilepsy and also schizophrenia. Being clear about the diagnosis may also affect the treatment. If your epileptic patient has paranoid, delusional, or hallucinatory symptoms, you may want to consider using carbamazapine (the anticonvulsant most commonly used for temporal lobe epilepsy) in addition to a trial of an antidepressant medication, lithium, or sometimes a small amount of antipsychotic medication. Psychopathology tends to be pleomorphic, and the treatment is the same.

Julie had experienced generalized tonic-clonic seizures and complex partial seizures since early childhood. Although she was taking anticonvulsant medication, she continued to have a seizure two or three times a year. Julie came for psychiatric evaluation because of depression, poor peer relationships, and academic underachievement. Julie became actively involved in an outpatient adolescent psychotherapy group and she benefitted from it. Her psychiatrist also saw her individually every other week and had family meetings about once a month.

After about a year of therapy Julie was functioning better in school and was more assertive with peers. One day during an individual therapy meeting she greatly surprised her psychiatrist by explaining in a matter-of-fact manner that the captain of the basketball team was in love with her, but that he was having a hard time expressing his true feelings to her. Julie said that she could use her thoughts to control the boy. For instance, if she were in the cafeteria line in back of him, she could mentally induce him to take a brownie instead of apple pie. She also felt that she had a special relationship with the boy's mother, who could communicate with the patient because she once been a guidance counselor.

At the next family meeting the psychiatrist asked Julie if she wanted to tell her parents about her feelings about her friend, the basketball player. She readily did so. Her parents asked a few questions and elicited, in a rather sensitive manner, a complicated delusional system. This schizophrenia-like mental disorder had apparently started during the course of psychiatric treatment, since the patient described it as a new development and it was news to both the therapist and to the parents. The psychiatrist prescribed perphenazine and the delusional thoughts abated.

Julie continued to improve in her functioning in school and also in her peer relations. As she felt more confidence in herself, Julie decided to exercise her sense of independence by discontinuing both her anticonvulsant and also her perphenazine. She did that without telling anybody, including her therapist. After a few weeks it became obvious that something was wrong, because she was having seizures and she also was ruminating again that the basketball player had a romantic interest in her. After the situation was investigated and the medications were reinstated, both the seizures and the delusions were controlled.

Temporal Lobe Syndrome, but No Seizures

It seems clear that adolescents who have temporal lobe epilepsy sometimes have personality traits and psychiatric symptoms which are caused by the seizure focus and its electrical activity. But is it possible for a patient to have temporal lobe personality traits without actually having epilepsy? In other words, is it possible to have temporal lobe dysfunction which is severe enough to have a chronic neurochemical effect on that part of the brain, but which is not severe enough to cause actual seizures? That idea is worth keeping in mind, especially when the adolescent's condition has been refractory to traditional treatments.

Kenny, age 14, was referred for inpatient psychiatric evaluation because of extraordinarily severe temper tantrums. Kenny would become frustrated over some minor disappointment, go into a violent rage that might last an hour, and be quite remorseful when it was over. He had cooperated in outpatient exploratory psychotherapy, which had no beneficial effect on the severe tantrums.

This youngster had a family history of documented temporal lobe epilepsy, in a paternal uncle. There was also a history of neonatal hypoxia. Since Kenny had been impulsive and distractible as a child, the pediatrician thought that he had attention-deficit hyperactivity disorder. He prescribed methylphenidate, which had been helpful. All in all, there were reasons to think about a neurological basis for Kenny's outrageous behavior.

Kenny's parents pointed out that it was not simply that he would become extremely angry. Kenny experienced many emotions and expressed many feelings in an extreme manner. When he was feeling good, he became frenzied with excitement. When he was disappointed, he became very sad very quickly. In clinical lingo, Kenny was overly intense and was not able to modulate affect along a number of parameters.

The neurological evaluation and the routine EEG were normal. In addition, however, it was arranged for Kenny to have a BEAM study, which stands for brain electrical activity mapping. The BEAM is a computerized EEG which is able to pick up very subtle changes and also compare the patient's pattern to a normal population. Kenny's BEAM study was markedly abnormal, in that it showed disorganized and impaired conduction in both temporal regions, as well as in other parts of the brain.

Although it is hard to be conclusive in these matters, the clinical history and the BEAM data seemed consistent with the diagnosis of organic personality disorder. Kenny was treated with carbamazapine with some success. Although the medication did not make him a whole new person, it did mean that the rages were less often and less severe. It also helped Kenny become more amenable to psychotherapy.

Pseudoseizures

Pseudoseizures or psychogenic seizures can come about in several ways. The easiest and probably the most common way is for a youngster who actually has epilepsy to discover that it is possible to have additional seizures through his own unconscious initiative and to achieve both primary gain and secondary gain. Sometimes patients are familiar with the epilepsy of a family member or a friend, so they borrow the symptom from the other individual. Finally, it may be that a frightened or anxious youngster starts by simply having a fainting spell. Thereupon, the concerned parents and concerned doctors investigate the fainting spell and may go so far as to conduct EEG's and other studies of the youngster's brain. That may plant the idea for future spells, which look more like seizures.

It sometimes is possible to distinguish between pseudoseizures and real seizures on clinical grounds (Riley, 1982; Rodin, 1984; Roy, 1989; Stevenson and King, 1988; Theodore, 1989). Goodyer (1985) described five adolescents with pseudoepileptic seizures. In comparing epilepsy with pseudoseizures, epilepsy is more likely to have stereotyped aura; to have cyanotic skin changes; to include self-injury, such as severe tongue biting; to cause incontinence; to be nocturnal; and to be followed by postictal confusion. In observing an episode, the body movements in epilepsy are stereotyped, with tonic and clonic phases. The movements in pseudoseizures are variable, random, asynchronous, and frequently involve truncal and pelvic thrusting.

If in doubt, the best solution may be to refer the youngster to a specialized inpatient epilepsy center which is able to diagnose the condition with certitude. The way it is done is to monitor the patient continually for several days. That is, the patient's EEG is recorded and the patient is videotaped continually. When an episode does occur, it is possible to correlate exactly the patient's behavior with any EEG changes.

TOURETTE'S DISORDER

Tourette's disorder has the distinction of being almost the only psychiatric condition in *DSM-III-R* to retain its eponym. That seems a suitable recognition for the man who was able to separate out this group of tiqueurs from all the other patients who visited the clinic at Salpétrière with involuntary movements. The role of Georges Gilles de la Tourette and the history of his syndrome was described by Lucas (1979).

The tic disorders are usually thought of as constituting a continuum from benign to serious conditions. If a child or adolescent has had a motor or vocal tic for less than two weeks, it does not merit a diagnosis in *DSM-III-R*. If the tics have continued nearly every day for at least two weeks, but less than a year, the diagnosis is transient tic disorder. If the youngster has experienced either vocal or motor tics, but not both, for more than a year, the diagnosis is chronic vocal tic disorder or chronic motor tic disorder. If the youngster has had both vocal and motor tics for more than a year, the diagnosis is Tourette's disorder.

This illness usually starts during childhood. Each patient may exhibit a variety of motor tics (such as eye blinking, grimacing, clenching the fists, shrugging shoulders, etc.) and vocal tics (coughing, making a barking sound, clearing throat, etc.). These tics come and go and one form of tic is replaced by another. The most striking symptoms, which occur infrequently and are not necessary for the diagnosis of Tourette's disorder, are echolalia (repeating the word or phrase of another person) and coprolalia (using obscene words and phrases) and copropraxia (using obscene gestures). By the time the youngster reaches adolescence he and his parents can usually list a number of tics which he has experienced.

The adolescent psychiatrist will occasionally see a patient who has had multiple tics for years and was never diagnosed as having Tourette's disorder. This happens less often than previously, because the Tourette Syndrome Association has greatly increased the awareness of this illness among the general public and among medical professionals. Several years ago Tourette's disorder was highlighted on a popular television program—a fictional medical examiner portrayed by Jack Klugman investigated the case of a person with this illness. Many people diagnosed themselves after seeing that show.

This is a neurological condition, so why is it in psychiatric textbooks at all? There have been at least three ways to account for the relationship between the neurological and the psychiatric aspects of Tourette's disorder. The first, exemplified by Margaret Mahler (1943), conceptualized Tourette's disorder as a psychosomatic condition. She considered the tic syndrome to be an organ neurosis of the neuromuscular apparatus. The second

Donald Cohen (1982, 1984) is a Renaissance psychiatrist. His medical education was at Yale, his psychiatric training was at Harvard, and he returned to New Haven to become a professor at his alma mater. He is Professor of Psychiatry, Pediatrics, and Neurology at Yale and the director of the Child Study Center. Dr. Cohen is a psychoanalyst with expertise in neurochemistry. His studies of autism and of Tourette's disorder have helped psychotherapists understand the relationship between the mind and the brain.

point of view is illustrated by Arthur Shapiro and Elaine Shapiro (1972). The Shapiros and their associates made an important contribution by showing that this disabling condition is treatable, by prescribing haloperidol. They held that Tourette's disorder is an organic condition which, in itself, did not have a psychological etiology or psychological manifestations. They felt that Tourette's disorder was not characterized by common psychopathological factors and that psychological symptoms that did sometimes occur were simply the patient's response to the illness. A third way to look at this condition has been developed by Donald Cohen (1982, 1984) and his colleagues at Yale. They feel that several neurochemical systems may dysfunction in Tourette's disorder and that the particular symptoms that occur in an individual patient may depend on the relative deficiencies or the balance between the dopaminergic system, the noradrenergic system, and the serotonergic system. They would say that the tics and the behavioral symptoms (restlessness, impulsivity) and mental symptoms (obsessions, compulsions, impaired concentration) are all caused by some basic organic pathology.

How can an adolescent therapist be helpful to a teenager with Tourette's disorder? You can certainly help by making the diagnosis and explaining the condition to the patient and to the parents. You can imagine how weird an adolescent must feel to find that his body insists on being out of control, sometimes in the most embarrassing manner. In one case, a youngster at a

Catholic boarding school found himself spouting off with, "Holy shit, Harry," in a loud, clear voice at morning prayers. An accurate diagnosis and scientific explanation would help the patient feel that he is neither crazy nor deviant.

The next step would be to discuss with the patient and the parents the pros and cons of medication to suppress the tics and also, perhaps, the obsessiveness, which can also be disabling. The available medications include haloperidol, pimozide, and clonidine. The indications, dosages, and side effects of these medications are readily available and have been summarized by Williams (1987). In general medication should not be used if the symptoms are mild and do not greatly interfere with school or with the youngster's peer relations. The physician certainly should discuss the possible side effects of chronic use, especially the possibility with haloperidol and pimozide of developing a whole new movement disorder, tardive dyskinesia. If you do agree to a trial of medication, start with a small dose and see what happens. You and the patient may be rewarded with a very satisfying result with only a small amount of medication.

The therapist can also be helpful by explaining this unusual condition to school personnel, since some of these patients have special educational needs. It may be that the teacher or the guidance counselor is baffled by the student because they don't know what Tourette's disorder is. Many children and adolescents with Tourette's disorder have learning disabilities, which may not fit into the typical categories used at the local schools. Sometimes the therapist may need to meet with school personnel to facilitate the youngster's placement in an appropriate program, which usually means a resource room for students with learning disabilities. If the patient has unusually severe behavioral or psychological symptoms associated with the Tourette's disorder, he may require placement in a school program for emotionally disturbed students.

The therapist can be supportive by referring the family to the Tourette Syndrome Association, 42-40 Bell Boulevard, Bayside, New York, 11361. Local chapters are in many cities and are quite helpful to families who are learning about this illness. The best part of the TSA newsletter is called "Tourette Victories," which are vignettes of members who have accomplished some goal, such as "graduating school, getting married, earning a scouting award, being elected Congressman."

Psychotherapy does not cure Tourette's disorder, but it may help the adolescent cope with his disability. If the youngster feels good about himself and is pursuing the tasks of adolescence, there is no point to proposing psychotherapy. But if the patient is chronically depressed and avoids social situations and can't make plans for the future, he would benefit from either individual counseling or a heterogeneous coed adolescent therapy group.

LOOKING FOR ZEBRAS

Now that Tourette's disorder is better known, it is recognized more and more often and many child and adolescent therapists treat several patients with that condition. There are other illnesses which occur much less frequently and it is not really possible to know the details of every obscure medical syndrome. However, it is possible to keep an open mind and to wonder actively whether there is something going on which is more than immediately meets the eye. It is a little like being a detective and looking for clues, even though no crime has been reported.

Oftentimes youngsters with physical illness first come to the attention of a psychotherapist, whom they reached through a school counselor or simply through the yellow pages. A girl was referred for "depression," manifested by tiredness and drooping eyes, and later was found to have myasthenia gravis. Another patient was underachieving and chronically depressed, and it turned out he had hypothyroidism. An older adolescent was hospitalized on a psychiatric unit because of a schizophrenic-like illness. The routine screening test for syphilis turned out to be positive, after the tests on a few thousand other patients had been negative. On rare occasions tumors and other mass lesions in the brain are found in psychiatrically hospitalized adolescents.

Take a Pediatrician to Lunch

It is not realistic to suggest that every adolescent who comes for counseling should have a physical examination. In fact, a pediatrician is likely to take a superficial history and run through a perfunctory physical examination when he is asked to see a patient for no particular reason. It makes more sense for the psychotherapist to refer the youngster to a pediatrician or some other specialist when a specific question needs to be addressed. It also makes sense to have an ongoing dialogue with pediatricians, so that patients do not slip between the cracks.

Howie, a 14-year-old boy, was referred for psychiatric evaluation by his pediatrician because of fainting spells. These incidents occurred at times of emotional excitement and were thought to be psychogenic. For instance, this shy youngster attended a school function and asked a girl to dance for the first time in his life. When the dance was over he "fainted" and was briefly unconscious. At the conclusion of the evaluation the psychiatrist said that there seemed to be a psychological basis for these spells and recommended outpatient therapy, but suggested that he and the pediatrician keep in touch to make sure that no physical problem was being overlooked.

The boy did not show up for his next appointment. The psychiatrist called the patient's mother, who apologized for not calling to cancel the appointment, but on the preceding day the youngster had been hospitalized for open-heart surgery. It turned out that the boy had a myoma in the wall of the heart. It was removed and that cured the fainting spells. The pediatrician had continued to follow the patient and heard a murmur that had not previously been present.

Kleine-Levin Syndrome

An interesting condition that ranks high in the annals of psychiatric trivia is the Kleine-Levin syndrome. This is a rare medical condition that presents with dramatic psychiatric symptoms. In the case described by Gillberg (1987), various specialists had labeled the patient as having drug addiction, schizophrenia, hysteria, and depression before the correct diagnosis was made. Orlosky (1982) reviewed the literature and tabulated the psychiatric symptoms which occurred in the thirty-three cases which he studied.

The Kleine-Levin syndrome usually occurs in male adolescents. It is characterized by recurrent episodes of sleepiness, compulsive eating, and psychiatric disturbances. The sleep disturbance is usually described as periods of profound sleepiness which may continue for several days, interrupted only by eating and trips to the bathroom. Unusual eating behavior was described. Although these patients do not crave food or seek it, they eat food compulsively when it is presented to them.

Patients with this illness manifested a variety of psychiatric symptoms, which Orlosky divided into three areas. The most common disturbances of behavior were sexual disinhibition, apathy, withdrawal, and agitation. He found disturbances of mood, such as irritability, depression, and euphoria. Most interesting were the disturbances of thought, which included confusion, amnesia, delusions, and hallucinations.

Here is something to think about. It was suggested by Young (1975) that the Kleine-Levin syndrome and anorexia nervosa are mirror images. The Kleine-Levin syndrome occurs in male adolescents and is characterized by decreased physical activity, increased eating, and hypersexuality. Anorexia nervosa occurs in female adolescents and is characterized by increased physical activity, decreased eating, and hyposexuality. Perhaps both illnesses are caused by hypothalamic dysfunction, but through opposing neuroendocrine systems.

CITED AND RECOMMENDED READINGS

Alexander, F. 1950. *Psychosomatic Medicine: Its Principles and Applications.* New York: W. W. Norton.

Bear, D., et al. 1982. Interictal behavior in hospitalized temporal lobe epileptics: relationship to idiopathic psychiatric syndromes. *Journal of Neurology, Neurosurgery, and Psychiatry.* 45: 481–488.

Bear, D., et al. 1984. Behavioral alterations in patients with temporal lobe epilepsy. In: *Psychiatric Aspects of Epilepsy*, edited by D. Blumer. Washington, D.C.: American Psychiatric Press.

Bear, D. M., and P. Fredio. 1977. Quantitative analysis of interictal behavior in temporal lobe epilepsy. *Archives of Neurology.* 34: 454–467.

Blumer, D., and D. F. Benson, editors. 1982. *Psychiatric Aspects of Neurologic Disease*. New York: Grune & Stratton.

Blumer, D., editor. 1984. *Psychiatric Aspects of Epilepsy*. Washington, D.C.: American Psychiatric Press.

Bruch, H. 1973. *Eating Disorders: Obesity, Anorexia and the Person Within*. New York: Basic Books.

Cohen, D., et al. 1982. Interaction of biological and psychological factors in the natural history of Tourette syndrome. In: *Advances in Neurology*, edited by A. Friedhoff and T. Chase. New York: Raven Press.

Cohen, D., et al. 1984. Tourette's syndrome. In: *Neuropsychiatric Movement Disorders*, edited by D. Jeste and R. Wyatt. Washington, D.C.: American Psychiatric Press.

Ferguson, S. M., and M. Rayport. 1984. In: *Psychiatric Aspects of Epilepsy*, edited by D. Blumer. Washington, D.C.: American Psychiatric Press.

Gillberg, C. 1987. Kleine-Levin syndrome: unrecognized diagnosis in adolescent psychiatry. *Journal of the American Academy of Child and Adolescent Psychiatry*. 26: 793–794.

Gold, P. W., et al. 1986. Abnormal hypothalamic-pituitary-adrenal function in anorexia nervosa. Pathophysiologic mechanisms in underweight and weight-corrected patients. *New England Journal of Medicine*. 314: 335–342.

Goodyer, I. M. 1985. Epileptic and pseudoepileptic seizures in childhood and adolescence. *Journal of the American Academy of Child Psychiatry*. 24: 3–9.

Halmi, K. A. 1988. Eating disorders. In: *American Psychiatric Press Textbook of Psychiatry*, edited by J. A. Talbott, et al. Washington, D.C.: American Psychiatric Press.

Halmi, K. A., editor. 1989. Eating disorders. In: *Treatments of Psychiatric Disorders*, by a Task Force of the American Psychiatric Association. Washington, D.C.: American Psychiatric Association.

Holland, A. J., et al. 1984. Anorexia nervosa: a study of 34 twin pairs and one set of triplets. *British Journal of Psychiatry*. 145: 414–419.

Kavanaugh, J. G., and A. Mattsson. 1979. Psychophysiologic disorders. In: *Basic Handbook of Child Psychiatry, Volume 2*, edited by J. D. Noshpitz. New York: Basic Books.

Lucas, A. R. 1979. Tic: Gilles de la Tourette's syndrome. In: *Basic Handbook of Child Psychiatry, Volume 2*, edited by J. D. Noshpitz. New York: Basic Books.

Mahler, M. S., and L. Rangell. 1943. A psychosomatic study of maladie des tics (Gilles de la Tourette's disease). *Psychiatric Quarterly*. 17: 579–603.

Miller, D., B. S. Carlton. 1985. The etiology and treatment of anorexia nervosa. *Adolescent Psychiatry*. 12: 219–232.

Minuchin, S. 1978. *Psychosomatic Families*. Cambridge, Mass.: Harvard University Press.

Orlosky, M. J. 1982. The Kleine-Levin syndrome: a review. *Psychosomatics*. 23: 609–621.

Riley, T., and A. Roy, editors. 1982. *Pseudoseizures*. Baltimore: Williams & Wilkins.

Rodin, E. 1984. Epileptic and pseudoepileptic seizures: differential diagnostic considerations. In: *Psychiatric Aspects of Epilepsy*, edited by D. Blumer. Washington, D.C.: American Psychiatric Press.

Roy, A. 1989. Pseudoseizures: a psychiatric perspective. *Journal of Neuropsychiatry*. 1: 69–71.

Shapiro, A. K., et al. 1972. The psychopathology of Gilles de la Tourette's syndrome. *American Journal of Psychiatry*. 129: 427–434.

Stevenson, J. M., and J. H. King. 1987. Neuropsychiatric aspects of epilepsy and epileptic seizures. In: *American Psychiatric Press Textbook of Neuropsychiatry*, edited by R. E. Hales and S. C. Yudofsky. Washington, D.C.: American Psychiatric Press.

Theodore, W. H. 1989. Pseudoseizures: differential diagnosis. *Journal of Neuropsychiatry*. 1: 67–69.

Thompson, T. L. 1988. Psychosomatic disorders. In: *American Psychiatric Press Textbook of Psychiatry*, edited by J. A. Talbott. Washington, D.C.: American Psychiatric Press.

Williams, D., et al. 1978. Neurogenic and hysterical seizures in children and adolescents. *American Journal of Psychiatry*. 135: 82–86.

Williams, D., and D. Mostofsky. 1982. Psychogenic seizures in childhood and adolescence. In: *Pseudoseizures*, edited by T. Riley and A. Roy. Baltimore: Williams & Wilkins.

Williams, D. T., et al. 1987. Neuropsychiatric disorders of childhood and adolescence. In: *American Psychiatric Press Textbook of Neuropsychiatry*, edited by R. E. Hales. Washington, D.C.: American Psychiatric Press.

Wilson, C. P., and I. L. Mintz, editors. 1989. *Psychosomatic Symptoms: Psychodynamic Treatment of the Underlying Personality Disorder*. Northvale, N.J.: Jacob Aronson.

Young, J. K. 1975. A possible neuroendocrine basis of two clinical syndromes: anorexia nervosa and the Kleine-Levin syndrome. *Physiol. Psychol.* 3: 322–330.

Part

Three

introduction

This section of the book is intended as an orientation to the inpatient psychotherapy of the adolescent. It focuses on general principles and basic concepts as does the remainder of the book and cannot serve as a comprehensive guide to inpatient care.

The goal of this section is to convey a sense of the basic role of hospital care. It is obvious to all of us that inpatient care cannot simply be considered a more intense version of outpatient therapy. There are profound differences in the two arenas of therapy due to the fact that hospitalization introduces a reality control over the patient's life which fundamentally alters the relationship between patient and therapist. In addition, much of the therapist's impact and influence is delegated to the remainder of the hospital staff in inpatient therapy. Understanding staff dynamics and hospital organization and policy within a therapeutic framework becomes an essential additional skill the therapist needs to acquire.

Part Three also addresses some of the specific problems associated with direct therapy of the adolescent and the family in a hospital setting.

As in the remainder of this book, the goal of Part Three is to present one possible orientation to a therapeutic approach. This orientation is not presumed to be the only possible view or even the best way to think of inpatient therapy. It is, at best, merely one coherent way to conceptualize the goals and techniques of inpatient care.

CHAPTER 23

the design of inpatient treatment centers

INTRODUCTION

The decision to remove an adolescent from his family or his surrogate family placement in order to provide residential treatment may be reached for a variety of reasons. Because of this wide range of indications, it is impossible to design any single treatment center in such a way that it can meet the needs of all youngsters who require inpatient treatment. In addition, facility design is often dictated to some extent by practical considerations including sources of funding, available physical plants, availability of potential staff members, community preferences, local population needs, and other external factors. It is obviously impractical and perhaps impossible to develop a small, long-term public facility for a community which has large numbers of troubled adolescents and no other treatment facility. The community and political pressures would probably require the development of a short-term evaluation center. Later the community might be willing to consider the development of long-term treatment facilities for some youngsters.

People who are planning inpatient programs for adolescents often have other practical questions. They want to know how you keep the kids from tearing the building down, maiming the staff, or otherwise creating complete chaos. They are concei ̣.ed, with good reason, about the techniques of behavioral control and safety. We will consider these questions later from a practical standpoint. The final answers to the overall success of an inpatient treatment program for adolescents are not simplistic or mechanical. Objective observations of existing programs suggest that many systems of clinical design can result in the successful treatment of emotionally disturbed adolescents. It is true that many

543

of these effective programs share common features (Noshpitz, 1976) but it is also evident that there is considerable diversity between programs. In some cases the differences between successful programs suggest that the crucial aspect of program design is the process by which it is achieved rather than the form of the final product.

BASIC PHILOSOPHY

When one reviews the successful programs mentioned above, one usually encounters strongly held theoretical opinions which the staff put forward to explain their effectiveness. When patients treated in these programs are interviewed, they often echo these ideas and may even appear to speak in the jargon language which is commonly used in the day-to-day activities of the treatment unit. Resistant patients often appear to be rejecting these common beliefs and phrasings while those patients who appear to be improving embrace them and offer them as an explanation for their better performance. After a few days spent talking with the staff and patients at one of these centers, an outside observer often feels an enthusiastic sense of conversion and acceptance of the guiding principles of the treatment program.

The therapeutic approach used at this center seems to be the answer!

Unfortunately, there are many catches to this simple solution to design problems. Very often if one takes the successful design and attempts to copy it in another setting, it is surprisingly unsuccessful. It is also rather confusing to study other successful programs and find that they embrace—with equal conviction—theories and ideas which differ markedly from those of the first treatment unit surveyed.

This puzzling and potentially discouraging observation is not so surprising if one remembers the need for diversity in inpatient treatment programs mentioned earlier. Different programs meet different needs, deal with different populations, and contain a complexity which defies the development of absolutes regarding the residential treatment of adolescents.

Like it or not, each adolescent residential treatment program must be custom designed to local conditions. Of course, the job of program planning is greatly assisted by familiarity with good programs. One can often draw valuable building blocks from the experiences of others. However, the final "whole" is somehow quite individual and always greater than the sum of its constituent parts.

The planning of any program begins with a careful survey of community needs, funding possibilities, and other practical issues which have been mentioned earlier. Once these have been determined, the next important step in clinical programming is the construction of a philosophical or conceptual skeleton—a clear, sharply outlined description of the purposes and goals of the treatment center. This basic formulation of program goals and approaches must be strong enough to bear the weight of emotional dissension which will inevitably arise to test it. This is a crucial point to remember!

Without a clear philosophy which is backed by a strong commitment, any adolescent program will show a frightening and eventually destructive instability. No program design can prevent verbal criticisms, acting out behavior, treatment failures, and periods of chaos and relative unproductivity. These distressing events are simply part of the reality of treating adolescents. If there is no strong philosophical direction in the program, one often attempts to eliminate the distressing occurrences by making programmatic changes. Since the problems will continue to reappear, there may be multiple confusing and disruptive false starts which can eventually lead to the collapse of the treatment effort.

This is not to say that blind faith in a theoretical position is the ideal basis for an adolescent treatment program. Long-term evaluation of treatment results and gradual program modifications when they seem clearly indicated should be welcomed in any program. However, there should be a sufficient degree of conviction regarding the philosophic directions of the program, hopefully based on the relevant literature, to provide an air of confidence and an attitude of conservativeness regarding basic changes in the program. Due to the revolutionary tendencies of disturbed adolescents as well as their propensity to externalize problems and seek personal solutions in social change, there is a great deal to be said for moving only grudgingly toward new attitudes and techniques in adolescent treatment programs.

In speaking of philosophic guidelines I am not referring to a highly theoretical or metapsychological construct of great subtlety and complexity. On the contrary, I am suggesting that one needs to think through in a very practical way, and in language that all staff—regardless of professional background—can understand, several basic questions regarding the nature of the proposed treatment center.

First of all one needs to designate the place that the treatment center plans to occupy in the world of the adolescent. This usually involves some effort to limit the scope of what the treatment program plans to achieve. Recognizing the program's limitations requires some thinking about a number of facets of the adolescent experience. This point can be illustrated by beginning with one simple question.

What is the treatment center's relationship to the adolescent's family?

Many philosophies of residential treatment imply that the treatment center's function is to serve as a substitute family. According to this view the emotionally disturbed youngster is considered to be suffering from inept or distorted parenting. His disability may then be corrected by providing substitute parent figures so that the adolescent can internalize more appropriate models. Subscribing to this viewpoint has obvious implications for program design. A plan must be devised which will wean the youngster from his pathological but intense tie to the original parents. Often this means that the facility should treat youngsters at some geographical distance from their family origin. Often it means that the program will severely restrict parental visits for a fairly prolonged period at the onset of treatment. Further, programming should provide every opportunity for one-to-one interactions between staff and patients, preferably utilizing and emphasizing natural alliances which may spring up between patients and particular staff members. Allowances must also be made for at least the possibility of extended periods of extreme regression so that earlier pathological parenting experiences can be re-worked with the new parent figure. In programs of this kind the original parents are often viewed as almost "toxic" and the youngster is often protected from extended unsupervised contact with this source of his difficulty. Staff members are encouraged to appreciate fully their tremendous importance to the patient and may be expected to take extensive responsibility for providing care and nurture to the young patients in their program. If parents are treated, this work is usually carefully separated from the direct treatment of the disturbed youngster. Perhaps the program that most closely exemplifies this paradigm is the Orthogenic School as conceptualized and directed by Doctor Bruno Bettelheim (1974).

Other treatment programs do not view themselves as substitutes for the family. They accept the family unit as their patient and feel that the adolescent is likely to show genuine improvement only if this entire social system of the family can be altered in a constructive way. These residential centers view themselves as a support system and a change agent for the family rather than as a substitute for it. In such a "family prosthesis" program, the design would be constructed to maximize direct parental involvement with the adolescent patients and with the treatment staff. In congruence with this view of the family as patient, treatment would include frequent visits home, relatively unrestricted parental visitation rights, and active encouragement of staff-parent cooperation around everyday management issues in the treatment facility. Such a program would also place certain restrictions on the patient population which could be served. Only those parents who lived in relatively comfortable commuting distance could be expected to have the degree of availability required by the treatment approach.

These brief and somewhat oversimplified illustrations are offered primarily to illustrate the process by which program design is evolved. If policies and procedures are determined in this way by the goals and purposes of the basic treatment approach, form can evolve naturally from function. By proceeding in this way, a multitude of important practical decisions are almost automatically shaped by a clear general and overriding conceptual framework. Having clinically determined reasons for program policies is extremely valuable in gaining consensual support from staff, administration, parents, and interested community members. This adds a basic consistency to program design and also provides a sensible answer to that constant question, "Why do the rules have to be as they are?"

Many other questions regarding a treatment center's place in the world of the adolescent patient must be answered in order to complete the philosophic design. The program must consider not only its relationship to the family but also its relationship to the community. For example, some treatment centers regard themselves as havens from a basically destructive and pathological larger society. These centers function almost as psychological convents or monasteries where the adolescent may be purified and perfected in preparation for eventual return to an imperfect world that he will then be strong enough to withstand. Centers of this kind often plan their activities to emphasize the difference between the protected treatment society and the larger world outside. Strong emphasis is placed on internal communal activities and there are carefully constructed buffers between the program and the outside world. The treated adolescent may initially be permitted social experiences outside of the confines of the treatment center only in company with other graduates of the program. For example, alcoholic adolescents may be transitioned outside of the residential alcoholism program by frequent and extensive contacts with Alcoholics Anonymous groups. Only when the youngsters seem to have formed close and comfortable attachments within these groups are they actually discharged home. Many drug rehabilitation programs are designed according to this principle. Some of these require an entering youngster to cut his hair as a symbolic renunciation of his previous mode of existence. The youngster may not be permitted to listen to rock music since that art form is associated with the larger youth culture's easy acceptance of drug usage. The important point is that the program design in these centers derives from a feeling that the youngster's disability results from negative and corrupting social influences which can be corrected through immersion in a more sensitive, healthy, and caring community in which all participants are embued with a deviant but nobler and superior value system.

Obviously another center which viewed its function to be a transmission of the best of community values and the reintegration of the youngster into the wider community as quickly as possible would be designed in a completely different way. For example a program with a strong community investment might use numerous community volunteers, the neighborhood public school, and a work program which attempted to build strong ties between the treatment unit personnel and local employers.

Basic program planning is also affected by other philosophical issues. Convictions regarding the nature of psychic structure and the process of emotional healing are central to program decisions. Program directors who subscribe to a view that emotional growth occurs as a result of insight and intrapsychic reorganization will derive a program design which is quite different from that which will be designed by a director who views behavior primarily as a response to external pressures and conditions. The dynamically oriented program will place greater emphasis on individualized treatment plans which are designed to maximize emotional expression and psychic exploration. Deviant behavior will be acceptable as a behavioral expression of the internal conflict which can be utilized in the process of exploration and resolution of previously internalized conflicts. Staff will be encouraged to deal with patient behavior within a framework of acceptance and psychological curiosity and may be helped to develop intense individual relationships with the patients. Strong peer group interactions may be viewed to some extent as a resistance to the treatment process and secondarily as a source of information which can be utilized in individual formal psychotherapy.

On the other hand, a program that emphasizes the concept that maladaptive behavior results from poor learning in the past or improper management in the present will require a greater emphasis on the necessity for following group norms and expectations. Staff will view their job primarily in terms of the entire patient group. They will be expected to maintain the unit's tra-

The history of residential and psychiatric inpatient programs for adolescents started before there was any such thing as a therapeutic milieu, antipsychotic medication, or diagnosis related group. The men mentioned here came from quite different backgrounds, but had something in common. Their writings suggest that each of them had a very strong sense of mission. They blended their philosophic ideals with personal charisma to create programs which changed the lives of their adolescent clients. Their books are interesting and hold nuggets of wisdom that are still pertinent.

August Aichhorn (1935) was a colleague of Sigmund Freud. In fact, Freud wrote the foreword to *Wayward Youth*. Aichhorn was an educator who became interested in psychoanalysis. He applied psychoanalytic principles to his work with adolescents at the Institute for Delinquents at Hollabrunn, Austria. Bruno Bettelheim (1974) was a survivor of the concentration camps at Dachau and Buchenwald. After his release in 1939, he came to the United States and eventually became a professor of psychology at the University of Chicago. He also was the director of the Sonia Shankman Orthogenic School, where he originated the residential treatment of autistic children. Fritz Redl and David Wineman (1952) were senior staff at a residential program in Detroit called Pioneer House. They specialized in treating angry, aggressive youth and endeavored "to stir the average citizen out of his amazing apathy toward the inexcusable and unfortunate amount of avoidable human waste."

ditions and values and to assist new patients in accepting these and in conducting themselves accordingly. Although individual difficulties may be viewed sympathetically, they are not pursued extensively due to the fear that the patient may use his internal problems as an excuse for failing to live up to group expectations. In addition to direct staff structuring, various sophisticated behavior modification techniques may be utilized to shape behavior in adaptive directions.

In practice, of course, most inpatient treatment centers are somewhat eclectic. That is, many centers utilize both insight psychotherapy and behavior modification. However, the ways in which these modalities are utilized and the relative centrality they occupy in the treatment program are dictated by an underlying sense of what is really important in the treatment process. For example, very few people would see value in allowing adolescents to act out in a totally uncontrolled manner within a treatment program. Control is necessary, but control may be viewed as an end in itself or merely as a way to prevent dissipation of anxiety which is needed for fruitful insight psychotherapy. In centers where acting out is viewed as learned maladaptive behavior, acting out is often actively and strenuously opposed even to the extent of using adversive stimuli. In centers where acting out is viewed as a defensive operation, programming tends to be designed to discourage the behavior through persuasion and appeals to the therapeutic alliance. In short, in the first kind of center the patient is told that his acting out is his illness, while in the second he is asked to desist from acting out so that he can be helped toward cure. The style and techniques of limit setting will be strongly influenced accordingly.

Even these philosophical issues may be influenced by practical considerations. One must look at staffing patterns, both in terms of numbers and in terms of the types of professional persons who will be available to implement a philsophical program. For example, it would be pointless to attempt to design an extremely sophisticated psychoanalytic program without staff members who were adequately trained in the intricacies of that theoretical model. The availability of sufficient funds to permit a high staff-to-patient ratio might allow a greater degree of behavioral freedom than that which would be practical in a program which could be only marginally staffed. Of course, one has to make a decision at some point as to whether a program is possible under existing conditions. There is no real service to adolescents in providing a facility which is improperly staffed or inadequately funded to the point that acceptable care is impossible.

THE DEVELOPMENT OF THE THERAPEUTIC PHILOSOPHY

So far we have spoken of this basic program design as though it could spring full-grown from the fertile brain of the program director. In fact, at inception the philosophic skeleton is often rather sketchy and still quite flexible in its details. The design usually emerges in a clear and stabilized form only in response to questions and issues raised by patients and staff when the program actually begins. However, some basic design must be present even at the outset and the elaboration of the finer points cannot be delayed indefinitely. As mentioned earlier, an adolescent program will be seriously stressed and will not exist for long unless it is protected by a strongly held philosophy. As a rule this philosophy will be quickly embodied in one individual who is viewed consciously or unconsciously by the entire staff as the emotional leader of the program. It is important that this leader have a strong conviction that the basic plan is a good one and that it will help adolescents to grow. This conviction must be strong since the purpose of the unit will be tested and shaken to its very foundation by adolescent rebelliousness and by the adolescent's relentless search for integrity, consistency, and meaning.

We are aware that this assertion regarding the importance of a central leader in an adolescent program may offend some mental health practitioners who believe strongly in a process of decision making by staff consensus. However, practical reality requires this kind of centralized leadership. Democracy is a great ideal for political organizations, but consensus alone can never provide the conceptual foundation, the necessary inner stability, and the consistency over time needed in an effective adolescent treatment center. However, to emphasize the need for a strong leader with a clear sense of purpose and basic techniques is not to suggest a dogmatic rigidity which rejects other opinions and ideas. On the contrary, it is extremely important to be able to hear and understand the ideas and innovations presented by staff members. This process is extremely valuable to the success of the program, not only because open communication helps other staff members to feel important and included in the decision-making process, but also because many specific suggestions will be valuable in their own right. The point is that all ideas should be tested against the basic understanding of what the treatment center is trying to accomplish so that policies do not change erratically in response to every clinical emergency, period of staff unrest, or other temporary expediency. As a matter of fact, comfort with one's overview of the program permits a relaxed consideration of any and all staff ideas, no matter how extreme they may sound at initial hearing. Since the stability of the program is based on "the big picture," it is possible to relax and consider many alternatives without excessive anxiety.

ASSEMBLING THE TREATMENT STAFF

If the conceptual framework described above provides the skeleton for the living organism of the treatment center, the staff provides the flesh and blood necessary for functioning. A great deal has been written and even more has been said regarding staff selection and qualifications for inpatient adolescent work. Many guidelines have been advanced, but anyone who works in the field sees daily exceptions to every rule. Unfortunately, it seems that the only real test of effectiveness as a staff member is to function for a period of time in that role. Even successful experience in other treatment centers is no guarantee that a staff member will work well in a new treatment program. For this reason most centers formalize a probationary period of three to four months during which the new staff member and the treatment center regard their relationship as tentative, temporary, and exploratory.

Although there is absolutely no proof, we have the personal feeling that there are advantages to having a staff composed of individuals of varying ages. The enthusiasm and empathy which young staff members bring to an adolescent program often need to be balanced by the wisdom and perspective of older staff members. However, a staff composed only of very mature people may lack the energy required to keep up with the almost frenetically active adolescent patient group. Needless to say, age requirements pale in importance compared to issues of professional qualifications and experience.

There are also advantages in having staff members of varying socioeconomic backgrounds if their professional credentials and experiences are comparable. In fact, a staff of divergent origins along many axes of human experience provides the widest possible range of empathy and potential identification models for the adolescent patients. However, the staff members must be able to respect one another's competence or personal diversity can lead to destructive dissension and splitting.

In this regard, some balances are difficult to achieve. Ideally, a unit would have similar numbers of males and females, for example, yet there are few available male nurses. In some parts of the country, racial and ethnic balance is difficult to achieve. The program director can only do what is possible, always using adequate professional qualifications as the primary selection criterion. In any case, staff training and supervision are always crucial.

Some mention should be made of the recurrent problem in the nursing staff structure of inpatient treatment centers. Those centers which are situated in hospitals usually have a patient-care staff composed partially of nurses and partially of non-medically trained attendants or psychiatric assistants. These two groups of individuals with their strongly divergent educational backgrounds frequently have problems working together. The background of most nurses is medical and highly professional. For some of them psychological mindedness comes with some difficulty, particularly when it seems to conflict with sensible behavioral standards. On the other hand, many young persons who are attracted to psychiatric work without professional training have had some training in psychology or other behavioral sciences and very little experience or even sympathy with the medical model. Often they feel that they know more about psychiatric care and psychological functioning than the nurses who are their superiors. This is equally true when nursing assistants are untrained and purely "intuitive." On the other hand, the nurses frequently feel saddled with unprofessional and maverick staff members who have no grasp of the real meaning of the therapeutic relationship or of proper conduct within the hierarchy of the treatment center. Since both groups have extremely valuable contributions to make to overall treatment, it is worth a great deal of effort to maintain mutual respect and cooperation between the two groups. This task usually falls to the program director, or if he is fortunate, to an experienced and skillful nurse to whom he can delegate the responsibility. The task is one of preventing either group from prematurely closing ranks with a polarized sense that they are correct and the other group is wrong. The value and contribution of both groups must be emphasized along with the crucial need to find a compromise position which everyone can accept. This is of obvious importance in an adolescent treatment program in view of the adolescent's tendency to split staff members as a defense. The program director must be alert to factions within the treatment staff and quick to utilize everyone's shared experience to demonstrate the need for unity and compromise. Paradoxically, this unity can often be achieved only after permitting a period of open disagreement and verbal dissension. As a rule, it is not the verbalized and recognized areas of staff disagreement that create the most serious problems in a treatment program. Covert and secret staff conflicts have the greatest potential for creating chaos and antitherapeutic disruption.

We shall return to this extremely important question of creating and maintaining open communication within the staff later in a more general context. At this point it is important to take a temporary detour to discuss staff training. The initial orientation of the staff and the continuing active educational programs provide the cornerstone for effective treatment throughout the life of any adolescent inpatient program.

STAFF TRAINING

Staff who are hired to work in an adolescent inpatient treatment center need many things. Even those who have received some formal education in the area of adolescent psychiatry are usually poorly prepared to utilize these basic skills effectively in any specific treatment setting before they have been trained in a program designed specifically for that treatment institution.

First of all the staff members need a great deal of information. This can often be best transmitted in a fairly didactic manner. However, since there is frequently a "combat patrol" mentality among workers in inpatient units, this didactic information must be given by individuals who are respected by the staff. As a rule this respect is given only to people who have worked successfully with inpatients. Specific examples are important, best drawn from recent experiences with patients known to the staff. If the staff regard a lecture as too theoretical or the lecturer as primarily "academic," they often discount the useful information which is being transmitted. Lecturers need to be brief and to the point, partly because many adolescent staff members are extremely practical and action oriented, but also because of the realistic need to staff the unit which precludes long hours of sitting in lecture halls. It is also wise to repeat basic lectures on a regular basis. New staff often cannot absorb certain information because they're not yet aware of its importance or relevance to their everyday work. In addition, because of the shift schedules, not all staff will be available at any given time a lecture is presented.

Examples of material which can be covered in lecture form include teaching the general philosophy of the treatment unit, its specific policies, basic characteristics of adolescent development, common psychopathological syndromes, psychopharmacology, and certain basic skills such as the fundamentals of interviewing techniques.

No effort will be made to suggest the specific content of these lectures. This will vary with the orientation of each program and with the teaching skills of those who are available to transmit the information. As implied earlier, the lectures should be kept as simple, practical, and as well illustrated as possible. The goal is to convey baseline information which can be used in everyday patient work. Many people even deprecate the value of didactic instruction of this kind in staff training. However, others, including the authors, feel that such instruction provides a basic security to staff, helps to prevent glaring gaps in knowledge, and saves a great deal of everyone's time by decreasing the need for individual repetition of basic information. The lecture series creates a shared body of knowledge which is available for reference in the future course of supervised experiential learning and general staff discussions regarding patient care.

In addition to information, staff members require assistance in gaining certain skills. For example, the format of instruction regarding interviewing techniques needs to be augmented with some opportunity to experiment through role playing or actual interview situations with adolescent patients. These training interviews may be observed or videotaped so that the staff member can receive immediate feedback. In reacting to these interviews it is important to reinforce strongly the positive aspects of the interview. One cannot ignore blatant errors in technique, but these can be approached with tact, understanding, and empathy for the anxiety of the neophyte staff member. It is important to avoid the impression that interviewing an adolescent is an arcane and intricate process best left only to the most highly trained professional. On balance, it is better for a staff member to conduct somewhat amateurish but sincere and comfortable interviews with the patients on the units than for the staff member to be afraid to talk to the patients for fear of "making things worse" through lack of skill. It is also important to remember that most actual staff interviews will occur in a very different situation than the one contrived for training purposes. Often in their day-to-day work on the unit the staff are much more comfortable in talking with the patients regarding routine unit activities and interactions than they will ever be in a formal interview setting. Nonetheless, teaching the staff to utilize nondirective approaches, comfortable silences, and emphatic responses to affective statements will increase the effectiveness of their interactions with the patients under any circumstances. Even more important than training in interview skills is staff training around behavioral control. One of the most disruptive and paralyzing aspects of a new staff member's feeling about working on an adolescent unit is the fear of violence. Many disturbed adolescents are extremely threatening and intimidating. The potential for actual violence of a dangerous degree is very real on any adolescent unit. Not only does the staff member face the prospect of a single youngster going out of control in a dangerous way, he must also contend with fantasies regarding group violence because of the propensity for contagion when an adolescent unit is angry and upset. The unit's policies in regard to dealing with situations of this kind must be concise and clear. The average staff member not only fears that he may be injured, but that his personal response to a violent situation may be nontherapeutic. Most staff members who choose to work in an adolescent setting accept the idea that a youngster's dangerous behavior is a product of his psychopathology and they desire to respond helpfully when this particular portion of the problem is evidenced. They can feel comfortable in this only if they are directed by a definite set of procedures which are utilized in situations of this kind. Because of the drama and intensity of the moment one cannot expect staff to be creative and flexible at a time when they must act quickly and decisively. It is important to be sure that all staff are totally familiar with the policies regarding control of dangerous behavior and that these policies are reviewed periodically.

Control of the violent patient is a subject which should not be taught only with words. The techniques of subduing and restraining a youngster who is out of control should be practiced in a role playing setting so that the proper approaches and procedures become second nature to the staff members. The staff person who is playing the role of the patient should be encouraged to be sufficiently resistant so that the new staff members get a realistic sense of the degree of physical effort which will be required to control a real patient.

This description of the importance of training in the control of physical violence is not meant to imply that restraining, subduing, and secluding adolescents are extremely common or desirable parts of their treatment. On the contrary, other techniques of behavioral control including the general atmosphere of the unit, skills in utilization of the relationship with the youngster, interviewing techniques for dealing with angry or frightened adolescents, and the appropriate utilization of patient group support are all more important on a day-to-day basis than are techniques for the physical management of the out-of-control adolescent. However, all of these approaches are utilized more comfortably and effectively if all staff members are quietly confident that, if necessary, they can handle any situation which occurs. The specific techiques for controlling violent behavior without injuring the patient or risking an injury to staff have been well described in the literature and will not be repeated here (Frost, 1972; Penningroth, 1975).

In addition to didactic training and the use of contrived experiential learning opportunities, all staff members deserve and need ongoing supervision of their daily work experience. As a rule, it is best if this can be provided by more experienced individuals of their own discipline who are now performing comparable tasks on the unit or who have done so in the past. When such individuals are not available, it is important to develop a supervisory atmosphere in which staff members feel comfortable in discussing their management of situations and their feelings regarding the patients and the treatment program. Supervision is useless if the staff member feels that it is directed primarily toward a critical review of every action. Anyone who has worked in the direct management of inpatient adolescents realizes that it is virtually impossible to avoid errors—even a multitude of errors. Decisions have to be made rapidly and often in settings which are at least noisy and distracting if not downright chaotic. Many factors, including the patient's basic illness, the current atmosphere of the entire unit, the particular group of staff who are on duty at the time, and an infinite variety of other variables all affect each decision. In the comfort and quiet of a supervision session, blessed with the clarity of the retrospectoscope, it is almost always easy to see how a situation could have been handled better than it was. Given these facts, a staff member would have every reason to resent a condescending or superior, carping, nitpicking attitude on the part of the supervisor.

On the other hand, there are many opportunities for spontaneous praise and even awe at the on-the-spot skill demonstrated by staff members in their daily dealings with adolescent patients. Needless to say, there is no reason for the supervisor to withhold this kind of feedback. There are many occupational hazards in working with inpatient adolescents, but a grandiose overevaluation of one's skills and abilities is not high on the list. As one staff member said, "One thing for sure, the kids will keep you humble."

It should be noted finally that the luxury of formal scheduled supervision is rarely available in an inpatient setting for adolescents. There is simply not time. Supervision tends to occur in conjunction with daily reports, casual conversations at the nursing station, and in other settings where the routine daily work is done. We have not been impressed with the value of having a staff member designated purely as a supervisor and teacher. The comradeship of a good treatment staff often works to exclude and isolate any individual who is not actively involved in patient care. In at least two treatment settings with which we are familiar, a unit "teacher" quickly became a professor who was scorned and actively avoided by the would-be students.

All of the training efforts described above are doomed to failure unless the training program teaches staff members how to recognize their own feelings and the influence of these feelings on their daily functioning. Staff members are likely to achieve this capacity for insight only if there is a strong sense of teamwork and group cohesion on the unit which supports an open, supportive, and realistic atmosphere. In our opinion, it is impossible for any individual to be so mature, well adjusted, and dedicated as to work effectively in an inpatient adolescent treatment program over an extended period of time without an active sense of involvement and mutual support from fellow staff members. The countertransference feelings stirred by disturbed adolescents are so intense that sooner or later one will make a serious error in dealing with a youngster. Tragic examples of competent staff members being actually seduced by patients or losing control of themselves and striking patients are all too common. Perhaps it is not surprising that these tragedies often happen to some of the most talented and skilled of the staff group. Perhaps outstanding individuals come to feel somewhat superior to their fellow workers and do not feel as much of a need for ventilation, discussion, and sharing of feelings as more average staff members might. Since they usually "know what to do," they feel little need to talk about it. In adolescent psychiatry, pride often comes before the fall.

Similar failures to communicate may occur with somewhat weak staff members who anticipate that they will be regularly criticized for their faltering efforts to help the patients. It is important for the program director to be especially alert to the vulnerability of individuals at both extremes of apparent competence.

One of the best safeguards for all staff members is the provision of regular opportunities for group discussion of patient management. It is difficult to attain the proper atmosphere for these group meetings. There is some tendency for them to degenerate into opportunities for the program director or other experienced staff members to hold forth on proper techniques, thereby demonstrating their skill and brilliance. On the other hand, if the meetings are equally worthless if they become "group therapy without a leader" during which staff members simply wallow in the range of feelings stirred in the crucible of an adolescent inpatient unit. Some structure is necessary but there must also be opportunities for sharing of intense and even professionally unacceptable feelings. Constructive learning can occur if one can establish a general attitude that professionalism is the goal at all times but that it cannot be achieved without many mistakes and false starts. One is also wise to encourage staff to teach one another and to share common and analogous experiences. Peer teaching both adds a richness of information and provides reinforcement of the team approach to the task of treatment. Rossman (1978) has described an excellent model of group staff training which he has evolved for his program.

LEADERSHIP AND PHILOSOPHIC EVOLUTION

Earlier we touched briefly on the management of tensions between nurses and psychiatric technicians. Of course, in adolescent inpatient treatment there are many other opportunities for cross-discipline conflict and other staff dissension. The leader's role in approaching these issues is very important. The proper management of conflicts of this kind is fairly obvious in theory. The program direction should be fair, impartial, and directed by the philosophy of the program. However, in practice, dealing with staff conflict can be highly problematic.

One of the main reasons for this is the peculiar emotional stress which falls upon the program director. We have just spent considerable time discussing the need for staff members to ventilate their feelings and discuss them openly. They also enjoy the opportunity for friendships outside of the work situation and for candid, even irresponsible cathartic outbursts regarding particular patients or other staff members. There are, in short, many opportunities for venting the intense emotions stirred by the work. On the other hand, the program director's position must be somewhat more lonely. He still must face the intense pressures and worries generated by conducting an adolescent inpatient treatment center. He is likely to be frequently harried and upset. In this situation there are many temptations to form confidential alliances with individual staff members who are seen by the director as unusually able, compatible, and sympathetic to his position. It is very easy with these trusted staff members to engage in cozy games of what Eric Berne would have called, "Ain't it awful!" These take the form of, "Ain't it awful how rigid and insensitive the teachers, nurses, or others are?" Obviously the program director must resist this temptation. One protection he can provide himself is to insist on discussing all staff differences in a group setting where favoritism is extremely unlikely to occur without detection. In these groups it is possible to stick to a policy of testing all disagreements against the basic philosophy of the unit. Of course, in dealing with all staff issues it is necessary to steer a careful course between arbitrary authoritarian control, which would defeat the sense of mutual commitment which we have said is essential to the success of the program, and the equally dangerous course of a rudderless permissiveness which would invite chaos. Let us consider a concrete example.

A new adolescent program is preparing to open and the staff members are considering the question of the appropriate involvement of parents. This will include many questions such as visiting hours, management of passes, staff response to parental phone calls, and staff reaction to patients' statements and queries regarding their relationships with their parents. Many other questions may be raised. Should the parents give their youngster an allowance or should the parents provide the treatment center with money which would be given to the youngster by staff? Should there be combined meetings of parents and staff in a "town meeting" format which would permit and encourage direct parental involvement in management decisions? Should the parents or the staff have the right to final decisions regarding the length of passes or even the question of whether a youngster should have a pass at all? Is it the parents' responsibility to approve visitors to the child or does the staff make the decision regarding who can come to the hospital?

These questions need to be debated openly in staff meetings. Discussions of this kind permit the staff to become aware of attitudes and prejudices which they may hold regarding parents in general or regarding parents of emotionally disturbed children. Talking out these decisions also allows the staff to think through their peculiar position as temporary substitute parents or as agents for a youngster's real parents. The program director will have the opportunity to evaluate his particular staff on their skills and interest in approaching parental involvement in particular ways. For example, some mental health workers are quite comfortable directing a town hall meeting which includes parents while others would feel hopelessly intimidated and overwhelmed by the task of attempting to deal with such a large group. This realistic appraisal of staff skills and limitations must be taken into account in choosing one or several of the potential techniques for involving parents actively in unit work.

However, many of the decisions would be determined by a previous basic philosophical position which the treatment program had decided earlier. That is, is this program designed to provide a substitute parenting experience for the adolescent or is it designed as a support to the present family structure? The implications of that decision have been described earlier.

What this example attempts to convey in a brief manner is the dynamic interaction between a relatively unchanging treatment concept and the rather fluid impact of staff and patients on everyday decision making. It is the interaction of these two elements which gradually weaves a distinct fabric of clinical planning individualized to the particular needs of a given center and the capabilities of its staff.

OTHER IMPORTANT ISSUES

To this point we have not talked in depth about the developmental needs of the adolescent and the influence that these have on clinical programming. It is obvious that these are overriding considerations since the adolescent must be provided with developmentally appropriate educational and social experiences, including such a simple and mundane thing as sufficient physical exercise. Adolescent programs cannot be totally serious, analytic, and intense 24 hours a day. Adolescents need fun, opportunities for social interaction, and the chance to perform activities which they can feel proud of. A well-designed adjunctive therapy program which not only permits outlets for the appropriate interest and energies of the adolescent, but also broadens skills of sublimation is crucial to the success of any inpatient treatment program. Educational programs which can provide a range of assistance from remedial education, challenging academics, and prevocational training for youngsters with very weak academic skills are also a crucial part of any treatment program.

The task of melding all of these components into a coherent, cooperative, and consistent design is an endless and challenging task. Accrediting agencies such as the Joint Commission on Accreditation of Healthcare Organizations (JCAHO) perform a necessary function by reminding us of the many necessary elements which go into quality patient care. They can also study programs to ensure that all the essential pieces are present. However, they can never really check the "heart" of any program. That almost indefinable portion of the puzzle is the esprit, confidence in the program, and sense of mutual endeavor which characterizes the effective treatment unit.

CITED AND RECOMMENDED READINGS

Aichhorn, A. 1935. *Wayward Youth.* New York: Viking Press.

Bettelheim, B. 1974. *A Home for the Heart.* New York: Knopf.

Frost, M. 1972. Violence in psychiatric patients. *Nursing Times.* 68: 748–749.

Lantz, J. E., and S. R. Thorward. 1985. Inpatient family therapy approaches. *Psychiatric Hospital.* 16: 85–89.

Noshpitz, J. D. 1976. The therapeutic aspect of residential treatment. *Journal of the Philadelphia Association of Psychoanalysis.* 3: 71–84.

Penningroth, P. E. 1975. Control of violence in a mental health setting. *American Journal of Nursing.* 75: 606–609.

Redl, F., and D. Wineman. 1952. *Controls from Within: Techniques for the Treatment of the Aggressive Child.* New York: The Free Press.

Rossman, P. G. 1979. A model for staff training in the psychiatric hospital treatment of adolescents. *Journal of the Academy of Child Psychiatry.*

Sanders, J. 1985. Principles of residential treatment: staff growth and therapeutic interaction. *Adolescent Psychiatry.* 12: 361–370.

CHAPTER 24

the process of inpatient treatment

THE THERAPEUTIC MILIEU

It is difficult to define precisely the concept of milieu therapy. The term refers for our purposes to the cumulative impact of all aspects of the treatment program aside from formally scheduled treatment sessions and adjunctive therapy activities. The milieu is composed of all the informal interactions between patients and between patients and staff in addition to the formal organization of the processes of daily life together.

Although this aspect of inpatient treatment may be difficult to define, it is of central importance. In fact, it is the milieu which cannot be duplicated outside of the residential treatment program. All other aspects of treatment such as individual therapy, group therapy, family therapy, psychopharmacology, and adjunctive therapy activities could be provided to patients without hospital care. Protective confinement and the structured life of a milieu program differentiate inpatient treatment from all other forms of care.

Some inpatient treatment programs have been organized with the conscious idea that the unit was to provide only humane protective confinement while the therapy occurred in formal psychotherapeutic interview situations. This concept of nursing care as glorified babysitting is not only demeaning to nursing staff personnel but an unrealistic denial of the true nature of life in a residential treatment center. The depreciation of nursing staff is an important issue since it tends to lead to a lack of investment in the program with resulting rapid turnover and general discontent. However, there are even more serious drawbacks to this approach.

566

Even if the program director does not realize it, both patients and staff are aware that scheduled psychotherapeutic time makes up a very small part of their life. Emotional involvements with fellow patients and with the staff who provide basic care are often much more intense than the involvement with the assigned psychotherapist. Attachments with this degree of importance will inevitably be structured in some way so that people can live together and relate with a reasonable degree of comfort. If a milieu is not planned, it will happen anyway and exert a powerful influence on the overall therapeutic thrust of the program. If the program director is unaware of this fact of inpatient living, he will be deprived of essential information and will lose the opportunity to direct this powerful therapeutic force.

It is realistic to view the inpatient treatment setting as a small society which has a somewhat unusual pattern of membership. Ostensibly this society is designed for the purpose of benefiting one subgroup of its population, namely the adolescent patient. By this very definition the adolescent patient is placed at some disadvantage in the social organization that he is joining. He is the citizen who is in need of help by reason of a presumed mental or behavioral deficiency. His wishes are suspect, his behavior is open to speculative interpretation, and his political actions are more to be understood than responded to. In addition to these disadvantages, the patient is likely to be the most transient member of the society, often leaving when his effectiveness in the small world of the inpatient unit reaches its maximum.

Another nonpermanent citizen group is composed of the parents of the adolescent inpatient. Their relationship to the social order is even more complex than that of the patient. They are not officially designated as ill and in some programs may not be viewed as needing the help of the treatment program. However, traditionally the parents of hospitalized adolescents are viewed with some suspiciousness by mental health professionals and may implicitly be regarded as the "real" source of the adolescent's psychopathology. This confusion is compounded by parental guilt regarding the adolescent's emotional difficulties. Often the parents carry the secret conviction that they are indeed responsible for the patient's difficulties. Although some parents are able to discuss this feeling openly and thus convert themselves into "patients," many of them defend themselves against these painful feelings. Defensive maneuvers may include rejection of the youngster, passive withdrawal, active hostility toward the treatment staff, and regressive identification with the adolescent patient so that the treatment staff is viewed as the bad, failing parent.

In addition to the confusion produced by these psychological currents, the parents must try to gain entry to the inpatient society while often having minimal contact with the staff. There may also be considerable confusion regarding the proper exercise of parental authority once an adolescent is hospitalized. Most parents view hospitalization as "turning over" the youngster to professionals. They may welcome this state of affairs and cheerfully relinquish parental authority or they may compete actively with the treatment staff in a way that is confusing and destructive to the adolescent patient.

The treatment staff members in an inpatient program often have equally confusing attitudes toward parents. This is particularly true if the program has not clarified its philosophy regarding its appropriate relationship to the patient's family. If the treatment staff view themselves as surrogate, corrective parents, the presence of the real parents may be viewed as an evil intrusion into their treatment efforts. This intrusion may or may not be regarded as a necessary evil. Unfortunately such a state of affairs sets the stage for defensive splitting in which all of the adolescent's difficulties are viewed as originating from the parents. This splitting permits the staff to avoid their feelings of anger and frustration with the adolescent patient so that these are never directly joined in the therapeutic process. Instead, the adolescent is viewed as all good—a helpless victim of parental destructiveness, who must always be understood and helped. Even if the parental destructiveness is charitably regarded as psychopathological in origin rather than malicious and willful, the adolescent still avoids all responsibility for his own problems.

The staff of an inpatient treatment unit also face a somewhat ambiguous status in the small society we are discussing. In some ways they are clearly the most powerful citizens in this world. They are relatively permanent residents who understand the traditions and laws of the country. By definition they are the ones who give the help to the needy patients. Ostensibly they are motivated by a healthy desire to be therapeutic. Their decisions are based on a righteous desire to assist and are not officially open to personal interpretations based on their life experiences. Their privacy is protected and their feelings and subjective responses are open to consideration only if they volunteer them.

On the other hand, this privileged position carries strong prohibitions against abuse, a noblesse oblige which in practice can lead to an almost masochistic and sacrificial role. Since staff must only do those things which will be helpful to adolescent patients, they may be reluctant to insist on conditions of life and unit policies which are openly and honestly based on staff convenience. If carried to extremes, this attitude can be extremely destructive in an adolescent treatment program. Unrealistic expectations of staff altruism can lead to resentment, burnout, and rapid staff turnover. In addition, staff "perfection" can have an infantalizing effect on the adolescent patient which merely reinforces a narcissistic, omnipotent defensive stance rather than promoting a responsible autonomy.

The opposite extreme is equally destructive. Programs which are designed to provide entirely for the comfort and well-being of staff may ignore the human and treatment needs of the adolescent patients. Since the patient has very little genuine political power in this small society, the result can be an unfeeling, calloused suppression of the rights of patients which is extremely destructive to any reasonable treatment goals.

Fortunately these potential inequities in the social structure of an inpatient treatment program are often outweighed by the humanity, common sense, and normal relatedness of the various individuals who comprise the populations described. Patients, for example, are often so obviously appealing and able that the staff will focus on their strengths and potentials rather than their defined social position. Many staff members are very comfortably aware that they receive as many emotional supplies from the adolescent patients as they give. Patients and parents usually have sufficient ego functioning to negotiate constructively within the framework of the treatment community. Still, it is important for both program director and staff to be aware of these potentially disruptive differences in status and position so that they can be controlled and utilized constructively in the treatment design.

It is also useful to consider the various interfaces where individuals of different political importance encounter one another. Obviously the interface between the staff and patient group is immediately apparent and is of extreme importance. It is also somewhat more delicate than is sometimes recognized. The staff's professionalism and their desire to function therapeutically are essential and laudable characteristics which must be supported and constantly reinforced as noted in the section on training. However, it is probably true that most pivotal staff-patient interchanges occur in a framework where the professional-patient boundary becomes slightly blurred and is then reconstructed on a new basis. For example, instances where staff become intensely and personally angry with a patient may, if appropriately resolved, lead to extensive emotional growth in both parties. It is also probably true that very personal positive attachments play an important role in fueling emotional reorganization. If staff members are able to remain cool, detached, and professional at all times, they may well be too defended or emotionally isolated to work well with adolescent patients. Adolescents demand and need a personal response. The delicate balance of permitting oneself this kind of involvement while retaining some degree of professional objectivity and focus on the therapeutic goals is the most difficult task faced by the treatment team. Staff frequently require support in recognizing and accepting as appropriate their individual and idiosyncratic responses to particular patients. As noted earlier, this can rarely be accomplished by "psychoanalyzing" the staff in either individual or group settings. The appropriate atmosphere of openness and sharing is most likely to be achieved when the program director sets an example of reflective awareness of his own responses and promotes a guilt-free atmosphere of emotional genuineness balanced by realistic limits of professional expectations regarding staff behavior. The staff need help in recognizing that it is entirely appropriate to have fantasies regarding adolescent patients which may be violent or erotic but that these must be entirely aim inhibited and utilized in the service of understanding and treating the adolescent.

The interface of patient-patient interactions is frequently underestimated in considering the important therapeutic occurrences within a treatment unit. In an informal followup of 50 former inpatients, this author (J.E.M.) found that over half of them mentioned a relationship with another patient on the unit as the most important and helpful aspect of their inpatient treatment experience. There is a great deal of apprehension regarding the potentially negative impact of patient-patient interactions in the hospital setting. Parents are often openly concerned that their youngster will be influenced by others who may be more ill or antisocial among the patient group. Staff members often recognize that intense one-to-one relationships between patients serve a defensive function. The followup study by Gosset et al. (1983) suggests staff are probably fundamentally wrong in opposing these pairings even though patients may use one another in the service of resistance or in order to gratify unhealthy and pathological or regressive drives. Obviously, these kinds of unhealthy interactions should be viewed both as potential impediments to the treatment process but also as a source of information and as an arena for therapeutic work. In a sense, they represent the externalization of internal pathological states which are the reason for the youngster's emotional difficulties. Staff should be equally alert, however, to the constructive potential of both dyadic relationships and the emotional interchanges in the patient group as a whole. It is only human for staff to occasionally feel twinges of envy in the recognition that members of the patient group are helping a particular youngster in a way that the staff have been unable to. The reaction is similar to that of the parents when they realize that their youngster is more invested in a peer relationship than in the parent-child bond.

We have already mentioned briefly the problems and interactions between staff and parents. This area requires constant attention and clarification if a constructive treatment effort is to be maintained. Staff require a great deal of help in understanding the motives and behavior of parents, particularly in programs that do not include extensive parental contact as part of their program design. The whole question of parent-patient interactions will be treated more extensively in the discussion of family therapy within inpatient settings.

In discussing the various aspects of the inpatient milieu of an adolescent unit, it is important to keep in mind a basic goal. All efforts to understand what is happening within the milieu are based on the desire to create a pro-therapy atmosphere which hopefully permeates the entire treatment program. This crucial element spells the difference between creating an extremely powerful treatment experience and the potential for strongly anti-therapeutic "mob" or gang behavior. A pro-therapy attitude is the most powerful deterrent against acting out and the strongest catalyst for production of relevant material in formal treatment settings. This pro-therapy atmosphere is difficult to describe. It does not imply a polyannish and superficial compliance seen only in the verbalization of the youngsters. In fact, most truly pro-therapy units are characterized by a great deal of grousing, challenges to authority, and other negative verbalizations. It should also be recognized that a pro-therapy atmosphere is not a static condition which can be once achieved and then forgotten. It is an elusive and delicate general attitude of anticipating and expecting growth which at the same time recognizes varying abilities within the patient group. Even though it is difficult to define or describe, it can be recognized in action. One observes youngsters speaking honestly with one another (in their own language and in a very practical way) about treatment goals, day-to-day behavior, and subjective personal responses to one another. In a program where a pro-therapy attitude is in the ascendency, patient A says to patient B, "Bill, I know you're pissed at your parents and the staff and maybe you've got reason, but breaking ashtrays is a stupid thing to do about it." It should also be noted that most inpatient adolescent programs develop a jargon which may be utilized in a "snow job" primarily aimed at conning the staff just as easily as it can be used as a legitimate shorthand for honest work. As in other aspects of psychotherapy, it is not so much the words as the affective tone which indicates the importance of what is being said. It is generally recognized that group sanctions and group responsibility are necessary in order to create a pro-therapy atmosphere in an adolescent program. The natural narcissism of adolescence and the cultural emphasis on individuality must be actively countered if one wishes to create mutual involvement and group cohesion. These techniques have been well described by Lewis et al. (1970). Although they are a necessary condition for creating a pro-therapy atmosphere, they are not a sufficient cause for that happy condition to result.

The single most important source of a pro-therapy atmosphere is the success of the treatment program.

Youngsters who have benefited from subscribing to the goals, techniques, and traditions of the treatment unit will become strong proponents of a positive pro-therapy attitude. The program has worked for them and they will make active efforts to convince new patients to accept the conditions of treatment as potentially effective for them. This advocacy is based not only on a genuine concern for the welfare of new patients but also on the human tendency to defend value systems which are of personal importance when they are challenged. Unfortunately for the equanimity of the treatment staff, those patients who are the most effective spokesmen in behalf of the treatment approach are forever being discharged because of the very improvement which makes them enthusiastic. The good news is that new leaders usually emerge to both benefit personally from the experience of leading and simultaneously to maintain the best aspects of the program.

You will notice that very little has been said regarding the specific organizational structure of the treatment community. This kind of consideration has been avoided because many different formal arrangements can accomplish the goals described above. For example, some units are organized around a government with elected officers who have a clearly defined relationship to staff sponsors. Other programs utilize the therapeutic community model where staff are included as members of the social system. Still other units are composed of several treatment teams, each of which sends representatives to some central governing body. The specific pattern is not as important as is the need for clarity regarding the functional mechanics of the specific organization. It is important that the unit have clearly established procedures by which decisions are made and conflicts are resolved. It is also important that these rules be followed scrupulously and that the small society of the treatment unit function as a government of laws rather than a government of people. That is, staff, as well as powerful or favored patients, must be law abiding within the organizational framework of the program. Even when this appears to work a hardship in the present, it can forestall more serious long-range difficulties which may result when special exceptions are granted.

THE DIRECT THERAPY OF THE ADOLESCENT
IN AN INPATIENT SETTING

Group Psychotherapy in the Inpatient Program

Almost all successful adolescent treatment centers utilize frequent group psychotherapy as an important constituent of their direct treatment program for the adolescent patient. Group therapy builds on the natural process of living together in the inpatient treatment center. It also provides a vehicle for shaping the group interactions of the entire unit in therapeutic directions. Because the youngsters live together 24 hours a day, inpatient group psychotherapy has the capacity for extreme intensity which may provide the opportunity for very profound emotional changes.

Because of the nature of most inpatient treatment programs, psychotherapy groups in an inpatient setting are almost invariably open-ended. This has many advantages, particularly for the newly admitted patient. Working in a group setting with individuals who have already progressed in the program and who have learned how to utilize the therapeutic facilities constructively smooths the entry process for the new youngster. In addition, many opportunities for dealing with issues of separation and loss are provided by the recurrent situation of discharge. Patients who are ready for discharge from the hospital are often very valuable members of the group and are themselves deeply invested in their relationships with other patients and staff on the unit. Working through these issues can be extremely valuable both to the departing patient and those that he leaves behind. This is particularly important in inpatient settings since so many hospitalized youngsters have significant difficulties in the area of separation-individuation.

It is often valuable to include nursing staff members as co-therapists in inpatient psychotherapy groups. Many relevant issues are raised around the behavioral activities of the patients. Nursing staff are often most familiar with these issues and are therefore in a position to bring them to the attention of the group. At the same time being part of the group psychotherapy permits the nursing staff members to view behavior in a wider context. The temptation to utilize group psychotherapy primarily as a behavioral control mechanism is offset in this way. For example, the nursing staff may have an opportunity to view directly the core depressive state in an individual which has expressed itself on the unit in the form of defensive acting out. The co-therapy relationship in the psychotherapy group forms a natural opportunity for liaison and a mutual working relationship which may avoid the extremes of dealing exclusively with either intrapsychic conflicts or their behavior manifestations. Obviously, the patient is best served by fusing these two views and recognizing their interdigitation.

The techniques of group psychotherapy in an inpatient setting are not basically different from those utilized in outpatient groups as described earlier in this book. However, there are a few differences which should be noted. First of all, the group has a great deal more information regarding each member than is typical of outpatient groups. Daily opportunities abound for observation and intimate discussion outside of the group setting. This can be either an advantage or a disadvantage. On the positive side, there is the potential for great richness of understanding based on the extreme intimacy of the living conditions of the group members. On the other hand, the lack of relative anonymity and the requirement to live together constantly may at times inhibit open interaction. For example, a youngster may be afraid to express strong feelings of anger toward a fellow group member when he knows that he must live with that person 24 hours a day over the next few weeks or months. Sexual feelings may also be blunted because of fears of overinvolvement. The potential for pairing and clique formation is also strengthened in an inpatient group.

Another way in which inpatient groups differ somewhat from their outpatient counterparts is the pattern of expression of anger. Because of the relative safety of the inpatient setting, open expressions of anger toward adults are usually much more free. The intense anger is amplified by the dual role of the mental health professional in an inpatient setting. That is, the therapist and other staff are viewed both as helpers and as "jailers." The fact that to some extent the youngster's freedom is being clearly restricted by the staff opens many opportunities for the expression of negative feelings. Much group therapy in an inpatient setting has to center around dealing with the issue of the patient's confinement, his hopes for discharge (which may in fact be extremely ambivalent), and his anger at being "forced" to remain in the treatment setting. Parenthetically, these feelings exist even in the treatment units where new "patient's rights" legislation has required all adolescents to sign in voluntarily in a very formal way. Even though the adolescent knows very well that he has admitted himself to the hospital and that he may leave on his own request at any time, he still may find ways to insist that staff are requiring him to remain. We feel that illusion of externally limited autonomy is so essential to the development phase of adolescence that these patently distorted assertions should be calmly accepted. Staff energy should be directed toward pointing out to the adolescent the appropriateness of the decision to retain him in the inpatient setting rather than wasting time in an effort to replace emotional reality with logic. The essential point is to insist that the restriction of freedom is a necessary and reasonable response to the youngster's behavior.

As mentioned briefly above, the issue of group termination with adolescents who are being discharged from the treatment program is extremely important in inpatient group psychotherapy. Although one occasionally feels that the process becomes somewhat ritualized (and certainly repetitive to the staff who continually expend their energy in assisting youngster after youngster to face directly his feelings about leaving), the process is so important that it must be pursued anyway. Naturally therapists should make every effort to avoid using cliches and falling into stereotyped comments regarding this important event. Simple concrete personal references to relationships between the departing patients and other individuals are much more useful than psychological generalizations in mobilizing genuine discussion of separation issues.

Individual Psychotherapy of the Hospitalized Adolescent

Some form of basic cooperation in the treatment effort is essential to success in the individual psychotherapy of any adolescent in any setting. This cooperativeness is based on an agreement between the therapist and the patient (which may not be verbalized directly) that there is a psychological problem and that the adolescent will permit the therapist to assist in its solution. Many features of inpatient treatment obscure and complicate the development of this basic understanding even beyond its obfuscation in the outpatient treatment of the adolescent.

We have already mentioned the issue of the patient's confinement. We have also already noted that often this confinement is more psychological than real. Still, we cannot deny that we do have unusual power and control over the adolescent in an inpatient setting. In some instances the adolescent is at least verbally opposed to this control and is in treatment only because the parents, the juvenile court, or other community agencies have forced his compliance. As noted above, even when the adolescent is a "voluntary" admission he will usually protest his status as an inpatient at some point in treatment. At these times if the therapist feels that inpatient treatment continues to be a necessity, the therapist is forced into a position of being the patient's "jailer" at the same time that he attempts to function as the patient's therapist. Obviously this is fertile ground for the popular adolescent defense against autonomy: the projection of personal responsibility. It is easy for an adolescent who is being held in hospital treatment against his verbalized wishes to insist that any observed problems that he may show are only the natural reaction to this abridgement of his civil rights. If this point is conceded, there is no therapeutic alliance since the treatment is clearly the therapist's responsibility and the patient can choose only between passively complying with expectations so that he can go home or bravely and independently resisting the ominous and unfair control being exercised by an institution over a helpless individual.

This set of circumstances requires modifications in the psychotherapeutic approach utilized in individual psychotherapy of the inpatient adolescent. Confrontation becomes more important since the patient must be continually faced with the internal origin of his problems. Fortunately, accurate confrontation is much easier in the inpatient setting than it is in the treatment of outpatient adolescents. There is a wealth of information available from the 24-hour observation of the patient's behavior and verbalizations. With this data, it is often possible to demonstrate convincingly to the patient that he cannot handle the demands of life outside of the hospital setting until certain problems are resolved. This process of confrontation is much more likely to succeed when one can obtain the support of the patient's peers in the inpatient group setting. The importance of creating and maintaining a pro-therapy atmosphere in the inpatient adolescent unit is of extreme importance. The techniques of creating this kind of atmosphere have been discussed earlier.

Another related feature of inpatient psychotherapy which often startles and confounds therapists inexperienced in that type of work is the intensity of anger routinely expressed by the patients. Often this is viewed as evidence of the more severe psychopathology present in the child who requires hospitalization. To some extent this is true but it does not account entirely for the phenomenon. In addition there are the interacting factors of the safety of the structured inpatient setting and the "legitimate complaint" of having one's life rather completely monitored and controlled. Regardless of its sources, it is important to recognize that this routinely observed intense and vehement anger in the treatment relationship does not suggest that the alliance is unworkable. To some extent all inpatient individual psychotherapy must be organized around a sometimes angry negotiation regarding the youngster's readiness for discharge. It should also be noted that the therapist too can afford a more open and firm expression of expectations regarding the level of behavior necessary for successful treatment to occur. Since the extended staff network of an inpatient setting provides considerable safety and support, it is rarely necessary to "pull punches." An intense interchange which might make it difficult for the youngster to continue in outpatient treatment is merely another rather routine "tough session" in inpatient psychotherapy.

An inpatient adolescent psychotherapy group was avoiding important and depressing treatment issues by clowning, interrupting one another, teasing the therapist, and generally producing chaos. The therapist made several efforts to comment on the defensive nature of the behavior and to deal with the problems in a more traditional psychotherapeutic way. These interventions were totally ineffective and in exasperation the therapist shouted, "If I had wanted to teach nursery school I would have gotten training for that instead of learning to be a psychiatrist. You're all behaving like a bunch of little brats."

The group did not take offense. They laughed, said "Wow, I've never seen you get so mad," and proceeded to settle down and work on important issues.

Similar, although less flamboyant, candor is possible in individual sessions also. These liberties can be taken because of the greater intimacy of the inpatient experience which makes it unlikely that patients will misunderstand the therapist's overall intentions toward them. Of course, as noted above, there is also much greater support both from the many other staff members and from patients with whom the patient relates.

Although the therapist should consistently confront the patient with his need for treatment and refuse to accept efforts to assign responsibility for the patient's welfare to himself, it should also be recognized that most adolescents cannot be expected to avow their need for treatment openly no matter how desperate that need may be. In fact, when patients speak too fluently of their need for psychotherapy, seasoned inpatient practitioners become suspicious that such talk is a maneuver to gain earlier discharge through an appearance of "insight."

Some comments should also be made regarding the importance and meaning of severe episodes of acting out which occur frequently in youngsters in inpatient psychotherapy. Often it is difficult to isolate any single factor, including the individual psychotherapeutic relationship, which can explain the youngster's behavior. The various concurrent important relationships which impinge on the youngster in inpatient treatment complicate one's efforts to gain a clear picture of the relative importance of each. The patient's relationship with his family, with significant nursing staff personnel, with other patients, and with friends outside the hospital must all be considered in trying to understand why a youngster has run away from the hospital, erupted into physical violence, brought drugs into the inpatient setting, or in some other way departed strikingly from treatment expectations.

The relationship with the individual psychotherapist is often underestimated in understanding the cause of these dramatic and disruptive behaviors. Acting out is a common form of resistance in the adolescent in outpatient psychotherapy. It becomes a much more potent method of avoiding further therapeutic work in the inpatient setting where the therapist is often viewed as "super parent" who can be angered, humiliated, or distanced by rejecting or disrupting the small universe that the therapist directs and controls, namely the inpatient treatment unit. In other words, the entire hospital situation may come to represent the therapist and thereby provide a broad stage for "acting in" an extended transference image.

It is obvious that episodes of severe acting out signal a disruption in the therapeutic alliance. They are drastic actions which are designed to force the therapist to assume roles with the patient aside from that of neutral therapeutic guide. It is often very difficult to be sure what the precise conscious or unconscious goal of the patient may be. One adolescent may be courting rejection in order to avoid a frightening growing closeness. Another patient may be attempting to elicit greater concern and protectiveness from the therapist in an effort to evade the unwanted psychological equality offered in the alliance. At other times the youngster may be tempting the therapist, attempting to provoke a punitive response which can be eroticized in sadomasochistic fashion. Often it is possible in an individual instance to gain enough information so that one can be reasonably sure of the dynamic forces which are in operation. However, even when the therapist understands some of the motives, there is rarely a good opportunity to interpret the meaning of the action in the period of time immediately following its occurrence. Since the alliance has been disrupted, the treatment situation is not ripe for genuine acceptance of interpretations. In addition, the chaos created in staff and family usually leads to a variety of theories regarding the youngster's motivation, most of which mainly reflect the anger which the patient has stirred.

For example, if the prevalent theory among the nursing staff is that a youngster went AWOL in order to "show off" and appear a hero to his fellow patients, the therapist's notion that the patient went AWOL because his growing affection for the therapist raised fears of homosexual attachment is likely to be viewed as psychiatric nonsense. In fact, the therapist may be accused of being hoodwinked by his young patient. Nursing staff may feel the therapist is trying to protect the patient from the just consequences of his behavior. It is particularly difficult to make the appropriate interpretation convincingly when the youngster's overt behavior during and after the AWOL fits the staff's description much more precisely than it fits the therapist's theories. The issue becomes very clouded if the patient himself states "candidly" that he ran away to prove that he could get away with it or "just for the hell of it."

In inpatient treatment it is particularly important to work backward from observable behavior and to raise questions which may
permit both staff and patient to expand their understandings of
the multiple causations of any particular act. In the example described above, the therapist may agree that the youngster was
"showing off " but may raise thoughtful questions about why he
might have the particular need at the present time to demonstrate
his bravery, contempt for authority, and resourcefulness. In both
the youngster's therapy sessions and in staff meetings it may become gradually more clear to everyone that the youngster's behavior was a counter-phobic defensive action.

In the effort to decipher the meaning of acting out in the
inpatient setting, the patient's expectations of the therapist's response can provide valuable clues. Has the patient anticipated
that the therapist would punish him, criticize him, withdraw affection from him? Or does the patient expect that the therapist
will now realize that the adolescent's complaints about the hospital were really serious and take better care of him? Often the
patient does not verbalize expectations but shows in his behavior
an anticipation of altered responses from the therapist. Commenting on these expectations may lead to a fruitful discussion
of those transference feelings which disrupted the therapeutic
alliance. The expectations often carry the fears and wishes which
the patient has not been able to put into words.

It should be emphasized that the therapist must simultaneously
support the behavioral controls to prevent continued acting out
at the same time that he is trying to understand the meaning of
the behavior. Both the staff and the patient have to be helped to
understand that recognizing the motives for an episode of acting
out does not justify the behavior or give license for its repetition.
This is a particularly important point with adolescents because
of their tendency to distort permissiveness and understanding of
feelings into an unjustified and dangerous permission to live out
all feelings regardless of reality consequences or the rights of
others.

It must also be recognized that some youngsters act out in ways
so dangerous to themselves, staff, or other patients, or to the

design and cohesion of the treatment program that continued psychotherapy becomes dangerous or impractical. However, this decision should always be considered very carefully. The acting-out adolescent produces intense negative feelings in both his therapist and in the nursing staff. As a rule of thumb, unless one can honestly say that the decision that a youngster is untreatable in a particular setting is genuinely reluctant and sad, the decision should be carefully reconsidered. If there are elements of satisfaction or even triumph in discharging a troublesome youngster from a treatment program, it suggests that the therapist or staff may be acting out anger, disappointment, or sadistic wishes toward the patient.

One must also remember in doing inpatient individual psychotherapy that the patient is intensely involved with many other staff members. Many of these other staff members have very different roles with the patient and the fact that their jobs are different may easily lead to problems. The nursing care staff and educational staff in an adolescent inpatient treatment unit have a difficult job. On balance they frustrate the adolescent patient much more frequently than they gratify him. Since they are entrusted with the behavioral management of the unit and with the education of young people who have frequently developed extremely negative attitudes toward school, these staff members cannot afford even the limited degree of permissiveness which the therapist can allow in his inpatient psychotherapy sessions. Frequently these staff members end up being the "bad guys" who do not "understand" that the patient is behaving badly only because he is angry, anxious, or in desperate need of a rebellious stance. In a very real sense these staff members cannot afford to "understand" these issues since they must first insist on a minimum level of appropriate behavior. In spite of the surging torrent of emotions and impulses which are stirred in the patients by the treatment process, nursing and teaching staff must reinforce ego control. They are the keepers of reality's demands, and that is frequently a thankless task on an inpatient adolescent psychiatric unit.

Because of these circumstances in hospital treatment, the opportunities for "splitting" abound. The patient may appear to have a warm and cooperative therapeutic relationship with his primary therapist while continuing to act out the negative side of his ambivalence with other staff members in an unexamined and guilt-free way. Needless to say, a pseudo-alliance of this kind does not actually benefit the patient since important areas of psychopathology are excluded from the treatment process and expressed uncritically toward other staff members in everyday life on the unit.

The patient's tendency to split his feelings in this way may easily be reinforced by unexpressed and unexamined splits between the various staff members. Therapists frequently view nursing staff as controlling and insensitive to dynamic treatment issues. Nursing staff may view therapists as overly permissive and naive regarding the patient's genuine motives. They may even view therapists as subtlely encouraging acting out against their efforts to maintain social control.

The educational staff is frequently the object of resentment. Nursing staff may be jealous of school holidays which regularly rekindle the chronic suspicion that teachers have a much easier life than they do. Therapists may view teachers as inflexible and overly concerned with the youngster's cognitive development and conventional educational expectations at the expense of emotional growth. Into present day efforts to work together collaboratively, staff members may carry consciously or unconsciously the fear and resentment of teachers which many of us develop during the anxiety of our personal educational experiences. These negative memories make it easy to identify with the adolescent's hostility toward teaching staff.

It is the responsibility of the therapist to understand and appreciate the contributions made by all disciplines and to recognize the interdependence of the entire treatment team. Opportunities for discussion of tensions and conflicts between staff members must be provided so that the patients are not used to act out staff problems.

In the direct individual psychotherapy with the adolescent patient it is crucial to insist on generalizing the therapeutic alliance. For example, the question of confidentiality in inpatient psychotherapy frequently provides a clue to the real strength of the alliance. Many patients try to create splits between the therapist and the remainder of the staff by offering to share information if the therapist will promise to keep it secret from nursing or teaching staff.

As a rule much more is lost than is gained by making such promises blindly. Of course, the therapist frequently makes choices regarding the kind of psychotherapy material which can be fruitfully shared with the extended staff. Often it is disruptive rather than helpful to discuss the patient's fantasies, dreams, and transference interactions in great detail with the staff. This is basically intrapsychic information which has its primary value in the one-to-one treatment situation. On the other hand, overt actions, interactions with other patients, family issues, and aspirations in the real world are important data for the entire staff to consider. Not only should the therapist insist on the freedom to use his own judgment in sharing material from individual psychotherapy with the remainder of the staff, he should strongly encourage the patient to share sensitive information with other staff members so that the alliance is generalized and its gains are moved closer to ordinary daily living. That is, if the patient can discuss distorted attitudes and conflicts with the staff members that he lives with 24 hours each day, he is one step closer to the capacity for self-observation and self-direction in ordinary family life and social interactions outside the home.

The therapist also needs to be alert to the relationships that the inpatient adolescent has with his fellow patients. A similar fragmentation of emotional experience may occur in relationships with fellow patients as well as with staff. Intense positive or negative interaction with other youngsters in the treatment program may represent the true focus of the patient's emotional investment, leaving the therapeutic alliance empty and bland though superficially cooperative and apparently constructive.

The patient may also utilize fellow patients to act out conflicts by proxy, collude with them in the avoidance of significant emotional issues, or use them to bolster up defenses in other ways. This is not to say that the therapist attempts to thwart these intense interpatient interactions. This would be an impossible task and probably not desirable in any event. However, it is important to be aware of what is happening between the adolescents on the unit and to utilize this information in formulating the patient's emotional patterns and intervening therapeutically.

Pharmacotherapy of the Inpatient Adolescent

Child psychiatrists have long had an extremely cautious attitude toward any psychoactive medication. This caution has extended to the adolescent patient. There is justifiable concern regarding the impact of a psychoactive drug on a developing organism. There is also concern that the drugs can be easily utilized to squelch annoying behavior even when this behavior is age appropriate and adaptive.

Although these concerns are realistic they have often led to an unfortunate situation in which talented and competent adolescent therapists are reluctant to use medication at all. This is unfair to the adolescent patients who could benefit from appropriate pharmacotherapy. The strong emotional attitudes have also led to some polarization between dynamic psychotherapists who do not use medication and other psychiatrists who utilize pharmacotherapy as the primary treatment approach. There has also been a tendency for well-staffed and dynamically oriented treatment programs to use little or no medication while poorly financed and minimally staffed institutions are grossly overmedicating adolescents. In these programs there is a scandalous use of medicine to obtund the youngsters in order to reduce management problems. The overall effect is to preclude any effective therapy or educational progress. Some of these situations have been brought to public awareness with the unfortunate side effect of producing in some sectors of the public a hysterical reaction toward even well-designed and appropriate pharmacotherapy.

It is obvious that some adolescents require psychoactive medication if their illness is to be adequately treated. Schizophrenic adolescents as well as those with manic-depressive illnesses should not be deprived of the indicated pharmacologic therapy (See chapters 12 and 20).

A text such as this one cannot deal with specific drugs and their precise dosages. Active research and clinical trials are going on constantly. It is necessary to read current journals in order to ensure appropriate and up-to-date use of medication. For this reason this section will deal primarily with general principles of pharmacotherapy. Occasionally we will mention specific medications which have proven their clinical efficacy, recognizing that they may well be supplanted by superior products at any time.

To begin with, most youngsters deserve a drug free period of evaluation when first admitted to an inpatient setting. If the patient has previously been medicated, the instructions for withdrawal of the specific medication should be followed carefully. Most drugs require a gradual reduction to avoid potential danger from rapid withdrawal. Even though the process of withdrawing a drug may be complicated by patient or parental anxiety, a drug free period can be extremely valuable. It is not unusual, for example, to encounter youngsters whose condition has been created or worsened by indiscriminate outpatient drug therapy. This iatrogenic portion of their illness cannot be identified unless medication is withdrawn for a period of time.

It is also important to see what impact the inpatient treatment program will have without the use of medication. This is important not only because all use of medication carries some risk, but because maintenance drug treatment in an outpatient setting is difficult. If a youngster can be treated successfully without medication this is preferable for many reasons. As a rule a period of ten days to two weeks without medication is a sufficient time period to provide an accurate baseline and clarify the need for medication.

Obviously, if a youngster's symptomatology poses an immediate serious threat to himself or to other persons living in the unit, medication cannot be withheld. In these instances adequate drug treatment should be instituted immediately. In addition, current pressures on hospital length of stay may not always permit an extended drug free trial.

Whenever medication is instituted it is important to be sure that it is prescribed in adequate dosage. Since, as described above, there is often a timidity in regard to drug usage among adolescent therapists there is the risk that small doses will be prescribed and that drug therapy will be prematurely interrupted when these amounts are insufficient to produce a therapeutic benefit. The therapeutic dosage level varies widely in individual adolescents and often is on the high side of acceptable dosage levels. On the other hand, some adolescents respond strongly to relatively small doses of medication. Proper management consists of beginning the adolescent on a very small dosage which should be raised fairly quickly to a level where either therapeutic benefit or side effects are observed. If a therapeutic response is achieved it may be possible to reduce the dosage and still continue the benefit. Obviously, the goal is to provide the patient with the lowest possible dosage that will maintain the desired therapeutic effect.

Most practitioners now agree that the phenothiazines can be administered in a single dose at bedtime. This not only provides a practical convenience to the nursing staff and the patient, but may prevent some side effects such as drowsiness from interfering with daily activities. Other people still prefer to prescribe two doses a day with two-thirds of the total medication given at night and one-third in the morning. Many inpatient centers prefer the liquid concentrated form of the drug since patients may develop considerable skill at pretending to take tablets while actually sequestering them for suicide attempts or abuse.

Oral medication should be used whenever possible except in situations where the patient's behavior is dangerous and his cooperation cannot be obtained. In very rare situations injection may be the preferred route of treatment in order to achieve a more rapid result.

One such situation where parenteral use is indicated is to provide rapid control of severely and acutely disorganized psychotic youngsters whose behavior is clearly dangerous. Chlorpromazine

50 to 100 mg IM is a time proven choice in this situation. Careful attention to the possibility of a hypotensive response is necessary, however. The same medication may be valuable for other youngsters who are dangerously out of control even though they are not psychotic. Other practitioners prefer to use a sedative drug such as a fast-acting barbiturate to control nonpsychotic patients.

The value of antidepressant medication in adolescents is less clear. Most depressive syndromes in adolescents are reactive and relatively unresponsive to antidepressant medication. These youngsters require psychotherapeutic approaches. However, some adolescents who show persistent severe depressive symptomatology, especially if it is accompanied with psychomotor retardation and somatic symptomatology, deserve a trial on the antidepressants.

Some inpatient treatment centers utilize PRN medications rather extensively. These may be given by nursing staff when they are concerned about the youngster's behavioral controls. The patient may also request the drug at times when he fears that he is losing control. Although this practice cannot be condemned totally, it is wise to review carefully the utilization of PRN medication. On an ad lib basis the medication may come to serve as a substitute for the psychological interventions which can often accomplish the same or better results. There is also the risk that the patient will come to depend on a pharmacological prop when, in fact, his own psychological resources could suffice.

Medication may be used at times with large numbers of youngsters when group contagion threatens to produce an outbreak of mass violence or extreme disruption within the treatment unit. Such a use of medication is certainly preferable to permitting a total destructive breakdown of the ward milieu. However, such a state of affairs calls for careful evaluation of the entire treatment program. Often the near riot conditions on the unit are the result of staff unrest, confused communications, or a general failure of appropriate treatment planning.

The question of utilizing medication in an effort to help youngsters who appear primarily characterological, immature, or impulsive is complex. There are reports in the literature of beneficial results from lithium and other psychoactive medications in this group of patients. On the other hand, it is with these patients that one can easily substitute chemical intervention for the more difficult but perhaps more valuable human interactions which could produce genuine emotional growth and maturation. For example, medication should never be used to suppress appropriate verbal anger even when the intensity of its expression is somewhat uncomfortable to the staff. It is also important to avoid using medication as a punitive control since "chemical warfare" of this kind not only fails to help the youngster involved but breeds an atmosphere of suspicion which will adversely affect the attitude of youngsters who actually need medication.

Although we now have available many potent medications, they can achieve their maximum benefit to the patient only if we remain sensitive to the psychological issues involved in their administration. Prescribing medication to an adolescent is a very important emotional event not only to the patient but to his parents. If the implications of using medicine are properly understood and supported by the adolescent and his parents, therapeutic benefit is maximized. On the other hand, even the most indicated medication may fail to produce the desired result if it is not administered in the proper psychological context.

As a rule medication is best presented as a supportive agent to the patient's efforts to benefit himself. The family or the patient should not be led to expect magical results which would obviate the need for continuing psychological treatment and efforts to improve family and individual functioning. As a rule it is possible to specify those symptomatic behaviors which are likely to benefit from medication. For example, a psychotic youngster may be told that a phenothiazine may help him think more clearly. An impulse ridden youngster may accept medication which is designed merely to allow him to delay action until he has considered various alternatives.

As a rule, except in emergency situations, it is unwise to administer medication when the youngster or the parents are intensely opposed to its use. If this resistance does not yield to psychotherapeutic efforts over a period of time it may be necessary to proceed without total support. This should be done only in cases where medication is clearly indicated and where other treatment approaches have been demonstrated insufficient.

These general suggestions by no means provide sufficient guidelines for the practitioner in the area of pharmacotherapy. By and large, it is advisable for the average psychiatrist to use only a few agents and to develop an in-depth knowledge of their indications, limitations, and side effects. Consultation with a practitioner who has made a special study of the use of medication is indicated in unusual or difficult cases whenever such expertise is available.

PSYCHOTHERAPY OF THE PARENTS OF THE HOSPITALIZED ADOLESCENT

The relationship between parents and inpatient treatment centers is notoriously troubled. There seems a natural tendency for competitiveness. Both parties seem to contribute to this negative interaction. Many mental health professionals tend to regard parents as the cause of emotional disturbance in adolescents. By and large the angry troubled adolescent is more than eager to support this hypothesis. On the other hand, many parents behave in ways that reinforce this bias.

The admission of an adolescent to an inpatient setting is invariably a complex emotional event for the adolescent's parents. To some extent they are relieved and grateful since the family's problems have usually become unbearable. At the same time, there are always elements of guilt and shame coupled with anxiety involved in the decision to turn over a portion of parental responsibility to the inpatient treatment staff. This complex set of emotions often leads to a regressive pattern in one or both parents. As a result the parents may appear childishly demanding, hopelessly inept, blindly critical, or in other ways rather irrational and unlikeable.

In spite of these inherent difficulties between the parent and the treatment program, they are forced to relate to one another. Most inpatient adolescent treatment programs insist on some parental involvement, feeling correctly that the adolescent's illness affects the entire family and may partially result from family psychopathology. The degree of involvement may depend to some extent on the program's philosophic decision regarding its appropriate role with the adolescent. If the program provides longterm care and is designed to substitute for the parents over an extended portion of the youngster's life, parental involvement becomes less crucial. Even in institutions of this kind, it is important to maintain parental support and cooperation at least to a minimal degree. Obviously, those programs that are designed to provide temporary support with the goal of returning the youngster to his family must provide much more active parental therapy. In any case, every effort should be made to respect the feelings of parents and to deal with them sympathetically and supportively. Even in situations where parental psychopathology interferes drastically with appropriate parenting, it is important for treatment staff to maintain a therapeutic attitude toward the parents rather than indulging in attitudes of critical reproach. Most parents are doing the best they can and need our help.

Adolescents who are disturbed enough to require residential treatment usually have reached a situation with their families which is a desperate one. The parents often feel defeated, confused, and totally ineffective in the parenting role. The adolescent patients often are extremely angry at their parents either for sins of commission or for less well-defined sins of omission. Both the parents and the adolescent are deeply disappointed in one another as a rule. These attitudes may be disguised by excessive solicitude and denial of conflict or they may be flagrantly apparent. Many different approaches have been utilized in approaching the family relationship of the hospitalized adolescent. Some programs insist on an initial period of separation with individual treatment for the adolescent and concurrent parent counseling. Other programs move immediately toward family therapy involving the adolescent with the parents. To some extent these decisions should be based on the clinical picture although elements of program design and practical necessity may also have to be considered. Regardless of the format one usually must eventually consider the family structure and determine the degree to which it allows for the adolescent's maturation.

It is impossible to consider the great varieties of family dysfunction which are encountered in inpatient treatment settings. Some families seem in temporary crisis and move toward a successful resolution without extensive alterations in family dynamics. We think it is safe to say, however, that most families encountered in inpatient practice have to face the need for extensive change in the course of inpatient care.

For example, some families include clearly deviant parents whose behavior plays a rather direct role in creating and maintaining the adolescent's aberrant behavior. One example is the antisocial parent of the severely acting-out adolescent. Some studies have shown that the adolescent is much more likely to improve if completely removed from the influence of such a parent (Steward et al., 1978). Another example would be the adolescent who by reason of brain damage or other biological defect is unable to function within an average normal family without creating intolerable strains for other family members.

As a rule family changes are more subtle. In the majority of cases this need for change must be directly addressed in a persistent manner. Inpatient staff often feel that a high percentage of their adolescent patients would benefit from placement outside the family. To some extent this probably reflects an overidentification with the adolescent and a competitive attitude toward the parents. As a matter of fact, the question is often academic. Most adolescents return to their families within a few months of discharge even when other placements have been recommended by the hospital staff.

Treatment staff should still feel free to address the question of whether the family is a potentially functional unit. For one thing, as noted above, some families are not viable and the difficult decision to reorganize the family with different members may be necessary. More important, this question is in some way at the back of everyone's mind in most cases. There are great advantages in addressing it directly since considering the possibility of dissolving the family both focuses the discussion on relevant issues and permits consideration of whole new ways of interacting. To some extent the question of leaving one's family is central in all adolescents. Considering concrete issues of emancipation often allows open discussion of more subtle emotional components of family functioning. It is important for treatment staff to remember that the inpatient adolescent is already temporarily separated from his parents. This reality factor undoubtedly partially explains the frequency with which the issue of actual family disruption is raised in the inpatient treatment of adolescents and their parents. In any case, the possibility of actual disruption of the family should be viewed as tentative and symbolic throughout the early phases of all such discussions.

One must also remember that families are typically resistant to psychological change. Even in situations where the family homeostasis is achieved at high group or individual cost, the prospect of altering the balance is frightening. One can anticipate not only the typical resistances encountered in outpatient family therapy, but extensive utilization of other opportunities for resistance which are offered in an inpatient setting. In inpatient programs which include an active family therapy component, family resistance is a frequent source of staff splits and conflicts. Harbin (1978) has described this phenomenon in detail.

In closing this discussion of family involvement in the inpatient psychotherapy of the adolescent, it should be emphasized again that not all problems with parents result from their individual psychopathology or from resistance to changing maladaptive family group dynamics. It is difficult to maintain a consistent and humane therapeutic approach in the face of the stresses involved in providing inpatient treatment for adolescents. The entire staff often feel strained and even overwhelmed by their task. Because the therapeutic commitment to the adolescent is more immediate, and perhaps to some extent because staff who have chosen work in such a unit have particular sympathies for people in the adolescent age group, the parents are perhaps the most likely scapegoat for our frustrations. We must confront parents in the process of helping them and their adolescent children. Before we confront too actively it is important for us to be sure that we have treated parents with the therapeutic understanding, tact, and simple humanity that we would desire for ourselves if we were in their shoes.

CITED AND RECOMMENDED READING

Berman, S. 1976. Hospitalization of children and adolescents: the role of the referring child psychiatrist. *Journal of the Philadelphia Association of Psychoanalysis.* 3: 5–15.

Fong, J. Y., et al. 1978. Multiple family group therapy with a tri-therapist team. *Nursing Clinics of North America.* 13: 685–699.

Gossett, J. T., et al. 1977. Follow-up of adolescents treated in a psychiatric hospital. Predictors of outcome. *Archives of General Psychiatry.* 34: 1037–1042.

Greenberg, L., et al. 1987. Countertransference during the acute psychiatric hospitalization of the adolescent. *Adolescent Psychiatry.* 14: 316–331.

Gunderson, J. 1978. Defining the therapeutic processes in psychiatric milieus. *Psychiatry.* 41: 327–335.

Harbin, H. T. 1978. Families and hospitals: collusion or cooperation? *American Journal of Psychiatry.* 135: 1496–1499.

Lewis, J. W., et al. 1970. Development of a pro-treatment group process among hospitalized adolescents. *Timberlawn Report.* No. 40.

Rabiner, E. L., et al. 1962. Conjoint family therapy in the inpatient setting. *American Journal of Psychotherapy.* 16: 618–631.

Saidel, D. H., and R. M. Sarles. 1988. Treatment considerations for children and adolescents. In: *Modern Hospital Psychiatry,* edited by J. R. Lion, et al. New York: W. W. Norton.

Stewart, M. A., et al. 1978. Unsocialized aggressive boys: a follow-up study. *Journal of Clinical Psychiatry.* 39: 797–799.

Stubblefield, R. L. 1978. Indications for hospitalization of adolescents. *Interaction.* 1: 20–27.

Trieschman, A. E. 1973. *The Other 23 Hours.* Chicago: Aldine Publishing.

index

597